Human Resource Management Resource Development in Contemporary Contex

Custom Publication

Human Resource Management / Human Resource Development in its Contemporary Context

Custom Publication

Compiled For
Dr Marian Crowley-Henry and Dr Paul Donovan

National University of Ireland Maynooth

Selection and editorial matter © Dr Marian Crowley-Henry and Dr Paul Donovan
The Sources list on page xi constitutes a continuation of this page.

All rights reserved. No reproduction, copy or transmission of this publication may be made without written permission.

No portion of this publication may be reproduced, copied or transmitted save with written permission or in accordance with the provisions of the Copyright, Designs and Patents Act 1988, or under the terms of any licence permitting limited copying issued by the Copyright Licensing Agency, Saffron House, 6–10 Kirby Street, London EC1N 8TS.

Any person who does any unauthorized act in relation to this publication may be liable to criminal prosecution and civil claims for damages.

The authors have asserted their rights to be identified as the authors of this work in accordance with the Copyright, Designs and Patents Act 1988.

First published 2013 by
PALGRAVE MACMILLAN

Palgrave Macmillan in the UK is an imprint of Macmillan Publishers Limited, registered in England, company number 785998, of Houndmills, Basingstoke, Hampshire RG21 6XS.

Palgrave Macmillan in the US is a division of St Martin's Press LLC, 175 Fifth Avenue, New York, NY 10010.

Palgrave Macmillan is the global academic imprint of the above companies and has companies and representatives throughout the world.

Palgrave® and Macmillan® are registered trademarks in the United States, the United Kingdom, Europe and other countries.

ISBN 978–1–137–30304–2

This book is printed on paper suitable for recycling and made from fully managed and sustained forest sources. Logging, pulping and manufacturing processes are expected to conform to the environmental regulations of the country of origin.

A catalogue record for this book is available from the British Library.

A catalog record for this book is available from the Library of Congress.

10 9 8 7 6 5 4 3 2 1
22 21 20 19 18 17 16 15 14 13

Printed and bound in Great Britain by
CPI Antony Rowe, Chippenham and Eastbourne

Contents

List of Figures	vii
List of Tables	ix
Sources	xi

PART ONE

1. The nature of contemporary HRM — 3
   Human Resource Management:
   John Bratton

2. Contextualizing human resource management — 49
   Human Resource Management in a Global Context:
   Jawad Syed and Dk Nur'Izzati Pg Omar

3. A critical perspective on strategic human resource management — 75
   Human Resource Management in a Global Context:
   Dima Jamali and Fida Afiouni

4. Organizational culture and HRM — 99
   Human Resource Management:
   John Bratton

5. Diversity Management — 139
   Human Resource Management in a Global Context:
   Nicolina Kamenou and Jawad Syed

6. Work–life balance in the 21st century — 165
   Human Resource Management in a Global Context:
   Nicolina Kamenou

APPENDIX A: The European Union Social Charter — 189
Human Resource Management in a Global Context

PART TWO

7. Workforce planning and talent management — 193
   Human Resource Management:
   Jeff Gold

8	Human resources planning *Human Resource Management in a Global Context:* Cathy Sheehan	243
9	Recruiting and selecting employees *Human Resource Management:* Jeff Gold	267
10	Recruitment and selection *Human Resource Management in a Global Context:* Olivia Kyriakidou	313
11	Performance management *Human Resource Management in a Global Context:* Jane Maley	351
12	Reward Management *Human Resource Management in a Global Context:* John Shields	385

PART THREE

13	The Nature and scope of HRD *Human Resource Development:* Jim Stewart, Jeff Gold, Paul Iles, Rick Holden and Julie Beardwell	431
14	Strategic HRD and the learning and development function *Human Resource Development:* Jim Stewart, Paul Iles, Jeff Gold, Rick Holden, Helen Rodgers and Hazel Kershaw-Solomon	443
15	The design and delivery of training *Human Resource Development:* Catherine Glaister, Rick Holden, Vivienne Griggs and Patrick McCauley	467
16	Evaluation of HRD *Human Resource Development:* David Devins and Joanna Smith	493
17	Workplace learning and knowledge management *Human Resource Development:* Jeff Gold, Rick Holden, Vivienne Griggs and Niki Kyriakidou	525
18	Continuing professional development and lifelong learning *Human Resource Development:* Jeff Gold and Joanna Smith	547

Index   571

List of Figures

1.1	The employment and psychological contract between employees and employers	15
1.2	HRM functions, contingencies and skills	19
1.3	The Harvard model of HRM	22
1.4	Ulrich's human resources business partner mode	30
2.1	Key factors of the macroenvironment	55
3.1	From traditional personnel management (TPM) to strategic human resource management (SRHM)	78
3.2	The resource-based view and human resource advantage	82
3.3	Linking human resources (HR) practices to competitive strategy	84
3.4	The Deloitte ME 'develop, deploy and connect' model	93
3.5	Deloitte ME value creation through strategic human resources	94
4.1	The dynamics of culture	101
4.2	The three levels of organizational culture	109
4.3	A strategy for changing organizational culture	122
4.4	A framework for analysing green HR practice–sustainability linkages. EI, employee involvement; PRP, performance-related pay	126
5.1	Usual approaches to managing diversity	142
7.1	Reconciling demand and supply	196
7.2	The diagnostic approach to manpower planning	198
7.3	Approaches to TM	218
7.4	A performance/potential chart	219
9.1	The stages of recruitment and selection	269
9.2	An attraction–selection–attrition framework	278
9.3	Job description format	282
9.4	Rodger's seven-point plan	282
9.5	Munro-Fraser's fivefold grading system	283
10.1	The recruitment and selection process	316
10.2	A model of the recruitment process	319
11.1	The performance management cycle	355
11.2	The purpose of performance management: the influences and implications	356
14.1	Incremental and transformational change	451
14.2	Shifting roles of the HRD professional	457

14.3	The business partner model in the UK civil service	457
14.4	The balance of expertise and influence	462
15.1	A training design framework	471
15.2	A model of the transfer of training	475
15.3	A framework of training and learning methods	480
16.1	Classic experimental design	496
16.2	The ROAMEF cycle	500
16.3	A four-stage training model	505
16.4	Levels of evaluation for training	506
16.5	Reaction-level evaluation sheet	508
16.6	Value and evaluation process	519
16.7	Measures of returns model	519
17.1	Contested possibilities in HRD	529
17.2	A model for informal and incidental learning	531
18.1	A CPD model	556

List of Tables

1.1	Selective UK Employment Statutes and Statutory Instruments, 1961–2007	14
1.2	The Storey model of HRM	27
2.1	An organization's macroenvironment	54
2.2	Hofstede's cultural dimensions	56
3.1	Definitions and differentiating attributes of strategic human resource management (SHRM)	80
3.2	Different competitive strategies and different employee competitive role behaviours	84
7.1	Headings for a typical HR module within ERP	206
9.1	Competencies in a financial services organization	276
9.2	Reasons for poor results from selection interviewing	290
10.1	External recruitment sources	320
10.2	Internal recruitment sources	322
11.1	Summary of performance appraisal approaches	366
12.1	Job-based versus person-based base pay	394
12.2	Options for base pay	394
12.3	Performance-related reward options	401
12.4	Collective incentives – pros and cons	404
15.1	Off-the-job methods	482
15.2	Integrated methods	484
16.1	Stakeholder objectives for training middle managers	504
16.2	Evaluation of development training for middle managers	512
18.1	Sample training record for solicitors	558
18.2	The revised 2004 National Qualifications Framework in the UK	562

Sources

This custom publication has been compiled for use in the National University of Ireland Maynooth. The chapters included are reproduced from the following works:

Chapter 1 from John Bratton and Jeff Gold: Human Resource Management 5th Edition © John Bratton 2012

Chapter 2 from Robin Kramar and Jawad Syed: Human Resource Management in a Global Context © Jawad Syed and Dk Nur'Izzati Pg Omar 2012

Chapter 3 from Robin Kramar and Jawad Syed: Human Resource Management in a Global Context © Dima Jamali and Fida Afiouni 2012

Chapter 4 from John Bratton and Jeff Gold: Human Resource Management 5th Edition © John Bratton 2012

Chapter 5 from Robin Kramar and Jawad Syed: Human Resource Management in a Global Context © Nicolina Kamenou and Jawad Syed 2012

Chapter 6 from Robin Kramar and Jawad Syed: Human Resource Management in a Global Context © Nicolina Kamenou 2012

Chapter 7 from John Bratton and Jeff Gold: Human Resource Management 5th Edition © Jeff Gold 2012

Chapter 8 from Robin Kramar and Jawad Syed: Human Resource Management in a Global Context © Cathy Sheehan 2012

Chapter 9 from John Bratton and Jeff Gold: Human Resource Management 5th Edition © Jeff Gold 2012

Chapter 10 from Robin Kramar and Jawad Syed: Human Resource Management in a Global Context © Peter Holland

Chapter 11 from Robin Kramar and Jawad Syed: Human Resource Management in a Global Context © Jane Maley

Chapter 12 from Robin Kramar and Jawad Syed: Human Resource Management in a Global Context © John Shields

SOURCES

Chapter 13 from Jim Stewart, Jeff Gold, Paul Iles, Rick Holden and Julie Beardwell Human Resource Development © Jim Stewart, Jeff Gold, Paul Iles, Rick Holden and Julie Beardwell

Chapter 14 from Jim Stewart, Jeff Gold, Paul Iles, Rick Holden and Julie Beardwell Human Resource Development © Jim Stewart, Paul Iles, Jeff Gold, Rick Holden, Helen Rodgers and Hazel Kershaw-Solomon

Chapter 15 from Jim Stewart, Jeff Gold, Paul Iles, Rick Holden and Julie Beardwell Human Resource Development © Catherine Glaister, Rick Holden, Vivienne Griggs and Patrick McCauley

Chapter 16 from Jim Stewart, Jeff Gold, Paul Iles, Rick Holden and Julie Beardwell Human Resource Development © David Devins and Joanna Smith

Chapter 17 from Jim Stewart, Jeff Gold, Paul Iles, Rick Holden and Julie Beardwell Human Resource Development © Jeff Gold, Rick Holden, Vivienne Griffs and Niki Kyriakidou

Chapter 18 from Jim Stewart, Jeff Gold, Paul Iles, Rick Holden and Julie Beardwell Human Resource Development © Jeff Gold and Joanna Smith

Every effort has been made to trace all copyright holders, but if any have been inadvertently overlooked the publishers will be pleased to make the necessary arrangements at the first opportunity.

PART ONE

CHAPTER 1
The nature of contemporary HRM

OUTLINE

- Introduction
- The development of HRM
- HRM in practice 1.1: A new role for HR professionals
- Management and HRM
- The nature of the employment relationship
- Scope and functions of HRM
- Theoretical perspectives on HRM
- HRM in practice 1.2: Twenty-first-century senior hr leaders have a changing role
- HRM and globalization: The HRM model in advancing economies?
- Studying HRM
- Critique and paradox in HRM
- Case study: Canterbury Hospital
- Summary, Vocab checklist for ESL students, Review questions and Further reading to improve your mark

OBJECTIVES

After studying this chapter, you should be able to:
- Explain the development of human resource management (HRM)
- Define HRM and its relation to organizational management
- Explain the central features of the contract in the employment relationship
- Summarise the scope of HRM and the key HRM functions
- Explain the theoretical issues surrounding the HRM debate
- Appreciate the different approaches to studying HRM

Introduction

This book is concerned with managing people, both individually and collectively, in the workplace. Emerging from the worst cyclical economic recession since 1945, human resource management (HRM) has assumed new prominence as concerns about global competitiveness, the demographics of ageing and climate change persist. It is argued that these global drivers of change require managers to adjust the way in which they manage in order to achieve innovation, sustainable growth and an effective use of employees. For some, HRM is associated with a set of distinctive 'best' practices that aim to recruit, develop, reward and manage people in ways that create what are called 'high-performing work systems'. For others, the HRM stereotype is simply a repackaging of 'good' personnel management practices – the 'old wine in new bottles' critique – or more fundamentally exposes enduring conflicts and paradoxes associated with labour management. As managers strive to reduce costs, most follow conventional wisdom – downsizing, restructuring and outsourcing work to ever cheaper labour markets – rather than looking to HRM in order to create competitive advantage or provide superior public services. Critical management theorists point to the need to address the conflict between the dual imperatives of competitiveness and control, and the cooperation and commitment of employees. Within the academic study of HRM, this conflict is often framed in terms of 'the rhetoric versus the reality' of HRM.

This chapter examines the complex debate surrounding the nature and significance of contemporary HRM. After defining HRM, we will examine the nature of the employment relationship and HRM functions. We will also explore some influential theoretical models that attempt to define HRM analytically. We will begin, however, by briefly examining the development of HRM.

> **reflective question**
>
> Based upon your reading or work experience, how important is HRM to individual performance at work or to organizational success?

The development of HRM

Despite the fact that 'human resource management' outwardly appears to be a relatively neutral management term, the language used to talk about it is imbued with ideologies that reflect radical changes in society over time. As understood in the approach we are taking here, innovations in management must be analysed within a framework of existing social relationships and interdependencies in society. The notion that HRM is *embedded* in society helps to capture and express the importance of culture, national politics, practising law and indigenous business-related institutions, for example employment tribunals, in explaining how work and people are managed. Thus, developments in HRM respond to and are shaped by changes in markets, social movements and public policies that are the products of the economic and political changes in society.

HRM in practice 1.1: A new role for HR professionals

There has been increased awareness and understanding of the impact that business activity has upon social and political systems as a result of high-profile corporate scandals, such as the alleged phone hacking at News International and the politicians implicated. Awareness has also been raised by global development initiatives such as the Business Leaders Initiative on Human Rights (a business-led organization aiming to find practical ways of implementing the Universal Declaration of Human Rights in a business context). As a result, organizations are increasingly being pushed to develop their business practices in order to operate within socially acceptable parameters. The 'triple bottom line' (Elkington, 1998) of *profit, people* and *planet* provides a convenient manifesto for the 'social contract' now expected from business. There is little doubt that there is tension between social obligations and the demands of shareholders. But who is awarded the daunting task of integrating the economic, social and environmental objectives into an organization's strategy, thus dealing with the complex task of balancing ethics and income? The need to define, balance and carry out these objectives has been intensified as the effects of the economic downturn are felt around the globe. A recent *People Management* article highlights this growing expectation that businesses will accept such responsibility:

> *The fallout from the world financial crisis continues unabated. For the first time since the Great Depression of the 1930s, some of the most sacred tenets of Western capitalism are being questioned in mainstream debate. Chief among these is our most basic assumption that growth is the primary goal of economic activity. There seems to be a widespread acceptance of the need for corporations to be more responsible as global tenants, to pay more attention to the broader consequences of economic activity and to adopt more sustainable practices ... While the recklessness of the financial services industry seems to have been pivotal, our research suggests that the crisis was the culmination of a far wider malaise affecting how organisations operate, what leaders do, and how they are developed ... Businesses are increasingly seen as participants in a wider ecology with responsibility for minimising their environmental impact and improving their contribution to social welfare. (Casserley and Critchley, 2010, p. 21)*

Much is made of the wide-ranging responsibilities of the human resources (HR) function. Alongside the strategic influence of their new role as a business partner in many

Source: Mat Coleman.

organizations, and the ongoing need for them to provide operational support, HR professionals are facing renewed and unrelenting pressure to act as moral and ethical compasses for organizations. This is rooted in the welfare role of the personnel function prior to the advent of HRM. The HR function has been awarded great responsibility as a guardian of the ethos and values that must be embedded in an organizational culture if HR specialists are to be successful. The changing expectations of organizational stakeholders can be attributed to notable cases of corporate mismanagement and stakeholders' growing awareness that their reputation could be damaged. This has led to a competitive need to justify not only what organizations do with their profits, but also how those profits are generated in the first place. Cross-border business and an emphasis on employee welfare and social, legal and philanthropic responsibilities have all forced organizations to nominate 'natural' leaders to be responsible for internal and external ethical responsibility.

> **Stop!** Should corporations behave in an ethical manner because it is morally right or because there is a 'business case' for management ethics? Should HR professionals act as the 'moral compass' for organizations?

Sources and further information:

For further information, see the Business Leaders Initiative on Human Rights website www.blihr.org. See also Casserley and Critchley (2010), Francis and Keegan (2005) and Watson (2007).

Note: This feature was written by Lesley McLean (née Craig) at Edinburgh Napier University.

Keynesianism: collectivism and personnel management

The roots of people management can be traced back to the Industrial Revolution in England in the late eighteenth century. However, we begin our discussion on this history with the economic and political conditions prevailing after the Second World War. The years 1950–74 were the 'golden age' of the Keynesian economic doctrine, as evidenced by the post-war Labour government's commitment 'to combine a free democracy with a planned economy' (Coates, 1975, p. 46). It was a period when both Conservative and Labour governments, anxious to foster industrial peace through conciliation, mediation and arbitration (Crouch, 1982), passed employment laws to improve employment conditions and extend workers' rights, which also encouraged the growth of personnel specialists. The Donovan Commission (1968) investigated UK industrial relations and recommended, among other things, that management should develop joint (trade union–management) procedures for the speedy settlement of grievances. The idea that there were both common and conflicting goals between the 'actors' – employers and trade unions – and the state's deep involvement in managing and regulating employment relations provided the *pluralist* framework for managing the employment relationship.

THE NATURE OF CONTEMPORARY HRM

> **HRM web links**
>
> Go to the website of the HR professional associations (for example, Australia www.hrhq.com; Britain www.cipd.co.uk; Canada www.hrpa.org; and USA www.shrm.org). Then click on the 'Mission statement' or 'History'. Evaluate the information you find in relation to the history of personnel management. What are the origins of the association?

Neo-liberalism: individualism and HRM

In the 1980s and 90s, there was a radical change in both the context and the content of how people were managed. Western economies saw the renaissance of 'market disciplines', and there was a strong belief that, in terms of economic well-being, too much government intervention was the problem. The new political orthodoxy focused on extending market power and limiting the role of the government, mainly to facilitate this laissez-faire agenda (Kuttner, 2000). The rise of the political ideology of Thatcherism in Britain represented a radical break from the consensual, corporatist style of government, which provided the political backcloth to this shift in managerial ideas and practices. Whereas it was alleged that traditional personnel management based its legitimacy and influence on its ability to deal with the uncertainties stemming from full employment and trade union growth, HRM celebrated the *unitary* philosophy and framework. Strongly influenced by the up-and-coming neo-liberal economic consensus, HRM subscribed to the idea that there was a harmony of goals and interests between the organization's internal members. The new approach was therefore to marginalize or exclude 'external' influences such as the state or trade unions.

The landmark publication *New Perspectives on Human Resource Management* (1989), edited by John Storey, generated the 'first wave' of debate on the nature and ideological significance of the normative HRM model. Debate focused on 'hard' and 'soft' versions of the HRM model. The 'hard' version emphasizes the term 'resource' and adopts a 'rational' approach to managing employees, that is, viewing employees as any other economic factor – as a cost that must be controlled. The 'soft' HRM model emphasizes the term 'human' and thus advocates investment in training and development, as well as the adoption of 'commitment' strategies to ensure that highly skilled and loyal employees give the organization a competitive advantage. For some academics, the normative HRM model represented a distinctive approach to managing the human 'input' that fitted the new economic order (Bamberger and Meshoulam, 2000); in addition, being much more concerned with business strategy and HR strategy linkages, it signalled the beginnings of a new theoretical sophistication in the area of personnel management (Boxall, 1992). For those who disagreed, however, the HRM stereotype was characterized as a cultural construct concerned with making sure that employees 'fitted' corporate values (Townley, 1994), even attempting to 'govern the soul' (Rose, 1999). In this way, the HRM model, among both its advocates and its detractors, became one of the most controversial topics in managerial debate (Storey, 1989). The displacement of personnel management by HRM can be seen as the outcome of neo-liberalism ideology, much as the 'social contract' of the 1970s was an outcome of Keynesian economic planning and the 'Old' Labour government–union partnership.

Management and HRM

HRM, in theory and in practice, encompasses a diverse body of scholarship and managerial activities concerned with managing work and people. An early definition of HRM by Michael Beer and his colleagues focuses on all managerial activity affecting the employment relationship: 'Human resource management (HRM) involves all management decisions and actions that affect the nature of the relationship between the organization and employees – its human resources' (1984, p. 1). Acknowledging HRM as only one 'recipe' from a range of alternatives, Storey (1995a, 2001) contends that HRM plays a pivotal role in sophisticated organizations, emphasizing the importance of the strategic dimension and employee 'commitment' in generating HR activities. In his view:

> Human resource management is a distinctive approach to employment management which seeks to achieve competitive advantage through the strategic deployment of a highly committed and capable workforce using an array of cultural, structural and personnel techniques. (Storey, 2007, p. 7)

Conceptualizing HRM as a high-commitment management strategy limits the discipline to the study of a relatively small number of distinct organizations as most firms continue to provide low wages and a minimal number of training opportunities (Bacon and Blyton, 2003). In contrast, Boxall et al. (2008, p. 1) define HRM as 'the management of work and people towards desired ends'. These authors advance the notion of 'analytical HRM' to emphasize that the primary task of HRM scholars is to build theory and gather empirical data in order to identify and explain 'the way management *actually behaves* in organizing work and managing people' (Boxall et al., 2008, p. 4, emphasis added).

This approach to HRM has three interrelated analytical themes. The first is a concern with the '*what*' and '*why*' of HRM, with understanding management behaviour in different contexts and with explaining motives. The second is a concern with the '*how*' of HRM, that is, the processes by which it is carried out. The third is concerned with questions of '*for whom and how well*', that is, with assessing the *outcomes* of HRM. The third characteristic in particular implies a critical purpose and helps us to rediscover one of the prime objectives of the social sciences – that of asking tough questions about power and inequality. It also reminds all of those who are interested in studying the field that HRM is 'embedded in a global economical, political and sociocultural context' (Janssens and Steyaert, 2009, p. 146).

Almost 50 years ago, sociologist Peter Berger wrote that the first wisdom of sociological inquiry is that 'things are not what they seem' (1963, p. 23). A deceptively simple statement, Berger's idea suggests that most people live in a social world that they do not understand. The goal of sociology is to shed light on social reality using what the late C. Wright Mills called the 'sociological imagination' – the ability to see the relationships between individual life experiences and the larger society, because the two are related (1959/2000, pp. 3–4). Sociologists argue that the sociological imagination helps people to place seemingly personal troubles, such as losing a job to outsourcing or local environmental degradation, into a larger national or global context. For Watson (2010), a critical approach to studying HRM provides inspiration and an invitation to apply Mills' 'sociological imagination' to matters of HRM 'outcomes' that have 'wider social consequences'. In the context of the post-2008 crisis and the search for the 'new economic philosophy', Delbridge and Keenoy (2010) provide a persuasive argument for critical HRM (CHRM), an intellectual activity, grounded in social science inquiry, that contextualizes HR practices within the prevailing capitalist society, challenges the maxims of what Alfred Schutz has called the 'world-taken-for-granted' and is more inclusive of marginal voices.

We need a definition of the subject matter that conceptualizes HRM in terms of employment or people management, one that distinguishes it from a set of 'neutral' functional practices, and one that conceives it as embedded in a capitalist society and its associated ideologies and global structures. The following attempts to capture the essence of what contemporary HRM is about:

> Human resource management (HRM) is a strategic approach to managing employment relations which emphasizes that leveraging people's capabilities and commitment is critical to achieving sustainable competitive advantage or superior public services. This is accomplished through a distinctive set of integrated employment policies, programmes and practices, embedded in an organizational and societal context.

Following on from this definition, CHRM underscores the importance of *people* – only the 'human factor' or labour can provide talent to generate value. With this in mind, it goes without saying that any adequate analytical conception of HRM should draw attention to the notion of *indeterminacy*, which derives from the employment relationship: employees have a *potential* capacity to provide the added value desired by the employer. It also follows from this that human knowledge and skills are a *strategic resource* that needs investment and skilful management. Moreover, the emergent environmental management literature provides a role for HRM in improving an organization's performance in terms of overall *sustainability*. Also implicit within our definition is the need for radical organizational and social change. Another distinguishing feature of HRM relates to the notion of *integration*. A cluster of employment policies programmes and practices needs to be coherent and integrated with the organization's corporate strategy. Finally, the 2008 global financial implosion and the 2011 nuclear crisis in Japan remind us that the economy and society are part of the same set of processes, and that work and management practices are deeply embedded in the wider sociocultural context in which they operate. The conception of CHRM put forward here resonates with analytical frameworks holding that HR practices can only be understood in the context of economic-societal factors that shape or direct those practices. The approach adopted can be summed up in the succinct phrase 'context matters'.

This book is oriented towards helping people manage people – both individually and collectively – more effectively, equitably and with dignity. It is plausible to argue that if the workforce is so critical for sustainability performance, HRM is too important to be left solely to HR specialists but should be the responsibility of *all* managers. Furthermore, human dignity *in* and *at* work is, or *ought* to be, at the heart of contemporary HRM (Bolton, 2007). The dignity dimension provides support for a reconceptualized HRM model of empowered, engaged and developed employees, the 'missing "human" in HRM' critique (Bolton and Houlihan, 2007). Recently, critics have voiced concerns regarding the 'moribund and limited' nature of mainstream HRM (Delbridge and Keenoy, 2010, p. 800). The demands for dignity in the workplace are a key dimension of CHRM that provides strong support for extending the analysis of HRM outcomes beyond employee performance and commitment to include the 'dignity' aspects of the employment relationship and equality. To grasp the nature and significance of HRM, it is necessary to understand the management process and the role of HRM within it. But before we do this, we should explain why managing people or the 'human' input is so different from managing other resources.

The meaning of 'human resource'

First and foremost, labour is not a commodity. It is people in work organizations who set overall strategies and goals, design work systems, produce goods and services, monitor quality, allocate financial resources and market the products and services. Human beings, therefore, become human capital by virtue of the roles they assume in the work organization. Employment roles are defined and described in a manner designed to maximize particular employees' contributions to achieving organizational objectives. Schultz (1981) defined human capital in this way:

> Consider all human abilities to be either innate or acquired. Every person is born with a particular set of genes, which determines his [sic] innate ability. Attributes of acquired population quality, which are valuable and can be augmented by appropriate investment, will be treated as human capital. (Schultz, 1981, p. 21; quoted in Fitz-enz, 2000, p. xii)

In management terms, 'human capital' refers to the traits that people bring to the workplace – intelligence, aptitude, commitment, tacit knowledge and skills, and an ability to learn. But the contribution of this human resource to the organization is typically variable and unpredictable. This indeterminacy of an employee's contribution to her or his work organization makes the human resource the 'most vexatious of assets to manage' (Fitz-enz, 2000, p. xii) and is helpful in understanding Hyman's (1987) assertion that the need to gain both *control over* and *commitment from* workers is the *leitmotiv* of HRM.

Managing people in a democratic market society extends beyond the issue of control. If the employer's operational goals and the employee's personal goals are to be achieved, there must necessarily be *cooperation* between the two parties. This reciprocal cooperation is, however, often accompanied by different forms of *resistance* and *conflict*. The nature of employment relations reminds us that people differ from other resources because their commitment and cooperation always has to be won: they have the capacity to resist management's actions and join trade unions to defend or further their interests and rights. At the same time, employment entails

These chefs provide an example of human capital in the context of a restaurant
Source: ©istockphoto.com/Huchen Lu.

an economic relationship and one of control and cooperation. This duality means that the employment relationship is highly *dynamic* in the sense that it is forged by the coexistence of control, cooperation and conflict in varying degrees (Brown, 1988; Edwards, 1986; Watson, 2004). Thus, HRM is inevitably characterized by structured cooperation and conflict.

The meaning of 'management'

The word *manage* came into English usage directly from the Italian *maneggiare*, meaning 'to handle and train horses'. In the sixteenth century, the meaning was extended to include a general sense of taking charge or directing (Williams, 1976).

The answer to the question 'Who is a manager?' depends on the manager's social position in the organization's hierarchy. A manager is an organizational member who is 'institutionally empowered to determine and/or regulate certain aspects of the actions of others' (Willmott, 1984, p. 350). Collectively, managers are traditionally differentiated horizontally by their function activities (for example, production manager or HR manager) and vertically by the level at which they are located in their organizational hierarchy (for example, counter manager or branch manager).

Management has been variously conceptualized as 'the central process whereby work organizations achieve the semblance of congruence and direction' (Mintzberg, 1973), as 'art, science, magic and politics' (Watson, 1986) and as a process designed to coordinate and control productive activities (see, for example, Thompson and McHugh, 2009). In his seminal work, Fayol (1949) envisioned management as a science. For Fayol, management is primarily concerned with internal planning, organizing, directing and controlling – known as the 'PODC' tradition. The creation of a formal organizational structure and work configuration is, therefore, the *raison d'être* for management. This classical stereotype presents an idealized image of management as a rationally designed system for realizing goals, but there are competing theoretical perspectives, as we will explain later in this chapter.

The nature of the employment relationship

The nature of the social relationship between employees and their employer is an issue of central analytical importance to HRM. The employment relationship describes an asymmetry of reciprocal relations between employees (non-managers and managers) and their work organization. Through the asymmetry of the employment contract, inequalities of power structure both the economic exchange (wage or salary) and the nature and quality of the work performed (whether it is routine or creative). In contemporary capitalism, employment relationships vary: at one end of the scale, they can be a short-term, primarily but not exclusively economic exchange for a relatively well-defined set of duties and low commitment; at the other, they can be complex long-term relationships defined by a broad range of economic inducements and relative security of employment, given in return for a broad set of duties and a high commitment from the employee.

The employment relationship may be regulated in three ways: unilaterally by the employer; bilaterally, by the employer and the trade unions, through a process of collective bargaining; and trilaterally, by employers, trade unions and statutes, through the intervention of the government or state (Kelly, 2005). What, then, is the essence of the employment relationship? Research into the employment relationship has drawn attention to economic, legal, social and psychological aspects of relations in the workplace.

At its most basic, the employment relationship embraces an *economic relationship*: the 'exchange of pay for work' (Brown, 1988). When people enter the workplace, they enter into a pay–effort bargain, which places an obligation on both the employer and the employee: in exchange for a wage or salary, paid by the employer, the employee is obligated to perform an amount of physical or intellectual labour. The pay–effort bargain is relevant for understanding how far the employment relationship is structurally conflictual or consensual. In the capitalist labour market, people sell their labour and seek to maximize their pay. To the employer, pay is a cost that, all things being equal, reduces profit and therefore needs to be minimized. Thus, as Brown (1988, p. 57) states, 'Conflict is structured into employment relations' as the benefit to one group is a cost to the other.

The 'effort' or 'work' side of the contract also generates tensions and conflict because it is inherently imprecise and indeterminate. The contract permits the employer to buy a potential level of physical or intellectual labour. The function of management is therefore to transform this potential into actual value-added labour. HR practices are designed to narrow the divide between employees' potential and actual performance or, in Townley's (1994, p. 14) words:

> Personnel practices measure both the physical and subjective dimensions of labour, and offer a technology which aims to render individuals and their behaviour predictable and calculable ... to bridge the gap between promise and

performance, between labour power and labour, and organizes labour into a productive force or power.

The second component of the employment relationship is that it involves a *legal relationship*: a network of contractual and statutory rights and obligations affecting both parties to the contract. Contractual rights are based upon case law (judicial precedent), and the basic rules of contract, in so far as they relate to the contract of employment, are fundamental to the legal relationship between the employer and the employee. It is outside the scope of this chapter to provide a discussion of the rules of contract. But, to use Kahn-Freund's famous phrase, the contract of employment, freely negotiated between an individual and her or his employer, can be considered to be the cornerstone of English employment law (Honeyball, 2010).

Statutory rights refer to an array of legislation that affects the employer–employee relationship and employer–union relationship: the 'right not to be unfairly dismissed' or the 'right to bargain', for example. Statutory employment rights provide a basic minimum or 'floor' of rights for all employees. A complex network of UK and European Union statutory rights regulates the obligations of employers and employees even though these are not (for the most part) formally inserted into the employment contract itself. If they are violated, legal rights can be enforced by some compulsory mechanisms provided by the state, for example a tribunal or the courts. Table 1.1 provides an overview of how UK employment legislation has helped to shape the legal regulation of employment relations. In broad terms, the employment laws of the 1979–97 Conservative government sought to regulate the activities of trade unions. Cumulatively, the changes marked 'a radical shift from the consensus underlying "public policy" on industrial relations during most of the past century' (Hyman, 1987, p. 93). The changes in the law tilted the balance of power in an industrial dispute towards the employer (Brown et al., 1997).

The influence of European Union (EU) law increased steadily during the same period. Although it is not a comprehensive body of employment legislation, EU employment law does draw on the Western European tradition, in which the rights of employees are laid down in constitutional texts and legal codes. Under the 1997 'New Labour' government, a plethora of legislative reform in employment law facilitated trade union organization and collective bargaining and extended protection to individual employees. For example, the 2006 Work and Families Act gave additional protections in relation to pregnancy – the right to maternity leave, time off for antenatal care and the right to maternity pay (Lockton, 2010).

The third distinguishing component of the employment relationship is that it involves a *social relationship*. Employees are not isolated individuals but members of social groups, who observe social norms and mores that influence their actions in the workplace. This observation of human behaviour in the workplace – which has been documented since the 1930s – is highly relevant given the increased

reflective question

Based on your own work experience or that of a friend or relative, can you identify three statutory employment rights?

Table 1.1 Selective UK Employment Statutes and Statutory Instruments, 1961–2007

Year	Act	Year	Act
1961	Factories Act (Safety)	1993	Trade Union Reform and Employment Rights Act
1963/72	Contract of Employment Act		
1965	Industrial Training Act	1996	Employment Rights Act
1968	Race Relations Act	1996	Employment Tribunals Act
1970	Equal Pay Act	1998	Employment Rights (Disputes Resolution) Act
1971	Industrial Relations Act		
1973	Employment and Training Act	1998	National Minimum Wage Act
1974	Health and Safety at Work etc. Act	1999	Employment Relations Act
1974/76	Trade Union and Labour Relations Act	2002	Employment Act
		2003	National Minimum Wage (Enforcement) Act
1975/86	Sex Discrimination Act		
1975	Employment Protection Act	2003	Employment Equality (Sexual Orientation) Regulations
1978	Employment Protection (Consolidation) Act		
		2003	Employment Equality (Religion or Belief) Regulations
1980	Employment Act		
1982	Employment Act	2004	Gender Recognition Act
1984	Trade Union Act	2004	Employment Relations Act
1986	Wages Act	2005	Disability Discrimination Act
1988	Employment Act	2006	Employment Equality (Age) Regulations
1989	Employment Act	2006	Work and Families Act
1990	Employment Act	2006	Equality Act
1992	Trade Union and Labour Relations (Consolidation) Act	2007	Corporate Manslaughter and Corporate Homicide Act

prevalence of work teams. Furthermore, unless the employee happens to be an international football celebrity, the employment relationship embodies an uneven balance of power between the parties. The notion in English law of a 'freely' negotiated individual agreement is misleading. In reality, without collective (trade union) or statutory intervention, the most powerful party, the employer, imposes the agreement by 'the brute facts of power' (Wedderburn, 1986, p. 106).

Inequalities of power in turn structure the nature of work. Most employees experience an extreme division of labour with minimal discretion over how they perform their tasks or opportunity to participate in decision-making processes. Thus, the social dimension is concerned with social relations, social structure and power – *people with power over other people* – rather than with the legal technicalities between the parties. As such, employment relations are deeply textured and profoundly sociological (Bratton et al., 2009). Looking at the development of the mainstream HRM canon over the last 25 years, it can be seen how little these inherent inequalities figure, despite the fact that they can be readily observed in the contemporary workplace.

In recent years, mainstream HRM scholarship has focused on another component of the employment relationship: the *psychological contract*. This is conceptualized as a dynamic two-way exchange of perceived promises and obligations between employees and their employer. The concept has become a 'fashionable' framework within which to study aspects of the employment relationship (Guest and Conway, 2002; Rousseau and Ho, 2000). The 'psychological contract' is a metaphor that captures a wide variety of largely unwritten expectations and understandings of the two parties about their mutual obligations. Rousseau (1995, p. 9) defines this

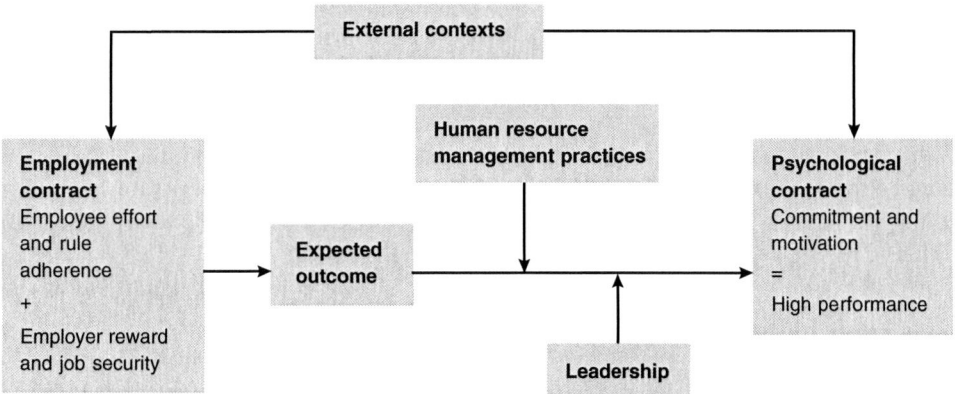

Figure 1.1 The employment and psychological contract between employees and employers

as 'individual beliefs, shaped by the organization, regarding terms of an exchange agreement between individuals and their organization'. Guest and Conway (2002, p. 22) define it as 'the perceptions of both parties to the employment relationship – organization and individual – of the reciprocal promises and obligations implied in that relationship'. At the heart of the concept of the psychological contract are levers for individual commitment, motivation and task performance beyond the 'expected outcomes' (Figure 1.1).

The psychological contract has a number of important features that employers need to appreciate. First, ineffective practices may communicate different beliefs about the reciprocal promises and obligations that are present (Guest and Conway, 2002). Thus, individuals will have different perceptions of their psychological contract, even when the legal contract is identical. Managers will therefore be faced with a multitude of perceived psychological contracts (PPCs) within the same organization (Bendal et al., 1998). Second, the PPC reaffirms the notion that the employment relationship is thought to be one of exchange – the promissory exchange of offers and the mutual obligation of the employer and employee to fulfil these offers. Third, PPCs are shaped in particular contexts, which includes HR practices. Rousseau argues that HR practices 'send strong messages to individuals regarding what the organization expects of them and what they can expect in return' (Rousseau, 1995, pp. 182–3). In the current post-crisis era, 'downsizing' has become a ubiquitous fact of organizational life (Datta et al., 2010; Mellahi and Wilkinson, 2010). Research suggests that those organizations downsizing can reduce the likelihood of psychological contract violation by ensuring that HR practices contribute to employees' perceptions of 'procedural fairness' (Arshad and Sparrow, 2010).

On any reading, the essence of the PPC thesis is the idea that a workforce is a collection of free, independent people, as though individual beliefs are fixed features of an employee's day-to-day behaviour. However, this addresses concerns of individual motivation and commitment within a *unitary* ideological framework. In doing this, in total contrast to critical paradigms, it neglects a well-established body of research grounded in sociology showing that people's beliefs and expectations about employment form *outside* the workplace. The work experiences of parents, for instance, shape the attitudes and career aspirations of their teenage children. The idea that family members and peer groups can influence expectations about career opportunities and the everyday reality of work is called 'orientation to work' (Goldthorpe et al., 1968; Hyman and Brough, 1975).

> **reflective question**
>
> What do you think of the concept of the psychological contract? Why does there appear to be more interest now in managing it? How important is it to manage the psychological contract for (1) non-managerial employees, and (2) managerial employees?

Scope and functions of HRM

HRM is a body of knowledge and an assortment of practices to do with the organization of work and the management of employment relations. The mainstream literature identifies three major subdomains of knowledge: micro, strategic and international (Boxall et al., 2008).

The largest subdomain refers to *micro HRM* (MHRM), which is concerned with managing individual employees and small work groups. It covers areas such as HR planning, job design, recruitment and selection, performance management, training and development, and rewards. These HR subfunctions cover a myriad of evidence-based practices, training techniques and payment systems, for instance, many of them informed by psychology-oriented studies of work (see, for example, Warr, 2008). The second domain is *strategic HRM* (SHRM), which concerns itself with the processes of linking HR strategies with business strategies and measures the effects on organizational performance. The third domain is *international HRM* (IHRM), which focuses on the management of people in companies operating in more than one country.

Drawing on the work of Squires (2001), these three major subdomains help us address three basic questions:

- What do HRM professionals do?
- What affects what they do?
- How do they do what they do?

To help us answer the first question, the work of Harzing (2000), Millward et al. (2000) and Ulrich (1997) identifies the key *MHRM* subfunctions of HR policies, programmes and practices that have been designed in response to organizational goals and contingencies, and have been managed to achieve those goals. Each function contains alternatives from which managers can choose. How the HR function is organized and how much power it has relative to that of other management functions is affected by both external and internal factors unique to the establishment. A regulation-oriented national business system, with strong trade unions, employment laws on equity and affirmative action, and occupational health and safety regulations, elevates the status of the HR manager and strengthens the corporate HR function. In contrast, a market-oriented corporate culture, with employee pay based on going market rates, minimum investment in employee training and shorter employment contracts, is associated with outsourcing and decentralization of the HR function, which weakens the corporate HR function (Jacoby, 2005).

The size of the organization also appears to negatively affect the extent to which HR services are provided internally by HR specialists from the central HR unit. Klass et al.'s (2005) study, for example, found that an increasing number of small and medium-sized organizations – defined as those with 500 or fewer employees – have established a business relationship with a professional employer organization that assumes responsibility for delivering their HR services and interventions, a process usually referred to as 'outsourcing'. Klass et al. argue that the choice is not between an internal HR department and outsourcing the HR services, but is one in which limited resources mean that it is a case of either obtaining HR expertise and services externally or foregoing such services. In addition, an increasing number of European organizations have transferred responsibility for their HR functions from the central HR department to line management. This process of 'decentralization' has occurred as HR has assumed a more strategic role (Andolšek and Štebe, 2005; CIPD, 2006a).

SHRM underscores the need for the HR strategy to be integrated with other management functions, and highlights the responsibility of line management to foster the high commitment and motivation associated with high-performing work systems. SHRM is also concerned with managing sustainability, including, for example, establishing a low-carbon work system and organization, communicating this vision, setting clear expectations for creating a sustainable workplace, and developing the capability to reorganize people and reallocate other resources to achieve the vision. As part of the integrative process, all managers are expected to better comprehend the strategic nature of 'best' or better HR practices, to execute them more skilfully, and at the same time to intervene to affect the 'mental models', attitudes and behaviours needed, for instance, to build a high-performing sustainable culture (Pfeffer, 2005). Furthermore, national systems of employment regulation shape SHRM: 'the stronger the institutional framework ... the less [sic] options a company may have to impose its own approach to regulating its HRM' (Andolšek and Štebe, 2005, p. 327).

HRM web links

Go to the website of the 2004 Workplace Employment Relations Survey (www.dti.gov.uk/employment/research-evaluation/grants/wers/index.html) for data on the job responsibilities of HR specialists. Has there been any change in the functions performed by HR specialists over the past decade? Are HR specialists involved in all the key areas of activity described in the text?

The peculiarities of national employment systems and national culture shape the employment relationship, and these forces and processes create different tendencies in HR practice operating across national boundaries. As such, they relate to the second question we posed earlier – what affects what managers and HR professional do? The HR activities that managers perform vary from one workplace to another depending upon the contingencies affecting the organization. These contingencies can be divided into three broad categories: external context, strategy and organization. The external category reinforces the notion that organizations and society are part of the same set of processes – that organizations are *embedded* within a particular market society that encompasses the economic and cultural aspects. The external variables frame the context for formulating competitive strategies. The internal organizational contingencies include size, work, structure and technology. Global as well as local factors can affect what managers do. For those managers in companies that cross national boundaries, *micro* HR policies and practices relating to global and local recruitment and selection, training and development, rewards and the management of expatriates will be affected by a particular country's institutional structure and cultural setting. These micro HR functions, when integrated with different *macro* contexts and overall strategy considerations, define the subdomain of *IHRM*.

It is important, therefore, to recognize that HR policies and practices are contingent upon external and internal contexts and are fundamentally interrelated. For example, a company responding to competitive pressures may change its manufacturing strategy by introducing 'self-managed' teams. This will in turn cause changes in recruitment and selection (for example, hiring people perceived to be 'team players'), and training and reward priorities (for example, designing crossfunctional training and designing a reward system that encourages the sharing of information and learning). HR practices, therefore, aim to achieve two objectives: to produce a synergy that improves employee performance and to enhance organizational effectiveness.

The third of our three basic questions – how do managers and HR professionals do what they do? – requires us to discuss the means or skills by which managers accomplish their HRM goals. Managers and HR specialists use technical, cognitive and interpersonal – such as mentoring and coaching – processes and skills to accomplish their managerial work (Agashae and Bratton, 2001; Senge, 1990; Squires, 2001; Yukl, 2005). Power is important because it is part of the influence process, as are legal procedures. In addition, communication practices and skills convey the formal and psychological contract to employees (Guest and Conway, 2002). Managing people is complex, and individual managers vary in terms of their capacity or inclination to use established processes and skills. These processes and skills therefore concern human relationships and go some way to explaining different management styles and the distinction between a manager and a leader (Bratton et al., 2004a). The micro, strategic and international domains, the contingencies influencing domestic and international HR policies and practices, and managerial skills are combined and diagrammatically shown in a three-dimensional model in Figure 1.2.

The model implies not only that HRM is a multidimensional activity, but also that its analysis has to be multidirectional (Squires, 2001). We might, for that reason, examine the effect of new technology (a contingency) on HR functions, such as training and development, and how HR functions are translated into action, such as learning processes. The model is useful in other ways too: it serves as a pedagogical device that allows its users to discover and connect a specific aspect of HRM within a consistent, general framework. It also helps to develop an 'analytical

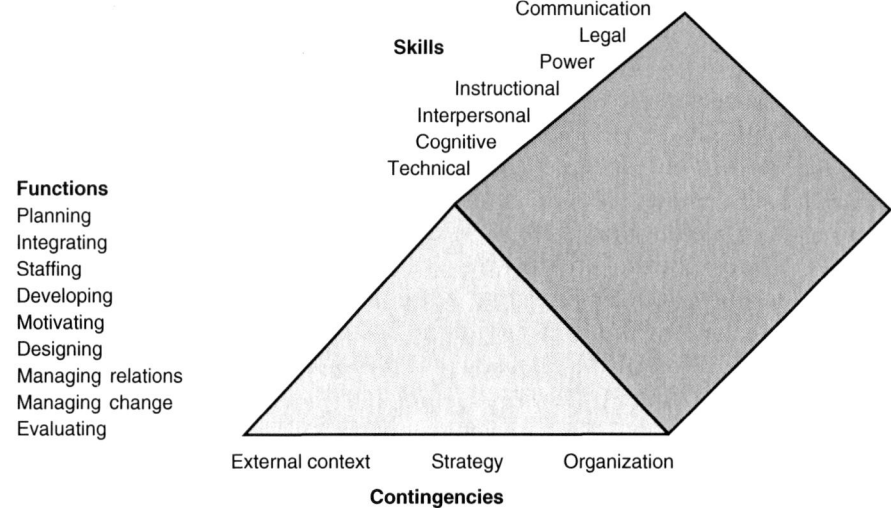

Figure 1.2 HRM functions, contingencies and skills
Source: Adapted from Squires (2001).

conception' of HRM by building theory and generating data based on managers' *actual* social actions in managing work and people across workplaces, sectors and different market societies (Boxall et al., 2008) – the classic rhetoric–reality gap notably highlighted by Legge (1995, 2005). It also offers HR specialists a sense of professional 'identity' by detailing professional functions, processes and skills. Finally, it helps HR specialists to look beyond their immediate tasks and to be aware of the 'totality of management' (Squires, 2001, p. 482).

HRM web links

Go to the website of the HR professional associations (for example Australia www.hrhq.com; Britain www.cipd.co.uk; Canada www.hrpa.org; or the USA www.shrm.org). Click on the 'Accreditation and/or certification' button. Using the information you find, compare the practices that HR professionals are formally accredited to practise with those practices listed in Figure 1.2. Does the information on the website give a comprehensive picture of 'What HRM specialists do'?

Theoretical perspectives on HRM

Practice without theory is blind. (Hyman, 1989, p. xiv)

So far, we have focused on the meaning of management and on a range of HRM practices used in the contemporary workplace. We have explained that HRM varies across organizations and market societies depending upon a range of external and internal contingencies. In addition, we have identified the skills by which managers accomplish their HRM goals. We will now turn to an important part of the

HRM in practice 1.2: Twenty-first-century senior hr leaders have a changing role

Early debate on HRM centred on the question 'How does HRM differ from personnel management?' For some, HRM represents a new approach to managing people because, in theory at least, it was envisioned to be integrated into strategic planning. HRM models also make reference to performance outcomes, predicting that a coherent 'bundle' of HR practices will enhance employee commitment and improve performance. To meet the challenges of the twenty-first century, it is argued, organizations therefore need a new senior manager, the chief human resources officer (CHRO). As one writer put it:

> *The modern CHRO is required increasingly to act as both strategist and steward. Jeff Schwartz, of Deloitte Consulting, said: 'The requirements and perception of HR are changing dramatically as this function's leadership is now expected to play a central role in building and shaping – not just staffing – the enterprise strategy.' 'The role of the CHRO as an enterprise business leader is still evolving – but this transformation has never been more timely or relevant.' 'This is an environment that HR leaders have longed for – where their executive peers would view HR as a business partner, rather than as a back-office administrator.'*[1]

In contrast, detractors argue that HRM is more a matter of repackaging 'progressive' personnel management. They emphasize that relatively few organizations have integrated HRM planning into strategic business planning, a central element in the HRM model. They also point to the incontrovertible evidence of a shift towards 'individually oriented' cultures that is symbolized by the growth of contingency pay, as well as the fact that a large proportion of UK firms are still preoccupied with traditional cost-focus strategies. The empirical

Source: ©istockphoto.com/Daniel Laflor.

evidence therefore suggests a lack of fit between knowledge of the normative HRM model and actual management practice.

> **Stop!** Debates on HRM offer an interesting perspective on the issues of state intervention in a market society. Among academics, HRM is highly contentious, and its antecedents, its defining characteristics and its outcomes are much disputed. What is your view? Is HRM different from personnel management?

Sources and further information:

[1]Deloitte Consulting's *Strategist and Steward* report, available at www.deloitte.com/us, and search for 'Strategist and Steward'. For a discussion on employee commitment and HRM, see Guest (1998); for evidence of the growth of 'individualism', see Kersley et al. (2005); and for further insight into the HRM debate, see Legge (2005).

Note: This feature was written by John Bratton.

---

mainstream HRM discourse – the search for the defining features and goals of HRM – by exploring the theoretical perspectives in this area.

Over the past two decades, HRM scholars have debated the meaning of the term 'human resource management' and attempted to define its fundamental traits by producing polar or multiconceptual models. A number of polar models contrast the fundamental traits of HRM with those of traditional personnel management, while others provide statements on employer goals and HR outcomes. These models help to focus debate around such questions as 'What is the difference between HRM and personnel management?' and 'What outcomes are employers seeking when they implement a HRM approach? Here, we identify six major HRM models that seek to demonstrate in analytical terms the distinctiveness and goals of HRM (Beer et al., 1984; Fombrun et al., 1984; Guest, 1987; Hendry and Pettigrew, 1990; Storey, 1992). These models fulfil at least four important intellectual functions for those studying HRM:

- They provide an analytical framework for studying HRM (for example, HR practices, situational factors, stakeholders, strategic choice levels and HR and performance outcomes).
- They legitimize HRM. For those advocating 'Invest in People', the models help to demonstrate to sceptics the legitimacy and effectiveness of HRM. A key issue here is the distinctiveness of HRM practices: 'it is not the presence of selection or training but a *distinctive approach* to selection or training that matters. It is the use of high performance or high commitment HRM practices' (Guest, 1997, p. 273, emphasis added).
- They provide a characterization of HRM that establishes the variables and relationships to be researched.
- They serve as a heuristic device – something to help us discover and understand the world of work – for explaining the nature and significance of key HR practices and HR outcomes.

The Fombrun, Tichy and Devanna model of HRM

The early HRM model developed by Fombrun et al. (1984) emphasizes the fundamental interrelatedness and coherence of HRM activities. The HRM 'cycle' in their model consists of four key constituent components: selection, appraisal, development and rewards. In terms of the overarching goals of HRM, these four HR activities are linked to the firm's performance. The weaknesses of Fombrun et al.'s model are its apparently prescriptive nature and its focus on four HR practices. It also ignores different stakeholder interests, situational factors and the notion of management's strategic choice. The strength of the model, however, is that it expresses the coherence of internal HR policies and the importance of 'matching' internal HR policies and practices to the organization's external business strategy. The notion of the 'HRM cycle' is useful as a heuristic framework for explaining the nature and significance of key HR practices that make up the complex field of HRM.

The Harvard model of HRM

As was widely acknowledged in the early HRM literature, the 'Harvard model' offered by Beer et al. (1984) provided one of the first comprehensive statements on the nature of HRM and the issue of management goals and specific HR outcomes. The Harvard framework (Figure 1.3) consists of six basic components:

1. Situational factors
2. Stakeholder interests
3. HRM policy choices

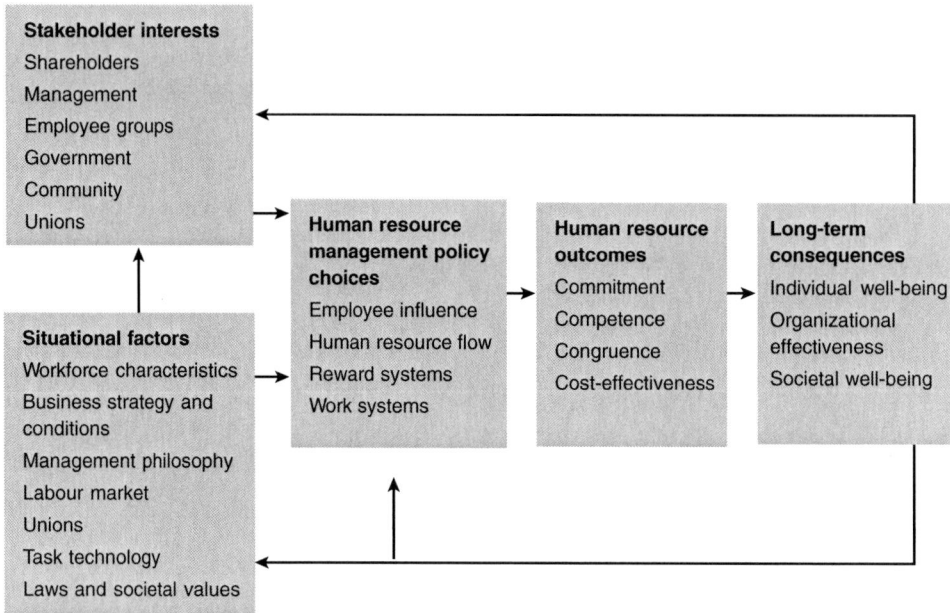

Figure 1.3 The Harvard model of HRM
Source: Beer, M. et al. (1984), Managing Human Assets, The Free Press.

4. HR outcomes
5. Long-term consequences
6. A feedback loop through which the outputs flow directly into the organization and to the stakeholders.

In the Harvard model of HRM, the *situational factors* influence management's choice of HR strategy. This normative model incorporates workforce characteristics, management philosophy, labour market regulations, societal values and patterns of unionization, and suggests a meshing of 'product market' and 'sociocultural logics' (Evans and Lorange, 1989). Analytically, both HRM scholars and practitioners will be more comfortable if contextual variables are included in the model because this reflects the reality of what they know: 'the employment relationship entails a blending of business and societal expectations' (Boxall, 1992, p. 72).

The *stakeholder interests* recognize the importance of 'trade-offs', either explicitly or implicitly, between the interests of business owners and those of employees and their organizations, the trade unions. Although the model is still vulnerable to the charge of 'unitarism', it is a much more pluralist frame of reference than is found in later models.

HRM policy choices emphasize that management's decisions and actions in HR management can be fully appreciated only if it is recognized that they result from an interaction between constraints and choices. The model depicts management as a real actor, capable of making at least some degree of unique contribution within the environmental and organizational parameters present and of influencing those parameters itself over time (Beer et al., 1984).

In terms of understanding the importance of management's goals, the *HR outcomes* of high employee commitment and competence are linked to longer term effects on organizational effectiveness and societal well-being. The underlying assumptions built into the framework are that employees have talents that are rarely fully utilized in the contemporary workplace, and that they show a desire to experience growth through work. Thus, HRM is indivisible from a 'humanistic message' about human growth and dignity at work. In other words, the Harvard framework takes the view that employment relations should be managed on the basis of the assumptions inherent in McGregor's (1960) classic approach to people-related issues, commonly called 'Theory Y', or, to use contemporary parlance, in conditions of human dignity at work.

The *long-term consequences* distinguish between three levels: individual, organizational and societal. At the level of the individual employee, the long-term HR outputs comprise the psychological rewards that workers receive in exchange for their effort. At the organizational level, increased effectiveness ensures the survival of the firm. In turn, at the societal level, as a result of fully utilizing people at work, some of society's goals (for example, employment and growth) are attained. The strength of the Harvard model lies in its classification of inputs and outcomes at both the organizational and the societal level, creating the basis for a critique of comparative HRM (Boxall, 1992). A weakness, however, is the absence of a coherent theoretical basis for measuring the relationship between HR inputs, outcomes and performance (Guest, 1997).

The sixth component of the Harvard model is a *feedback loop*. As we have discussed, situational factors influence HRM policy and choices. Conversely, however, long-term outputs can influence the situational factors, stakeholder interests and HR policies, and the feedback loop in Figure 1.3 reflects this two-way relationship.

As was observed by Boxall (1992), the Harvard model clearly provides a useful analytical basis for the study of HRM. It also contains elements that are analytical (that is, situational factors, stakeholders and strategic choice levels) and prescriptive (that is, notions of commitment, competence, and so on).

The Guest model of HRM

In David Guest's (1989, 1997) framework, different approaches to labour management are examined in the context of goals, employee behaviour, performance and long-term financial outcomes. According to this HRM model, managers are advised to consider the effects of a core set of integrated HR practices on individual and organizational performance.

For Guest, HRM differs significantly from personnel management, and he attempts to identify the major assumptions or stereotypes underpinning each approach to employment management. Personnel management seeks 'compliance', whereas HRM seeks 'commitment' from employees. In personnel management, the psychological contract is expressed in terms of a 'fair day's work for a fair day's pay', whereas in HRM it is 'reciprocal commitment'. In the area of employee relations, personnel management is said to be pluralist, collective and 'low trust', whereas HRM is unitarist, individual and 'high trust'. The points of differences between personnel management and HRM are also reflected in the design of organizations. Thus, organizations adopting the personnel management model exhibit 'mechanistic', top-down and centralized design features, whereas firms adopting HRM are allegedly 'organic', bottom-up and decentralized. Finally, the policy goals of personnel management and HRM are different. In the former, they are administrative efficiency, standard performance and minimization of cost. In contrast, the policy goals of HRM are an adaptive workforce, an improvement in performance and maximum utilization of human potential.

According to these stereotypes, HRM is distinctively different from personnel management because: (1) it integrates HR into strategic management; (2) it seeks employees' commitment to organizational goals; (3) the HR perspective is unitary with a focus on the individual; (4) it works better in organizations that have an 'organic' structure; and (5) employer goals prioritize the full utilization of human assets.

Implicit in the contrasting stereotypes is an assumption that the dominant HRM model is 'better' (allowing enhanced commitment and flexibility) within the current more flexible labour markets and in decentralized, flexible, empowering and organic organizational structures. However, as Guest correctly states, 'variations in context ... might limit its effectiveness' (1987, p. 508). The central hypothesis of Guest's (1997) framework is that managers should adopt a distinct set or 'bundle' of HR practices in a coherent fashion; the outcome will be superior individual and organizational performance.

Guest's model has six components:

1. An HR strategy
2. A set of HR policies
3. A set of HR outcomes
4. Behavioural outcomes

5. Performance outcomes
6. Financial outcomes.

The model acknowledges the close links between HR strategy and the general business strategies of differentiation, focus and cost. The 'core' hypothesis, however, is that HR practices should be designed to lead to a set of HR outcomes of 'high employee commitment', 'high quality' and 'flexibility'. Like Beer et al., Guest sees high employee commitment as a critical HR outcome, concerned with the employer's goals of binding employees to the organization and obtaining the behavioural outcomes of increased effort, cooperation and organizational citizenship. 'Quality' refers to all aspects of employee behaviour that relate directly to the quality of goods and services. Flexibility is concerned with how receptive employees are to innovation and change. The model focuses on the link between HR practices and performance. Only when all three HR outcomes – commitment, quality and flexibility – are achieved can superior performance outcomes be expected. As Guest (1989, 1997) emphasizes, these HRM goals are a 'package': 'Only when a coherent strategy, directed towards these four policy goals, fully integrated into business strategy and fully sponsored by line management at all levels is applied will the high productivity and related outcomes sought by industry be achieved' (1990, p. 378).

Guest (1987, 1989, 1997) recognizes a number of conceptual issues associated with the dominant HRM model. The first is that the values underpinning the model are predominantly individualist-oriented: 'There is no recognition of any broader concept of pluralism within society giving rise to solidaristic collective orientation' (Guest, 1987, p. 519). The second concerns the status of some of the concepts, such as that of commitment, which is suggested to be 'a rather messy, ill-defined concept' (Guest, 1987, pp. 513–14). A third issue is the explicit link between HRM and performance. This raises the problem of deciding which types of performance indicators to use in order to establish the links between HR practices and performance. It has been argued elsewhere that Guest's model may simply be a polar 'ideal type' towards which organizations can move, thus proposing unrealistic conditions for the practice of HRM (Keenoy, 1990, p. 367). It may also make the error of criticizing managers for not conforming to an image constructed by academics (Boxall, 1992). Furthermore, it presents the HRM model as being inconsistent with collective approaches to managing the employment relationship (Legge, 1989).

In contrast, the strength of the Guest model is that it clearly maps out the field of HRM and classifies its inputs and outcomes. The model is useful for examining the key employer goals usually associated with the normative models of HRM: strategic integration, commitment, flexibility and quality. The constituents of the model hypothesizing a relationship between specific HR practices and performance can be empirically tested by research. Guest's constructed set of theoretical propositions can also provide a framework for a critical dialogue on the precise nature, tensions and contradictions of HRM.

The Warwick model of HRM

The Warwick model emanated from the Centre for Corporate Strategy and Change at the University of Warwick, UK, and with two particular researchers: Hendry and

Pettigrew (1990). The Warwick framework extends the Harvard model by drawing on its analytical aspects. The model takes account of business strategy and HR practices, the external and internal context in which these activities take place and the processes by which such changes take place, including interactions between changes in both context and content. The strength of the model is that it identifies and classifies important environmental influences on HRM. It maps the connections between the outer (wider environment) and the inner (organizational) contexts, and explores how HRM adapts to changes in context. The implication is that those organizations achieving an alignment between the external and internal contexts will experience superior performance. A weakness of the model is that the process whereby internal HR practices are linked to business output or performance is not developed. The five elements of the model are as follows:

1. Outer context – socioeconomic, technical, political-legal, competitive
2. Inner context – culture, structure, leadership, task-technology, business outputs
3. Business strategy content – objectives, product market, strategy and tactics
4. HRM context – role, definition, organization, HR outputs
5. HRM content – HR flows, work systems, reward systems, employee relations.

The Storey model of HRM

The Storey framework attempts to demonstrate the differences between what John Storey terms the 'personnel and industrials' and the HRM paradigm by creating an 'ideal type'. He devised the model by reconstructing the 'implicit models' conveyed by some managers during research interviews. We should note that the usage of an 'ideal type' is a popular heuristic tool in the social sciences. It is a 'mental image' and cannot actually be found in any real workplace. Its originator Max Weber wrote in *The Methodology of the Social Sciences,* that 'In its conceptual purity, this mental construct [*Gedankenbild*] cannot be found empirically anywhere in reality' (Bratton et al., 2009, p. 216). An ideal type is not a description of reality; neither is it an average of something, or a normative exemplar to be achieved. It is a *Utopia*. Its purpose is to act as a comparison with empirical reality in order to establish the differences or similarities between the two positions, and to understand and explain causal relationships.

Storey posits that the HRM model emerged in the UK as a 'historically situated phenomenon' and is 'an amalgam of description, prescription, and logical deduction' (Storey, 2001, p. 6). The four main elements in his HRM framework (Table 1.2) are:

- Beliefs and assumptions
- Strategic aspects
- Role of line managers
- Key levers.

According to the stereotypes depicted in Table 1.2, the HRM 'recipe' of ideas and practices prescribes certain priorities. In this framework, the most fundamental *belief and assumption* is the notion that, ultimately, among all the factors of production, it is labour that really distinguishes successful firms from mediocre

Table 1.2 The Storey model of HRM

Personnel and industrial relations (IR) and human resource management (HRM): the differences

Dimension	Personnel and IR	HRM
Beliefs and assumptions		
Contract	Careful delineation of written contracts	Aim to go 'beyond contract'
Rules	Importance of devising clear rules/mutuality	'Can do' outlook; impatience with 'rules'
Guide to management action	Procedures/consistency/control	'Business need'/flexibility/commitment
Behaviour referent	Norms/custom and practice	Values/mission
Managerial task vis-à-vis labour	Monitoring	Nurturing
Nature of relations	Pluralist	Unitarist
Conflict	Institutionalised	De-emphasised
Standardisation	High (for example 'parity' an issue)	Low (for example 'parity' not seen as relevant)
Strategic aspects		
Key relations	Labour–management	Business–customer
Initiatives	Piecemeal	Integrated
Corporate plan	Marginal to	Central to
Speed of decision	Slow	Fast
Line management		
Management role	Transactional	Transformational leadership
Key managers	Personnel/IR specialists	General/business/line managers
Prized management skills	Negotiation	Facilitation
Key levers		
Foci of attention for interventions	Personnel procedures	Wide-ranging cultural, structural and personnel strategies
Selection	Separate, marginal task	Integrated, key task
Pay	Job evaluation; multiple fixed grades	Performance-related; few if any grades
Conditions	Separately negotiated	Harmonisation
Labour–management	Collective bargaining contracts	Towards individual contracts
Thrust of relations with stewards	Regularised through facilities and training	Marginalised (with exception of some bargaining for change models)
Communication	Restricted flow/indirect	Increased flow/direct
Job design	Division of labour	Teamwork
Conflict handling	Reach temporary truces	Manage climate and culture
Training and development	Controlled access to courses	Learning companies

Source: Storey (1992).

ones. It follows logically from this that employees ought to be nurtured as a valued asset and not simply regarded as a cost. Moreover, another underlying belief is that the employer's goal should not merely be to seek employees' compliance with rules, but to 'strive' for 'commitment and engagement' that goes 'beyond the contract' (Storey, 2001). The *strategic qualities* contained in Storey's framework show that HRM is a matter of critical importance to corporate planning. In Storey's words, 'decisions about human resources policies should ... take their cue from an explicit alignment of the competitive environment, business strategy and HRM strategy' (p. 10).

HRM AND GLOBALIZATION
The HRM model in advancing economies?

Contemporary globalization is the defining political economic paradigm of our time. In terms of HR strategy, HRM policies and practices have to be aligned to the global activities of transnational enterprises, and must be able to attract and retain employees operating internationally but within different national employment structures. The word 'globalization' became ubiquitous in the 1990s. It was, and still is, a thoroughly contested concept depending on whether scholars view it as primarily an economic, a political or a social phenomenon.

In the economic sphere, globalization is understood as a worldwide process of integration of production and consumption resulting from the reduction of transport and communication costs – a global system of economic interdependences. Arguments that build only on these technical conceptions emphasize the positive aspects of globalization, and draw attention to the outsourcing of manufacturing jobs to China and India from high-wage Western economies. The economic argument is captured by this extract from a Foresight2020 research report:

> On a per-capita basis, China and India will remain far poorer than Western markets and the region faces a host of downside risks,' Laza Kekic, director of forecasting services at the Economist Intelligence Unit, says. 'Asia will narrow the gap in wealth, power and influence, but will not close it.' The report assumes that world economic growth depends on the pace of globalization. Labour-intensive production will continue to shift to lower-cost countries but the report concludes that fears of the death of Western manufacturing are premature. Workers in the low-cost economies will

Source: ©istockphoto.com/Jessica Liu.

> *benefit but Chinese average wages, for example, will rise only to about 15% of the developed-country average in 2020 compared with today's 5%.*
>
> Writers who conceptualize globalization in terms of politics and power argue that 'big business' has relegated national governments to being the 'gatekeepers' of free unfettered markets. Because there is little competition from alternative ideologies, twenty-first century capitalism 'is more mobile, more ruthless and more certain about what it needs to make it tick' (Giddens and Hutton, 2000, p. 9). Modern capitalism has been called a 'febrile capitalism' that is serving the needs of Wall Street and the financial and stock markets.
>
> > **Stop!** Critics charge that national governments have lost power over their own economies as a handful of large corporations are being permitted to control natural resources and social life. In other words, civil society is perceived principally through the 'prism of economics'. Take a moment to assess critically the various standpoints in the globalization debate. What economic and political forces encourage outsourcing? What are the implications of outsourcing for HRM?
>
> **Sources and further information:**
>
> See Giddens and Hutton (2000), Hoogvelt (2001), Chomsky (1999), and Gereffi and Christian (2009). To download Foresight2020 free of charge, visit www.eiu.com/foresight2020.
>
> *Note:* This feature was written by John Bratton.

The third component, *line management*, argues that general managers, and not HRM specialists, are vital to the effective delivery of HRM practices (Purcell et al., 2009). Research evidence from 15 UK 'core' organizations suggests that line managers have emerged in almost all cases as the crucial players in HR issues (Storey, 1992).

The *key levers* element in the model focuses on the methods used to implement HRM. In researcher–manager interviews on HRM, Storey found considerable unevenness in the adoption of these key levers, such as performance-related pay, harmonization of conditions and investment to produce a work-related learning company. What is persuasive about the HRM narrative, observes Storey (2007), is evidence of a shift away from personnel procedures and rules as a basis of good practice, to the management of organizational culture as proof of avant-garde practice.

Ulrich's strategic partner model of HRM

To overcome the traditional marginalization of the personnel function and to strengthen the status of the profession, the UK Chartered Institute for Personnel and Development (CIPD) has long sought to demonstrate the added value of HR activities in business terms. Such a position requires a transition from the functional

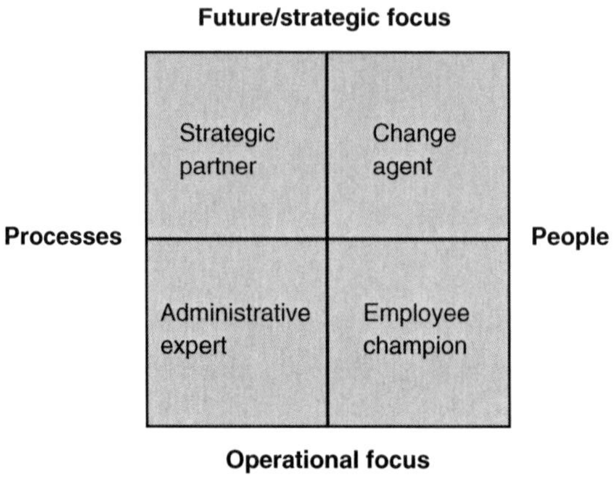

HRM / HRD IN ITS CONTEMPORARY CONTEXT

Future/strategic focus

	Processes	People
	Strategic partner	Change agent
	Administrative expert	Employee champion

Operational focus

Figure 1.4 Ulrich's human resources business partner model

HR orientation, with the HR department primarily involved in administering policies, towards a partnership orientation, with the HR professional engaged in *strategic* decisions that impact on organizational design and organizational performance. In the last decade, the HRM model most favoured to support such a move has been provided by David Ulrich's (1997) 'business partner' model. Ulrich presents a framework showing four key roles that HR professionals must accomplish in order to add the greatest value to the organization (Figure 1.4). The two axes represent focus and activities. HR professionals must focus on both the strategic and the operational, in the both the long and the short term. Activities range from managing processes to managing people. Therefore these two axes delineate four principal roles:

- *Strategic partner* – future/strategic focus combined with processes
- *Change agent* – future/strategic focus combined with people
- *Administrative expert* – operational focus combined with process
- *Employee champion* – operational focus combined with people.

A later variant of the model integrates the change agent role into the strategic partner role, and gives greater emphasis to HR professionals playing a leadership role (Ulrich and Brockbank, 2005). As such, the first two roles require a strategic orientation; for example, as a strategic partner, HR professionals work with other managers to formulate and execute strategy, and as a change agent, they facilitate transformation and significant change. During the 2000s, the Ulrich business partner model was widely espoused in the mainstream HRM literature, partly because of the perceived increase in status and prestige of HRM, because the strategic partner and change agent roles proved highly attractive to many ambitious HR practitioners, and because of its rhetorical simplicity (Brown et al., 2004). Furthermore, the administrative role provides for processes to 're-engineer' the organization towards great efficiency, while the employee champion relates to listening to employees and providing resources for employees. Research shows, however, that, of the small sample surveyed, few HR practitioners considered their primary roles to be those of the 'less trendy' employee champion and administrative expert (Guest and King, 2004; Hope-Hailey et al., 2005).

Although it has been influential, the way in which this model has been implemented would suggest a degree of pragmatism, probably to reduce cost, with the four roles being combined into three, but with implications for how HR departments are structured (Reilly et al., 2007). For example, administrative roles would be structured into a shared services centre, with the task of providing cost-effective processes to run transactional services such as payroll, absence monitoring and simple advice for employees. Centres of excellence provide specialist knowledge and development to produce innovations in more complex areas such as talent, engagement and leadership and management development. Strategic business partners take on the work with managers and leaders, influencing and helping the formation of strategy, perhaps as members of a management team.

Perhaps inevitably, the role of the strategic business partner attracts most attention, while the employee champion role, which concerns the well-being of staff, tends to be left to line managers and is therefore likely to be neglected (Francis and Keegan, 2006). With the recession following the 2008 financial crisis, there has been concern with sustaining organizational performance through leadership, shared purpose, engagement, assessment and evaluation, agility and capacity-building (CIPD, 2011). It is, however, suggested that none of these can be achieved without a good process of learning and development for HR practitioners. Despite the popularity of the business partners' model, a survey of managers revealed that only 47 per cent polled believed that Ulrich's model was successful in their organization, and 25 per cent said the model was ineffective (Pitcher, 2008).

HRM web links

For more information on Ulrich's HRM model, go to: http://hrmadvice.com/hrmadvice/hr-role/ulrichs-hr-roles-model.html.

reflective question

Reviewing the six models, what beliefs and assumptions are implied in them? What similarities and/or differences can you see? How well does each model define the characteristics of HRM? Is there a contradiction between the roles of 'change agent' and 'employee champion' as outlined in Ulrich's model? Is it realistic to expect HR professionals to be 'employee champions'?

Studying HRM

It has become commonplace to point out that HRM is not a discipline in its own right, but a field of study drawing upon concepts and theories from core social science disciplines including anthropology, psychology, sociology, law and political science. This provides relatively elastic boundaries within which to analyse how the employment relationship is structured and managed. In addition, these elastic boundaries generate multiple ways of making sense of the same organizational phenomenon or the differing standpoints found in the HRM canon.

How we understand work and HRM is very much influenced by key social discourses, a discourse being a number of ideas that together form a powerful body of thought that influences how people think and act. Management in the twenty-first century is being influenced by multiple social discourses that include globalization, environmental destruction, social injustice and fundamental neo-liberal economic failure. We should also note that management research and education is going through a process of post-crisis reflexivity (Currie et al., 2010).

In understanding the recent debate that management education and pedagogy should be more reflexive and critical, it is crucial to develop a knowledge base of competing ideological perspectives or paradigms. For our purposes here, we will define paradigms as established frameworks of interrelated values, beliefs and assumptions that social science scholars use to organize their reasoning and research. Each paradigm in the social sciences makes certain bold assertions about the nature of social reality and, in turn, provides legitimacy and justification for people's actions (Babbie and Benaquisto, 2010). When people ask, 'What paradigm are you using?' they might just as well be asking, 'What is your own bias on this aspect of social life?', as each paradigm has a particular bias based on a particular version of knowing about social reality (Hughes, 1990). Paradigms are a 'lens' through which we view the world of work. Thus, when we refer to a particular paradigm to study the HRM phenomenon, we are speaking of an interconnected set of beliefs, values and intentions that legitimize HR theory and practice. For the purpose of developing a critical, analytical conception of HRM, we will in this section compare and contrast three major paradigms – *structural-functionalism*, *conflict* and *feminism* – that have emerged to make sense of work, organizations and HRM.

The intellectual roots of the *structural-functional paradigm* can be traced to the work of the French philosopher Auguste Comte (1798–1857) and French sociologist Emile Durkheim (1858–1917). Comte believed that society could be studied and understood logically and rationally, and he used the term *positivism* to describe this research approach. Durkheim studied social order and argued that the increased division of labour in modern societies created what he called 'organic solidarity', which maintained social harmony: 'The division of labour becomes the chief source of social solidarity, it becomes, at the same time, the foundation of moral order' (Durkheim, 1933/1997, p. 333).

The popularity of the structural-functionalist approach is commonly attributed to the US sociologist Talcott Parsons (Mann, 2011). For Parsons, organizations can function in a stable and orderly manner only on the basis of shared values. In his words: 'The problem of order, and thus the nature of the integration of stable systems of social interaction … thus focuses on the integration of the motivation of actors with the normative cultural standards which integrate the action system' (1951, p. 36). Although there are variations and tensions, the structural-functional paradigm takes the view that a social entity, such as a whole market society or an organization, can be studied as an organism. Like organisms, a social system is composed of interdependent parts, each of which contributes to the functioning of the whole. A whole society or an organization is held together by a consensus on values, or a value system. The view of an organization as a social system thus looks for the 'functions' served by its various departments and members and the common values shared by its members.

It is frequently assumed that managerial functions and processes take place in organizations that are rationally designed to accomplish strategic goals, that organizations are harmonious bodies tending towards a state of equilibrium and order, and that the basic task of managers is to manage resources for formal organizational ends. Thus, the structural-functionalism paradigm, sometimes also known as 'social systems theory', becomes inseparable from the notion of efficiency. The focus of much of the research and literature on management using this 'lens' is about finding the 'winning formula' so that more managers can become 'effective' (Thompson and McHugh, 2009). Common to all variations of structural-functionalism, which is often seen as the dominant or mainstream perspective, is a failure to connect management processes to the 'master' public discourse on market-based societies and globalization.

The intellectual roots of the *conflict paradigm* are most obviously found in the works of the German philosopher Karl Marx (1818–1883). The German sociologist Max Weber (1864–1920) also devoted much research to work and organizations within advanced capitalist societies. In his early manuscripts of 1844, Marx analysed the fundamental contradiction of capitalism that arose from structured tensions between capital (employers) and labour (employees). Specifically, he made the assumption that these two social classes have competing interests. For Marx, the relationship between capitalists and workers was one of contradiction. Each is dependent upon the other, and the two must cooperate to varying degrees. Yet there is a fundamental conflict of interest between capital and labour: the capitalist seeks to minimize labour costs; the workers seek the opposite. As a result, economic forces compel employers and employees to cooperate, but also there are forces that simultaneously cause conflict between the two groups.

Equally importantly, workers experience alienation or 'estrangement' through the act of labour. Marx describes alienation explicitly as an absence of meaning or self-worth. Alienated workers are people 'robbed' of the unique characteristic or the 'essence' of human beings – their ability to be creative through productive work. Marx's analysis of alienation continues to inform contemporary studies of work and the prerequisites for dignity *in* and *at* work (see, for example, Bolton, 2007).

Similar to Marx, Weber's analyses of advanced capitalist societies centre on work and organizations, especially large bureaucracies. Two themes within Weber's work are especially relevant to understanding contemporary theories of work and management. One is the notion of *paradox* in market societies. In *The Protestant Ethic* (1904–05/2002), Weber pessimistically warns of creeping rationalization and of the tendency of people to experience a debilitating *'iron cage'*. The process of rationalization is, according to Weber, unremittingly paradoxical (Bratton et al. 2009). He, and subsequent writers in the Weberian tradition, focused on the notion of *'paradox of consequences'* – two or more positions that each sound reasonable yet conflict or contradict each other. For example, an organization invests in new technology and achieves higher levels of efficiency, and ultimately rising profits. However, the performance benefits of the technology are accompanied by behaviours that reduce long-term efficiency as work becomes increasingly devoid of meaning or dignity for the employees. Thus, a paradox of consequence results when managers, in pursuit of a specific organizational goal or goals, call for or carry out actions that are in opposition to the very goals the organization is attempting to accomplish.

A second theme that lies at the centre of Weber's sociology is his analysis of *power* and domination by social elites (Bratton et al., 2009, p. 235). In *Economy and Society* (1922/1968), Weber stresses that power is an aspect of virtually all social relationships. However, Weber was primarily interested in legitimate forms of domination or power, or what he called 'legitimate authority', which allocates the right to command and the duty to obey. He argued that every form of social elite attempts to establish and cultivate belief in its own legitimate authority. For example, *legal-rational* domination, which Weber defined as 'a belief in the legality of enacted rules and the right of those elevated to authority under such rules to issue commands' (Weber, 1922/1968, p. 215), is exercised through bureaucracy, itself a product of the systematic rationalization of work and society. Weber viewed bureaucratic domination with some apprehension. The more perfectly bureaucracy is developed, 'the more it is 'dehumanized' (p. 975) as it 'reduces every worker to a cog in this [bureaucratic] machine and, seeing himself in this light, he will merely ask how to transform himself from a little into a somewhat bigger cog' (p. iix).

Critical scholars draw heavily on the works of Marx, and to a lesser extent Weber, to explain management activities in terms of basic 'logics' underlying capitalist production and society: goods and services are produced for a profit; technology and bureaucratic principles provide new opportunities for increasing both the quantity and the quality of work; and the agents acting for the capitalists – the managers – decide how and where goods and services are to be produced within the context of powerful economic imperatives that do not allow for substantial differences in management style or approach. Thus, managerial control is a *structural* imperative of capitalist employment relations, causing what Edwards' (1986) calls '*structural antagonism*'. Labour process analysis is part of the conflict school of thought. It represents a body of theory and research that examines 'core' themes of technology, skills, control and worker resistance, as well as, more recently, new 'postmodern territories' with a focus on subjectivity, identity and power (Thompson and Smith, 2010). The conflict paradigm, when applied to work organizations, sets out to discover the ways in which power, control, conflict and legitimacy impact on contemporary employment relations. It emphasizes that HRM can only be understood as part of a management process embedded within the wider sociocultural and political economy order of a capitalist society, which determines the nature of work and employment practices. The various critical approaches to HRM attempt to demystify and contextualize the situation of HRM by focusing on the interplay of economic, social and political forces, power and systematic inequality, and structured antagonism and conflict (see Delbridge and Keenoy, 2010; Thompson and Harley, 2008; Watson, 2010).

The third social science paradigm examined here, the *feminist paradigm*, traces its intellectual roots to eighteenth-century feminist writings, such as Mary Wollstonecraft's *A Vindication of the Rights of Woman* (1792/2004) and, in the 1960s, to Betty Friedan's *Feminine Mystique* (1963). Whereas Marx chiefly addressed the exploitation of the working class, the early feminist writers provided a 'sophisticated understanding into gender-based, persistent, and pervasive injustices that women continue to experience in all areas of life' (Bratton et al., 2009, p. 11). Researchers looking at the market society from a feminist perspective have drawn attention to aspects of organizational life that are overlooked by other paradigms. In part, feminist scholarship has focused on gender differences and how they relate to the rest of society. Over the decades, gender has become a concept to be wrestled with, but here we use the word to refer to a set of ideas that focuses on the processes of gender roles, inequalities in society and in the workplace, problems of power, and women's subordination and oppression.

Theoretically, one of the most important consequences of gender analysis is its power to question the research findings and analysis that segregate studies of HRM from those of gender divisions in the labour market (Dex, 1988), patriarchal power (Witz, 1986), issues of workplace inequality (Phillips and Phillips, 1993) and 'dual-role' and work–life issues (Knights and Willmott, 1986; Platt, 1997; Warhurst et al., 2008). More importantly, however, including the dimension of gender in the study of contemporary HRM has the potential to move the debate forward by examining the people who are deemed to be the 'recipients' of HRM theory and practice (Mabey et al., 1998a). For example, Dickens (1998) has noted that the equality assumption in the HRM model, which emphasizes the value of diversity, is part of the rhetoric rather than the reality. Reinforcing this observation, a large-scale Canadian study showed that women face a gender bias when it comes to career advancement. In addition, women from visible minorities face a 'double bias' favouring white men at all levels, from entry-level to middle managers right up to chief executive officers (Yap and Konrad, 2009). The feminist paradigm takes it as self-evident that gender inequality in the workplace can only be understood by developing a wider gender-sensitive understanding of society and employment practices.

> **reflective question**
>
> It is important to explore your own values and views and therefore your own perspective on HRM. What do you think of these social science paradigms? How do they help us to explain the actions and outcomes of behaviour in organizations? Which perspective seem to you to be more realistic, and why? How do these paradigms help us to understand the uncertainties and conflicts evident in contemporary workplaces?

Critique and paradox in HRM

Since Storey's (1989) landmark publication, the HRM canon has been subject to 'external' and 'internal' criticism (Delbridge and Keenoy, 2010). The external critique has come from academics within the broad field of critical management studies and labour process theory. These critics include Alvesson and Willmott (2003), Godard (1991), Thompson and McHugh (2009) and Watson (2004). They expose structured antagonisms and contradictions, and contend that HR practices can only be understood in the context of the wider cultural and political economy factors that shape or direct those practices. Critical management theorists also argue that mainstream HRM researchers have routinely neglected or marginalized those most directly impacted by HR practices – the employees. Generally, there has been an intellectual failure to engage in the process of 'denaturalization' – of questioning 'taken-for-granted' beliefs and assumptions and 'unmasking' the questionable results of HRM research. Finally, critics hold that most HRM researchers have largely failed to subject employment practices to a critical scrutiny of 'unintended consequences', 'contradictions' or the 'collateral damage' resulting from their application (Delbridge and Keenoy, 2010, p. 803).

The principal 'internal' critics of HRM include Karen Legge (2005), who provides a sustained critique with respect to the divide between what she describes as the 'rhetoric' and the 'reality' of HRM. Similarly, Barbara Townley (1994) offers a sustained Foucauldian analysis and critique of HRM, and Winstanley and Woodall (2000) present a sustained ethical critique of HRM. More generally, Keenoy and Anthony (1992) have sought to explore the ambiguity associated with the term 'human resource management' itself. This relates to the question of where the emphasis of strategic management policy is placed: is it on the word '*human*' or on '*resource*' in management? This ambiguity generated the notion of 'soft' and 'hard' HRM and, more recently, provoked a collection titled *Searching for the 'H' in HRM* in the 'moral' market society (Bolton and Houlihan, 2007).

Analytically, critical commentaries of the HRM phenomenon echo the belief that the contemporary workplace mirrors the capitalist society at large: a social entity that may be characterized by creativity, innovation, wealth, but also one that exhibits constant change, strategic variation, human degradation, inequality, social power, differential interests, contradiction and paradox. Charles Dickens (1859/1952), in *A Tale of Two Cities*, nicely captures the existence of paradox in modernity: 'It was the best of times, it was the worst of times, it was the age of wisdom, it was the age of foolishness …'. This duality of creativity and wealth alongside degradation and inequality in the workplace is neatly captured by a well-known drawing found in first-year psychology textbooks, an image that can be seen at the same time as a beautiful young woman and an old crone.

Drawing upon Weber's work, the 'internal' critics of HRM have used the paradox of consequence to encourage their audiences to view the reality of HRM differently. For example, new job and work designs were promoted to revitalize organizations in order to enlist workers' knowledge and commitment, but what have emerged are downsizing and work intensification. A similar contradiction emerges in new reward systems with the introduction of variable pay arrangements, but what can emerge is a 'bonus culture' that undermines other espoused employer goals such as loyalty and commitment, or, as the 2008 banking crisis attests, risk-aversion. Legge's incisive critique identifies the basic paradox that the dominant HRM model simultaneously seeks both control over and the commitment of employees, the tensions in the 'soft' and 'hard' schools of HRM, and the rhetoric that asserts 'we are all managers now'. Paradoxically, the inclusion of the HR director in the strategic management team, the process of 'decentralization' or the act of 'giving away HR management' to line managers, as well as the outsourcing of HR activities, might ultimately lead to the demise of the HR professional, thereby undermining the ongoing quest of HRM specialists for centrality and credibility (Legge, 2005).

Critical accounts of HRM also suggest a paradox of consequence arising from new networked organizational designs (Rubery et al., 2002). The short-lived nature of multiemployer networks, differentiated by employer, business contracts and employment contracts, encourages subcultures that may counter any efforts to create a 'high-commitment' culture and/or violate the psychological contract. As Legge explains, in discussing interfirm relationships: 'When flexibility is the justification and watchword ... pragmatism ... is likely to moderate, if not supplant, a truly strategic approach to HR' (2007, p. 54). Furthermore, when employers are urged to adjust to Britain's ageing workforce (Brindle, 2010), investment in work-based learning is at odds with the reality of 'HRM's organizationally sponsored ageism' (Lyon and Glover, 1998, p. 31).

In our view, studying HRM remains relevant. The global and environmental drivers of change that are reshaping Western economies and societies will cast a long shadow over contemporary organizations as managers struggle to control work and employment activities. Analytical HRM is, therefore, highly relevant given that its *raison d'être* is, using a variety of approaches or styles, to leverage people's knowledge and capabilities and manage employment relationships. In particular, given the need for organizations to develop sustainably oriented strategies, a reflexive, critical analysis of HRM is increasingly important to understanding organizational life.

Furthermore, with regard to concerns about an absence of reflexive critique in business schools, Delbridge and Keenoy's (2010) contribution elaborating what constitutes CHRM is both important and timely. In writing this text, we have found concepts from the social science paradigms to be highly relevant, albeit through the lens of our own cultural bias. As in previous editions of *Human Resource Management: Theory and Practice*, we are concerned with developing a context-sensitive understanding of work and practices of HRM. Throughout the book, we emphasize that paradox and antagonism is structured into the employment relationship. Many mainstream HRM writers have not been realistic about the nature of capitalism (Thompson and Harley, 2008). From our perspective, it goes without saying that different work systems and HR strategies and practices can only be understood in the context of the wider cultural-political economy, technological, environmental and market factors that direct or influence work regimes.

We are aiming to provide a more critical, nuanced account of the realities of the workplace in market societies, one that encourages a deeper understanding and sensitivity with respect to employment and HR-related issues. We hope that *Human Resource Management: Theory and Practice* captures the range of change evident in today's workplaces, and will moreover lead to the kind of sensibilities that encourage the reader to question, to be critical and to seek multicausality when analysing contemporary HRM.

CASE STUDY

Canterbury Hospital

Setting

In the twenty-first century, New Zealand is tackling environmental issues similar to those of many countries: the more sustainable use of water, managing marine resources, reducing waste and improving energy efficiency. The country is particularly concerned about the decline of its unique plants, animals and ecosystems.

The country is striving to build a positive image of New Zealand through exporting environmentally sensitive products and maintaining a reputation of being sustainable at home and abroad. The government has therefore recognized that there is a need to increase reporting on sustainable practices among New Zealand businesses in order to raise the profile of New Zealand globally on this important issue.

For the last few years, the Ministry for the Environment has promoted several grant-funding programmes to support environmental initiatives. In an attempt to control administration costs and improve the evaluation of the programme's outcomes, a decision was recently made to combine the funds supporting environmental initiatives at the community level. It is hoped that merging these funds will mean that the programme will be more streamlined and that there will be more flexibility to meet government priorities.

The combined funding programme, called the Community Environment Fund (CEF), aims to support community groups, businesses and local government in taking environmental actions. To be eligible for funding, applicants have to demonstrate that their projects will support one or more of the following objectives:

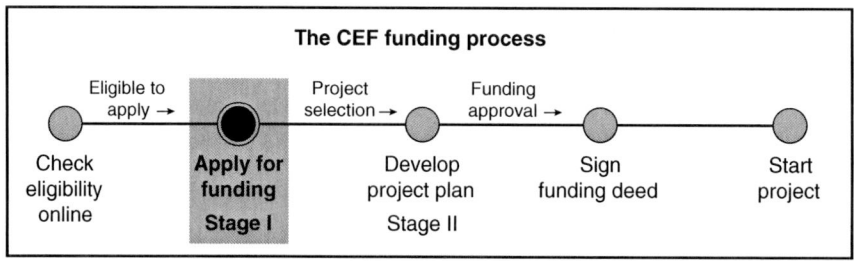

Source: www.mfe.govt.nz/withyou/funding/community-environment-fund/; Ministry for the Environment (New Zealand) (2011).

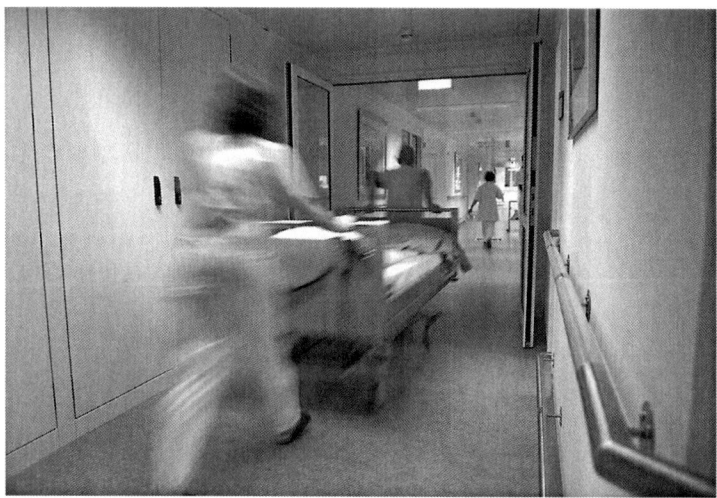

Source: ©istockphoto.com/Dr. Heinz Linke.

- Raise awareness of environmental damage
- Support and strengthen partnerships between community, industry, Maori populations and local government on practical environmental initiatives
- Involve the community in practically focused action for the environment
- Empower the community to take action that improves the quality of the environment
- Increase community-based advice, educational opportunities and public information about environmental legislation.

Eligible environmental projects will be considered for a minimum of $10,000 and up to a maximum of $300,000 of funding per financial year.

The problem

Canterbury Hospital, located near the city of Christchurch, provides a wide range of complex medical, surgery and mental health services, and is not only one of New Zealand's largest healthcare centres, but also its oldest. The hospital has a poor reputation in terms of its HRM and struggles with adversarial union relations. Workers are given low autonomy in their jobs, and the organizational structure contains several layers of management. Decision-making is primarily centralized.

The hospital's administration recently became aware of the funding provided by the government's new environmental initiative. Subsequently, in a public meeting, Chief Executive Officer Heather Nicol announced the creation of an Environmental/Sustainability Innovation Committee, made up of staff members chosen by management from the various hospital departments: 'Environmental stewardship is a key component of our hospital's strategic and operational planning, and through this new committee we will be contributing to our organization's and the country's goals to become more sustainable.' The committee, she said, would recommend and develop projects that would meet the funding criteria outlined by the government.

This new and revolutionary approach by the hospital administration took most of the staff by surprise. Although many were eager to learn about the environmental issues and contribute their ideas through this experience, others were suspicious of management's motives in involving staff members when they had never been asked to participate in such a public initiative before. Shortly before the initial meeting of the selected group, the HR department received an angry call from the union executive questioning why they had not been asked to sit on the committee and asking what criteria had been used to select the employees who were to participate. The union demanded a meeting with management to discuss how workloads and jobs would be impacted by the employees' involvement.

Assignment

Working either alone or in a study group, prepare a report drawing on this chapter and other recommended material addressing the following:

1. Using one of the five major HRM models, identify which aspects of the case illustrate traditional personnel management and HRM approaches.

2. What contribution can a set of 'best' HR practices make to this organization?
3. Reflecting upon the national business system, discuss how the effectiveness of HR practices depends on the context of an organization.

Note: Your report may be written to fit your own national business and legal context.

Essential reading

Dunphy, D. C., Griffiths, A. and Benn, S. (2003) *Organizational Change for Corporate Sustainability: Understanding Organizational Change*. London: Routledge.

Enhert, I. (2009) Sustainability and human resource management: reasoning and applications on corporate websites. *European Journal of International Management,* **3**(4): 419–38.

Jones, G. (ed.) (2011) *Current Research in Sustainability*. Prahan: Tilde University Press.

Tyler, M. and Wilkinson, A. (2007) The tyranny of corporate slenderness: 'corporate anorexia' as a metaphor for our age. *Work, Employment and Society,* **21**(3): 537–49.

For more on New Zealand's Community Environment Fund, go to: www.mfe.govt.nz/withyou/funding/community-environment-fund.

Note: This feature was written by Lori Rilkoff, HR Manager at City of Kamloops, BC, Canada.

Visit the companion website at www.palgrave.com/business/bratton5 for guidelines on writing reports.

Summary

- In this introductory chapter, we have emphasized the importance of managing people, individually and collectively, over other 'factor inputs'. We have examined the history of HRM and emphasized that, since its introduction, it has been highly controversial. The HRM phenomenon has been portrayed as the historical outcome of rising neo-liberalism ideology, closely associated with the political era of Thatcherism.

- We have conceptualized HRM as a strategic approach, one that seeks to leverage people's capabilities and commitment with the goal of enhancing performance and dignity *in* and *at* work. These HRM goals are accomplished by a set of integrated employment policies, programmes and practices within an organizational and societal context. We suggest that the HRM approach as conceptualized here constitutes CHRM, extending the analysis of HRM outcomes beyond performance to include equality, dignity and social justice.

- To show the multiple meanings of the term 'human resource management', we have examined five theoretical models. We have discussed whether HRM now represents a new orthodoxy; certainly, the language is different.

- We have explained that tensions are omnipresent. These include tensions between profitability and cost-effectiveness and employee security; between employer control and employee commitment; and between managerial autonomy and employee dignity. Throughout this book, we illustrate and explain some of these tensions and inevitable paradoxes to encourage a deeper understanding of HR-related issues.

- Finally, workplace scholars use a variety of theoretical frames of reference or paradigms – here the focus has been on structural-functionalism, conflict and feminist paradigms – to organize how they understand and conduct research into HRM.

Vocab checklist for ESL students

- analyse (v), analysis (n), analytical (adj)
- arbitrate (v), arbitrator (n), arbitration (n)
- bureaucrat (n), bureaucracy (n), bureaucratic (adj)
- capitalize (v), capital (n), capitalist (n), capitalism (n)
- conflict (n), conflict perspective (n)
- contract (v), contract (n), contractor (n), contractual (adj)
- controversy (n), controversial (adj)
- criticize (v), critic (n), critical (adj)
- downsize (v), downsizing (n)
- economize (v), economics (n), economy (n), economist (n), economical (adj)
- employ (v), employee (n), employer (n), employment (n)
- equity (n), equitable (adj), equal (adj)
- globalize (v), globe (n), globalization (n), global (adj)
- idea (n), ideology (n), ideological (adj)
- interdepend (v), interdependencies (n), interdependent (adj)
- international human resource management (IHRM) (n)
- liberalize (v), liberalism (n), liberal (n) (adj)
- manage (v), manager (n), management (n), managerial (adj)
- mediate (v), mediator (n), mediation (n)
- micro human resource management (MHRM) (n)
- norm (n), normative (adj), normal (adj)
- oblige (v), obligation (n), obligatory (adj)
- outsource (v), outsourcing (n)
- paradigm (n)
- paradox (n), paradoxical (adj), paradoxically (adv)
- recruit (v), recruit (n), recruitment (n)
- restructure (v), restructuring (n)
- rhetoric (n), rhetorical (adj)
- sociology (n), sociologist (n), sociological (adj)
- stakeholder (n)
- stereotype (v), stereotype (n), stereotypical (adj)
- strategic human resource management (SHRM) (n)
- strategize (v), strategy (n), strategist (n), strategic (adj)
- sustain (v), sustainability (n), sustainable (adj)
- theorize (v), theory (n), theorist (n), theoretical (adj)
- unionize (v), union (n), unionization (n)

Note: some words are denoted as nouns (n) when in fact the word is a gerund; for example, 'restructuring' is in the gerund form; however, gerunds function grammatically as nouns, so the general term of noun (n) is used.

Visit www.palgrave.com/business/bratton5 for a link to free definitions of these terms in the Macmillan Dictionary, as well as additional learning resources for ESL students.

Review questions

1. What is 'human resource management' and what role does it play in work organizations?
2. To what extent does the emergence of HRM reflect the rise and ideology of neo-liberalism?
3. To what extent is HRM different from conventional personnel management – or is it simply 'old wine in new bottles'?

Further reading to improve your mark

Reading these articles and chapters can help you gain a better understanding and potentially a higher grade for your HRM assignment.

- The changing role of HRM is explored in R. Caldwell (2001) Champions, adapters, consultants and synergists: the new change agents in HRM. *Human Resource Management Journal*, **11**(3): 39–52.

Critical studies are also found in the following:

- Delbridge, R. and Keenoy, T. (2010) Beyond managerialism? *International Journal of Human Resource Management*, **21**(6): 799–817.
- Dickens, L. (1998) What HRM means for gender equality. *Human Resource Management Journal*, **8**(1): 23–45.
- Kochan, T. (2008) Social legitimacy of the HRM profession: a US perspective. In P. Boxall, J. Purcell and P. Wright (eds) *The Oxford Handbook of Human Resource Management* (pp. 599–619). Oxford: OUP.
- Legge, K. (2005) *Human Resource Management: Rhetorics and Realities*. London: Palgrave Macmillan.
- Storey J. (ed.) (2007) Human resource management today: an assessment. In J. Storey (ed.) *Human Resource Management: A Critical Text* (pp. 3–20). London: Thompson Learning.
- Thompson, P. and Harley, B. (2008) HRM and the worker: labour process perspectives. In P. Boxall, J. Purcell and P. Wright (eds) *The Oxford Handbook of Human Resource Management* (pp. 147–65). Oxford: OUP.
- Watson, T. (2010) Critical social science, pragmatism and the realities of HRM. *International Journal of Human Resource Management Studies*, **21**(6): 915–31.

Visit www.palgrave.com/business/bratton5 for lots of extra resources to help you get to grips with this chapter, including study tips, HRM skills development guides, summary lecture notes, and more.

References

Agashae, Z. and Bratton, J. (2001) Leader–follower dynamics: developing a learning organization. *Journal of Workplace Learning*, 13(3): 89–102.

Alvesson, M. and Willmott, H. (eds) (2003) *Studying Management Critically*. London: Sage.

Andolšek, D. M. and Štebe, J. (2005) Devolution or (de)centralization of HRM function in European organizations. *International Journal of Human Resource Management*, 16(3): 311–29.

Arshad, R. and Sparrow, P. (2010) Downsizing and survivor reactions in Malaysia: modelling antecedents and outcomes of psychological contract violations. *International Journal of Human Resource Management*, 21(11): 1793–815.

Babbie, E. and Benaquisto, L. (2010) *Fundamentals of Social Research* (2nd edn). Toronto, Ontario: Nelson.

Bacon, N. and Blyton, P. (2003)The impact of teamwork on skills: employee perceptions of who gains and who loses. *Human Resource Management Journal*, 13(2): 13–29.

Bamberger, P. and Meshoulam, I. (2000) *Human Resource Management Strategy*. Thousand Oaks, CA: Sage.

Beer, M., Spector, B., Lawrence, P. R., Quin Mills, D. and Walton, R. E. (1984) *Managing Human Assets*. New York: Free Press.

Bendal, S. E., Bottomley, C. R. and Cleverly, P. M. (1998) Building a new proposition for staff at NatWest UK. In P. Sparrow and M. Marchington (eds) *Human Resource Management: The New Agenda* (pp. 90–105). London: Financial Times/Pitman.

Berger, P. L. (1963) *Invitation to Sociology*. New York: Anchor Books.

Bolton, S. C. (ed.) (2007) *Dimensions of Dignity at Work*. Amsterdam: Elsevier.

Bolton, S. C. (ed.) (2007) *Dimensions of Dignity at Work*. Amsterdam: Elsevier.

Bolton, S. C. and Houlihan, M. (eds) (2007) *Searching for the Human in Human Resource Management: Theory, Practice and Contexts*. Basingstoke: Palgrave Macmillan.

Bolton, S. C. and Houlihan, M. (eds) (2007) *Searching for the Human in Human Resource Management: Theory, Practice and Contexts*. Basingstoke: Palgrave Macmillan.

Boxall, P. (2008) The goals of HRM. In P. Boxall, J. Purcell and P. Wright (eds) *The Oxford Handbook of Human Resource Management* (pp. 48–67). Oxford: Oxford University Press.

Boxall, P. F. (1992) Strategic human resource management: beginnings of a new theoretical sophistication? *Human Resource Management Journal*, 2(3): 60–79.

Bratton, J. Denham, D. and Deutschmann, L. (2009) Capitalism and Classical Sociological Theory. Toronto, Ontario: University of Toronto Press.

Bratton, J., Grint, K. and Nelson, D. (2004a) *Organizational Leadership*. Mason, OH: Thomson/South-Western.

Brindle, D. (2010) Embrace the grey workforce, scheme urges employers. *The Guardian*, June 5, p. W2.

Brown, D., Caldwell, R., White, K., Atkinson, H., Tansley, T., Goodge, P. and Emmott, M. (2004). *Business Partnering: A New Direction for HR*. London: CIPD.

Brown, W. (1988) The employment relationship in sociological theory. In D. Gallie (ed.) *Employment in Britain* (pp. 33–66). Oxford: Blackwell.

Brown, W. (1988) The employment relationship in sociological theory. In D. Gallie (ed.) *Employment in Britain* (pp. 33–66). Oxford: Blackwell.

Brown, W., Deakin, S. and Ryan, P. (1997) The effects of British industrial relations legislation. *National Institute Economic Review*, 161: 69–83.

Casserley, T. and Critchley, B. (2010) Sustainable leadership: perennial philosophy. *People Management,* August 12: 20–4.

Chartered Institute of Personnel and Development (2006a) *Offshoring and the Role of HR*. London: CIPD.

Chartered Institute of Personnel and Development (2011) *Sustainable Organisation Performance*. London: CIPD.

Chomsky, N. (1999) *Profit over People*. New York: Seven Stories Press.

Coates, D. (1975) *The Labour Party and the Struggle for Socialism*. Cambridge: Polity Press.

Crouch, C. (1982) *The Politics of Industrial Relations* (2nd edn). London: Fontana.

Currie, G., Knights, D. and Sgtarkey, K. (2010) Introduction: a post-crisis critical reflection on business schools. *British Journal of Management*, 21: 1–5.

Datta, D., Guthrie, J., Basuil, D. and Pandey, A. (2010) Causes and effects of employee downsizing: a review and synthesis. *Journal of Management*, 36(1): 281–348.

Delbridge, R. and Keenoy, T. (2010) Beyond managerialism? *International Journal of Human Resource Management*, 21(6): 799–817.

Dex, S. (1988) Gender and the labour market. In D. Gallie (ed.) *Employment in Britain* (pp. 281–309). Oxford: Blackwell.

Dickens, C. (1859/1952) *A Tale of Two Cities*. London: HarperCollins.

Dickens, L. (1998) What HRM means for gender equality. *Human Resource Management Journal*, 8(1): 23–45.

Donovan, Lord (1968) *Royal Commission on Trade Unions Employers' Association*. Cmnd 3623. London: HMSO.

Durkheim, E. (1933/1997) *The Division of Labor in Society*. New York: Free Press.
Edwards, P. K. (1986) *Conflict at Work: A Materialist Analysis of Workplace Relations*. Oxford: Blackwell.
Edwards, P. K. (1986) *Conflict at Work: A Materialist Analysis of Workplace Relations*. Oxford: Blackwell.
Elkington, J. (1998) Enter the triple bottom line. In A. Henriques and J. Richardson (eds) *The Triple Bottom Line: Does it All Add Up?* (pp. 1–16). London: Earthscan.
Evans, A. L. and Lorange, P. (1989) The two logics behind human resource management. In P. Evans, Y. Doz and A. Laurent (eds) *Human Resource Management in International Firms: Change, Globalization, Innovation* (pp. 144–62). Basingstoke: Palgrave Macmillan.
Fayol, H. (1949) *Administration Industrielle et Générale/General and Industrial Management*. London: Pitman.
Fitz-enz, J. (2000) *The ROI of Human Capital*. New York: AMACOM.
Fombrun, C. J., Tichy, N. M. and Devanna, M. A. (eds) (1984) *Strategic Human Resource Management*. New York: John Wiley & Sons.
Francis, H. and Keegan, A. (2005) Slippery slope. *People Management*, June 30: 26–31.
Francis, H. and Keegan, A. (2006) The changing face of HRM: in search of balance. *Human Resource Management Journal*, 16(3): 231–49.
Gereffi, G. and Christian, M. (2009) The impacts of Wal-Mart: the rise and consequences of the world's dominant retailer. *Annual Review of Sociology*, 35: 573–91.
Giddens, A. and Hutton, W. (2000) In conversation. In W. Hutton and A. Giddens (eds) *On the Edge: Living with Global Capitalism* (pp. 1–51). London: Jonathan Cape.
Godard, J. (1991) The progressive HRM paradigm: a theoretical and empirical re-examination. *Relations Industrielles/Industrial Relations*, 46(2): 378–99.
Goldthorpe, J. H., Lockwood, D., Bechhofer, F. and Platt, J. (1968) *The Affluent Worker: Industrial Attitudes and Behaviour*. Cambridge: Cambridge University Press.
Guest, D. and King, Z. (2004) Power, innovation and problem solving: the personnel managers' three steps to heaven? *Journal of Management Studies*, 41(3): 401–23.
Guest, D. E. (1987) Human resource management and industrial relations. *Journal of Management Studies*, 24(5): 503–21.
Guest, D. E. (1989) HRM: implications for industrial relations. In J. Storey (ed.) *New Perspectives on Human Resource Management* (pp. 41–55). London: Routledge.
Guest, D. E. (1997) Human resource management and performance: a review and research agenda. *International Journal of Human Resource Management*, 8(3): 263–76.
Guest, D. E. (1998) Beyond HRM: commitment and the contract culture. In P. Sparrow and M. Marchington (eds) *Human Resource Management: The New Agenda* (pp. 37–51). London: Financial Times/Pitman.
Guest, D. E. and Conway, N. (2002) Communicating the psychological contract: an employer perspective. *Human Resource Management Journal*, 12(2): 22–38.
Harzing, A. W. (2000) An empirical analysis and extension of the Bartlett and Ghoshal typology of multinational companies. *Journal of International Business Studies*, 31(1): 101–20.
Hendry, C. and Pettigrew, A. (1990) Human resource management: an agenda for the 1990s. *International Journal of Human Resource Management*, 1(1): 17–44.
Honeyball, S. (2010) *Honeyball and Bower's Textbook on Employment Law (11th edn)*. Oxford: Oxford University Press.
Hoogvelt, A. (2001) *Globalization and the Postcolonian World* (2nd edn). Basingstoke: Palgrave Macmillan.
Hope-Hailey, V., Farndale, E. and Truss, C. (2005) The HR department's role in organizational performance. *Human Resource Management Journal*, 15(3): 49–66.
Hughes, J. (1990) *The Philosophy of Social Research* (2nd edn). Harlow: Longman.
Hyman, R. (1987) Trade unions and the law: papering over the cracks? *Capital and Class*, (31): 43–63.
Hyman, R. (1987) Trade unions and the law: papering over the cracks? *Capital and Class*, (31): 43–63.
Hyman, R. (1989) *The Political Economy of Industrial Relations*. Basingstoke: Palgrave Macmillan.
Hyman, R. and Brough, I. (1975) *Social Values and Industrial Relations*. Oxford: Blackwell.

Jacoby, S. M. (2005) *The Embedded Corporation: Corporate Governance and Employment Relations in Japan and the United States.* Princeton, NJ: Princeton University Press.

Janssens, M. and Steyaert, C. (2009) HRM and performance: a plea for reflexivity in HRM studies. *Journal of Management Studies*, 46(1): 143–55.

Keenoy, T. (1990) Human resource management: rhetoric, reality and contradiction. *International Journal of Human Resource Management*, 1(3): 363–84.

Keenoy, T. and Anthony, P. (1992) HRM: metaphor, meaning and morality. In P. Blyton and P. Turnbull (eds) *Reassessing Human Resource Management* (pp. 233–55). London: Sage.

Kelly, J. E. (2005) Industrial relations approaches to the employment relationship. In J. A.-M. Coyle-Shapiro, L. Shore, S. Taylor and L. Tetrick (eds) *The Employment Relationship: Examining Psychological and Contextual Perspectives* (pp. 48–64). Oxford: Oxford University Press.

Kersley, B., Alpin, C., Forth, J., Bryson, A., Bewley, H., Dix, G. and Oxenbridge, S. (2005) *Inside the Workplace: First Findings from the 2004 Workplace Employment Relations Survey (WERS 2004).* London: DTI/ESRC/ACAS/PSI.

Klass, B., Gainey, T., McClendon, J. and Yang, H. (2005) Professional employer organizations and their impact on client satisfaction with human resource outcomes: a field study of human resource outsourcing in small and medium enterprises. *Journal of Management*, 31(2): 234–54.

Knights, D. and Willmott, H. (eds) (1986) *Gender and the Labour Process.* Aldershot: Gower.

Kuttner, R. (2000) The role of governments in the global economy. In W. Hutton and A. Giddens (eds) *On the Edge: Living with Global Capitalism* (pp. 147–63). London: Jonathan Cape.

Legge, K. (1989) Human resource management: a critical analysis. In J. Storey (ed.) New Perspectives on Human Resource Management (pp. 21–36). London: Routledge.

Legge, K. (1995) *Human Resource Management: Rhetorics and Realities.* Basingstoke: Macmillan.

Legge, K. (2005) *Human Resource Management: Rhetorics and Realities* (anniversary edn). Basingstoke: Palgrave Macmillan.

Legge, K. (2007) Networked organizations and the negation of HRM? In J. Storey (ed.) *Human Resource Management: A Critical Text* (3rd edn) (pp. 39–56). London: Thomson Learning.

Lockton, D. J. (2010) *Employment Law* (7th edn). Basingstoke: Palgrave Macmillan.

Lyon, P. and Glover, I. (1998) Divestment or investment? The contradictions of HRM in relation to older employees. *Human Resource Management Journal*, 8(1): 56–68.

Mabey, C., Skinner, D. and Clark, D. (eds) (1998a) *Experiencing Human Resource Management.* London: Sage.

McGregor, D. (1960) The Human Side of Enterprise. New York: McGraw-Hill.

Mellahi, K. and Wilkinson, A. (2010) Slash and burn or nip and tuck? Downsizing, innovation and human resources. *International Journal of Human Resource Management*, 21(13): 2291–305.

Mills, C. Wright (1959/2000) *The Sociological Imagination.* Oxford: Oxford University Press.

Millward, N., Bryson, A. and Forth, J. (2000) *All Change at Work: British Employee Relations 1980–1998.* London: Routledge.

Mintzberg, H. (1973) *The Nature of Managerial Work.* London: Harper & Row.

Parsons, T. (1951) *The Social System.* Glencoe, IL: Free Press.

Pfeffer, J. (2005) Changing mental models: HR's most important task. *Human Resource Management*, 44(2): 123–8.

Pfeffer, J. (2005) Changing mental models: HR's most important task. *Human Resource Management*, 44(2): 123–8.

Phillips, P. and Phillips, E. (1993) *Women and Work: Inequality in the Canadian Labour Market.* Toronto, Ontario: Lorimer.

Pitcher, G. (2008) Backlash against human resource management partner model as managers question results. Personnel Today, September 17. Available at www.personneltoday.com/articles/2008/01/28/44126.

Platt, L. (1997) Employee work–life balance: the competitive advantage. In F. Hesselbein, M. Goldsmith and R. Beckhard (eds) *The Drucker Foundation, the Organization of the Future* (Chapter 32). San Francisco, CA: Jossey-Bass.

Purcell, J. (1989) The impact of corporate strategy on human resource management. In J. Storey (ed.) *New Perspectives on Human Resource Management* (pp. 67–91). London: Routledge.

Reilly, P., Tamkin, P. and Broughton, A. (2007) *The Changing HR Function: Transforming HR?* London: Chartered Institute of Personnel and Development.

Rose, N. (1999) *Governing the Soul: The Shaping of the Private Self* (2nd edn). London: Sage.

Rousseau, D. M. (1995) *Psychological Contracts in Organizations: Understanding Written and Unwritten Agreements.* Thousand Oaks, CA: Sage.

Rousseau, D. M. and Ho, V. T. (2000) Psychological contract issues in compensation. In S. L. Rynes and B. Gerhart (eds) *Compensation in Organizations: Current Research and Practice* (pp. 273–310). San Francisco, CA: Jossey-Bass.

Rubery, J. Earnshaw, J., Marchington, M., Cooke, F. L. and Vincent, S. (2002) Changing organizational forms and the employment relationship. *Journal of Management Studies*, 39(5): 645–72.

Schultz, T. W. (1981) *Investing in People: The Economics of Population Quality*. Berkeley, CA: University of California Press.

Senge, P. (1990) *The Fifth Discipline*. New York: Doubleday.

Squires, G. (2001) Mangement as a professional discipline. *Journal of Management Studies*, 38(4): 473–87.

Storey, J. (1992) *Developments in the Management of Human Resources*. Oxford: Blackwell.

Storey, J. (1995a) Human resource management: still marching on or marching out? In J. Storey (ed.) *Human Resource Management: A Critical Text* (pp. 3–32). London: Routledge.

Storey, J. (2001) Human resource management today: an assessment. In J. Storey (ed.) *Human Resource Management: A Critical Text* (2nd edn) (pp. 3–20). London: Thompson Learning.

Storey, J. (ed.) (1989) *New Perspectives on Human Resource Management*. London: Routledge.

Storey, J. (ed.) (2007) Human resource management today: an assessment. In J. Storey (ed.) *Human Resource Management: A Critical Text* (pp. 3–20). London: Thompson Learning.

Thompson P. and McHugh, D. (2009) *Work Organisations: A Critical Approach* (4th edn). Basingstoke: Palgrave Macmillan.

Thompson, P. and B. Harley, B. (2008) HRM and the worker: labour process perspectives. In P. Boxall, J. Purcell and P. Wright (eds) *The Oxford Handbook of Human Resource Management* (pp. 147–65). Oxford: Oxford University Press.

Thompson, P. and Smith, C. (2010) (eds) *Working Life*. Basingstoke: Palgrave Macmillan.

Townley, B. (1994) *Reframing Human Resource Managment*. London: Sage.

Townley, B. (1994) *Reframing Human Resource Managment*. London: Sage.

Ulrich, D. (1997) Human resource champions. *The Next Agenda for Adding Value and Delivering Results*. Boston, MA: Harvard Business School Press.

Ulrich, D. and Brockbank, W. (2005) *The HR Value Proposition*. Boston, MA: Harvard Business School Press.

Warhurst, C., Eikhof, D. R. and Haunschild, A. (2008) *Work Less, Live More? Critical Analysis of the Work–Life Boundary*. Basingstoke: Palgrave Macmillan.

Warr, P. (2008) Work values: some demographic and cultural correlates. *Journal of Occupational and Organizational Psychology*, 81: 751–75.

Watson, S. and Harmel-Law, A. (2010) Exploring the contribution of workplace learning to an HRD strategy in the Scottish legal profession. *Journal of European Industrial Training*, 34(1): 7–22.

Watson, T. (1986) *Management, Organization and Employment Strategy*. London: Routledge & Kegan Paul.

Watson, T. (2004) HRM and critical social sciences. *Journal of Management Studies*, 41(3): 447–67.

Watson, T. (2007) HRM, ethical irrationality, and the limits of ethical action. In A. Pinnington, R. Macklin and T. Campbell (eds) *Human Resource Management. Ethics and Employment* (pp. 223–36). Oxford: Oxford University Press.

Watson, T. J. (2010) Critical social science, pragmatism and the realities of HRM. *International Journal of Human Resource Management Studies*, 21(6): 915–31.

Weber, M. (1922/1968) *Economy and Society*. New York: Bedminster.

Wedderburn, Lord (1986) *The Worker and the Law* (3rd edn). Harmondsworth: Penguin.

Williams, R. (1976) *Keywords: A Vocabulary of Culture and Society*. New York: Oxford University Press.

Willmott, H. (1984) Images and ideals of managerial work. *Journal of Management Studies*, 21(3): 349–68.

Winstanley, D. and Woodall, J. (eds) (2000) *Ethical Issues in Contemporary Human Resource Management*. Basingstoke: Palgrave Macmillan.

Witz, A. (1986) Patriarchy and the labour market: occupational control strategies and the medical division of labour. In D. Knights and H. Willmott (eds) *Gender and the Labour Process* (pp. 14–35). Aldershot: Gower.

Yap, M. and Konrad, A. (2009) Gender and racial differentials in promotions: is there a sticky floor, a mid-level bottleneck, or a class ceiling? *Relations Industrielle/Industrial relations*, 64(4): 593–620.

Yukl, G. (2005) *Leadership in Organizations* (6th edn). Englewood Cliffs, NJ: Prentice Hall.

CHAPTER 2
Contextualizing human resource management
Jawad Syed and Dk Nur'Izzati Pg Omar

- Introduction
- Contextualizing HRM in a global village
- Contextual influences on HRM
- Critical discussion and analysis
- Conclusion
- For discussion and revision
- Further reading
- Case study: HRM in Brunei's public sector
- References

After reading this chapter, you should be able to:
- Understand the importance of local context and its implications for HRM
- Identify the external contexts that affect the policies and actions involved in HRM
- Learn how to design context-appropriate HRM
- Understand the pros and cons of a crosscultural transfer of HRM practices
- Identify future directions for contextualizing HRM

Introduction

Human resource management (HRM) as a management concept originated in the 1950s in North America with the seminal works of Drucker (1954) and McGregor (1957), and has subsequently been adopted and widely used across the world. HRM is defined as the managing of people within employer–employee relationships.

This usually involves maximizing employees' performance (Harris, 2002), and human resources need to be effectively utilized in order to obtain maximum productivity and performance. By the 1980s, the concept of HRM had gained wider international recognition, particularly in English-speaking countries (Sparrow and Hiltrop, 1994).

The theories and practices of HRM have since made inroads into continents other than North America and Europe, such as their adoption and integration into Asia and Africa (see, for example, Bennington and Habir, 2003; McCourt and Foon, 2007). However, despite more than two decades of academic research and practice, the HRM literature has been only partly successful in offering a universal solution for the complexities of managing people that can transcend national, institutional, cultural and economic divides. Özbilgin's (2004) survey of academic scholarship and journals in the field of international HRM points towards a limited geographical coverage by the 'mainstream' scholarship in HRM, which remains dominated by North American and Western European theorization and empirical studies. In other words, HRM is not culturally neutral. The limited geographical reach of HRM is also highlighted by other authors, such as Baruch (2001) and Clark et al. (2000), who have argued for an ethical duty on the part of HRM scholars and journals to widen their geographical spread. Critical Thinking 2.1 highlights the parochial nature of HRM resulting from its geographical and theoretical limitations.

Although HRM is today an international phenomenon, the nature and scope of its links with local institutions, labour laws, corporate strategies and industrial relations vary greatly across national borders (Özbilgin, 2004). Despite the fact that the mainstream HRM theories, which were overwhelmingly formulated in management schools in North America (see, for example, Beer et al., 1985; Schuler and Jackson, 1987) and the UK (Storey, 1992) in the 1980s, quickly found their way to other developed countries (Maurice et al., 1986; Tung, 1993) and later to developing countries (Budhwar and Debrah, 2001), few models of HRM found in the mainstream literature derive from outside the English-speaking world. This is despite an increasing consensus that mainstream human resources theories and practices are inadequate in addressing the human resource issues facing international and multinational companies (Clark et al., 2000). As a result, and also because of a growing pursuit of effective ways of managing human resources in crosscultural contexts (Taylor et al., 1996), it is important to develop a contextualized understanding and operationalization of HRM. The interest of scholars and practitioners in this topic is expected to grow further due to the relevance of issues such as crossnational and comparative HRM, expatriate management and diversity management (Caligiuri, 1999).

This chapter begins with a literature review on the adoption and implementation of HRM and the contextual forces that influence it. We also consider certain latent tensions between globalization and HRM. The case study at the end of the chapter presents an empirical study of HRM practices in Brunei Darussalam, describing the influence of the macroenvironmental context on the design and implementation of HRM strategies, policies and practices in government sector organizations in Brunei.

> **Critical Thinking 2.1**
>
> **Parochialism in the HRM literature**
>
> In the 'mainstream' English-language texts on HRM, there are hardly any references to resources in other languages (Özbilgin, 2004). Exceptions to this rule are some European languages, for example French-, German- and Spanish-language publications, which are also only very occasionally cited in English-language texts. The inclusion of materials not written in English is hardly encouraged and is often left to the linguistic competence of individual authors. As a consequence, the mainstream writing in the field of HRM remains influenced and dominated by the English-speaking world.
>
> Adler (1991) refutes any claims of universal reach and offers the notion of 'parochialism' in management writing. Clark et al. (1999) identify two forms of parochialism in the international HRM texts: (1) that a sole reliance on English-language sources poses a major challenge; and (2) that the texts often fail to acknowledge the methodological complexities of studying crossnational and international management issues. The limiting impact of the English language appears to be the most insidious as it simply demarcates our knowledge of and imagination related to HRM practice to those geographies where the English language is spoken.
>
> Similarly, the difficulty of formulating overarching conceptual frameworks, theoretical models and critical approaches is a recurring theme in the international HRM literature. Large-scale empirical studies in this field are rare, and such studies come with long descriptions of the limitations of their method and analysis. However, due to their rarity, great significance is attributed to the studies that are available, and their findings are often overstated, misinterpreted or used out of context. For example, although Hofstede's work in the 1960s and 70s challenged the assumption that the theoretical frameworks developed in the USA would be universally applicable (Schneider, 2001), Hofstede's IBM studies were later quoted as a clear indicator of the convergence and divergence of management practices, without much questioning of the nature of his study.
>
> **Questions**
> 1. What are the implications of the dominance of English-language literature for theories and practices in HRM?
> 2. How can scholars and practitioners of HRM benefit from the literature on HRM that has been published in languages other than English?
>
> *Source*: Adapted from Özbilgin (2004).

Contextualizing HRM in a global village

Global integration has driven dramatic changes in the economic and institutional contexts of HRM. Globalization refers to the shift to a more integrated and interdependent world economy (Hill, 2009). It focuses on the maximization of profits and, as an economic driver, has had a significant effect on the way in which human resources are managed. Globalization has also changed the image of a company. Companies have become multinational, each one seeking to attain the competitive advantage, and the human resources of a company may just be the key to that. For this reason, HRM policies are changing in order to better respond to different cultural and institutional contexts.

Context is multilayered, multidimensional and interwoven (Collin, 2007), and different contexts may have dynamic and divergent influences on the organization of work within their sphere of influence. Globalization has steadily and gradually created a world in which:

> barriers to cross-border trade and investment are declining; material culture is starting to look similar the world over; and national economies are merging into an interdependent, integrated global economic system. (Hill, 2009: 4)

During current times, when the world economy and businesses are shaped and structured by the process of globalization, it is imperative to understand and contextualize the policies and practices of HRM.

Although it is no longer possible to divide the world economy into separate, distinct national economies isolated from foreign markets and influences, it would be wrong to ignore the fact that employment relationships in almost all countries remain largely shaped by national systems of employment legislation and the cultural contexts in which they are operationalized. Critical Thinking 2.2 highlights the case of varying perspectives on working hours in the European Union (EU).

Although factors such as culture, history and language underlie much of the variation in management practices, the practice of HRM is, more than that of any other business function, closely linked to national culture (Gaugler, 1988). Culture can mean many different things for people with different backgrounds. Culture, according to Tylor (1924: 1), is 'that complex whole which includes knowledge, belief, art, morals, law, custom, and any other capabilities and habits acquired by man as a member of society'. Within employment contexts, there is ample evidence that people's behaviours are affected by specific national cultures. Hofstede (1991) suggests that the significance of national culture is that most inhabitants of a country share the same mental program. Based on that, other researchers have sought to discover to what extent individuals' national culture influences their way of working and thinking, and to identify how people in different countries may have a collective programming, that is, a predisposition to behave in a certain way (Stredwick, 2005).

Although globalization is pervasive, it is not without serious criticism. Critics argue that globalization has demoted national governments as regulators of the free market system (Chomsky, 1999). Among other things, globalization may at times create inequality and environmental challenges. In 1996, the United Nations reported that the assets of the world's 368 billionaires exceeded the combined incomes of 45 per cent of the planet's population (Faux and Mishel, 2001). The Kyoto Protocol in 1997 and subsequent agreements at the Copenhagen climate summit in 2009 have highlighted issues (the need to reduce emissions of carbon dioxide and greenhouse gases) that directly affect the behaviour of organizations and countries. Organizations will lobby their governments to prevent the ratification of such treaties and lessen other external pressures that may affect their economic interests. For example, in 2002, Canada potentially faced unemployment losses through plant closures and costs in the manufacturing sector relating to curbing their emissions (Chase, 2002). When firms seek foreign investment or outsourcing to take advantage of economies of scale, lay-offs of workers in the home country may drain the economy through welfare benefits, and the demand for cheaper services in the host country of globalizing firms may entail making adjustments in the local labour markets.

Globalization has created dynamic alternatives for multinational firms. Corporations can outsource production and services to more economically viable locations, allowing multinational enterprises to drive down costs and increase their efficiency. For example, several clothing giants in the UK and the USA now outsource much of their manufacturing to South Asia, where production costs are much lower. And the displacement of workers caused by transferring resources away from Europe to Asia is not occurring just in the clothing industry. Many telecommunication firms too are transferring their back-office operations to India and other countries where costs are cheaper. This adversely affects the labour market in home countries that may face unemployment of the manual working classes.

In recent years, it has become increasingly evident that the global economic crisis that began in 2008 may leave many nations in recession. Many firms have reacted to this by making thousands of workers redundant, especially in sectors where the recession has hit hardest, for example financial services and the construction industry in 2009. This approach places pressure on organizations in terms of issues outside of their control, at times forcing them to relocate or restructure their operations. In these circumstances, it is essential to consider how HRM can be contextualized in its design and implementation.

Critical Thinking 2.2

Geographical variation in philosophy

Scholars and scientists list a large number of variations between countries and point towards a 'wide diversity in philosophies of people management' (Price, 1997: 122). When comparing one country with another, certain tasks that need to be completed within a line of work are given different priorities and are completed in a different way (Price, 1997). An example of this is the EU voting for a decree stating that its Member States should introduce legislation to decrease the number of working hours for employees. Every country then had to set a chosen number of hours, and it was apparent that the number of working hours thought suitable was different between different countries: the UK believed that 48 hours was reasonable, whereas France decided 35 hours was enough (Stredwick, 2005).

Questions
1. Why is it important to consider a country's sociocultural context when designing HRM?
2. What factors affect the number of working hours per week in a country?

Contextual influences on HRM

This section highlights different contextual forces that may influence HRM – we will start with a discussion of sociocultural context. Hofstede (1980) identified five dimensions of culture, and culture serves as an umbrella for all other contexts: legal, political, economic and technological contexts are all influenced by the role culture plays in a society. Noe et al. (2008) state that culture shapes people's respect and obedience for laws and regulations, hence affecting a country's legal and political system. And the way in which human capital and technology are valued by a particular society influences the economy of that country. Various HRM practices, such as recruitment and selection, training and development, compensation systems, performance appraisal and the employment relationship, are affected by the macrocontextual factors that this section will cover (Table 2.1).

Table 2.1 suggests that the strategies and practices of human resources ought to be examined in a broader context, and that social, legal, economic, political and technological influences all have a different impact when putting HRM into a context. For example, the global economic crisis and the near collapse of the banking system in 2008 are powerful contextual events that affect both national economies and organizations. Macrocontextual analysis will lay the groundwork for an investigation of the extent to which and how local cultural and institutional contexts affect HRM (Figure 2.1).

Table 2.1 An organization's macroenvironment

Legal and political factors	*Economic factors*
National legislation (current and future)	Home economy
International legislation	Trends in the economy
Regulatory bodies and processes	Overseas economies
Government policies	General taxation
Government term and change	Taxation specific to the product/service
Trading policies	Seasonality issues
Funding, grants and initiatives	Market/trade cycles
Home market pressure groups	Specific industry factors
International pressure groups	Distribution trends
Ecological/environmental issues	Customer/end-user drivers
Wars and conflicts	Interest/exchange rates
	International trade and monetary issues
Sociocultural factors	*Technological factors*
Lifestyle trends	Information and communications
Demographics (age, gender, literacy)	Development of competing technology
Language	Associated/dependent technologies
Ethnicity/race	Replacement technology/solutions
Religion/sect	Maturity of technology
Ethical issues	Manufacturing maturity and capacity
Social policy	Research funding
Technology	Technology legislation
Media views	Innovation potential
Consumer attitudes and opinions	Intellectual property issues
Company image	Global communications
Fashion, brand, role models	
Major events and influences	

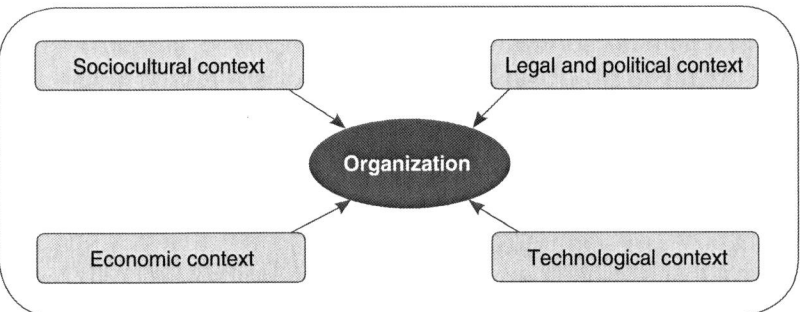

Figure 2.1 Key factors of the macroenvironment

Sociocultural context

Several elements in the sociocultural context have consequences for the design and efficacy of HRM. Culture dynamics and population demographics affect many aspects of the business environment. Rousseau (1990) argues that culture is a set of common values, beliefs, expectations and understandings that are obtained through socialization; it is learnt and shared by the members of the community (Noe et al., 2008). Culture can be defined as a system of values and norms that are shared among a group of people (Hill, 2009). It is dynamic and changes over time, for example when a nation becomes more affluent.

According to Tayeb (2005), HRM is a 'soft' aspect of an organization. Hence it is more influenced by culture than are financial and technical matters, which are considered to be the 'hard' aspects of an organization. Culture has a significant role in attracting, motivating and retaining individuals in organizations. Other key areas that are usually influenced by culture are training, performance management and compensation.

Hofstede's (1984) five dimensions of culture can influence management practices and the culture of organizations. The five categories are outlined in Table 2.2 and are also discussed below.

Individualism versus collectivism

This dimension describes the strength of the relationship between individuals in a society, that is, the degree to which people act as individuals rather than as members of a group, or the extent to which the individuals are integrated into groups. In individualist cultures such as the USA, the UK and The Netherlands, people are expected to look after their own interests and the interests of their immediate families. South-East Asian countries are more collectivist – they look after the interests of the larger community. Collectivist cultures tend to owe total loyalty to their group.

Low versus high power distance

This cultural dimension concerns hierarchical power relationships and refers to the unequal distribution of power. It describes the degree of inequality among people

Table 2.2 Hofstede's cultural dimensions

Individualism	The degree to which individuals are integrated into groups
Power distance	The extent to which the less powerful members of organizations and institutions accept and expect that power is distributed unequally
Uncertainty avoidance	A society's tolerance for uncertainty and ambiguity
Masculinity	The distribution of emotional roles between the genders
Long-term orientation	Long-term-oriented societies foster pragmatic virtues oriented towards future rewards, in particular saving, persistence and adapting to changing circumstances. Short-term-oriented societies foster virtues related to the past and present, such as national pride, respect for tradition, preservation of 'face' and fulfilment of social obligations

Source: Adapted from http://www.geerthofstede.nl/culture/dimensions-of-national-cultures.aspx (accessed July 2011).

that is considered to be normal in different countries. For example, Denmark and Israel have a small power distance, whereas India and the Philippines have a larger one. Another obvious example is the way people are addressed. In a business context, Mexican and Japanese people always address each other using titles, for example Señor Smith or Smith-San, but in the USA, first names are preferred. The reason for this is to minimize power distance.

Low versus high uncertainty avoidance

This dimension deals with the fact that the future is not perfectly predictable. For example, in Singapore and Jamaica, cultures of weak uncertainty avoidance, individuals are socialized to accept uncertainty and take each day as it comes. However, Greek and Portuguese culture socializes people to seek security through technology, law and religion.

Masculinity versus femininity

This dimension indicates the extent to which the dominant values in a society tend to relate to assertiveness and a greater interest in things than in people and quality of life. A 'masculine' culture is one in which dominance and assertiveness are valued, as is evident in the USA, Japan and Venezuela, for example. A 'feminine' culture, as can be found in The Netherlands and Sweden, promotes values that have been traditionally regarded as feminine, leaning more towards quality of life and relationships in society. Hofstede (1984) notes that most South-East Asian countries fall the between the masculine and feminine poles.

Long-term versus short-term orientation

Long-term orientation focuses on the future and holds values in the present that will not necessarily provide an immediate benefit; examples of countries adopting this approach are Japan and China. The USA, Russia and West Africa have a short-term orientation, being oriented towards the past and present, and promoting respect for tradition and the fulfilment of social obligations.

It is, however, important to acknowledge the criticism raised by some authors who view Hofstede's conceptualization of culture as static and essential. For example, Ailon (2008) and McSweeney (2002) caution against an uncritical reading of Hofstede's cultural dimensions, particularly because of their allegedly ethnocentric interpretations, which may lead to stereotyping.

Other scholars have identified additional dimensions of culture, including its informal, material or dynamic orientation (Adler, 1991; Ronen, 1994). They have compared HRM across countries and observed that cultural values and orientations are determinants of the differences found between them (see, for example, Arvey et al., 1991; Brewster and Tyson, 1991; Triandis et al., 1994; Brewster, 2007). However, culture may not explain all the differences in HRM found across countries (Lincoln, 1993; Jackson and Schuler, 1995) – such differences may also be an outcome of variations in economic and political conditions (see, for example, Carroll et al., 1988), laws and social policies (see, for example, Florkowski and Nath, 1993), industrial relations systems (Strauss, 1982) and labour market conditions (see, for example, Levy-Leboyer, 1994).

Legal and political context

The legal and political context is represented by national laws and sociopolitical policies and norms. Given that culture is a codification of right and wrong that exists in a country's laws, political systems and laws often reflect what constitute the legitimate behaviour and norm of a particular country (Tayeb, 2005; Noe et al., 2008). These contexts have the power to shape the nature of the employment relationship and the way in which HRM practices and policies are enacted (Bratton and Gold, 2007). Jackson and Schuler (1995) claim that almost all aspects of HRM are influenced by political and legal regulations, and Noe et al. (2008) have identified training, compensation, hiring and lay-offs as some of the HRM practices most commonly affected by this context.

The UK, the USA and most European countries, for example, place a strong emphasis on eliminating discrimination in the workplace; hence, equal employment regulations are put into effect. To focus on one example, in the UK the Sex Discrimination Act 1975, the Disability Discrimination Act 1995, the Race Relations Act 1976, the Employment Equality (Age) Regulations 2006, the Employment Equality (Religion or Beliefs) Regulations 2003 and the Equality Act (Sexual Orientation) Regulations 2007 are the laws that are included under the heading of Equality Employment Regulations. These regulations play a major role in developing HRM policies in relation to recruitment and dismissal procedures (Noe et al., 2008). Not only that, but pay and compensation can also be affected, with the setting of minimum wages for employees and a determination of the extent to which unions have the legal right to negotiate with the management.

The role of the state and its political system is crucial in determining the nature of employment relations in a country. Tayeb (2005) points out that workers in Germany have a legal right to 'co-determination', in which their participation in management is ensured; therefore, any HRM matter must abide by such laws (Noe et al., 2008). The Brunei case study at the end of this chapter provides another example of how the state impacts on employment relations. Furthermore, the

European Economic Community can also affect the political-legal system relating to HRM because it provides workers' fundamental social rights. These rights include freedom to be fairly compensated, freedom of association and collective bargaining, and equal treatment for men and women.

Legal influences affecting HRM practices can take the form of how local regulations affect the labour market (see Critical Thinking 2.3). Different countries will impose regulations on minimum wages and working hours as well as the involvement of trade unions, as has been seen in most Western developed economies. In the UK, government legislation has gradually worn down the power of trade unions and given rise to managerial flexibility and decentralized employment regulation. Although it is employers who control the design of HRM practice at an organizational level, managers need to be aware or informed of external developments in the legal context.

Politically related external conflicts may have acute implications for firms operating in a particular country, and managers need to be aware of political manoeuvrings relevant to their interests. The state does not, however, have a monopoly of control over the conduct of business – firms too can lobby and influence state policies to meet their needs (Needle, 2004). This was the case with the USA's mohair farmers, who were paid numerous cash payments from the Federal budget (Wheelan, 2003). The mohair agricultural subsidy has now disappeared, but it highlights the importance and power of organized institutions.

External pressures in the global political environment may directly affect how business and employee relationship are conducted. The collapse of the Communist system in 1989 in East Europe and Central Asia paved the way for new market economies based on the Western capitalist market system. Employment regulation and managerial responsibility were taken away from government and replaced by the power of institutions and organizations.

Critical Thinking 2.3

Employment relations in India

Labour unrest haunts auto sector in Tamil Nadu *Madhu Bharati, May 4, 2010 (Chennai)*

In recent decades, the Indian State of Tamil Nadu has been attracting enormous investment into automobile and accessories manufacturing. However, investors and manufacturers have of late become quite worried about repeated labour unrest, which is also impeding future investment in the state.

Hyundai, the second largest car maker in the country, is facing a similar situation. In May 2010, Hyundai employees threatened a sit-in strike after the company refused to reinstate 35 employees who had been dismissed for alleged misconduct. According to a news report, the company was not able to meet the agreed deadline to reinstate the dismissed workers. The company has been making frantic efforts for a possible settlement with the dismissed employees, offering them certain financial compensation as a part of the settlement.

If the strike announced in May 2010 does go ahead, it will be the third strike at Hyundai over the past year. Previously, in April 2009, employees went on strike for 18 days after the company laid off 65 workers. Then again, in July 2009, employees went on strike protesting at a wage agreement that had allegedly been signed by a minority union (or pocket union).

However, Hyundai is not the only company suffering as a result of labour unrest. In May 2009, workers at MRF struck work for several months, demanding recognition of their union. In September 2009, a senior official at Pricol was killed in workers' unrest in the auto-ancillary hub of Coimbatore, which resulted in a work closure lasting more than a month.

According to Abdul Majeed, an auto sector leader at PWC, labour laws are to be blamed: 'Our labour laws need an amendment. No one wins when it comes to dealing with labour. There has to be a give and take to some level amongst everyone. But our labour laws are the biggest of problems.'

The existing labour laws in India require large companies to seek prior permission from state governments before laying off workers or hiring workers on contract. These laws have been blamed by managers for encouraging workers to go on frequent strikes. With India positioning itself as the hub of small car production, such labour unrest may not send the right message to international investors.

Questions
1. In the light of this example, is it correct to blame laws for encouraging workers to strike?
2. Is it always possible to reconcile the ethical and business implications of labour laws?

Source: Adapted from NDTV Profit, May 4 2010.

Economic context

Although the economic context of a country is hardly predictable and stable, it is most likely to have long-term consequences for HRM (Tayeb, 2005). The attitudes and values that are embedded in every individual are formed by culture (Noe et al., 2008), hence the claim of human capital theory that a culture that encourages continuous learning is most likely to contribute to the success of the economy. Jackson and Schuler (1995) argue that skills, experience and knowledge are of significant value for the economy, and enhancing them can make individuals more productive and more adaptable to changing economic conditions.

The need to improve human capabilities relates back to whether the economic system supplies sufficient incentives for developing human capital. For example, Tayeb (2005) found that socialist economies offer a free education system, which provides an opportunity for human capital to be developed, thus enabling employees to obtain greater monetary rewards based on their competencies. This is evident in the USA, where levels of human capital are reflected in the differences in individuals' salaries, higher skilled employees, for example, earning better compensation than lower skill ones (Noe et al., 2008). In fact, it has been discovered that for each additional year of schooling, individuals' wages increase by about 10–16 per cent (Noe et al., 2008). Conversely, the opportunity to enhance human capital is smaller in capitalist systems due to the high costs of training employees; hence, human resource development is lower in capitalist countries (Tayeb, 2005).

Tayeb (2005) highlights the role of market conditions in determining employees' rights in capitalist countries that have 'centre right' policies. According to Flamholtz and Lacey (1981), investments in human capital are usually made in anticipation of future returns; besides improving employees' competencies, the costs also include factors such as motivating, monitoring and retaining these employees in order to benefit from their gains in productivity (Jackson and Schuler, 1995). In this book offers a detailed discussion of HRM in contemporary transnational businesses.

Of course, different forms of political capitalism, for example in terms of their socialist or free-market orientation, will have different effects on the way in which HRM is practised domestically as well as internationally. Even the most global of companies may be deeply rooted in the national business systems of their country of origin. For example, Edwards (2004), Hu (1992) and Ruigrok and van Tulder (1995) have argued that, on several dimensions, multinational corporations exhibit national characteristics.

There are various ways in which HRM can increase organizations' human capital, for instance offering attractive compensation and benefits packages to individuals, what Jackson and Schuler (1995) claim is 'buying' human capital, which is apparent in recruitment and selection processes. Creating equal opportunities in training and development can also help to 'make' human capital in an organization; at times of tight labour supply, this method is usually adopted. Training and developing existing employees' capabilities, as well as enhancing their wages, benefits and working conditions, can help in retaining them, especially when there is a scarce supply of human capital in the economy.

At times of economic boom and similarly in times of recession, the supply and demand of labour forces may vary in relation to a country's unemployment level. When the economy is booming and the level of unemployment is low, employees have much greater power and influence over their working conditions, pay and other employment rights (Tayeb, 2005). Having said that, managers in return gain more prerogatives during recessions and periods of high unemployment by controlling employees' working conditions and compensation, thus weakening the power and influence of both workers and trade unions. Jackson and Schuler (1995) note that it is common in such periods for absenteeism and turnover rates to fall because competition for jobs is more intense and employees' poor performance may result in retrenchment. It has been identified that, in the USA, excess demand typically relates to low unemployment, whereas high unemployment is reported to be associated with excess supply (Jackson and Schuler, 1995).

Technological context

Technology has evolved along with globalization, which is often associated with advances in communication and information technology. The way people throughout the world communicate, exchange information and learn about their world has changed as computer usage has become more prevalent in almost every part of the globe, further enhanced by the increase in the number of information technology-literate individuals (Burton et al., 2003). The influence of technology is also apparent in HRM (Critical Thinking 2.4), especially with the transformation of traditional HRM to IT-based HRM, or what is known as e-HRM (Bondarouk and Ruel, 2009), as a result of the growing sophistication of IT.

e-HRM, for example, deals with the implementation of HRM strategies, policies and practices through the full use of web-based technologies. Bondarouk et al. (2009) believe that e-HRM can reduce the cost of traditional methods of processing and administration of paperwork, as well as speeding up transaction processing, reducing information errors and improving the tracking and control of human resources actions. However, the effectiveness of e-HRM may depend upon the types and levels of knowledge that are required by the system and the extent to which tasks and people are interdependent (Jackson and Schuler, 1995).

When face-to-face HRM services become obsolete, higher levels of motivation and commitment are required (Othman and Teh, 2003). This is because employees are expected to work independently with little supervision, so the supervisor's role is greatly reduced as control over employees' work behaviour can no longer be exerted through direct observation. According to Bondarouk and Ruel (2009), e-HRM eliminates the 'human resources middleman' who is initially responsible for dealing with human resources matters.

Besides ensuring independent work through the introduction of e-HRM, IT also enables organizational learning to help employees improve their capability, adaptation, knowledge and understanding (Othman and Teh, 2003) because the use of teams is practised, which helps the transfer of learning from the individual to the organization. Othman and Teh claim that, with the growing usage of IT, people are expected to think critically, be able to solve problems, communicate and work in teams, creatively and proactively, as well as bring diverse and newer perspectives to their work. This requires a change in organizational structures and processes, for example selection processes, training, performance appraisals and rewards. Put simply, this means that the way employee performance is monitored has to rely on data interpretation and on assessing outputs.

There are, however, some critiques of the usage of IT in organizations. Based on findings from Othman and Teh (2003), the workforce is deskilled and controlled by managers through the use of IT. There is less chance for employees to develop their intellectual skills when their role has already been weakened by IT. Additionally, while most management invests heavily in acquiring technology, insufficient resources tend to be allocated to managing the organizational change process; thus HRM issues are neglected, and technology usage fails to meet expectations.

Critical discussion and analysis

HRM is constantly being reshaped by new economic, sociocultural and political realities. Changes in the levels of unemployment, structural transformation (for example, privatization and deindustrialization) and social trends (an ageing population) will all shift the balance of power in individual and collective contract negotiations.

Critical Thinking 2.4

Technological context and HRM

The correlation between new technology and work can be identified in many different forms. Academics have, however, pinpointed three specific areas in which HRM practices are directly affected (Millward and Stevens, 1986):

- *Advanced technology change:* new plant machinery and equipment that has incorporated microprocessor technology.
- *Conventional technological change:* machinery and equipment not aided by microprocessor technology.
- *Organizational change:* substantial changes in work organizations not involving new plant, machinery or equipment (Bratton and Gold, 2007).

Across many workplaces, microprocessor technology plays an active role: in 1998, 87 per cent of manufacturing workplaces in the UK used microprocessor-based technology, a large jump from 44 per cent in 1984 (Bratton and Gold, 2007). This reflects how great an influence the technological context may have on designing HRM. Entire organizations are administered based on their information system. In addition, manufacturing process concepts are part of the technological context that are able to directly impact upon organizations. Similarly, performance enhancement and organizational restructuring have vigorously shaped business processes in order to gain a competitive advantage.

Total quality management (TQM) focuses on maximizing profits by increasing service and product quality and decreasing costs (Hill, 2005). TQM and other quality management innovations such as Six Sigma are ground-breaking institutional approaches to improving organizations and are an example of how the technological context has influenced the design of HRM. However, quality management may also pose a problem for managers and organizations: although the system welcomes key aspects of quality – between suppliers and customers – it demands mutual commitment from every party involved in the organization and requires rigorous implementation and corporate governance, which may cause a hegemonic conflict between top and mid-level management and the workforce whom they direct.

Questions
1. Do technological advances always have positive implications for employees in organizations?
2. What role can HRM play in coping with changes in the technological context of an organization?

Furthermore, increasing globalization and advances in information and communication technologies are fast transforming the world into a global village in which management practices cannot remain isolated from external influences. As demonstrated in this chapter, we will be ill-advised to believe that globalization will cause organizations to become isolated or aloof from the society in which they operate.

Conversely, local contexts will remain a key influence on the way in which human resources are treated and managed.

It is, however, a fact that some types of HRM system may be used effectively across countries that are culturally quite dissimilar (Wickens, 1987; MacDuffie and Krafcik, 1992), and that organizational and industry characteristics remain key determinants of managerial practices and employee behaviours (Hofstede, 1991). Our understanding of the role of national culture in HRM could also benefit from investigations examining how multinational corporations develop HRM systems that are simultaneously consistent with multiple and distinct local cultures and yet internally consistent in the context of a single organization (cf. Heenan and Perlmutter, 1979; Tung, 1993; Jackson and Schuler, 1995).

From an academic perspective, certain specialized fields, for example industrial-organizational psychology and social work psychology, may be very useful in advancing our understanding of HRM in context. In this age of unprecedented internationalization as well as sociocultural specificity, the dearth of comparative publications in HRM is both surprising and alarming (Özbilgin, 2004). Several shifts in approach may be required: from treating organizational settings as sources of error variance to attending as closely as possible to individual characteristics; from focusing on individuals to treating social systems as the target for study; from focusing on single practices or policies to adopting a holistic approach to conceptualizing HRM systems; from research conducted in single organizations at one point in time to research comparing multiple organizations across time, space and culture; and from a search for the 'one best way' to a search for the many possible ways to design and maintain effective HRM systems (Jackson and Schuler, 1995) .

Conclusion

In conclusion, it is imperative that local contextual factors are considered when designing and operationalizing HRM policies. Although HRM and organizations are currently evolving due to the evolving nature of globalization, culture continues to have a vital effect on people and organizations. As Stredwick notes 'indeed to the observer in one country, the workplace practices in another might seem downright absurd ... any attempt to impose the ways and methods that he or she knows best in that other national context might be doomed to failure' (2005: 442).

The chapter has demonstrated that the field of HRM will have limited value if it does not adequately take into account cultural and institutional contexts. Global policies may seem an easy solution, but the issue of the expatriate workers, diversity and institutional and cultural variances must not be neglected. As Sparrow and Hiltrop (1994) suggest, care must be taken to escape the trap of ignoring significant differences between national cultures.

In this chapter, we have identified a number of elements in the macrolevel environment, that is, the sociocultural, legal, political, economic and technological contexts, that affect HRM in different ways. Economy is an important context that influences the design and outcomes of HRM; the financial crisis occurring at the time of writing this book has affected employment environment across many nations, and this is in turn affecting the behaviour of local labour markets.

Similarly, cultural values, such as age and gender traditions and stereotypes, are significant social contexts relevant to HRM.

Managers also need to be aware of legal contexts that have the potential to affect employment relations. Local culture and other external pressures will influence the design of HRM, but institutions can, in their turn, influence the contexts affecting them – political leveraging and lobbying has, for example, been conducted by corporations against agreements that have had the potential to affect employment behaviour, such as the Kyoto agreement.

External contexts can also be linked to the pursuit for competitive advantage, as is usually emphasized in organizations in industrialized Western economies linking HRM strategy to competitive advantage. Towards that end, HRM practitioners will need to analyse and respond to external contextual issues and deal with them in a coherent and strategic manner.

FOR DISCUSSION AND REVISION

1. How do macrocontextual factors affect the design and operationalization of the following HRM functions:
   - Recruitment and selection
   - Training
   - Performance management
   - Reward management
   - Career management.

2. Make a study of HRM policies and practices in a specific company. Identify the various ways in which the HRM policies and practices in that company are affected by its sociocultural, political, legal and economic contexts.

3. What are various tensions between the globalization and contextualization of HRM? What are implications of such tensions for the future of HRM?

4. Identify at least one resource in a language other than English which deals with issues related to HRM. Feel free to seek help from a friend who speaks a language other than English. What can you learn from this resource?

5. How does the dominance of US and UK literature in the field of HRM affect the contextualization of HRM?

6. According to Hofstede (1991), organizational and industry characteristics may be more important than national cultures as determinants of managerial practices and employee behaviours. Discuss.

Further reading

Books

Dowling, P. J., Festing, M. and Engle, A. D. (2008) *International Human Resource Management. Managing People in a Multinational Context* (5th edn). London: Thomson Publishing.

Price, A. (2007) *Human Resource Management in a Business Context* (3rd edn). London: Thomson Learning.

Quinn, J. B., Mintzberg, H. and James, R. M. (eds) (1988) *The Strategy Process: Concepts, Context, and Cases*. Englewood Cliffs, NJ: Prentice Hall International.

Journals

Budhwar, P. and Khatri, P. (2001) HRM in context: the applicability of HRM models in India. *International Journal of Cross Cultural Management*, 1(3): 333–56.

Jackson, S. E. and Schuler, R. S. (1995) Understanding human resource management in the context of organizations and their environment. *Annual Review of Psychology*, 46: 237–64.

Kamoche, K. (2002) Introduction: human resource management in Africa. *International Journal of Human Resource Management*, 13(7): 993–7.

Khatri, N. (1999) Emerging issues in strategic HRM in Singapore. *International Journal of Manpower*, 20(8): 516–29.

Schmidt, V. (1993) An end to French economic exceptionalism? The transformation of business under Mitterand. *California Management Review*, (Fall), 75–98.

Selmer, J. and Leon C. D. (2001) Pinoy-style HRM: human resource management in Philippines. *Asia Pacific Business Review*, 8(1): 127–44.

Wan, D. (2003) Human resource management in Singapore: changes and continuities. *Asia Pacific Business Review*, 9(4): 129–46.

Other resources

Institut Perkhidmatan Awam (2008) About IPA. Available from: http://ipa.gov.bn/ipaonline/ipa_information/ipa_history.aspx [accessed 31 December 2009].

Laman Rasmi Jabatan Pekhidmatan Awam (n.d.) Hal Ehwal JPA. Available from: http://jpa.gov.bn/hal_ehwal/index.htm [accessed 31 December 2009].

CASE STUDY

HRM in Brunei's public sector

Brunei is a monarchical government that is governed by Sultan Haji Hassanal Bolkiah Mu'izzaddin Waddaulah, who has executive authority and is assisted and advised by five constitutional bodies. The concept of 'Malay Islamic Monarchy' (MIB) is often thought of as a 'national philosophy', incorporating both the official Malay language, culture and customs and the importance of Islam as a religion and a set of guiding values.

Brunei, situated in South-East Asia, has an estimated population of 390,000, of whom 67 per cent are Malay and 15 per cent are Chinese, the remaining 18 per cent comprising indigenous groups, expatriates and immigrants. About 54 per cent of the overall population is made up of the 20–54-year age group, which is the economically productive group. The main source of income for Brunei is the oil and gas industry, followed by the private and government sectors. The public sector is the main employer for the majority of citizens and residents of Brunei (Brunei Economic Development Board, n.d.).

Owing to Brunei's distinct political system, it has different employment structures from those of other South-East Asian countries. Brunei is ruled by a strict essence of conformity and consensus that does not allow organization or individuals to challenge the government and its policies. Brunei's public sector may be seen as a 'model employer' (Beattie and Osborne, 2008), in the sense that the public sector sets an example to the private sector in terms of the fair treatment of employees and providing good conditions of service – this includes high levels of job security, better leave entitlement and generous pensions (Black and Upchurch, 1999). In this case study, we seek to explore how HRM policies and practices in the public sector are shaped by contextual influences in Brunei.

In the public sector, the *General Order and State Circulars* shape HRM practices. The General Order dates back to 1962; its content covers many key elements of HRM, for example appointments, promotions, benefit entitlement, work etiquette and discipline, although certain current issues related to HRM may not be present in the booklet. State Circulars cover more current HRM issues not addressed in the General Order, including those which have just arisen. All government bodies are sent Circulars whenever any new issues arise. Circulars often call upon the command of the Sultan of Brunei, who holds the absolute power in the way Brunei should be managed.

All civil servants are required to have a detailed knowledge of – and abide by – both the General Order and State Circulars in order to carry out their jobs and to progress in their careers. Every officer, supervisor or clerk who is aspiring towards promotion or a rise in salary will have to sit a written examination based on the content of both these sets of government policies.

A recent innovation within HRM in the Brunei public sector is the *Government Employee Management System* (GEMS), which is currently being trialled. This is a web-based system that enables efficient data input and greater transparency, which allows a better management of HRM practices such as recruitment and selection, compensation and benefits, as well as human resources administration. In addition, this will reduce paper usage and help Brunei to become more 'green'. Human resources administrators, government employees and the public are the three main stakeholders that GEMS is focusing on.

GEMS allows human resources administrators to manage job advertisements, and update and approve allowance and benefit applications. Government employees can apply for allowances and benefits online, retrieve useful information such as the latest policies that have been introduced, check their balance of leave entitlement and participate in surveys and forums where they can express their suggestions for how to improve the civil service. The public, on the other hand, can check job vacancies online, submit job applications and track their progress (Government Employee Management System, 2010).

Interviews conducted with a number of mangers and non-managerial staff in three departments within the Brunei public sector have provided an insight into how the local context has an impact on the design and implementation of HRM practices.

Socioculture

Many interviewees felt that Brunei's close-knit socioculture was an important factor in HRM practices. In particular, family relationships have a significant impact on workplace relations with supervisors and colleagues alike. As one interviewee stated:

> Working in the public sector, we are expected to respect our supervisors and officers. Supervisors and officers, regardless of their age, are like a father or leader to us; we share an informal relationship and talk to them in person if we have any issues or problems. A very family-like relationship is what motivates me, in particular, because it gives me a feeling of belonging and security. Although we have an informal relationship, it does not mean that we respect our superiors any less.

Previous research in other countries has highlighted that close-knit relationships often result in subjective and informal recruitment and selection processes (see, for example, Myloni et al.'s [2004] research in Greece). The majority of the employees interviewed for this case study claimed that family connections do not influence the way people are employed. This is evident in the following except:

> Yes we have a very close relationship in our culture, but I must say that it has no direct influence on the way we recruit and select applicants. Because everyone goes through the same procedure, that is, a written exam and then interviews for short-listed applicants. Furthermore, there are guidelines and procedures that need to be followed when recruiting people. Also, there is a group of committee members who decides on the final result'; this is based on consensus agreement. There is no room for favouritism. ... Personally, when the one who is newly recruited happens to be the son/daughter of an authority figure in the public sector, it is because he/she is qualified for the position, he/she might have already been trained with the kind of traits and skills that we are looking for. That is not nepotism.

However, the above account contradicts statements made by at least three other participants, who felt that 'nepotism' is still the essence of recruitment and selection, particularly in the government sector. Overall, the interviews suggest that close-knit social relationships in Brunei society have an impact on employment relationship in the workplace. However, the impact is moderated in HRM practices, particularly in recruitment and selection, because governmental regulations still affect HRM policies.

Law and politics

The national philosophy of MIB has an important influence on the way HRM works in the public sector. One interviewee noted that:

> Malay culture teaches us to be respectful and courteous to others. Islam instils honesty, trust, loyalty and good faith in oneself. Monarchic government means that His Majesty the Sultan holds the ultimate power in decision-making; no one is allowed to go against His Majesty's command. So, basically MIB influences us, in terms of the way we bring ourselves, the way we perform our work as a loyal subject of His Majesty. Every aspect of government affairs revolves around the concept of MIB.

The political influence of the state has in other studies been shown to either strengthen or undermine the role of HRM (Tayeb, 2005): a more cooperative government will have a better chance of adopting HRM efficiently, and vice versa. When asked whether monarchical government hinders employee participation in decision-making, one interviewee stated that:

> Any grievances, complaints or suggestions that are made by employees are attended to by respective supervisors or officers. Obviously in a monarchical government like Brunei, His Majesty holds the absolute powers in major decisions. But other than that, we do value employees' suggestions and points of view. We always take their opinions into consideration. In my position as an officer, I make sure that

my door is always open for them to come in and express any problem or suggestion that they may have. We ensure that we include them into any problem-solving and decision-making, because it is important that they feel included.

When asked about how the General Order and State Circulars are dealt with by public sector workers, managers underlined the critical importance of these, not only for their own careers, but also to provide a basis for all government servants for what should and should not be done while working in the public sector. As one interviewee noted:

Every circular is by command of His Majesty The Sultan; we are obliged to obey them. Officers are directed to encourage and make employees aware of existing circulars.

Non-managerial staff, however, tended to take a less rigorous approach and were sometimes unfamiliar with the content of these documents. Regulations were still poorly enforced regardless of the availability of the General Order and State Circulars.

With regards to the content of the General Order, benefits entitlements and working hours are usually included and practised in workplace policies. Participants generally felt that the policies adopted by the government are flexible and family-friendly. For example, one married female participant stated that:

Yes it is very family-friendly. One of the most obvious aspect is the working hours in the government sector. In the regulation book, General Order, it states that one should work maximum 8 hours from 7.45 am to 4.30 pm, but there is some flexibility when it comes to family responsibility, such as sending or picking up children to/from school. Also, in terms of leave entitlement, a married woman can take unpaid leave to follow her husband who was sent to work abroad and her job is still available when she comes back.

Economics

Research suggests that, for individuals to be more productive and adaptable to changing economic conditions, experience and knowledge have to be significantly valued (Jackson and Schuler, 1995). In the Brunei public sector, this valuation of education and human capital seems to have been achieved. When asked whether different economic situations influenced the need for educated or experienced workforce, one manager noted that:

In the government sector education plays a very important role because we believe fresh graduates have new ideas, which would ultimately benefit the organization over a person with experience who might not have anything new to bring to the organization.

From an economic perspective, Brunei is currently facing an excess supply of labour in the job market. An officer thus explained this:

This is a very challenging issue Brunei is facing. The demand for jobs is overwhelmingly high but the supply of jobs to accommodate the demand is rather low. This is because a new post will only be available when someone retires, resigns, there is end of contract of an employee or a budget is allocated to create new posts.

This is consistent with Jackson and Schuler's observation that a country is likely to experience high unemployment in times of oversupply of its labour force. Brunei is currently experiencing this problem, and thus many students are sponsored to study abroad to temporarily alleviate the number of workers currently seeking jobs. The problem with an oversupply of labour is that very few vacant positions are usually available in the government sector. For example, in response to a recent advertisement (at the time of this research) for a clerical position, 1,000 applications were received for only four vacancies.

Technology

Technology is a new element in the government sector in Brunei. The Sultan has allocated billions of dollars for IT to be used effectively. In particular, the introduction of GEMS, described above, is indicative of a new approach to technology in HRM practice. Public sector workers have mixed reactions to this new system. One manager noted that:

> It's very convenient because there's less paperwork and sharing of documents will be easier as it is computerised. Leave applications, benefits entitlement, car and house loans, all are accessible any time and anywhere.

Another, less positively, argued that:

> We currently have an online method of inputting data called SIMPA; it is in Malay and it is very straightforward. But it is only for data entry and nothing else. Well, GEMS from what I have tried is a bit too complex for me because there are so may folders to click on and most importantly, it is in English. To be honest, I am not good in English language, so I don't know how I will be able to get used to the changes.

Officers in general tend to agree with the technological changes that the government intends to implement, whereas the staff are slightly hesitant about the changes. For example, a training officer stated that:

> Every human resources development representative of each government department is given courses to train their respective employees on the usage of this new system. Emphasis is given to clerical positions as they are the ones who handle most paperwork.

From the interview data, one obvious challenge facing HRM in Brunei relates to how well individuals can adjust themselves to technological changes. Moving away from the traditional face-to-face HRM services may cause some difficulty and stress for some employees. Training, on the other hand, may assist staff and officers to adapt effectively to such changes.

Conclusion

This study of HRM in Brunei makes clear that the macroenvironmental context has a huge impact on the way HRM polices are designed and implemented. Culture serves as the overarching umbrella for all the other contexts, such as the legal and political system, the economy and adaptation to technology. In the main, HRM in Brunei revolves around the MIB ideology, which signifies the extent to which Western-originated HRM practices are customized and applied in the country. Human capital is given great importance and has high value in the job market; incentives are, therefore, given to improve human capital. However, the monarchical government of Brunei limits the ability for freedom of speech, freedom of associations and collective bargaining.

A hierarchical relationship is present in the government sector, but power distance is not a key concern, as is evident from the interview data. These show that Brunei does have a hierarchical relationship as claimed by Hofstede (1984) but that the power distance is not very great and is often a sign of respect for authority and for one's superiors. The relationship shared between officers and subordinates positively affects employees' participation rates in problem-solving and decision-making. However, close-knit relationships seem not to excessively influence the recruitment and selection process, which is regulated by state laws and procedures.

From a legal and political context perspective, the MIB ideology seems to have a visible impact on HRM. It enhances the initiatives of various departments in ensuring that everyone gets 100 hours of training and development. It also prohibits employees from setting up or joining trade unions, instead encouraging a more peaceful and harmonious negotiation with officers and supervisors. The General Order and State Circulars are still weakly enforced, although superiors tried to stress their importance. In addition, MIB and state laws help to create a family-friendly policy that is flexible for working parents and employees with dependants.

From an economic context perspective, human capital, education, knowledge and skills are encouraged through continuous learning for all employees and officers. The benefits offered by the public sector create the perception of its being the most stable and secure workplace, and hence provide an advantage when recruiting and retaining human capital. Oversupply of the workforce is a prominent issue in Brunei. This affects HRM processes in making sure that the public sector recruits the right people for the right jobs.

Technology seems to be an upcoming aspect in the government sector. Not much information could be gleaned, except for the perceptions of older workers that there is a shift towards an online-based system of HRM. Some older workers find it difficult to adjust to this, but they are still able to do so slowly. Also, when officers and staff were asked whether this would increase convenience, most participants answered positively, saying that IT is helping to speed up their work and lessen their workload.

It can be concluded that local culture and politics (MIB) have a much greater impact on the implementation of HRM in Brunei. We recommend that further research be conducted on a larger scale to explore the contextualization of HRM in Brunei and other national contexts. Preferably, academia–industry partnership-based research in these government departments might allow for a deeper understanding of the topic.

Questions

1. How do culture and politics affect the design and implementation of HRM in Brunei?
2. Culture serves as the overarching umbrella for all the other contexts, such as the legal and political system, the economy and adaptation to technology. Critically discuss this.
3. How can HRM enable individual employees to adjust themselves to technological changes in their organizations?
4. How does HRM in Brunei different from HRM in a Western country?

References

Adler, N. J. (1991) *International Dimensions of Organizational Behavior*. Boston, MA: PWS-KENT Publishing.
Ailon, G. (2008) Mirror, mirror on the wall: culture's consequences in a value test of its own design. *Academy of Management Review*, 33(4): 885–904.
Arvey, R. D., Bhagat, R. S. and Salas, E. (1991) Cross-cultural and cross-national issues in personnel and human resources management: where do we go from here? *Personnel and Human Resource Management*, 9: 367–407.
Baruch, Y. (2001) Global or North American top management journals? *Journal of Cross-cultural Management*, 1(1): 131–47.
Beattie, R. S. and Osborne, S. P. (2008) *Human Resource Management in the Public Sector*. London: Routledge.
Beer, M., Lawrance, P. R., Mills, D. Q. and Walton, R. E. (1985) *Human Resource Management*. New York: Free Press.
Bennington, L. and Habir, A. D. (2003) Human resource management in Indonesia. *Human Resource Management Review*, 13(3): 373–92.
Black, J. and Upchurch, M. (1999) Public sector employment. In Hollinshead, G., Nicholls, P. and Tailby, S. (eds) *Employee Relations*. London: Financial Times Management.
Bondaruk, T. V. and Ruel, H. J. M. (2009) Electronic human resource management: challenges in the digital era. *International Journal of Human Resource Management*, 20(3): 505–14.
Bondaruk, T., Ruel, H. and Heijden B. V. D. (2009) e-HRM effectiveness in a public sector organization: a multi-stakeholder perspective. *International Journal of Human Resource Management*, 20(3): 578–90.
Bratton, J. and Gold, J. (2007) *Human Resource Management: Theory and Practice* (4th edn). New York: Palgrave Macmillan.
Brewster, C. (2007) Comparative HRM: European views and perspectives. *International Journal of Human Resource Management*, 18(5): 769–87.
Brewster, C. and Tyson, S. (eds) (1991) *International Comparisons in Human Resource Management*. London: Pitman.
Brunei Economic Development Board (n.d.) Introducing Brunei. [Online]. Available from: http://www.bedb.com.bn/ [Accessed 9 November 2009].
Budhwar, P. S. and Debrah, Y. A. (2001) *Human Resource Management in Developing Countries*. London: Routledge.
Burton, J. P., Butler, J. E. and Mowday, R. T. (2003) Lions, tigers and alley cats: HRM's role in Asian business development. *Human Resource Management Review*, 13(3): 487–98.
Caligiuri, P. M. (1999) The ranking of scholarly journals in international human resource management. *International Journal of Human Resource Management*, 10(3): 515–19.
Carroll, G. R., Delacroix, J. and Goodstein, J. (1988) The political environments of organizations: an ecological view. *Research in Organizational Behavior*, 10: 359–92.

Chase, S., 2002. Ratifying Kyoto. *Globe and Mail*, 27 February, p. B6.
Chomsky, N. (1999). *Profit over People: Neoliberalism and the Global Order*. New York: Seven Stories Press.
Clark, T., Gospel, H. and Montgomery, J. (1999) Running on the spot? A review of twenty years of research on the management of human resources in comparative and international perspective. *International Journal of Human Resource Management*, 10(3): 520–44.
Clark, T., Grant, D. and Heijltjes, M. (2000) Researching comparative and international human resource management. *International Studies of Management and Organization*, 29(4): 6–17.
Collin, A. (2007) Contextualising HRM: developing critical thinking. In Beardwell, J. and Claydon, T. (eds) *Human Resource Management: A Contemporary Approach*. Harlow: FT Prentice Hall, pp. 83–116.
Drucker, P. (1954) *The Practice of Management*. New York: Harper & Row.
Edwards, T. (2004) The transfer of employment practices across borders in multinational companies. In Harzing, A.-W. and Ruysseveldt, J. V. (eds) *International Human Resource Management*. London: Sage, pp. 389–410.
Faux, J. & Mishel, L. (2001) Inequality and the global economy. In Hutton, W. and Giddens, A. (eds.) *On the Edge: Living with Capitalism*. London: Vintage Books.
Flamholtz, E. G. and Lacey, J. M. (1981) Personnel management, human capital theory, and human resource accounting. Cited in Jackson, S. E. and Schuler, R. S. (1995) Understanding human resource management in the context of organizations and their environments. *Annual Review of Psychology*, 46: 237–64.
Florkowski, G. W. and Nath, R. (1993) MNC responses to the legal environment of international human resource management. *International Journal of Human Resource Management*, 4: 305–24.
Gaugler, E. (1988) HR management: an international comparison. *Personnel*, (August): 24–30.
Government Employee Management System (2010) About GEMS: GEMS Background. [Online]. Available from: http://www.jpa.gov.bn/gems/EN/About_GEMS/background.htm [Accessed 10 January 2010].
Harris, L. (2002) The future for the HRM function in local government: everything has changed – but has anything changed? *Strategic Change*, 11(7): 369–78.
Heenan, D. A. and Perlmutter, H. V. (1979) *Multinational Organization Development*. Reading, MA: Pearson Addison Wesley.
Hill, T. (2005) *Operations Management*. Basingstoke: Palgrave Macmillan.
Hill, C. (2009) *International Business: Competing in the Global Marketplace* (7th edn). New York: McGraw-Hill.
Hofstede, G. (1980) *Culture's Consequences: International Differences in Work Related Values*. Beverly Hills: Sage.
Hofstede, G. (1984) Cultural dimension in management and planning. *Asia Pacific Journal of Management*, 1(2): 81–99.
Hofstede, G. (1991) *Cultures and Organizations*. London: McGraw-Hill.
Hu, Y.-S. (1992) Global or stateless corporations are national firms with international operations. *California Management Review*, (Winter): 107–26.
Jackson, S. E. and Schuler, R. S. (1995) Understanding human resource management in the context of organizations and their environments. *Annual Review of Psychology*, 46: 237–64.
Levy-Leboyer, C. (1994) Selection and assessment in Europe. In Triandis, H. C., Dunnette, M. D. and Hough, L. M. (eds) *Handbook of Industrial and Organizational Psychology* (2nd edn, Vol. 4). Palo Alto, CA: Consulting Psychology Press, pp. 173–90.
Lincoln, J. R. (1993) Work organization in Japan and the United States. In Kogut, B. (ed.) *Country Competitiveness: Technology and the Organizing of Work*. Oxford: Oxford University Press, pp. 93–124.
McCourt, W. and Foon L. M. (2007) Malaysia as model: policy transferability in an Asian country. *Public Management Review*, 9(2): 211–29.
MacDuffie, J. P. and Krafcik, J. (1992) Integrating technology and human resources for high performance manufacturing. In Kochan, T. and Useem, M. (eds) *Transforming Organizations*. New York: Oxford University Press, pp. 210–26.

McGregor, D. (1957) *The Human Side of Enterprise. Fifth Anniversary Convocation of the MIT School of Industrial Management.* Cambridge, MA: MIT Press.

McSweeney, B. (2002) Hofstede's model of national cultural differences and their consequences: a triumph of faith – a failure of analysis. *Human Relations*, 55(1): 89–118.

Maurice, M., Sellier, F. and Silvestre, J.-J. (1986) *Bases of Industrial Power.* Cambridge, MA: MIT Press.

Millward, N. and Stevens, M. (1986) *British Workplace Industrial Relations 1980–1984.* Aldershot: Gower.

Myloni, B., Harzing, A. K. and Mirza, H. (2004) Host country specific factors and the transfer of human resource management practices in multinational companies. *International Journal of Manpower*, 25(6): 518–34.

Needle, D. (2004) *Business in Context* (4th edn). London: Thomson.

Noe, R. A., Hollenbeck, J. R., Gerhart, B. and Wright, P. M. (2008) *Human Resource Management: Gaining a Competitive Advantage* (6th edn). New York: McGraw Hill.

Othman, R. and The, C. (2003) On developing the informated work place: HRM issues in Malaysia. *Human Resource Management Review*, 13: 393–406.

Özbilgin, M. (2004) Inertia of the international human resource management text in a changing world: an examination of the editorial board membership of the top 21 IHRM journals. *Personnel Review*, 33(2): 205–21.

Price, A. (1997) *Human Resource Management in a Business Context.* London: International Thomson Business Press.

Ronen, S. (1994) An underlying structure of motivational need taxonomies: a cross-cultural confirmation. In Triandis, H. C., Dunnette, M. D. and Hough, L. M. (eds) *Handbook of Industrial and Organizational Psychology* (2nd edn, Vol. 4). Palo Alto, CA: Consulting Psychology Press, pp. 241–70.

Rousseau, D. M. (1990). Assessing organizational culture: the case for multiple methods. In Schneider, B. (ed.), *Organizational Climate and Culture.* San Francisco: Jossey-Bass, pp. 153–92.

Ruigrok, W. and van Tulder, R. (1995) *The Logic of International Restructuring.* London: Routledge.

Schneider, S. (2001) Introduction to the international human resource management special issue. *Journal of World Business*, 36(4): 341.

Schuler, R. S. and Jackson, S. E. (1987) Linking competitive strategies with human resource management practices. *Academy of Management Review*, 1(3): 207–19.

Sparrow, P. R. and Hiltrop, J.-M. (1994) *European Human Resource Management in Transition.* London: Prentice Hall.

Storey, J. (1992) *Developments in the Management of Human Resources: An Analytical Review.* Oxford: Blackwell.

Strauss, G. (1982) Workers participation in management: an international perspective. *Research in Organizational Behavior*, 4: 173–265.

Stredwick, J. (2005) *An Introduction to Human Resource Management* (2nd edn). London: Elsevier.

Tayeb, M. H. (2005) *International Human Resource Management: A Multinational Company Perspective.* New York: Oxford University Press.

Taylor, S., Beechler, S. and Napier, N. (1996) Toward an integrated model for strategic international human resource management. *Academy of Management Review*, 21(4): 959–71.

Triandis, H. C., Dunnette, M. D. and Hough, L. M. (eds) (1994) *Handbook of Industrial and Organizational Psychology* (2nd edn, Vol. 4). Palo Alto, CA: Consulting Psychology Press.

Tung, R. L. (1993) Managing cross-national and intra-national diversity. *Human Resource Management Journal*, 23(4): 461–77.

Tylor, E. B. (1924). *Primitive Culture* (7th edn, Vols 1 and 2). New York: Brentano's.

Wheelan, C. (2003) *Naked Economics: Undressing the Dismal Science.* New York: W. W. Norton.

Wickens, P. (1987) *The Road to Nissan.* London: Macmillan.

CHAPTER 3
A critical perspective on strategic human resource management

Dima Jamali and Fida Afiouni

- Introduction
- From personnel management to SHRM: an evolutionary road map
- Differentiating attributes, key contributions and underlying theories
- Critical analysis and discussion
- Conclusion
- For discussion and revision
- Further reading
- Case study: Strategic human resource management: insights from Deloitte ME's experience
- References

After reading this chapter, you should be able to:
- Recognize recent transformations and dynamic change in the human resources management (HRM) field
- Demonstrate good knowledge of the various theoretical approaches to strategic HRM
- Discuss how human resources can be a source of sustainable competitive advantage
- Critically examine choices and contingencies in the HRM field
- Recognize the significant advances brought about by the strategic HRM paradigm, as well as lingering challenges, particularly the gap that remains between human resources policies and practices

Introduction

Over the past two decades, there has been a vibrant change and evolution in the field of human resource management (HRM). Schuler and Jackson (2007) categorize changes in the field into two major transformations. The first has entailed a transformation from personnel management to HRM, and the second constituted a leap forward into what is commonly referred to today as strategic HRM (SHRM). According to its proponents, SHRM constitutes a new orthodoxy and is mainly differentiated by its macro or strategic orientation, as well as its focus on outcomes and performance (Delery and Doty, 1996). Although it is certainly a discipline that is still taking shape and form, SHRM has enjoyed an astounding ascendancy in recent years, and has attracted significant interest from the academic and practitioner community (Becker and Huselid, 2006).

The aim of this chapter is to provide a critical assessment of SHRM, shedding light on its differentiating attributes and theoretical foundations, as well as the persistent gaps and challenges in this rapidly growing field. SHRM undoubtedly presents significant advances and new insights in relation to people management, but it is not a panacea and there is still no consensus on an exact definition of SHRM among scholars. These challenges, coupled with the difficulty of translating theory into practice, are possible stumbling blocks in the way of the fully fledged maturation of SHRM and will be fleshed out and discussed further in the sections below.

The structure of this chapter is as follows. First, we will explore the evolutionary road map from personnel management to SHRM and examine the various theoretical approaches to SHRM, namely the universalist, contingency and resource-based views (RBVs). This exploration will be enriched by practical exercises and critical questions that allow for a better understanding of the strategic role of HRM. Finally, we will adopt a critical perspective that aims to reveal the global and ethical issues that underpin SHRM and sensitize the reader to the potential gaps that remain between the policy and practice of SHRM.

From personnel management to SHRM: an evolutionary road map

The traditional personnel management approach was prevalent in the first part of the 20th century and reflected management currents revolving around Weberism, Taylorism and scientific management. The focus was on maximizing labour productivity and efficiency, and in response to this, the personnel management function adopted a uniquely inward and operational focus, with an obsessive concern with legal compliance and streamlining basic administrative and personnel processes. Personnel management was therefore commonly characterized as a transactional, low-level, record-keeping and maintenance function with a short-term micro-orientation and a preoccupation with operational issues, practices and policies, to the neglect of broader business issues and the overall direction of the organization (Guest, 1987; Redman and Wilkinson, 2009). This approach to the management of people was essentially anchored in a view of labour as a commodity to be used efficiently and discarded as appropriate.

The first major transformation or turning point came about in the 1970s and reflected the ascendancy of the human relations and organizational behaviour paradigms (Mahoney and Deckop, 1986; Anthony et al., 2002). These new theoretical traditions highlighted the complexity of human behaviour and the importance of soft aspects of management, including leadership and motivation, in impacting work outcomes in a positive way. The challenge for HRM was therefore to reposition 'employees as valued organizational resources' (Dunn, 2006: 71) and to better orchestrate policies and practices that affected their behaviour and productivity at work (Schuler and Jackson, 2007).

Although HRM retained essentially its tactical short-term orientation, it was heralded as 'a new era of humane people oriented employment management' (Keenoy, 1990: 375) capitalizing on systematic and professional management practices, and the improved coordination and integration of human resources practices. Valuing employees as an important human capital – an investment rather than a cost (Wright et al., 2001) – was the prevailing assumption permeating this first transformation of the function. This transformation of the HRM function was in turn accompanied by the emergence of the total quality management (TQM) paradigm. Despite differences in the nature of and approaches to TQM and HRM, both concepts share the paramount importance of people-focused organizational efforts. These shared characteristics of the two concepts suggest a resurgence of the value attached to managing human resources, as both focus on a systematic and careful approach to the recruitment of employees, the use of teamwork and group problem-solving, egalitarian work structures, a commitment to training, and performance and reward systems.

The second major transformation in the field occurred more recently, starting in the 1990s in response to large-scale organizational change and an intensely competitive global economic environment (Calakoglu et al., 2006). In the context of new trends including organizational transience, corporate restructuring (for example, mergers and acquisitions, and downsizing), a renewed focus on quality and customers, and the war for talent among others (Conner and Ulrich, 1996; Amit and Belcourt, 1999; Pilbeam and Corbridge, 2006), the need for agility and efficiency has been accentuated. In addition, the role of human resources has been brought to the fore as it has been realized that employees can have a significant impact on the overall success of the organization. SHRM is therefore anchored in a recent appreciation that human resources and the effective management of people are critical to profitability (Boxall and Purcell, 2011) and the overall ability of a firm to thrive and compete (Meilich, 2005). As suggested by Boxall and Purcell (2011), the adjective 'strategic' implies a concern with the ways in which HRM is critical to the firm's survival and relative success', and SHRM has come to denote 'a strategic and coherent approach to the management of an organization's most valued assets – the people working there, who individually and collectively contribute to the achievement of its objectives' (Armstrong, 2006: 3).

Figure 3.1, adapted from Pilbeam and Corbridge (2006) and Brockbank (1999), outlines this ongoing process of transformation or evolution from traditional personnel management to SHRM. Figure 3.1 also highlights interesting nuances at both sides of the continuum. On the left-hand side, we can note nuances between reactive and proactive operational orientations with an operationally reactive human resources function focused on day-to-day demands and implementation of the regular and

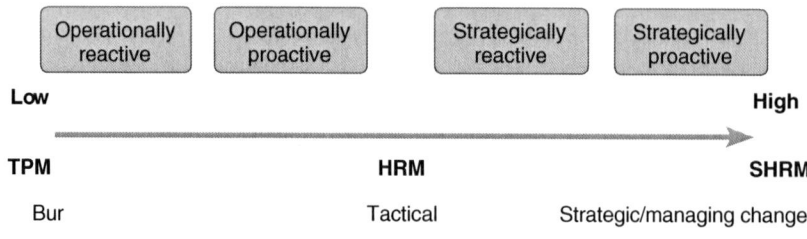

Figure 3.1 From traditional personnel management (TPM) to strategic human resource management (SRHM)
Source: Adapted from Pilbeam and Corbridge (2006), Bockbank (1999).

Mini Case Study 3.1

HRM at Algorithm: good strategic alignment

Algorithm is a pharmaceutical plant operating in the Middle East, having existed under this name since 1989. The firm's business line is manufacturing pharmaceutical products and sending them to its distributors and exporters (it does not handle any distribution activities itself). Algorithm belongs to a group of three sister companies employing a total of 320 employees, 170 of whom are employed by Algorithm. It manufactures products under license, as well as its own generic products. It has a development laboratory – the Product Development Lab – but this mainly copies generic products and designs new products without creating molecules. The organization does not outsource any technical or production activities as it has all the necessary departments and assets. This means that it manufactures, analyses and registers all its products. The plant's production includes over-the-counter (OTC) and prescription drugs, but no cosmetic products.

An interview was conducted with Mrs Nicole Bakhache, the HR and administration manager at Algorithm Lebanon and a member of Algorithm's strategy-setting team. The human resources function at Algorithm has been given much greater importance over the past 5 years, and no major decision related to people or structure is taken without human resources input. Mrs Bakhache explained that some personnel activities involve a more reactive role (for example, benefits and payroll), whereas other human resources activities, such as recruitment, training and career planning, involve a more proactive and strategic role.

At Algorithm, the human resources department also plays a substantial role in ensuring the success of general business strategies, and helping to accomplish business goals. It is expected to translate business strategy into action, and to focus on aligning human resources strategies and practices with business strategies. The department has forged a partnership with line managers, and together they formulate and manage processes to help meet business objectives. Furthermore, line managers now view human resources as a partner and are themselves involved in the management of human resources – working along with the human resources function on activities such as recruitment, people development and personnel-related issues.

The human resources manager explained that the strategies of the human resources function are aligned with the general business strategies, and that line management involves human resources in meetings where future strategies are being formulated. They are, for example, involved in strategic meetings discussing company expansion (since they will have to recruit the qualified staff needed for this), budgeting and planning. Mrs Bakhache explained that the technical departments do not have regular meetings with human resources, but hold periodic meetings to discuss budgets, management reviews, expansion plans, recruitment and a review of training needs. The input of human resources is required when discussing issues related to staff, such as filling internal vacancies and retaining key staff if ever they should consider leaving the company.

Questions

1. How does the human resources department at Algorithm help to accomplish its business goals?
2. Use Figure 3.1 to evaluate the role of the human resources department in terms of its strategic/operational orientation as well as proactive/reactive orientation.

mundane; this contrasts with a more proactive orientation concerned with improving the basics, as suggested by Brockbank (1999). We can also highlight interesting nuances between strategically reactive and strategically proactive human resources orientations on the right-hand side of the continuum, with the strategically reactive human resources generally concerned with implementing and realizing strategy, and more strategically proactive human resources concerned with creating and forging strategic alternatives (Brockbank, 1999).

Differentiating attributes, key contributions and underlying theories

At the heart of SHRM lies the idea that the way in which people are managed is one of the most crucial factors in the array of competitiveness-inducing variables, with a view that labour is an asset that should be leveraged in the pursuit of competitive advantage (Boxall and Purcell, 2011). Strategic choices associated with labour processes in turn reflect on the firm's performance. Hence, human resource policies need to be integrated with each other, as well as linked to the strategies and overall direction of the organization (Schuler and Jackson, 2007). In this context, the core differentiating attributes of SHRM have come to be theorized as revolving around commitment, flexibility, quality and integration (Guest, 1987), a strategic thrust informing decisions about people management and a new set of levers to shape the employment relationship (Storey, 2001). Armstrong (2006) identifies core differentiating features of SHRM revolving around strategic orientation, commitment, people as a core asset and business values/results. Some of these core themes are reflected in Table 3.1.

In essence, SHRM is more fluid, organic and strategy-driven practice and is associated with *commitment*-based systems of control (Guest, 1990: 152). SHRM is therefore based on the assumption that people are not only assets, but also have value-creating properties. This insight derives essentially from the RBV of the firm, a concept that emerged in 1984 and has enjoyed increasing popularity within the strategic management and HRM literatures. According to Wright et al. (2001), the RBV has been clearly instrumental to the development of the SHRM field of study, primarily because it has promoted a rebalancing of the strategy literature away from external factors (such as industry position) towards the firm's internal resources as sources of competitive advantage.

Indeed, one of the key contributions of the RBV to date has been a theory of competitive advantage and how firms can achieve and sustain their competitive advantage (Fahy, 2000). The RBV contends that the answer to this question lies in the nurturing and deployment of certain key resources. From an RBV perspective, not all resources are of equal importance – certain resources have an edge in terms of creating competitive advantage (Fahy, 2000). Barney (1991) posits that desirable resources must meet four conditions, namely value, rareness, inimitability and non-substitutability. Collis and Montgomery (1995) suggest along the same lines that value-creating resources are characterized by inimitability, durability, appropriability, non-substitutability and competitive superiority. The RBV has therefore contributed significantly in terms of putting people on the strategy radar screen and highlighting the importance of people to competitive advantage.

Table 3.1 Definitions and differentiating attributes of strategic human resource management (SHRM)

Author(s)	Definition of SHRM
Boxall and Purcell (2000)	A concern with the ways in which HRM is critical to organizational effectiveness
Buyens and De Vos (2001)	The linking of the human resources function with the strategic goals and objectives of the organization in order to improve business performance and develop organizational cultures that foster innovation and flexibility
Redman and Wilkinson (2009)	A concept entailing strategic integration and a positive approach to the management of employees, with an emphasis on staff as a resource rather than a cost
Guest (1987)	SRHM has four key dimensions: commitment, flexibility, quality and integration
Armstrong (2006)	SHRM is differentiated by its strategic thrust, emphasis on integration, commitment orientation, belief that people are core assets and focus on business values and results
Storey (2001)	Four key aspects of SHRM entailing a particular constellation of beliefs and assumptions, a strategic thrust informing decisions about people management, the central involvement of line managers, and a reliance upon a new set of levers to shape the employment relationship

> **Exercise**
>
> Barney (1991) posits that desirable resources must meet four conditions – value, rareness, inimitability and non-substitutability – in order to be a source of sustainable competitive advantage. Based on these characteristics, critically examine how human resources are a possible source of competitive advantage.
>
> - Where does the advantage come from?
> - Is it a human capital advantage deriving from the quality of the employees, or is it a human process advantage deriving from the set of human resources policies and practices that has been applied?

Following the logic of the RBV, human capital constitutes a very important intangible asset or resource that is resistant to duplication by competitors. However, what is equally important from this perspective is the way in which this asset is deployed and managed, which has been captured through the notion of 'capabilities' that was introduced by Leonard-Barton as early as 1992. Capabilities are the tangible and intangible assets that firms use to develop and implement their strategies (Wernerfelt, 1995). Essentially, capabilities encompass the skills of individuals and groups, as well as the organizational routines and interactions through which all the firm's resources are coordinated (Grant, 1991). Typical of the latter are, among others, teamwork, communication, collaboration, learning, knowledge management, work design, organizational culture, trust between management and workers, and leadership. In this respect, human resources is not limited to its effects on employee skills and behaviour. Instead, its effects are more encompassing in that they help weave those skills and behaviours within the broader fabric of organizational systems, processes and ultimately competencies (Wright et al., 2001).

Capabilities that give an organization a strategic advantage over its competitors have been called core capabilities (Leonard-Barton, 1992), although a number of alternative terms have been used to refer to the same or similar concepts. An important article by Prahalad and Hamel (1990) that helped to disseminate the RBV refers to developing core competence within an organization. Core competence develops from collective learning in an organization, especially from being able to coordinate diverse sets of skills and integrate different technologies. Teece et al. (1997) define dynamic capabilities as the ability to integrate, build and reconfigure internal and external competencies to address rapidly changing environments. Similarly, Leonard-Barton (1992) posits that dynamic capabilities reflect an organization's ability to achieve new and innovative forms of competitive advantage given path dependencies and market positions.

In other words, human resources do not automatically confer a sustainable competitive advantage, and the managerial role is critical in nurturing, deploying and protecting key firm resources over time (Williams, 1992). Whereas exceptional human talent confers human capital advantage (HCA), firms need to supplement or pair the latter with what has been referred to as human process advantage

(HPA), through the nurturing of specific processes, routines and practices, and their constellation, operation and application over time (Boxall, 1996). Therefore, organizations face a dual challenge – or the management of mutuality (Wright et al., 2001) – that entails the creation of a committed and talented workforce, as well as nurturing the right processes that support this talent and shape its competencies, cognitions and attitudes (Boxall, 1996). The contemporary theories of job design, are important in conferring such a HPA in the sense that they focus on human needs and psychological aspects of job content. In other words, SHRM needs to take into account job design aspects relating to variety and challenge, continuous learning, decision-making autonomy and social relationships, particularly in creating HPA.

These two sources of competitive advantage, when effectively combined, reinforce the systemic quality of highly effective human resources architectures and confer human resource advantage, as illustrated in Figure 3.2. SHRM posits in turn a relationship between a firm's human resources architecture and that firm's performance (Becker and Huselid, 2006).

The link between the human resources architecture and the firm's performance is not direct but is usually mediated by an appropriate match between the human resources architecture and strategic choice – what is commonly referred to as the human resources–strategy fit (Schuler and Jackson, 1987). In other words, the human resources architecture needs to be aligned with the larger competitive strategy of the firm. As Mohrman and Lawler (1997: 160) write, 'in order for the human resources function to contribute to its organization's performance, it must ensure that all of its human resources practices "fit with each other and with the strategy and design of the organization".' Although the latter has tended to be a salient underlying premise of SHRM – that firms adopting a particular strategy require human resources practices that are different from those required by organizations

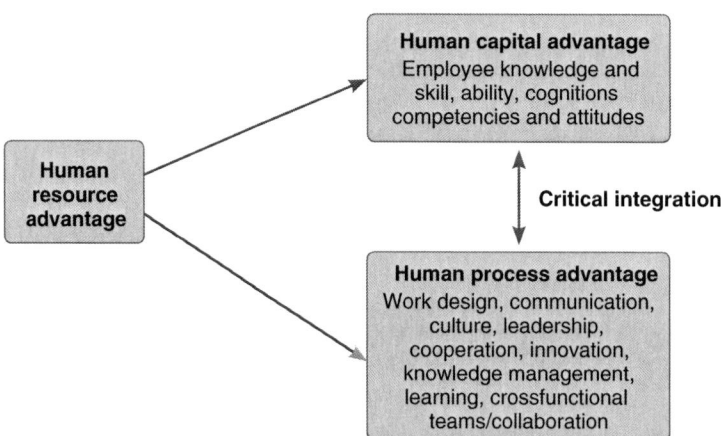

Figure 3.2 The resource-based view and human resource advantage
Source: Adapted from Boxall (1996).

adopting alternative strategies (Delery and Doty, 1996) – there is no consensus on this point. This is reflected in the emergence of three different modes of theorizing in the field of SHRM:

- the universalistic perspective;
- the contingency perspective;
- the configurational approach.

These are described briefly below.

The universal approach, also commonly referred to as the best practice approach, to SHRM posits that some human resources practices are always better than others, and that all organizations should adopt these best practices (Delery and Doty, 1996). The logic is that all firms are likely to see improvements in their performance if they identify and implement best practice, and that the link between human resources and the firm's performance is universal across the population of organizations. The most renowned model in the best practice approach is that of Pfeffer (1994), who argued that the greater adoption and use of 16 management practices, such as employment security, selectivity in hiring, incentive pay, high wages, empowerment, participation, training and skill development and promotion from within, would result in higher productivity and profit across firms. Osterman (1994) similarly suggested that innovative work practices, such as teams, quality circles, job rotation and TQM, stimulate productivity gains across companies. These practices identified by Pfeffer (1994) and others have been labelled as high-performance work practices as they induce higher performance (Delery and Doty, 1996).

Contingency theorizing, or what is commonly referred to as the best fit approach, argues that the human resources strategy will be more effective when it is appropriately integrated with its specific organizational and broader environmental context (Boxall and Purcell, 2011). For example, the rate of product, service or market innovation has frequently been treated as a critical contingency, with firms that are highly innovative considered as prospectors, firms that are moderately innovative considered as analysers, and firms that rarely innovate considered as defenders (Miles and Snow, 1984). Basically, the successful implementation of any of those business strategies relies heavily on human resources and its moulding of appropriate employee behaviour (Delery and Doty, 1996). Schuler and Jackson (1987), for example, argue that human resources practices should be designed to reinforce the behavioural implications of the various generic strategies defined by Porter (1985), as illustrated briefly in Figure 3.3 and Table 3.2. Therefore, to the extent that an organization's strategy demands behavioural requirements for its success, the use of human resources practices can reward and control employee behaviour (Delery and Doty, 1996).

A third approach, the configurational approach to HRM, bridges the gap between the universal and the contingency approaches and suggests that a firm will perform better through an appropriate internal fit between its HRM practices (the configuration fit) and an appropriate external fit between the firm's business strategy and its HRM practices. MacDuffie (1995) argues that the appropriate unit of analysis for studying the strategic link between different HRM practices and performance does not involve individual practices as much as interrelated and internally

HRM / HRD IN ITS CONTEMPORARY CONTEXT

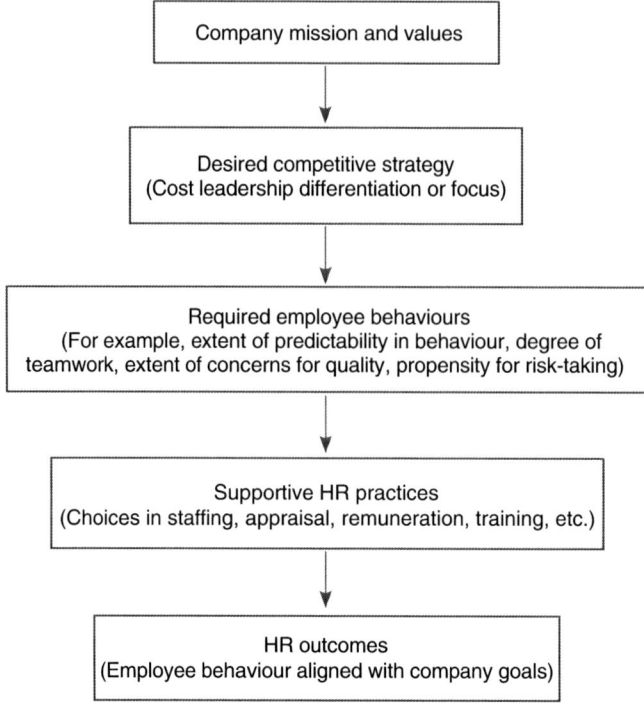

Figure 3.3 Linking human resources (HR) practices to competitive strategy
Source: Adapted from Schuler and Jackson (1987: 208).

Table 3.2 Different competitive strategies and different employee competitive role behaviours

Strategy	Employee role behaviours needed
Innovation	• Highly innovative behaviour • Very long-term behaviour • Highly cooperative behaviour • Moderate concern for quality • Moderate concern for quantity • Equal concern for process and results • Flexibility for change and risk-taking • High tolerance for ambiguity and unpredictability
Cost leadership	• Repetitive and predictable behaviour • Short-term behaviour or focus • Autonomous or individual acti vity • Modest concern for quality • High concern for quantity of outputs • Primary concern for results • Low risk-taking activity • High degree of comfort with stability

Source: Adapted from Schuler and Jackson (1987: 209).

Mini Case Study 3.2

HRM at Fattal: a continuous improvement journey

Fattal Holding is a regional organization operating in the Middle East and North Africa region, with a total of 932 employees in Fattal Lebanon, 220 in Syria, 140 in Jordan, 110 in Iraq, 50 in the UAE and 50 in Sudan. It specializes in distribution, sales and marketing. The human resources director at Fattal, Mr Samir Messara, has worked there for 24 years, for the last 6 years as human resources director, reporting to the chief operating officer, and previous to that as a line manager.

The human resources department at Fattal has existed since 1982, and has developed from a personnel department in charge of administrative activities to a strategic human resources department that started off in 1996–1997. There are currently seven employees in the human resources department working in the following divisions: personnel administration, training, compensation and benefits, recruitment, and communication and bonding – better known in Fattal as 'the five pillars of human resources', as Mr Messara describes them.

In the past 3 years, the human resources function has shifted its techniques and adopted a competency-based approach in which all functions (for example, recruitment, selection and performance appraisal) are linked back to core skills and competencies. Mr Messara explained that Fattal's CEO has announced to all the directors that the human resources department is the most strategic asset in the company because it deals with people. Mr. Messara asserted that senior management, as well as line management, at Fattal recognize the significance of the human resources function and appreciate its added value, considering it to be as important as the other functions in contributing to the organization's performance. He also stressed that the operational and strategic pillars are equally important parts of the human resources department: 'operational does not mean that it is not important, and strategic does not mean that it is theoretical'. Subdividing functions into operational and strategic is thus a secondary issue as one without the other does not work or succeed – in other words, there is a 'duality'.

The human resources function therefore plays both a reactive and a proactive role. A reactive role is adopted when a decision is taken and the human resources department 'cascades it' through its systems and procedures; human resources monitors its execution and follows it to completion or finalization. Human resources operations are now expanding in terms of new people – new assignments and recruitment for human resources in Syria and Iraq – a reactive role in which human resources has been deeply involved.

The proactive role comes from the strategic part of human resources. Human resources is always invited to be part of the 'think-tank' of the company and is invited by the CEO and Director to join in the decision-making about the next steps to be taken. Human resources is involved in the organization's major business decisions and takes part in strategy-setting meetings wherein they offer their own input. Their input is considered in the final outcome, and the department also maintains open lines of communication with the Chairman, CEO, and all the general managers and country managers.

> The proactive role of human resources can therefore be seen to be quite important in Fattal. For example, the firm had an issue regarding whether or not to open a subsidiary in Libya – this would need investment, the country was new to the firm's operations, and it would need new suppliers. Mr Messara explained that the human resources department was involved from day one in discussing the viability, feasibility and implications of opening up in Libya, as well as in how to go about it.
>
> **Questions**
>
> 1. How has the human resources department evolved at Fattal during the last 28 years?
> 2. Mr Messara stressed that the operational and strategic pillars are equally important parts of the human resources department: 'operational does not mean that it is not important, and strategic does not mean that it is theoretical.' Critically examine this statement and elaborate more on the 'duality' of HRM's role, as well as on factors critical to success.

consistent practices, called 'bundles'. He explains that a bundle creates the multiple, reinforcing conditions that support employee motivation, given that employees have the necessary knowledge and skills to perform their jobs effectively.

Critical analysis and discussion

The succinct review presented above clearly highlights new directions and a significant advance in the scholarship of SHRM. SHRM has partly evolved in response to a dramatically more competitive economic environment. But there are those who argue that the ascendancy of SHRM should be viewed in the context of the long-standing battle that the human resources function has faced in justifying its position and demonstrating its value to business firms (Wright et al., 2001). At the heart of SHRM is the question of how much of a difference HRM can make in terms of organizational performance, and more specifically how the management of human capital can make this difference (Colakoglu et al., 2006). SHRM has certainly matured over the past few years, and has benefited from some empirical support and from the reinforcement provided by the RBV; however, there are lingering issues that are worth accounting for when discussing SHRM, most notably the frequently raised criticism that the field still lacks a solid theoretical foundation, as highlighted below (Dyer, 1984; Delery and Doty, 1996). According to Wright and McMahan (1992: 297):

> Without good theory, the field of SHRM could be characterized as a plethora of statements, regarding empirical relationships and prescriptions for practice that fail to explain why these relationships exist or should exist.

The RBV of the firm has provided a core theoretical rationale for the potential role of human resources as a strategic asset in the firm, and has broadened the foundation for exploring the impact of human resources on strategic resources. Several authors have, however, expressed concern about the level of abstraction in RBV theory and in SHRM theory in general (Priem and Butler, 2001; Becker and Huselid, 2006). According to Becker and Huselid (2006), the link between the human resources architecture and most RBV concepts remains too abstract and too indirect to explain the link between that architecture and a firm's subsequent performance, or how human resources contributes to a firm's sustained competitive advantage. Implementation from this perspective should be given more attention in SHRM theory because the link between the human resources system and the firm's performance is not as direct as suggested by previous SHRM literature (Wright and Sherman, 1999). There are also intermediate outcomes that are central and crucial to a more complete understanding of how the human resources architecture drives a firm's performance, and very few attempts have been made to demonstrate that the human resources practices actually impact the skills or behaviours of the workforce, and that these skills or behaviours are related to concrete performance measures (Wright et al., 2001; Becker and Huselid, 2006).

Another common criticism is the reliance in the RBV on constructs that are difficult to operationalize in practice, which limits the prescriptive value of the theory for managers (Priem and Butler, 2001). What we need, according to Priem and Butler (2001), is a more careful delineation of the specific mechanisms purported to generate competitive advantage and more actionable prescriptions. According to Wright et al. (2001), a major step forward in the SHRM literature will be simply to move beyond the application of RBV logic to human resource issues, and towards research that directly tests the core concepts of the RBV. According to Fahy (2000), the vast majority of contributions within the RBV have been of a conceptual rather than an empirical nature, with the result that many of its fundamental tenets remain to be validated. Colbert (2007) posits that although the RBV has been helpful and relevant to the field of SHRM, there are aspects of the view that scholars have deemed critical but that are difficult to deal with in research and practice. Another important and salient criticism relates to the preoccupation of the RBV with internal resources, undermining the fact that countries provide variable contextual inputs and resources in terms of physical infrastructure, sociopolitical systems, and educational and technical infrastructure. Hence, there is a danger of becoming too absorbed with the firm as the unit of analysis (Boxall and Purcell, 2011).

There is also a continuing debate and various expressed concerns about best practice (universal) versus best fit (contingency) streams of theorizing in SHRM. A common concern with the best practice approach is whether there is indeed a best human resources architecture that creates value for all firms. Despite the appeal of the notion of universally applicable HRM practices, some problems persist including the following:

- subjectivity and a lack of agreement on a definitive prescription of the best bundle;
- the implicit assumption that a particular bundle of practices is feasible for all organizations;
- the way in which best practices sometimes become ends in themselves dissociated from company goals (Boxall and Purcell, 2011).

Moreover, research suggests that national contexts matter, and the wide variations in labour laws and unionism across nations undermine support for best practice models. There are also salient differences across sectoral and organizational contexts (for example, sectors exposed to international competition). Generally, the evidence points to the adoption of innovative human resources bundles or high-performance work systems in sectors where quality is a major competitive factor and where firms need to exploit advanced technology. Cost-effectiveness is also certainly an important consideration in the limited diffusion of best practice models (Boxall and Purcell, 2011).

There is also a parallel set of concerns with best fit or contingency models. The most important concern relates to the purported simplicity of arranging a firm's assets and resources given a specific choice of strategy (Wright et al., 2001). Specifically, according to Cappelli and Singh (1992), most SHRM models based on fit assume: (1) that a certain business strategy demands a unique set of behaviours and attitudes on the part of employees; and (2) that certain human resources policies produce a unique set of responses from employees. But both assumptions are simplistic. There is also a lack of sophistication in existing descriptions of competitive strategy in the sense of concrete evidence that resilient firms in some sectors tend to successfully and simultaneously pursue different kinds of strategy (for example, cost leadership and differentiation). In addition, there are concerns that best fit models emphasizing the alignment of HRM and competitive strategy tend to overlook employee interests (Boxall and Purcell, 2011). In other words, the strategic goals of HRM are plural. Although they do involve supporting the firm's competitive objectives, they also involve meeting employee needs and complying with social requirements for labour management (Boxall and Purcell, 2011). Multiple fits are required, and there is always a strategic tension inherent in a changing environment between performing optimally in the present context and building the capacity of the organization and preparing for the future.

Exercise

Many qualified human resources managers often fail to manage the function strategically. Who is to blame? The human resources manager? Organizational factors? Environmental factors? List and discuss all possible factors that might impede proper SHRM initiatives.

One of the main reasons for lingering ambiguity and complexity in this area is that the choice of performance measures used in SHRM research studies varies widely. SHRM tries to link and synthesize multiple metrics, but this has been neither simple nor straightforward. Whereas traditional HRM research has tended to focus on individual-level outcomes such as job performance, job satisfaction and motivation, SHRM has focused on firm-level outcomes related to labour productivity, sales growth, return on assets and return on investment. This latter category of financial and accounting outcomes is more distal to human resources practices than individual-level employee outcomes (Colakoglu et al., 2006). Although corporate- or firm-level performance metrics are important to examine, they are, according to some authors, not definitely and necessarily more important than others. The focus on organizational performance is illuminating and convincing for managers looking for concrete evidence of a significant impact of human resources on distal outcomes such as market or financial performance (Colakoglu et al., 2006). But these organizational performance outcomes are inevitably rooted in lower level outcomes to which SHRM does not seem to accord enough attention.

These complexities become even more accentuated in the context of international SHRM research, which considers the growing importance of multinational corporations (MNCs) and the influence of complex global strategic business decisions on the human resource activities of these MNCs (Sparrow and Braun, 2007). Complexity arises from the multiplicity of independent variables as influencing factors, and from the importance of linking HRM policies and practices with the organizational strategies of the MNC. This is rooted in the realization that MNCs are geographically dispersed and vary in their goals, and that different levels of integration and responsiveness are also invariably affected by whether or not the parent company actually has a global strategy, or more specifically 'a strategic international HRM system orientation'. In addition, it comes from the degree of similarity of affiliates' human resources systems to those of the parent company, and the extent to which top management believes that HRM capability is indeed a source of strategic advantage (Sparrow and Braun, 2007).

On a final note, there is also enduring concern about whether human resources strategy theories developed in Western countries do actually apply to other cultures, and how human resources strategies may be made to apply better in other cultures, which has been the domain of comparative HRM research. The answer to the first part of the question is clearly no, in the sense that human resources theories developed in Western countries do not necessarily apply universally, and there are important contingency variables and institutional realities and multilevel factors that affect the practice of SHRM. Generally, the conclusion reached is that companies are not as global or international as is often assumed, and that a clear country of origin effect is still evident (Sparrow and Braun, 2007). US MNCs, for example, tend to be more formalized and centralized than others in the management of HRM issues ranging from pay systems to collective bargaining and employee recognition. There is also a stream of literature that considers how the transfer of human resources practices can happen successfully, with convergence of practice depending, according to Kostova (1999), on internationalization and the implementation of human resources rules by subsidiaries.

Looking back on the last two decades, Paauwe and Boselie (2005) point to major similarities between the development of HRM and the developments in strategic management theorizing. In the 1980s, HRM was influenced by Porter-like outside–in approaches, for example reflected in the work of Schuler and Jackson (1987), emphasizing the necessity of strategic fit – the fit between the overall strategy (based on the external environment) and the human resources strategy. The introduction of the RBV in the 1990s also led to a transition from the former outside–in approaches (based on contingency assumptions) to an inside–out approach, in which human resources play a key role in the search for the sustained competitive advantage of an organization (Paauwe and Boselie, 2005).

Recently, institutional theory has been increasingly used as a framework to analyse human resource practices. It looks at the influence that environmental factors and institutions such as social and political systems, legislation and the power of labour unions and trade associations have on the adoption of human resources practices (Chow, 2004). The rationale of institutional theory is, according to Paauwe and Boselie (2003), that organizations are embedded in a wider institutional context that plays a role in shaping HRM practices and policies. Institutional mechanisms (for example, legislation with respect to conditions of employment, collective bargaining agreements, employment security, trade union influence and employee representation) shape employment relationships and human resources decision-making in organizations. Paauwe (2004) acknowledges institutional differences at both a country level and an industry level. Institutional mechanisms (mimetic, normative and/or coercive) affect the relationship between HRM and performance and should therefore be taken into account in future research (Paauwe and Boselie, 2003).

Conclusion

The aim of this chapter was to provide a critical assessment of SHRM, shedding light on its differentiating attributes and theoretical foundations, as well as on the lingering gaps and challenges in this field. The opening sections highlighted the evolution in the field from personnel management to HRM and, most recently, SHRM. Although some suggest that the changes in the field are revolutionary (Storey, 1993; Hope-Hailey et al., 1997; Hoque and Noon, 2001), it is more accurate to characterize the change process as one of metamorphosis, evolution or adaptation rather than of completely new creation (Torrington et al., 2002; Redman and Wilkinson, 2009). Each phase basically constitutes an improvement that has effectively leveraged or built on, rather than replaced, the preceding knowledge base of the discipline (Schuler and Jackson, 2007).

SHRM is essentially posited as constituting the highest level of sophistication or maturation in the field, and as an apt response to existing business trends and challenges. It has brought to the fore a set of new assumptions relating to strategic thrust, an emphasis on integration, an orientation towards commitment, a belief that people are the core assets, and a focus on business values and results. In the process, SHRM has raised and addressed an array of important questions, probing the link between HRM and organizational effectiveness. For example, which human resources practices lead to greater organizational performance? How does a firm ensure that its human resources practices fit with its strategy? How does it ensure that its individual human resources practices fit with each other? The key constructs and central debates in SHRM have grown out of the above questions: best practice versus best fit, horizontal and vertical fit, fit versus flexibility, univariate and multivariate effects, and appropriate theoretical frames (Colbert, 2007). What is common to all this work though is a focus on the links between human resources practices, the human resource pool and organizational outcomes (Colbert, 2007).

The applications and implications of the RBV within the SHRM literature have clearly led to an increasing convergence between the fields of strategic management and SHRM (Snell et al., 2001). In relation to both areas of the literature, the RBV has helped to put people on the radar screen and to highlight the importance of human knowledge and a firm's processes and capabilities in general as sources of competitive advantage. With its emphasis on the firm's internal resources as sources of competitive advantage, the RBV has gained increasing popularity within SRHM and has become by far the most often used theory within SHRM, both for the development of theory and for the rationale underlying empirical research. The RBV has triggered at the very least a deeper understanding of the interplay between HRM and competitive advantage, as well as a substantial advance in the SHRM literature.

But although the RBV has formed an integrating ground or backdrop for most of the work in SHRM over the past decade, it offers little in an explicit sense in the way of prescriptions for managers, thus not answering the 'how' questions central to SHRM. Delery (1998) notes that while the RBV provides a nice backdrop explaining the importance of human resources to a firm's competitiveness, it does not specifically deal with how an organization can develop and support the human resources it needs for competitive advantage.

Although many continue to refer to best practice versus best fit, perhaps a broader conceptualization, as suggested by Wright et al. (2001) and also nicely captured in Figure 3.2 above, is to focus on the people management system within an organization. The word 'system' denotes attention to the importance of understanding the multiple practices that impact employees, rather than focusing on a single practice. The term 'people', rather than 'human resources', expands the relevant practices to those beyond the direct control of the human resources function, such as to communication, work design, culture, leadership and a host of others that affect employees and shape their competencies, cognitions and attitudes. In other words, sustained competitive advantage is not just a function of single or isolated components, but rather a combination of human capital elements such as the development of stocks of skills, strategically relevant behaviours and supporting people management systems. The recognition of the systemic quality of highly effective human resources and people management systems has been a key insight brought to the fore through the RBV and SHRM paradigm.

FOR DISCUSSION AND REVISION

1. Explain the evolutionary road map from personnel management to SHRM. What are the factors that triggered this evolution?
2. Why is the application of 'best practice' models of SHRM in organizations problematic?
3. In what way have the contingency and the configurational approaches to HRM contributed to your understanding of SHRM?
4. How does the RBV contribute to your understanding of SHRM?
5. The link between HRM practices and organizational performance is not direct, and HRM scholars often refer to the existence of a 'black box' between the two concepts. Divide the class into groups of three. Each group should discuss what this black box entails. Then share your findings with other groups and discuss them.

6. Defining the effective human resource manager:

- What does an effective human resources manager look like? What skills, competencies and knowledge do they require to become a business partner? Try to collect information from a range of sources, for example corporate websites, human resources practitioner journals (*HR magazine, Personnel Today, People Management*), other journals (*Human Resource Management Journal, International Journal of Human Resource Management, Personnel Review*), the Chartered Institute of Personnel Development and The Society for Human Resource Management websites and HRM textbooks to develop a profile of an effective human resources manager in the 21st century.
- Discuss your findings with other students in your class. What conclusions can you draw?

Further reading

Books

Boxall, P. and Purcell, J. (2011) *Strategy and Human Resource Management* (3rd edn). New York: Palgrave Macmillan.

This book is a classic work integrating HRM and strategic management, explaining the latest theoretical and practical developments in this fascinating area and bridging the gap between theory and practice. It also integrates both HRM and employment relations in a critical and constructive way.

Schuler, R. and Jackson, S. (2007) *Strategic Human Resource Management* (2nd edn). Malden, MA: Blackwell Publishing.

This book provides students with a complete and updated guide to the latest work in the field. This selection of important and highly readable articles from authors around the world charts key developments that have changed the theory and practice of SHRM over the last decade.

Journals

Legnick-Hall, M. L., Legnick-Hall, C. A., Andrade, L. S. and Drake B. (2009) Strategic human resource management: the evolution of the field. *Human Resource Management Review*, 19: 64–85.

This article takes an evolutionary and chronological perspective on the development of the SHRM literature. The authors trace how the field has evolved to its current state, articulate many of the major findings and contributions, and discuss how they believe it will evolve in the future. This approach contributes to the field of SHRM by synthesizing work in this domain and by highlighting areas of research focus that, while promising, have remained largely unexamined.

Paauwe, J. and Boselie, P. (2003) Challenging 'strategic HRM' and the relevance of the institutional setting. *Human Resource Management Journal*, 13(3): 56–70.

In this article, the authors use the theory of new institutionalism as a better way to understand the shaping of human resources policies and practices in different settings. After a concise review of the latest debates in the area of SHRM, in which the RBV is the dominant perspective, they turn to an analysis of HRM in different institutional settings, which suggests the need for additional theory – that is, new institutionalism.

Wright, P. M., McMahan, G. C. and McWilliams, A. (1994) Human resources and sustained competitive advantage: a resource-based perspective. *International Journal of Human Resource Management*, 5(2): 301–26.

The RBV of the firm has influenced the field of SHRM in a number of ways. This paper explores the impact of the RBV on the theoretical and empirical development of SHRM. It explores how the fields of strategy and SHRM are beginning to converge around a number of issues, and proposes a number of implications of this convergence.

A CRITICAL PERSPECTIVE ON STRATEGIC HUMAN RESOURCE MANAGEMENT

CASE STUDY

Strategic human resource management: insights from Deloitte ME's experience

The Deloitte Middle East Firm (Deloitte ME) is a member of the global professional services firm Deloitte Touche Tohmatsu, which employs 169,000 people in 140 countries and had revenues of US$27 billion in the 2009 fiscal year. Deloitte ME is one of the longest established professional services firms in the region and has been operating since 1926 in 15 countries with 26 offices and a team of over 2,300 professionals. It has enjoyed a compounded revenue growth rate of 31 per cent in the region over the 3 years to 2010.

This case study is based on several rounds of interviews with Mrs Rana Ghandour Salhab, the first woman admitted as partner in the Middle East in the 80-year history of the firm in the region. She is currently the partner in charge of human resources and communications in the Middle East and a member of the Deloitte ME Board Advisory Council and the Deloitte ME Partner Screening Committee. It is worth noting that, in April 2009, Deloitte ME was recognized as one of the best 10 employers in the Middle East by Hewitt Associates, the global human resources consulting firm that runs best employer surveys across the world.

Based on a recent survey asking Deloitte employees what they expect from their employer, Deloitte ME adopted a 'develop, deploy and connect' model as a talent strategy and a Career Value Map tool to reinforce the steps that individuals can take to own their careers and leverage Deloitte's resources and tools within each of the model areas. According to Mrs Salhab, organizations can, by focusing on these three elements, generate capability, commitment and alignment in key workforce segments (Figure 3.4), which in turn improves business performance: 'When this happens, the attraction and retention of skilled talent largely take care of themselves'.

Deloitte has an interesting regional Talent Attraction Program and e-recruitment, revolving around a Middle East referral scheme, university relationships, an alumni and experienced hire programme, supplier relations, web and social networks

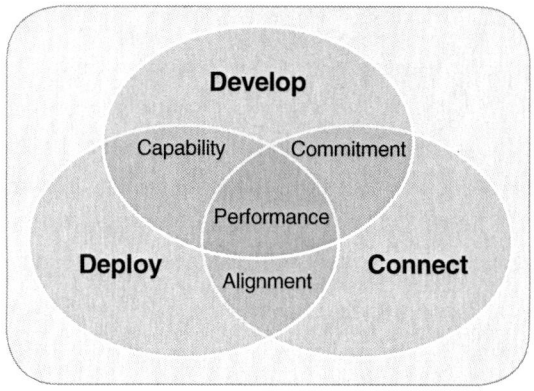

Figure 3.4 The Deloitte ME 'develop, deploy and connect' model

sourcing, and Google ad words. The Deloitte Invites Top Talent programme also aims to attract top students from leading universities around the region to source offices with nationals of the Gulf Cooperation Council and Arabic-speaking professionals. Their screening techniques focus on assessment centres, competency-based behavioural interviewing, psychometric testing and a global development programme for their workforce. The Deloitte performance management system is the key development employee tool, with a technical and shared skills competency model that facilitates year round career conversations and a coaching culture. Through the ME Deloitte Retention and Advancement for Women Program, the firm is committed to creating an environment where high achieving women and men both reach leadership roles.

Deloitte ME has been striving for a balance between a strategic human resources agenda with a long-term impact and operational day-to-day human resources activities. The company realizes that the drivers and challenges for the business are transitioning the core efforts of human resources towards providing the business with a competitive advantage. This will happen by moving away from a focus on administration (for example, payroll, benefits, compliance and record-keeping), or what they refer to as value maintenance, to a focus on value creation through the selection and design of human resources practices that support the firm's strategy (Figure 3.5). Mrs Salhab recognizes that assuming the human resources partner role depends on the level of maturity of the organization; it also illustrates nicely how the Deloitte ME function has made a successful transition from roles revolving around analyst and advisor to human resources roles entailing effective advocacy and partnering. This transformation has, according to Mrs Salhab, required a proactive approach combining flexible and specialist human resources orientations, combined with the redirecting of administration queries and a more active involvement of line managers in different sorts of people management activities.

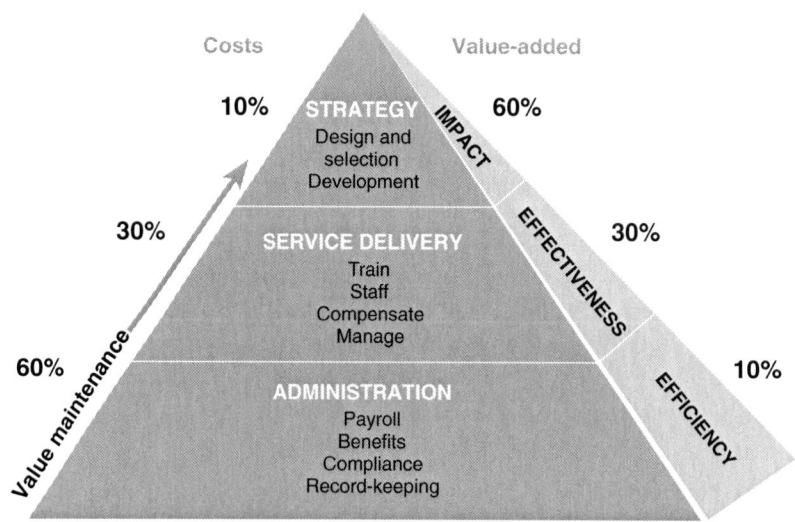

Figure 3.5 Deloitte ME value creation through strategic human resources

Mrs Salhab admits that the transformation of human resources into strategic roles is not always easy and may in some companies be typically undermined by a number of risks and pitfalls that have to be avoided. These may be, for example:

- reduced client satisfaction (in the sense that a one-size-fits-all approach to service delivery may not recognize the diversity of employees);
- insufficient market insight into and innovation in human resources policies;
- low morale in human resources, with no clear career path or longer term development programme for some human resources professionals;
- overly expensive running costs and poor-quality outsourcing contracts;
- ineffective human resources business partners who are unable and ill-equipped to deliver the level of business advice expected;
- a continued erosion of data quality, and therefore human resources credibility, as a result of poorly constructed processes;
- dissatisfaction with self-service technologies due to their low-quality implementation and the poor education of line managers.

These failings have led the business to question whether human resources is best placed to fix the issues or whether the business itself should take control and address them. Mrs Salhab also admits that, despite the global change in paradigms of SHRM, human resources professionals are still spending too much time on low-impact activities (for example, responding to queries, responding to complaints, enforcing policies, managing conflicts and basic administrative transactions) as opposed to forging strategy, developing metrics and nurturing talent and leaders.

According to Mrs Salhab, human resources cannot just become strategic overnight. They have to drive a strategic agenda around things that matter, strengthen leadership capability, create an adaptable workforce and advise on strategies that can maintain and enhance performance. This requires a number of key organizational and cultural changes that need to be crafted together, revolving around establishing the role of the chief human resources officer, optimizing shared service centres, measuring success through value operation centres, and freeing business partners and the chief human resources officer to reflect the strategic focus. Other important changes revolve around adjusting human resources strategies to respond to changing needs, identifying critical human resources metrics and business strategies, identifying talent issues and prioritizing human resources needs, redesigning structures around strategic objectives and, importantly, understanding the talent needs of the business. In this context, the onus also falls on human resources to nurture the right skills and competencies, including, among others, the following:

- behavioural competencies as in leadership skills, negotiation and conflict resolution, change leadership and communication skills;
- technical competencies, as in functional human resources knowledge, project management and the management of strategic resources;
- business competencies, as in business acumen, industry and organizational awareness, strategy and business planning, and consulting skills.

In conclusion, for Mrs Salhab, human resources is clearly at a turning point. For a decade now, it has been undergoing a process of transformation. But for many, this has been a process that has increasingly failed to produce the results expected of it: 'During these times of rapidly changing economics, we believe human resources is faced with a stark choice. It can either evolve and make a significant contribution, or be diminished and dispersed in the business.'

Questions

1. Mrs Salhab stated that 'During these times of rapidly changing economics, we believe human resources is faced with a stark choice. It can either evolve and make a significant contribution, or be diminished and dispersed in the business.' Use Figures 3.4 and 3.5 to explain how the human resources department at Deloitte adds value to the business.
2. Mrs Salhab is the first woman admitted as a partner in the Middle East in the 80-year history of the firm in the region. What additional challenges and opportunities can this provide for the successful development of the human resources department?
3. Do some further research and investigate whether the same human resources practices and policies are applied at Deloitte in various regions of the world. What lessons can you draw?

References

Amit, R. and Belcourt, M. (1999) Human resources management processes: a value-creating source of competitive advantage. *European Management Journal*, 17(2): 174–81.

Anthony, W., Kacmar, M. and Perrewe, P. (2002) *Human Resource Management: A Strategic Approach* (4th edn). Cincinnati, OH: South-Western.

Armstrong, M. (2006) *Strategic Human Resource Management: A Guide to Action* (3rd edn). London: Kogan Page.

Barney, J. (1991) Firm resources and sustained competitive advantage. *Journal of Management*, 17(1): 99–120.

Becker, B. and Huselid, M. (2006) Strategic human resources management: where do we go from here?' *Journal of Management*, 32(6): 898–925.

Boxall, P. (1996) The strategic HRM debate and the resource based view of the firm. *Human Resource Management Journal*, 56(3): 59–75.

Boxall, P. and Purcell, J. (2000) Strategic human resource management: where have we come from and where should we be going? *International Journal of Management Reviews*, 2(2): 183–203.

Boxall, P. and Purcell, J. (2011) *Strategy and Human Resource Management* (3rd edn). New York: Palgrave Macmillan.

Brockbank, W. (1999) If HR were really strategically proactive: present and future directions in HR's contribution to competitive advantage. *Human Resource Management*, 38(4): 337–52.

Buyens, D. and De Vos, A. (2001) Perceptions of the value of the HR function. *Human Resource Management Journal*, 11(3): 70–89.

Cappelli, P. and Singh, H. (1992) Integrating strategic human resources and strategic management. In Lewin, D., Mitchell, P. and Sherer, P. (eds) *Research Frontiers in Industrial Relations and Human Resources*. Madison, WI: IRRA, pp. 165–92.

Chow, I. (2004) The impact of institutional context on human resource management in three Chinese societies. *Employee Relations*, 26(6): 626–42.

Colakoglu, S., Lepak, D. and Hong, Y. (2006) Measuring HRM effectiveness: considering multiple stakeholders in a global context. *Human Resource Management Review*, 16: 209–18.

Colbert, B. (2007) The complex resource based view: implications for theory and practice in strategic human resource management. In Schuler, R. and Jackson, S. (eds) *Strategic Human Resource Management* (2nd edn). Malden, MA: Blackwell Publishing, pp. 98–123.

Collis, D. and Montgomery, C. (1995) Competing on resources: strategy in the 1990s. *Harvard Business Review*, 73: 118–28.

Conner, J. and Ulrich, D. (1996) Human resource roles: creating value, not rhetoric. *Human Resource Planning*, 19(3): 38–49.

Delery, J. (1998) Issues of fit in strategic human resource management: implications for research. *Human Resource Management Review*, 8: 289–309.

Delery, J. and Doty, D. (1996) Modes of theorizing in strategic human resource management: tests of universalistic, contingency, and configurational performance predictions. *Academy of Management Journal*, 39(4): 802–35.

Dunn, J. (2006) Strategic human resources and strategic organization development: an alliance for the future? *Organizational Development Journal*, 24(4): 69–76.

Dyer, L. (1984) Linking human resource and business strategies. *Human Resource Planning*, 7(2): 79–84.

Fahy, J. (2000) The resource based view of the firm: some stumbling blocks on the road to understanding sustainable competitive advantage. *Journal of European Industrial Training*, 24: 94–104.

Grant, R. (1991) The resource based theory of competitive advantage: implications for strategy formulation. *California Management Review*, 33: 114–35.

Guest, D. (1987) Human resource management and industrial relations. *Journal of Management Studies*, 24(5): 503–21.

Guest, D. (1990) Personnel management: the end of orthodoxy? *British Journal of Industrial Relations*, 29(2): 149–75.

Hope-Hailey, V., Gratton, L., McGovern, P., Stiles, P. and Truss, C. (1997) A chameleon function: HRM in the '90s. *Human Resource Management Journal*, 3(3): 5–18.

Hoque, K. and Noon, M. (2001) Counting angels: a comparison of personnel and HR specialists. *Human Resource Management Journal*, 11(3): 5–22.

Keenoy, T. (1990) HRM: rhetoric, reality, and contradiction. *International Journal of Human Resource Management*, 23(1): 363–84.

Kostova, T. (1999) Transnational transfer of strategic organizational practice: a contextual perspective. *Academy of Management Review*, 24(2): 308–24.

Leonard-Barton, D. (1992) Core capabilities and core rigidities: a paradox in managing new product development. *Strategic Management Journal*, 13: 111–25.

MacDuffie, P. (1995) Human resource bundles and manufacturing performance: organizational logic and flexible production systems in the world auto industry. *Industrial and Labor Relations Review*, 48(2): 197–221.

Mahoney, T. and Deckop, J. (1986) Evolution of concept and practice in personnel administration/human resource management. *Journal of Management*, 12(2): 223–41.

Meilich, O. (2005) Are formalization and human asset specificity mutually exclusive: a learning bureaucracy perspective. *Journal of American Academy of Business*, 6: 161–9.

Miles, R. and Snow, C. (1984) Designing strategic human resource systems. *Organizational Dynamics*, 13(1): 36–52.

Mohrman, S. and Lawler, E. III (1997) Transforming the human resource function. *Human Resource Management*, 36(1): 157–62.

Osterman, P. (1994) How common is workplace transformation and who adopts it? *Industrial and Labor Relations Review*, 47: 173–88.

Paauwe, J. (2004) *HRM and Performance: Unique Approaches for Achieving Long-term Viability*. Oxford: Oxford University Press.

Paauwe, J. and Boselie, P. (2003) Challenging 'strategic HRM' and the relevance of the institutional setting. *Human Resource Management Journal*, 13(3): 56–70.

Paauwe, J. and Boselie, P. (2005) HRM and performance: what's next? *Human Resource Management Journal*, 15(4): 68–83.

Pfeffer, J. (1994) *Competitive Advantage Through People: Unleashing the Power of the Workforce*. Boston, MA: Harvard Business School Press.

Pilbeam, S. and Corbridge, M. (2006) *People Resourcing: Contemporary HRM in Practice* (3rd edn). London: Prentice Hall.

Porter, M. (1985) *Competitive Advantage*. New York: Free Press.

Prahalad, C. K. and Hamel, G. (1990) The core competence of the corporation. *Harvard Business Review*, (May–June): 79–91.

Priem, R. and Butler, J. (2001) Is the resource based view a useful perspective for strategic management research? *Academy of Management Review*, 26(1): 22–40.

Redman, T. and Wilkinson, A. (2009) *Contemporary Human Resource Management: Text and Cases* (3rd edn). Harlow: Prentice Hall.

Schuler, R. and Jackson, S. (1987) Linking competitive strategies with human resource management practices. *Academy of Management Executive*, 1(3): 207–19.

Schuler, R. and Jackson, S. (2007) Preface. In *Strategic Human Resource Management* (2nd edn). Malden, MA: Blackwell Publishing.

Snell, S., Shadur, M. and Wright, P. (2001) The era of our ways. In Hitt, R., Freeman, R. and Harrison, J. (eds) *Handbook of Strategic Management*. Oxford: Blackwell Publishing, pp. 627–9.

Sparrow, P. and Braun, W. (2007) Human resource strategy in international context. In Schuler, R. and Jackson, S. (eds) *Strategic Human Resource Management* (2nd edn). Malden, MA: Blackwell Publishing, pp. 162–99.

Storey, J. (1993) The take-up of human resource management by mainstream companies: key lessons from research. *International Journal of Human Resource Management*, 4(3): 529–33.

Storey, J. (2001) *Human Resource Management: A Critical Text* (2nd edn). London: Routledge.

Teece, D. J., Pisano, G., and Shuen, A. (1997) Dynamic capabilities and strategic management. *Strategic Management Journal*, 18(7): 509–33.

Torrington, D., Hall, L. and Taylor, S. (2002) *Human Resource Management*. London: FT/Prentice Hall.

Wernerfelt, B. (1995) The resource based view of the firm: ten years after. *Strategic Management Journal*, 16: 171–4.

Williams, J. (1992) How sustainable is your competitive advantage? *California Management Review*, 34: 29–51.

Wright, P. and McMahan, G. (1992) Theoretical perspectives for strategic human resource management. *Journal of Management*, 18: 295–320.

Wright, P. and Sherman, W. (1999) Failing to find fit in strategic human resource management: theoretical and empirical problems. *Research in Personnel and Human Resources Management*, Supplement 4: 53–74.

Wright, P., McMahan, G., Snell, S. and Gerhart, B. (2001) Comparing line and HR executives' perceptions of HR effectiveness: services, roles, and contributions. *Human Resource Management*, 40(2): 111–23.

CHAPTER 4
Organizational culture and HRM

OUTLINE

- Introduction
- Culture and modernity
- Organizational culture
- HRM and globalization: Multiculturalism's magic number
- HRM as I see it: Keith Stopforth, Bupa Health and Wellbeing
- Perspectives on organizational culture
- HRM in practice 4.1: Management surveillance: someone's watching you …
- Managing culture through HRM
- Sustainability and green HRM
- HRM in practice 4.2: Can we measure changes in organizational culture?
- Paradox in culture management
- Case study: Big Outdoors
- Summary, Vocab checklist for ESL students, Review questions and Further reading to improve your mark

After studying this chapter, you should be able to:
- Explain the relationship between national culture and organizational culture
- Define organizational culture and be aware of notions of dominant culture, cultural diversity, subcultures and countercultures
- Explain different theoretical perspectives on organizational culture
- Understand how senior managers strive to change the culture of their organization and the role of human resource management (HRM) in the change process
- Explain the role of HRM in creating low-carbon sustainable work systems

Introduction

In 2010, the consultancy company Baringa Partners won Britain's Best Workplace Award largely because of its organizational culture, which emphasized open communications and the nurturing of talented employees. In the same year, research reported increased incidences of a 'binge-working culture' (Campbell, 2010), a 'long-hours culture' in which employees regard 'busyness' as 'voluntary' behaviour or overtime, and long hours as 'a badge of honour' (Chatzitheochari and Arber, 2009). And in 2011, a report by the UK House of Commons Justice Select Committee reported that their probation officers spent 75 per cent of their time on form-filling and responding to centrally driven emails, which they described as a 'tick-box culture' (Travis, 2011).

Workplace norms of work and leisure activities can be seen as an expression of organizational culture and power. The work–life balance discourse can illustrate that the different ways in which we *experience* work are shaped by a form of hegemony, and by what we believe, what we value and what we see as legitimate (Kärreman and Alvesson, 2009; Schneider, 2000). These intangible informal structures or 'ways of doing' work can be thought of as 'organizational culture'. Culture management is becoming important for thinking in strategic human resource management (HRM) because it is increasingly perceived to be a 'key lever' to release consensus, flexibility and commitment (Storey, 2007). Culture can also create a context in which employees 'follow the flow', where 'compliance is not only desirable: it is almost irresistible' (Kärreman and Alvesson, 2009, p. 1141). In the HRM canon, organizational culture has been described as a transformation process to unlock the 'holy grail' of commitment by appealing to employees' desire to contribute to 'goals beyond immediate self-interest' (Beer et al., 1984, p. 181). Critical management scholars, however, are highly sceptical about claims of managing cultures, regarding such claims as naive and as doing little to remove the 'structured antagonism' found in the employment relationship (Edwards, 1986, 1995).

To understand the contemporary workplace, we must consider not only job design and underlying structure, but also cultures related to the workplace. This chapter begins by introducing the concept of national culture and discusses its relevance to the contemporary workplace. We will then explore the complex concept of organizational culture – what it is, and how it manifests itself within the modern workplace. We examine different theoretical perspectives on organizational culture, and finally we will take a critical look at the clusters of HRM practices that are used to change and manage culture. This analysis then provides us with the opportunity to take a critical look at the organizational culture–performance relationship, with particular reference to sustainable low-carbon work cultures.

> **reflective question**
>
> Based upon your own experience of work or of being a customer of an organization, is it possible to recognize a different tone or 'feel' within organizations? How do the intangible 'ways of doing' things at your university compare, for instance, with your employment experience?

Culture and modernity

The word 'culture' is one of the most complicated words in the English language (Williams, 1983). In everyday language, the word 'culture' is loaded with evaluative connotations related to social class, power and status (Parker et al., 2003). The complexity of its modern usage can be appreciated when, in everyday speech, we refer to rock music as 'popular culture' and opera as 'high culture'. In the latter case, culture is associated with the arts, refinement and a privileged education. When anthropologists and sociologists use the term 'culture', it includes such social activities, but it also emphasizes that a national culture has a 'collectivizing effect' and creates differences between populations.

A 'culture' refers to an imperfect collection of interrelated understandings and behaviours shared by a people, which are shaped by ways of thinking and acting, by identities and by the material artefacts that together shape a people's way of life. As such, culture includes all the things people learn while growing up among a particular group: attitudes, beliefs about how people should act in particular situations, how females and males should interact, perceptions of reality and so forth. By definition, culture is collective, it is shared by a group of people, and it is socially learned and transmitted from one generation to the next (Giddens, 2009; Macionis and Gerber, 2011). You might think of culture as a societal tapestry of woven threads that makes each society unique or, on a larger scale, as a national characteristic such as 'Englishness'. The central implication for human resources (HR) practice is that culture constrains and enables social action, conditioning social structure or relatively stable patterns of individual behaviour and motivations (Figure 4.1).

Cultural scholars contend that the culture of a human society is a manifestation of a complex interplay of symbols, laws, values, beliefs and practices that are learned and exhibited by its members (Adler and Gundersen, 2008). In the postmodernism discourse, now that the sacred and the 'spiritual' seem to be extinct, it

> **HRM web links**
>
> Visit www.new-paradigm.co.uk/Culture.htm for a description of organizational culture, and www.tnellen.com/ted/tc/schein.html for an article on culture and leadership.

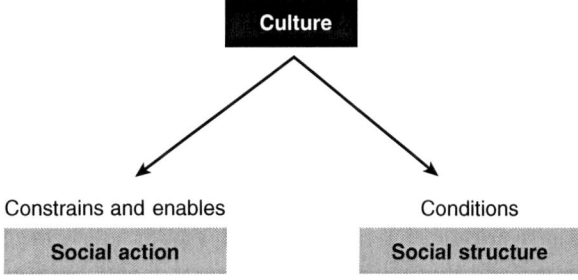

Figure 4.1 The dynamics of culture
Source: Adapted from Parker et al. (2003).

is plausibly argued that culture has become material or materialistic in terms of its structures and functions (Jameson, 1991).

Symbols, for example, in languages, intellectual life and religion, are ideas that convey meaning between individuals and groups. One important aspect of culture is language. Words and utterances can have different meanings depending on the context. In Japan, for example, some utterances may be lost in translation. When government officials or business people say that they will take something 'into serious consideration', they mean 'no' (Buruma, 2011), but this is not always understood by expatriate managers. Take also the symbol of the cross, which has a powerful meaning for Christians but little for Buddhists. The Confederate flag, however, has a powerful meaning for Christians and non-Christians alike, as a searing symbol of the nineteenth-century American slave-holding states (Manji, 2010).

Symbols also influence the essential *values* that people hold about society and the world around them. Values have profound, although partly unconscious, effects on people's behaviour in different situations. A *norm* is a shared ideal (or rule) about how people ought to act in certain situations, or about how particular people should act toward particular other people. The different ways in which people act and interact with others, and the tendency for people to view their own way of life as 'natural', can cause personal disorientation or 'culture shock' for tourists and immigrants experiencing a new country (Macionis and Gerber, 2011). Shared symbols, values and behaviour, however, change over generations. The process by which each generation or other new members of society learn the way of life of their society is called *socialization*.

A mixture of factors distinguish 'capitalist modernity'. This term has come to define the vast and largely unregulated expansion of the production and consumption of commodities, their related national markets, individualism and secularization over the last 200 years (Sayer, 1991). Late modernity is associated with the production of information, conspicuous consumption, especially in the area of leisure, global markets and social networks. The dynamics of late modernity, it

Symbols come in all shapes and sizes. What does this well-known symbol mean to you?
Source: ©istockphoto.com/Anthony Seebaran.

is argued, have brought an 'extensification of contemporary culture' (Lash, 2010, p. 2). Take, for example, the iconic coffee chain Starbucks: there are many stores not just in every European capital, but in seemingly every district of Beijing, Delhi, Johannesburg and Buenos Aires too. This growing extensification of contemporary urban life is being driven by multinational corporations and global inter-governmental organizations such as the International Monetary Fund, the United Nations and the World Bank, as well as non-governmental organizations such as Oxfam. Moreover, 'time' and 'space' have taken on a new meaning in contemporary culture with today's global capitalism. City-dwellers increasingly face the choices and uncertainties of a globalized market society, with experiences that cut across all spatial boundaries of social class and nationality or ethnicity, of religion and ideology, and whose reference point is both global and local (Giddens, 1990; Harvey, 1994).

In this context of seismic shifts in how contemporary societies are organized and an increasing extension of social structures – the patterns of social relations that bind people together and give shape to their lives – people acquire new values, beliefs and practices from the groups to which they belong. A national culture has a number of essential features: it is *collective, socially learned, transmitted, shared* and a product of human socialization and social interaction. These defining aspects of national culture are important in understanding the complexity of culture and how people seek to assert their social uniqueness over time and place; moreover, they help us to see how a society's beliefs and values can guide and shape the employment relationship.

Europe, North America and Asia are culturally diverse. Within their borders lie many cultures and subcultures formed by divisions such as social class, ethnicity and gender, this tapestry of multiple subcultures being in turn locally differentiated. A stream of studies describes the cultural traits found in Eastern and Western societies, perhaps the best known being Hofstede's (2010) study, which measured national culture in 64 countries. Hofstede's data, based on one global corporation, IBM, initially identified four independent dimensions of national cultural differences:

- *Power distance* – the extent to which those who are less powerful accept that power is distributed unequally
- *Individualism* versus *collectivism* – the degree to which members of society are integrated into communities
- *Masculinity* versus *femininity* – the general acceptance of sex-biased values and the sexual division of labour
- *Uncertainty avoidance* – society's tolerance for ambiguity and uncertainty, which ultimately deals with the search for truth.

HRM web links

Visit Geert Hofstede's website – http://geert-hofstede.com/website – which includes his publications and a link to a symposium video. Also visit http://tinyurl.com/2ndzbj, which includes critiques of Hofstede's work.

Since early modernity, the moral values of societies on both sides of the Atlantic have had a strong influence on the management of people. The value-loaded notion of 'fairness', for example, underwrites the structure of rewards and work obligations. This is illuminated by the maxim 'A fair day's wage for a fair day's work' (Hyman and Brough, 1975). Changing 'life' values have also changed participation rates in the labour market and challenged traditional gender roles in the workplace. In addition, different national cultures have influenced Western scholars' thinking on the best way to motivate employees, and on how to close the 'commitment gap'. In Maslow's theory of work motivation, for instance, higher order self-actualization is seen as the supreme human need. But this assumption presupposes an *individualist* culture in which the ties between individuals are loose and everyone is expected to look after themselves and their immediate families.

Renewed interest in the culture–performance link has generated studies comparing North American and East Asian cultural values. Faced with reports of superior Japanese management practices, researchers examined whether the 'commitment gap' between North American and Japanese workers can be attributed to differences in cultural values and national character (Lincoln and Kalleberg, 1992). In some national cultures, the values of *collectivism* and sharing are cited as a defence against an ideology seeking to lower taxes and privatize public services:

> It's the difference between being human beings and animals. With animals, when one of them gets old, they let it die, they eat it. We want to take care of our people, our youths, our students, our elderly. We are the most egalitarian society [Quebec] in North America and we want to keep it that way. (Séguin, 2010, p. A16)

Hofstede's argument for cultural homogeneity has attracted considerable criticism. The empirical basis for his proposal is a statistical averaging of his quantitative data – survey responses from IBM's employees. But an average of personal values claiming to measure the values of a national culture is about as meaningful as an average of personal income. As has been well established elsewhere, in the same way as there is a wide variance in personal income in any population, so there is a wide dispersion in the personal values of that population (McSweeney, 2002).

Among the developed countries in the global economy, few are likely to exhibit a singular culture, being more likely to be plural, with hyphenated identities such as African-American, Chinese-Canadian, French-Canadian, Anglo-Indian and so on. In support of the cultural diversity argument, experts document almost 7000 languages worldwide, suggesting the existence of that many distinct cultures (Macionis and Gerber, 2011). In the countries located in the Asian region, there are at least seven major official languages, and the people believe in widely different religions and philosophies, ranging from Buddhism and Hinduism to Islam and Christianity. Within the European Union, there are 23 official and working languages. And within the UK, the question of whether or not Scotland, Wales, Northern Ireland or England has its own distinct culture evokes strong responses. Scotland, for example, as a land of lochs, mountains and tartan, forms a compelling image that transmits 'potent resonances for culture' (McCrone, 2001, p. 37).

The empirical evidence at the centre of Hofstede's argument for a 'national culture' contains contradictions and paradoxes. In reality, people live and work in multiple cultures. The quest for a 'unified' culture is therefore doomed to ignore the fragmentation and complexities of contemporary society. To argue that research on the relationship between national values and organizational cultures is 'loose' (Hofstede et al., 2010) is not to imply that cultural undercurrents do not structure human behaviour in subtle but highly regular ways, or that as citizens and as employees, we do not carry our cultural heritage and social identities into the workplace. We talk and act in a particular way that reflects both our collective unconsciousness and our ethical standards (Saul, 2008). In other words, cultural plurality does not mean that Western societies do not function without national or regional norms. Amidst the plurality, national culture translates into organizations by influencing the core values and beliefs that constitute their organizational cultures (see, for example, Zhang and Begley, 2011).

> **reflective question**
>
> The problem of identifying a national culture is soon apparent when we examine values. Take Britain, for example. Just what are core 'British values'? How do we complete the phrase 'as British as ...?' Is it possible to identify Indian or Canadian values?

Organizational culture

In the current organizational literature, the word 'culture' is used to capture various 'ways of doing' and employees' interactions, as in 'bonus culture', 'binge-working culture' or 'masculine culture'. When academics and executives debate the merits of transforming or managing 'organizational culture', what exactly is it that they are trying to change or manage? The notion of organizational culture is equally as complex as that of national culture, and equally it lends itself to very different uses. In the literature, the terms 'corporate culture' and 'organizational culture' are common. The distinction between the two is that the former is devised and transmitted downwards to subordinates by senior management as part of a strategy of mobilizing employee commitment and portrays the workforce as 'culture-takers'. Organizational culture, on the other hand, is a product of employees' creativity and portrays the participants as 'culture-makers' (Linstead and Grafton Small, 1992).

The terms *culture* and *climate* are used interchangeably by some culture researchers (Schneider, 2000). These are complementary constructs, but they reveal overlapping nuances in the social and psychological life of complex organizations. Culture scholars tend to use qualitative methodology derived from anthropology to examine symbolic and cultural forms of organizations. Climate researchers, however, attempt to measure individuals' perceptions of workplace conduct and the meaning they assign to it using quantitative methods, such as regression analysis. The distinction between culture research and climate research therefore lies in the different methodology traditions, what they consider to be significantly meaningful and the agenda underlying each approach. More critical interpretations contend that the psychological treatment of culture largely reflects 'a neo-human relations agenda' (Parker, 2000).

HRM AND GLOBALIZATION
Multiculturalism's magic number

In the first decade of the new millennium, questions have been raised about the so-called multiculturalism experiment. In Europe, Chancellor Angela Merkel has claimed that German multiculturalism has 'utterly failed', and The Netherlands, the UK and France have all, to differing degrees, blamed multiculturalism for weakening their national social cohesion. Even in Canada, one of the world's most multicultural societies, 'its reality remains complex and at times volatile' (Peritz and Friesen, 2010, p. A14).

High levels of immigration in the last three decades have transformed Canada from a bilingual – English and French – two-culture society to a cultural mosaic. Immigration statistics reveal just how much Canada has changed. Before 1961, about 91 per cent of immigrants to Canada came from Western Europe, especially the UK, and less than 5 per cent came from Asian and Middle Eastern countries. Canadians celebrated their European cultural inheritance but gave 'scarcely a nod, let alone a meaningful nod, in the direction of the First Nations, the Métis, the Inuit' (Saul, 2008, p. 4).

Between 1991 and 2001, however, European immigrants constituted 20 per cent of total immigration, while immigrants from Asia and the Middle East made up 58 per cent. This change in the pattern of immigration was the result of a deliberate change in public policy. Now Canadian society is officially multicultural in that this aim is embodied in government social policy designed to encourage ethnic or cultural heterogeneity. Quebec has become the crucible for a Canadian debate over identity, values and how far newcomers should be accommodated at work and in other areas of life. In 2008, Quebec established a telephone 'hotline'

Source: ©kbrowne41/Shutterstock.com.

to tackle matters of linguistic, ethnic and religious accommodation. The following three cases provide a window into managing the multicultural workplace:

- *Case 1* – A Sikh employee in a food warehouse wants to wear a kara – a bangle-type metal bracelet that represents an expression of the Sikh faith. The warehouse has a ban on jewellery for employees who handle food, for hygiene purposes. The company wants to know if it should accommodate the employee's request.
- *Case 2* – A college student wears a Muslim face veil, or niqab, that covers her entire body except for a slit for her eyes. She has agreed to pose for her student ID bare-faced, but does not want the image to be entered into a college-wide computer database. The college is seeking a policy that will balance its security needs with the student's wishes.
- *Case 3* – A Muslim schoolteacher requests each Friday afternoon off to attend prayers at his mosque. The school board wants to know how to accommodate him.

Multiculturalism has generated controversy because people need to rethink their core values and norms. The issue of reasonable accommodation in multicultural workplaces has become a microcosm of the diversity dilemma: it affects the psychological contract, it is linked to the topic of dignity at work (Bolton, 2007), and it has repercussions for HRM.

Stop! If you were the HRM manager employed at these three workplaces, what advice would you give to each? What types of cultural knowledge might be common in a workplace in your home country? How would you react if you were asked by an employer to remove an article of faith, for example a cross or a kara?

Further reading and other resources:

See Peritz and Friesen (2010), Saul (2008) and Taylor and Bain (2005). View the film *Slumdog Millionaire* (2009) for an insight into culture training at Indian call centres. And go to this book's website for information on how Quebec's Multiculturalism Commission advised the three organizations mentioned in this feature.

Note: This feature was written by John Bratton.

The different approaches generate different definitions of organizational culture. An early definition by Smircich focuses on values that guide employees' conduct at work and shape their interactions. Organizational culture (Smircich, 1983, p. 344) is the:

Social or normative glue that holds an organization together ... The values or social ideals and the beliefs that organization members come to share. These values or patterns of beliefs are manifested by symbolic devices, such as myths, stories, legends and specialized language.

In contrast, a definition focusing on shared meanings and symbolism is articulated by Alvesson (2002, pp. 3–4):

> For me values are less central and less useful than meanings and symbolism in cultural analysis ... Culture is not primarily 'inside' people's heads, but somewhere 'between' the heads of a group of people where symbols and meanings are publicly expressed, for example, in work group interactions, in board meetings but also in material objects. Organizational culture then is central in governing the understanding of workplace interactions, events and processes. It is the context in which these phenomena become comprehensible and meaningful.

A synthesis of the definitions captures the essential elements of organizational culture. It concerns the importance of shared values, beliefs and language that shape and perpetuate organizational reality, so that employees' work conduct is more predictable and governable.

reflective question

Reading the two definitions of organizational culture, does your university have a culture? How does this differ within and between the different faculties, schools or departments of the university?

To understand organizational culture, we must examine its parts, even though any organizational culture is greater than the sum of its parts. Drawing on the work of Edgar Schein (2010), Figure 4.2 shows three fundamental levels of organizational culture: *artefacts*, *values* and *basic assumptions*. These can be imagined as an iceberg. The uppermost subtriangle might be viewed as the 'tip of the iceberg', representing the observable parts of organizational culture, which are embedded in shared values, basic assumptions and beliefs that are invisible to the human eye. Each level of culture influences another level.

The first level comprises the visible, the *artefacts* and material objects such as buildings, technology, art and uniforms that the organization 'uses' to express its culture. For example, when a company uses only email for internal communication, the cultural message is that IT is a highly valued resource. Displaying art on office walls signals to members and visitors that creating a stimulating cultural context in which employees can explore ideas and aesthetics is highly valued (Harding, 2003). Other examples are the wearing of professorial apparel, the doctor's white coat in the National Health Service (NHS) and the black gown worn by academics at official university ceremonies. The visible culture also includes *language*.

How managers describe other employees is an example of using symbols to convey meaning to each other. For example, Walmart refers to its employees as 'associates', and at Disneyland they are known as 'cast members'. Social *behaviour* is another aspect of observable organizational culture, including rituals and ceremonies. *Rituals* are collective routines that 'dramatize' the organization's culture. For example, the office party can be viewed as a ritual for *integrating* new members into

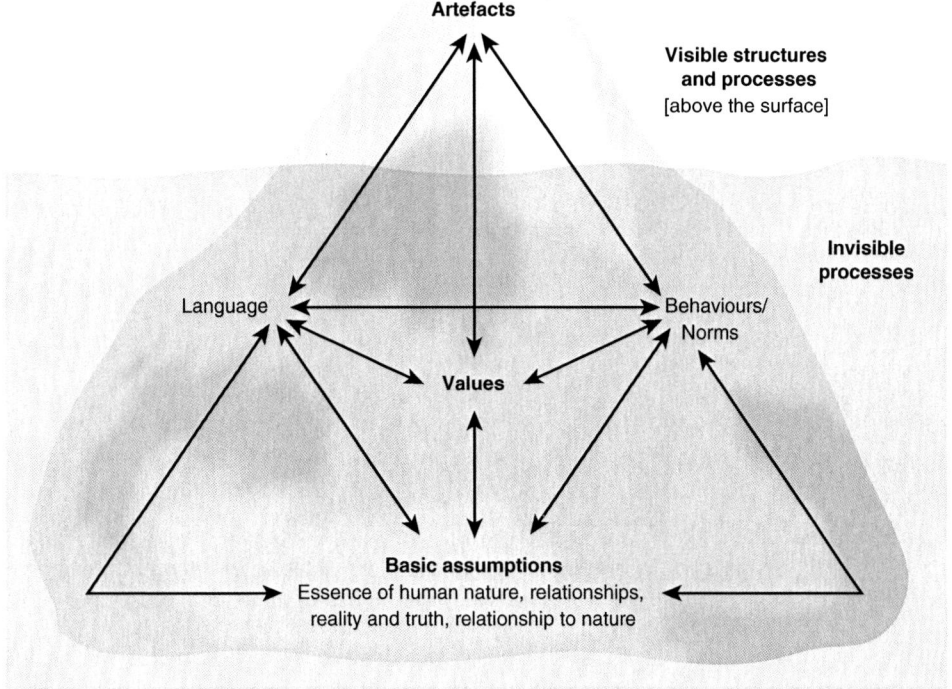

Figure 4.2 The three levels of organizational culture

Leather, tattoos and long hair could be considered an expression of this motorcycle club's visual culture

Souce: ©istockphoto.com/Luca Cepparo.

the organization. *Ceremonies* are planned and represent more formal social artefacts than rituals, as in, for example, the 'call to the bar' ceremony for graduating lawyers.

The second level of organizational culture comprises perceived shared work-related *values*, which are invisible. Previous studies suggest that perceived organizational ethical values refer to workers' beliefs concerning what practices are acceptable or appropriate in their organization (Biron, 2010). Perceived organizational values are therefore the standards of desirability by which employees evaluate aspects of their work or profession and make choices between options (Warr, 2008). For example, in healthcare, standard medical practice is influenced by a belief in evidence for practice or by a commitment to patient-centred care. In many universities, practice is influenced by the espoused value 'We are a teaching-centred institution'. Employment-related espoused values possess six characteristics (Warr, 2008):

- They involve a moral or ethical statements of 'rightness'.
- They pertain to desirable modes of behaviour at a given point in time.
- They directly influence employees' behaviour and experiences, and act as significant moderators.
- They are typically associated with strategic goals and address questions such as 'What are we doing?' and 'Why are we doing this?'
- They guide the selection and evaluation of the organization's members.
- They may vary with respect to male/female, demographic and cultural differences.

The term 'shared' in cultural analysis implies that organizational members are a whole. Each member has been exposed to a set of dominant values, although not every member may internalize and endorse these. Despite the substantial evidence that perceived organizational values influence the behaviour of workers, the practical application of the insights generated by this research has been limited (Biron, 2010).

The third level of organizational culture relates to *basic assumptions*, which are invisible, unconscious, taken for granted, difficult to access and highly resistant to change. These are the implicit and unspoken assumptions that underpin everyday choices and shape how members perceive, think and emotionally react to social events. For example, in the NHS, assumptions about the relative roles of doctors and nurses, about patients' rights or about the sources of ill-health underpin everyday decisions and actions (Davies, 2002). The basic assumptions or beliefs about human nature, human relationships, relationships to nature and how the world works form the base from which employees, who enter the workplace as social beings with life histories and experiences, build their values of how the world *should* be. Assumptions and values then guide employees' workplace conduct and shape their interactions, as do the artefacts with which members surround themselves. Organizational culture manifests itself most clearly through the organization's policies and practices (Zhang and Begley, 2011).

HRM web links

Visit http://web.mit.edu/scheine/www/home.html, which is Schein's official website.

reflective question

Thinking about your own university or college, does the culture manifest itself through policies or practices? For instance, do you expect and experience a student-centred focus? Do teaching staff primarily focus on their teaching or their research interests? Is there a 'publish or perish' culture? Try to assess your answer at three levels: observable artefacts, shared values and basic assumptions of the culture.

HRM as I see it

Keith Stopforth
Head of Talent and Development, Bupa Health and Wellbeing
www.bupa.co.uk

Bupa is an international private healthcare company with bases on three continents and over 10 million customers in over 200 countries. Bupa provides health insurance, care homes, health assessments, occupational health services and child care, and runs its own hospital, Bupa Cromwell Hospital, in London. The company also owns several healthcare companies overseas, including Sanitas in Spain and IHI Danmark in Denmark.

Keith Stopforth has been with Bupa since 2001. He now works in Bupa Health and Wellbeing in the UK, having previously worked as a sales manager and then branch training manager at Prudential. Keith is currently developing his skills in executive coaching and mentoring. He is a member of the Talent Forum 2011.

Visit www.palgrave.com/business/bratton5 to watch Keith talking about talent management, organizational culture and diversity at Bupa, and then think about the following questions:

1. What is Keith's view of organizational culture and the role of the HR department in 'shaping' culture?
2. What are the role of competencies in this process?
3. How does BUPA embrace diversity? What opportunities are provided to encourage prospective employees, and how do you think these could be applied in other companies?

Perspectives on organizational culture

The family tree of the different perspectives on organizational culture is rooted in classical sociological theory. The work of the German sociologist Max Weber is representative of the canonical literature on understanding employees' work conduct as a cultural phenomenon: individuals behave 'not out of obedience, but either because the environment approves of the conduct and disapproves of its opposite, or merely as a result of unreflective habituation to a regularity of life that has *engraved itself as a custom*' (Weber, 1922/1968, p. 312, emphasis added). Much contemporary writing in culture analysis can be divided into two schools of thought: managerialist and critical.

Managerially oriented perspectives

This body of writing examines culture from the premise that it can play a role in building organizational consensus and harmony, and can improve performance. From this viewpoint, organizational culture is a *variable* – an attribute that an organization possesses or *'has'* and, as such, can be created by corporate managers.

This standpoint is associated with the *structural-functionalist* approach to cultural analysis. Its theoretical roots date back to Auguste Comte (1798–1857) and Emile Durkheim (1858–1917) and, in the twentieth century, to the US sociologist Talcott Parsons (1902–1979). The central premise of the structural-functionist approach is that cultural processes can create organizational stability and consensus. The task of senior management is therefore to focus on how culture can be managed and disseminated downwards to organizational members.

Within this genre, Peters and Waterman's influential book *In Search of Excellence* is probably the best well-known example of the 'has' school. These gurus view culture as an elixir that binds together the specific human qualities that lead to a maximizing of employees' commitment to providing a high-quality service or product – what is sometimes called a 'commitment-excellence organization'. Thus, mainstream theorists are said, in Martin's (1992) words, to follow an *'integration'* perspective. In this sense, management-inspired cultural processes and interventions attempt to alleviate the many forms of the ever-present conflict that arises from managing the labour process. This approach focuses on building a culture that binds members together around the same core values, beliefs and norms, which are considered to be prerequisites for achieving the organization's strategic goals. For integration or functionalism theorists, culture is conceptualized as 'organization-wide agreement with values espoused by top management' (Martin and Frost, 1996, p. 600). The notion of 'cultural engineering' – creating the 'right' kind of culture to align with strategic goals – is seen as a 'lever' for fostering commitment and loyalty in the workforce.

What constitutes the 'right culture' for excellence is, however, a matter of debate. A popular approach is the contingency theory, which is based on the belief that senior managers need to consider both external and internal variables when deciding what kind of culture best fits their organization. Deal and Kennedy (1982), for example, identify important contingencies such as the level of risk, the size and design of the organization, ownership and governance, technology and the need for innovation. In the leadership literature, a connection between leadership, culture and employees' commitment to the organization has often been theoretically proposed. Employee organizational commitment is the degree to which employees identify with the organization's goals and values, their willingness to exceed a minimum level of effort on behalf of the organization, and their intention to remain with the organization.

Specifically, recent studies have found that 'transformational' leadership behaviour is an antecedent variable in regard to employee commitment. For example, Simosi and Xenikou (2010, p. 1611) conclude that both transformational leadership behaviour and contingent reward were found to be 'significantly and positively related to affective and normative commitment' as well as to employees' feeling of obligation to remain in the organization. Champy contends that 'values are our moral navigational devices' and that, for real change to occur, leaders need 'cultural warriors' at every level of the organization to communicate new values to their peers (1996, p. 79). Whereas management gurus such as Peters and Waterman, Deal and Kennedy, and Champy focus on values that foster 'strong' corporate cultures, researchers have in recent years argued that cultural diversity and the changing nature of the employment relationship have heightened how important it is to understand the dynamics of employee commitment as a potential determinant of motivation (see, for example, Becton and Field, 2009; Mathew and Ogbonna, 2009; Su et al., 2009).

Contingency studies do draw attention to cultural heterogeneity, and Martin (1992) refers to these as the *differentiated* perspective. An organization such as the NHS might have one dominant culture expressing its core values, but it also has sets of *subcultures* defined by professions, function and space. An image of professional groups with strong norms and values potentially challenging aspects of the organization's core values is associated with Ouchi's (1980) concept of the 'clan', itself drawn from Durkheim's theory of mechanical solidarity. A study of healthcare providers revealed that 'complex multiple cultural values are often hierarchical and are commonly interpreted in ways that ascribe differentiated, fragmented and collective meaning' (Morgan and Ogbonna, 2008, p. 61). Healthcare professionals may collectively interpret the espoused value of providing the 'best possible care' for patients, but that 'care' will be delivered differently by the various professional groups. For doctors, this may mean eradicating the cause of illness, whereas for occupational therapists it may mean helping patients achieve greater mobility (Fitzgerald and Teal, 2004). In contrast, a macho and aggressive subculture might exist among male workers doing mundane or unpleasant work (Ackroyd and Crowdy, 1990).

Subcultures help to bind workers together, to cope with shared frustrations and to preserve a distinctive identity (Bolton, 2005). The analyses of subcultures reveal a wide variation in values, work conduct and assumptions – these are, however, a normal part of organizational life.

reflective question

Do you think a complex organization like the UK's NHS has subcultures? What are the implications for HRM practices if core subcultures exist?

A sociologically informed analysis of culture also acknowledges the existence of *countercultures* in work organizations. These create their own form of organizational reality through a subculture that actively opposes the dominant values and norms (Martin and Siehl, 1983). For example, a policy change focusing on 'putting customers first' may produce countercultures as some staff may be reluctant to abandon professional or trade norms and may strongly reject service-oriented values. Mergers and acquisitions may also produce countercultures. There may be a 'clash of corporate cultures' when the values, beliefs and norms held by members of an acquired organization are inconsistent with those of the acquiring organization. The debate on the existence of subcultures and countercultures emphasizes the complexities and interwoven character of organizational culture and avoids an overly static and monolithic picture of everyday organizational life.

Critically oriented perspectives

Critical cultural scholars share a similar view that values and norms are deeply embedded in society. In contrast to the structural-functionalist perspective that understands culture as something an organization '*has*', critical workplace theorists proceed from the idea that the organization '*is*' a culture. The central premise is that, at its roots, the work organization is a manifestation of human consciousness, a source of power, a socializing and controlling force. Moreover, adherents of the 'is' view of culture are likely to play down any outcomes in terms of efficiency that result from changes in the culture (Alvesson, 2002). Here, three critically oriented perspectives – symbolic-interactionist, conflict and feminist – will serve as alternative lenses through which to understand organizational culture.

The *symbolic-interactionist* approach understands organizational culture as the sum of all the employees' interactions. In this school of thought, culture plays the role of a 'carrier' for shared meaning (hence 'symbolic') and is produced by workers and managers in face-to-face encounters (hence 'interactionist') as they go about their everyday workplace activities. The culture of the organization is created by its members and reproduced by the networks of symbols and meanings that employees share and that make shared work conduct possible. The analysis of organizational culture can therefore occur through studying observable artefacts, language, action and the beliefs and values of organizational members.

In the realm of shared *artefacts*, displayed mission statements, framed photographs of individuals and ceremonies, technology and displayed art are all manifestations of culture. *Language* is explored to see how it is used to communicate effectively in order to make work conduct possible. Story-telling touches all of us, reaching across cultures and generations (Fulford, 1999). In workplaces, shared *stories*, *myths* and *legends* serve to construct a common ground for understanding work behaviour. For example, an account of a dramatic event in the past history of the company serves to create a shared meaning of how workers are expected to handle problems in the present.

Also scrutinized is shared work *action*. Rites commonly found in the workplace are those of recognition (for example, an employee of the month award) and of conflict (for example, a disciplinary hearing). Shared *beliefs* and *values* are examined too. In workplace talk, the espousal of 'values' or perceived 'ethical values'

The office water cooler is a well-known location for sharing workplace stories
Source: ©iofoto, 2011. Shutterstock Images.

is omnipresent; this can concern either legislative provisions that are not always heeded (for example, antidiscrimination laws) or values that are not adequately supported or funded by the organization. Employee groups will wrap their proposals around a 'values' rhetoric to elevate these demands over more pedestrian ones. By highlighting day-to-day social interaction, this analysis explains why organizational cultures are enduring. However, research suggests that a lack of organizational support and mistreatment and indignity at work can undermine the normative influence of perceived ethical values (Biron, 2010). Furthermore, a common critique of this approach relates to its underemphasis of how larger social structures cause disagreement on meanings.

Unlike the integration perspective, the *critical perspective* explores how values, beliefs and norms develop to sustain inequalities and the power of employers. It sets out to develop an understanding of organizational culture by situating it in the context of capitalist relations of domination and control. The intellectual roots of this analysis are found in the canonical text written by Karl Marx and Friedrich Engels. In the 1859 preface to *The Critique of Political Economy*, Marx wrote: 'The mode of production of material life conditions the social, political and intellectual life process in general. It is not the consciousness of men that determines their being, but, on the contrary, their social being that determines their consciousness' (Tucker, 1978, p. 4). For Marx, cultural knowledge is socially produced on the basis of particular structures of economic relationships. Furthermore, in *The German Ideology*, Marx and Engels (1998) reiterate the point that ideas about how the world works, perceptions of reality and so forth are cultural constructs that reflect constellations of class interests – typically those of society's most powerful social elite. Moreover, dominant ideas in society are directly interwoven with the economy and with work-related activities. Many conflict theorists agree with Marx's assertion that social elites use *ideology*, a non-material element of culture, to shape the thoughts and actions of other social classes, as, for example, in the popular idea that markets can best decide society's economic priorities because 'governments cannot pick winners'. Public discourse often supports these views, since no alternatives are debated or offered.

Conflict perspectives call attention to the perpetual tension, conflict and resistance that exists between different employee groups. The structured antagonism between capital and labour, and, in tandem with this, managerial control, focuses on the '*who*' of power over other people and the '*how*' of employee commitment. Here, the focus is on 'strong' corporate cultures as an employment strategy to develop a sense of 'community' and to activate employee emotion, which might lead to enhanced loyalty and commitment to the company (Ray, 1986; Thompson and McHugh, 2009). Around this thesis, a body of literature has developed which argues that cultural control overlaps and exists alongside, rather than replaces, more traditional forms of management control strategies, such as bureaucracy, technology and the more traditional HRM policies and practices, for example completing forms or 'punching in' at the start of a working day. In this sense, systems of cultural hegemony do not replace but instead *complement* other employment strategies adopted over time that aim to increase the loyalty and control of employees, and ultimately their efficiency.

reflective question

What national (macro) and global forces drive the development of employment strategies? To what extent have the reverberations of the 2008–12 economic crises caused managers to change the mix of employment strategies, including cultural control, with which they experiment?

The picture represented by critical workplace scholars is one that represents contradictory and unstable organizational cultures. Drawing on the postmodernist discourse, this approach has been referred to as the *fragmentary* perspective (Martin, 2002). As such, organizational culture is characterized by ephemerality, ambiguity and change, and exposes claims of unified corporate cultures. Culture is 'a loosely structured and incompletely shared system that emerges dynamically as cultural members experience each other, events, and the organization's contextual features' (Martin, 1992, p. 152). The value of this fragmentary approach lies in its exposure of the naivety of using a culture metaphor to describe the organization – it is naive to think that there is no ambiguity in what cultural members believe and do. For example, it might expose claims of truth such as 'We are an equal opportunity employer' while masking the gender or race inequality arising from a male-dominant or white-dominant workplace (Martin, 2002).

The *feminist perspective* argues that gender is a central aspect of work and organizations. Why, 35 years after the passing of the UK Sex Discrimination Act, and in an age of alleged equality of opportunity (in developed economies at least), is the gender gap so enduring in the workplace? Understanding the gender problem in organizational culture analysis is important for at least four reasons:

- First, virtually every human culture known to exist has been dominated by the men, and *external* societal values associated with notions of masculinity and femininity are often reflected in work-related processes. For example, it is common to find processes that privilege the rationality and 'objectivity' associated with masculine attributes while suppressing emotion, which is associated with family and other feminine attributes.
- Second, gender inequality is supported by ideology that seeks to 'naturalize' gender roles. As Eagleton (1983, p. 135) remarks, 'Ideology seeks to convert culture into Nature'. The idea that a woman's place is in the home, or a woman is incapable of performing the duties of a firefighter, illustrates the existence of this ideology.
- Third, *inside* the workplace, practices involved in recruitment, selection and appraisal often conform to and extend the sex-biased societal values that reinforce job segregation – the tendency for men and women to work in different occupations – as well as systemic discrimination against women.
- Finally, some organizations (for example, schools and the media) play a direct part in the socializing processes by which people acquire gender identities (Aaltio-Marjosola and Mills, 2002). For example, the social association between masculinity and physical hazards contributes to the gendered nature of 'the way things are done' in an organization, justifying 'masculine occupations'.

HRM in practice 4.1: Management surveillance: someone's watching you ...

Management have always felt the need to observe and monitor employees' work – a management function that can be traced from the 'overseers' in the first factories of eighteenth-century Britain to the foremen and supervisors of the twentieth century. Since the last two decades of that century, however, the rapid diffusion of information technology has created systems of monitoring and surveillance that seem, to many, to be all-embracing.

As a recent newspaper account put it:

From 'mystery shoppers' to swipe cards, from CCTV to phone, email and Internet monitoring, today's workforce is under constant surveillance. ('Work' Supplement, The Guardian, May 7, 2011)

The article goes on to report that such surveillance can even extend outside the workplace, with some organizations hiring private investigators to check up on cases of suspected employee absenteeism.

In addition to the long-standing management desire to monitor actual performance, it is clear that there is a perceived need to monitor employee time-use to avoid what has in the USA been termed 'cyberloafing'. There is a rather fuzzy line here between management prerogative and employee privacy: under human rights legislation, employees are entitled to a 'reasonable' amount of personal communication, although they should not expect to be able to use company equipment for this purpose. If the line is crossed, it can be costly: the European Court of Human Rights awarded more than £6000 to an employee of a Welsh college whose emails, telephone and Internet usage had been secretly monitored.

The apparent omnipresence and scope of electronic monitoring led in the 1990s to a renewed interest in French philosopher Michel Foucault's claim that contemporary society had become characterized by surveillance. Foucault resurrected the term 'panopticon' ('all-seeing'), first invented for the design of a model prison by the eighteenth-century economist Jeremy Bentham. In a panopticon, the subject – in Bentham's example, the prisoner – never knows whether he is being watched or not but, because he *might* be, he suitably modifies his behaviour. One can see how the spread of CCTV and the electronic counting of throughput at supermarket checkouts seems to validate Foucault's claim.

However, as part of their long-standing work on call centres, Peter Bain and Phil Taylor (Bain and Taylor, 2000) showed that this model ignores the agency of both employees and managers. The call centre in their case study was characterized by intensive, repetitive and often acutely stressful work. The agents' performance was monitored in a variety of ways, including supervisors listening in and the recording of calls (remote observation), in addition to 'mystery shopper' calls in which the responses of customer service agents were assessed. Bain and Taylor found that experienced customer service agents knew when they were being monitored and often manipulated the call flow, logging on and off to get small breaks. There were also variations in the degree to which individual managers pursued remote observations, since overintensive monitoring led to stressed and demoralized employees who could not deliver a good quality of service. Also, as the supervisors' bonuses were calculated on their team's performance, they did not want the team to have too many 'red' observations. Finally, during the period of the research project, the call-centre workers successfully took the issues of working conditions and health and safety to the trade union, and the union was subsequently able to contest many of the daily instances of management control.

> **Stop!** Count the number of ways in which your actions are known to others who are not your direct acquaintances (for example, when using your cash card, shop loyalty card or Internet log-on, or being seen on a town-centre CCTV). If our general social privacy is being eroded, how much privacy should we expect in the workplace?

Sources and further information:

See Bain and Taylor (2000), Sewell (1998) and Sewell and Wilkinson (1992).

Note: This feature was written by Chris Baldry at the University of Stirling.

Feminist perspectives have brought about a major shift in our ways of thinking about culture and knowledge, and also about the way in which the political impinges upon and permeates all of our ways of thinking and acting, both public and private. The argument is that, with notable exceptions, mainstream analysis has generally reflected dominant social beliefs about gender roles that men inhabit the 'public' domain of action, decision-making, power and authority, while women inhabit the 'private' domestic world. Thus, critical feminist scholars have contended that the standard treatment of organizational culture neglects how gender, a patriarchal system, subtle stereotyping, social networks that unintentionally exclude women, systemic discrimination, female-hostile banter and sexuality, that is, sexual characteristics and sexual conduct in the workplace, profoundly shape work cultures. Although sexuality serves to affirm men's sense of shared masculinity, it can serve to make women feel uncomfortable, and leaving the organization is often seen as the only alternative (Brewis and Linstead, 2000). Organizational culture is often a crucial determinant of sexual harassment (Chamberlain et al., 2008) that can be an entrenched feature of workplaces through pornographic pin-ups, taunting and innuendo, and predatory conduct.

National culture, with its societal value system and norms, is deeply intertwined with organizational culture in a dialectical relationship, each being fashioned and refashioned by the other. Including the gender-sexuality paradigm in the study of organizational culture has pushed the boundaries of the differentiation approach by addressing concerns of inequality and discriminatory workplace practices. As sociologist Judy Wajcman observes, the contemporary workplace is not gender neutral; indeed, 'gender is woven into the very fabric of bureaucratic hierarchy and authority relations' (Wajcman, 1998, p. 47). In broad terms, work cultures can be studied from three perspectives, those of *integration, differentiation* and *fragmentation*. Joanne Martin (1992) argues that all three are necessary to fully understand how culture operates in the workplace. Each of the major perspectives we have examined can be used as a theoretical compass for navigating through the myriad and competing views found in the organizational culture and HRM literature.

> **reflective question**
>
> Which of these perspectives do you consider most useful for understanding the nature of contemporary organizations and why?

Managing culture through HRM

Organizational cultures are amazingly stable and enduring. From an integrationist perspective, a strong culture can produce a common value system that is consistent with organizational goals such as higher productivity. From this point of view, corporate culture functions as the ultimate form of management control – a self-controlled, committed workforce dedicated to management's expectations and goals. Thus, developing a 'strong' culture in which members of the organization develop a fierce loyalty to the organization offers the possibility to close the 'commitment gap' in the employment relationship, thereby releasing the workers' creative and productive capacity).

An important goal of HRM is to manage the psychological contract, to change the employment relationship from a binary *low-trust* and *low-commitment* relationship to a participatory *high-trust* and *high-commitment* relationship, as well as to capture, manage and control emotion in the organization (Bolton, 2005; Legge, 2005). Contemporary workplace scholars, drawing heavily on Erving Goffman's (1967) work comparing human interactions with drama, argue that a robust corporate culture provides normative and behavioural 'scripts' for employees to follow. The 'scripts' are written by management and reflect the big issues of productivity, organizational flexibility, social legitimacy and 'strategic tensions'. The scripts may also provide clear expectations of work behaviour for new initiatives such as high-performance work systems, or may be used to capture and manage employees' emotional labour (du Gay, 1996).

The role of HRM in translating and crafting an organization's culture has received substantial attention in both the popular and the academic HRM literature. It has been argued, for example, that 'the HR professional must recognize, articulate, and shape a company's culture' (Brewster et al., 2008, p. 312). Several researchers have examined the phenomenon of organizational culture in multinational corporations. The issue they have focused on is whether the subsidiaries of multinational corporations generate 'third cultures', that is hybrid versions of their home and host country cultures (Hui and Graen, 1997; Zhang and Begley, 2011). Amid culturally diverse environments, although an organizational culture may be partly crafted by senior managers, it is not effortlessly manipulated by them. Indeed, as HRM is one of the main transmitters of company policies and practices, changes in HR policies and practices that run counter to, or do not blend with, perceived organizational values will usually meet with resistance from managers and other employees, and may fail (Biron, 2010; Gahan and Abeysekera, 2009; Zhang and Albrecht, 2010). In this context, leadership and HRM theorists have tried to identify effective ways to change manifestations of organizational culture: visible *artefacts*, including language and shared behaviour; work *values*, which are invisible, but can be espoused; and various sets of HRM practices that reinforce the culture. This section reviews strategies of planned culture change:

- Leadership processes that create the motivation to change behaviour, with a particular emphasis on their symbolic content
- Reframing social networks of symbols and meanings through artefacts, language, rituals and ceremonies
- Initiating new HRM practices to change work conduct.

A careful review of the literature shows that all three strategies implicitly adhere to Lewin's (1951) three-stage model of planned change, which involves 'unfreezing' present inappropriate employees' work conduct, 'changing' to new behaviour patterns and positive reinforcement to 'refreeze' the desired change.

Leading cultural change

The role of leadership in generating employees' support for cultural change is rooted in the leadership literature (see, for example, Bass and Riggio, 2006). There are, however, sociologically informed writers who recognize that cultures can be changed to match strategic goals. In contrast to the crudely prescriptive functional approach, Morgan (1997, p. 152) cautiously argues that:

> Managers can influence the evolution of culture by being aware of the symbolic consequences of their actions and by attempting to foster desired values. But they can never control culture in the sense that many management writers advocate.

The guiding maxim for implementing successful strategies for cultural change is that of meeting 'complexity with complexity' (Bate, 1995, p. 5). One mainstream approach acknowledging complexity is John Kotter's (1996) sequential model, which focuses on what specific work behaviours leaders should engage in when managing change, typically involving Lewin's 'unfreezing', 'changing' and 'refreezing' stages. Kotter's model attempts to change culture through an empiricist-rational strategy, that is, by assuming that employees make rational choices if provided with the 'correct' information. In an economic crisis, Canadian writer Naomi Klein (2007) reminds us that 'unfreezing' and organizational change may occur through 'shock therapy', as witnessed by the 2008 banking crisis, as well as by skilful management.

Reframing of social networks and meanings

One strategy to change an organizational culture is by reframing social networks of symbols and meanings in order to increase the commitment that individual employees show to their organization's mission. This can be done by changing physical artefacts, for example displaying a framed copy of the organization's new mission statement, or by redesigning work systems, such as creating work teams that have greater autonomy. Many organizations have reframed shared symbols and meanings by changing the language to promote high levels of discretionary employee behaviour. Stories and story-telling are pervasive in culture management. Stories often contain, both explicitly and implicitly, arguments for and against work-related values; they help members to locate work experiences and develop new insights, which in turn promote sense-making or sense-giving and new ways of behaving (Boyce, 1997; Gold et al., 2002).

Notable examples of language and narrative strategies to achieve cultural change can be seen with British Airways and their mission of 'Putting People First', as well as in 'corporate' universities, where students are increasingly conceptualized as 'clients', and professors as 'service providers' who must 'brand' their institutions and sell their 'products', as do car and beer manufacturers, for example. The general gist of this cultural change strategy is that, if it is properly introduced, the reframing of cultural artefacts is potentially very effective in disconfirming the appropriateness of employees' present behaviours, providing employees with new behavioural models and affirming new ways of doing things.

HRM practices to change culture

People are key carriers of values into the workplace. Thus, one way to change or reinforce a particular culture is through the 'individual–organizational fit' (Purcell et al., 2009, p. 23). Evidence suggests that a strong culture can be created by a galaxy of HR practices directed towards individual employees. HR *selection* practices are an important means of 'knowing' and managing a culture change (Townley, 1994). Personality- and competency-based tests represent the psychological calculation of suitability and enable managers to find talented individuals who seem to 'fit' the new culture. Changing and managing culture involves formal and informal work-related learning, a process sociologists call *socialization*. By means of socialization, employees learn the symbols and meanings and shared practices of an organization.

In addition, the performance appraisal system is a systematic HR practice used to classify and rank employees hierarchically according to how well they integrate the newly defined set of beliefs, values and actions into their normal ways of doing things. The newly espoused values are incorporated into the appraisal system to enable employees to be compared with each other, to render them 'known' and to reinforce the desired cultural change. HR *reward* practices can have a reinforcing or 'refreezing' effect when the appraisal system connects desired work behaviours with rewards. For example, given the general *commodification* of education, new contracts in universities reinforce a 'research culture' in which promotion and pay are tied to research productivity rather than teaching excellence. Administrators or managers can furthermore reinvigorate the culture change process and increase discretionary behaviour with new formal *training* and, importantly, the informal learning of organizational values and routines.

Drawing upon leadership and HRM studies, the three strategies of planned culture change are shown in Figure 4.3. Steps 1 and 2 represent Lewin's 'unfreezing' stage, steps 3 and 4 represent the 'changing' stage, and step 5 represents the 'refreezing' or consolidation process. The cluster of HR practices mentioned above is a conduit through which dominant shared values can be both carried into the organization and enacted (Purcell et al., 2009). The most sceptical detractors claim that HR practices can help to sustain 'cultural doping' so that individual employees exhibit

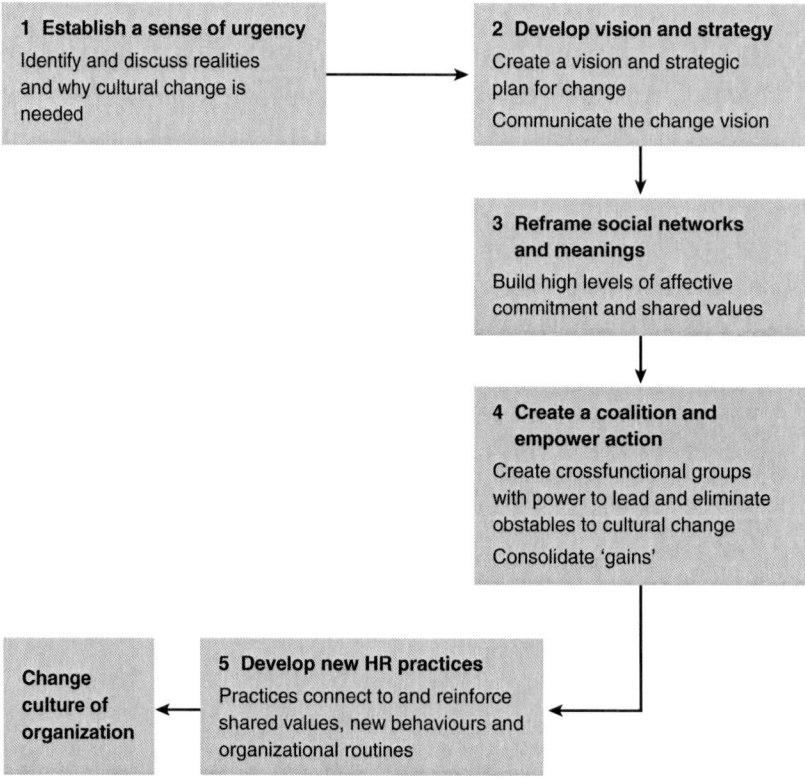

Figure 4.3 A strategy for changing organizational culture

shared values and routines – how work is performed – congruent with those of their organization (Alvesson and Willmott, 1996). In strong cultures, a metaphorical 'glue' therefore bonds employees and encourages each to internalize the organization's culture because it fulfils their need for social affiliation and identity.

Sustainability and green HRM

The meaning of sustainability was explored when we examined the concept as part of a corporate strategy. In this chapter, we have explained that values pervade all areas of human life and strongly influence the way in which work and people are managed. The different ways of thinking about sustainability vie for legitimacy in the public discourse and also challenge human values both outside and inside the workplace. In mainstream management, economic sustainability is defined in terms of maintaining the expansionist economic cycle, an approach based on money values. On the other hand, broader definitions underscore a variation of what is called the 'quadruple mix'. In management parlance, this refers to the pursuit of *quadruple bottom line* performance, which is a balance of economic, environmental, social and cultural goals. This perspective represents a shift away from economic values towards life values.

The debate that shapes much of what we hear, think and decide about sustainability is, by and large, dominated by economists, partly because of the money-value logic of our market society, but also, it is argued, because 'economists are clear and ecologists are muddled' on the meaning of sustainability (Sumner, 2007, p. 92). Unsurprisingly, then, it is the economic perspective that tends to influence patterns of organizational decision-making.

In mainstream definitions of the term, sustainability is seen as a strategic goal or mission that is underpinned by values and a strong culture expressing what the organization is and its relationship with its customers and employees. To borrow from Purcell et al. (2009), it can be the 'Big Idea'. If long-term sustainability is to go beyond quaint rhetorical notions of 'going green', several scholars maintain that organizations have to develop a 'sustainability-oriented organizational culture' (see, for example, Chen, 2011; Jabbour et al., 2010; Linnenluecke and Griffiths, 2010). The concept of a sustainable culture involves developing a set of values consistent with sustainability that are 'embedded' into all activities, such as purchasing, work systems, distribution and HR management. As part of a move towards corporate sustainability, sustainability-based values should 'interconnect' the relationships between suppliers and customers and the organizational culture. Sustainability-based values should be 'enduring' to provide a stable base for both the achievement of flexibility and the management of performance. It is a form of organizational learning in which a series of interrelated behaviours create a collective sense-making (Weick, 2001).

A sustainable workplace is a 'collective endeavour' and has the same attributes as strong corporate cultures where the culture acts as a metaphorical 'glue' that bonds employees and work processes together. As Purcell and his colleagues observe, although ad hoc HR practices can easily be replicated, 'it is the mix of these practices with well-developed routines underpinned by values collectively applied and

HRM in practice 4.2: Can we measure changes in organizational culture?

Much cultural analysis is framed within a workforce commitment–performance relationship in which a configuration of a 'strong' culture produces a loyal workforce and superior performance. The new recognition that in order to provide superior services, especially in service-oriented, team-based workplaces, managers need to enlist the know-how of all their employees places a premium on interpersonal communication (Guirdham, 2011). A culture that emphasizes communication and trust helped Baringa Partners, a management consultancy firm, to win the top award of Best Workplace in Britain (Widget Finn, 2010). In one employee's inimitable words:

> 'I love this place and I love the job I do. I believe we are all exceptionally proud to work for such a unique, encouraging and fair company.' According to Mohamed Mansour, managing partner, Baringa has a company culture that focuses on supporting and growing talented and motivated staff: 'All our senior people are involved in every recruiting decision we make. We use personal networks, selecting the best people we have worked with, alongside more traditional methods of finding new talent.' Recruiting in this way makes a difference to the psychological contract Baringa has with its employees: the emphasis is not just on ensuring staff are suitable for the organization, but also that the organization is suitable for staff.
>
> Communication and trust are essential to Baringa's success, claims Mr Mansour. 'We have no big central office where everyone gets together round the coffee machine. Our consultants spend most of their time at client sites, so we use regular company meetings every six weeks to catch up with colleagues, meet new joiners, get up to date with strategy and achievements, and give everyone an opportunity to have their say.' The meetings contribute to the open, honest and consistent communication needed to build trust. As one staff member says: 'Everyone is open, honest and approachable, with a can-do attitude to getting things done as a team. Nobody is left to do things on their own, which is excellent and a vast improvement on previous places I have worked.'
>
> Celebrating success is a key way to motivate staff. The company gives a quarterly award of £500 to an employee who has demonstrated an exceptional contribution to the company's core values, with annual awards for Team of the Year, the Star Player, One to Watch and Cheerleader. (Great Place to Work® Institute UK)

Despite these impressive accounts of culture management, demonstrating a relationship between a 'strong' culture and superior performance is not without its problems. Ideally, the methodology would permit a calculation of how different cultures – 'weak' versus 'strong' – affect performance, while controlling the other factors influencing performance. The data must demonstrate the extent to which the staff internalize new core values, using a particular set of performance variables over a period of time.

> **Stop!** What HR practices did Baringa use to create a successful culture? How can we be confident about the culture–performance link? What credible evidence do we need to explain the impact of culture on performance?

Sources and further information.

See Widget Finn (2010). Also review Chapter 3, 'HRM and Performance', and look at Ashkanasy et al. (2000).

Note: This feature was written by John Bratton.

embedded which is so hard to imitate' (2009, p. 26). Scholarship on organizational sustainability affirms the importance of the efficient management of finite natural resources, the need to consult and 'engage' the entire workforce, and the effective management of people (Quaddus and Siddique, 2011). Moreover, it confirms the importance of convergence between low-carbon sustainable strategies, an organizational culture based on ecological values and integrated HR practices (Bratton, 2009; Fernandez et al., 2003). The established use of HR processes in workplace health and safety, lean regimes, minimum waste production and cultural management makes HRM well positioned to coordinate the goal of a green, sustainable strategy (Jabbour et al., 2010).

A cluster of HR practices is both a carrier through which dominant values are expressed and enacted and also, by their outcomes, an expression of deep-rooted values (Purcell et al., 2009). The extant literature on organizational culture and business strategy highlights how important it is for the prevailing business strategy and organizational culture to be consistent with each other – 'internal fit' – and with the wider operation of the organization – 'external fit' (see, for example, Hau Siu Chow and Liu, 2009). Extending the 'best fit' debate, a 'green' HR strategy should coincide with the organization's business strategy and create an appropriate culture to enhance sustainable organizational performance. The emergent literature on 'green HRM' emphasizes that a set of integrated HR practices covering recruitment, performance management and appraisal, learning and development, rewards and employment relations can build a more sustainable workplace culture (Renwick et al., 2008). Broadly speaking, the role of green HRM in sustainable strategy is to develop and support the organization's low-carbon and sustainable initiatives (Wehrmeyer, 1996). Figure 4.4, an extension of Fombrun et al.'s (1984) model, suggests five broad categories of HRM functions in which the role of green HRM in sustainable management can be analysed.

An obvious way to build a low-carbon workplace is through self-selection by prospective employees. Given a choice, people are attracted to 'green' employers that are keenly attuned to climate change issues and have a strong ecological approach (Philips, 2007). Environmentally sensitive job previews combined with an accurate portrayal of the organization's culture can attract talented people with values that match and sustain sustainability (Jabbour, 2011; Wehrmeyer, 1996). Another obvious way to embed a new 'Big Idea' based on ecological values in the workplace is through the *selection* process. Employment selection tests based on attitudinal and behavioural profiling can be used to screen applicants for green values. However, the validity and predictive power of these assessment techniques have all been subject to challenge. Emergent studies in environmental management suggest that, in those organizations with proactive sustainability programmes, the sustainability criteria are systematically integrated further than just in the recruitment and selection process, reaching into employee performance appraisal and the rewards and training dimension.

The reward system is a good indicator of the seriousness of an organization's commitment to sustainability management (Wehrmeyer, 1996). Employee *performance appraisal*, for example, can incorporate low-carbon performance standards related to material and energy waste, recycling and air and water emission indicators. A shift to ecological values and sustainable processes can further be reinforced when

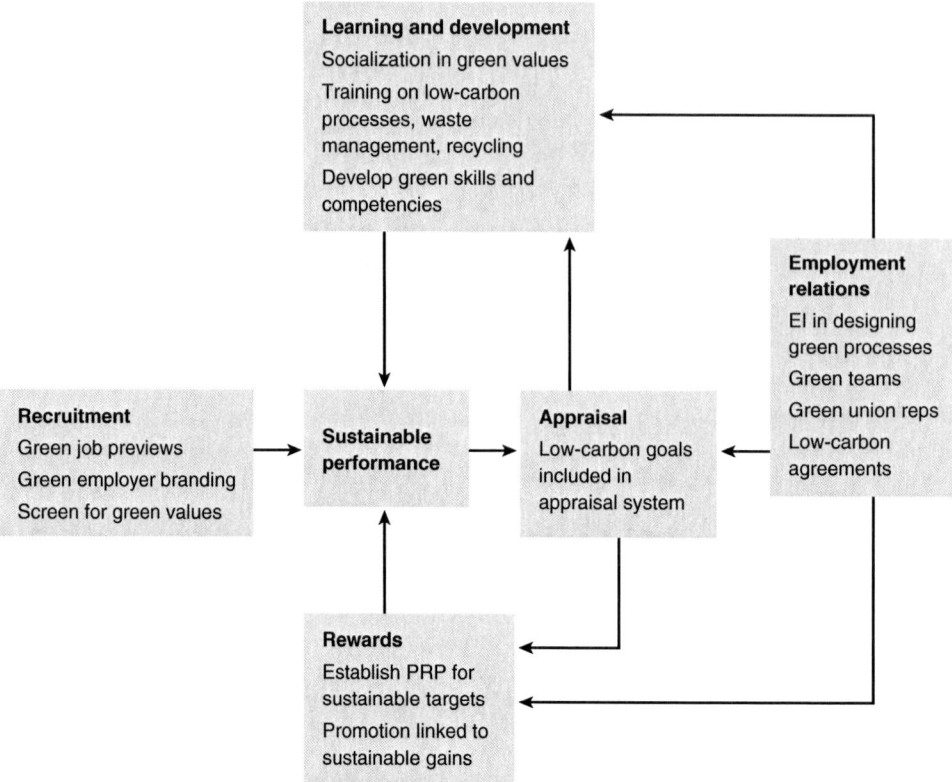

Figure 4.4 A framework for analysing green HR practice–sustainability linkages. EI, employee involvement; PRP, performance-related pay

employee *rewards* are linked to low-carbon and sustainable performance goals. For example, monetary rewards can be related to acquiring designated green skills and competencies, and ecological knowledge, meeting energy-saving or waste reduction targets and achieving sustainable performance goals.

Non-union and union employee voices can be heard via *employment relations* practices designed to allow employees or their representatives some 'say' in how their workplace is managed. Employee voice mechanisms such as suggestion schemes, employee involvement teams and self-managed teams are seen by many observers as a major element of the green HRM strategy, largely because they provide workers with an opportunity to use their intimate knowledge *of* work and discretion *at* work to generate creative ecofriendly initiatives rather than rely solely on managers. The rationale for employee voice processes can be partly explained by the necessary human input into a successful sustainable strategy, a strategy based on low levels of carbon emissions, product differentiation and high levels of value added and quality.

Sustainability *training* and *workplace learning* are considered to be the main HR interventions that work towards developing a low-carbon work system (Garavan and McGuire, 2010; Jabbour, 2011; Jabbour et al., 2010; Sarkis et al., 2010). Much of this training is related to improving employee health and safety, saving energy and waste management. For example, the US company 3M has encouraged employees to find creative ways to reduce pollution through their Pollution Prevention Pays (3P) programme, which has already saved the company close to $300 million (Renwick et al., 2008, p. 7). European trade unions have extended their traditional occupational health and safety concerns by strongly supporting environmental improvements and green skills training. In the UK, the Trades Union Congress (TUC) has included the environmental and sustainability issue in its training for union representatives, and has called for investment in training as a cardinal principle in creating decent and green jobs. The TUC position is nicely summed up by Frances O'Grady (2010): 'Without green skills, there can be no decent green jobs; without decent green jobs, no flourishing green industries; and without these green industries, we will not – cannot – build a green economy'.

In the European Union, trade unions have attempted to strengthen engagement in sustainable work at workplace level by calling for major investments in energy efficiency and renewable technologies, asking for mandatory environmental audits and bringing sustainability issues forward into 'mainstream' bargaining agendas (Trades Union Congress, 2010). For trade unions, the low-carbon agenda is rooted in their long-standing aspirations for healthy working conditions, social justice, high-skill jobs and decent work (Mayer, 2009; Storey, 2004). The link between green working conditions and social justice is perhaps not self-evident. But, as analysis suggests, exposure to toxic health hazards disproportionately affects blue-collar workers. As Mayer (1996) reminds us, workers are on the front line of the fight to remove toxic substances that threaten the health of workers *inside* the workplace and members of local communities *outside* it.

Conflict between environmental groups and trade unions is not, however, uncommon. For example, in North America, Keystone XL, the proposed 2673 kilometre pipeline that would carry oil sands crude from Canada to US refineries on the Gulf Coast, has stirred fierce emotion between local communities and US unions. Opponents fear that leaks from the pipeline will endanger the underground water reservoir beneath the Nebraska Sandhills, which lie in the proposed path of Keystone XL. Local unions, on the other hand, support the project because it will generate jobs: 'The message is jobs. That's pretty much as simple as it is,' said Ron Kaminski, representative for Laborers Local 1140 (Vanderklippe, 2011).

Overall, a review of the environmental management literature notes the importance of aligning HR practices: 'companies that are able to align practices and human resource dimensions with the objective of environment management can be successful in the organizational journey towards environmental sustainability', writes Jabbour (2011, p. 104). This section has offered a potentially fruitful framework for examining HR interventions to create sustainable workplaces. Future research may provide insight into whether green HRM theory is matched with green HRM action and improved eco-performance.

HRM web links

Go to www.tuc.org.uk and search for 'green jobs and green skills', which will bring up TUC policy statements on these issues.

Paradox in culture management

Is the Big Idea always a Good Idea? And assuming that top managers are able to change to a strong one-culture organization, is this necessarily desirable? If the central premise of the 'has' theory is that ideas within a social work group are homogeneous, unified and uncontested, a strong one-culture organization can have unintentional consequences. It can give members an organizational identity, reinforce complex friendship networks and employee engagement, and strongly influence designated behaviour without the need for costly bureaucratic controls. However, if fundamental changes are needed, a strong corporate culture can be an impediment to a management mantra of creative thinking, informal learning and innovation. Although the prescriptive literature presents organizational culture as a variable that can be easily manipulated to produce ideal types of coherence and integration to 'fit' new organizational goals, careful consideration should be given to the unintended or paradoxes of such a strategy.

These tensions surface in the relevant literature. Management scholars, who primarily understand the one-culture phenomenon as a unifying force, focus on the counterforces that challenge strong corporate cultures. The lay-off of workers in response to the recession and deep cuts in government expenditure are, however, a compelling reinforcement of the two-culture, or 'us and them', organization. Employment laws legitimating workplace unionism and collective bargaining have a similar unintended consequence of reinforcing the adversarial duo or multicultures (Beer et al., 1984). The rationales for investing in training and enlisting employees' tacit knowledge to create sustainable workplaces have a similar unintended consequence for managers. Fernandez et al. (2003), for example, argue that green initiatives stem from the synergy between an empowered, engaged and creative workforce and a new context of unsustainable growth and business practices. The learning-creativity paradigm as a source of competitive advantage and high-quality services is based upon critical reflection and open dialogue activities that might be considered to be deviant behaviour (Coopey, 1996). Eco-initiatives are often the result of workers challenging conventional ideas and solutions and effectively 'rule-breaking'. In other words, the creation of green initiatives requires a nurturing and celebration of the creative potential of deviant thinking and action (Bratton and Garrett-Petts, 2008) and can, as such, be viewed as a counterforce to cultural homogeneity.

Despite attempts by the trade union movement in Britain to build alliances to produce sustainable, low-carbon growth, there is evidence that many employers consider union involvement as a challenge to the one-culture system and management prerogative. The 'green bargaining agenda' based on ecofriendly principles and insights is not without contradiction. The trade union movement can potentially act as the pivotal agency of environmental and social change (Mayer, 2009; Storey, 2004), but unions face barriers to playing this role because they can find themselves representing workers on opposite sides of conflicts related to environmental protection and job security. For environmental movements, for example, the generation of nuclear energy and the importation of hazardous waste is unsustainable, yet job security is a major issue for the unions representing workers at nuclear power plants and at incineration plants processing imported toxic waste (Oates, 1996; Storey, 2004).

Organizational culture is embedded in powerful informally shared social interactions and norms. For this reason, the most sceptical detractors argue that culture *as a whole* cannot be 'created, discovered or destroyed by the whims of management' (Meek, 1992, p. 209). Willmott (1993) notes a potentially manipulative intent of corporate agendas for culture change, and details the resistance to strong cultures, or what he calls 'corporate culturalism', found among powerful professional groups. For example, a 'Big Idea' that expected professional engineers to 'sell their services to clients' caused many to resist and threaten resignation (Schein, 2010). Similarly, in the public sector domain, it is suggested that professionals, may 'evade commercial feeling rules' (Bolton, 2005, p. 108). Sociological studies describe all kinds of unusual and idiosyncratic employee conduct that creates small spaces of 'uncolonized terrain, a terrain which is not and cannot be managed' (Gabriel, 1995, p. 478). The scope for employees to offer 'empty performances' and to be indifferent to officially sponsored values is nicely captured by Goffman's classic study (1961, p. 267; also quoted in Bolton, 2005, p. 138):

> Whenever we look at a social establishment ... we find that participants decline in some way to accept the official view of what they should be putting into and getting out of the organization ... Where enthusiasm is expected, there will be apathy, where loyalty, there will be disaffection; where attendance, absenteeism; ... where deeds are to be done, varies of inactivity.

Furthermore, Ackroyd and Thompson's (1999) concept of 'misbehaviour' emphasizes not only the messy reality of conflict in the workplace, but also the fact that employee resistance to new 'Big Ideas' can be less overt, less familiar, less observable and barely manageable.

Not surprisingly therefore, critical workplace scholars tend to be highly sceptical about claims of managing cultures, regarding such claims as naive. In particular, the preoccupation with culture obscures enduring structural inequalities, antagonism and conflict (Edwards, 1995). As demonstrated in the recent recession, culture does nothing to remove the need for top management to try to reduce labour costs, intensify the pressure of work and render employees redundant. The binary conflict of interest between capital and labour that exists within a 'negotiated order' of mutual cooperation suggests that the significance of organizational culture cannot be grasped unless it is related to structures of power – *power over other people* – within a context of market exigencies.

These arguments stress that the work values of managers and other employees are shaped by outside variables such as class, gender, race and profession or trade. Furthermore, that culture can never be wholly managed because it emerges from complex processes involving how employees construct their sense of identity in ways that are beyond management's control. At the very best, culture-change interventions are only successful at the observable behavioural level rather than the subconscious level (Ogbonna, 1993). Finally, adding to the complexity of managing culture is the omnipresent Internet. It has, for example, been argued that the Internet adds a 'space dimension' that may undermine a prevailing configuration of norms and values or culture in new ways (Ogbonna and Harris, 2006).

CASE STUDY

Big Outdoors

Setting

Despite being one of the largest and most developed markets in the world, the retail industry for sports and camping goods in the UK has faced several challenges in recent years. This has come as a result of rising consumer debt, unemployment and demographic shifts causing a movement away from traditional competitive sports. However, the consumer's continued focus on recreational activities, as well as the development of 'extreme' sports such as rock-climbing, ice-climbing and caving, has helped to maintain growth levels. The rising participation of retirees in hill-walking has also helped to protect the market from more serious reversals. Many retail outlets are now offering specialized services and specific brands to attract this new demographic and lure back their cautious loyal customers.

Source: ©istockphoto.com/Juanmonino.

The problem

Established in 1984, Big Outdoors is an outdoor and sporting goods retail firm specializing in hiking and camping equipment. It currently employs 13 full-time workers with an additional 18 part-time workers to assist with increased sales on weekends. As the firm sells to the low end of the market, most of the employees are students supplementing their income to pay for their education who have very little training or experience in the activities the store sells supplies for. The majority of the staff are between the ages of 18 and 23 years old. The hourly pay rate is only slightly more than the minimal wage, and staff turnover is high.

Recently, Big Outdoors was sold to a new owner, Jonathan Tempest, an avid rock-climber, who plans to introduce better quality merchandise with a focus on the high end of the market. His personal business philosophy is 'Focus on high-quality merchandise and excellent customer service, and profit will take care of itself.' With his strong background in the recreational retail industry, Jonathan recognizes that this will require a new business plan as well as a shift in the organization's culture. As the firm is too small to have an in-house HR department to help make these changes, Jonathan decides to hire a local HR consulting firm. He also creates a team of the most experienced employees to provide input into any changes that will be made.

At the first meeting with the consultant Kelly Maynard, Jonathan introduces the team members and lays out his plan to change the firm's merchandise and market focus. However, he admits he is struggling over how to approach changing the overall culture to fit the new direction of the company. Jonathan stresses he wants the team to take a lead role in this aspect. Kelly asks to have some time to study the firm's current HR practices, including its recruitment, training and reward processes, before she makes any recommendations to Jonathan.

Assignment

Acting as the consultant, prepare a report drawing on the material from this chapter addressing the following:

1. What change interventions can Jonathan introduce in order to create a culture at Big Outdoors that is more aligned with the new strategic vision?
2. What do you think of Jonathan's decision to create an employee team? What role, if any, should members of that team play in implementing a cultural change in the organization?

Essential reading

Burke, W. (2011) *Organizational Change: Theory and Practice*. Los Angeles: Sage.
Schein, E. (2010) *Organizational Culture and Leadership*, 4th edn. San Francisco: Jossey-Bass.
Tushman, M. and O'Reilly, C. (1996) Ambidextrous organizations: managing evolutionary and revolutionary change. *California Management Review*, **38**(4): 8–30.

To learn more about the role of leadership in culture change in a retail environment, go to www.icmrindia.org/casestudies/catalogue/Human%20Resource%20and%20Organization%20Behavior/HROB063.htm.

Note: This case was written by Lori Rilkoff, HR manager at City of Kamloops, BC, Canada.

Visit the companion website at www.palgrave.com/business/bratton5 for guidelines on writing reports.

Summary

- In this chapter, we have explored the nature of organizational culture – a unique configuration of shared artefacts, common language and meanings and shared values that influences ways of doing things in the workplace. The culture of an organization influences what employees should think, believe or value.

- We have discussed how national culture and organizational culture are deeply intertwined – each influencing the other, with the latter embedded in society. Yet we have noted that standard accounts of organizational culture have tended to neglect how gender, patriarchy and sexuality in society and in the workplace profoundly influence the dynamics of organizational culture.

- We explained that culture analysis can be divided into different schools of thought. The functionalist perspective stresses that culture can play a role in building consensus and harmony, and emphasizes how this can improve performance. It views organizational culture as a variable – it is something that an organization 'has' and can, as such, be produced and managed.

- The prescriptive literature tends to present too uniform a view of organizational culture. Alternative approaches point out the existence of subcultures and counterculture. These concepts are important if we believe that organizations consist of individuals and work groups with multiple sets of values and beliefs.

- The critical perspective focuses on a sociological concern to describe and critically explain cultural processes, how culture emerges through social interaction, power relations, communities of practice and norms. It also focuses on connections between social inequalities and patriarchal systems *outside* the workplace, and socialization processes and conduct *inside* it. Viewed through a sociologist's lens, culture is something that a work organization '*is*'.

- We have emphasized that a set of integrated HR practices is both a carrier through which dominant values are expressed and enacted and also, by their outcomes, an expression of deep-rooted values. The well-established use of HR practices to promote health and safety, minimize waste and manage culture makes HRM well positioned to lead and coordinate the goal of a green sustainable strategy.

- We make no claims of originality, but we do offer a potentially fruitful framework for exploring how a set of integrated green HR practices – covering recruitment, performance management and appraisal, learning and development, rewards and employment relations – can help to build more sustainable work practices. Finally, we have emphasized that managers must be aware of the messy realities that shape complex organizations.

Vocab checklist for ESL students

- appraise (v), appraisal (n)
- artefact (n)
- assume (v), assumption (n)
- binge (n)
- collectivize (v), collectivism (n), collective/collectivizing (adj)
- counterculture (n)
- culture (n), cultural (adj)
- diversity (n), diverse (adj)
- dominate (v), domination (n), dominant (adj)
- expatriate (v), expatriate (n)
- feminist (n) (adj), feminine (adj)
- heterogeneity (n), heterogeneous (adj)
- idealize (v), ideology (n)
- individualism/individual (n)
- integrate (v), integration (n)
- International Monetary Fund (n)
- multiculturalism (n), multicultural (adj)
- non-governmental organization (n)
- pluralism/plurality (n), plural/pluralistic (adj)
- ritualize (v), ritual (n), ritualistic (adj)
- secularize (v), secularization (n)
- socialize (v), socialization (n)
- subculture (n)
- United Nations (n)

Visit www.palgrave.com/business/bratton5 for a link to free definitions of these terms in the Macmillan Dictionary, as well as additional learning resources for ESL students.

Review questions

1. How does national culture relate to organizational culture?
2. Review the functionalist and critical perspectives on organizational culture described in this chapter. Which perspective do you find most appealing and plausible? Why?
3. What impact do expectations about gender have upon workplace activities and HR practices? To what extent, if at all, do notions of masculinity and femininity reinforce or challenge traditional notions of organizational culture?
4. What role can HRM play in creating a more sustainable low-carbon work system?

Further reading to improve your mark

Reading these articles and chapters can help you gain a better understanding and potentially a higher grade for your HRM assignment.

- Mats Alvesson's (2002) *Understanding Organizational Culture*. London: Sage emphasizes the importance of avoiding 'quick fixes' when it comes to organizational culture.
- The links between work values in countries with a different cultural heritage are explored in Peter Warr's (2008) article Work values: Some demographic and cultural correlates. *Journal of Occupational and Organizational Psychology*, **81**: 751–75. See also H. de Cieri (2008) Transnational firms and cultural diversity. In P. Boxall, J. Purcell and P. Wright (eds) *The Oxford Handbook of Human Resource Management* (pp. 509–29). Oxford: OUP.
- For insight into 'green' workplaces, see P. Docherty, M. Kira and A. B. Shan (2009) *Creating Sustainable Work Systems* (2nd edn). London: Routledge; C. J. C. Jabbour (2011)

How green are HRM practices, organizational culture, learning and teamwork? A Brazilian study. *Industrial and Commercial Training,* **43**(2): 98–105; and W. Wehrmeyer (1996) *Greening People: Human Resources and Environmental Management.* Sheffield: Greenleaf Publishing.

- More critical accounts of culture management can be found in Karen Legge's chapter, HRM: from compliance to commitment, pp. 209–40 in *Human Resource Management: Rhetorics and Realities* (2005), Basingstoke: Palgrave Macmillan; B. McSweeney (2002) Hofstede's model of national cultural differences and their consequences: a triumph of faith – a failure of analysis. *Human Relations,* **55**(1): 89–118; P. I. Morgan and E. Ogbonna (2008) Subcultural dynamics in transformation: a multi-perspective study of health care professionals. *Human Relations,* **61**(1): 39–65; and M. Parker (2000) *Organizational Culture and Identity.* London: Sage.

Visit www.palgrave.com/business/bratton5 for lots of extra resources to help you get to grips with this chapter, including study tips, HRM skills development guides, summary lecture notes, and more.

References

Aaltio-Marjosola, I., and Mills, A. J. (Eds) (2002). *Gender, Identity and the Culture of Organizations.* London: Routledge.
Ackroyd, S. and Crowdy, P. A. (1990) Can culture be managed? Working with 'raw' material: the case of the English slaughtermen. *Personnel Review,* **19**(5): 3–13.
Ackroyd, S. and Thompson, P. (1999) *Organizational Misbehaviour.* Thousand Oaks, CA: Sage.
Adler, N. J. and Gundersen, A. (2008) *International Dimensions of Organizational Behavior* (5th edn). Mason, OH: Thomson/South-Western.
Alvesson, M. (2002) *Understanding Organizational Culture.* London: Sage.
Alvesson, M. and Willmott, H. (1996) *Making Sense of Management: A Critical Analysis.* London: Sage.
Ashkanasy, N. M. , Broadfoot, L. E. and Falkus, S. (2000) Questionnaire measures of organizational culture. In N. M. Ashkanasy, C. P. M. Wilderom and M. F. Peterson (eds) *Handbook of Organizational Culture and Climate* (pp. 131–45).Thousand Oaks, CA: Sage.
Bain, P. and Taylor, P. (2000) Entrapped by the electronic panopticon? Worker resistance in the call centre. *New Technology, Work and Employment,* **15**(1): 2–18.
Bass, B. M. and Riggio, R. (2006) *Transformational Leadership* (2nd edn). Mahwah, NJ: Lawrence Erlbaum.
Bate, P. (1995) *Strategies for Cultural Change.* Oxford: Butterworth-Heineman.
Becton, J. B. and Field, H. S. (2009) Cultural differences in organizational citizenship behaviour: a comparison between Chinese and American employees. *International Journal of Human Resource Management,* **20**(8): 1651–69.
Beer, M., Spector, B., Lawrence, P. R., Quin Mills, D. and Walton, R. E. (1984) *Managing Human Assets.* New York: Free Press.
Biron, M. (2010) Negative reciprocity and the association between perceived organizational ethical values and organizational deviance. *Human Relations,* **63**(6): 875–97.
Bolton, S. C. (2005) *Emotion Management in the Workplace.* Basingstoke: Palgrave Macmillan.
Bolton, S. C. and Houlihan, M. (eds) (2007) *Searching for the Human in Human Resource Management: Theory, Practice and Contexts.* Basingstoke: Palgrave Macmillan.
Boyce, M. (1997) Organizational story and storytelling: a critical review. *Journal of Organizational Change Management,* **9**(5): 5–26.
Bratton, A. J. (2009) HRM Practices and Environmental Management: An Exploratory Case Study of a UK City Council. Unpublished MSc dissertation, University of Edinburgh.
Bratton, J. and Garrett-Petts, W. (2008) Art and workplace learning: innovation, and the economic development of Canadian small cities. In D. Livingstone, K. Mirchandani and

P. Sawchuk (eds) *The Future of Lifelong Learning and Work: Critical Perspectives*. Rotterdam: Sense Publishers.

Brewis, J. and Linstead, S. (2000) *Sex, Work and Sex Work: Eroticizing Organization*. London: Routledge.

Brewster, C., Carey, L., Grobler, P., Holland, P. and Warnich, S. (2008) *Contemporary Issues in Human Resource Management*. Cape Town, South Africa: Oxford University Press.

Buruma, I. (2011) Political aftershock: public trust breakdown. *Globe and Mail*, April 8, p. A15.

Campbell, D. (2010) The binge working culture is taking its toll. *The Observer*, May 16, 37.

Chamberlain, L. J., Crowley, M., Tope, D. and Hodson, R. (2008) Sexual harassment in organizational context. *Work and Occupations*, **35**(3): 262–95.

Champy, J. (1996) *Reengineering Management: The Mandate for New Leadership*. New York: HarperCollins.

Chatzitheochari, S. and Arber, S. (2009) Lack of sleep, work and long hours culture: evidence from the UK Time Use Survey. *Work, Employment and Society*, **23**(1): 30–48.

Chen, Y.-S. (2011) Green organizational identity: sources and consequence. *Management Decision*, **49**(3): 384–404.

Coopey, J. (1996) Crucial gaps in the 'learning organization'. In K. Starkey (ed.) *How Organizations Learn* (pp. 348–67). London: International Thomson Business.

Davies, H. (2002) Understanding organizational culture in reforming the National Health Service. *Royal Society of Medicine Journal*, **95**(3): 140–2.

Deal, T. E. and Kennedy, A. A. (1982) *Organization Cultures: The Rites and Rituals of Organization Life*. New York: Addison-Wesley

du Gay, P. (1996) *Consumption and Identity at Work*. London: Sage.

Eagleton, T. (1983) *Literary Theory: An Introduction*. Minneapolis: University of Minnesota Press.

Edwards, P. K. (1986) *Conflict at Work: A Materialist Analysis of Workplace Relations*. Oxford: Blackwell.

Edwards, P. K. (1995) The employment relationship. In P. K. Edwards (ed.) *Industrial relations: Theory and Practice in Britain*. Oxford: Blackwell.

Fernandez, E., Junquera, B., and Ordiz, M. (2003) Organizational culture and human resources in the environmental issue. *International Journal of Human Resource Management*, **14**(4): 634–56.

Fitzgerald, A. and Teal, G. (2004) Health reforms, professional identity and occupational sub-cultures: the changing interprofessional relations between doctors and nurses. *Contemporary Nurse*, **16**: 9–19.

Fombrun, C. J., Tichy, N. M. and Devanna, M. A. (eds) (1984) *Strategic Human Resource Management*. New York: John Wiley & Sons.

Fulford, R. (1999) *The Triumph of Narrative*. Toronto, Ontario: Anansi.

Gabriel, Y. (1995) The unmanaged organization: stories, fantasies and subjectivity. *Organizational Studies*, **16**(3): 477–501.

Gahan, P. and Abeysekera, L. (2009) What shapes an individual's work values? An integrated model of the relationship between work values, national culture and self-construal. *International Journal of Human Resource Management*, **20**(1): 126–47.

Garavan, T. and McGuire, D. (2010) Human resource development and society: human resource development's role in embedding corporate social responsibility, sustainability, and ethics in organizations. *Advances in Developing Human Resources*, **12**(5): 487–507.

Giddens, A. (1990) *The Consequencies of Modernity*. Cambridge: Polity Press.

Giddens, A. (2009) *Sociology* (6th edn). Cambridge: Polity Press.

Goffman, E. (1961) *Asylums: Essays on the Social Situation of Mental Patients and Other Inmates*. New York: Doubleday Anchor.

Goffman, E. (1967) *Interaction Ritual: Essays on Face-to-Face Behavior*. New York: Doubleday Anchor.

Gold, J., Holman, D. and Thorpe, R. (2002) The role of argument analysis and story telling in facilitating critical thinking. *Management Learning*, **33**(3): 371–88.

Guirdham, M. (2011) *Communicating Across Cultures at Work* (3rd edn). Basingstoke: Palgrave Macmillan.

Harding, K. (2003) A leap of faith. *Globe and Mail*, January 8, p. C1.

Harvey, D. (1994) *The Conditions of Postmodernity: An Enquiry into the Origins of Cultural Change*. Oxford: Blackwell.

Hau Siu Chow, I. and Liu, S. S. (2009) The effect of aligning organizational culture and business strategy with HR systems on firm performance in Chinese enterprises. *International Journal of Human Resource Management*, **20**(11): 2292–310.

Hofstede, G. Hofstede, Gert Jan and Minkov, M. (2010) *Cultures and Organizations: Software of the mind* (3rd edn). London: McGraw-Hill.

Hui, C. and Graen, G. (1997) Guanxi and professional leadership in contemporary Sino-American joint ventures in mainland China. *Leadership Quarterly*, **8**(4): 451–65.

Hyman, R. and Brough, I. (1975) *Social Values and Industrial Relations*. Oxford: Blackwell.

Jabbour, C. J. C. (2011) How green are HRM practices, organizational culture, learning and teamwork? A Brazilian study. *Industrial and Commercial Training*, **43**(2): 98–105.

Jabbour, C. J. C., Santos, F. C. A., and Nagano, S. M. (2010) Contributions of HRM throughout the stages of environmental management: methodological triangulation applied to companies in Brazil. *International Journal of Human Resource Management*, **21**(7): 1049–89.

Jameson, F. (1991) *Postmodernism, or The Cultural Logic of Late Capitalism*, London: Verso.

Kärreman, D. and Alvesson, M. (2009) Resisting resistance: counter-resistance, consent and compliance in a consulting firm. *Human Relations*, **62**(8): 1115–44.

Klein, N. (2007) *The Shock Doctrine*, Toronto, Ontario: Vintage Canada.

Kotter, J. (1996) *Leading Change*. Boston, MA: Harvard Business.

Lash, M. L. (2010) *Intensive Culture: Social Theory, Religion and Contemporary Capitalism*. London: Sage.

Legge, K. (2005) *Human Resource Management: Rhetorics and Realities* (anniversary edn). Basingstoke: Palgrave Macmillan.

Lewin, K. (1951) *Field Theory in Social Science*, New York: Harper.

Lincoln, J. and Kalleberg, A. (1992) *Culture Control and Commitment*. Cambridge: Cambridge University Press.

Linnenluecke, M. and Griffiths, A. (2010) Corporate sustainability and organizational culture. *Journal of World Business* **45**: 357–66.

Linstead, S. and Grafton Small, R. (1992) Corporate strategy and corporate culture: the view from the checkout. *Personnel Review*, **19**(4): 9–15.

McCrone, D. (2001) *Understanding Scotland*. London: Routledge.

Macionis, J. and Gerber, L. M. (2011) *Sociology* (7th Canadian edn). Toronto, Ontario: Pearson.

McSweeney, B. (2002) Hofstede's model of national cultural differences and their consequences: a triumph of faith – a failure of analysis. *Human Relations*, **55**(1): 89–118.

Manji, I. (2010) How complex the culture of fear. *Globe and Mail*, November 26, p. A21.

Martin, J. (1992) *Cultures in Organizations: Three Perspectives*. New York: Oxford University Press.

Martin, J. (2002) *Organizational Culture: Mapping the Terrain*. Thousand Oaks, CA: Sage.

Martin, J. and Frost, P. (1996) The organizational culture war games: a struggle for intellectual dominance. In S. R. Clegg, C. Hardy and W. R. Nord (eds) *Handbook of Organizational Studies* (pp. 599–621). London: Sage.

Martin, J. and Siehl, C. (1983) Organizational culture and counterculture: an uneasy symbiosis. *Organizational Dynamics*, **122**: 52–65.

Marx, K. and Engels, F. (1998) *The German Ideology*. New York: Prometheus Books.

Mathew, J. and Ogbonna, E. (2009) Organizational culture and commitment: a study of an Indian software organization. *International Journal of Human Resource Management*, **20**(3): 654–75.

Mayer, B. (1996) *Blue-Green Coalitions: Fighting for Safe Workplaces and Healthy Communities*. Ithaca, NY: Cornell University Press.

Mayer, B. (2009) *Blue-Green Coalitions: Fighting for Safe Workplaces and Healthy Communities*. Ithaca, NY: Cornell University Press.

Meek, L. (1992) Organizational culture: origins and weaknesses. In G. Salaman (ed.) *Human Resources Strategies* (pp. 198–229). London: Sage.

Morgan, G. (1997) *Images of Organization*. London: Sage.

Morgan, P. I. and Ogbonna, E. (2008) Subcultural dynamics in transformation: a multi-perspective study of healthcare professionals. *Human Relations*, **61**(1): 39–65.

Oates, A. (1996) Industrial relations and the environment in the UK. In W. Wehrmeyer (ed.) *Greening People: Human Resources and Environmental Management* (pp. 117–40) Sheffield: Greenleaf Publishing.

Ogbonna, E. (1993) Managing organizational culture: fantasy or reality. *Human Resource Management Journal*, **3**(2): 211–36.

Ogbonna, E. and Harris, L. C. (2006) Organizational culture in the age of the internet: an exploratory study. *New Technology, Work and Employment*, **21**(2): 162–75.

O'Grady, F. (2010) 'Keynote address to TUC green Growth Conference', October 13. Available at: www.tuc.org.uk/social/tuc-18662-f0.cfm (accessed October 15, 2010).

Ouchi, W. G. (1980) Markets, bureaucracies, and clans. *Administrative Science Quarterly*, **25**(1): 129–41.

Parker, J., Mars, L., Ransome, P. and Stanworth, H. (2003) *Social Theory: A Basic Tool Kit*. Basingstoke: Palgrave Macmillan.

Parker, M. (2000) *Organizational Culture and Identity*. London: Sage.

Peritz, I. and Friesen, J. (2010) Multiculturalism's magic number. *Globe and Mail*, October 2, pp. A14–15.

Philips, L. (2007) Go green now to combat climate change. *People Management*, August 23.

Purcell, J., Kinnie, N., Swart, J., Rayton, B. and Hutchinson, S. (2009) *People Management and Performance*. London: Routledge.

Quaddus, M. A. and Siddique, M. A. B. (eds) (2011) *Handbook of Corporate Sustainability*. Cheltenham: Edward Elgar.

Ray, C.A. (1986) Corporate culture: the last frontier of control? *Journal of Management Studies*, **23**(3): 287–97.

Renwick, D., Redman, T. and Maguire, S. (2008) *Green HRM: A Review, Process Model, and Research Agenda*. Discussion Paper Series No. 2008.01 April. Sheffield: University of Sheffield Management School.

Sarkis, J., Gonzalez-Torre, P. and Adenso-Diaz, B. (2010) Stakeholder pressure and the adoption of environmental practices: the mediating effect of training. *Journal of Operations Management*, **28**: 163–76.

Saul, J. R. (2008) *A Fair Country*. Toronto, Ontario: Viking.

Sayer, D. (1991) *Capitalism and Modernity: Excursus on Marx and Weber*. London: Routledge.

Schein, E. (2010) *Organizational Culture and Leadership* (4th edn). San Francisco, CA: Jossey-Bass.

Schneider, B. (2000). The psychological life of organizations. In N. Ashkanasy, C. Wilderon and M. Peterson (eds) *Handbook of Organizational Culture and Climate* (pp. xvii–xxi). Thousand Oaks, CA: Sage.

Séguin, R. (2010) Quebec labour, student groups unite to fight to right. *Globe and Mail*, November 6, p. A16.

Sewell, G. (1998) The discipline of teams: the control of team-based industrial work through electronic and peer surveillance. *Administrative Science Quarterly*, **43**: 397–428.

Sewell, G. and Wilkinson, B. (1992) Someone to watch over me: surveillance, discipline and the just in time labour process. *Sociology*, **26**(2): 271–89.

Simosi, M. and Xenikou, A. (2010) The role of organizational culture in the relationship between leadership and organizational commitment: an empirical study in a Greek organization. *International Journal of Human Resource Management*, **21**(10): 1598–616.

Smircich, L. (1983) Concepts of culture and organizational analysis. *Administrative Science Quarterly*, **28**(3): 339–58.

Storey, R. (2004) From the environment to the workplace ... and back again? Occupational health and safety activism in Ontario, 1970s–2000+. *Canadian Review of Sociology and Anthropology*, **41**(4): 419–47.

Storey, J. (ed.) (2007) Human resource management today: an assessment. In J. Storey (ed.) *Human Resource Management: A Critical Text* (pp. 3–20). London: Thompson Learning.

Su, S., Baird, K. and Blair, B. (2009) Employee organizational commitment: the influence of cultural and organizational factors in the Australian manufacturing industry. *International Journal of Human Resource Management*, **20**(12): 2494–516.

Sumner, J. (2007) *Sustainability and the Civil Commons*. Toronto, Ontario: University of Toronto Press.

Taylor, P. and Bain, P. (2005) Indian calling to the far away towns. *Work, Employment and Society*, **19**(2): 261–82.

Thompson P. and McHugh, D. (2009) *Work Organisations: A Critical Approach* (4th edn). Basingstoke: Palgrave Macmillan.

Townley, B. (1994) *Reframing Human Resource Management*. London: Sage

Trades Union Congress (2010) 'TUC Green Growth Conference'. Available at: www.tuc.org.uk/social/tuc.

Travis, A. (2011) Probation officers spend 75% of time on red tape, report finds. *The Guardian*, July 27, p. 7.

Tucker, R. C. (1978) *The Marx–Engels Reader*. New York: Norton.

Vanderklippe, N. (2011) Keystone faces 'last stand'. *Globe and Mail*, September 26, p. B1.

Wajcman, J. (1998) *Managing Like a Man*. University Park, PA: Pennsylvania State University Press.

Warr, P. (2008) Work values: some demographic and cultural correlates. *Journal of Occupational and Organizational Psychology*, **81**: 751–75.

Weber, M. (1922/1968) *Economy and Society*. New York: Bedminster.

Wehrmeyer, W. (1996) *Greening People: Human Resources and Environmental Management*. Sheffield: Greenleaf Publishing.

Weick, K. E. (2001) *Making Sense of the Organization*. Oxford: Blackwell.

Widget Finn (2010) 'Best Workplaces 2010'. Barinnga Partners, UK's Best Workplaces, May. Available at: www.greatplacetowork.co.uk.

Williams, R. (1983) *Keywords*. New York: Oxford University Press.

Willmott, H. (1993) 'Strength is ignorance: freedom is slavery': managing culture in modern organizations. *Journal of Management Studies*, **30**(4): 515–52.

Zhang, Y. and Albrecht, C. (2010) The role of cultural values on a firm's strategic human resource management development: a comparative study of Spanish firms in China. *International Journal of Human Resource Management*, **21**(11): 1911–30.

Zhang, Y. and Begley, T. M. (2011) Perceived organizational climate, knowledge transfer and innovation in China-based research and development companies. *International Journal of Human Resource Management*, **22**(1): 34–56.

CHAPTER 5
Diversity management
Nicolina Kamenou and Jawad Syed

- Introduction
- Key concepts of diversity management
- The diversity management discourse and its limitations
- A relational framework for diversity management
- Advantages of diversity
- From positive discrimination to positive action
- Strategies to manage diversity
- Methodological considerations in conducting research on diversity management: the case of ethnic minority women
- Conclusion
- For discussion and revision
- Further reading
- Case study: Samina's Experiences in Retail Co.
- References

After reading this chapter, you should be able to:

- Understand and distinguish between diversity management and equal employment opportunity
- Understand how demographic transformation of the population and the workforce affects the future of diversity management in the workplace
- Understand various forms of employment stereotypes and discrimination
- Know about various laws and regulations in place in several countries to tackle workplace discrimination
- Distinguish between the business case and social equity approaches to diversity management
- Understand methodological considerations in diversity management research

Introduction

The aim of this chapter is to introduce students to the concepts of managing diversity and equal opportunities in employment. Given the demographic transformations of the general population and the labour force in many countries, workforce diversity is a major issue facing managers and organizations. There is, however, evidence of unrelenting stereotypes and discriminatory attitudes and behaviours that not only permeate the workplace, but are also found in abundance on a societal and an institutional level.

This chapter will introduce students to various forms of employment discrimination, as well as legislation in various countries to tackle discrimination. With respect to theorizing diversity management, two key approaches will be discussed: the business case approach and the social equity approach. The chapter also discusses some methodological issues related to conducting research on diversity and equal opportunity, and presents a case study on ethnic minority women in the UK.

Key concepts of diversity management

In the last few decades, diversity management has been gaining increasing attention within the field of human resource management (HRM) and international HRM. Cox (1994) noted that diversity management was initially seen to be a 'North American affair', and that the emphasis in other countries (for example, Canada and the UK) was on learning lessons from the US experience. Local context, however, remains a major determinant of the approach to diversity and diversity management in any country. For example, British identity or Britishness is a key factor in diversity management in the UK 'because most of the disadvantaged women and men in our society have ancestral roots in the colonies of Britain's erstwhile empire, and it is they who bear the brunt of racism and discrimination' (Lorbiecki, 2001: 2).

Most definitions of and discussions related to diversity management focus on the organizational benefits it can provide, that is, the business case for diversity. A large number of organizations in the US, UK and elsewhere are now attempting to 'embrace diversity', both as a result of the advocated benefits of having a diverse group of staff, but also because of demographic changes. Legislative pressures are also crucial in organizations' attempts to present themselves as diversity-friendly.

In the UK, there is extensive legislation covering diversity, including the Race Relations Act 1976, the Race Relations Amendment Act 2000 and the Sex Discrimination Act 1975, as well as EU discrimination provisions that cover religion or belief, sexual orientation and age. The new UK single Equality Act, which came into force in October 2010, brings together a number of existing laws and includes age, disability, gender reassignment, marriage and civil partnership, pregnancy and maternity, race, religion and belief, gender and sexual orientation. The general equality duty in the public sector is set out in the Equality Act 2010 (Equality and

Human Rights Commission, 2011), which states that those subject to the equality duty must make efforts to:

- eliminate unlawful discrimination, harassment and victimization and other conduct prohibited by the Act;
- advance equality of opportunity between people who share a protected characteristic and those who do not;
- foster good relations between people who share a protected characteristic and those who do not.

In New Zealand, institutions concerned with a single group in society have recently been replaced by an overarching human rights body that is concerned with various equality strands (Parker and Douglas, 2010).

With some notable exceptions, mainly in the US (for example, Thomas, 1992; Nkomo and Cox, 1996; Thomas and Ely, 1996) but also with some UK examples (Dickens, 1994, 1999; Liff, 1997, 1999; Lorbiecki and Jack, 2000; Kamenou, 2003; Kirton and Greene, 2005; Kamenou and Fearfull, 2006), diversity management has received limited attention from academic scholars. There has been more sociological work on the effects of discrimination and prejudice in organizations and society as a whole (see, for example, Anthias, 1992; Afshar and Maynard, 1994; Brah, 1994; Blackstone et al., 1998) than on diversity management research within business or management schools, although this situation has slowly improved over the last few years. There is a dire need for more academic research on diversity and equality within the 'human-focused' management topics, such as HRM, and organizational behaviour, but also within more general management and business areas such as strategic management, economics and critical accounting. Discussions surrounding equality should be mainstream in both management research and teaching, instead of being considered as a 'soft extra' within more sociological aspects of the curriculum and of research.

The diversity management discourse and its limitations

In the literature addressing specific approaches to diversity and their limitations, 'equal employment opportunity' (EEO), 'affirmative action' and 'diversity management' are frequently used terms (see, for example, Deluca and McDowell, 1992; Syed and Kramar, 2009). Demographic changes in both the population in general and the labour market in many countries mean that employers today need to manage a far broader diversity of groups in their current employment practices compared with the numbers managed in the past (Pool and Sceats, 1990). Accordingly, much literature is now available to organizations informing them how best to handle a diverse workforce (see, for example, Ferris et al., 1994; Thomas and Ely, 1996; Härtel and Fujimoto, 2000; Ely and Thomas, 2001; Ashkanasy et al., 2002; Murray and Syed, 2005; Bell, 2007).

Figure 5.1 offers three popular approaches to workforce diversity in various international contexts. It highlights the key features of each approach, for example:

- the emphasis of EEO on eliminating discrimination in human resources policies and practices;
- the emphasis of affirmative action on equality of outcomes;
- the emphasis of diversity management on the inclusion of all forms of diversity and business outcomes.

All of these approaches have their origins in the US labour market. Whereas the first two approaches are generally legally mandated, the diversity management approach is based on voluntary corporate measures. Diversity management was adopted as an alternate approach to affirmative action because the realities facing organizations were 'no longer the realities affirmative action was designed to fix' (Thomas, 1990: 107). Affirmative action failed to 'deal with the root causes of prejudice and inequality and did little to develop the full potential of every man and woman in the company' (1990: 117).

Within the Australian context, diversity management has been described as 'second-generation' EEO opportunity that followed a wave of antidiscrimination legislation (Teicher and Spearitt, 1996). The diversity agenda has been described as one that 'has come to Australia from the USA as an HRM workplace strategy'

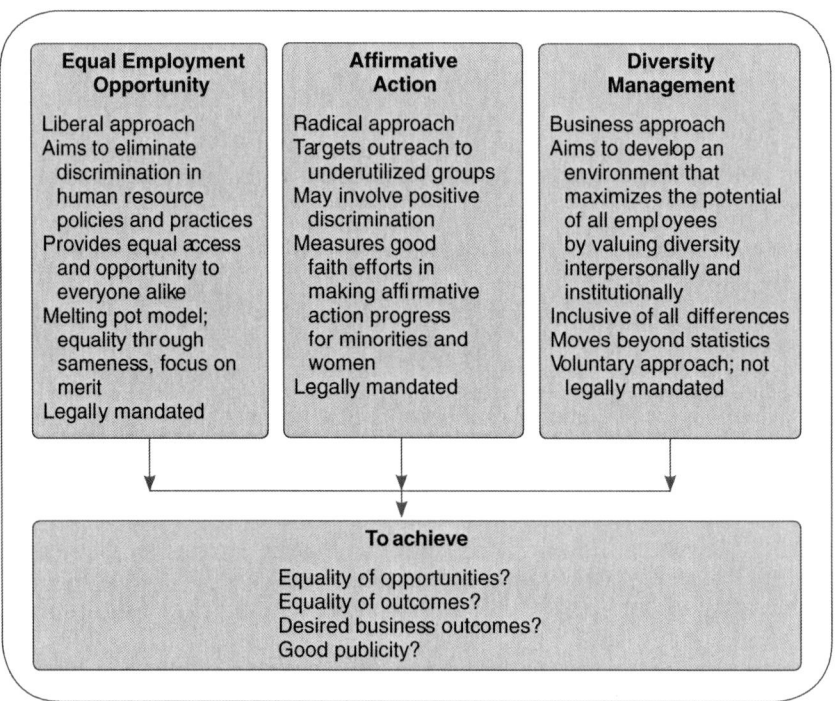

Figure 5.1 Usual approaches to managing diversity
Source: Based on University of California (1999) and Gagnon and Cornelius (2000).

(Strachan et al., 2004: 199), an agenda that has traditionally focused on gender (De Cieri and Kramar, 2005). However, certain other groups of people, such as indigenous Australians and persons from non-English speaking backgrounds, continue to be disadvantaged in employment (Syed and Ali, 2005).

Traditionally, diversity policies have been externally driven, influenced by social responsibility doctrines. However, since the mid-1990s, there has been a shift in public policy towards the business case of diversity. Managing a diverse workforce is now closely linked to business performance (that is, it is internally driven) and is generally considered to be a part of corporate strategy (Bertone and Leahy, 2003). Accordingly, diversity management is described as a programme that was 'needed, not only to meet employee needs, but to reduce turnover costs and ensure that customers receive the best service possible' (De Cieri and Kramar, 2005: 28–9).

Critical Thinking 5.1

The discourse of diversity management

Some scholars suggest that managers now talk about diversity both to keep on the right side of the law, and to ensure the commitment of diverse employees to the organization and its objectives (Antonios, 1997). Employers' approaches generally range from a straight lack of interest to a more inclusive approach and positive potential for a long-term business strategy. Some organizations devote little attention to the area, whereas others devote much. There is also some evidence of a negative reaction against EEO endeavours. In particular, the emphasis on affirmative action has sparked most resistance (D'Netto et al., 2000). Previous research suggests that, in most organizations, diversity policies appear to represent a renaming of EEO rather than being an integrated management approach in their own right (Kramar, 2004). An integrated approach is, however, hard to achieve through single-level conceptualizations of diversity management (Syed and Kramar, 2009; Syed and Özbilgin, 2009).

Scholars have expressed some concern that a shift from social-equity driven EEO to business-benefits driven diversity management may exacerbate the debatable employment conditions of women, ethnic minorities and other disadvantaged groups. For example, Humphries and Grice (1995) argue that while diversity management may be seen as a new social division between the core, the periphery and the unemployed, it ignores the categories that 'illustrate women and other people as not having achieved proportionate representation in the statistics of privilege' (1995: 30–1). The replacement of the discourse of equity with the discourse of diversity may relegate many people from diverse backgrounds to the 'insecure periphery' (1995: 31). In other words, there are serious concerns about the direction and scope of diversity management in improving the conditions of disadvantaged people in the workplace.

There are also some concerns about a predominant emphasis on individuality within the discourse of diversity management. Social identity theory proposes that individuals identify with groups that positively affect their self-esteem, and evaluate their own groups by social comparisons to other groups (Tajfel and

Turner, 1986). Previous research also suggests that organizational interventions that fail to address the underlying problem of cultural disintegration will not be able to alleviate social disadvantage within and outside organizations (Appo and Härtel, 2003).

Although collective identity is generally ignored in employment contexts, employers are reportedly more concerned about legal regulations. Managers generally seem to be driven by a legal compliance approach (Antonios, 1997), but legislation is generally limited in its ability to bring about cultural and attitudinal change in organizations (Pyke, 2005). Most probably, this is because of the narrow, single-level conceptualizations of diversity management, so that issues related to national culture, structural conditions, and multiple and intersectionality (overlapping) of various forms of identity remain generally neglected.

Questions
1. Is diversity management a repackaging of EEO to make it more attractive to business organizations while paying lip-service to disadvantaged workers?
2. What tangible differences in outcomes may be identified as a result of the change from EEO to diversity management?

A relational framework for diversity management

In order to enable organizations to pursue an integrated approach, Syed and Özbilgin (2009) propose a relational framework that treats diversity management from a layered and intersectional perspective. The framework is informed by Bourdieu's relational sociology, which treats social reality as being layered across agency and structure (see, for example, Bourdieu, 1998). Syed and Özbilgin discuss the need for a relational framework with which equality of opportunities could be studied in dynamic (that is, always evolving), overlapping (in terms of structure and agency and of various forms of identity) and context-specific (instead of universalistic) terms. They argue that single-level conceptualizations of equal opportunities fail to capture the interplay between agentic and structural concerns of equality. Therefore, they propose a relational framework that bridges the divide between large-scale macro-national, medium-sized meso-organizational and small-scale micro-individual insights to arrive at a realistic conceptualization of diversity management.

At the *macro-national* level, the relational framework of diversity management discusses the impact of national structures and arrangements, such as laws, social organization, national culture, and gender and race relations. At the *meso-organizational* level, the framework takes into account the organizational processes, rituals and routinized behaviours at work that establish the rules of middle-level gender and race relations. An absence of debate on equality of rights at work and a lack of recognition of multicultural traditions mean that meso-level relationships may reflect a hierarchical organization of discriminatory practices, embedded within broad social relations. At the *micro-individual* level, the relational framework deals with issues related to individual identity, aspirations and agency that affect change, these phenomena also being viewed in terms of gender and race.

Advantages of diversity

Cox and Blake (1991) identify six dimensions that can help organizations to create a competitive advantage from effectively managing the diversity of their workforce, namely cost, human resource acquisition, marketing, creativity, problem-solving and organizational flexibility.

Cost

Issues such as high employee turnover rates and absence from work cost businesses significant amounts of money. A recent survey by Kronos and Mercer (2008) showed that unplanned and extended absences cost companies 9.2 per cent of their payroll. According to Cox and Blake (1991), women and racial minority groups had high turnover rates and absenteeism in the workplace due to issues such as pregnancy and fixed work schedules. However, studies prove that organizations have reduced women's turnover rates by 63 per cent as a result of providing in-house childcare facilities (Youngblood and Cook, 1984), and that introducing flexible working times has significantly reduced absenteeism (Kim and Campagna, 1981).

Resource acquisition

Organizations today are involved in a persistent struggle to attract and retain top-quality employees. Cox and Blake (1991) suggest that by using positive publicity to recruit women and individuals from racial minorities, companies can indirectly boost their recruiting efforts.

Marketing and creativity

Markets are becoming more diverse (Cox and Blake, 1991), and each market has its own cultural preferences and sensitivities (Hill, 2008). From a team perspective, a diverse mix of team members is likely to be more creative than a group of identical individuals. A diverse team holds different attitudes and perspectives that are not possessed by an identical team. Therefore, discussions within a diverse group are likely to result in a higher level of analysis and lower conformity in thought, whereas the members of a group who are identical may have little to talk about or may commit identical mistakes (Cox and Blake, 1991). Diversity encourages more creativity and innovation, which can in turn lead to more effective decision-making (Gibson and Gibbs, 2006).

Problem-solving and system flexibility

Companies such as HSBC Bank and Proctor and Gamble (P&G) have achieved global success by hiring talented employees and making sure they gain international experience by relocating them to countries with cultural identities completely different from their own (Ready and Conger, 2007). In this way, employees exchange information about each other's cultures. The knowledge gained in this way can help employees to understand subtle details such as valuable cultural dimensions and how business deals are negotiated (Hofstede, 1984). This can in turn lead to greater flexibility in the system and better problem-solving in organizations (Ready and Conger, 2007).

> **Critical thinking 5.2**
>
> **The challenges of managing diversity**
>
> Managing diversity is not an easy task. Several issues, such as conflict, isolation and discrimination, may exist within diverse work groups.
>
> In certain situations, diversity may trigger social isolation, which is probably caused by not only social stereotypes, but also unique individual dispositions (Putnam, 2007). Kreitz (2008) suggests that managers in organizations should be able to identify whether people are keeping to themselves and rectify this by promoting an organizational culture in which each group is enabled to embrace each other's identities rather than trying to 'make everyone the same' (Putnam, 2007).
>
> In addition, conflict may arise in diverse groups. In-groups and out-groups can be created as a result of racial and gender differences (Richard et al, 2004). Richard et al. explain that strong identification between people of the same race and gender results in 'poor intergroup communication' and increased conflict during group work.
>
> Research has also suggested that the majority group may feel resentful towards diversity initiatives, especially if these initiatives are not communicated sensitively and constructively by organizations. This often leads to resistance and tensions among different groups, and also to a reluctance on the part of minority groups to engage with diversity initiatives, such as positive action, in case they are seen as 'tokens' (Kamenou, 2003).
>
> **Questions**
> 1. If the majority group remains resentful towards disadvantaged employees, is it at all useful to implement diversity management in the workplace?
> 2. What can organizations do to alleviate any apprehensions in the majority group?

Discrimination is a major issue in organizations with a diverse workforce. International Labour Organization (2004) studies show that qualified migrants in Western industrialized countries face a discrimination rate of 35 per cent (that is, one in three are unfairly excluded in employment procedures). The social identity of employees is reported to be responsible for differing career path trajectories and significant income differences, for instance, for migrant workers who face both 'glass door' and 'glass ceiling' discrimination based on their race and gender (Syed, 2008).

From positive discrimination to positive action

Although positive discrimination (or affirmative action) is now disallowed in many countries (for example, Australia, the UK and the USA) because it allegedly violates the principle of merit and equality, there is evidence of governmental initiatives in order to encourage employment of the previously disadvantaged groups. Positive action may take many forms, as seen, for example, in targeted advertising campaigns encouraging ethnic minority candidates to join the police force.

From a legal perspective, section 47 of the Sex Discrimination Act 1975 in the UK allowed for the use of 'positive action' in a number of specific circumstances. Similarly, sections 37 and 38 of the Race Relations Act 1976 allowed an employer to give special encouragement and provide specific training for a particular racial group. These two Acts have now been replaced by the Equality Act 2010, which also provides for positive action in recruitment and promotion. From an organizational perspective, positive action may include initiatives such as the introduction of non-discriminatory selection procedures and training programmes, or policies aimed at preventing sexual harassment.

Box 5.1 provides some examples of positive action in organizations and also a guide to assess the need for positive action.

Box 5.1 Does your company need positive action?

Before deciding to introduce positive action to encourage underrepresented groups to apply for jobs, employers must look at their own employees to establish how many underrepresented groups have been doing the kind of work in question during the previous 12 months. If the number of underrepresented groups is comparatively small, consideration can be given to encouraging them to apply for the relevant vacancies. For example:

- A local government authority in the UK used 'statements of encouragement' in adverts to women to encourage applications in areas where women had traditionally been underrepresented.
- London's Metropolitan Police has a positive action team who are undertaking a series of job fairs to encourage ethnic minority and female candidates to join their service.

Useful contacts

- See http://www.equalityhumanrights.com/ for further information on gender-positive action and other equality related policies and actions
- For resources on Age Positive, a diversity-related initiative from the UK government, see http://www.dwp.gov.uk/age-positive/

Sources: Equality Advice Centre; http://www.equality-online.org.uk/equality_advice/index.html

Strategies to manage diversity

Managing diversity is not a 'one-off problem'. Hence, organizations need a coherent strategy to understand and manage it, for example in the shape of top management commitment, training and extensive organizational knowledge (Kreitz, 2008). To be more specific, organizations need to create respect for all identity groups by valuing and respecting diversity (Cox and Blake, 1991). Moreover, diversity should be represented in all levels and networks across the organization (Ely and Thomas, 2001). Box 5.2 provides some examples of best practices in diversity management.

> **Box 5.2 Successful business stories of diversity management**
>
> It's not that difficult to find examples of good diversity practice. Here are a few.
>
> - UK supermarket giant Tesco does not impose an age limit on its employees. They say that 'It's attitude not age that creates customer satisfaction'. Tesco recruits people from all ages since they believe that customers love people from different age groups dealing with them. Tesco's employees also report that they prefer working in an age-diverse team (Chartered Institute of Personnel and Development, 2005).
> - BC Tel, a telephone company in Canada, set up an Indo-Canadian phone line. This helped the company to provide Indian- and Chinese-language services and fostered their relationship with diverse customers (Affiliation of Multicultural Societies and Service Agencies of BC, 2000).
> - Ebco Industries, Ltd., a Canadian manufacturing company, has received several prestigious awards, for example the federal government's Excellence in Race Relations Award and the Boeing Company's Eagle Award for Outstanding Cost Reduction and Quality Performance. The company has 900 employees from 48 nationalities. Hugo Eppich, the founder of the company, says that their philosophy is to respect individuals and their uniqueness; he also says that they focus more on strengths rather than differences. Among the diversity practices of this company are multicultural food festivals for all employees and displaying flags of all nationalities in the reception area (Affiliation of Multicultural Societies and Service Agencies of BC, 2000).
> - Corporate Rabobank (based in The Netherlands) has an intranet site that is dedicated to diversity management. This site gives information about the bank's policies, improvements and planned activities. The most interesting thing about this site that it has a page called 'intercultural management', which talks about the reasons behind Rabobank choosing to adopt a multicultural environment (Subeliani and Tsogas, 2005).
> - The military of a country usually reflects its society. The social composition of the US Air Force has altered in recent years as a result of increasing diversity of the USA's population. The military leadership is devoted to education and training on equal opportunities and non-discrimination. Several short courses are offered on sexual harassment, equal opportunities and cultural diversity.

> Moreover, 2-day courses are offered to senior management on areas such as racism, crosscultural socialization and others.
>
> The US Air Force's leadership encourages contributions from all people without any regard to their origins (Moon, 1997).
>
> **Questions**
>
> Undertake the following as a class exercise. Based on your personal knowledge or research, identify a successful story of diversity management in a local or international organization.
>
> 1. What works well in that organization?
> 2. Where is there room for improvement?

The US Government Accountability Office (2005) has consulted experts on diversity and suggested nine leading practices organizations that should follow, as described below.

1. Leadership commitment

A good leader's commitment to diversity should be visible based on how well he or she communicates the vision of diversity in an organization. The Government Accountability Office (2005) further recommends that an organization's support for diversity should be communicated in the form of policies, procedures, speeches, meetings and newsletters. Moreover, this support should exist throughout the organization all the way from senior management to the lowest level (Kreitz, 2008). Roosevelt (2006) identifies the following three skills a leader should have for managing diversity, namely the ability to:

- recognize and analyse diversity in a group;
- determine whether action is required with respect to a particular group;
- respond appropriately to a problem.

2. Diversity as part of an organization's strategic plan

Managing diversity is not an isolated issue (Kreitz, 2008): it can take 5–7 years for an organization to successfully integrate its related policies into the strategic plan (Government Accountability Office, 2005). The strategic plan to manage diversity should be in line with the organization's goals (Jayne and Dipboye, 2004).

3. Diversity linked to performance

Managing diversity should be effectively focused on increasing productivity and innovation. For example, positive promotion of diversity can boost an organization's overall recruiting effort (Cox and Blake, 1991) and help a company to extend its services to a more diverse customer base (Ely and Thomas, 2001).

4. Measurement

Organizations can measure the impact of diversity on their performance by collecting and analysing empirical data drawn from interviews, focus groups and surveys (Government Accountability Office, 2005). In order to successfully measure the impact (for example, cost and effort) of diversity, managers must set goals at the start of the year and then review them at the end (Roosevelt, 1999).

5. Accountability

In order to promote the achievement of an organization's diversity goals, managers should be rewarded through adequate performance management and reward systems (Government Accountability Office, 2005). According to the Government Accountability Office, this implies that managers at all levels of the organization should be reviewed based on their ability to manage diverse teams and achieve diversity-specific goals.

6. Succession planning

Organizations should actively identify diverse talent pools and develop them into potential future leaders (Government Accountability Office, 2005). For example, Ready and Conger (2007) explain how the banking organization HSBC has a system of talent pools that tracks the careers of employees with good potential within the organization. The selected candidates are first trained by local managers or business heads, after which they are given assignments overseas. Managers then identify the most capable candidates, who are put in a higher level pool of talent. These candidates can become executive managers in 3–5 years and may in the long term reach top management level.

7. Recruitment

In order to keep up with international competition and a growing diverse market place (Kreitz, 2008), firms need to attract a skilful and diverse workforce. This may help organizations to solve problems and achieve their goals using the multicultural exchange of knowledge, innovation and creativity (Cox and Blake, 1991; Richard et al., 2004).

8. Employee involvement

Organizations should involve employees in their diversity management efforts. According to the Government Accountability Office (2005), this will lead employees to form networks, task forces, councils and committees that help an organization to identify issues, raise opinions and so on, which will ultimately lead the organization to recommend actions while keeping its employees' interest first.

9. Diversity training

To reap the benefits of diversity, organizations need to ensure that management and staff understand the advantages and challenges of diversity (Government Accountability Office, 2005). According to Jayne and Dipboye (2004), the training provided needs to emphasize that a diverse group brings with it new skills and perspectives that can be used to improve task performance. Moreover, team-building exercises should be carried out in such a way that members are able to understand each other's cultural background. Training is essential as team members who are unaware of diversity and its complexities may not work together effectively, and may instead contribute to negative stereotypes and discrimination in the workplace (Ely and Thomas, 2001).

So far, this chapter has provided an overview of key areas of diversity and equality, engaging with key concepts, frameworks and the advantages and challenges faced when managing diversity. The next section will focus on methodological issues that researchers should consider when conducting research on diversity management.

Methodological considerations in conducting research on diversity management: the case of ethnic minority women

This section presents some key methodological considerations to be taken into account when conducting research in the diversity management area. The discussion will engage with the career experiences of ethnic minority women as a means of illustrating key issues related to methodology and the position of the researcher and the researched. Reflexivity on the researchers' role and influence must be considered, particularly in situations where one group is historically seen as more dominant than another. Lorbiecki and Jack (2000: S22) have argued that reflexivity:

> encourages social actors, be they academics or practitioners, to look more deeply at what they are doing and to consider the political, cultural and social implications of the knowledge they are constructing.

Ethnic minority women are seen as social actors within organizational and social group structures and cultures, which may affect their strategies and plans; in turn, they may also be affected by these structures and cultures. In the same vein, researchers are also seen as social actors placed within a specific context at a specific point in time, where their experiences may be informed by a number of factors including their ethnicity, gender, class, education and geographical location. An ethnic minority woman may have different realities from those of a white woman, a white man, an ethnic minority man or an ethnic minority woman of a different ethnic group or class. At the same time, one should avoid essentializing (that is, stereotyping) groups as having specific traits – the above argument should be extended to remind researchers that ethnic minority women of the same ethnic group or class can still have different experiences.

If we acknowledge the fact that there is a need for a better understanding of how researchers can conduct work within diversity management, it is important to examine and identify appropriate methodologies that are sensitive to our topic of investigation and overcome biased perspectives that limit the validity and usefulness of the research.

By focusing on the career experiences of ethnic minority women, one should be aware of the dangers of adopting a feminist research methodology, since the second-wave Western feminist literature has been accused of ignoring the experiences of ethnic minority women (hooks, 1981, 1984, 1989, 1991; Collins, 1990; Maynard, 1994). For example, Finch (1984) and Oakley (1981, 1987) have been criticized for assuming unity by gender and ignoring other divisive factors (Lee, 1993). In some respects, however, a feminist methodology may be appropriate as it is open to giving participants voices to express themselves in their own words, and to setting up non-hierarchical relations between the researcher and the participants.

It is important to identify and engage with non-ethnocentric feminist methodologies, which have been sensitive to multicultural studies and have allowed for an interaction of gender with other subidentities such as class, race, culture and religion. The work of Edwards (1990, 1993) is especially useful in this respect as she has provided a detailed discussion of feminist research methodologies that need to be sensitive to racial and class divisions. She has also discussed her own position as a white woman interviewing Caribbean women, and has engaged with debates on how white researchers can conduct sensitive research on minority groups without imposing their own power or privilege.

Most feminist research writers agree that there is no one method that can be deemed '*the* feminist methodology' – to use Edwards' (1993: 182) original emphasis. It seems that there is not one specific feminist philosophy or methodology, but rather a number of overlapping feminist methodologies. Thus, there are no feminist 'how-to-recipes' (Duelli Klein, 1983: 90). Nevertheless, Edwards (1990: 479) has argued that even though there is no single feminist methodology, there are certain elements that characterize the overall approach: 'a feminist methodology has as its base a critique of objectivity, of the supposedly rational, detached, value-free research as traditionally espoused'. Edwards goes to present three key principles that guide feminist research:

1. Women's lives need to be addressed in their own terms: 'women's round lives have been pushed into the square holes of male-defined theories, and where their experiences do not fit those experiences have been invalidated, devalued, or presented as deviant' (Edwards, 1990: 479).
2. Feminist research should not just be '*on* women' but '*for* women' (Edwards' original emphasis). Edwards (1990) argues that the final aim of research should be to improve women's situations, and this raises concerns on the relationship between the researcher and the researched. The researched should not be treated as 'objects' of research, and their voices and concerns should be heard.
3. The researcher should locate herself (Edwards wrote from a perspective that women should interview women and therefore only acknowledges the female in her discussions) in the research and the process of production of results. She should do this by making explicit the reasoning procedures she has used in carrying out the research and, on a reflexive level, by focusing on the 'researcher's effect upon the actual process of the research, her class, race, assumptions,

and beliefs', as well as the effect these have upon the research and its analysis (Edwards, 1990: 479).

Carrying out a study across racial and ethnic lines raises certain issues for the researcher, for example practical, strategic, ethical and epistemological concerns (Stanfield and Dennis, 1993, cited in Kamenou, 2007). Andersen (1993) has argued that research focusing on race has often been distorted as it has been centred on the perspectives and experiences of dominant group members. This could have the unwelcome consequence that the production of knowledge has been 'ideologically determined and culturally biased' (Stanfield, 1993: 4).

Alvesson and Willmott (1992) argue that it is important, when conducting research, to allow people to speak for themselves through ethnographic studies. This 'is a vital means of moderating "totalizing" accounts of management and organization' (p. 442) and of allowing a detailed analysis of perceptions of cultural life through the eyes of the participants (Hammersley and Atkinson, 1995). With regard to interviewing women from ethnic minority groups, some feminists have attributed to the open-ended interview 'an ability to help counter any implicit racism on the part of white researchers' (Edwards, 1993: 184). Open-ended interviews allow women to speak for themselves, and this can avoid the production of data that 'pathologize' women (Edwards, 1993, p. 184) and treat them as passive agents.

Edwards (1993: 184), however, goes on to discuss possible dangers if the female researcher and the female participant(s) derive from a different race or class:

> if we accept that there are structurally based divisions between women on the basis of race and/or class that may lead them to have different interests and priorities, then what has been said about woman-to-woman interviewing may not apply in all situations.

In terms of women interviewing women, Minister (1991) argued that women are not comfortable with hierarchical same-sex systems, and that researchers should therefore attempt to minimize the hierarchical relationship. This argument is perhaps simplistic as it falls into the trap of stereotyping all women as behaving in a similar way and having similar preferences and goals. Some women may be comfortable in a given scheme of hierarchies and may even encourage a power relationship with other women, whereas some may not see themselves as having a bond with other women, or as feeling any need to provide them with help or support.

It is important to look at some of the arguments proposed by black feminists who have criticized white feminists for attempting to involve themselves in research into black people's experiences. Black feminists have argued that white researchers are not capable of, and should not be, conducting research involving ethnic minority men and women as they do not have first-hand experience, insight or understanding. Carby (1982) was a main voice in black feminism and argued that studies by white researchers involving black people are operating within white Western supremacist assumptions. A central argument lies in whether white researchers can contribute to the understanding of the experiences of different racial groups, and whether dominant groups can comprehend the experiences of outsiders (Andersen, 1993). Andersen (1993: 41), a white female researcher, suggested that there are certain problems in conducting research involving ethnic minority groups because of the social distance imposed by class and race relations when the interviewers are white and middle-class and those being interviewed are not:

> How can white scholars study those who have been historically subordinated without further producing sociological accounts distorted by the political economy of race, class and gender?

Standpoint feminists (that is, scholars who propose that feminist social science should be practised from the standpoint of women instead of men) have advocated that members of subordinated groups have unique viewpoints on their own experiences and on society as a whole, arguing that one's race, class and gender are both the origin and the object of sociological knowledge (Andersen, 1993). Kamenou (2002, 2007) has contended, however, that people may be able to gain knowledge without having first-hand experience, and be able to produce research and 'represent the other' (Kitzinger et al., 1996), provided they adopt reflexivity, being sensitive to their own position and the ways in which that position can affect their perceptions and attitudes.

When attempting to conduct culturally sensitive research, there are concerns over how researchers' identities and positions might affect their understanding of situations in which they are not involved. Andersen (1993) has contended that white academics conducting research on race and ethnicity need to acknowledge the influence of institutional racism in their research. This is a great challenge for researchers in white-dominated academic institutions. Academic scholars wanting to conduct research within the diversity management area need to understand the sensitivity of the topic if they want to embark on research involving groups that are diverse in terms of ethnicity, gender, culture, religion and so on. In addition, this research needs to be placed within the broader historical and geographical context in which it is taking place.

To conduct research within the diversity management field and examine the work and life experiences of ethnic minority groups, we advocate for a non-hierarchical, empathy-driven approach in which participants are given a voice to express their opinions and discuss their experiences (Kamenou, 2002, 2007; Syed and Pio, 2010). One cannot deny that profit-making organizations will inevitably focus on any benefits they can accrue from diversity, as well as on cost–benefit analysis in relation to legal sanctions if they do not adhere to equality policies and practices. Management academics, however, need to look beyond the narrow spectrum of conducting research on yet another management topic and recognize that this research needs to be placed within its historical context and geographical location (Kamenou, 2007; Syed, 2009).

There is an urgent need for more work exploring *how* research in equality and diversity should be conducted. Again, work has been conducted in this area of studying 'others' (Davis et al., 2000) in anthropological and cultural studies (see, for example, Rosaldo, 1989; Alcoff, 1991/1992), but this has not occurred to any great extent within management studies. It is not suggested that there is one best model to be adopted when conducting research in this area, but it is important to highlight the fact that there are some methodological considerations that scholars ought to be aware of when working in the field of diversity management.

Conclusion

This chapter has demonstrated that the current ongoing demographic transformation of both the workforce and the general population in many countries has immense implications for the future of HRM, including diversity management, in the workplace. The chapter discussed key concepts of diversity management and distinguished between the EEO and diversity management approaches to managing workforce diversity. It also discussed the distinction between affirmative action and positive action, and identified a gradual transition to the latter in many countries.

In our theorization of diversity management, we criticized the usual organization-focused approaches to diversity management and instead argued for a multilevel approach to diversity that takes into account the overlapping (macro-national, meso-organizational and micro-individual) dimensions of diversity. We discussed the issue of the various laws and regulations in place in several countries to tackle workplace discrimination. Finally, we offered a detailed case study of ethnic minority women in the UK in order to highlight important methodological considerations in understanding and researching diversity management.

An understanding of or interest within management research on equality and diversity, although fundamental, needs to be informed by historical, sociopolitical and economic factors, as well as by an understanding of post-colonialism and institutional racism in organizations. We explored here the methodological considerations of conducting research within the diversity management field, illustrating the key points through a focus on the work and career experiences of ethnic minority women. Certain issues have a universal appeal, for example:

- the need for an informed understanding of the context in which research is conducted;
- an acknowledgement of how this context affects participants from diverse social groups, in terms of, for example, gender, ethnicity, culture, age and disability;
- an understanding of the issues surrounding reflexivity and self-awareness within research.

Conducting sensitive research within diversity management is therefore dependent on context, but the methodological process allows for some elements of convergence across locations and populations. There is a real need for more work in this area that will improve the baseline of diversity and equality-related research within management settings so that such research will adopt a relevant and context-specific methodology and acknowledge the historical, political and geographical context within which it functions.

FOR DISCUSSION AND REVISION

Questions

1. Why is it inappropriate to treat diversity management as an organization-specific issue?

2. Critically review the legislative framework of diversity management in your country. What are its strengths and weaknesses?
3. What key steps can an organization take in order to manage diversity effectively?
4. Why is it important to understand the local context in order to manage or research diversity?
5. What are current best practices in organizations in your country to manage diversity?

Exercises

1. What are the pros and cons of affirmative action? Debate your answers.
2. Study diversity management policies and practices in a specific company. Identify the various ways in which diversity management policies and practices in that company are affected by its sociocultural, political, legal and economic contexts.
3. Through an Internet search, identify and compare the diversity management policies or visions of at least three companies. Which policies or visions do you prefer, and why?

Further reading

Books

Anthias, F. and Yuval-Davis, N. (1992) *Racialized Boundaries: Race, Nation, Gender, Colour and Class and the Anti-racist Struggle*. London: Routledge.
Bell, M. (2007) *Diversity in Organizations*. Mason, OH: Thomson/South-Western.
Bhavnani, R. (1994) *Black Women in the Labour Market: A Research Review*. London: Organization Development Centre, City University.
Blaine, B. E. (2007) *Understanding the Psychology of Diversity*. London: Sage.
Davidson, M. J. (1997) *The Black and Ethnic Minority Woman Manager: Cracking the Concrete Ceiling*. London: Paul Chapman.
Harvey, C. and Allard, M. J. (eds) (2005) *Understanding and Managing Diversity: Readings, Cases, and Exercises* (3rd edn). New York: Prentice Hall.
Konrad, A., Prasad, P. and Pringle, J. (eds) (2006) *Handbook of Workplace Diversity*. London: Sage.
Modood, T., Berthoud, R., Lakey, J., Nazroo, J., Smith, P., Virdee, S. and Beishon, S. (1997) *Ethnic Minorities in Britain: Diversity and Disadvantage. Fourth National Survey on Ethnic Minorities*. London: Policy Studies Institute.
Özbilgin, M. (2009) *Equality, Diversity and Inclusion at Work: A Research Companion*. Cheltenham: Edward Elgar.
Özbilgin, M. and Syed, J. (eds) (2010) *Managing Cultural Diversity in Asia: A Research Companion*. Cheltenham: Edward Elgar.
Özbilgin, M. and Tatli, A. (2008) *Global Diversity Management: An Evidence-based Approach*. New York: Palgrave Macmillan.

Journals

Amos, V. and Parmar, P. (1984) Challenging imperial feminism. *Feminist Review*, 17: 3–20.
Fearfull, A. and Kamenou, N. (2006) How do you account for it?: a critical exploration of career opportunities for and experiences of ethnic minority women. *Critical Perspectives on Accounting*, 17(7): 883–901.

Kamenou, N. (2008) Reconsidering work–life balance debates: challenging limited understandings of the 'life' component in the context of ethnic minority women's experiences. Special Issue on Gender in Management: New Theoretical Perspectives. *British Journal of Management*, 19: S99–S109.

McGuire, G. M. (2000) Gender, race, ethnicity and networks: the factors affecting the status of employees' network members. *Work and Occupations*, 27: 500–23.

McGuire, G. M. (2002) Gender, race and the shadow structure: a study of informal networks and inequality in a work organization. *Gender and Society*, 16(3): 303–22.

Mason, D. (1996) Themes and issues in the teaching of race and ethnicity in sociology. *Ethnic and Racial Studies*, 19(4): 789–806.

White, Y. E. (1990) Understanding the black woman manager's interaction with the corporate culture. *Western Journal of Black Studies*, 14(3): 182–6.

CASE STUDY

Samina's Experiences in Retail Co.

Samina has been working in Retail Co. for almost 8 years. She rose through the organizational ranks and has recently been appointed store manager for the company's newest store. Today was a rare occasion on which she actually had some time to take a quick lunch break so was picking at her sandwich and sipping her coffee. She was in a reflective mood.

She remembered arriving on her first day at work as a shopfloor-level assistant aged 24. She had planned to work at Retail Co. over that summer as she had just completed her university degree. She had wanted to apply for a 'proper job' after the summer. But her plans changed when she was selected early on by her line manager, Mark, as 'someone with a lot of potential', as he put it. He had supported her in getting a position on the organization's fast-track management scheme a year after she had been recruited. Samina always fondly remembered Mark, who took her under his wing and showed her the ropes. He had retired 2 years ago, and they had spoken only occasionally since then. She missed their chats and the support that Mark had always provided. He was great for bouncing ideas off, and he 'always had her back', as he used to say.

Samina was proud of her achievements and for succeeding in reaching her own career goals. With the help of Mark and some of the other managers, she had developed a clear career plan, and she had clearly stated her ambition of becoming a store manager before she reached 34. Colleagues often joked that she was a well-oiled machine, always efficient, very organized and very focused. This sometimes created conflict with some of her workmates, who had not adopt the same management style. At times, she found that upsetting, but it had no an effect on her drive to succeed.

Her family, especially her mother, often told her how proud they were of her work achievements. Samina was the daughter of a Pakistani family who had migrated to the north of England in the 1970s. There were always high expectations of Samina and her two brothers to do well professionally. In the last couple of years, however, her parents had started hinting that maybe she had been focusing 'too much' on her career, at the expense of other areas. Samina knew his really meant having a husband and children!

Samina was aware that, at the moment, she was focusing solely on her career, but she felt she did not have a choice. As a new store manager, her days were very demanding and made up of long hours in the store. She felt the pressure to succeed and prove her critics wrong. Although she had a good working relationship with most of the staff and managers, she was very aware of some resentment, especially from some older white managers, who had assumed they would be made this store's manager once it opened.

The focus of Retail Co. on equality and diversity issues over the last few years had been great and, in Samina's opinion, much needed. There were very few ethnic minority staff in any management positions, but they were especially sparse at senior management levels. The Chief Executive had clearly communicated her commitment to equality in all areas such as gender, ethnicity, disability and age. She had focused on the benefits that diversity could bring to the organization and the need for the stores to represent local communities. As part of these diversity initiatives, stores were given 'aspirational targets' to reach within 2 years, including a higher representation of ethnic minority male and female staff at management levels. Samina knew she had all the right credentials for a store manager's post as she had gained the required management experience in her time at Retail Co.

Increasingly, however, she was feeling like an outsider. Discussions would suddenly halt once she entered the staff canteen; staff would be whispering after she had passed them in the corridor. Indeed, some comments were loud enough for her to hear. 'She is so young; what does she know about managing a whole store?' The most recent comment she had heard the day before was from a Bakery manager, Tom, who had worked for Retail Co. for 20 years: 'Everyone knows she was placed in that position to reach ethnic targets. Actually, it's one tick for race and one tick for gender. It's not right. Why can't they just promote people on merit?'

Samina knew that Tom was very resentful of the organization's diversity initiatives as he perceived these as positive discrimination, despite clear communication from senior managers that they could not lawfully positively discriminate in favour of any group. Thankfully, she was aware that not everyone shared his views and that some staff at least were in support of the initiatives and her promotion. But the negative comments still dominated in her mind.

Anna, a shopfloor-level assistant in her 50s, had come to see her the day before and congratulated her on her promotion. Samina felt touched by this as most staff did not openly wish her well, which she saw that as another sign of resentment or assumptions of tokenism. Her good mood quickly vanished though as Anna went on to say: 'I think it's a great achievement Samina, don't get me wrong … But I think you are now at an age that you should be focusing on marriage and having kids; you're not that young any more!' Samina felt she could never win. She was worn down by people's expectations, especially her family's views of what it meant to be a single woman in her 30s, focusing on her career. Despite all her achievements in the workplace, she was often made to feel less of a woman – that is, when she was not made to feel like a token promoted to make up Retail Co.'s aspirational targets.

Samina's lunch break was now over and she still had a long day ahead of her. She emptied her tray and started walking back to her office, reluctantly passing three of her colleagues chatting in the corridor. The last thing she needed was more 'well-meaning' comments …

Questions

1. What are some of the issues that Samina seems to be facing in relation to her work and recent promotion?
2. What are your views on the positive action initiatives that Retail Co. has put in place?
3. What challenges is Samina facing in balancing her work and personal life demands?
4. Could these challenges be influenced by different factors (for example, race, religion, gender or age)?
5. Do you think Samina's experiences may be different from those of white women or ethnic minority men in her organization? Why or why not?
6. During her lunch break, Samina was reflecting on her early experiences in Retail Co. and on having a mentor. How important is mentoring in one's career? What issues could people from minority groups face in selecting a mentor?

References

Affiliation of Multicultural Societies and Service Agencies of BC (2000) Cultural Diversity in Organizations and Business: Gaining a Competitive Advantage. Vancouver, Canada. Available from: http://www.amssa.org/pdf/diversity2000.pdf [accessed 10 May 2010].

Afshar, H. and Maynard, M. (1994) (eds) *The Dynamics of Race and Gender*. London: Taylor & Francis.

Alcoff, L. (1991/1992) The problem of speaking for others. *Cultural Critique*, 20: 5–32.

Alvesson, M. and Willmott, H. (1992) On the idea of emancipation in management and organization studies. *Academy of Management Review*, 17(3): 432–64.

Andersen, M. L. (1993) Studying across difference: race, class and gender in qualitative research. In Stanfield, J. H. II and Dennis, R. M. (eds), *Race and Ethnicity in Research Methods*. California: Sage, pp. 39–52.

Anthias, F. (1992) Connecting race and ethnic phenomena. *Sociology*, 6(3): 421–38.

Antonios, Z. (1997) Speech delivered by the Race Discrimination Commissioner at the Women, Management and Industrial Relations Conference, 29 July. Available from: http://www.humanrights.gov.au/speeches/race/managing_diversity.html [accessed 10 June 2006].

Appo, D. and Härtel, C. E. J. (2003) Questioning management paradigms that deal with Aboriginal development programs in Australia. *Asia Pacific Journal of Human Resources*, 41(1): 36–50.

Ashkanasy, N. M., Härtel, C. E. J. and Daus, C. S. (2002) Diversity and emotion: the new frontiers in organizational behavior research. *Journal of Management*, 28: 307–38.

Bell, M. P. (2007) *Diversity in Organizations*. Mason, OH: South-Western.

Bertone, S. and Leahy, M. (2003) Multiculturalism as a conservative ideology: impacts on workforce diversity. *Asia Pacific Journal of Human Resources*, 41(1): 101–15.

Blackstone, T., Parekh, B. and Sanders, P. (eds) (1998) *Race Relations in Britain: A Developing Agenda*. London: Routledge.

Bourdieu, P. (1998) *Practical Reason: On the Theory of Action*. Cambridge: Polity Press.

Brah, A. (1994) Race and culture in the gendering of labour markets: South Asian young Muslim women and the labour market. In Afshar, H. and Maynard, M. (eds), *The Dynamics of Race and Gender*. London: Taylor and Francis, pp. 151–71.

Carby, H. V. (1982) White women listen! Black feminism and the boundaries of sisterhood. In Centre for Contemporary Cultural Studies, *The Empire Strikes Back*. London: Hutchinson, pp. 45–54.

Chartered Institute of Personnel and Development (2005) *Diversity Management: Linking Theory and Practice to Business Performance*. London: CIPD.

Collins, P. H. (1990) *Black Feminist Thought*. London: Unwin Hyman.

Cox, T. (1994) A comment on the language of diversity. *Organization*, 1(1): 51–7.

Cox, T. H. and Blake, S. (1991) Managing cultural diversity: implications for organizational competitiveness. *Academy of Management Executive*, 5(3): 45–56.

Davis, O. I., Nakayama, T. K. and Martin, J. N. (2000) Current and future directions in ethnicity and methodology. *International Journal of Intercultural Relations*, 24: 525–39.

De Cieri, H. and Kramar, R. (2005) *Human Resource Management in Australia: Strategy, People, Performance*. Sydney: McGraw-Hill.

Deluca, J. M. and McDowell, R. N. (1992) Managing diversity: a strategic 'grass-roots' approach. In Jackson, S. E. and Associates (eds), *Diversity in the Workplace: Human Resources Initiatives*. New York: Guilford Press, pp. 227–47.

Dickens, L. (1994) The business case for equal opportunities: is the carrot better than the stick? *Employee Relations*, 16(8): 5–18.

Dickens, L. (1999) Beyond the business case: a three-pronged approach to equality action. *Human Resource Management Journal*, 9(1): 9–19.

D'Netto, B., Smith, D. and Pinto, C. (2000) *Diversity Management: Benefits, Challenges and Strategies*. DIMA Project No. 1. Carlton, Victoria: Mt Eliza Business School, Victoria.

Duelli Klein, R. (1983) How to do what we want to do: thoughts about feminist methodology. In Bowles, G. and Duelli Klein, R. (eds), *Theories of Women's Studies*. London: Routledge & Kegan Paul, pp. 88–102.

Edwards, R. (1990) Connecting method and epistemology: a white woman interviewing black women. *Women's Studies International Forum*, 13(5): 477–90.

Edwards, R. (1993) An education in interviewing: placing the researcher and the research. In Renzetti, C. M. and Lee, R. M. (eds), *Researching Sensitive Topics*. California: Sage, pp. 181–96.

Ely, R. J. and Thomas, D. A. (2001) Cultural diversity at work: the effects of diversity perspectives on work group processes and outcomes. *Administrative Science Quarterly*, 46: 229–73.

Equality and Human Rights Commission (2011) Public Sector Duties. Available from: http://www.equalityhumanrights.com/advice-and-guidance/public-sector-duties/ [accessed 31 March 2011].

Ferris, G. R., Frink, D. D. and Galang, M. C. (1994) Diversity in the workplace: the human resources management challenges. *Human Resource Planning*, 16: 41–51.

Finch, J. (1984) 'It's great to have someone to talk to': the ethics and politics of interviewing women. In Bell, C. and Roberts, H. (eds), *Social Researching: Politics, Problems, Practice*. London: Routledge & Kegan Paul, pp. 166–80.

Gagnon, S. and Cornelius, N. (2000) Re-examining workplace inequality: a capabilities approach. *Human Resource Management Journal*, 10(4): 68–87.

Gibson, C. B. and Gibbs, J. L. (2006) Unpacking the concept of virtuality: the effects of geographic dispersion, electronic dependence, dynamic structure, and national diversity on team innovation. *Administrative Science Quarterly*, 51(3): 451–95.

Government Accountability Office (2005) Diversity Management: Expert-identified Leading Practices and Agency Examples. Available from: http://www.gao.gov/new.items/d0590.pdf [accessed 10 June 2010].

Hammersley, M. and Atkinson, P. (1995) *Ethnography: Principles in Practice*. London: Routledge.

Härtel, C. E. J. and Fujimoto, Y. (2000) Diversity is not a problem to be managed by organizations but openness to perceived dissimilarity is. *Journal of Australian and New Zealand Academy of Management*, 6(1): 14–27.

Hill, C. W. L. (2008) *International Business Competing in the Global Market Place* (7th edn). New York: McGraw-Hill.

Hofstede, G. (1984) Cultural dimensions in management and planning. *Asia Pacific Journal of Management*, 1(2): 81–98.

hooks, b. (1981) *Ain't I a Woman?* London: Pluto.

hooks, b. (1984) *Feminist Theory: From Margin to Center*. Boston: South End Press.
hooks, b. (1989) *Talking Back: Thinking Feminist, Thinking Black*. London: Sheba Feminist Publishers.
hooks, b. (1991) *Yearning*. London: Turnaround.
Humphries, M. T. and Grice, S. (1995) Equal employment opportunity and the management of diversity: a global discourse of assimilation? *Journal of Organizational Change Management*, 8(5): 17–32.
International Labour Organization (2004) Facts on Migrant Labour. Available from: http://www.ilo.org/public/english/bureau/inf/download/factsheets/pdf/migrants.pdf [accessed 15 February 2010].
Jayne, M. E. A. and Dipboye, R. L. (2004) Leveraging diversity to improve business performance: research findings and recommendations for organizations. *Human Resource Management*, 43(4): 409.
Kamenou, N. (2002) Ethnic Minority Women in English Organizations: Career experiences and Opportunities. Unpublished PhD thesis, University of Leeds.
Kamenou, N. (2003) Critical issues in the implementation of diversity strategies: a case study of UK organizations. *International Journal of Knowledge, Culture and Change Management*, 3: 507–20.
Kamenou, N. (2007) Methodological considerations in conducting research across gender, 'race', ethnicity and culture: a challenge to context specificity in diversity research methods. *International Journal of Human Resource Management*, 18(11): 1995–2009.
Kamenou, N. and Fearfull, A. (2006) Ethnic minority women: a lost voice in HRM. *Human Resource Management Journal*, 16(2): 154–72.
Kim, J. S. and Campagna, A. F. (1981) Effects of flexitime on employee attendance and performance: a field experiment. *Academy of Management Journal*, (December), 729–41.
Kirton, G. and Greene, A.-M. (2005) *The Dynamics of Managing Diversity: A Critical Approach* (2nd edn). Oxford: Elsevier.
Kitzinger, D. P., Bola, M., Campos, A. B., Carabine, J., Doherty, K., Frith, H., McNulty, A., Reilly, J. and Winn, J. (1996) The spoken work: speaking of representing the other. *Feminism and Psychology*, 6(2): 217–35.
Kramar, R. (2004) Does Australia really have diversity management? In Davis, E. and Pratt, V. (eds), *Making the Link 15: Affirmative Action and Employment Relations*. Sydney: CCH Australia, pp. 19–26.
Kreitz, P. A. (2008) Best practises for managing organizational diversity. *Journal of Academic Librarianship*, 34(2): 101–20.
Kronos and Mercer (2008) The Total Financial Impact of Employee Absences. Available from: http://www.kronos.com/AbsenceAnonymous/media/Mercer-Survey-Highlights.pdf [accessed 1 December 2009].
Lee, R. M. (1993) *Doing Research on Sensitive Topics*. London: Sage Publications.
Liff, S. (1997) Two routes to managing diversity: individual differences or social group characteristics. *Employee Relations*, 19(1): 11–26.
Liff, S. (1999) Diversity and equal opportunities: room for a constructive compromise? *Human Resource Management Journal*, 9(1): 65–75.
Lorbiecki, A. (2001) Openings and Burdens for Women and Minority Ethnics Being Diversity Vanguards in Britain. Gender, Work and Organization Conference, University of Keele, June 2001.
Lorbiecki, A. and Jack, G. (2000) Critical turns in the evolution of diversity management. *British Journal of Management*, 11, Special Issue, S17–S31.
Maynard, M. (1994) 'Race', gender and the concept of 'difference' in feminist thought. In Afshar, H. and Maynard, M. (eds), *The Dynamics of Race and Gender*. London: Taylor & Francis, pp. 9–25.
Minister, K. (1991) A feminist frame for the oral history interview. In Gluck, S. and Patai, D. (eds), *Women's Worlds: The Feminist Practice of Oral History*. New York: Routledge, pp. 27–42.
Moon, M. M. K. (1997) Understanding the impact of cultural diversity on organizations. The Research Department Air Command and Staff College, Research Paper No. AU/ACSC/0607C/97-03. Maxwell, AB: Air University.

Murray, P. and Syed, J. (2005) Critical issues in managing age diversity in Australia. *Asia Pacific Journal of Human Resources*, 43(2): 210–24.

Nkomo, S. and Cox, T. Jr (1996) Diverse identities in organizations. In Clegg, S. R. et al. (eds), *The Handbook of Organization Studies*. London: Sage, pp. 338–56.

Oakley, A. (1981) Interviewing women: a contradiction in terms. In Roberts, H. (ed.) *Doing Feminist Research*. London: Routledge & Kegan Paul, pp. 30–61.

Oakley, A. (1987) Comment on Malsteed. *Sociology*, 21: 63.

Parker, J. and Douglas, J. (2010) The role of women's groups in New Zealand, UK and Canadian trade unions in addressing intersectional interests. *International Journal of Comparative Industrial Relations and Labour Law*, 26(3): 295–319.

Pool, I. and Sceats, J. (1990) Population: human resource and social determinant. In Green, P. F. (ed.) *Studies in New Zealand Social Problems*. Palmerston North: Dunmore Press, pp. 31–53.

Putnam, R. D. (2007) E pluribus unum: diversity and community in the twenty-first century. The 2006 Johan Skytte Prize Lecture. *Scandinavian Political Studies*, 30: 137–74.

Pyke, J. (2005) Productive Diversity: Which Companies are Active and Why? Master's thesis, Victoria University, Melbourne, Australia.

Ready, D. A. and Conger, J. A. (2007) Make your company a talent factory. *Harvard Business Review*, 85(6): 68–77.

Richard, O. C., Barnett, T., Dwyer, S. and Chadwick, K. (2004) Cultural diversity in management, firm performance, and the moderating role of entrepreneurial orientation dimensions. *Academy of Management Journal*, 47(2): 255–66.

Roosevelt, T. R. Jr (1999) Diversity management: some measurement criteria. *Employer Relations Today*, 25: 49–62.

Roosevelt, T. R. Jr (2006) Diversity management: an essential craft for leaders. *Leader to Leader*, 41 (Summer): 45–9.

Rosaldo, R. (1989) *Culture and Truth: The Remaking of Social Analysis*. Boston: Beacon Press.

Stanfield, J. H. (1993) Epistemological considerations. In Stanfield, J. H. II and Dennis, R. M. (1993) (eds), *Race and Ethnicity in Research Methods*. London: Sage, pp. 16–36.

Stanfield, J. H. and Dennis, R. M. (eds) (1993) *Race and Ethnicity in Research Methods*. California: Sage.

Strachan, G., Burgess, J. and Sullivan, A. (2004) Affirmative action or managing diversity: what is the future of equal opportunity policies in Australia? *Women in Management Review*, 19(4): 196–204.

Subeliani, D. and Tsogas, G. (2005) Managing diversity in the Netherlands: a case study of Rabobank. *International Journal of Human Resource Management*, 16(5): 831–51.

Syed, J. (2008) Employment prospects for skilled migrants: a relational perspective. *Human Resource Management Review*, 18, 28–45.

Syed, J. (2009) Contextualising diversity management. In Özbilgin, M. (ed.) *Equality, Diversity and Inclusion at Work: A Research Companion*. Cheltenham: Edward Elgar, pp. 101–11.

Syed, J. and Ali, F. (2005) Minority ethnic women in the Australian labour market. In Davis, E. and Pratt, V. (eds), *Making the Link: Affirmative Action and Employment Relations*. Sydney: CCH Australia, pp. 48–54.

Syed, J. and Kramar, R. (2009) Socially responsible diversity management. *Journal of Management and Organization*, 15(5): 639–51.

Syed, J. and Özbilgin, M. (2009) A relational framework for international transfer of diversity management practices. *International Journal of Human Resource Management*, 20(12): 2435–53.

Syed, J. and Pio, E. (2010) Veiled diversity: workplace experiences of Muslim women in Australia. *Asia Pacific Journal of Management*, 27(1): 115–37.

Tajfel, H. and Turner, J. C. (1986) The social identity theory of intergroup behaviour. In Worchel, S. and Austin, W. G. (eds), *Psychology of Intergroup Relations*. Chicago: Nelson, pp. 7–24.

Teicher, J. and Spearitt, K. (1996) From equal employment opportunity to diversity management: the Australian experience. *International Journal of Manpower*, 17(4/5): 109–33.

Thomas, D. and Ely, R. (1996) Making differences matter: a new paradigm for managing diversity. *Harvard Business Review*, 74(5): 79–90.

Thomas, R. R. (1990) From affirmative action to affirming diversity. *Harvard Business Review*, (March–April), pp. 107–17.

Thomas, R. R. (1992) Managing diversity: a conceptual framework. In Jackson, S. E. (ed.) *Diversity in the Workplace: Human Resource Initiatives*. New York: Guilford.

University of California (1999) *Staff Affirmative Action Office Policy*. Berkeley: University of California.

Youngblood, S. A. and Cook, K. C. (1984) Child care assistance can improve employee attitudes and behaviour. *Personnel Administrator*, (February), 93–5.

CHAPTER 6
Work–life balance in the 21st century
Nicolina Kamenou

- Introduction
- The changing face of employment
- Work–life balance initiatives and flexible working arrangements
- The legal framework
- Employee well-being and health
- International and contextual considerations in work–life balance debates
- Conclusion
- For discussion and revision
- Further reading
- Case study: Balancing work and life in a non-Western economy
- References

After reading this chapter, you should be able to:

- Understand the changing nature of the workplace and its effects on work–life balance in a global context
- Review the changing nature of employment in relation to issues of work–life balance for different social groups, focusing on gender, age, disability, ethnicity, religion and sexuality
- Outline the range of work–life balance initiatives and flexible working practices
- Outline the legislative context for work and family balance, as well as key equality legislation
- Evaluate the societal and economic benefits and costs in relation to balancing work and life
- Outline key current debates on work–life balance issues in a global context

- Acknowledge, and engage in debates relating to, cultural specificity and variation across countries and regions in terms of issues of work–life balance
- Critically engage with key work–life balance issues through examples, questions and an end-of-chapter case study

Introduction

Globalization, increased competition, a long-hours working culture, people living longer, changes in family structures and evolving legal provisions related to employment and working conditions have a direct effect not only on individuals' workplace experiences, but also on their private and social life experiences.

This chapter engages in key debates on work–life balance (WLB) by taking a global perspective, acknowledging national and cultural differences in how WLB is perceived and how flexible working arrangements are negotiated, and noting diverse legal frameworks and workplace practices dealing with work and employment, rights for parents, carers, and so on. The experiences of social groups, including among others women, older workers and ethnic minority groups, in relation to WLB issues are also explored. A range of WLB organizational initiatives and flexible working types are presented, together with the legal protection associated with these practices. A discussion on the social and economic benefits of a healthy, fulfilled workforce is presented, as is an evaluation of the costs of inaction on the part of organizations and the government, such as the costs of high absenteeism and work-related stress. Key concepts will be evaluated and examples and exercises will be provided throughout the chapter, along with an end-of-chapter case study, in order to help readers engage with critical issues and debates on WLB in varied contexts.

Changing demographics such as the ageing population trend experienced in most developed economies, the increasing number of women in the labour market, renegotiated social roles, the rise in single-parent families and an increased awareness of diversity and legislative changes have had an impact on WLB and governmental and organizational initiatives related to WLB. The increased importance placed on the public image of organizations and the drive to engage in corporate social responsibility initiatives indicate an understanding from the employers' view of the need to engage with well-being and WLB initiatives. Coupled with legal regulation and an acknowledgment of the business case argument – that is, the argument that treating employees with respect, providing flexible working arrangements and acknowledging external-to-work responsibilities can be linked to increased productivity and commitment – this makes a compelling case for treating WLB initiatives as key to organizational success. The Sunday Times 100 Best Companies to Work For, a large-scale survey that focuses on best practice initiatives in relation to people management, includes as some of its key areas 'well-being', which relates to WLB, and 'giving something back', which focuses on whether the organization contributes to its local community and society (http://www.bestcompanies.co.uk, as cited in Bolton and Wibberley, 2007).

It should be noted at this point that the term 'balance' is often deceiving as it implies distinct lives that can be experienced as finite and separate from each other. A central critique, therefore, of discussions on WLB surrounds the problematic notion that a well-balanced approach between paid work and life outside work is assumed to be feasible (Sparrow and Cooper, 2003). The term 'balance' assumes a trade off between work and life, whereas in reality there is great overlap between these two worlds, with 'no clear-cut distinction between the world of work and the work of family, friends and social networks and community' (Taylor, 2002: 17).

Despite this critique, as well as discussions on wide-ranging issues in WLB, most debates in the area have typically assumed a naive view of the 'life' aspect of the WLB equation (Kamenou, 2008). The focus has typically been placed on working mothers and family-friendly policies, but more recently the experiences of fathers and their 'contribution to the home' have been gaining increasing attention (see, for example, Featherstone, 2003; Clarke and O'Brien, 2003). Discussions on juggling work and personal demands have typically ignored issues faced by other groups, for example disabled or older workers or the carers of older or disabled people (Equal Opportunities Commission, n.d.; Gardiner et al., 2007). With few exceptions (see, for example, Rana et al., 1998; Healy et al., 2004; Bradley et al., 2005; Dale, 2005; Kamenou, 2008), issues around ethnicity, culture and religion have also been absent from the majority of discussions around WLB debates and initiatives.

One cannot assume that employment experiences are universal across the world or, indeed, universal within a country or region. Economic, sociopolitical and cultural factors, education systems and family structures will have an effect on individuals' experiences in the workplace, on the centrality of work in people's lives, on how work and family responsibilities are negotiated and on how childcare responsibilities are divided.

The following sections will engage with key issues in relation to work and life, and will critically review changing trends in employment in relation to a number of social groups who have been historically disadvantaged in the labour market. Key equality legislation for the protection of each group will also be cited.

The changing face of employment

Gender

The number of women entering employment has been steadily increasing since World War II, with the male participation rate slowly falling. From 1971 to 2008, the female participation rate increased from 56 per cent to 70 per cent. Within the same period, the male participation rate fell from 92 per cent in 1970 to 79 per cent in 2008 (Office for National Statistics, 2008). This trend is predicted to continue, and some argue that the number of women in the labour market will be higher than that of their male counterparts in the next decade. This has been stated as a key driver for WLB and family-friendly policies in organizations (Kodz et al., 2002; Torrington et al., 2008).

There has also been a rise in the number of single-parent families, with most of these families being headed by women rather than men. The number of dual-career couples is increasing, and this trend makes the effort to 'balance' work and personal life more challenging. It is argued that today's fathers are more 'hands-on' than their own fathers and grandfathers were, and are more willing to share childcare responsibilities. Interestingly, some recent research has indicated that, in dual-career households where women earn the same as or more than their male counterparts, men are willing to help with childcare but are reluctant to support their partners with domestic work (Crompton and Lyonette, 2009). Research indicates that women typically do three-quarters of the domestic work even when they are in paid employment: they do an average of 18.5 hours a week, whereas their male counterparts typically undertake 6 hours a week of domestic work (Kan, 2001).

As stated earlier, the majority of discussions on WLB have focused on women, mainly working mothers. Although this should be acknowledged as a shortcoming in the literature as the experiences of other social groups have, in the majority, been absent, it has to be recognized that gender is a key component of WLB debates – women in the workplace still face disadvantage in employment and career progression, and are still subjected to stereotypical gendered assumptions.

Some seminal research in the UK in the 1990s brought to the forefront the shortcomings of existing organizational cultures in relation to family-friendly policies and WLB issues. Lewis (1997) and Liff and Cameron (1997) argued that there is an underlying assumption that women are not as committed to work and to their careers as their male counterparts, and women are often seen as 'the problem' (Liff and Cameron, 1997). The writers have argued that notions of commitment are therefore gendered, commitment being assessed on male standards such as hours of work and a linear career path with no career breaks. This ignores the unequal distribution of domestic and childcare responsibilities and focuses on inputs (that is, hours at work) rather than outputs (that is, productivity and end results). Moreover, Lewis (1997) argued that two main barriers to effective family-friendly policies are a low sense of entitlement to these policies by employees who do not feel they can utilize them, and organizational discourses of time, which:

> obscure the advantages of alternative ways of working, for the organization as well as for individual employees and their families, and perpetuate organizational structures which interfere with family life, and help to maintain gender inequalities. (Lewis, 1997: 21)

In the UK, a statutory Gender Equality Duty had been enforced from 2007, which required all British public authorities to actively promote gender equality and to eliminate unlawful discrimination and harassment. Such as the UK Equality Act 2010, combine previous equality legislation, including the Sex Discrimination Act 1975.

It has been argued that some countries have made further progress in renegotiating traditional gender roles. Scandinavian countries are often cited as best-practice examples of employment practices, welfare systems and initiatives on well-being. For example, Lamb (2009) contends that gender roles have successfully changed at work and home in Sweden. Swedish social policies presume that couples adopt the dual breadwinner model, which then places the onus on the government and organizations to enable both men and women to be part of the labour force. Through a number of cultural or societal changes, Lamb argues that Sweden has redefined the notion of a 'good father' by emphasizing the need for men to be involved in their children's care. Critical Thinking 6.1 explores some key issues in relation to WLB and fathers in Britain in some more detail, including some questions for readers to consider.

> ### Critical Thinking 6.1
>
> ### Fathers and WLB
>
> An Equality and Human Rights Commission (EHRC) Report has highlighted the tensions that British fathers experience in attempting to balance work and family. It touches on the lack of confidence of many fathers to request flexible working as they fear this would have a negative effect on their career as they could be perceived to be less committed to their organization. The report also states that 45 per cent of men fail to take 2 weeks' paternity leave after their child is born, citing financial reasons for not taking advantage of this policy.
> Andrea Murray, Acting Group Director of Strategy from the EHRC has stated:
>
> Two-thirds of fathers see flexible working as an important benefit when looking for a new job. This highlights an opportunity for British businesses to use flexible working as an incentive for attracting and retaining the most talented of employees. [Such policies have been associated with] increased productivity, reduction in staff turnover, reduced training costs and an ability to respond better to customer requirements.
> Source: Equality and Human Rights Commission (2009).
>
> ### Questions
> 1. What are the longer term implications of fathers not spending time with their children? Think of the impact this situation can have for both home life and organizations.
> 2. Imagine you are an human resources manager. Your organization has well-developed policies on WLB initiatives and flexible working arrangements, but you are aware that the 'take-up' of these initiatives is much lower for male than female staff. You will head a group meeting to discuss ways to encourage all staff who might benefit from these initiatives to utilize them. What would be your main recommendations? What barriers could you envisage facing?

Age

WLB is central to all individuals and should not always be equated with balancing work with family or childcare demands. As discussed earlier in the chapter, developing economies are faced with an ageing population, and this has a profound effect on issues to do with care, retirement and pensions. In the UK, the proportion of people over the age of 65 to people of working age is 21 to 100 (Torrington et al., 2008). It is also predicted that by 2030 more than a quarter of the population will be over 65 (Torrington et al., 2008).

With the age structure of the population changing, the competition for young employees can intensify, and the increase in the group of 35-year-olds and older will increase demand for WLB policies as men and women in this group are likely to have family commitments (Bunting, 2004). With the removal of the compulsory retirement age, the proportion of people over 60 who stay economically active will also increase, and Bunting (2004) argues that this group includes individuals who are disillusioned with work and experience low job satisfaction:

> Meanwhile, those at the beginning of their working lives will increasingly have to consider how they can maintain the intensity of work over the long haul; retirement no longer beckons at sixty, but at seventy or even beyond. (Bunting, 2004: 305)

There are age-related stereotypes labelling older workers as less able to learn and adapt to technology, and younger workers as unmotivated and not experienced. Torrington et al. (2008) argue, however, that, in relation to older workers, there is evidence that people over the age of 50 can perform well and be highly motivated if the appropriate systems and support structures are in place. It is argued that the availability of flexible working arrangements, training, clear performance targets and proactive avoidance of discriminatory practices are central factors in older workers having a positive employment experience, accompanied by job satisfaction and high productivity. Platman (2002)'s study investigated the adoption of 'portfolio' careers as a means in retaining older workers in organizations. The research investigated portfolio careers in the media industry for people over the age of 50, the findings suggesting that this type of career is seen as attractive to this age group as it provides high flexibility in terms of hours and type of work, and does not impose a retirement threshold.

There is legal protection against age discrimination in the European community through the European Union's (EU) Framework Directive for Equal Treatment in Employment and Occupation (2000). This was adopted in the UK in 2006 as the Employment Equality (Age) Regulations. These Regulations cover workers of all ages and all employers, encompassing employment and vocational training, flexible working, retirement, redundancy and pay. Through this legislation, there is now no official retirement age in the UK. The 'standard' or 'default' age is 65, but this is not mandatory. The EU Directive, and subsequently the UK legislation, is seen as a response to the trend of an ageing population and therefore as capitalizing on the available pool of candidates, as well as addressing concerns about labour shortages and about age discrimination in the labour market. Interestingly, protection for age discrimination in the USA, through the Age Discrimination in Employment Act (1967) only protects individuals who are 40 years of age or older. Box 6.1 presents some good practice examples of British organizations that have actively attempted to recruit and develop employees of diverse ages.

Disability

Despite extensive policies and initiatives in the UK focusing on disability, mainly developed under the Labour government, discrimination and disadvantage are

> **Box 6.1 Age-positive British organizations**
>
> - A recent staff survey at supermarket chain Somerfield showed that 80 per cent of employees over the age of 50 felt strongly committed to the company, compared with 62 per cent overall. Similarly, older workers were more likely than others to say they were proud to work for the company.
> - Home improvement company B&Q experienced 39 per cent less short-term absenteeism after employing older workers at one of their locations.
>
> *Source*: Department for Work and Pensions (2007).

still faced by people with disabilities. A lack of understanding and engagement with the varied forms of disability has been exacerbating the marginalization of disabled people. People who have a disability are a highly disparate group in that their disability can vary in terms of its severity, stability and type (Woodhams and Danieli, 2000) and also include mental health issues, learning difficulties and sensory impairments.

Legal protection against disability discrimination was formalized in the UK with the Disability Discrimination Act in 1995 (extended in 2005), which placed the onus on employers to have to make 'reasonable adjustments' to the workplace environment and working arrangements in order to accommodate people with disabilities. Since 2006, the public sector has had specific responsibilities through the Disability Equality Duty. This duty requires employers in public sector organizations to proactively promote equality for disabled people and to carry out equality impact assessments on their policies. Disability discrimination is now covered as part of the New Equality Act 2010, mentioned above.

In terms of the need to balance work and personal life demands, it is important for employers to recognize the needs of staff with a disability or impairment. Staff who have health problems, especially long-term illnesses, are 'in particular need of working practices that facilitate a balance between work demands and life needs' (Hogarth et al., 2001: 253).

Sexual orientation

Falling outside the heterosexual (and male, white, able-bodied) norm is still a challenging situation for lesbian, gay, bisexual and transgender (LGBT) people in employment and society. Discrimination based on sexual orientation is often difficult to identify and challenge as members of the LGBT community may not disclose their sexuality due to fear of exclusion and discrimination. There is legal protection for EU Member States, and the UK's sexual orientation regulations give effect to the requirement in the Equal Treatment Framework Directive through the Employment Equality (Sexual Orientation) Regulations 2003.

The USA does not have federal legislation in place to protect lesbian, gay and bisexual people on sexual orientation grounds (Sargeant, 2009), despite a long-running campaign for national legislation. States and municipalities had the option to enforce legislation at that level, but they also had the option not to; 15 states actually have anti-gay partnership laws in place (Howenstine, 2006).

Sargeant (2009: 639) argues that lesbians, gay men, bisexuals and transgender people are placed in one category mainly for convenience in terms of identifying 'the discriminatory treatment that they jointly suffer as a result of not conforming to the expectations of a heterosexist society'. The author argues that the life experiences and discrimination faced by the 'LGBT group' are not identical and that there is a distinction in law between lesbians, gay men and bisexuals as a group and transgender people as a separate group. Sargeant's (2009) paper explores issues of LGBT elders from a UK and a US perspective. There is very limited research on LGBT elders, and this paper argues that this group experience particular discrimination that is unique and different from the experiences of elders in general and heterosexual elders in particular.

There is little academic research on lesbian and gay parents and their experiences in the workplace and society. A report by the American Psychological Association (2005) cited research comparing the children of lesbian and gay parents with the children of heterosexual parents, and indicated that common stereotypes of the effect of gay parenting on children's sexuality and development were not supported. Early studies focused on middle-class, well-educated families, but recent research has acknowledged differences in terms of ethnicity, socioeconomic statues and regions (American Psychological Association, 2005).

Race, ethnicity, culture and religion

Protection from race discrimination in the UK came in the form of the Race Relations Act 1976 and the Race Relations (Amendment) Act 2000, and there is now protection through the Equality Act 2010. The UK public sector also has specific responsibilities through the Race Equality Duty. In terms of religion or belief, the EU's Employment Equality (Religion or Belief) Regulations 2003 provide protection for groups or individuals on the grounds of their religion or belief. An important effect of this legislation is the fact that religious groups who do not share a common ethnicity are now protected from discrimination.

As mentioned earlier in this chapter, when engaging in debates on WLB, an understanding of the diversity of forms of life and life experiences is crucial. Factors such as race, religion and culture may have an effect on how individuals conceptualize and experience key issues in terms of both their work and their personal life. Issues such as religious responsibilities, caring for extended families, and priorities in different regions and countries in relation to WLB are very important to consider. At the same time, one should not generalize and assume that specific ethnic or religious groups would behave in a specific way – the main point is that diversity should be acknowledged both within and across groups.

An area that has been receiving more attention in recent years is the impact of the interaction of gender with race, culture and religion on work and societal experiences. This section will present some key literature and key arguments in relation to ethnic minority women, focusing on their experiences in terms of work and life.

In relation to domestic labour and household structures, Gardiner (1997) has proposed that there are different experiences across racial and ethnic groups. Carby

(1982) argued, for example, that the experiences of African-American and Black Caribbean women were shaped by the history of slavery and colonialism. Gardiner (1997) also contended that full-time motherhood was never dominant for this group of women as there was a necessity to work full time to support their families. More recent data support these views, with Duncan and Irwin (2004: 394) suggesting that Caribbean mothers are more likely to see 'substantial hours in employments as a built-in component of good mothering' and to accept that they have the primary responsibility for childcare and domestic responsibilities as well as taking the necessity to work for granted.

Bhopal (1997: 4) contended that South Asian women's experiences may be different from those from African and Caribbean communities in that 'the specific cultural norms and standards of South Asian families may be reinforced through different forms of patriarchy experienced by women'. In addition, South Asian women may experience oppression 'by the form of marriage they participate in, the giving of dowries, participating in domestic labour and the degree of control they have in domestic finance'. She argued that although South Asian communities are diverse, there are similarities that place them in a different setting from white communities: 'there is the primacy of family over the individual ... with emphasis on child rearing and family interaction patterns for both males and females' (Bhopal, 1997: 7).

Research supports the contention that a major factor of stress for ethnic minority women is their perception of living two separate lives (Bell, 1986; Denton, 1990; Davidson, 1997; Kamenou, 2008). Thomas and Aldefer (1989: 135) define this as 'bicultural stress': 'the set of emotional and physical upheavals produced by a bicultural existence'. Bell et al. (1993: 118–19) have argued that 'circumstances often dictate that, for women of colour to be successful managers, they must adopt a new identity and abandon commitment to their old culture [of racial or ethnic community]'. The bicultural stress can be intensified by the fact that the ethnic minority women's own communities may perceive them as 'traitors' when they try to fit in the white dominant culture of their organizations (Bell et al., 1993).

It is important, therefore, to acknowledge the diversity of experiences when focusing on work and life debates as placing all women – and men – in predetermined groups, regardless of their ethnicity, socioeconomic status, age or other factors, which assumes a naive understanding of the different societal and work experiences. Acknowledging different forms of life is crucial in order to engage in a realistic analysis that can inform organizational policy and practice (Kamenou, 2008).

Critical Thinking 6.2 engages in a key discussion on the interaction between choice and structural constraints in the context of employment and career development.

Work–life balance initiatives and flexible working arrangements

The chapter now turns to a review of a number of WLB initiatives and flexible working arrangements.

The majority of WLB initiatives focus on arrangements to help parents or carers with children or older and disabled family members. These initiatives typically include a number of flexible working arrangements, as discussed below, as well as

Critical Thinking 6.2

All about choice?

There have been ongoing debates on the importance of agency and the strategies that women and other social groups employ in determining their own career path. Hakim (1991, 1995, 2004) has argued that agency is central to women's choices in terms of decisions on whether they focus on their job or career, or whether they choose to focus on their family. Hakim has been heavily criticized for assuming that everyone can make free choices without acknowledging structural constraints (Devine, 1994; Ginn et al., 1996; McRae, 2003).

On the other side of the debate, some writers analysing women's position in the labour market have focused on the limitations imposed by structures for women's opportunities and advancement (see, for example, Walby, 1983, 1986; Bhopal, 1997). Walby's theory of patriarchy (1983, 1986) has been criticized for its indifference to the practices and motivation of individuals. As Collinson et al. (1990: 48) have argued, Walby is 'unable to explain how these social structures are constituted, and this inevitably results in a theory of patriarchy which is heavily deterministic as well as economistic'.

A number of writers have argued that an acknowledgement of the interaction of structure and agency, as well as culture, is needed when examining the impact of gender on employment (see, for example, Devine, 1994; Evetts, 2000) and of ethnicity and gender on career development (see, for instance, Kamenou, 2002, 2008).

Questions

1. In the context of the agency versus structure debate, reflect on key issues discussed in this chapter in relation to WLB. How important to do you think women's and men's choices are in relation to balancing work and life?
2. What would you consider to be the key constraints in taking up flexible working and other WLB initiatives offered in organizations?
3. Do you think there are issues or concerns that may affect some social groups more than others? Extend your discussions beyond a focus on gender, to include other groups such as ethnic minority or disabled groups.

---

the possibility of on-site crèche facilities and childcare allowances. There is, however, a trend, mainly for larger organizations, to provide programmes that can benefit all of their employees; these typically centre around well-being, reducing stress and providing support. Free or subsidized health club memberships are now common in larger organizations, as are health insurance provisions. Some organizations also provide opportunities for counselling for staff who may be facing work and also personal problems. There is a wide range of flexible working arrangements, the most common being:

- part-time work;
- flexible hours;

- job-sharing;
- career breaks;
- working from home/working remotely (teleworking);
- seasonal hours;
- term-time work;
- shift-swapping;
- compressed working time;
- unpaid leave/unpaid sabbatical.

Box 6.2 provides an insight into some key WLB policies at IBM Corporation.

Dieckhoff and Gallie (2007) cite flexible working arrangements as being high on the EU agenda of economic inclusion and adaptability. The UK government policy on flexible working focuses on the business case argument; that is, the focus is on the benefits to employers and business. Policy and practice in relation to WLB and flexible working in EU countries have in the main focused on the parents of young children, but as discussed earlier in the chapter, there has been more attention recently on other groups, such as older workers and carers.

'Flexible work' is typically seen as work outside the 'standard' arrangements of permanent, fixed daytime work of between 30 and 48 hours a week and working 'on site' (Tomlinson and Gardiner, 2009). Booth and Frank (2005), as cited in Tomlinson and Gardiner (2009), found that only two-fifths of male and female

---

Box 6.2 WLB policies at IBM

IBM is a multinational computer, technology and IT consulting corporation with its headquarters in New York, USA. It is a company often cited for its progressive WLB policies and flexible work initiatives. Some of the more innovative policies at IBM include:

- **The Self Funded Leave policy**: as stated on the IBM website, this 'policy provides scope for employees to "purchase" one to four weeks additional leave in a calendar year. This ... is in addition to normal annual entitlements. All participants in the program need to take their annual leave entitlements as well as this additional leave.'
- **Men@Work:** the Men@Work program is a 2-day program allowing men to address issues such as balancing work and family issues, physical and psychological concerns, discussions on relationships, and so on.
- **Work Life Essentials:** this online portal assists IBM staff in sourcing information to help manage their work and life. The portal offers access to a wide variety of information on childcare, eldercare, multimedia resources, useful readings, seminars and educational resources, divided into three sections: Caring for the Family, Caring for Me and Caring for My Employees.

Source: IBM website, Work Life Flexibility Programs; http://www-07.ibm.com/au/diversity/work_life_balance_programs.html (accessed April 2010).

employees have 'standard' jobs in the UK. As a number of writers have argued (see, for example, Lewis, 1997; Liff and Cameron, 1997), the notion of 'standard' work assumes a male model of work characterized by continuous employment with no career breaks. There is, however, a gender dimension as research indicates that women are less likely to have this linear career model and more likely to work on a casual basis or in part-time contracts, to have career breaks and to work from home. Tomlinson and Gardiner (2009) also argue that there are gender differences in terms of the requests for flexible working. Men typically request 'flexi-time', while women more often request a reduction in hours, be it permanent or temporary.

Existing research alerts us to the dangers of flexible working arrangements as they often reinforce gendered working patterns rather than challenge them. The rhetoric, therefore, of flexible working assuming more engagement from a wider talent pool, and consequently increased productivity and commitment, may be conflated by the reality of employers using arrangements that suit them and their business, with no real impact on the gendered culture of organizations.

Guest's (1987, 1989) normative model of human resource management (HRM), based on four key dimensions (strategic integration, commitment, flexibility – numerical and functional – and quality) has been criticized in relation to equality. HRM appears to promote equality as the emphasis is on attracting, retaining and fostering the commitment of the 'best people' for the job, regardless of irrelevant characteristics such as gender or race. The critique focuses on the argument that, in reality, HRM may be a barrier to equality as individuals may foster their own interests, there are power relations at play, and there may be a desire to maintain the status quo of inequality in order to utilize people for the benefit of the organization. For example, organizations may benefit from a system in which peripheral labour is cheaper and available on demand, with fewer benefits for individuals working at lower levels of the organization or on casual or fixed-term contracts. Such a system reinforces existing inequalities and horizontal and vertical segregation.

Exercise

- What issues do women – and men – face in employment today in relation to balancing work and personal life commitments?
- There may be additional concerns for other social groups (that is, ethnic minority groups, people with disabilities and so on) in relation to balancing work and life. Discuss.

The legal framework

The legal framework has been developing in the area of employment and work practices, and legislation has been a key driver for developing organizational policies on family-friendly policies and, more widely, on WLB. UK legislation has been mostly driven by EU Directives, and a number of legal provisions were significantly extended in April 2003. The UK government introduced a 10-year strategy for childcare in 2004, which included proposals to extend existing statutory provisions on maternity and paternity leave. These provisions resulted in the Work and Families Act 2006 (Box 6.3), mostly effective from April 2007 onwards.

Continental Europe provides more comprehensive and equitable childcare arrangements than the UK. France, Denmark and Sweden offer publicly funded childcare, which has an effect in increasing female participation rates. The provision of parental leave is higher than in Britain, with 3 years offered in France, Sweden

---

Box 6.3 Provisions of the UK Work and Families Act 2006

- Annual leave: all staff are entitled to a minimum of 28 days' paid annual holiday, and from April 2009 Bank Holidays could be counted towards this.
- Working time: this is limited to 48 hours, unless 'opted out'. The Working Time Regulations provide for minimum rest periods and have provisions for night work.
- Parental leave: there is a right to 13 weeks' unpaid parental leave for men and women at any time up to their child's fifth birthday.
- Time off for dependant care (for family emergencies, elderly dependants, children, etc.) can be granted.
- Maternity leave: all women are entitled to 9 months' paid leave with the option of an 3 additional months on an unpaid basis. In terms of paternity leave, fathers under this Act were initially entitled to 2 weeks' paid paternity leave. In April 2010 it was announced that Additional Paternity Leave and Pay (APL&P) would enable eligible fathers to take up to 26 weeks' additional paternity leave. The leave may be paid if taken during the mother or partner's Statutory Maternity Pay period, Maternity Allowance period or Statutory Adoption Pay period, but leave taken after this period has ended will be unpaid. (http://www.bis.gov.uk/policies/employment-matters/strategies/paternity-leave)
- Adoption leave: there is entitlement to 26 weeks' ordinary adoption leave and 26 weeks' additional adoption leave.
- Right to request flexible working: employees with children under the age of 17 (under the age 18 if child is disabled) and those with caring responsibilities for adults can request a change to their working arrangements. The employer can refuse such a request on business grounds but needs to follow procedures to do so.
- Part-time work: part-timers are entitled to the same hourly rate of pay and have the same entitlements to annual leave and maternity/parental leave as full-timers on a pro-rata basis. There is the same entitlement to sick pay and the same treatment in terms of access to training.
- Detriment: an employer cannot subject an employee to a detriment because he or she has attempted to exercise the rights mentioned above. This can be taken to an employment tribunal.

Source: Chartered Institute of Personnel and Development. Work–Life Balance Factsheet; http://www.cipd.co.uk/subjects/health/worklifebalance/worklifeba [accessed March 2010].

and Denmark, and with higher levels of pay. In Norway, a component of parental leave is only available to fathers in order to encourage men to take it up. Bunting (2004) cites a remarkable rise in the take-up rate of this, which increased from a mere 2 per cent in 1990 to 85 per cent in 2000. The author also cites examples from Italy, Spain and Belgium, where parents have the flexibility to spread out parental leave over a number of years.

Employee well-being and health

The implications of a long-hours culture in which commitment is often linked to inputs rather than outputs can have a negative effect on employees. As Noon and Blyton (1997) have argued, individual working hours do not always equate to an organization's operating hours, and more flexibility is demanded to serve a '24/7 society'. There is wide evidence of work intensification over the last couple of decades and of increased levels of stress. Stress is now seen as a common phenomenon in the workplace, with wide-ranging negative implications for both workers and employers. Studies have indicated that individuals in employment have been suffering from anxiety and have been experiencing work overload, loss of control and insufficient personal time (Holbeche and McCartney, 2002).

Other writers have argued that employers will occur 'costs of inaction' (see, for example, Liff and Cameron, 1997; Sparrow and Cooper, 2003) if they do not attempt to challenge the long-hours, input-driven work cultures. Some of these costs include poor health, overwork resulting in stress and stress-related illnesses, dissatisfaction, family conflicts, higher absenteeism, lower productivity and high staff turnover. Existing work cultures implicitly demand that work takes priority over everything else, including family. Bunting (2004), in her book *Willing Slaves: How the Overwork culture is Ruling our Lives*, warns about the dangers of the British overwork culture (Box 6.4) and its negative effects on our own health and the health of our children, as well as the negative impact on relationships between parents and their children.

> **Box 6.4   Working hours: overly committed or overly stretched?**
>
> Coats (2007) argues that the UK government may need to adopt an interventionist stance and reconsider its position in relation to the EU Working Time Directive (1993) and the UK's Working Time Regulations 1998. Coats contends that the UK government should consider a phased approach to the removal of the opt-out from the 48-hour maximum working week that the EU Working Time Directive advocates. He argues that this initiative was adopted in the Republic of Ireland with no adverse impact on economic growth or employment.
>
> Bunting (2004: 304) argues that, in many European countries, long hours at work are considered as 'a sign of inefficiency or incompetence, rather than of commitment as it is in overwork cultures'. A number of the UK's neighbours, such as Austria, Finland, Spain and Sweden, have limits of 39- or 40-hour weeks.

> Bunting also cites Australia and New Zealand as countries with an 'overwork culture' and states this is mainly due to the deregulation of the labour market: 'the number of male employees working more than eleven hours a day jumped from one in eighteen to one in eight between 1974 and 1997' (2004: 302).

International and contextual considerations in work–life balance debates

Throughout the chapter, examples were cited in countries outside the UK, mainly in Europe and in the USA, in relation to their involvement with work and life issues. This section will provide further discussion and some illustrations of key issues in different contexts, including non-Western societies such as Africa, India and Japan, as well as issues facing employees, including expatriates, in multinational corporations (MNCs) around the world.

Within international HRM research, issues are intertwined with the theories and practices of cross-cultural management and diversity management. As Özbilgin (2005: 164) argues 'the international level, by definition, embodies a greater level of diversity than the national level'. At the international level, Stephens and Black (1991), as cited in Özbilgin (2005), noted the significance of WLB issues in a study on 67 American expatriate managers and argued that recognizing the career aspirations of the expatriates' spouses and partners was an important area to consider within international HRM.

Shaffer et al. (2001) explored the impact of perceived organizational support and of work–family conflict on the psychological withdrawal of expatriates, and identified that both these factors have a direct effect on their decision to quit international assignments. These two studies highlight the importance of a better understanding of work–family issues and of the needs of family members accompanying expatriates on international assignments. This understanding of and sensitivity to key issues can provide organizations with an important insight into the issues faced by international staff, and in turn to higher chances of the international assignments being successfully completed.

De Cieri and Bardoel (2008), in their study of 13 MNCs, identified key tensions in relation to the management of work–life issues. Participants in their research, mainly human resources and diversity managers, contended that WLB was important for talent management and for developing a high-performing workforce. As the authors state (p. 31): 'Managers and employees are beginning to recognize the strategic role of global work–life policies and practices in managing a global workforce; this presents several challenges for the [human resources] function in MNCs.'

As stated earlier in the chapter, it is important, when engaging with debates on balancing work and personal life, to recognize the diversity of experience in terms of regions, culture and nationality. Lewis et al. (2007) argue, however, that the WLB concept originated in a Western, neo-liberal context, particularly in the USA and the UK. This is not to argue that issues and tensions in balancing work and family/personal lives are not universal concerns. However, the context in which one operates should be kept in mind when attempting to understand these concerns as a model based on a Westernized, developed economy setting, with a reliance on market forces, may not be applicable to a developing, non-Westernized emerging economy. In the latter situation, other issues, such as rapid industrialization, security and efforts to maintain traditional family structures may be at play (Box 6.5). Recent work on the negotiated self and work identities of Indian call-centre workers has highlighted WLB tensions and stress for these workers, in the context of global outsourcing (see, for example, Aryee et al., 2005; D'Cruz and Noronha, 2008).

> **Box 6.5 WLB in non-Western economies**
>
> Lewis et al.'s (2007) study of WLB tensions involved interviews with participants in seven countries, including India, South Africa and Japan. They argue that work intensification is becoming a global phenomenon, in which long hours are equated with commitment in the context of a 'new economy'. The authors cite a participant in a South African country meeting as stating: 'You work long hours, and then you are seen as really making a difference.' An Indian management consultant is also cited as arguing that the long-hours culture 'has become so entrenched ... especially in the new economy ... we've got to work hard and ... literally give up our personal lives' (Lewis et al., 2007: 366). There is increasing attention to work–life balance challenges in Japan, partly due to the context of very low birth rates, and there are ongoing debates on how to further engage men in domestic and childcare work. One female participant argued however that:
>
> There is a two-tier workforce in Japan. One, which is very highly career orientated, which is described as full-time work and is largely dominated by men. The second is part-time work, which lacks any of the benefits associated with full-time work and is largely dominated by women. [Men] are seen as the breadwinners and they are desperate to get jobs that enable them to provide economically for current or future families. (p. 364)

Conclusion

This chapter has critically reviewed key WLB theories, debates and pertinent issues. It has been argued that most WLB debates have assumed a naive view of the 'life' aspect, and this chapter has attempted to provide a more balanced perspective on key issues. It has engaged with changing trends in the workplace, acknowledging the diversity of experiences across social groups and across regions. It has been highlighted throughout that both researchers and managers should be sensitive to this diversity and should not attempt to prescribe a 'one-size-fits-all' approach when offering suggestions and solutions to balancing work and personal life demands.

Some areas emerging through the discussions have focused on the dangers of equating commitment and productivity with a long-hours culture, where input is considered as more important than output. The Work Foundation (Chartered Institute of Personnel and Development, 2003) contends that managers need to shift the way they measure staff, focusing on performance and outputs. A shake-up of the existing organizational cultures and a shift to a more supportive environment, where all individuals are valued irrespective of characteristics such as gender, race and age, is crucial. In addition, the involvement of human resources as well as line managers in supporting this change and leading by example cannot be overestimated.

Glynn et al. (2002) suggest a range of management skills needed in promoting and managing flexibility, including planning, delegating fairly, understanding the capacity and skills of their staff, and being able to resist pressure from other parts of their organization when demands are deemed unrealistic. In addition to these skills, there is a need to identify a business case for WLB initiatives as this should provide organizations and staff with a clear rationale for the benefits to themselves and, in the latter case, their employers. Adapting policies to operational needs, monitoring progress and highlighting success stories are also positive steps that organizations can take in the quest for a better balance between work and life (whatever form that life may take).

As indicated through international examples, managers should be aware of differences in terms of priorities and perspectives in different regions across the world. An understanding of socioeconomic, political and cultural settings is fundamental in devising and implementing appropriate WLB policies that employers and employees can embrace and benefit from.

FOR DISCUSSION AND REVISION

1. What areas do WLB debates seem to be focusing on?
2. Would you consider this to be limiting? If so, in what way?
3. What can be the costs of an 'overwork' culture to both employees and organizations?
4. What key legislation can you cite which protects social groups from discrimination?
5. What legislation can you cite in relation to employment and work and life?
6. Highlight key differences in how employers and employees may be dealing with WLB in different regions. Think of examples in the Western, developed economies and also in non-Western, emerging markets.
7. If you were a senior human resources manager in an MNC who has been transferred to the Chinese office, how would you attempt to implement the flexible working arrangements and family-friendly policies designed at the parent company? What issues would you need to consider?

Further reading

Books

Burke, R. J and Cooper, C. L. (2008) *The Long Hours Culture: Causes, Consequences and Choices.* Bingley: Emerald Group.
An edited collection of chapters on key issues of WLB, divided into three sections of causes, consequences and choices.

Chartered Institute of Personnel and Development (2000) *Getting the Right Work–life Balance*. London: CIPD.

This research report by M. Coussey from the University of Cambridge engages with a number of real-life case studies focusing on work and life and family-friendly practices.

Felstead, A. and Jewson, N. (1999) *Global Trends in Flexible Labour*. London: Macmillan Business.

An edited book with chapters from numerous authors on flexible work and non-standard forms of employment. It includes discussions and research from European countries, such as Germany, Spain, Sweden and the UK.

Heery, E. and Salmon, J. (2000) *The Insecure Workforce*. London: Routledge.

An edited collection of chapters focusing on the 'insecurity thesis' and looking at this in a variety of contexts, such as the public sector, 'gendered employment', the psychological contract, trade unions and so on.

Houston, D. M. (2005) *Work–Life Balance in the 21st Century*. Basingstoke: Palgrave Macmillan.

An edited collection of chapters on a wide range of WLB issues including gender, careers, fatherhood, job insecurity, ethnicity and organizational cultures.

Other resources

Readers are also encouraged to utilize the following relevant websites that provide numerous articles, statistics and information on WLB issues:

- The Chartered Institute of Personnel and Development (CIPD): www.cipd.co.uk
- The Equality and Human Rights Commission (EHRC): http://www.equalityhumanrights.com/
- The HRM guide: http://www.hrmguide.co.uk/

CASE STUDY

Balancing work and life in a non-Western economy

Adesuwa woke up at 5:15 am to start getting ready for her job as a human resources manager in a large Nigerian bank in the busy city of Lagos. If she wanted to avoid the hectic Lagos traffic jam, she would need to leave the house by 6 am. At this time, it would only take her 20 minutes to reach the office, but if she set off any later, it could take more than 2 hours to cover the short distance. She was already dreading another long day; the return journey would be quicker if she stayed at work till about 7 pm. Her husband, Osagie, was also up and getting ready for a similar day.

Their two daughters were still peacefully asleep. They were growing up so fast: Itohan was 2 and Egie was 4 years old. She was very thankful to her parents, especially her mother, for all their help and support with the girls. Her mother and father were staying with her and Osagie, and were often relied upon to help with the kids. She couldn't help feeling guilty, though, for missing out on her children's everyday life. She wasn't sure her mum was aware of it, but she would make comments that made Adesuwa feel like a bad parent. She would often say, as Adesuwa came through the front door after a hard day at work, 'Oh, you are home … the girls kept crying and asking for you all day.' But her mum would never say anything similar to Osagie. Comments from both her parents that she never has the time to fulfil her home responsibilities didn't help the tension she constantly felt when she was in the office.

When she arrived at work to start another day in the bank, her boss, Mr Adebayo, was standing by her desk with a large pile of staff appraisals that she need to review and countersign. They were needed by lunchtime, he mentioned on his way out. After the consolidation of Nigerian banks a few years before, competition had increased in the industry, and senior managers in her bank kept reminding staff 'how lucky' they were to have a job. This didn't really help the already tense situation, and there was a feeling of insecurity and competitiveness. The old culture of support and encouragement, which she had encountered before the consolidation, was no longer present, and Adesuwa felt that everyone was out for themselves and wanted to showcase their own individual achievements.

Adesuwa had been working as a human resources manager in this bank for 2 years, but she didn't feel she connected with her colleagues: everyone was always so busy and focused on their work. She could see, however, that staff were not necessarily productive, although they were very keen to be 'seen to be working'. Her relationship with her boss, although always courteous and professional, was sometimes strained as she felt he was not willing to listen to anything critical about the company or its processes or procedures. They had been working together for the 2 years Adesuwa had been at the bank, but he had never asked her any questions about her personal circumstances. He probably didn't even know she had young children, he never asked where she lived, whether she was driving into work or anything to do with her life outside her work. It was clear to all of his staff that he just expected everyone, men and women, to be committed to the organization, and he would often be overheard saying 'we need to put the company first'. Adesuwa knew that Mr Adebayo had teenage sons and that his wife never worked but took care of the home.

She didn't like complaining about how stressed and guilty she often felt, though, as she thought it made her sound selfish. She had a good job, security and a good enough salary. She knew of other friends and colleagues who were really struggling to make ends meet, and some had lost their jobs. She craved, however, for an organization that would at least acknowledge staff's non-work responsibilities and demands. Flexibility or flexible policies were never discussed as an option at the bank. When you were hired, it was assumed you would work full time – although it often felt like she working two days in one, from 6:30 am to 7:30 pm. There was never any acknowledgment or explicit appreciation of her hard work and the long hours she put in.

Her husband was starting to get frustrated with the demands Adesuwa's job was placing on her. He kept mentioning that he had married her and not her mother. Her mum, he would say, was the one taking care of their children and the home. Adesuwa felt Osagie didn't appreciate that this was not a clear-cut choice for her; it wasn't as if she didn't want to spend more time with her children or even just have time to rest and unwind. She sometimes contemplated looking for another job with more flexibility, but from her preliminary investigations, she knew the salary would not be as good – and they needed the money.

Adesuwa was almost half way through the appraisal forms. It was 10:30 am and she was already exhausted. She had four meetings scheduled in the afternoon and still had to prepare for two of them, but her mind was elsewhere. Her mum had told her the previous night that she and her father were 'too old to be full-time parents for the second time'. Adesuwa didn't know what to do. She had been talking to another female human resources manager, Grace, who had been facing similar issues, but neither of them could find a way round their problems and recurring guilt. Adesuwa enjoyed her job, she knew she was good at it, and she prided herself in being known as conscientious and reliable. She had ambitions to progress further, but she also felt she was missing out on so much at home. Her husband had mentioned a couple of times recently that if he started making more money, she could stop working, but she didn't want that. It was now 12 pm and she had finished countersigning all the forms. She had about 15 minutes for a quick early lunch, and then she would need to go straight into her meetings.

Her boss was still at work when she started getting ready to leave at 7:15 that evening. He had another couple of hours of work to get through before he could leave. Adesuwa looked exhausted when he saw her leaving. She was a hard worker and he valued her contribution to his team. He knew she was struggling with the long hours at work and with having two young girls at home. A few times he thought of chatting to her about it and telling her that she was working 'over and above the call of duty', but he was unsure about acknowledging this openly. He didn't want her to start thinking that she could get a better job elsewhere as this would mean losing one of his best employees.

Adesuwa opened the front door to her home at 8 that evening. Her mum had managed to keep the girls awake so she could at least hold them and play with them for the next 20 minutes or so. They were tired though, so they were fast asleep by 9. Her husband walked in as her mum was laying the table for them to eat. Adesuwa could hardly hold a conversation as she was eating her dinner. She could feel her mum's disapproving stare on her, but she chose not to acknowledge it or say anything. She and Osagie got up, said goodnight to her parents and went to bed exhausted, knowing that the next day would be very similar to the one they had just had.

Some background/context for guidance

A consolidation exercise of Nigerian banks took place in 2005, and a number of banks merged at that point. The case study uses this background as the relevant context in order to acknowledge tensions, job insecurities and increased competition that might have developed following this change.

Some key issues to be considered relate to the culture of the organization and the hesitation experienced by Adesuwa's boss, Mr Adebayo, in acknowledging the demands of Adesuwa's life outside work. It seems that his situation is different as he has a wife at home and older children, and he may be lacking an understanding of the demands on a dual-career couple. His views with regard to recognizing his employees' hard work is also a concern as this management style can create alienation, resentment and eventually a higher turnover, which is what Adesuwa's boss is trying to avoid. There are no flexible policies in the organization, and students should discuss this as well as the culture of the organization, where 'presenteeism' seems to equate to commitment.

In the home, Adesuwa is expected to 'take care of the home', and both her husband and parents seem – implicitly or explicitly – to have that expectation. Her work is not considered to be as important as her home demands, and although she receives much practical support, mainly from her mum, this does not always alleviate the tension and guilt she is feeling.

Students should engage with both work and personal life experiences, discuss the context/background to the case study, and acknowledge potential cultural differences in terms of the region/country in which this case study is situated. They should suggest organizational developments, such as the development of flexible work and/or family-friendly policies in the organization. There is no 'one solution' to the problems presented here, but instead a critical engagement, using material, literature and examples from the chapter, should guide students in answering the questions below.

Questions

1. What are the key issues Adesuwa is facing at work and at home?
2. Is she receiving support from her organization? What is her relationship with her manager?
3. What areas could be improved at work to help her better balance her work and personal life demands?
4. Is she receiving support from her family? What is the form of this support? Could her husband and parents further support her in order to alleviate her stress?
5. Could the long work hours that both Adesuwa and Osagie experience have an impact on their relationship with their daughters? In what ways?
6. Could there be any cultural elements that readers need to be sensitive in when offering their suggestions?

Guided reading

Ituma, A. and Simpson, R. (2007) Moving beyond Schein's typology: individual career anchors in the context of Nigeria. *Personnel Review*, 36(6): 978–95.

Lewis, S., Gambles, R. and Rapoport, R. (2007) The constraints of a work–life balance approach: an international perspective. *International Journal of Human Resource Management*, 18(3): 360–73.

Kamenou, N. (2008) Reconsidering work–life balance debates: challenging limited understandings of the 'life' component in the context of ethnic minority women's experiences. Special Issue on Gender in Management: new theoretical perspectives. *British Journal of Management*, 19(S1): S99–109.

References

American Psychological Association (2005) *Lesbian and Gay Parenting*. Washington: APA.

Aryee, S., Srinivas, E. S. and Tan, H. H. (2005) Rhythms of life: antecedents and outcomes of work–family balance in employed parents. *Journal of Applied Psychology*, 90(1): 132–46.

Bell, E. L. (1986) The power within: bicultural life structures and stress among black women. Unpublished PhD dissertation, Case Western Reserve University.

Bell, E. L., Denton, T., C. and Nkomo, S. (1993) Women of color in management: towards an inclusive analysis. In Larwood, L. and Gutek, B. (eds), *Women in Management: Trends, Issues, and Challenges in Managerial Diversity*. California: Sage.

Bhopal, K. (1997) *Gender, 'Race' and Patriarchy: A Study of South Asian Women*. Farnham: Ashgate.

Bolton, S. C. and Wibberley, G. (2007) Best companies, best practice and dignity at work. In Bolton, S. C. (ed.), *Dimensions of Dignity at Work*. Burlington: Butterworth-Heinemann, pp. 134–53.

Booth, A. L. and Frank, J. (2005) Gender and work–life flexibility in the labour market. In Houston, D. M. (ed.), *Work–life Balance in the 21st Century*. Basingstoke: Palgrave Macmillan, pp. 11–28.

Bradley, H., Healy, G. and Mukherjee, N. (2005) Multiple burdens: problems of work–life balance for ethnic minority trade union activist women. In Houston, D. (ed.), *Work–life Balance in the 21st Century*. Basingstoke: Palgrave Macmillan, pp. 211–29.

Bunting, M. (2004) *Willing Slaves: How the Overwork Culture is Ruling Our Lives*. London: HarperCollins.

Carby, H. V. (1982) White women listen! Black feminism and the boundaries of sisterhood. In Centre for Contemporary Cultural Studies. *The Empire Strikes Back: Race and Racism in 70s Britain*. London: Hutchinson, pp. 212–35.

Chartered Institute of Personnel and Development (2003) Managers obstruct flexibility. *People Management*, 9(18): 9.

Clarke, L. and O'Brien, M. (2003) Father involvement in Britain: the research and policy evidence. In Day, R. and Lamb, M. (eds), *Reconceptualising and Measuring Fatherhood*. Mahwah, NJ: Lawrence Erlbaum, pp. 34–52.

Coats, D. (2007) Respect at work: just how good are British workplaces? In Bolton, S. C. (ed.), *Dimensions of Dignity at Work*. Burlington: Butterworth-Heinemann, pp. 53–70.

Collinson, D., Knights, D. and Collinson, M. (1990) *Managing to Discriminate*. London: Routledge.

Crompton, R. and Lyonnette, C. (2009) Partners' Relative Earnings and the Domestic Division of Labour. Paper presented at the Gender Inequalities in the 21st Century, Queen's College, Cambridge, 26–27 March.

Dale, A. (2005) Combining family and employment: evidence from Pakistani and Bangladeshi women. In Houston, D. (ed.), *Work–Life Balance in the 21st Century*. Basingstoke: Palgrave Macmillan, pp. 230–45.

Davidson, M. J. (1997) *The Black and Ethnic Minority Woman Manager: Cracking the Concrete Ceiling*. London: Paul Chapman.

D'Cruz, P. and Noronha, E. (2008) Doing emotional labour: the experiences of Indian call centre agents. *Global Business Review*, 9: 131–47.

De Cieri, H. and Bardoel, E. A. (2008) Tensions for HR: Who Takes Responsibility for Work–Life Management in Multinational Corporations? Final Report to the Society for Human Resource Management (SHRM) Research Foundation. Based on a paper presented to the Academy of International Business Annual Conference, June 30 – July 4, Milan, Italy.

Denton, T. C. (1990) Bonding and supportive relationships among black professional women: rituals of restoration. *Journal of Organizational Behavior*, 11: 447–57.

Department for Work and Pensions (2007) Flexible Retirement and Retirement: Age Positive Guide. Available from: http://www.dwp.gov.uk/docs/AP_Retirement_Guide.pdf [accessed 9 September 2011].

Devine, F. (1994) Segregation and supply: preferences and plans among 'self-made' women. *Gender, Work and Organization*, 1(2): 94–109.

Dieckhoff, M. and Gallie, D. (2007) The renewed Lisbon strategy and social inclusion policy. *Industrial Relations Journal*, 38(6): 480–502.

Duncan, S. and Irwin, S. (2004) The social patterning of values and rationalities: mothers' choices in combining caring and employment. *Social Policy and Society*, 3(4): 391–9.

Equality and Human Rights Commission (2009) Fathers Struggling to Balance Work and Family: Working Dads Want More Time with Their Children. Available from: http://www.equalityhumanrights.com/media-centre/october-2009/fathers-struggling-to-balance-work-and-family/ [accessed 9 September 2011]

Equal Opportunities Commission (n.d.) Policy Statement: Carers and Work–Life Balance. Available from:http://www.eoc.org.uk/Default.aspx?page=15440 [accessed August 2006].

Evetts, J. (2000) Analysing change in women's careers: culture, structure and action dimensions. *Gender, Work and Organization*, 7(1): 57–67.

Featherstone, B. (2003) Taking fathers seriously. *British Journal of Social Work*, 33: 239–54.

Gardiner, J. (1997) *Gender, Care and Economics*, Basingstoke: Macmillan.

Gardiner, J., Stuart, M., Forde, C., Greenwood, I., MacKenzie, R. and Perrett, R. (2007) Work–life balance and older workers: employees' perspectives on retirement transitions following redundancy. *International Journal of Human Resource Management*, 18(3): 476–89.

Ginn, J., Arber, S., Brannen, J., Dale, A., Dex, S., Elias, P., et al. (1996) Feminist fallacies: a reply to Hakim on women's employment. *British Journal of Sociology*, 47(1): 167–74.

Glynn, C., Steinberg, I. and McCartney, C. (2002) *Work–Life Balance: The Role of the Manager*. Horsham: Roffey Park Institute.

Guest, D. E. (1987) Human resource management and industrial relations. *Journal of Management Studies*, 24(5): 503–21.

Guest, D. E. (1989) Personnel and HRM: can you tell the difference? *Personnel Management*, (January): 48–51.

Hakim, C. (1991) Grateful slaves and self-made women: fact and fantasy in women's work orientations. *European Social Review*, 7(2): 102–21.

Hakim, C. (1995) Five feminist myths about women's employment. *British Journal of Sociology*, 46(3): 429–55.

Hakim, C. (2004) *Key Issues in Women's Work: Female Diversity and the Polarisation of Women's Employment*. London: Glass House Press.

Healy, G., Bradley, J. and Mukherjee, N. (2004) Inspiring Union women – black and minority ethnic women in trade unions. In Healy, G., Heery, E., Taylor, P. and Brown, W. (eds), *The Future of Worker Representation*. London: Palgrave, pp. 103–26.

Hogarth, T., Hasluck, C., Pierre, G. Winterbotham, M. and Vivian, D. (2001) *Work–Life Balance 2000: Results from the Baseline Study*. Norwich: Department of Education and Employment Institute for Employment Research with IFF Research.

Holbeche, L. and McCartney, C. (2002) *The Roffey Park Management Agenda*. Horsham: Roffey Part Institute.

Howenstine, D. W. (2006) Beyond rational relations: the constitutional infirmities of anti-gay partnership laws under the equal protection clause. *Washington Law Review*, 81(2): 417–46.

Kamenou, N. (2002) Ethnic minority women in English organisations: career experiences and opportunities. Unpublished PhD thesis, Leeds University Business School, University of Leeds.

Kamenou, N. (2008) Reconsidering work–life balance debates: challenging limited understandings of the 'life' component in the context of ethnic minority women's experiences. Special Issue on Gender in Management: New Theoretical Perspectives. *British Journal of Management*, 19(S1): S99–109.

Kan, M. (2001) *Gender Asymmetry in the Division of Domestic Labour. Who Does the Housework? Report*. Colchester: University of Essex Institute for Social and Economic Research.

Kodz, J., Harper, H. and Dench, S. (2002) *Work–Life Balance: Beyond the Rhetoric*. Institute for Employment Studies Report No. 384. Brighton: Institute for Employment Studies.

Lamb, M. (2009) Mothers, Fathers, or Parents at Home and at Work. Paper presented at Gender Inequalities in the 21st Century, Queen's College, Cambridge, 26–27 March.

Lewis, S. (1997) 'Family friendly' employment policies: a route to changing organizational cultures or playing about at the margins? *Gender, Work and Organization*, 4(1): 13–23.

Lewis, S., Gambles, R. and Rapoport, R. (2007) The constraints of a work–life balance approach: an international perspective. *International Journal of Human Resource Management*, 18(3): 360–73.

Liff, S. and Cameron, I. (1997) Changing equality cultures to move beyond 'women's problems'. *Gender, Work and Organization*, 4(1): 35–46.

McRae, S. (2003) Choice and constraints in mothers' employment careers: McRae replies to Hakim. *British Journal of Sociology*, 54(4): 585–92.

Noon, M. and Blyton, P. (1997) *The Realities of Work*. London: Macmillan Business.

Office for National Statistics (2008) Working Lives: Employment Rates Higher for Men, ONS focus on gender. Available from: http://www.sigmascan.org/Live/Source/ViewSource.aspx?SourceId=7373 [accessed 15 September 2011].

Özbilgin, M. (2005) *International Human Resource Management: Theory and Practice*. London: Palgrave Macmillan.

Platman, K. (2002) Matured assets. *People Management*, 8(24): 40–2.

Rana, B. K., Kagan, C., Lewis, S. and Rout, U. (1998) British South Asian women managers and professionals: experiences of work and family. *Women in Management Review*, 13(6): 221–32.

Sargeant, M. (2009) Age discrimination, sexual orientation and gender identity: UK/US perspectives. *Equal Opportunities International*, 28(8): 634–45.

Shaffer, M. A., Harrison, D. A., Gilley, K. M. and Luk, D. M. (2001) Struggling for balance amid turbulence on international assignments: work–family conflict, support and commitment. *Journal of Management*, 27(1): 99–121.

Sparrow, P. R. and Cooper, C. L. (2003) *The Employment Relationship: Key Challenges for HR*. Oxford: Butterworth-Heinemann.

Stephens, G. K. and Black, S. (1991) The impact of spouse's career orientation on managers during international transfers. *Journal of Management Studies*, 28: 417–28.

Taylor, R. (2002) *The Future of Work–Life Balance*. Swindon: Economic and Social Research Council.

Thomas, D. A. and Aldefer, C. P. (1989) The influence of race on career dynamics: theory and research on minority career experiences. In Arthur, M., Hall, D. T. and Lawrence, B. S. (eds), *Handbook of Career Theory*. Port Hope, ON: Cambridge University Press, pp. 133–58.

Tomlinson, J. and Gardiner, J. (2009) Organisational approaches to flexible working: perspectives of equality and diversity managers in the UK. *Equal Opportunities International*, 28(8): 671–86.

Torrington, D., Hall, L. and Taylor, S. (2008) *Human Resource Management*. Harlow: Prentice Hall.

Walby, S. (1983) Patriarchal structures: the case of unemployment. In Gamarnikow, E., Morgan, D., Purvis, J. and Taylorson, D. (eds), *Gender, Class and Work*. London: Heinemann.

Walby, S. (1986) *Patriarchy at Work*. Oxford: Polity Press.

Woodhams, C. and Danieli, A. (2000) Disability and diversity – a different too far? *Personnel Review*, 29(3): 402–17.

APPENDIX A
The European Union Social Charter

The Social Charter was adopted by all member states, except the UK, in December 1989. The Social Charter is not a legal text. It is a statement of principles by which governments agree to abide. They will be required each year to present a report on how they are implementing the Charter. Its aim is to highlight the importance of the social dimension of the single market in achieving social as well as economic cohesion in the European Community.

The preamble of the Social Charter gives added weight to other international obligations such as International Labour Organization conventions. The preamble also includes a commitment to combat every form of discrimination, including discrimination on grounds of sex, colour, race, opinions and belief.

Summary of the rights set out in the Social Charter:

1. Freedom of movement throughout the Community with equal treatment in access to employment, working conditions and social protection.
2. Freedom to choose and engage in an occupation, which shall be fairly remunerated.
3. Improvement of living and working conditions, especially for part-time and temporary workers, and rights to weekly rest periods and annual paid leave.
4. Right to adequate social protection.
5. Right to freedom of association and collective bargaining.
6. Right to access to lifelong vocational training, without discrimination on grounds of nationality.
7. Right of equal treatment of men and women, especially in access to employment, pay, working conditions, education and training and career development.
8. Right to information, consultation and participation for employees, particularly in conditions of technological change, restructuring, redundancies, and for transfrontier workers.
9. Right to health protection and safety at the workplace including training, information, consultation and participation for employees.
10. Rights of children and adolescents, including a minimum working age.
11. Right for the elderly to have a decent standard of living on retirement.
12. Right of people with disabilities to programmes to help them in social and professional life.

PART TWO

CHAPTER 7
Workforce planning and talent management

OUTLINE

- Introduction
- People and planning
- Manpower planning
- Human resource planning
- Workforce planning
- HRM in practice 7.1: Planning the headcount on the policy roller-coaster
- Flexibility
- Talent management
- HRM as I see it: Sarah Myers, Sky
- Diversity management
- HRM and globalization: What to do about macho?
- Human resource accounting
- Case study: TNNB Ltd
- Summary, Vocab checklist for ESL students, Review questions and Further reading to improve your mark

OBJECTIVES

After studying this chapter, you should be able to:
- Explain the place of planning in human resource management
- Explain the difference between manpower planning, human resource planning and workforce planning
- Give details of the use of ICT in workforce planning
- Explain the various meanings of and approaches to flexible working
- Understand developments in the idea and practice of talent management
- Understand the requirements for diversity management
- Outline key ideas in human resource accounting

Introduction

How certain are you that you can make a plan for the future? What was the impact on your planning of the UK Government's announcement in October 2010 of spending cuts in the public sector, which will lead to the loss of 490,000 jobs in the public sector by 2014/15 (as quoted in the *Guardian*, October 19, 2010)? As you might imagine, similar questions need to be asked in organizations to ensure that the right number of people, with the right kind of talent and skill combinations, get into the right positions at the right time. A plan that achieves this is called a *workforce plan*, and its purpose is to provide some degree of certainty and control over future events. However, as we all know very well, plans do not always work out as intended.

The global economic crisis and the consequent recession in the late 2000s has made the process of planning for the recruitment and deployment of a workforce increasingly precarious. The decisions involved in making such plans rely on data that can be used to make forecasts about the future. First, there are forecasts relating to the demand for the workforce, based on the requirements of the organization in relation to its environment. Second, there are forecasts for the degree to which the supply of the workforce will match demand for it. In both instances, however, the ability to forecast with any kind of certainty will be reduced, and uncertainty and complexity will be increased. This could mean that plans made through an analysis of past data might become no more than a way of making sense of the past – in other words, they will fail to account for future events, and workforce planners will need to become more creative. The shocks and disturbances of the late 2000s have increased the need for planning to become both an analytical process for predictability and a creative process for working with unpredictability, unknowable shocks and complexity. It also needs to become a continuous process with as much emphasis on doing the planning as having a plan.

People and planning

At the start of the twenty-first century, it was claimed that the route to competitive advantage is achieved through people (Gratton, 2000). There was growing evidence that effective human resources (HR) practices could enhance a company's sustainability and profitability if there was integration with business purpose (Guest et al., 2003), although there was also evidence of a failure by many senior managers to recognize this (Caulkin, 2001). Furthermore, according to the resource-based view of the firm, an organization can derive competitive advantage from its resources through the development of human resource management (HRM) systems and routines that are unique to that organization (Barney et al., 2001). Thus, any organization could plan how it would deploy and combine a range of HR practices and achieve high commitment and enhanced performance (Wall and Wood, 2005).

At this time, prior to the economic downturn that started in 2008, there was a concern about skills shortages and competition between organizations to attract and develop people who could add most to an organization's performance. This became known as the 'war for talent' (Michaels et al., 2001), with many organizations adopting policies for *talent management* (TM). For HR practitioners, TM represents another opportunity to attain credibility and a status as professionals (Chuai et al., 2008) by presenting a rational and coherent argument for specific HR practices that contribute directly to the outcomes the organization desires. This supports the idea of 'HRM as a modernist project' (Legge, 2005, p. 337), pushing to address the traditional weaknesses of personnel managers by constructing a 'hard' version of HRM that is more strategic. Finding a more strategic role has been a long-running feature of HR's story over the last 20 years, requiring a variety of approaches to achieve it (Tamkin et al., 1997). In some cases, this involves supporting business strategy by developing appropriate policies and procedures. In others, it means being proactive and playing a leading role in driving strategy.

The ability to formulate plans has been one of the requirements for joining strategic discussions and, as we will show in this chapter, this ability is connected to priorities for people in organizations. Thus, in times of relatively full employment, people and their skills were important because of their scarcity. For example, in the 1960s, the main concerns of manpower planning were an emphasis on the quantities, flows and mathematical modelling of people. During the years of recession in the 1970s and 80s and then the 1990s, manpower planning was used to reduce or 'downsize' the workforce. A more qualitative view of people underpinned *human resource planning* (HRP), which involved the development and provision of a framework that would allow an organization to integrate key HR practices so that it could meet the needs of its employees, enhance their potential and meet the performance needs of the business strategy. The uncertainty and complexity of organization and business conditions in the late 2000s is resulting in more varied approaches and methods relating to planning, which we will call *workforce planning*. This will include putting together TM strategies that aim to develop more people in house and retain key employees (Chartered Institute of Personnel and Development [CIPD], 2009a), as well as searching for new ways to reduce staffing numbers in the face of business recession and cuts in government funding.

> **reflective question**
>
> From your experience or reading, how much importance do you think is given to plans for people in organizations? Can small organizations engage in workforce planning?

Manpower planning

What we now call workforce planning was originally referred to as 'manpower planning'. During the twentieth century, this represented a response by personnel and HR managers to ensure that the necessary supply of people was forthcoming to allow targets to be met. In theory at least, a manpower plan could show how the demand for people and their skills within an organization could be balanced by supply. The key stages of this approach are shown in Figure 7.1.

The idea of balance between demand and supply reflects the influence of the language of classical labour economics, in which movement towards an 'equilibrium'

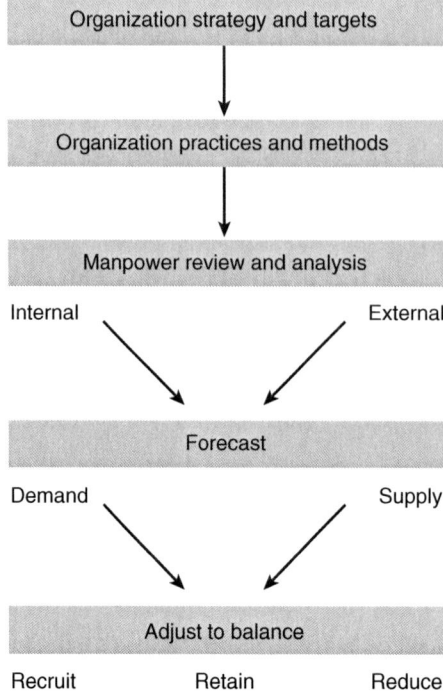

Figure 7.1 Reconciling demand and supply

serves as an ideal. Such influences can be found in some of the definitions and explanations of manpower planning put forward over the past 50 years. For example, in 1974, the UK's Department of Employment defined manpower planning as a 'strategy for the acquisition, utilization, improvement and preservation of an organization's human resources.' Four stages of the planning process were outlined:

1. An evaluation or appreciation of the existing manpower resources
2. An estimation of the proportion of currently employed manpower resources that were likely to be within the firm by the forecast date
3. An assessment or forecast of labour requirements needed if the organization's overall objectives were to be achieved by the forecast date
4. Measures to ensure that the necessary resources were available as and when required, that is, the manpower plan.

Stages 1 and 2 were linked in the 'supply aspect of manpower', with stage 1 being part of 'normal personnel practice' (Department of Employment, 1974). Stage 3 represents the 'demand aspect of manpower'. There were two main reasons for companies to use manpower planning: first, to develop their business objectives and manning levels; and second, to reduce the 'unknown' factor. Stage 4 requires an interaction between demand and supply so that skills are utilized to the best possible advantage, and the aspirations of the individual are taken into account (Smith, 1980).

Because of the complexity of interaction of these factors within a context that included aims of optimization and overall equilibrium, manpower planning became a suitable area of interest for operational research and for the application of statistical techniques (Bartholomew, 1971). In this process, organizations could be envisaged as a series of stocks and flows, and as part of an overall system of resource allocation. Models of behaviour could be formulated in relation to labour turnover, length of service, how quickly promotions occurred and age distribution. These variables could be expressed as mathematical and statistical formulae and equations that would allow solutions to manpower decisions to be calculated. With the growing use of computers, the techniques and models became more ambitious and probably beyond the comprehension of most managers (Parker and Caine, 1996). In large organizations, there was, however, a growth in the number of specialist manpower analysts who were capable of dealing with the complex processes involved.

reflective question

Do you think a manpower system can be adequately represented as a series of stocks and flows?

Emphasizing statistical models of manpower supply and demand at the expense of the reality of managing and interacting with people was bound to be met with suspicion, certainly by employees and their representatives, as well as by managers 'forced' to act on the results of the calculations. Hence, during the 1970s and 80s, manpower planning acquired a poor reputation as a system with few benefits and only a few examples of when 'comprehensive and systematic manpower planning [was] fully integrated into strategic planning' (Cowling and Walters, 1990, p. 6). There were a number of attempts to make manpower planning techniques more 'user-friendly' to non-specialists. Thus, the fall-out from theoretical progress in manpower analysis was the application of techniques to help with 'real' manpower problems (Bell, 1989), for example why one department in an organization seemed to suffer from a dramatically higher turnover of labour, or why graduate trainees were not retained in sufficient number. Personnel managers were able to build up a 'toolkit' of key manpower measures relating to, for example, employee turnover, retention, stability and absenteeism. All of these could be relatively easily calculated, either monthly or quarterly, and expressed graphically to reveal trends and future paths.

Through the 1990s, such techniques were incorporated into PC-based computerized personnel information systems. As the software became more user-friendly, personnel departments were able to take advantage of this and make themselves more responsive to business needs. Most large and medium-sized organizations will now employ some form of computerized personnel system, and there are many providers of suitable software; we will explore such developments later in this chapter.

HRM web links

Go to www.acas.org.uk/index.aspx?articleid=1183 for access to a booklet published in the UK by the Advisory, Conciliation and Arbitration Service – *Managing Attendance and Employee Turnover* – which provides assistance to organizations that have labour turnover and absenteeism problems. You will also find examples of formulae used to measure absenteeism and turnover. Go also to www.softwaresource.co.uk, a site established by the CIPD, which provides information on and access to many HR software products and suppliers.

Diagnosing manpower problems

The use of manpower planning techniques within computerized personnel information systems can be seen as part of a continuing search by the personnel function to find areas of expertise to legitimize its position and prove its value by 'adding to the bottom line'. Thus, there is an attempt to use manpower information as a way of understanding problems so that action can be taken as appropriate. In this way, HR managers have been practising what Fyfe (1986, p. 66) referred to as 'the diagnostic approach to manpower planning'. This approach built on and broadened the demand and supply approach outlined in Figure 7.1 in order to identify problem areas and understand why they were occurring. This is shown in Figure 7.2.

The idea of an equilibrium between demand and supply can occur only on paper or on the computer screen; the more probable situation is one of continuous imbalance as a result of the dynamic conditions facing any organization, people's behaviour and the imperfections of manpower models. A diagnostic approach would mean becoming aware of manpower problems by monitoring statistics such as turnover and stability, as well as by obtaining qualitative data from interviewing staff. Such interviews might reveal concerns with job satisfaction and the career

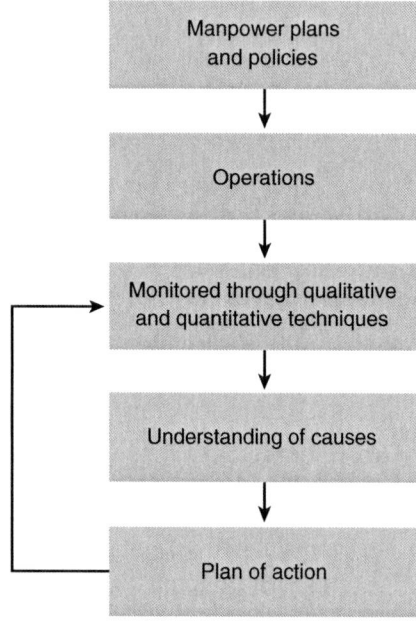

Figure 7.2 The diagnostic approach to manpower planning

paths open to staff, reflecting the fact that aspirations they hold that are not being met by current practices. Rather than express these aspirations openly for fear of conflict with management, many staff may prefer to seek employment elsewhere. The loss of talented staff has important cost implications, and a diagnostic approach to retention can provide a significant pay-off.

Employee turnover

The reasons for employee turnover are based on complex factors often requiring solutions that are specific to the context of each organization. Morrell et al. (2001) suggested that explanations of voluntary employee turnover fall into two categories:

- *Economic or labour market reasons* – the emphasis being on external factors such as market conditions
- *Psychological reasons* – the emphasis being on feelings and perceptions relating to job satisfaction, involvement and commitment within the psychological contract.

Research on employee turnover has focused on the latter, seeking to explore more closely why voluntary turnover occurs, which is particularly important given the costs of replacing and recruiting new staff, as well as the pressure on the remaining staff to cover the work. For example, employee turnover may rise in times of organizational change; that is, the 'shock' of changes in patterns of work may lead to decisions to quit (Morrell et al., 2004). A better understanding of the psychological features of turnover can allow for more focused interventions and avoid the unnecessary costs involved. Morrell et al. (2004) suggest the use of certain measures to minimize the effects of change, including:

- Surveys
- Consultation processes
- Intra- and extra-firm career guidance
- Exit interviews
- Leaver profiling.

In the 2000s, the loss of staff is also seen as the loss of intellectual capital and experience, and the replacement of 'knowledge workers' can be both expensive and time-consuming (Buckingham, 2000; Ton and Huckman, 2008). In addition, Des and Shaw (2001) highlight the importance of social capital – the value of relationships between people, embedded in network links that facilitate the trust and communication that are vital to an organization's overall performance. Social capital is reduced when people leave, with a negative impact on organizational performance (Shaw et al., 2005).

We would usually expect high employee turnover to have a negative impact on performance, but recent research has proved that this is not always the case. Siebert and Zubanov (2009) completed an analysis of employee turnover in a large retail organization in the UK and found differences in commitment among full-time core sales assistants compared with part-timers, these differences affecting the turnover–performance relationship. With the full-time staff, there was a negative relationship between turnover and performance, but with the part-timers, the relationship was positive. This suggested a need to consider differences between work systems for different groups in organizations. Thus, full-time or core staff would benefit from high-involvement approaches to their management including less monitoring and control of their performance and more training and career development; part-time or secondary staff would, however, be allocated more routine tasks, more control and less training and career development.

A similar result was found in Budhwar et al.'s (2009) study of high turnover in Indian call centres, where many staff were college graduates with little experience and little intention of staying, so their commitment to working in the organization was limited. Much of the work was considered 'monotonous' and, along with night shifts, affected 'quality of life' and 'work–life balance'. It is hardly surprising that such a work system results in high turnover, but presumably there is a ready supply of staff that can be recruited as substitutes, with only low levels of training needed.

Human resource planning

HRM seeks to make an explicit link between strategy, structure and people. During the 1990s, the plan to bring this about was referred to as the HR plan. This also symbolized the intention to link HR practices to superior performance at work. There has been an ongoing debate on the benefits of adopting a 'high-road' HRM strategy of high training, high involvement, high rewards and quality commitment (Cooke, 2000) versus a 'low-road' strategy characterized by low pay, low job security and work intensification. Furthermore, research suggested the importance of introducing HR practices together in a 'bundle' so that they would enhance and support each other. For example, a plan to introduce performance appraisal on its own will be far less effective without a consideration of training, reward, careers and the attitudes and styles of managers.

It is also important to coordinate the implementation (Hoque, 1999), although any plan to do this will be subject to local culture and everyday meanings, which support the 'strength' of the HRM system (Bowen and Ostroff, 2004). For example, if the organization is pursuing a strategy of increasing its exports, the staff's perception of what they feel the organization is like, based on such factors as policies, rewards and how managers behave towards the staff, will affect how HRM activities such as training and career development will affect overall performance. More recent research highlights how different pressures from both within and outside any organization will affect how HRM is implemented (Boon et al., 2009); in the UK, case study research has highlighted the need for an integrated system of HRM covering skills, recruitment, absenteeism, reward and encouragement to be innovative in order to achieve superior performance (Department of Trade and Industry, 2005a).

A high-road HRM strategy linked to a high-performing organization requires a belief by management that engagement with people represents the key source of competitive advantage because an organization's route to success is based on having a distinctive product and/or service quality as well as price (MacLeod and Clarke,

2009). Furthermore, the continuing development of those people will be a vital feature of both the formation and the implementation of a business strategy.

> **HRM web links**
>
> Go to www.bis.gov.uk/policies/employment-matters/strategies/employee-engagement. This is the UK's Department of Business site on Employee Engagement.

While there is evidence of a correlation between high-road HRM and business performance (Wall and Wood, 2005), such evidence may not always convince managers in their decision-making. A resource-based view of organizations would suggest that the distinctive expertise and skills of people are a first-order element of strategy-making and therefore a key element in planning (Liff, 2000). However, HRM is in many cases still a third-order strategic issue (Coleman and Keep, 2001), so that when difficulties arise, many organizations swiftly move towards a version of HRM in which HR activities are designed to respond to strategy, with people viewed as a resource whose cost must be controlled. We know from experience that, in sectors such as retail banking, when competition and deregulation created conditions of continuous flux, it became easier to adopt a low-road version of HRM resulting in branch closures and the loss of many jobs (Storey et al., 1997).

Another example can be found in the implementation of business process re-engineering (Hammer and Champy, 1993) during the 1990s. As discussed earlier, this involved a radical change in business processes by applying IT to integrate tasks and produce an output of value to the customer. As the change unfolded, unnecessary processes and layers of bureaucracy were identified and removed, and staff became more empowered to deliver high-quality service and products. Business process re-engineering has, however, almost always been accompanied by unemployment (Grey and Mitev, 1995), a fact that HRP may attempt, with difficulty, to disguise. Downsizing by reducing staff numbers is seen by many organizations as a means of improving their efficiency, productivity and overall competitiveness (Cross and Travaglione, 2004), but, as we will explore below, redundancy can also have many negative consequences for organizations.

> Visit www.palgrave.com/business/bratton5 for a bonus case study on downsizing at the Royal Bank of Scotland.

In the UK, specific historical, social, political and institutional contextual features make for a business environment that is largely incompatible with high-road HRM (Cooke, 2000). Thus, with the pressure to sustain or increase profits, employees are more likely to be treated as a 'number' in the quest to reduce costs. This has been a continuing pattern, so that HRP has become a framework to accommodate the 'multifarious practices' of 'pragmatic and opportunistic' organizations (Storey, 1995b). It is perhaps for these reasons that, during the 2000s, the term 'workforce planning' came to be preferred, particularly as organizations began to face growing uncertainty towards the end of the decade (Cappelli, 2009).

> **reflective question**
>
> Can an organization claim a high-road approach to HRM while adopting low-road practices? What are the consequences of this?

Workforce planning

In 2008, the bank Northern Rock was nationalized as a consequence of a strategy that failed during the financial crisis. Around 6500 people worked for the bank in 2008, but by June 2010 this figure was close to 4000, with more job losses planned. Like many other organizations, the bank was seeking to plan for the future while facing uncertainty and unpredictability. So the notion of 'right people, right skills, right place and right time' was fraught with difficulty. The trade union suggested that the job cuts were 'short-termist' and likely to worsen unemployment in the UK's North East, where the bank was based. The then CEO, Gary Hoffman (who resigned in November 2010, intending to join another bank in 2011), said 'There is still a challenging economic environment and in order to meet our objectives, we must align our staffing level to match the smaller size of the business, increase efficiency and reduce our cost base' (as quoted in the *Guardian*, June 9, 2010).

But, of course, it had not been always like this, and pre-2008, Northern Rock, like many other organizations, had faced a different problem: that of finding the right kind of people to support its delivery of services and growth. The search was on to find 'high-potential' individuals in the so-called 'war for talent' (Michaels et al., 2001) as part of a growing interest in TM (see below). Workforce planning is the process of forecasting the supply and demand of skills against the requirements of future production and services delivery in a situation of uncertainty and change. It is a process that must be set in a particular context, and can cover many different activities, including the formulae involved in manpower planning such as employee turnover, and the diagnostic and strategic understanding of HRP (Curson et al., 2010); it can also be broader in scope than either of these.

Cappelli (2009) suggest two types of forecast. First, there are internal forecasts to consider the future workforce in terms of numbers and skills or competencies and how these will be affected by competition for staff and the requirements of the work. Any organization will need to understand the talent of its workforce, how such talent will occupy particular roles, and the relationship between roles. A future perspective will consider the preparation for and movement between roles, including succession planning and the management of careers. The second type of forecast is the prediction of demand, which has to be considered against the demand for products and services. The latter determines skill requirements for the future and is considered be significant in national efforts to move towards high-value/high-skill production in the UK (UK Commission for Employment and Skills, 2009).

HRM in practice 7.1: Planning the headcount on the policy roller-coaster

In June 2011, the General Teaching Council for Scotland reported that only 1 in 5 of the 2009–10 cohort of newly qualified teachers had secured a permanent full-time job. All Scottish probationary teachers are guaranteed a post for 1 year after qualifying, but after that employment in the education sector is not guaranteed. The proportion of new teachers with no job at all had risen from 13.5 per cent to 16.2 per cent, and the numbers being offered full-time or part-time temporary and supply teaching had also risen (BBC News, 2011).

This is a good example of the difficulties of workforce planning in a large heterogeneous sector such as primary and secondary education, with the additional problem of the time lag between entering a programme of initial professional education and the state of the labour market on completion. The number of teachers required in any year is dependent on a range of factors such as the number and composition of the school-age population, policy decisions on maximum and minimum class sizes, the rate of teachers leaving the profession and the state of public sector finances. The teaching degree, like most initial degrees in Scotland, is a 4-year course, during which time any of these variables can change. In any part of the public sector, such changes are likely to be a direct result of fluctuations in policy – the 2010 cohort of new teachers had the misfortune to be looking for work at a time of impending cutbacks in public sector financing and of economic conditions that had led many older teachers to postpone early retirement.

Another example of how state policy directly affects workforce planning and composition is given by Stephen Bach's detailed analysis of the use of immigrant nursing staff in the NHS (Bach, 2010). This was driven by government's perception of a staffing crisis (in relation to policy targets set for the service) and a manipulation of immigration policy to meet the crisis. In the early years of the twenty-first century, the government of the day had pledged to increase the nursing workforce in England by 20,000 additional posts by 2004 and then, in a revised plan, by 35,000 by 2008. Because of the lags in bringing UK-trained nurses into employment, for similar reasons to those we have seen for teachers, the response was actively to step up recruitment from overseas. The government was thus susceptible to criticism that it was poaching trained nursing staff from developing nations.

However, by 2005, staff targets had been exceeded, after which policy priorities changed from staff expansion to curbing expenditure. In the meantime, the number of domestic nurse training places had expanded by a third, so overseas recruitment was drastically reduced. The government changed the immigration points system and removed most nursing grades from the shortage occupation list. This meant that an employer would have to prove it had a vacancy and had been unable to recruit UK or European Economic Area nurses. It also meant that existing work permit-holders were deterred from changing employer in case they lost the right to work in the UK.

Bach's study shows, first, that the supply of immigrant workers has not been the result of an inexorable process of globalization, as is often inferred by populist discussions of immigration. More importantly, it indicates that, in the public sector, workforce planning and the supply and demand of labour are inevitably going to be critically affected as much by state policy as by the normal labour market interplay of supply and demand for suitably qualified people.

> **Stop!** What do you think public sector managers can do to secure a stable and suitably qualified workforce?

Sources and further information:

See BBC News (2011) and Bach (2010) for background reading.

Note: This feature was written by Chris Baldry at the University of Stirling.

Visit the companion website at www.palgrave.com/business/bratton5 for bonus HRM in practice features on Ernst and Young's maternity coaching scheme, and flexible shifts and part-time staff at Kwik Fit.

But it is not just organizations that undertake workforce planning. Governments, for example, are to a greater or lesser extent interested in the supply of skills to match forecasts in demand. Green et al. (1999) have shown how countries such as South Korea, Singapore and Taiwan – the 'tiger economies' – consider skill requirements against targets for growth, which in turn sets the direction for the supply of skills obtained in schools, colleges and universities. Information for planning is gathered systematically in combination with efforts to persuade employers to demand skills at higher levels.

In sectors such as the UK's National Health Service (NHS), workforce planning faces significant complexities due to the large variety of skill classifications and needs. Curson (2006) sees medical workforce planning as analogous to crystal-ball gazing, and Parsons (2010) views it as both a science and an art since predictions for the future, based on the analysis of trends, can hardly be relied upon when future requirements based on need rather than demand are likely to change so rapidly. Part of the art of workforce planning is the utilization of tools such as simulations and scenarios to create conversations between different stakeholders that then set the direction for action (Micic, 2010).

The use of ICT in workforce planning

As we indicated earlier, workforce planning can be supported through the use of information and communication technology (ICT). It is argued that human resource information systems (HRISs) can enhance a more systemic consideration of HR activities and their linkage with the organization's vision and goals (Mayfield et al., 2003). Indeed, generating, capturing, tracking and disseminating organizational knowledge, in all its manifestations in software packages and online, are key features of knowledge management and organizational learning, and both can be facilitated by a HRIS. HRIS has become a form of organizational intelligence, enabling the production of various forecasts and scenarios for future possibilities and unexpected shocks (Hurley-Hanson and Giannantonio, 2008).

During the 1990s, there was a widespread use of HRISs for transaction applications in operational areas such as employee records, payroll and absence control. This suggests that its primary use was as a means of collecting data for others to use in decision-making, and that it was used much less in expert systems and decision support applications (Kinnie and Arthurs, 1996). Ball (2001, p. 690) concluded at the end of this period that 'HRM still seems to be the laggard in running its own systems' to support decision-making and strategy.

A crucial element in any HRIS is how the information is used, especially in decisions concerning how people are employed at work. It is suggested (Liff, 1997a) that a HRIS can be seen from different viewpoints that in turn affect its use. These viewpoints are that its purpose is:

- To provide an objective view of an organization in which the information used is comprehensive and accurate, allowing the best decisions to be made
- To construct organization realities, including the categories and classifications determining the information that should be collected
- To make sense of what is going on within an organization and what needs to be done, according to how information is interpreted by each person, based on his or her view of life at work.

In three case studies, Liff (1997a) found that each view could be used to explain managers' use of a HRIS. Managers were most attached to an objective view of a HRIS and viewed the information it represented as neutral; that is, skills were defined from a 'rational reassessment of current labels' (Liff, 1997a, p. 27). In addition, there was a belief that the HRIS categories could construct a new approach to managing staff and play a role in 'serving dominant business strategy'. The third view could, however, also be found, especially in the way in which apparent discrepancies in information produced by the system could be understood on the basis of existing knowledge of life at work.

In the 2000s, there has been an extension of HRISs towards e-HR (Kettley and Reilly, 2003), with many HR departments using the Internet and web-enabled technologies to create an organizational network of HR data and information. In addition, there has been a development of new approaches to HR activities such as e-recruitment, e-learning and e-reward. Another approach is to allow staff to access information on HR issues, for example how much holiday they have left for the year, via a business-to-employee (B2E) portal. Advanced B2E solutions include attempts to influence ways of working and relationships, such as enhancing e-working by developments in telephony, shared collaboration spaces, online meeting rooms and shared access to intelligence and knowledge management applications. Furthermore, making such information available on the Internet allows it to be accessed by staff from a PC anywhere in the world.

Other ICT developments provide an opportunity for HR departments to work strategically with other functions. Many large and medium-sized organizations have, for example, attempted to integrate all information flows through enterprise resource planning (ERP) software – a typical HR module within ERP might include the items listed in Table 7.1 (see Jackson, 2010). Each heading in the module provides access to a database requiring data to be entered. Once

Table 7.1 Headings for a typical HR module within ERP

Application screening	Salary administration
Payroll	Work schedule
Planning	Travel expenses
Recruitment	Benefits administration
Compensation management	Personnel development
Funds and position management	Personnel time management
Time evaluation	Shift planning, training
Event management	

entered, information can then be processed and re-presented for appropriate use. Furthermore, most ERP systems allow for an integration between modules and units within modules, which forms parts of an organization's knowledge management system. Jackson (2010) argues that ERP allows routine HR functions to be consolidated to support business processes, saving cost and securing competitive advantage. However, like all software and technology innovations, it is necessary to consider how change is implemented to secure the benefits and full use of ERP's functionality.

HRM web links

You can examine ERP software for use in HR at the following web links: www.lawson.com/Solutions/Software/Human-Capital-Management and www.sageabra.com/products_and_services/why_sage_abra_hrms.

reflective question

Do you think that all communications at work can be settled via e-HR and B2E? Is there a 'solution' for HR issues?

Flexibility

In planning how to respond to rapid technological and global change, and customer demands, many organizations invoke the idea of 'flexibility'. This is a term with a variety of different meanings and a variety of implications for workforce planning.

reflective question

How many definitions of flexibility can you think of? As you consider these different definitions, examine the implications for skills, the hours and location of work, the type of contract and the overall motivation and satisfaction of people at work.

Stredwick and Ellis (2005) suggest some key advantages of flexible working. For businesses, there is the chance to exploit the 24-hour economy and open new labour markets that avoid traditional working patterns. Employees seem to like flexible working too, achieving 'far more in the flexible mode' with no 'desire to go back to traditional working patterns' (p. 5). Flexibility can also be seen by employees as means of achieving a more satisfactory work–life balance (Jones et al., 2007), allowing for greater control over their working time, especially for women and those with caring responsibilities (McDonald et al., 2005).

The ambiguity in the definitions of flexibility has allowed a number of interpretations to justify a variety of organizational activities. A key idea is Atkinson and Meager's (1985) model of a 'flexible firm', which identified four types of flexibility that could be implemented:

- *Functional* – 'a firm's ability to adjust and deploy the skills of its employees to match the tasks required by its changing workload, production methods and/or technology' (Atkinson and Meager, 1985, p. 2)
- *Numerical* – a firm's ability to adjust the level of labour inputs to meet fluctuations in output
- *Distancing strategies* – the replacement of internal workers with external subcontractors, that is, putting some work, such as running the firm's canteen, out to contract (now referred to as 'outsourcing')
- *Financial* – support for the achievement of flexibility through the pay and reward structure.

These flexibilities are achieved through a division of employees into the core workforce and the peripheral workforce. Flexibility here is something done *to* the workforce (Alis et al., 2006). The core group is composed of those workers expected to deliver functional flexibility and includes those with firm-specific skills and high discretionary elements in their work. The peripheral group is composed of a number of different workers, such as those directly employed by a firm as secondary workers to perform work with a low discretionary element, or those employed as required on a variety of contracts, for example part-time, temporary and casual workers. This category of employee might also include highly specialized workers such as consultants. The final category comprises trainees, some of whom may be being prepared for eventual transfer to the core group. It is important to remember, when considering the issue of flexibility, that organizations have a choice about the type of flexibility that can be adopted.

The idea of the flexible firm has been recognized for many years, although not without criticism (see Pollert, 1988), and is often accepted as a 'panacea of restructuring' as it combines different changes in the organization of work, such as multiskilling, job enlargement, teamwork, labour intensification and cost control (Pollert, 1991).

HRM web links

Go to www.flexibility.co.uk and use this site to explore different ideas of flexibility.

Flexible working today

It has been argued that the hard HRM approach, with its emphasis on people as numbers within a framework of cost control, has held most sway in the practice of flexibility (Richbell, 2001). Thus, the 2004 Workplace Employment Relations Survey (Kersley et al., 2006) revealed that 30 per cent of workplaces had employees on temporary or fixed-term contracts in 2004, a similar proportion to that found in 1998 (32 per cent; Department of Trade and Industry, 2005b). The survey showed that 83 per cent of workplaces had part-time employees, a rise from 79 per cent in 1998 (Department of Trade and Industry, 2005b). Part-time employees made up more than half the workforce in 30 per cent of workplaces, and in 44 per cent of workplaces that employed part-time staff, women made up all the part-time staff.

Recent times have seen the acceptance of a range of terms and practices that come under the umbrella of the idea of 'flexibility', with all its definitions and implications. In the UK, partly as a response to European Union directives on working time, parental leave and part-time work, and partly as a stimulus to policies on work–life balance, parents of children under the age of 6 years and parents of disabled children have the legal right under the 2002 Employment Act to request more flexible working with respect to hours worked, time and possibly location. The Work and Families Act 2006 extended maternity, paternity and carers' rights. Thus, there has been a shift towards a more employee-friendly approach in the UK and to

Working from home is one definition of flexibility. How many others can you think of?
Source: ©istockphoto.com/diego cervo.

flexibility that allows more choice over where and when work can be done. This has resulted in a range of possible 'ways of working' such as:

- *Annualized hours* – working time is organized on the basis of the number of hours to be worked over a year rather than a week; it is usually used to fit in with peaks and troughs of work
- *Compressed hours* – which allows individuals to work their total number of agreed hours over a shorter period. For example, employees might work their full weekly hours over 4 rather than 5 days
- *Flexi-time* – employees have a choice about their actual working hours, usually outside certain agreed core times
- *Home-working* – either on a full-time basis or on a part-time basis where employees divide their time between home and office
- *Job-sharing* – involves two people employed on a part-time basis, but working together to cover a full-time post
- *Shift-working* – gives employers the scope to have their business open for longer periods than an 8-hour day
- *Staggered hours* – employees can start and finish their day at different times
- *Term-time working* – employees can take unpaid leave of absence during the school holidays.

Research by Kelliher and Anderson (2008) suggests that such practices are perceived by employees as enhancing job quality, particularly with respect to control, autonomy and work–life balance. There are, however, some downsides to these practices in relation to opportunities for learning and development because remote working means less visibility at work.

The onset of the financial crisis has meant a strong association of flexibility with short-term working, which has been shown to have played a key role in preserving jobs, especially among staff with permanent contracts. The effect of this has been to increase the labour market segmentation between permanent and temporary staff (Hijzen and Venn, 2011).

> **reflective question**
>
> Considering the next 10 years of your working life, which form of flexible working most appeals to you, and how do you expect employers to respond in terms of pay, conditions and opportunities for learning and development?

> Visit www.palgrave.com/business/bratton5 to read HRM in practice features on Ernst and Young's maternity coaching scheme, and flexible shifts and part-time staff at Kwik Fit.

Teleworking

One of the most significant choices for flexible working has been teleworking, telecommuting and/or home-working. According to Duxbury and Higgins (2002, p. 157), such work is 'performed by individuals who are employed by an organization but who work at home or at a telecenter for some portion of their working time during regular business hours'.

Huws (1997) identified five main types of teleworking:

- *Multisite* – an alternation between working on an employer's premises and working elsewhere, usually at home, but also in a telecottage or telecentre
- *Tele-home-working* – work based at home, usually for a single employer and involving low-skilled work performed by people tied to their homes
- *Freelancing* – work for a variety of different clients
- *Mobile* – work carried out using communication technology such as mobile phones, fax machines and PC connections via the Internet, often by professional, commercial, technical and managerial staff who work 'on the road'
- *Relocated back functions (call centres)* – specialist centres carrying out activities such as data entry, airline bookings, telephone banking, telephone sales and helpline services.

The trend towards greater home-working and teleworking is being driven by a variety of factors: technology with the impact of email, the Internet and cheaper and faster ICT; employees demanding and expecting more flexibility and a better work–life balance; and employer initiatives to use home-working to boost productivity, retention and loyalty, and to reduce costs (Dwelly and Bennion, 2003).

> **HRM web links**
>
> Go to www.flexibility.co.uk/viewers/homeworkers.htm, a site that provides resources for individuals working (or wanting to work) from home. The home page of the Telework Association is www.telework.org.uk, which provides advice to workers and managers, and includes an online magazine, job information and a teleworking handbook.

It is claimed that there are a variety of benefits from teleworking, including a reduction or elimination of travelling to work accompanied by a reduction of stress, which can in turn increase productivity. As technology has moved from basic PC and telephones, home-workers can now teleconference and hold interactive problem-oriented meetings using advanced software such as Windows Meeting Space. One claim is that parents have more time for family responsibilities and so achieve a better work–life balance (Tremblay 2003), although many mothers would claim that time with children creates its own pressures and stresses (Hilbrecht et al., 2008). In addition, working at home can also mean an imbalance towards work because it is always present (Scott-Dixon, 2004).

Telework is inevitably mainly devoted to information and knowledge-based services, including professional work. Among such workers, there is the potential for feelings of isolation because there is not the constant presence of others to provide social contact, points of comparison and feedback. Golden et al. (2008) completed research on such workers but found that isolation was not related to lower commitment, intention to leave or loyalty to an organization, perhaps because of the benefits of being at home. There was, however, an impact on job performance, especially where workers spent significant time without face-to-face interactions, although some people are likely to benefit from the lack of distractions.

One significant feature of telework has been the growth of call or contact centres, which have been regarded as one of the 'success stories' of the UK economy, employing around 800,000 people (Department of Trade and Industry, 2004). Since 2008, however, call centres have also been the focus of significant job losses both in the UK and elsewhere. The operation of call centres is based on the idea that customers can be serviced at a lower cost through the use of telephones and other ICT links, with the possibility of also learning about customers in order to enable cross-selling.

Within this process, there are two key but usually contradictory aims – the needs to be cost-efficient but customer-oriented (Korczynski, 2002). Thus, customers may appreciate staff's time in dealing with their enquiries, but, simultaneously, the length of time taken to respond to customers is being monitored, with pressure to minimize cost. This can place stress on staff and has led to the view of call centres as opportunities for job intensification in which managers can tightly monitor and control staff performance and limit their autonomy (Stredwick and Ellis, 2005). One consequence of this is high rates of absenteeism and turnover, with terms such as 'sweatshop' and 'slave labour' frequently being applied (Deery and Kinnie, 2004). There is also evidence that long work hours can lead to fatigue and ill-health when balanced against domestic requirements (Bohle et al., 2011; Hyman et al., 2003).

> **HRM web links**
>
> Go to www.bullyonline.org/related/callcntr.htm, which examines the problem of bullying in call centres.

Although there is concern about working conditions in call centres, alternatively, through attention to the design of jobs, call centres can become locations of high-performance work systems, which can positively affect motivation and performance. This allows staff more autonomy as there is less staff monitoring and more focus on team work and leadership (Russell, 2008). The potential here is that, as information and knowledge workers, call staff can significantly enhance the services that call centres provide, although the tension with cost savings can often limit customer interactions with actual employees.

HR practices can play a key role in supporting the creation of high-performance work systems in work cultures, but, as we have already suggested, the 'strength' of an HRM system is demonstrated in the everyday relationships between staff and management. As argued by Wood et al. (2006), there are significant links between the opportunity for relationship-building within call-centre work design and performance, and crucially management's orientation towards these. Interestingly, in comparisons across different countries, it was those countries with coordinated or 'social market' economies, such as Austria, Denmark, Germany, Sweden and The Netherlands, all with more regulated labour markets and institutions, that were associated with better quality jobs and lower turnover in call centres. In countries with liberal market economies, such as the USA and UK, there was a tendency for lower job discretion for workers in call centres (Holman et al., 2007).

> **HRM web links**
>
> Go to www.ilr.cornell.edu/globalcallcenter for details of the Global Call Center Project.

Offshoring and outsourcing

Although call centres have been an apparent success, many organizations have in recent years sought even further cost savings from flexible working by moving their call centres to countries with low wages but similar or even higher skills. Once the customer is used to the lack of face-to-face contact, why not take the process a step further, removing the now irrelevant geographical boundary? This process is referred to as offshoring.

It is argued that offshoring can create wealth even when workers may lose their jobs in their home country. Farrell (2005, p. 68) argues that the 'price' of an organization's ability to cut costs and create new markets is 'continuous change and higher turnover for workers', which can cause 'pain and dislocation'. To avoid this, it is claimed, labour markets need to become more flexible so that workers can benefit from the gains of globalization as well as suffer the costs. Organizations can include training for re-employment, career guidance and reasonable severance packages in their HR plans. One argument is that although jobs may be lost to low-wage economies, displaced workers can retrain and move to higher valued-added jobs. Offshoring has, therefore, become linked to claims of increasing productivity (Amiti and Wei, 2009).

There is, however, some doubt that highly skilled jobs are safe when economies such as India also aspire to high value-added work (for example, in ICT development). Levy (2005) argues that organizations are developing the ability to integrate geographically dispersed operations, which can mean skilled workers in one location competing with skilled workers in different parts of the world. It is also possible that, where there are shortages of skilled and qualified staff, an organization may prefer to offshore some activities such as innovation to locations where qualified staff are more readily available (Lewin et al., 2009).

In addition to offshoring, an organization can seek to slice up or 'disaggregate' its value chain by outsourcing (Contractor et al., 2010); in this process, an organization seeks to source aspects of its production or service processes by setting up a contractual relationship with an external provider. This allows an organization to focus on its core capability and obtain supporting services such as sales, administration (including HR – see below) and ICT at a lower cost from providers who are in turn able to concentrate on their core capability. According to Harland et al. (2005), in addition to focusing on core activities, the principal drivers for outsourcing are freeing up assets, reducing costs and the potential benefits of working with a supplier or partner who is able to exploit advanced technologies. For example, in the pharmaceutical industry, specialist contract research organizations provide outsourced services in areas such as data management, medical coding and marketing, allowing companies to focus on high-value activities.

As a consequence, it has in many organizations become more difficult to speak of a unified entity; instead, in such companies, it is best to consider the working of relationships both internally and externally. Among these relationships will be those characterized by a tight specification of contracts with outsourced service providers, with low trust and pressure to lower costs and compete on price. Colling (2005, p. 95) refers to these as 'distanced' relationships that can also create difficulties for the contracting organization.

An example here might be the relationship between British Airways (BA) and its outsourced catering supplier, Gate Gourmet. In 2005, under pressure to reduce costs in the UK, Gate Gourmet sought to make redundancies and change working conditions. This resulted in a dispute with the trade union, which escalated in August 2005 when the company attempted to bring in 130 temporary workers to cope with the peak travel season. This was followed by an unofficial or 'wildcat' strike by workers and the dismissal of 800 staff. There were a number of consequences for BA: first, they could provide no in-flight food; second, some flights were cancelled; and third, around 1000 BA staff, many of them friends and family members of the staff at Gate Gourmet, stopped work in solidarity with them – this led to the delay or cancellation of around 900 flights, at an extra cost of around £45 million.

In contrast, other relationships are more 'engaged', characterized by mutual trust and joint approaches to planning and working via projects and high value-added services in which the outsourced supplier can play a vital role in enhancing decision-making and performance capability through innovation and knowledge production – a typical claim of many consultancies involved in knowledge process outsourcing (Mudambi and Tallman, 2010). Because such relationships are based on a mutual recognition of the contribution of talented staff, it also becomes possible to consider more strategic possibilities for collaboration and cooperation.

HRM activities are among the services that have been outsourced in recent years. For example, since 2000, telecommunications company BT has outsourced significant HR services to Accenture (see Saunders and Hunter, 2007). Outsourcing in HR is based on the view that administrative work and operations can be carried out by outside suppliers, leaving HR staff to concentrate on strategic and high value-added work. Sako and Tierney (2005) examined the growth of HR outsourcing, finding that although operations such as payroll administration have been more susceptible to outsourcing, there have been more deals that have bundled processes together with moves towards a transformational view of HR outsourcing in which an organization seeks consulting and systems integration as part of the bundle. It is argued that because HR suppliers are outside the organization, they are more accountable, can take a more objective view and can gain a more complete understanding of performance.

Interestingly, research by Woodall et al. (2009) found that, especially in larger organizations, the decision to outsource HR was usually taken because of the success of outsourcing other activities. That is, it was not especially made on the basis of a full understanding of the costs and benefits. It was also found that reductions in core HR staff meant significant challenges in providing a quality service, partly because there was insufficient understanding of the role and activities of HR practitioners.

HRM / HRD IN ITS CONTEMPORARY CONTEXT

The effect on British Airways of strikes at catering supplier Gate Gourmet provides one example of the difficulties that can arise for the contracting organization in a distanced relationship
Source: ©istockphoto.com/DNY59.

Attitudes to work

With a growing number of temporary, fixed-term and outsourced service contract workers, there has been some interest in the effect of employment status on motivation and commitment to work.

> **reflective question**
>
> What do you think would be the effect of being given a fixed-term contract? How would it affect your motivation and satisfaction at work?

Research by Guest et al. (1998) into the views of workers in a variety of different settings found that people on fixed-term contracts generally had a positive psychological contract. Reasons given for this were that employees on fixed contracts had more focused work to complete and did not have to engage in organizational politics or complete administrative duties. They might also face lower work demands than permanent staff, avoiding stress and taking less work home. Such employees perhaps benefit from a better work–life balance (Hogarth et al., 2001).

McInnis et al. (2009) explored different understandings of contracts and the relation to commitment. They suggested that staff on short-term contracts could be faced with contracts that were also organization-centred and set clear terms to define the work to be done – but such contracts had little connection to commitment. Evans et al. (2004), however, examined the work of highly skilled technical contractors in the USA over a period of two and a half years. It was observed that their work was cyclical, involving periods of contract work on projects, and often involved intense activity and pressures from contracting organizations to use their expertise to solve problems, at any time of day. There were also periods between contracts, or 'downtime' – sometimes referred to as 'beach time', 'bench time' or even 'dead time'. They did not consider themselves unemployed at such times – this was normal for contracting. It was found that contractors, even though they were free from normative pressure for permanent employment, did not necessarily enjoy a desirable flexible lifestyle. The contractors often worked longer hours when contracted, and when they were not, they had to continue working to ensure the next contract, using past work to promote their reputations. They had little time to relax.

One of the most persistent findings is the significance of the psychological contract for gaining commitment. How staff perceive their obligations affects their attitudes, motivation and feelings of justice (Battisti et al., 2007). Part of such perceptions relates to the way in which HR practices are employed in combination with an opportunity to innovate within a role. These findings reinforce the view that, in planning to become more flexible, organizations are faced with a choice. Taking an ad hoc approach that is nevertheless driven by cost reduction may produce improved short-term financial results, but is likely to have a negative impact on motivation, innovation and commitment. Although the use of outsourcing and temporary and fixed-term contracts may have positive results, a consistent finding in the research is, however, that high-road HR practices lead to a positive psychological contract and positive organizational outcomes. Organizations may be tempted by the 'wrong sort of flexibility' (Michie and Sheehan-Quinn, 2001, p. 302), which does not improve productivity or competitiveness. However, many organizations have during the 2000s been persuaded of the need to focus on their relationship with talented staff, even though the recession has put a different emphasis on such a stance, as we will now consider.

Redundancy

Workforce planning is always a contingent process and, clearly, one of the contingent factors is economic conditions. The CIPD (2010a) also identified this factor as a barrier to diversity management, and, in spite of claims that recession provides an opportunity to focus on the talent within organizations, the late 2000s have been characterized by job losses in all sectors, the emphasis shifting from the private to the public sector in the UK following the Comprehensive Spending Review in October 2010. However, redundancy, or 'employee downsizing' as it is sometimes referred to, has also been a feature of many economies in the face of global pressures, cost competition and shifts in demand. As Datta et al. (2010, p. 282) argue, it has 'become the norm in many countries'.

In the UK, the legal framework for redundancy provides for payments, introduced in 1965, and minimum standards set by the European Union relating to consultation, compensation, selection and periods of notice.

> **HRM web links**
>
> Go to www.direct.gov.uk/en/Employment/RedundancyAndLeavingYourJob/Redundancy/DG_10029835 for information on redundancy consultation and notification.

Losing staff has negative consequences for organizations, as well as for those made unemployed. First, and perhaps most obviously, redundancy is a violation of the psychological contract based on a build-up of mutual expectations and obligations between employees and the organization, in which the greater the degree of employees' involvement in their work, the more negative is their feeling of violation (Stoner and Gallagher, 2010). Second, there is a loss of skill, knowledge, wisdom and social capital – the talent that employees accumulate over years of practice at work. The result of downsizing may thus be a loss of productivity (Yu and Park, 2006).

Third, there is an effect on those employees who remain at work after a period of downsizing. If they respond sympathetically towards those made redundant, they may experience effects such as guilt, lower motivation and commitment, mistrust and insecurity (Thornhill et al., 1997); this is referred to as 'survivor syndrome'. A further effect, according to Appelbaum and Donna (2000), is that compromising productivity by downsizing is detrimental to the survivors, leading to an increase in absenteeism (Travaglione and Cross, 2006). Managers may suffer, particularly when 'delayering' occurs, through 'burnout' as a consequence of changing workloads and loss of opportunities for progression (Littler et al., 2003). There might also be a decline in loyalty and 'even increases in white collar crime' (p. 226). Fourth, redundancy is stressful for those made unemployed, possibly due to the process of being made redundant itself and then through the experience of unemployment (Pickard, 2001; see also Richard Sennett's *The Corrosion of Character* [1998] for an extensive consideration of the debilitating effects of downsizing and job insecurity).

In their wide-ranging review of research, Datta et al. (2010) found that the negative outcomes of redundancy have as much to do with the manner of implementation as with the fact of having been made redundant itself. The way in which change is conducted during downsizing, along with contextual factors such as organizational culture and climate, will affect the outcomes (Self et al., 2007). Forde et al. (2008) explore the idea of 'socially responsible restructuring' during a period of mass lay-offs in the UK steel industry. This idea is based on the need to engage with the interests of all stakeholders during the process of restructuring and redundancy as part of an organization's corporate social responsibility agenda, as suggested by the European Union (European Commission, 2008).

It was found, however, that there were significant gaps between what was said and what was done about the process of restructuring. For example, socially responsible restructuring would suggest allowing time for access to job counsellors and external support agencies, but these were often found to be blocked by managers. In addition, fair and objective criteria for lay-off and redeployment might have been stated, but they were interpreted as inequitable and subjective by employees. It is suggested that HR has a key role to play to ensure 'ethical stewardship' (Forde et al., 2008, p. 22) in situations such as these.

> **HRM web links**
>
> Read more about socially responsible restructuring at http://ec.europa.eu/employment_social/equal/news/200708-cede1_en.cfm.

Talent management

During the 1990s and for most of the 2000s, there has been competition between organizations to find and develop 'high-potential' staff as part of a 'war for talent' (Michaels et al., 2001). As a consequence, TM has become a significant area of policy activity, accompanied by a growing list of books, conferences and techniques. More recently, focusing on the importance of knowledge workers and knowledge creation and sharing, Whelan and Carcary (2011) have suggested that organizations need to adopt a 'smart' version of TM in order to retain staff and their knowledge. There is, however, also a concern that TM is another repackaging of HR practices as 'old wine in new bottles' (Chuai et al., 2008).

There has been some evidence of how TM is practised in organizations and how recession has altered the focus (CIPD, 2009a; Tansley et al., 2007a) towards developing talent in house and concentrating on essential development. One response has been to strengthen relationships through TM. For example, at BT, a 'talent deal' sets out commitments to a 'talent pool' consisting of career planning, networking opportunities and mentoring.

> **reflective question**
>
> What is your understanding of talent? Is TM necessary in a recession?

TM policies need to be set against the context and situation of each organization. This can lead to variety of approaches, as shown in Figure 7.3. In this figure, the two dimensions of Exclusive/Inclusive and People/Position provide four possible patterns. First, the 'exclusive people' approach rests on the assumption that key individuals or stars are necessary for the organization's success (Groysberg, 2010). As a consequence, attention is given to those people considered to be 'high potential' and/or 'high performing' (Incomes Data Services, 2010). In contrast, an 'exclusive position' approach starts from the question, 'What key positions are needed to meet the strategy?' People with the right skills and attributes can then be found to fill those positions. Huselid et al. (2005) refer to strategically critical jobs as 'A' positions, filled by 'A' players. Such positions are supported by 'B' positions and 'C' positions – the latter might be seen as jobs that can be outsourced or eliminated. The crucial argument is that improving the performance of 'A' players in

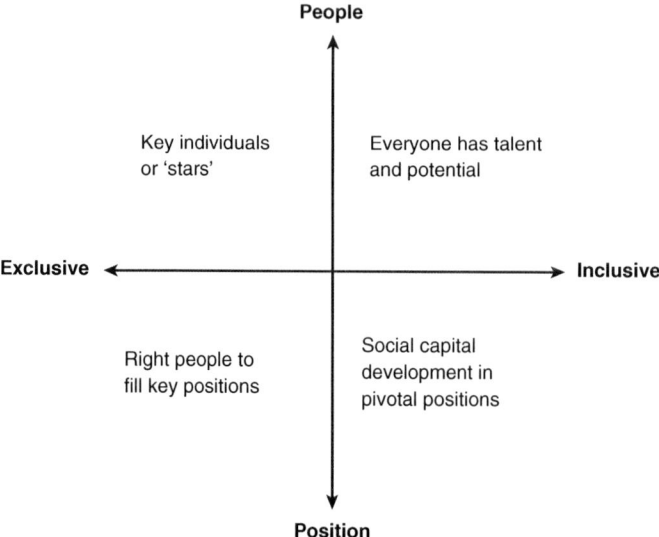

Figure 7.3 Approaches to TM

'A' positions will have a more than proportionate impact on the overall performance of the organization. An example might be the performance of customer service staff who have direct interactions with customers.

The 'inclusive people' approach is a recognition that everyone in an organization has talent and the potential for high performance. For example, according to the Learning and Development Manager of the restaurant chain Nando's, their approach to TM is based on the assumption that 'everyone who works for us is talented' and that everyone can 'grow and develop in their own environment' (quoted in *People Management*, May 3, 2007, p. 16). This approach also gives more attention to the relationships between people and to how work is often organized through teams, for example in legal work and software development. So giving attention to the 'stars' could actually reduce performance overall (Groysberg et al., 2004). The inclusive position approach highlights the importance developing relationships based on cooperation, trust and goodwill, and accessing networks – referred to as *social capital development* (McCullum and O'Donnell, 2009). Relationships with others both inside and outside an organization give strategic importance to pivotal positions in providing above-average impact (Collings and Mellahi, 2009).

Succession planning

Succession planning has traditionally been concerned with ensuring a smooth replacement for senior managers and leaders, so that there will be less disruption to performance (Giambatista et al., 2005). More recently, succession planning has been presented as the purpose of TM, although there may still be some disconnection between TM and succession processes (Tansley et al., 2007a) if both processes are completed without sharing information. The key link focuses on a plan that considers the organization's future direction and requirements against the capabilities and potential of those selected for a 'talent pool'. Membership of a pool is determined by a selection process including interviews, 360-degree feedback and other assessments. In larger organizations, there can be different pools for different levels. Tansley et al. (2007a, p. 26) identify four levels:

- Entry level
- Emerging talent
- Rising stars
- Executive talent.

The connections between the levels are referred to as the 'talent pipeline', and this provides an organization with a plan for flexible succession, as well as with a way of motivating internal staff (CIPD, 2009a). There can also be lateral movement between roles, departments and projects. Talent pools and pipelines allow a strategic view of a flow of the right people at the right time, what Ready and Conger (2007) refer to as a 'talent factory'. Part of the planning involves identifying who the right people are for each pool. Succession sometimes has to occur quickly, perhaps in response to an emergency or an absence. At such moments, Rothwell (2011) points to the importance of replacement plans carrying the implication that replacements are not needed on a permanent basis.

A typical approach might be to chart high performers against high potential, as shown in Figure 7.4. Each combination of performance and potential can be used to identify staff for talent pools. The top right corner identifies high performers with high potential, whereas the bottom right corner identifies high performers with low potential. This chart is frequently presented as a 3 × 3 matrix with nine boxes, allowing for more differentiation. Crucially, however, this allows a strategic view of talent from which a plan for succession and development can be made. There are also software solutions to help with this process. Pollitt (2007) showed how one organization used software including functions for succession planning and identifying future blockages to track 300 managers in a global talent pool.

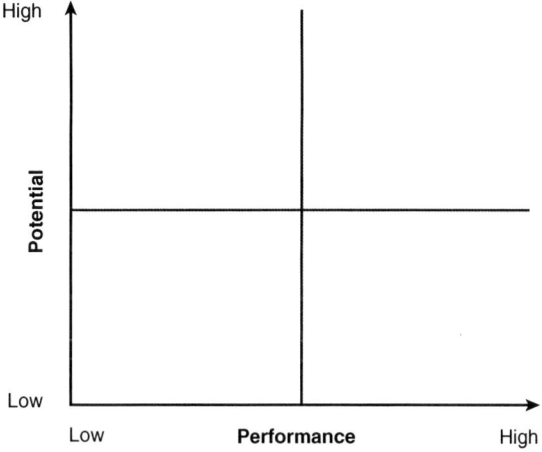

Figure 7.4 A performance/potential chart

reflective question

What approach would you adopt for someone in the top left segment of the chart – that of low performance and high potential?

HRM as I see it

Sarah Myers
Director of Talent Management, Sky
www.sky.com

Sky entertains and excites more than 10.1 million homes through the most comprehensive multichannel, multiplatform television service in the UK and Ireland. It continues to break new ground with its own portfolio of channels, which includes Sky 1, Sky Living, Sky Arts, Sky Atlantic, Sky Sports, Sky News and Sky Movies.

Sky also works with dozens of other broadcasters on the satellite platform, online and mobile. Sky is now leading the UK into the age of high-definition television with Sky+ HD, and has launched Europe's first 3DTV channel, Sky 3D, as well as Sky Anytime+, its Internet-delivered video on-demand service. The company is also the UK's fastest-growing broadband and home phone provider.

Sarah Myers joined Sky in 2003. She is a Fellow of the CIPD and has an MSc in Human Resources from the London School of Economics. She is also a member of the HR Leadership Alliance for the Heads of Talent Management, an alumna of the School of Coaching and a member of the Editorial Board of *People Management* magazine.

Visit www.palgrave.com/business/bratton5 to watch Sarah talking about TM at Sky, how it has been affected by the recession and its relationship to business strategy. Then think about the following questions:

1. What does Sarah mean by looking 'end to end' in TM?
2. How is development related to talent groups at Sky?
3. In Sarah's view, how is talent linked to succession?

Career management

TM strategies are increasingly required to take a more long-term view, which means focusing on the retention of committed staff, who in turn expect their careers to be considered (Scott and Revis, 2008). In the past, the term 'career' was one that was usually applied to managerial and professional workers, and HR practices provided support for career development along a 'well-made road' via which individual desires for status and fulfilment could be reached (Sennett, 1998, p. 120). Along the way, of course, many employees encountered blocks to their careers, such as a lack of opportunities and support and, for women, cultural and structural prejudices to career progress referred to as the 'glass ceiling' (Davidson and Cooper, 1992). Graduates too might find their aspirations unsatisfied as they experienced a gap between what they expected and what their organizations provided (Pickard, 1997). In addition, those from ethnic minorities might find themselves 'ghettoed' into certain sectors of work (Singh, 2002). For many employees, however, it was indeed possible to embrace the idea of an organizational career that could be planned for the course of a working life, and theoretical models supported a view that careers could be planned and managed (Grzeda, 1999).

Through the 1990s and into the 2000s, there were significant changes in the way in which careers were explained, understood and managed. Various tensions – such as competition, recession and short-term financial pressures, a breakdown in functional structures in favour of process structures such as project teams and even the loss of bureaucratic personnel systems that planned career moves – have combined, in some companies, to 'dump the basic idea of the corporate career' (Hirsh and Jackson, 1997, p. 9). Many employees still, however, regard their job as a career step (Taylor, 2002).

Adamson et al. (1998) suggested that there have been three changes in organizational career philosophy:

- An end to the long-term view of the employer–employee relationship
- An end to movement through the hierarchy being seen as career progression
- An end to logical, ordered and sequential careers.

One of the manifestations of these changes is that fewer organizations would now claim to offer careers for life, with some evidence that employees are unhappy with the ways in which their careers are developing (CIPD, 2003). If neither individuals nor organizations can plan for the long term, this suggests that the term 'career', with its implication of predictable progression, may have lost its commonly understood meaning. Instead, the career path becomes 'multidirectional' (Baruch, 2004).

An alternative view is that of the 'portfolio career' (Templer and Cawsey, 1999), in which individuals might expect, over the course of their working lives, to work for a variety of different organizations in a variety of positions; as a result of this, they will need a range of skills, learning new ones as required to enhance their employability. Included in the sequence might be periods of leisure, education and domestic tasks. A related view is that of the 'boundaryless career' (Arthur and Rousseau, 2000), during which individuals can consider movements between jobs, locations and occupations. Sullivan and Arthur (2006) also refer to psychological mobility, which considers how people perceive their abilities in making career choices in the light of current realities. This reflects an interest in what Khapova et al. (2007, p. 115) see as the 'subjective career' based on an 'individual's interpretation of his or her career situation at any given time'.

Similarly, it reflects the 'protean career' (Hall, 2002), in which individuals are proactive in directing their careers, using personal values to evaluate their success. These images are part of a general move towards all of us accepting responsibility for our own career development through acquiring employability skills and developing life-long learning (O'Donoghue and Maguire, 2005). Research by De Vos and Soens (2008) suggests that a 'protean career attitude' is related to career success, but this requires skills of career self-management, supported by organizational culture and HR practices including the development of career competencies (Ball, 1997) that should include a balance between work and non-work. Sturges et al. (2010) show the importance of perceptions of the organization's support for career management, especially relationships with managers and others, if staff are to be retained and developed. Furthermore, if such support is absent, staff are more likely to manage their careers in order to take them away from the organization.

These views of career learning are not, however, universally accepted. For example, Mallon and Walton (2005), in a study of career learning among local government and health workers in the UK and New Zealand, found that few were actively engaging in this. Furthermore, most still saw their careers in terms relating to their employment within their organizations (or previous organizations where workers were now working for themselves). It was still very much the case that definitions of careers were organizationally situated, and that this affected what was deemed relevant to learn. In addition and more generally – as a consequence of the expansion of higher education – there is a growing number of graduates with higher levels of knowledge and skills, but these do not automatically make them employable. Employability, skills and knowledge require a valued response from employing organizations (Elias and Purcell, 2003).

> **reflective question**
>
> The notion of careers is subject to change and flux. Who do you think should be responsible for the development of people's working lives? How are you making yourself employable, and what are the skills of employability and life-long learning? To help you, examine the HRM web link www.ics.heacademy.ac.uk/Employability/index.htm, which will take you to a site devoted to employability.

These varying images of what constitutes a career point to a 'pendulum of ownership of career development' by which responsibility swings between the organization and the individual (Hirsh and Jackson, 1997, p. 9). Over the last 20 years, many organizations have engaged in restructuring activities that have led to 'delayering' and the removal of grades. The spread of career development initiatives could thus be seen as a way of empowering and motivating staff who have remained in place as part of a core workforce, and this extends now to TM strategies. Given the different approaches to TM we considered above, it is not entirely clear how these will affect patterns of career development. However, we can suggest a segmented pattern encompassing career development for everyone at work, but with different patterns for different work groups:

- Managers and 'high-potential/high performance' staff – careers managed by the organization, not always for life, but with succession-planning to fill senior positions
- Highly skilled workers – attempts to attract and keep key workers by offering career development paths
- The wider workforce – more limited development opportunities often caused by and resulting in uncertainty over career paths; there is an expectation that these workers should look after themselves.

Research suggests a mixed picture of career management practice. In the UK, the CIPD (2003) carried out a survey of over 700 organizations relating to their current and emerging practice on career management. There was good practice in some organizations, but fewer than one-half had a written strategy for career management, with only around a quarter having a strategy for all staff. The greatest focus was on developing and retaining managers and key staff, with only 9 per cent aiming to provide employees with a better understanding of career opportunities and expectation. There was, however, an overwhelming espousal of the philosophy of a partnership approach to career management for all employees, even though the reality suggested a focus on particular groups of staff.

Lips-Wiersma and Hall (2007) have provided a case study of careers in an organization during change, finding evidence that staff were taking more responsibility for careers but that this was shared with the organization. Thus, where staff were setting their own career goals and aiming to find opportunities such as secondments, HR either helped or initiated projects with secondments, seeking to link the individuals' career aspirations with the culture and direction of the organization. According to Lips-Wiersma and Hall (p. 789):

> Career management and development has a significant role to play in achieving mutuality of organizational and individual interests.

For those selected into talent programmes and talent pools, it would seem that the benefits include development opportunities that enable career enhancement. Research by the CIPD (2010a) based on surveys and interviews showed, not surprisingly, that selection for such programmes was likely to increase engagement and help employees see a future with their organization, so a career path was clearer. In addition, coaching, mentoring and networking – thus increasing social capital – were more highly valued. The HR function was important in ensuring that the programme was well run and considered effective for the organization.

reflective question

How do think those not selected for talent pools might respond, and what impact is there on their careers?

Finally, in this section, it is useful to consider Sullivan et al.'s (2007) kaleidoscope career model, which takes a lifespan approach and suggests that each person can seek a best fit of choices based on the parameters of:

- *Authenticity* – an alignment of internal values with those of the place of work
- *Balance* – between work and non-work demands, including family, friends and personal interests
- *Challenge* – of stimulating work and career advancement.

These parameters are interpreted differently over a lifespan and between generations in organizations. For example, those considered to be part of Generation X (born between 1965 and 1983) have a higher preference than baby-boomers (born 1946–1964) for authenticity and balance (Sullivan et al., 2009). We await further research on those born after 1983, or Generation Y, who appear to seek high rewards but want flexibility to do so, being very information-savvy and well networked. Will they seek more challenges but also more of a work–life balance, and will they therefore be difficult to satisfy?

Diversity management

One of the most important trends in recent years has been an interest in the benefits to be achieved by planning for a diverse workforce, known as 'diversity management', and its connection with business and organizational success (Tatli et al., 2007). Furthermore, it is argued that diversity and TM actually need to be completely integrated and should be seen as 'one and the same thing' (CIPD, 2010b, p. 19).

This move towards diversity can be seen as an extension of, but simultaneously a contrast to, the promotion of equal opportunities during the 1970s and 80s. Equal opportunities is the view that people should be treated equally regardless of race, ethnic origin, gender, sexual orientation and other social categorizations, so that 'individuals are enabled freely and equally to compete for social rewards' (Jewson and Mason, 1986, p. 307). Jewson and Mason set equal opportunities within a free-market tradition, and the purpose of legislation and policies was seen as removing obstacles within and distortions to the working of markets. They pointed to a liberal approach based on 'positive action' to ensure fair and meritocratic procedures in organizations, underpinned by antidiscrimination legislation. They contrasted this with a more radical view, highlighting the embedded nature of discrimination, which could not be corrected through fair procedures alone. Instead, disadvantaged groups would need 'positive discrimination' to achieve fairness, although this still remains unlawful in the UK.

There has, however, been a general recognition that equal opportunities based on 'sameness' has not fulfilled its promise, and that while overt discrimination has been largely removed, prejudice and stereotyping remain embedded within organizations and society at large. One of the crucial difficulties is that debates on equality are based on ethical arguments, often framed in terms of either social justice or a business case, which Gagnon and Cornelius (2000) suggest tends to produce sterility when it comes to practice.

Diversity, according to Schneider (2001, p. 27) is 'about creating a working culture that seeks, respects, values and harnesses difference'. The basic contrast with

For Barclays Bank, valuing the diversity of its employees is the key to success
Source: Courtesy of Barclays Bank PLC.

equal opportunities is an acceptance that there are differences between people, that such differences can be valued, and that they are the source of productive potential within an organization. It is suggested that diversity can provide an organization with a valuable resource in competing both globally and locally. Thus, Singh (2002) highlights a business case for diversity, claiming that inclusion and the development of people 'to the best of their abilities' (p. 3) will result in commitment, creativity and competitive advantage for the organization. For example, Barclays Bank (http://group.barclays.com/Citizenship/Diversity-and-our-people) declares the following:

> Our people are the foundation of Barclays success. It's as simple as that. We want the most talented, whatever their style, personality, age, race, gender, sexual orientation, or disability.

reflective question

How do you think that Barclays can achieve such a vision of diversity?

Like Barclays, many organizations are seeking to manage diversity, and this requires organizations to recognize differences. According to Liff (1997b), there are four approaches to managing diversity based on the degree of commitment to social group equality as an organizational objective, and on the perceived relevance of differentiation between social groups for policy-making:

- The first approach might be to dissolve differences in order to 'stress individualism' (Liff, 1997b, p. 13) so that everyone's needs and desires for effective working are recognized. This tends to minimize differences, giving little recognition to the value of difference – rather like traditional equal opportunities approaches.

HRM AND GLOBALIZATION
What to do about macho?

A basic assumption of HR theory is that the performance of a work organization is linked to its people, and that an individual's job performance is a function of his or her human capital (knowledge and skill). It follows that the link between human capital and earnings should be strong: those who possess human capital should be rewarded with good jobs and high earnings.

But what if a particular segment of the population were systematically excluded from good jobs and did not receive the earnings one would expect given their human capital? This is the situation of women in many parts of the world. While in some nations (or groups of nations), there has been significant progress in reducing work-related gender inequalities, in other parts of the world such inequalities persist.

Take the case of Latin America. Recent research by economist Hugo Nopo indicates that while the earnings gap between men and women has narrowed, it still favours men. The gap persists despite the gains that women have made in the acquisition of human capital. 'It is somewhat paradoxical' writes Nopo, 'that besides having more schooling, women still earn less than men' (2011, p. 80).

There are obviously many factors at work here. Traditional gender roles and gender discrimination may still exert a powerful influence in Latin American cultures. However, according to Nopo, gender biases diminish when employers have access to accurate information about productivity (2011, p. 81):

> *In the absence of information ... individuals use observable characteristics such as gender, skin colour, and height as proxies for productivity. When real information about productivity is revealed, individuals do not use these proxies anymore and base their decisions on the productivity data instead.*

Rational arguments may be sufficient to alter the views of those who discriminate against women in the workplace. At home, however, in the private world of the family, things may be different. Nopo points out that the women devote 70–80 per cent of their time to domestic work in Latin American households – 'far more than women's contribution in other societies' (2011, p. 81). To free up the time necessary to complete this domestic work, women must look for flexibility in their paid work arrangements. Women therefore 'choose' 'part-time work, small firms, and informal jobs' (p. 81). This helps to explain the earnings gap and the fact that women are not adequately rewarded for their human capital. It also points to barriers that prevent work organizations from making optimal use of available human capital.

> **Stop!** The word 'macho' captures some of the qualities associated with the masculine gender role in Latin America. What does macho mean to you? Is there a word that captures the qualities associated with the feminine gender role in Latin America?

> Do HR professionals have any business thinking about the home life of their employees? And what could be done to change gender roles in Latin America, especially in households where traditional ways of doing things are taken for granted?
>
> Are traditional gender roles uniformly strong or weak in countries such as the USA or UK, or is there some variation within these countries? Among which groups, or in which parts of the country, might the influence of traditional gender roles remain strong?
>
> *Note*: This feature was written by David MacLennan at Thompson Rivers University.

- In contrast, a second approach is to value differences. Crucial here is the recognition that past practices have reinforced inequalities and led to under-representation and disadvantage. This may mean that there needs to be a change in practice to create a culture reinforcing the fact that everyone has a valued role in an organization.
- The third approach of accommodating differences seeks not to waste talent but to ensure that everyone has an equal chance. This could mean, for example, targeting recruitment for under-represented groups that have the necessary qualifications.
- A fourth approach is to utilize differences, recognizing their usefulness and developing policies that value them. Liff uses the example of a career track for 'family' women with career breaks, gradual promotion and part-time work. The crucial feature of the policy would be that this track would be valued in the same way as the traditional track.

It might be argued that the idea of managing diversity is not a great deal more in advance of traditional approaches to equal opportunities. Indeed, many organizations espouse a commitment to equality and diversity that could easily be translated into a focus on 'sameness', rather than tackling the complexity of 'difference'. However, in contrast to the preventive stance of equal opportunities, managing diversity takes a more positive line in which an organization seeks to avoid accusations of treating people unequally (Kirton and Greene, 2000). There is also a widening of the coverage beyond traditional concerns with race and gender, and this echoes legislative and regulative support related to age, sexual orientation and disability.

Probably the most important feature is, however, the encouragement from senior management to put diversity at the forefront of its concerns. Some organizations, for example Ford and BT, have indicated this by the appointment of diversity directors or diversity champions. Thus, there is value to be gained from being diverse, in terms of both orientation towards the external context, by appreciating the diversity of cultures and ethnic backgrounds of staff and customers, and recognition of the variety within an organization.

Diversity needs to be seen strategically, as part of a cultural change process (Singh, 2002) and one that is good for organizational performance (Pilch, 2006). Recently, in the UK, the Confederation of British Industry, the Trades Union Congress and the Equality and Human Rights Commission all joined forces to argue that meeting legal and moral requirements on diversity can have clear business benefits (Confederation of British Industry, 2008). Research in Ireland for 132 companies clearly showed a link between high-performance working and organizational outcomes when factors such as diversity were managed in an integrated and cohesive manner (Flood et al., 2008).

There are, however, also doubts. Foster and Harris (2005), for example, identified that employers and employees are often confused by the simultaneous focus on equality and the valorization of difference in the workplace, and question whether diversity is just equality repackaged or genuinely represents something new. In addition, there is a critical engagement with the concept of diversity and its origins (Lorbiecki and Jack, 2000) and a warning against the dangers of a 'utilitarian' business argument (Western, 2008).

For diversity to be taken seriously, it has to be more than checking possible prejudice in the recruitment literature or expecting line managers to take responsibility for implementing plans. It needs to be recognized that historical tradition plays a vital role, usually below the surface of consciousness, in maintaining normative value sets that will prevent the agenda of diversity advancing. There needs to be a challenge to and a critique of the attitudes and background assumptions that individuals implicitly hold and that are also embedded in everyday objects and activities that form the commonality of our lives and to which we are bound (Wood et al., 2004). Thus, greater attention to socialization and the development of a culture of tolerance is required if the positive benefits of diversity are to be gained.

There is, however, also a potential for greater conflict based on the misunderstandings that are caused when people from different backgrounds and cultures have different points of view and different values; this can, in turn, lead to lower job satisfaction and higher staff turnover (McMillan-Capehart, 2005). The CIPD (2010b) found a range of barriers to integrating talent and diversity, such as unsuccessful previous experiences, an exclusive orientation towards talent and a lack of boardroom diversity. However, their research also pointed to some excellent examples of practice in managing diversity in such organizations as BT, the Guardian Media Group and the NHS in the London borough of Tower Hamlets. There is an argument for organizations to appreciate the value that can be provided through the talents of a diverse workforce. However, as Ford et al. (2009) found, such an argument needs to work with the interests of leaders and managers. Although compliance with the law is expected, many people do not like to be told what to do, and the area of diversity often falls into this category.

HRM web links

Go to www.nhsemployers.org/EmploymentPolicyAndPractice/EqualityAndDiversity/Pages/Home.aspx, which provides an overview of NHS strategy for equality and diversity. Also check out the Employers' Forum on disability at www.efd.org.uk, which provides guidance on recruiting and retaining disabled employees, and the Employers' Forum on Age at www.efa.org.uk.

Human resource accounting

Making people redundant would appear to contradict claims that 'people are our greatest asset' and the fact that people as human capital are a crucial asset in the knowledge economy (Pilch, 2000). However, the need to show the value of people has led to various attempts use the language of accounting to represent this value in an organization's financial statement. We refer to such efforts as *human resource accounting* (HRA), which we define as the process of identifying, quantifying, accounting and forecasting the value of human resources in order to facilitate effective HRM. HRM needs to be measured and expressed in financial terms to gain credibility (Toulson and Dewe, 2004), and a failure to do this has been a key factor in reducing the importance of decisions related to HR.

Unlike capital items and materials, people cannot be owned by an organization. They can, however, be said to 'loan' their abilities to perform in return for rewards from the organization (Mayo, 2002). Organizations will seek to obtain the most from such a loan by combining people's knowledge and skills with other resources to add value. Furthermore, such value-adding can increase over time through the knowledge and skills that employees develop from performing their work, and from specific activities such as training and development. An organization might therefore claim that it is important to include such value-adding capability on its balance sheet. There have for many years been attempts to account for the value of people in organizations, with a tendency to treat people in financial terms, 'the dominant image of HRA for many people' (Flamholz, 1985, p. 3) being putting 'people on the balance sheet'. Valid and reliable models of measurement have, however, been lacking, and HRA has 'progressed at something less than a snail's pace' (Turner, 1996, p. 65).

More enthusiasm for HRA has been found in Sweden, where many organizations have used its key ideas in decision-making, leading to a 'changed way of thinking' about the management of HR (Gröjer and Johanson, 1998, p. 499). HRA was, for example, integrated into the management control process of three companies researched by Johanson and Nilson (1996) in which managers were trained and information systems adjusted. Furthermore, HRA statements were included in the companies' annual reports. It was found that HRA techniques were useful as management tools, but management were also ambivalent towards HRA since the techniques could also be used to assess the efficiency of the managers themselves (Johanson, 1999).

As a tool that management can use to control costs, HRA can be accused of contributing to a narrow view of people in organizations as being an expense to be minimized and cut when necessary. This view can significantly underrate the value of people in terms of their accumulation of knowledge and understanding as they learn at work, which makes them difficult to replace as well as difficult to copy. People therefore have a value that is greater than simply the cost of their employment. Although that value is difficult to capture in financial terms, knowledge and understanding in an organization form part of its intangible assets or intellectual capital, which includes features such as brand names, as well as knowledge and understanding. Edvinsson and Malone (1997) suggest that intellectual capital in an organization is composed of two factors. First, there is structural capital, such as hardware and software, trade and brand names, and relationships with customers and suppliers – as Edvinsson and Malone (1997, p. 11) have put it, 'everything left at the office when the employees go home'. Second, there is human capital, which is the knowledge and skills of employees at work as well as their values and culture. In combination, human capital plus structural capital equals intellectual capital.

> **reflective question**
>
> What is the intellectual capital of your course? How is this intellectual capital valued?

Mayo (2002, p. 38) suggests the use of a 'human capital monitor' to calculate the added value of people in an organization. The key idea is that added value, in the form of both financial and non-financial contributions, can be assessed by considering:

- *People as assets* – composed of employment costs, capability, potential, alignment of values and contributions

plus

- *People's motivation/commitment* – which is affected by factors in the work environment such as leadership, practical support, reward and recognition, and learning and development.

What is significant about intellectual capital is that, as the knowledge economy advances, more organizations will need to invest in knowledge-creating activities, in which the production of new knowledge is a vital differentiator between different organizations (Garvey and Williamson, 2002). However, the difficulty has always been how to value intangible assets within the accountancy profession (Cleary, 2010), although there have been moves to find such an understanding in recent years – albeit with limitations. In the UK, following the report of the Accounting For People Task Force (2003), a central recommendation was that organizations producing annual operating and financial reviews should include information on 'human capital management'. There was an acceptance that the lack of agreed measurements and definitions would require an evolutionary approach, and that this could, of course, be used as an excuse to avoid any effort to produce human capital information on management. Toulson and Dewe (2004) have called for HR managers to become familiar with a range of measurement practices and tools in order to enhance their understanding of different points of view.

The CIPD (2005a) has provided a guide on human capital reporting covering a range of measuring tools and methodologies, ranging from simple and subjective anecdotes about the value of people's performance to internal and external benchmarking, through to the identification of the human capital drivers of performance. Sánchez et al. (2009) recently developed a model for universities to enable the reporting of intellectual capital. However, there continues to be uncertainty over the requirement for organizations to provide a more wide-ranging report beyond finances. Verma and Dewe (2008), for example, found, in a survey of UK organizations, that there was recognition of the importance of measuring human resources, but that there had been little progress in doing so due to lack of support as well as uncertainty over what to measure.

> **HRM web links**
>
> You may wish to consult Lev Baruch's work on the measurement of intangible assets at www.baruch-lev.com, where his research papers can be obtained. Go to http://www.iasplus.com/standard/ias38.htm for a summary of IAS 38, the International Accounting Standard for intangible assets. And look at http://annualreport.marksandspencer.com/financial-review/financial-review.aspx for the Operating and Financial Review of Marks and Spencer, with a report on 'People' at http://annualreport.marksandspencer.com/financial-review/people.aspx.

CASE STUDY

TNNB Ltd

Setting

TNNB is a family-owned engineering business producing electrohydraulic systems for a wide range of customers, mostly for export. It has won two Queens Awards for Export and is regarded as a leader in its sector. Each system is built to order, with a salesperson obtaining the initial details before a design engineer builds a portfolio of images that can be presented to the customer. On approval, which can take anything up to 6 months, a contract is established and the order is handed over to project managers.

The principal tasks of the project managers are to build a relationship with the customer, to draw up a plan with key dates for completion, to ensure safe delivery and check installation, and to make sure that resources are allocated at the right time in the right combination. Project management is complex work, and to ensure delivery against the terms of the contract with the customer, where delays can result in a loss of revenue, it is necessary to establish a strong network of relationships with everyone involved in the completion of an order. Although a project plan will contain the key details and requirements for completion, it is up to a project manager to track performance, often in parallel streams, so that any disconnections can be prevented or dealt with. As Lewis (2000) identifies, it is always necessary for a project manager to know:

- Where we are
- Where we should be
- How can we get on track again.

The problem

TNNB employs two project managers who can between them be responsible for several projects at a time, usually at different stages of completion. During a period when six projects were in process, it became evident early on that some key stages were not being completed against schedule, the company managers being alerted by the prospect of penalty clauses. Further evidence revealed that one of the project managers had a reputation for being too slow and measured, spending too much time in his office, apparently making a paper plan that seemed to be out of step with events on the ground. He could identify where the project should be, but could seldom identify the current status of the project. The second project manager was more likely to have the opposite problem – good on the live situation of the project but poor at planning, often resulting in reactive scheduling.

Source: ©istockphoto.com/endopack.

TNNB had two managers, cousins within the owning family, and after a brief meeting together, they decided to take a closer look at what was happening. It soon became clear that there were tensions between the systems engineers and the mechanical design and service engineers. In addition, the project managers were not dealing with this effectively, with the main systems engineer claiming he was 'being let down' and was feeling 'frustrated' through the 'incompetence' of the project managers. He argued that neither project manager seemed to have the necessary skills or talent for the job, and that both were associated with missed deadlines or crisis meetings to get things done at the last minute because no advance information had been provided.

The two project managers were defensive about their work, arguing that management had not prepared them sufficiently for the role. Furthermore, they said that the company's shift to project-based working had, despite its success in the market, not been properly thought through.

The family managers felt threatened by what they found. First, they believed that project-based working with good project managers was the only way they could ensure continued progress in the company. Second, systems engineering added a distinctive feature to the product, and any possibility of losing engineers from this section would cause difficulties. But losing any of their engineers would not be helpful since they were difficult to find, had learnt a lot on the job, which took time, and had mostly been with the company for several years (with some not far from retirement).

Assignment

Working either alone or in a study group, prepare a report drawing on this chapter and other recommended material addressing the following:

1. How would a TM strategy help this company?
2. What perspective or approach to talent would be appropriate?
3. What policies and practices for talent development are needed now?
4. What policies and practices for talent development are needed in the future?

Essential reading

Lewis, J. P. (2000) The *Project Manager's Desk Reference: A Comprehensive Guide To Project Planning, Scheduling, Evaluation, and System.* New York: McGraw Hill.

Note: This feature was written by Jeff Gold.

Visit the companion website at www.palgrave.com/business/bratton5 for a bonus case study on downsizing at the Royal Bank of Scotland, and for guidelines on how to write a report.

Summary

- Manpower planning in the 1960s and 70s emphasized quantities, flows and mathematical modelling to ensure that the necessary supply of people was forthcoming to allow targets to be met.

- Personnel specialists were able to utilize manpower measures of labour turnover, absenteeism and stability to diagnose and solve problems, increasingly aided by PC-based software packages. Manpower planning could play a vital role in the management of the employment relationship.

- HRP could be seen to be a continuation and extension of this process, which fully recognizes the potential of people and their needs in the development of strategies and plans. Integrated systems of HR activities are associated with superior performance in high-performing organizations.

- Workforce planning is a process of forecasting the supply of and demand for skills against the requirements of future production and services delivery in a situation of uncertainty and change. It is a process supported by the use of ICT enabling the production of

- various forecasts and scenarios for future possibilities and unexpected shocks. Such systems can also be provided over the Internet as a feature of e-HR.

- In many organizations, the language of flexibility and a range of different practices have been employed, often without consideration for their effect on employment relations. There has been a growth in the number of part-time and tele-home-working employees, with government backing for flexible working, as well as in the outsourcing and offshoring of services. There is, however, little evidence of the overall impact on business performance and people's motivation.

- TM has become a significant area of policy activity accompanied by a growing list of books, conferences and techniques. Patterns of TM can vary according to inclusivity and the attention given to people or positions.

- Fewer organizations offer careers for life, and career planning has become more difficult. Each person will need a range of skills to develop a portfolio career, and there has been a growing emphasis on people accepting responsibility for developing their own careers and making themselves employable.

- There is growing interest in managing diversity at work. Diversity is a means of creating heterogeneity in the workforce, a variety of experiences, backgrounds and networks enhancing the ability to solve complex problems. Managing diversity needs to be seen as part of cultural change.

- The late 2000s have been characterized by job losses in all sectors. Negative outcomes of redundancy have as much to do with the manner of its implementation, and contextual factors such as the organization's culture and the climate will affect the outcomes.

- HRA has been advocated as presenting the value of people as assets, but there has been a lack of a valid and reliable model of measurement.

Vocab checklist for ESL students

- business process re-engineering (n)
- business-to-employee (B2E) (n)
- corporate social responsibility (n)
- discretion (n), discreet/discretionary (adj)
- diversity (n), diverse (adj)
- enterprise resource planning (ERP) (n)
- equal opportunity (n)
- flexibility (n), flexible (adj)
- human capital (n)
- human resource accounting (HRA) (n)
- human resource infrastructure system (HRIS) (n)
- human resource planning (HRP) (n)
- information and communication technology (ICT) (n)
- intellectual capital (n)
- kaleidoscope career model (n)
- knowledge process outsourcing (n)
- manpower planning (n)
- offshoring (v), offshore (n) (adj)
- outsourcing (v) (n)
- redundancy (n), redundant (adj)
- retain (v), retention (n)

- second (v), secondment (n)
- social capital (n)
- succeed (v), succession (n)
- talent (n), talented (adj)
- talent management (TM) (n)
- telecommute (v), telecommuting (n)
- teleworking (n)
- turnover (n)

Visit www.palgrave.com/business/bratton5 for a link to free definitions of these terms in the Macmillan Dictionary, as well as additional learning resources for ESL students.

Review questions

1. 'When an organization is mapping out its future needs, it is a serious mistake to think primarily in terms of number, flows and economic models.' Discuss.
2. How is workforce planning linked to strategic planning?
3. What would be your response to the publication of figures that showed an above-average turnover of students in a university/college department?
4. What are the various approaches to managing talent in times of recession?
5. Can negative outcomes associated with redundancy be avoided?

Further reading to improve your mark

Reading these articles and chapters can help you gain a better understanding and potentially a higher grade for your HRM assignment.

- Peter Cappelli has written a range of papers and books on talent and workforce planning. In A supply chain approach to workforce planning, *Organizational Dynamics*, **38**(1): 8–15, he charts the decline of manpower planning but shows how, in the face of uncertainty, forecasts for supply and demand for talent are still very necessary.
- For a more critical perspective on flexibility based on extensive interviews in eight case studies around 60 organizations in various forms of interorganizational relationship, read M. Marchington, D. Grimshaw, J. Rubery and H. Willmott (eds) (2005) *Fragmenting Work: Blurring Organizational Boundaries and Disordering Hierarchies*. Oxford: Oxford University Press.
- A critical review of interest in TM is taken by Robert E. Lewis and Robert J. Heckman (2006) in Talent management: a critical review, *Human Resource Management Review*, **16**(2): 139–54.
- For a recent update on theories and practice of career management and development, the 4th edition of *Career Management* by Jeffrey H. Greenhaus, Gerard A. Callanan and Veronica M. Godshalk (2010), published by Sage, Thousand Oaks, CA, is recommended.
- Gill Kirton and Anne-Marie Greene (2010) provide a critical view of diversity management in *The Dynamics of Managing Diversity: A Critical Approach (3rd edn)*. Oxford: Butterworth-Heinemann.

Visit www.palgrave.com/business/bratton5 for lots of extra resources to help you get to grips with this chapter, including study tips, HRM skills development guides, summary lecture notes, and more.

References

Adamson, S. J., Doherty, N. and Viney, C. (1998) The meanings of career revisited: implications for theory and practice. *British Journal of Management*, **9**(4): 251–9.

Alis, D., Karsten, L., and Leopold, J. (2006) From gods to goddesses. *Time and Society*, **15**(1): 81–104.

Amiti, M. and Wei, S.-J. (2009) Service off-shoring and productivity: evidence from the US. *World Economy*, **32**(2): 203–23.

Appelbaum, S. H. and Donna, M. (2000) The realistic downsizing preview: a management intervention in the prevention of survivor syndrome. Part I. *Career Development International*, **5**(7): 333–50.

Arthur, M. B. and Rousseau, D. M. (eds) (2000) *The Boundaryless Career*. Oxford: Oxford University Press.

Atkinson, J. S. and Meager, N. (1985) Introduction and summary of main findings. In J. S. Atkinson and N. Meager, *Changing Work Patterns* (pp. 2–11). London: National Economic Development Office.

Bach, S. (2010) Managed migration? Nurse recruitment and the consequences of state policy. *Industrial Relations Journal*, **41**(3): 249–66.

Ball, B. (1997) Career management competences – the individual perspective. *Career Development International*, **2**(2): 74–9.

Ball, K. (2001) The use of human resource information systems: a survey. *Personnel Review*, **30**(6): 677–93.

Barney, J., Wright, M. and Ketchen, D. J. (2001) The resource-based view of the firm: ten years after 1991. *Journal of Management*, **27**: 625–41.

Bartholomew, D. J. (1971) The statistical approach to manpower planning. *Statistician*, **20**: 3–26.

Baruch, Y. (2004) Transforming careers: from linear to multidirectional career paths. *Career Development International*, **9**(1): 58–73.

Battisti, M., Fraccaroli, F., Fasol, R. and Depolo, M. (2007). Psychological contract and quality of organizational life: an empirical study on workers at a rest home. *Industrial Relations*, **62**, 664–88.

BBC News (2011) 'Fewer new Scottish teachers find permanent jobs', June 15, 2011. Available at: www.bbc.news/uk-scotland-13773708 (accessed November 30, 2011).

Bell, D. (1989) Why manpower planning is back in vogue. *Personnel Management*, July: 40–3.

Bohle, P., Willaby, H., Quinlan, M. and McNamara, M. (2011) Flexible work in call centres: working hours, work-life conflict and health, *Applied Ergonomics*, **42**(2): 219–24.

Boon, C., Paauwe, J., Boselie, P. and Den Hartog, D. (2009) Institutional pressures and HRM: developing institutional fit. *Personnel Review*, **38**(5): 492–508.

Bowen, D. E. and Ostroff, C. (2004) Understanding HRM–firm performance linkages: the role of the 'strength' of the HRM system. *Academy of Management Review*, **29**(2): 203–21.

Buckingham, G. (2000) Same indifference. *People Management*, **6**(4): 44–6.

Budhwar, P., Verma, A., Malhotra, N. and Mukherjee, A. (2009) Insights into the Indian call centre industry: can internal marketing help tackle high employee turnover. *Journal of Services Marketing*, **23**(5): 351–62.

Cappelli, P. (2009) A supply chain approach to workforce planning. *Organizational Dynamics*, **38**(1): 8–15.

Caulkin, S. (2001) The time is now. *People Management*, **7**(17): 32–4.

Chartered Institute of Personnel and Development (2003) *Managing Careers Survey*. London: CIPD.

Chartered Institute of Personnel and Development (2005a) *Human Capital Reporting: An Internal Perspective*. London: CIPD.

Chartered Institute of Personnel and Development (2009a) *Fighting Back Through Talent Innovation*. London: CIPD.

Chartered Institute of Personnel and Development (2010a) *The Talent Perspective. What Does It Feel Like To Be Talent-Managed?* London: CIPD.

Chartered Institute of Personnel and Development (2010b) *Opening Up Talent For Business Success*. London: CIPD.

Chuai, X., Preece, D. and Iles, P. (2008) Is talent management just 'old wine in new bottles'? *Management Research News*, **31**(12): 901–11.

Cleary, P. (2010) Human Resource Accounting. In D. McGuire and K. M. Jorgensen (eds) *Human Resource Development* (pp. 44–54). London, Sage.

Coleman, S. and Keep, E. (2001) 'Background literature review for PIU project on workforce development'. Available at: www.cabinet-office.gov.uk/innovation/2001/workforce/literaturereview.pdf.

Colling, T. (2005) Managing human resources in the networked organization. In S. Bach (ed.) *Managing Human Resources* (pp. 90–112). Oxford: Blackwell.

Collings, D. and Mellahi, K. (2009) Strategic talent management: A review and research agenda. *Human Resource Management Review*, **19**(4): 304–13.

Confederation of British Industry (2008) *Talent Not Tokenism: The Business Benefits of Workforce Diversity*. London: CBI/TUC/EHRC.

Contractor, F. J., Kumar, V., Kundu, S. K. and Pedersen, T. (2010) Reconceptualizing the firm in a world of outsourcing and offshoring: the organizational and geographical relocation of high-value company functions. *Journal of Management Studies*, **47**(8): 1417–33.

Cooke, F. L. (2000) *Human Resource Strategy to Improve Organisational Performance: A Route for British Firms?* Working Paper No. 9. Economic and Social Research Council Future of Work Programme. Swindon: ESRC.

Cowling, A. and Walters, M. (1990) Manpower planning – where are we today? *Personnel Review*, **19**(3): 3–8.

Cross, B. and Travaglione, A. (2004) The times they are a-changing: who will stay and who will go in a downsizing organization? *Personnel Review*, **33**(3): 275–90.

Curson, J. (2006) Crystal-ball gazing: planning the medical workforce. *British Journal of Hospital Medicine*, **67**(8): 1141–7.

Curson, J. A., Dell, M. E., Wilson, R. A., Bosworth, D. L. and Baldauf, B. (2010) Who does workforce planning well? *International Journal of Health Care Quality Assurance*, **23**(1): 110–19.

Datta, D., Guthrie, J., Basuil, D. and Pandey, A. (2010) Causes and effects of employee downsizing: a review and synthesis. *Journal of Management*, **36**(1): 281–348.

Davidson, M. J. and Cooper, C. L. (1992) *Shattering the Glass Ceiling*. London: Paul Chapman.

Deery, S. and Kinnie, N. (2004) *Call Centres and Human Resource Management: A Cross-national Perspective*. Basingstoke: Palgrave Macmillan.

Department of Employment (1974) *Company Manpower Planning*. Manpower Papers No. 1. London: HMSO.

Department of Trade and Industry (2004) *The UK Contact Centre Industry: A Study*. London: DTI.

Department of Trade and Industry (2005a) *People, Strategy and Performance: Results from the Second Work and Enterprise Business Survey*. London: DTI.

Department of Trade and Industry (2005b) *Inside the Workplace: First Findings from the 2004 Workplace Employment Relations Survey* (WERS 2004). London: DTI.

Des, G. G. and Shaw, J. D. (2001) Voluntary turnover, social capital and organizational performance. *Academy of Management Review*, **26**: 446–56.

De Vos, A. and Soens, N. (2008) Protean attitude and career success: the mediating role of self-management. *Journal of Vocational Behavior*, **73**: 449–56.

Duxbury, L. and Higgins, C. (2002) Telework: a primer for the millennium introduction. In Cooper, C. L. and Burke, R. J. (eds) *The New World of Work: Challenges and Opportunities* (pp. 157–200). Oxford: Blackwell.

Dwelly, T. and Bennion, Y. (2003) *Time To Go Home: Embracing the Home-working Revolution*. London: Work Foundation.

Edvinsson, L. and Malone, M. S. (1997) *Intellectual Capital*. London: Piatkus.

Elias, P. and Purcell, K. (2003) *Measuring Change in the Graduate Labour Market*. Research Paper No. 1. Bristol: Employment Studies Research Institute.

European Commission (2008) *Restructuring in Europe*. Brussels: European Commission.

Evans, J. A., Kunda, G. and Barley, S. A. (2004) Beach time, bridge time, and billable hours: the temporal structure of technical contracting. *Administrative Science Quarterly*, **49**: 1–38.

Farrell, D. (2005) Offshoring: value creation through economic change. *Journal of Management Studies*, **42**(3): 675–83.

Flamholz, E. (1985) *Human Resource Accounting*. Los Angeles, CA: Jossey-Bass.

Flood, P. Mkamwa, T., O'Regan, C., Guthrie, J. P., Liu, W., Armstrong, C. and MacCurtain, S. (2008) *New Models of High Performance Work Systems: The Business Case for Strategic HRM, Partnership and Diversity and Equality Systems*. Dublin: NCPP and Equality Authority.

Ford, J., Tomlinson,, J., Sommerlad, H. and Gold, J. (2009) "'Just don't call it diversity': Developing a programme for the business case for diversity in west yorkshire", paper presented at the HRD conference, Newcastle-upon-Tyne.

Forde, C., Stuart, M., Gardiner, J., Greenwood, I., MacKenzie, R. and Perett, R. (2008) *Socially Responsible Restructuring in an Era of Mass Layoffs*. CERIC Working Paper No. 5. Leeds: Leeds University.

Fyfe, J. (1986) Putting people back into the manpower planning equation. *Personnel Management*, October: 64–9.

Gagnon, S. and Cornelius, N. (2000) Re-examining workplace equality: the capabilities approach. *Human Resource Management Journal*, **10**(4): 68–87.

Garvey, B. and Williamson, B. (2002) *Beyond Knowledge Management*. Harlow: Pearson Education.

Giambatista, R. C., Rowe, W. G. and Riaz, S. (2005) Nothing succeeds like succession: a critical review of leader succession literature since 1994. *Leadership Quarterly*, **16**: 963–91.

Golden, T., Veiga, J. and Dino, R. (2008) The impact of professional isolation on teleworker job performance and turnover intentions: does time spent teleworking, interacting face-to-face, or having access to communication-enhancing technology matter? *Journal of Applied Psychology*, **93**(6): 1412–21.

Gratton, L. (2000) A real step change. *People Management*, **6**(6): 26–30.

Green, F., Ashton, D. N., James, D. and Sung, J. (1999) The role of the state in skill formation: evidence from the Republic of Korea, Singapore and Taiwan. *Oxford Review of Economic Policy*, **15**(1): 82–96.

Grey, C. and Mitev, N. (1995) Reengineering organizations: a critical appraisal. *Personnel Review*, **24**(1): 6–18.

Gröjer, J.-E. and Johanson, U. (1998) Current development in human resource accounting and costing. *Accounting, Auditing and Accountability*, **11**(4): 495–505.

Groysberg, B. (2010) *Chasing Stars: The Myth of Talent and the Portability of Performance*. Princeton, NJ: Princeton University Press.

Groysberg, B., Nanda, A. and Nohria, N. (2004) The risky business of hiring stars. *Harvard Business Review*, **82**(5): 93–100.

Grzeda, M. M. (1999) Re-conceptualizing career change: a career development perspective. *Career Development International*, **4**(6): 305–11.

Guest, D. E. (1998) Beyond HRM: commitment and the contract culture. In P. Sparrow and M. Marchington (eds) *Human Resource Management: The New Agenda* (pp. 37–51). London: Financial Times/Pitman.

Guest, D. E., Michie, J., Conway, N. and Meehan, M. (2003) Human resource management and corporate performance in the UK. *British Journal of Industrial Relations*, **41**(2) 291–314.

Hall, D. T. (2002) *Careers In and Out of Organizations*. Thousand Oaks, CA: Sage.

Hammer, M. and Champy, J. (1993) *Reengineering the Corporation*. London: Nicholas Brealey.

Harland, C., Knight, L., Lamming, R. and Walker, H. (2005) Outsourcing: assessing the risks and benefits for organisations, sectors and nations. *International Journal of Operations and Production Management*, **25**(9): 831–50.

Harris, A. (2008) Distributed leadership: according to the evidence. *Journal of Educational Administration*, **46**(2): 172–88.

Hijzen, A. and Venn, D. (2011) *The Role of Short-time Work Schemes During the 2008–09 Recession*. OECD Social, Employment and Migration Working Paper No. 115. Brussels: OECD Publishing.

Hilbrecht, M., Shaw, S., Johnson, L. C. and Andrey, J. (2008) 'I'm home for the kids': contradictory implications for work–life balance of teleworking mothers. *Gender, Work and Organization*, **15**(5): 454–76.

Hirsh, W. and Jackson, C. (1997) *Strategies for Career Development: Promise, Practice and Pretence*. Report No. 305. Brighton: Institute for Employment Studies.

Hogarth, T., Hasluck, C., Pierre, G., Winterbotham, M. and Vivien, D. (2001) *Work–Life Balance 2000: Results from the Baseline Study*. Department for Education and Employment Research Report No. 249. London: DfEE.

Holman, D., Batt. R. and Holtgrewe, U. (2007) 'The Global Call Centre Report: international perspectives on management and employment'. Available at: www.ilr.cornell.edu/globalcallcenter (accessed December 1, 2010).

Hoque, K. (1999) Human resource management and performance in the UK hotel industry. *British Journal of Industrial Relations*, **37**(3): 419–43.

Hurley-Hanson, A. and Giannantonio, C. (2008) 'Human resource information systems in crises', paper presented at Academy of Strategic Management Conference, Tunica.

Huselid, M. A., Beatty, R. W. and Becker, B. E. (2005) A players or A positions? The strategic logic of workforce management. *Harvard Business Review*, **83**(12): 110–17.

Huws, U. (1997) Teleworking: *Guidelines for Good Practice*. Report No. 329. Brighton: Institute for Employment Studies.

Hyman, J., Baldry, C., Scholarios, D. and Bunzel, F. (2003) Work–life imbalance in call centres and software development. *British Journal of Industrial Relations*, **41**(2): 215–39.

Incomes Data Services (2010) *Talent management. HR studies*. No. 918. London: IDS.

Jackson, L. (2010) Enterprise resource planning systems: revolutionizing lodging human resources management. *Worldwide Hospitality and Tourism Themes*, **2**(1): 20–9.

Jewson, N. and Mason, D. (1986) The theory and practice of equal opportunities policies: liberal and radical approaches. *Sociological Review*, **34**(2): 307–34.

Johanson, U. (1999) Why the concept of human resource costing and accounting does not work. *Personnel Review*, **28**(1/2): 91–107.

Johanson, U. and Nilson, M. (1996) *Human Resource Costing and Accounting and Organisational Learning*. Report No. 1995:1. Stockholm: Personnel Economics Institute.

Kelliher, C. and Anderson, D. (2008) For better or for worse? An analysis of how flexible working practices influence employees' perceptions of job quality. *International Journal of Human Resource Management*, **19**(3): 421–33.

Kersley, B., Alpin, C., Forth, J., Bryson, A., Bewley, H., Dix, G. and Oxenbridge, S. (2006) *Inside the Workplace: Findings from the 2004 Workplace Employment Relations Survey*. London: Routledge.

Kettley, P. and Reilly, P. (2003) *e-HR: An Introduction*. Report No. 398. Brighton: Institute of Employment Studies.

Khapova, S. N. Arthur, M. B. and Wilderom, C.P.M (2007) The subjective career in the knowledge economy. In H. Gunz and M. Peiperl (eds) *Handbook of Career Studies* (pp. 114–30). Thousand Oaks, CA: Sage.

Kinnie, N. J. and Arthurs, A. J. (1996) Personnel specialists' advanced use of information technology. *Personnel Review*, **25**(3): 3–19.

Kirton, G. and Greene, A. (2000) *The Dynamics of Managing Diversity*. Oxford: Butterworth Heinemann.

Korczynski, M. (2002) *Human Resource Management in Service Work*. Basingstoke: Palgrave Macmillan.

Legge, K. (2005) *Human Resource Management: Rhetorics and Realities* (anniversary edn). Basingstoke: Palgrave Macmillan.

Levy, D. L. (2005) Offshoring in the new global political economy. *Journal of Management Studies*, **42**(3): 685–93.

Lewin, A., Massini, S. and Peeters, C. (2009) Why are companies offshoring innovation? The emerging global race for talent. *Journal of International Business Studies*, **40**: 901–25.

Lewis, J. P. (2000) The *Project Manager's Desk Reference: A Comprehensive Guide To Project Planning, Scheduling, Evaluation, and System*. New York: McGraw Hill.

Liff, S. (1997a) Constructing HR information systems. *Human Resource Management Journal*, **7**(2): 18–31.

Liff, S. (1997b) Two routes to managing diversity: individual differences or social group characteristics. *Employee Relations*, **19**(1): 11–26.

Liff, S. (2000) Manpower or human resource planning – what's in a name? In S. Bach and K. Sisson (eds) *Personnel Management* (3rd edn) (pp. 93–110). Blackwell: Oxford.

Lips-Wiersma, M. and Hall, D. T. (2007) Organizational career development is not dead: a case study on managing the new career during organizational change. *Journal of Organizational Behavior*, **28**: 771–92.

Littler, C. R., Wiesner, R. and Dunford, R. (2003) The dynamics of de-layering: changing management structures in three countries. *Journal of Management Studies*, **40**(2): 225–56.

Lorbiecki, A. and Jack, G. (2000) Critical turns in the evolution of diversity management. *British Journal of Management*, **11**: S17–31.

McCullum, S. and O'Donnell, D. (2009) Social capital and leadership development. *Leadership and Organization Development Journal*, **30**(2): 152–66.

McDonald, P., Brown, K. and Bradley, L. (2005) Explanations for the provision utilisation gap in work–life policy. *Women in Management Review*, **20**(1): 37–55.

Macleod, D. and Clarke, N. (2009) *Engaging for Success: Enhancing Performance Through Engagement*. London: Department of Business.

McMillan-Capehart, A. (2005) A configurational framework for diversity: socialization and culture. *Personnel Review*, **34**(4): 488–503.

Mallon, M. and Walton, S. (2005) Career and learning: the ins and the outs of it. *Personnel Review*, **34**(4): 468–87.

Mayfield, M., Mayfield, J. and Lunce, S. (2003) Human resource information systems: a review and model development. *Advances in Competitiveness Research*, **11**(1): 139–51.

Mayo, A. (2002) A thorough evaluation. *People Management*, **8**(7): 36–9.

Michaels, E., Handfiled-Jones, H. and Axelrod, B. (2001) *The War for Talent*. Boston, MA: Harvard Business School Press.

Michie, J. and Sheehan-Quinn, M. (2001) Labour market flexibility: human resource management and corporate performance. *British Journal of Management*, **12**(4): 287–305.

Mićić, P. (2010) Developing leaders as futures thinkers. In J. Gold, R. Thorpe and A. Mumford (eds) *The Gower Handbook of Leadership and Management Development* (p. 547–66). Aldershot: Gower.

Morrell, K. M., Loan-Clarke, J. and Wilkinson, A. J. (2001) Unweaving leaving: the use of models in the management of employee turnover. *International Journal of Management Reviews*, **3**(1): 219–44.

Morrell, K. M., Loan-Clarke, J. and Wilkinson, A. J. (2004) Organisational change and employee turnover. *Personnel Review*, **33**(2): 161–73.

Mudambi, S. M. and Tallman, S. (2010) Make, buy or ally? Theoretical perspectives on knowledge process outsourcing through alliances. *Journal of Management Studies*, **47**(8): 1434–56.

Nopo, H. (2011) The Inter-American Development Bank presents ... pushing for progress. Women, work, and gender roles in Latin America. *Harvard International Review*, Summer: 78–83.

O'Donoghue, J. and Maguire, T. (2005) The individual learner, employability and the workplace. *Journal of European Industrial Training*, **29**(6): 436–46.

Parker, B. and Caine, D. (1996) Holonic modelling: human resource planning and the two faces of Janus. *International Journal of Manpower*, **17**(8): 30–45.

Parsons, D. (2010) Medical-workforce planning: an art or science? *Human Resource Management International Digest*, **18**(5): 36–8.

Pickard, J. (1997) Vacational qualifications. *People Management*, 10 July: 26–31.

Pilch, T. (2000) *Dynamic Reporting for a Dynamic Economy*. London: Academy of Enterprise.

Pilch, T. (2006) *Diversity and Economy*. London: Smith Institute.

Pollert, A. (1988) Dismantling flexibility. *Capital and Class*, (34): 42–75.

Pollert, A. (1991) *Farewell to Flexibility?* Oxford: Blackwell.

Pollitt, D. (2007) Software solves problem of global succession planning at Friesland Foods. *Human Resource Management International Digest*, **15**(6): 21–23.

Ready, D. and Conger, J. (2007) Make your company a talent factory. *Harvard Business Review*, **85**(6): 68–77.

Richbell, S. (2001) Trends and emerging values in human resource management. *International Journal of Manpower*, **22**(3): 261–8.

Rothwell, W. J. (2011) Replacement planning: a starting point for succession planning and talent management. *International Journal of Training and Development*, **15**(1): 87–99.

Russell, B. (2008) Call centres: a decade of research. *International Journal of Management Reviews*, **10**(3): 195–219.

Sako, K. and Tierney, A. (2005) *Sustainability of Business Service Outsourcing: The Case of Human Resource Outsourcing (HRO)*. AIM Working Paper. London: Advanced Institute of Management.

Sánchez, M. P., Elena, S. and Castrillo, R. (2009) Intellectual capital dynamics in universities: a reporting model. *Journal of Intellectual Capital*, **10**(2): 307–24.

Saunders, J. and Hunter, I. (2007) *Human Resource Outsourcing: Solutions, Suppliers, Key Processes and the Current Market*. London: Orion Partners.

Schneider, R. (2001) Variety performance. *People Management*, **7**(9): 26–31.

Scott, B. and Revis, S. (2008) Talent management in hospitality: graduate career success and strategies. *International Journal of Contemporary Hospitality Management*, **20**(7): 781–91.

Scott-Dixon, K. (2004) *Doing IT: Women Working in Information Technology*. Toronto, Ontario: Sumach Press.

Self, D. R., Armenakis, A. A., and Schraeder, M. (2007) Organizational change content, process, and context: a simultaneous analysis of employee reactions. *Journal of Change Management*, **7**: 211–29.

Sennett, R. (1998) *The Corrosion of Character*. New York: Norton.

Shaw, J. D., Duffy, M. K., Johnson, J. L. and Lockhart, D. E. (2005) Turnover, social capital losses and performance. *Academy of Management Journal*, **48**(4): 594–606.

Siebert, W. S. and Zubanov, N. (2009) Searching for the optimal level of employee turnover: a study of a large U.K. retail organization. *Academy of Management Journal*, **52**(2): 294–313.

Singh, V. (2002) *Managing Diversity for Strategic Advantage*. London: Council for Excellence in Management and Leadership.

Smith, A. R. (1980) *Corporate Manpower Planning*. London: Gower Press.

Stoner, J. S. and Gallagher, V. C. (2010) Who cares? The role of job involvement in psychological contract violation. *Journal of Applied Social Psychology*, **40**(6): 1490–514.

Storey, J. (ed.) (1995b) *Human Resource Management: A Critical Text*. London: Routledge.

Storey, J., Cressey, P., Morris, T. and Wilkinson, A. (1997) Changing employment practices in UK banking: case studies. *Personnel Review*, **26**(1): 24–42.

Stredwick, J. and Ellis, S. (2005) *Flexible Working* (2nd edn). London: Chartered Institute of Personnel and Development.

Sturges, J., Conway, N. and Liefooghe, A. (2010) Organizational support, individual attributes, and the practice of career self-management behavior. *Group and Organization Management*, **35**(1): 108–41.

Sullivan, S. and Arthur, M. (2006) The evolution of the boundaryless career concept: examining physical and psychological mobility. *Journal of Vocational Behavior*, **69**: 19–29.

Sullivan, S. E., Forret, M. L., Carraher, S. M. and Mainiero, L. A. (2009) Using the kaleidoscope career model to examine generational differences in work attitudes. *Career Development International*, **14**(3): 284–302.

Tamkin, P., Barber, L. and Dench, S. (1997) *From Admin to Strategy: The Changing Face of the HR Function*. Report No. 32. Brighton: Institute for Employment Studies.

Tansley, C., Turner, P. and Foster, C. (2007a) *Talent: Strategy, Management, Measurement. Research into Practice*. London: Chartered Institute of Personnel and Development.

Tatli, A., Mulholland, G., Ozbilgin, M. and Worman, D. (2007) *Managing Diversity in Practice: Supporting Business Goals*. London: Chartered Institute of Personnel and Development.

Taylor, R. (2002) *Britain's World of Work – Myths and Realities*. Swindon: Economic and Social Research Council.

Templer, A. J. and Cawsey, T. F. (1999) Rethinking career development in an era portfolio careers. *Career Development International*, **4**(2): 70–6.

Thornhill, A., Saunders, M. N. K. and Stead, J. (1997) Downsizing, delayering – but where's the commitment. *Personnel Review*, **26**(1): 81–98.

Ton, Z. and Huckman, R. S. (2008) Managing the impact of employee turnover on performance: the role of process conformance. *Organization Science*, **19**(1): 56–68.

Toulson, P. K. and Dewe, P. (2004) HR accounting as a measurement tool. *Human Resource Management Journal*, **14**(2): 75–90.

Travaglione, A., and Cross, B. (2006) Diminishing the social network in organizations: does there need to be such a phenomenon as "survivor syndrome" after downsizing? *Strategic Change*, **15**: 1–13.

Tremblay, D.-G. (2003) Telework: a new mode of gendered segmentation? Results from a study in Canada. *Canadian Journal of Communication*, **28**(4): 461–78.

Turner, G. (1996) Human resource accounting – whim or wisdom? *Journal of Human Resource Costing and Accounting*, **1**(1): 63–73.

UK Commission for Employment and Skills (2009) *Ambition 2020, World Class Skills and Jobs for the UK*. London: UKCES.

Verma, S. and Dewe, P. (2008) Valuing human resources: perceptions and practices in UK organisations. *Journal of Human Resource Costing and Accounting*, **12**(2): 102–23.

Wall, T. D. and Wood, S. J. (2005) The romance of human resource management and business performance, and the case for the big science. *Human Relations*, **58**(4): 429–61.

Western, S. (2008) *Leadership: A Critical Text*. London: Sage.

Whelan, E. and Carcary, M. (2011) Integrating talent and knowledge management: where are the benefits? *Journal of Knowledge Management*, **15**(4): 675–87.

Wood, I., Rodgers, H. and Gold, J. (2004) 'Picturing prejudice: learning to see diversity', paper presented at the Fifth HRD Conference, Limerick University, May.

Wood, S., Holman, D. and Stride, C. (2006) Human resource management and performance in UK call centres. *British Journal of Industrial Relations*, **44**(1): 99–124.

Woodall, J., Scott-Jackson, W., Newham, T. and Gurney, M. (2009) Making the decision to outsource human resources. *Personnel Review*, **38**, (3):236–52.

Yu, G. and Park, J. (2006) The effect of downsizing on the financial performance and employee productivity of Korean firms. *International Journal of Manpower*, **27**: 230–50.

CHAPTER 8
Human resources planning
Cathy Sheehan

- Introduction
- Approaches to HRP
- The strategic role of HRP
- Conclusion
- For discussion and revision
- Further reading
- Case study: The Australian Cladding Company
- References

After reading this chapter, you should be able to:
- Discuss the rise of human resource planning (HRP) as a strategic priority
- Explain the techniques associated with forecasting the supply and demand of human resources
- Outline the role of job analysis in the HRP process
- Describe and analyse the impact of restructuring on HRP responses
- Explain the role of HRP in talent management
- Discuss international HRP considerations

Introduction

In the Introduction to this book, Syed and Kramar emphasized the increasing globalization of the world of work and the capacity of events in one country to impact on others. International social and economic change and resultant changes in the international labour market pose particular challenges for the human resource management (HRM) function. The global financial crisis of 2008–09 was a good example of a situation in which the HRM function had to provide leadership in managing potential workforce reductions while still attracting and retaining critical talent in order to maintain businesses' viability.

At a time when many organizations internationally were struggling to manage skill shortages (see Rudd et al., 2007), economic uncertainty created a further level of complexity. The Corporate Leadership Council (2008) advised that those companies which avoided reactionary approaches to HRM and managed to maintain morale and retain skilled employees during the period of downsizing would come through the crisis in a stronger competitive position. These circumstances require innovative responses and careful HRM planning. As custodians of the people resource in organizations, it is the role of the HRM function to assist in the development of human resource planning (HRP) initiatives that match changes in the supply and demand for labour, and also manage initiatives to retain and attract talent strategically rather than reactively.

The purpose of this chapter is, first, to broadly review approaches to HRP, and second, to critically analyse some of the strategic responses to issues associated with the supply and demand of labour. The chapter starts with a discussion of the stages that the HRP activity has moved through and of the emerging recognition of the strategic importance of this area. Techniques for HRP are then explored, including quantitative and qualitative approaches. Following on from this, a discussion of job analysis highlights the connections between the analysis of what a job involves and the HRP requirements for it. Having explained HRP techniques, the discussion will then move on to an examination of the more strategic issues associated with HRP, such as HRP as part of restructuring initiatives and the role of HRP in decisions related to talent management and globalization.

Approaches to HRP

The evolution of HRP

Huselid (1993: 36) has explained that HRP essentially matches 'projected human resource demand with its anticipated supply, with explicit consideration of the skill mix that will be necessary throughout the firm'. HRP is a dynamic process affected by both predictable and unpredictable forces. The economic change experienced during the global financial crisis, for example, in 2008–09 impacted on markets and resulted in swings in consumer demand that affected the level of labour required to meet the product output thus needed. These unplanned changes in the demand for labour occurred at a time when there were ongoing forecasted demographic shifts in the profile of the available workforce (Rudd et al., 2007). These environmental challenges potentially pose major threats to organizational viability, but careful management of the HRP process can make a substantial contribution to the ultimate success or failure of the business.

Jamali and Afiouni consider the change and evolution that has occurred in the field of HRM and the increasing awareness of the value of strategic HRM for improving organizational outcomes that has become apparent in the past two decades. HRP activity is a good example of how HRM can provide this strategic value. Industry shifts away from manufacturing to a greater focus on service and knowledge work have led to a recognition of the potential for human capital to make a substantial and lasting impact on sustainable competitive advantage (Wright et al., 1994; Barney and Wright, 1998; Zula and Chermack, 2007).

Historically, the manufacturing industry has provided a large source of work, but its contribution to the number of employed people has been in decline. As a result, the primary focus of employment in many developed countries has increasingly become service-oriented. By the late 1980s, for example, more than 60 per cent of employees in the Organisation for Economic Co-operation and Development as a whole were working in the services sector (Blyton, 1989). In Australia in 1990–91, the manufacturing industry was the main source of employment, but in 2004–05 manufacturing was ranked third after retail trade and the property and business services industries (Australian Bureau of Statistics, 2006).

The impact of this shift towards services has implications for the type of employee who is now in demand:

- As most service work requires *face-to-face or voice-to-voice interaction* with customers (Macdonald and Sirianni, 1996), the service interaction may involve high levels of emotional labour or 'the management of feeling to create a publicly observable facial and bodily display' (Hochschild, 1983: 7).
- Another feature of employment conditions in the service sector is *flexibility in work arrangements* (Smith, 2005). Australian studies suggest evidence of the common pattern also seen in other industrialized countries: employment is moving from the 'traditional' forms of full-time, permanent work towards a wider variety of working arrangements, including part-time work, temporary employment and contract employment (Van den Heuvel and Wooden, 1997; Kalleberg, 2000).

The growth in the service sector has therefore changed expectations of the type of worker who is now in demand and the structure of working arrangements. Firms that can effectively adjust their human capital base to meet these economic challenges and maintain a workforce mix that supports strategic priorities are well placed to maintain their competitive advantage.

Despite the current priority given to HRP, it has in fact moved through a number of stages to get to this position. Initially, in the *'regulation'* phase, HRP activity ensured that managerial behaviour and organizational systems were compliant with government regulations. The role of HRP was to ensure alignment with laws in areas such as industrial relations, equal employment opportunity, minimum wages and salaries, and employment conditions. The compliance element at this stage actually meant that HRP at times worked against strategic planning rather than with it. In the period spanning the 1960s, 70s and 80s, the compliance activity that dominated HRP meant that activities were confined to operational and reactive activities that did not factor in the need to be strategic (Ulrich, 1987).

As global proactive strategic initiatives were given greater priority, *ntrol'* phase. During this period, HRP was used vidual behaviour strategy. Performance management and reward systems, for exan to develop human behaviour in line with strategic priorities. Alth connected to strategic planning, it was still largely an implementation tool.

It was not until phase three, the *'shape'* phase, that HRP effectively became a potential source of strategic competitive advantage. Ulrich (1987) explains that it was during this stage that key stakeholders such as employees, customers and unions agreed on HRM configurations that would create strategic unity.

Before moving on to a discussion of some of these strategic issues, it is useful to consider how the HRP process actually works. The next section will therefore review how an organization can approach matching human resource demand to supply, before moving into a broader discussion of the strategic impact of HRP activity.

Techniques of HRP

Demand forecasting in HRM determines the quantity and quality of employees required to meet the organization's goals. These forecasts are usually associated with particular job categories and skill areas that support the organization's current and future goals. There are a variety of approaches that provide useful data, differing in their approach and level of sophistication. Demand forecasting may be undertaken either *quantitatively* or *qualitatively*.

Quantitative demand forecasting

Quantitative approaches rely on statistical techniques and mathematical modelling, whereas qualitative approaches gather expert opinions to determine possible changes in demand. Two forms of quantitative analysis include trend projections and multiple regression.

Trend projection is time series analysis that processes past and present information on the number of people hired in various departments, job categories or skills areas and, based on any observed increases or decreases, forms predictions into the future. Although such information is quite easy to understand, the underlying assumption is that previous trends will determine future trends, which does not take into account unexpected environmental developments.

The aim of the *multiple regression* approach is to broaden the determinants of future demand to determine reliable indicators of future demand. Specific independent variables, or predictors, may include variables such as sales in a retail store, student numbers in a school or hospital bed capacity in a hospital. In the situation facing Holden, outlined in Box 8.1, labour demand was affected by adjustments to internal operating decisions as well as changes in consumer taste. The greater the number of independent variables that can be used to predict the labour demand, the more accurate will be the prediction. The restrictions on using multiple regression are, however, the availability of the data and also the size of the sample, with larger datasets providing more accurate information. There is also an expectation that those working in the HRM area are comfortable dealing with both datasets and the computer programs that accompany the technique.

Qualitative demand forecasting

An alternative to the quantitative approach is provided by qualitative techniques that draw in information from key stakeholders. Data collection can be quite informal or can be structured in a formal manner using approaches such as the Delphi technique.

Using a Delphi survey, HRM planners contact a group of expert informants and ask them to respond anonymously to some questions on HRP. Responses are collected and fed back to respondents together with another set of questions. The process continues until a consensus has been obtained (Rothwell, 1995). The benefits of this approach are that expert information is gathered without face-to-face pressure within the group to conform to a particular line of thinking. The approach is also useful when conditions are changing and there are few existing precedents on how to proceed.

Exercise

Under what conditions would a qualitative approach to demand forecasting be more feasible or appropriate than a quantitative approach?

Box 8.1 Factors impacting on labour demand at Holden

During March 2007, car maker Holden made a decision to cut 600 jobs at its assembly operations in Adelaide, Australia. The fall in labour demand was associated with a range of demand determinants including adjustments to internal operating decisions as well as changes in broader consumer demand.

With respect to the internal operating changes, Director of Manufacturing Rod Keane said that the decision to reduce the workforce at the Elizabeth plant followed a major investment at the plant that had increased efficiencies and allowed the car maker to maintain production levels with fewer staff. It also came as the company moved to end the production of its older VZ range of vehicles and concentrate on the new VE models.

Broader reasons for the decline in labour demand were related to a slide in sales of the locally built Commodore range in 2006, with sales down 15.4 per cent. Holden had also cut 1,400 jobs in August 2005, when it axed its third shift at Elizabeth due to a falling local and global demand for large cars.

Ian Jones, federal secretary of the Australian Manufacturing Workers Union vehicle division, commented on environmental pressures that had contributed to this decline in sales. 'Petrol pricing, currency costs, unabated entry of imported products, declining assistance and increased cost of finance are all factors that by themselves would cause major problems for industry,' Mr Jones said.

Federal Industry Minister Ian Macfarlane confirmed that the global automotive industry was going through challenging times and that Australian car producers were not immune from this.

Source: Adapted from http://theage.drive.com.au/motor-news/holden-axes-600-jobs-in-adelaide-20070305-140fo.html [accessed 15 August 2011].

Supply forecasting

Supply forecasting draws from both internal and external sources of HRM information related to supply of employees. Internal labour supply information considers the range of people within the organization who can be promoted, transferred or developed to meet supply needs. When undertaking such a review, a skills inventory – a system for keeping track of employee skill development – is a useful source of information. These data can be kept manually, especially in smaller organizations, but in larger organizations well-developed human resources information systems and detailed performance management information may assist in identifying employees with high potential and the appropriate skills. Along with internal sources of supply, organizations scan labour supply sources external to the organization. This sort of analysis takes into account environmental analysis relating to demographic trends in order to assess the qualitative and quantitative impacts.

In terms of the usefulness of efforts to match the demand and supply of labour, evidence suggests that firms adopting clear HRM planning objectives and a formal planning process obtain useful information for strategic planning (Huselid, 1995; Lam and Schaubroeck, 1998). Despite the logic of external and internal labour scanning, there is evidence that people planning is not always formally developed and implemented. The impact of unplanned environmental events, for example, means that it is frequently difficult to estimate internal labour demand. Indeed, Huselid (1993) established that environmental volatility had an important impact on the adoption of HRP approaches. The most common use of HRP occurred in firms that were experiencing moderate levels of workforce volatility. Firms characterized by high or low levels of workforce volatility, however, tended to have a lower use of HRP. Huselid (1993) observed that higher levels of volatility may render HRP ineffective, whereas low levels of volatility make it unnecessary.

Rothwell (1995) also commented on the lack of HRP within the development of human resource strategy. Consistent with Huselid (1993), the argument is made that the rate of environmental change renders HRP so problematic that it becomes infeasible. Plans are developed but fail to be implemented as further internal or external changes negate the relevance of any proposed initiatives. Policy priorities may also shift as competing interest groups vie for primacy and existing plans are sidelined in the process.

Rothwell (1995) also suggests that the abilities and skills of those who are expected to take on these planning tasks may impact on the quality of HRP. Line managers, for example, who are given the task of making planning projections may not have the background skills or the time to dedicate to developing labour models. Kulik and Bainbridge (2006), in a survey of both HRM professionals and line managers covering a range of HRM responsibilities, established that, with respect to HRP, the collective view confirmed that HRP is best managed centrally by HRM rather than by the line. Although this assigns responsibility to those who may have the skills, line managers often still need to be involved as the decisions ultimately impact on the capacity of line management to complete the organization's output requirements.

Job analysis

Within the HRP process, matching the demand and supply of labour informs decision-makers about potential trends and changes in labour requirements, and also provides information about the best labour mix. Job analysis refines and complements this information to determine exactly what each job involves and who is required before specific staffing decisions can be made (Schneider and Konz, 1989).

Broadly speaking, job analysis refers to the process of getting detailed information about jobs (Brannick et al., 2007). Organizational conditions often change in response to new technology and machinery, as well as legislative and market requirements. Job analysis therefore becomes important in interpreting what the job currently involves. Having identified the objective of the job analysis, the HRM analyst must determine the type of information that needs to be collected, the source of the information, the method of data collection and how the data will be analysed.

The type of information that is collected is usually associated with the development of a job description, or the list of tasks, duties and responsibilities of the job. Additionally, a job specification, or person specification, is derived that lists the knowledge, skills, abilities and other characteristics that an individual must have to successfully perform the job. The most common source of information is the person already in the job. There are limits to the usefulness of this source, however, when the views of the present incumbents differ from those of their supervisors (O'Reilly, 1973). Employees may, for example, exaggerate their duties, especially if the process is associated with a review of remuneration, and it may become necessary to seek out additional information. When the job is a new position or when the incumbent has actually left the organization, further input is usually sought. Under these conditions, for example, it becomes necessary to bring in the views of supervisors or co-workers.

Common methods of data collection include observation, interviews, questionnaires, diaries and critical incident approaches. The choice of the method depends largely on the purpose of the analysis and the nature of the job, and a number of methods are often used together:

- *Observation* is useful when the job involves standardized repetitive jobs and manual work: when jobs have actions, observation is a good way to track what needs to be done. More complex positions involving internal thought processing, such as the work of an accountant, are, however, difficult to measure through observation. Similarly, when a job involves irregular work, as, for example, with the role of a manager, observation becomes less useful.
- *Interviews* are more appropriate in these situations and overall are one of the most commonly used job analysis data collection methods.
- *Diaries* are also helpful when the responsibilities of a job do not form a regular pattern. If diaries are reliably maintained over an extended period, they are especially useful in tracking irregular and infrequent duties.
- Finally, critical incident approaches are employed to provide specific explanations for effective and ineffective job performance. This approach is usually used to track what is required and what is to be avoided for the success or failure of the job. The process can be onerous as it requires fairly detailed descriptions of what the employee did during a particular incident and explanations of why the

performance was effective or ineffective; for this reason, it is not commonly used across routine tasks.

In addition to these qualitative approaches, quantitative questionnaires such as the position analysis questionnaire provide useful data that can be used to compare information across a range of jobs (Jeanneret and Strong, 2003). These quantitative surveys usually break jobs down into standardized dimensions that are rated; the information obtained can then be used to differentiate jobs with respect to levels of complexity, processing and responsibility.

> ### Exercise
>
> When would quantitative approaches to job analysis be more suitable than qualitative approaches?

Despite the usefulness and importance of job analysis, a number of writers have explained that the rational approach described above – which breaks each job down and produces specific job descriptions and specifications – may no longer be viable. As the rate of technology changes and work becomes more knowledge-based, task boundaries created by traditional job classifications are dissipating. Jobs have become more flexible, and their boundaries are vague and dynamic (Brannick et al., 2007).

Stewart and Carson (1997) have argued that, along with the move away from traditional hierarchical structure and control towards flexible, team-based designs, employees have become more than simple components that fit a series of static job descriptions. A key idea is the development of emerging relationships that may create new networks between employees. These emerging networks do not, however, always have a comfortable fit with traditional structures. The more fluid connections mean that what needs to be done and who does it becomes a product of what each person brings into the organization and how they connect with existing staff. Therefore, rather than work roles being planned and fixed, they become indefinite. It is more likely that jobs will develop around individuals rather than the reverse. Therefore, as well as impacting on job content, environmental pressures have led to re-evaluations of who is employed and how the employer–employee relationship is managed.

The following section shifts our discussion away from a review of how HRP is approached, to a broader discussion of managing the strategic issues associated with an over- or undersupply of labour and with attempts to maintain the employee–employer relationship during these periods.

The strategic role of HRP

Restructuring and downsizing

Over the last two decades, technological and market changes have prompted major reviews of organizational processes and structure. During periods of economic uncertainty, firms struggle to find ways to cut costs and become more efficient and effective. Payroll expenses and employee downsizing are often targeted during periods of recession, for example, as a way to boost company profits (Cascio and Wynn, 2004). Indeed, the Corporate Leadership Council (2008) reported that, by the end of 2008, 20 per cent of Australian and New Zealand firms were preparing for the inevitable downturn in 2009 and had indicated that they might either freeze or downsize their staffing levels in the 6-month period following the financial crisis alert in the October.

The promise of workforce reduction is an immediate reduction of costs, coupled with increased levels of efficiency, productivity and competitiveness (Farrell and Mavondo, 2004; Iverson and Zatzick, 2007). Unfortunately, the expectations of economic benefits following employee reductions are often not realized (Gandolfy, 2008). In an analysis of the financial impact of downsizing, Cascio and Wynn (2004) compared employers adopting a stable position with those who chose to downsize and found no consistent evidence to support the notion that employment downsizing led to an improvement in financial indicators such as return on assets.

The economic premise that profit is driven by either a reduction in costs or an increase in revenues is complicated by the human reactions associated with a reduction in the workforce. Organizations face problems with diminished productivity and loyalty, and loss of critical organizational knowledge. The negative consequences of an organizational downsizing response can include heightened levels of stress, conflict, role ambiguity and job dissatisfaction among employees (Appelbaum et al., 1999).

Downsizing survivors – those employees who remain in the organization – generally find themselves with increased workloads and responsibilities without the necessary training and support. These stresses result in a range of mental and physical illness that impact on the quality of their work. Indeed, Gandolfy (2008), in a review of the research in the area, has shown that the 'victims', or those who are involuntarily downsized out of the job, report more positive outcomes than employees who stay. Victims commonly received transition packages and outplacement services and support, felt lower levels of stress in the job and experienced fewer negative effects than survivors. Such conditions may also encourage talented employees who are already comfortable with mobility to leave organizations that do not offer the appropriate opportunities for development and advancement.

A primary reason given for the negative consequences associated with downsizing is the poor execution and management of these reduction initiatives (Appelbaum et al., 1999). It is possible, however, to strategically manage workforce reductions and tensions during periods of economic stress through effective HRM approaches. Cascio and Wynn (2004) similarly argue that downsizing remains a viable and sometimes necessary response to environmental pressure, but reinforce that how the process is executed is critical (Box 8.2). Specifically, employees' involvement and input are key in creating a sense of psychological control over events that have such major personal consequences. Avoiding rumours by honest, consistent and regular communication from the executive group can also assist in reducing stress levels.

> **Box 8.2 Clever HRP responses to tough economic conditions**
>
> Cascio and Wynn (2004) have argued that pressures to downsize *can* be managed effectively. Staged responses to economic pressure involving pay cuts, reduced working hours and using up outstanding leave can stave off immediate action to downsize.
>
> In response to the global financial crisis, a number of Australian companies avoided immediate wide-scale lay-offs and employed less invasive tactics. Alcoa, the world's largest integrated bauxite mine, froze the wages of its Australian workforce of 6,400 and capped the salary of its managing director for 2 years.
>
> In the banking sector, Ralph Norris, the Commonwealth Bank chief executive, took a 10 per cent pay cut in his base salary, and middle management roles, which were paid more than $100,000 per year, were subject to a 12-month freeze on both base salaries and short-term incentives. The bank also gave a commitment to avoid moving any jobs offshore for the following 3 years and to retain its call centres and operations processing centres in Australia for the next 3 years (*The Australian*, April 21, 2009).
>
> GM Holden also responded to the global downturn by trimming shifts to avoid lay-offs. In May 2009, it moved its Adelaide factory to single-shift operation to avoid job cuts among its production workers (*The Australian*, April 3, 2009).
>
> These companies made it clear that these actions were deliberate attempts to save jobs and maintain viability.

Ethical factors in downsizing

Wilcox and Lowry, if not all, areas of HRM practice involve ethical considerations, and the following discussion highlights how the area of downsizing, as an HRP initiative, is not a morally neutral event.

The argument can be made that resource munificence, or abundance, may be grounds for judging whether a particular instance of downsizing is morally or socially responsible (Van Buren, 2000). In other words, an organization's resource base can be used to evaluate the extent of its obligations to 'downsized' employees. Based on assumptions made about relationships within the psychological and social contracts between employers and their employees, the expectation is that employment should be stable and secure if firms are doing well. When organizations engage in downsizing merely to increase an already adequate rate of profit, however, they are likely to be held more culpable for such actions than when environmental forces such as technological change or competitive conditions constrain them. Consistent with this, when organizations are characterized by declining resource munificence, downsizing is more ethically justifiable.

Zyglidopoulos (2003) empirically investigated the impact of downsizing on a firm's reputation for corporate social performance (RCSP) and found not only that downsizing had a negative impact on the firm's reputation, but also that firms that experienced higher financial performance prior to downsizing suffered a greater negative impact on their RCSP. The research therefore indicated that, despite the apparent validity of downsizing as a structural response to economic stress, managers have implicit psychological and social contracts with and ethical responsibilities towards their employees, and these are carefully monitored by stakeholders. When these contracts are broken, the impact on the company's reputation can be such that companies that want to re-hire qualified employees after a downsizing cycle may find it more difficult to do so because of the damage done to their RCSP.

Later, Zyglidopoulos (2005) compared downsizing with 'downscoping', in which the structural response is to divest or sell off organizational divisions. Within downscoping, employees swap employers but do not necessarily lose their jobs. A comparison between these approaches revealed that although both restructuring attempts have negative impacts on corporate reputation, downsizing has more damaging ramifications within the market.

A further important ethical consideration within downsizing is how the process is carried out. Issues associated with procedural justice – the fairness and equity of the procedures that are used to make decisions – are critical and have important consequences for employees' behaviours and attitudes. Fair processes encourage organizational citizenship behaviour or discretionary behaviours lying outside the employees' formal roles that support and assist an organization during a period of economic stress rather than work against it. These approaches provide survivors with a reason to stay and, importantly, give future prospective new hires a reason to join (Cascio and Wynn, 2004).

Zatzick and Iverson (2006) reinforce the ongoing impact that careful HRM practices can make during a period of downsizing. They have established that firms that continue to invest in their employees through the use of HRM practices designed to provide employees with skills, information, motivation and latitude can assist in maintaining workforce productivity during periods of reduction in the workforce. The argument is made that investment in these practices lessens perceived contract breaches as employees continue to receive opportunities for skill development as well as reassurance of their value in the workplace.

Meeting HRP challenges through flexibility

The preceding discussion has highlighted the HRP techniques that can be employed to match supply and demand. In reality, however, environmental factors such as economic uncertainty, technological change, demographic changes and shifts in values often pose substantial difficulties that limit the success of the HRP process. HRP approaches that do not build in adaptive labour responses may therefore fail to meet environmental challenges. These realities have led to the emergence of flexible options within HRP as a way of managing fluctuations in the supply and demand of labour.

The concept of the flexible model of the firm was developed by Atkinson (1984) as an alternative to traditional hierarchical structures. The model redefines the organization's workforce into two main segments: the *core* and the *periphery*. The core workforce is made up of permanent, highly skilled workers, and the peripheral workforce is made up of a range of temporary employment arrangements. Flexibility options underpin the management of these labour classifications.

- *Functional flexibility* involves opportunities for role and task variety and is normally associated with the core workforce. Higher levels of training and development in these core workers mean that they tend to experience higher levels of job security (Burgess, 1997).
- *Numerical flexibility*, as the name suggests, refers to techniques to vary the quantity of labour on hand, rather than being related to investments in the range and scope of the employee skill base. Internal numerical flexibility refers to the amount and time of labour input required of existing employees; overtime and flex-time are examples of this type of flexibility (Rimmer and Zappala, 1988). Alternatively, external numerical flexibility involves changing the actual number of employees as well as the hours that they work. This latter type of numerical flexibility covers the arrangements made with casual or temporary workers who are called in when needed but do not benefit from a permanent contractual relationship with the employer.

Both functional and numerical flexibility are facilitated by financial and procedural flexibility:

- *Financial flexibility* refers to the compensation system that builds in variations in wages for different types of worker (Atkinson, 1984). These arrangements allow organizations to reward and therefore encourage skill development in the core workforce.
- Finally, *procedural flexibility* is critical in that it provides the consultative mechanisms for introducing the other forms of flexibility through changes in both legal and traditional practices covering employment (Boyer, 1988).

The promise of these forms of flexibility to help organizations respond more easily to environmental fluctuations and match labour resources more closely with variations in supply and demand have led to major shifts in the workforce profile. Spain, France, The Netherlands, Finland and Australia are examples of countries that have shown a large growth in the use of temporary employment conditions (Campbell and Burgess, 2001). In the Australian setting in 2003, for example, over a quarter (28 per cent) of all wage and salary earners were employed on a casual basis, and in the period since 1988 more than half of all new jobs created have gone to casual workers (Kryger, 2004). Despite the benefits in terms of flexibility that are offered by alternative forms of work, the arrangements create numerous challenges for both employees and organizations.

For the employee, casual work is closely associated with poor working conditions, including low hourly rates of pay, low and irregular earnings, reduced employment security, lack of access to notice and severance pay, reduced access to unfair dismissal rights, vulnerability to changes in schedules, loss of skill- and age-related pay increments, and lack of representational rights (Pocock et al., 2004). For the employer, although using this category of worker is associated with flexibility and often reduced costs, the arrangement does have potentially negative ramifications (Buultjens, 2001). For example, casual workers are, owing to the transient nature of their terms of employment, less likely to identify strongly with the organization

(Hall, 2006); as a result, they may not absorb and display appropriate organizational values and behaviours.

The limited organizational investment in casual workers also means that these employees may have less opportunity to develop the skills necessary for the job, and therefore the contribution that they make may be limited to generic industry tasks rather than adding real value in terms of the specialized tasks expected by some service providers. Lowry's (2001) investigation of the work arrangements for casual employees within the registered club industry in New South Wales indicated that casual workers are employed on a primarily transactional basis and that their employment conditions are characterized by an underinvestment in employee development (Buultjens, 2001; Lowry, 2001). The impact of an underinvestment in HRM activities such as training and feedback has ramifications for the quality of the service delivery provided by these workers. Lowry's (2001) findings, for example, indicated that some employees were so dissatisfied with the lack of feedback and recognition that they made a conscious decision not to improve the quality of their service. This finding is consistent with the previous research by Schneider et al. (1998), who established a relationship between HRM practices, including training and supportive supervision, and the quality of the service.

There is evidence, however, that the move to a greater reliance on non-standard types of worker – those without set hours or the expectation of continued employment – does have benefits for the organization. Ghosh et al. (2009) have established that the greater use of non-standard workers is positively associated with increased financial performance on the part of the firm. As well as having cost-saving benefits, non-standard arrangements allow firms to give workers a trial of employment before assigning them permanent status.

Moreover, Ghosh et al.'s research indicates that non-standard forms of work are associated with a greater financial impact when firms are operating in less uncertain but more competitive environments. Once uncertainty rises, reliance on non-traditional workers becomes less effective, and when uncertainty is high, a permanent workforce becomes more valuable. Permanent staff's high level of task flexibility and knowledge and expertise specific to the firm help an organization to sustain itself at a time when conditions are in flux. The argument is that, during periods of greater uncertainty, the core workforce assist the organization in protecting its technical edge, and consolidate activities that are considered important for organizational success (Ghosh et al., 2009). Although flexible forms of work allow companies to shed workers when they are not needed, the attraction and retention of a talented core workforce remains a priority, and it is this issue that is addressed in the following section (see also Mini Case Study 8.1).

Talent management

Vaiman and Vance (2008: 3–4) define talent as including 'all of the employed people within an organization who may differ dramatically in levels of knowledge, skill and ability.' Although there will be a variation in the critical strategic nature of this talent within an organization, these authors argue that all employees represent potential sources of valuable knowledge.

> **Mini Case Study 8.1**
>
> **Casual workers at the *BankInfo* Call Centre**
>
> *BankInfo* is a new call centre currently being set up by a small regional bank. The purpose of the call centre is to process a broad range of customer queries ranging from simple account questions to much more complex financial planning matters.
>
> Brad Ellis, the manager of the new centre, is focused on cost minimization and, as people are going to be his major expense, he is considering the use of a primarily casual workforce as a way of keeping costs down. By using more casual workers, he can take people on and off work as he needs them and avoid having a permanent workforce that he has to employ consistently even when demand drops. When the bank introduces new financial products, for example, he will need more staff, but at other times he simply will not require as many people.
>
> Brad thought he should talk about his staffing idea with the human resources manager at head office, Sylvia Waters. He had heard that she was a difficult character who was always going on about how HRM was not involved enough in strategic decisions. But he nevertheless decided to give her a ring and at least hear what she had to say. When he made the phone call, he was surprised by how enthusiastic Sylvia was to hear from him. Sylvia started by saying 'Well, thanks for ringing Brad. I appreciate the opportunity to have some input here – a lot of the managers think that HRM is really just about hiring and firing. What sort of employee profile are you thinking about using?'
>
> Brad outlined his view, and Sylvia seemed to be listening closely. When he had finished, however, he found himself becoming frustrated as she started to warn him about the dangers of relying primarily on a casual workforce, especially for more complex customer interactions. Sylvia made the following comment: 'Think about the ongoing training costs, the problems with retention and the continuous recruitment issues that you are going to face. It may not actually be the best way of keeping costs down in the long run.' At this point, Sylvia had to cut the conversation short to go to an appointment, but she urged Brad to contact her again so that they could come up with a solution.
>
> After the call, Brad could not help thinking that the human resources department sometimes simply got in the way and created more problems than solutions. On the other hand, he felt that Sylvia had made some good points, so perhaps he should set up a meeting with her and try to plan this out more carefully.
>
> **Question**
>
> 1. How can HRP in the call centre be configured to achieve cost-effectiveness but also ensure that more complex customer enquiries are dealt with appropriately?

Ulrich (2006) provides a more specific definition and characterizes 'talent' in two ways. The first is as competence, or an individual's knowledge, skills and values that are required for both the present and the future. Second, Ulrich specifies that such employees have commitment, as shown through their capacity to work hard, put the time in to do what they are asked to do and give their discretionary energy to the firm's success. Finally, these employees make a real contribution and find meaning and purpose in their work.

The recognition of the value of talent comes at a time when, as indicated above, companies are adopting more flexible work practices and moving away from traditional commitments involving permanent work status. These shifts have been accompanied by a changing psychological contract within the employment relationship such that employees will increasingly look for employability rather than employment and will often want to change jobs (Losey, 2005). Indeed, these transitions often occur across borders as international employment markets offer advanced opportunities for development. Firms may therefore need to refocus their HRM practices on what employees are looking for in order to attract and retain valuable staff.

Although HRM recognizes the value of people as assets, this does not mean that HRM approaches always adopt an employee focus (Guest, 2002). The unitarist underpinnings of HRM assume that what is good for the organization is also good for its employees (Legge, 2005). In times of economic stress, however, when organizations may constrict employees' conditions and benefits, it may become increasingly difficult for employees to see any evidence of alignment between the employer's and employee's goal. The view of people as a compliant organizational resource is further challenged by an increasingly well-educated workforce and generational shifts in the values of the workforce that now emphasize both challenging work and an acceptable work–life balance (Guest et al., 2003). Uncertain economic conditions may therefore heighten the need to become more employee-focused in order to retain existing talented employees.

Guest (2002) has previously provided some guidance on how to test for employee-focused HRM approaches by exploring the impact of various HRM approaches on employees' reports of work satisfaction. Results indicated that key HRM practices related to work satisfaction included those associated with the high-performance work systems approach discussed by Zatzick and Iverson (2006). Notably, these included efforts to design or make work more interesting and challenging, direct participation and the extensive provision of information. Guest (2002) also identified the importance of a further set of more bureaucratic employee-oriented practices including family-friendly, equal opportunity and anti-harassment initiatives. Pocock (2005) similarly makes the business case for a link between work–life balance and the attraction and retention of a firm's workers. The increase in the number of women in the workforce, coupled with an ageing population base that requires carers, increases the need for companies to support valued employees who have family responsibilities.

Along with these HRM practices, employees' expectations for personal growth, as reported by both Edgar and Geare (2005) and Boxall et al. (2003), are useful in designing employee-focused HRM. Boxall et al. (2003) identified training opportunities as a factor determining employees' decisions to leave their employer. This is consistent with the changing psychological contract that focuses individuals on their own personal development needs (Sheehan et al., 2006). Employees now tend to have a greater appreciation of opportunities to upgrade their knowledge, skills and abilities so that they can remain in demand in the wider employment market (Holland et al., 2007).

Beechler and Woodward (2009) have identified a number of organizations that are implementing new practices to retain valuable employees. Within the accounting profession, where the supply of new talent is well below the anticipated demand and where professional service firms are finding it difficult to retain young associates who are focused on self-development, Deloitte, one of the 'Big Four' global accounting and consulting firms, is engaging in what it calls 'mass career customization'. This programme assists employees to map their careers through a series of interactive exercises and online resources. Other organizations have increased their emphasis on formal training. Goldman Sachs, for example, has set up the Goldman Sachs University. Australia's Macquarie Group, the international investment house, has similarly displayed a commitment to formal training, creating a partnership with INSEAD in 2006 in order to provide the first corporate-specific Masters degree from a top-tier business school. Despite the changing psychological contract and the current tendency for employees to move more freely between organizations, it is clear that many companies are taking quite specific steps to engage and retain talented employees.

Exercise

It could be argued that employee retention should not always be a priority – an important aspect of talent management may instead lie in acknowledging the fact that employees may at some point need to leave the organization. Perhaps the focus should be on employees' engagement in their job while they are in the organization rather than on employee retention for its own sake.

- What situational factors are likely to promote this argument?

International considerations

One of the developments resulting from new forms of work organization as an HRP response has been an increase in the outsourcing of work and the resultant 'offshoring' of tasks to overseas providers. Offshoring refers to work that is not constrained by a need for actual customer contact or local knowledge, meaning that it can therefore be provided remotely or globally (Farrell et al., 2005). The key benefit from offshoring is the economic return of replacing high-wage labour costs with lower costs. Offshoring is also seen as a way of enabling organizations to focus their resources on their core business (Domberger, 1994).

The HRP decision to source labour from international sites is not without its complications. Often, the complexity or idiosyncratic nature of a particular set of tasks makes the move offshore difficult. A further issue is the lack of maturity in the newly developing offshoring market. Middle management skills, for example, may still be under development in the target countries, and services may not meet the expectations of the companies that are choosing to relocate their operations overseas (Farrell et al., 2005). Connected with this is a generalized concern about the suitability of labour to fit with the quality of service demanded by customers. Key suitability factors include problems with language skills, an educational system that does not emphasize interpersonal skills and attitudes towards teamwork, and cultural fit. Tangible savings could be lost if these issues associated with quality and service are not managed (Nash et al., 2004).

These issues require additional monitoring to ensure that quality and service are being delivered in an appropriate manner. Shiu (2004) concludes that the aforementioned issues of culture, language, service integration and maintenance will require time for clients and customers to adjust, and this may not always be an option for a firm that is trying to make strategic headway in a timely manner.

Conclusion

This chapter has provided an overview of technical approaches to HRP as well as a discussion of some of the strategic challenges that are now being incorporated into HRP thinking. HRP has evolved through a series of stages from legal compliance and application as a control mechanism, to more recently being considered as a valuable strategic tool. As a strategic mechanism, HRP is not simply a matter of ensuring that a firm meets swings in the supply and demand of labour, but rather that the process adds real value when addressing the strategic needs of the company. The strategic imperative has been heightened by environmental changes associated with increasing levels of uncertainty and competition.

These forces have alerted companies to the value of the people resource and have led to a rethink of traditional responses to an over- or undersupply or demand for labour. Downsizing to deal with a drop in labour demand, for example, has in the past been adopted as a necessary cost-cutting measure. Although this response is still used, the process is now more likely to factor in the impact on employees and ensure that workers are informed and have some sense of personal control. Such an approach assists in keeping employees engaged inthe strategic goals of the company and also enhances the firm's corporate reputation.

Changes in the flexibility of work organization have also been used to deal with variations in the supply and demand of labour, and have resulted in a shift in the expectations of workers in terms of permanent work arrangements. Although this helps companies to deal with changes in demand patterns, it has also raised issues relating to employee loyalty and commitment. Revised expectations on the part of the workforce's employees have led companies to think more carefully about the relationships that they develop with their workers, especially those who provide critical talent resources. Even during periods of a slow-down in labour demand, as was experienced during the 2008–09 global financial crisis, firms have become more mindful of the importance of attracting and retaining talent. Overall, HRP has evolved considerably, and has moved beyond a mere matching of labour needs with output requirements to incorporate a strategic view of the people resource and the impact that can be ultimately made on sustained competitive advantage.

> **FOR DISCUSSION AND REVISION**
>
> 1. What are the HRP implications associated with an increase in the services sector?
> 2. Under what conditions is a qualitative approach to demand forecasting preferable?
> 3. Do you agree that environmental changes render HRP so problematic that it becomes infeasible? Is there a way to approach HRP under volatile conditions that still adds value?
> 4. Discuss why some commentators argue that job descriptions have become redundant.
> 5. How can an organization's resource munificence (abundance) be used to assess whether downsizing is a morally or socially appropriate response?
> 6. If an organization is committed to retaining talented workers, what sort of HRM initiatives may assist in the retention of valuable workers?
> 7. Further reading

Further Reading

Books

Berger, L. A. and Berger, D. R. (2011) *The Talent Management Handbook: Creating a Sustainable Competitive Advantage by Selecting, Developing, and Promoting the Best People, 2.* New York: McGraw-Hill.

Boxall, P. and Purcell, J. (2011) *Strategy and Human Resource Management.* Basingstoke: Palgrave Macmillan.

Caplan, J. (2011) *The Value of Talent: Promoting Talent Management Across the Organization.* London: Kogan Page.

Cascio, W. (2010) *Managing Human Resources: Productivity, Quality of Work Life, Profits.* Boston: McGraw-Hill/Irwin.

Delahaye, B. (2011) *Human Resource Development: Managing Learning and Knowledge Capital.* Prahran: Tilde University Press.

Hartel, C. E. J., Fujimoto, Y., Strybosch, V. E. and Fitzpatrick, K. (2007) *Human Resource Management. Transforming Theory into Innovative Practice.* French's Forest, NSW: Pearson.

Kramar, R., Bartram, T., De Cieri, H., Noe, R., Hollenbeck, J., Gerhart, B. and Wright, P. (2010) *Human Resource Management in Australia* (4th edn). Sydney: McGraw-Hill.

Teicher, J., Holland, P. and Gough, R. (eds) (2006) *Employee Relations Management: Australia in a Global Context* (2nd edn). Frenchs Forest, NSW: Prentice Hall.

Withers, M., Williamson, M. and Reddington, M. (2010) *Transforming HR: Creating Value Through People* (2nd edn). Amsterdam: Butterworth-Heinemann.

Journals

Burgess, J. and Campbell, I. (1998) Casual employment in Australia: growth, characteristics, a bridge or trap? *Economic and Labour Relations Review*, 9(1): 31–54.

Grant, R. (2003) Strategic planning in a turbulent environment: evidence from the oil majors. *Strategic Management Journal*, 24(6): 491–517.

Guest, D. (2004) Flexible employment contracts, the psychological contract and employment outcomes: an analysis and review of the evidence. *International Journal of Management Reviews*, 5/6(1): 1–19.

Lepak, D. and Snell, S. (2002) Examining the human resource architecture: the relationships among human capital, employment and human resource configurations. *Journal of Management*, 28(4): 517–43.

Tsui, A., Pearce, J., Porter, L. and Hite, J. (1995) Alternative approaches to the employee-organizational relationship: does investment in employees pay off? *Academy of Management Journal*, 44: 1089–121.

CASE STUDY

The Australian Cladding Company

The Australian Cladding Company (ACC) was started in 1998 by Jim Hackett. With a background in engineering, Hackett created a new light-weight, low-cost house cladding product that found a ready market in Australia. The company grew dramatically, and although ACC had located its headquarters in Sydney, the company supplied its product into a number of states, as well as attracting international customers. The cladding product was very popular in major building projects, as well as in home building and extension work.

The general health of the Australian economy and initiatives such as the First Home Owner Grant scheme (a one off payment of $7,000 that was introduced by the government in mid-2000 to offset the effect of the Goods and Services Tax) ensured that the construction industry remained buoyant. ACC had also been involved with the supply and installation of the product in a large number of large building projects in Western Australia, where the mining boom had had a positive flow-on effect to the construction industry.

To staff the venture, Hackett initially used contacts from the building industry, and he hand-picked the members of his management team. This group was very small, and it still consists of just:

- Jim Hackett as Managing Director;
- Ben Harper, Engineering and design;
- Reg Grundy, Marketing and sales;
- Arthur Seymour, Financial controller;
- Ted Clark, Production manager;
- Jill Hackett (Jim's wife), Personnel (wages and salary/personnel admininstration).

The growth of the company was quite remarkable. At first, it employed about 20 crew, but as demand increased the business went from a small operation to a much larger concern employing nearly 150 production staff and a further 25 staff working in support roles such as logistics, engineering, personnel, sales, and accounting and finance.

Despite healthy sales figures, profits during 2007 and into the first part of 2008 were down. At the time, Arthur Seymour explained to Hackett that profit was falling because costs were increasing. The cost management figures were showing increased scrap and wastage rates, and labour costs were rising. Along with these cost increases, there were further issues that were of a concern to Hackett.

First, there were efficiency problems with the production staff: at times, they were waiting around not doing anything, yet at other times they were stressed and working flat out. Second, despite a history of long staff tenure, the company was now having problems with employee retention. This was particularly an issue with the skilled staff on the floor, but several key engineering people had also left, along with an IT specialist who had only been with the company for 6 months.

Finally, the number of workplace accidents was on the rise, and Sandra, one of the machine operators, had approached Jill Hackett to suggest that some of the workers were failing to take enough care around the machinery. She also pointed out that the increasing cohort of female workers at times felt uncomfortable with the way in which some of the men spoke to them, and if the issue was not dealt with appropriately, the company could have a number of sexual harassment cases to deal with.

By mid-2008, Jim Hackett had become so worried about declining performance and the staffing problems that he employed a consultant to find out what was going on. In September, Hackett met with the consultant, Terry Wild. Terry explained that most of the problems seem to be connected with the very quick growth of the company, and, as is often the case with companies that expand at an accelerated rate, the human resources approach had not kept up with the expansion. For example, ACC had not really planned its workforce around peak demand periods. In addition, whether or not Hackett realized it, the workforce that he had in place was quite different from the workforce that he had had years before, when most of the workers were male tradesmen. Jill, who was in charge of hiring new staff, had introduced a large number of women, and these new employees were not prepared to put up with the 'boys club' approach. Terry also observed that there was discontent within the skilled workforce, who felt that they were not receiving enough professional development. Furthermore, all of the senior positions were taken up by the existing management group, and other employees could not see a career path for themselves in the organization.

Hackett took offence at the suggestion that Jill was not managing the personnel issues, and responded to Terry that Jill worked really hard and did a great job. Terry submitted his final report in late October 2008. Hackett briefly read through the executive summary; it seemed to him that Terry was basically pushing for 'a more strategic approach to human resources'. The report sat on Hackett's desk for a while. Then, in late October and early November, news of the international credit crisis hijacked discussions at ACC management level, and Hackett did not get back to reading the rest of the report.

As 2009 began, the fall-out from the international economic situation really started to hit ACC. Construction on a number of big projects in Western Australia came to a halt, and orders were cancelled. Furthermore, although the government was dropping interest rates to encourage household spending and the First Home Owners Grant had been increased to $21,000, the construction industry was feeling the impact of the economic downturn. During this time, Arthur Seymour reminded Hackett that one of the major cost blowouts in 2008 had been associated with labour, and if the company was going to survive it was going to have to cut its labour force – basically, the company was going to have to downsize until economic conditions improved.

Hackett realized the practicality of this suggestion but was still concerned about the impact of such a message, especially in view of the comments that had been made by Terry Wild in late 2008. So Hackett decided to invite Terry to come along to the next management meeting to discuss the company's response to the economic downturn and provide some insights based on Terry's investigation from the previous year.

Hackett rang Terry to ask him if he would attend the management meeting, and Terry was pleased to be involved. Hackett explained that ACC were considering downsizing the workforce, and Terry agreed that this was a reasonable and necessary response. He also made the observation, however, that in light of the staff problems from the previous year, any downsizing approaches would have to be handled extremely carefully. Terry made the comment:

> Prior to the economic downturn, you already had problems with the workforce. The lack of an effective human resources approach that kept up with your expansion was becoming a major problem. You really needed at that time to look at your work flows and how your jobs were designed. You were also losing important staff. Now, if you inform staff that they are going to lose their jobs, existing problems might be made worse. When I come to see you next week, we need to rethink how you are managing some key human resources issues.

As he rang off, Hackett wondered whether getting Terry Wild involved was actually going to be a good idea – it might just complicate matters. He thought to himself that people either wanted to work for the company or they didn't. If they weren't happy at ACC, they would have to find work elsewhere – at least if they went, it would get rid of some of the labour cost problems.

Questions

1. What are the immediate and underlying problems facing ACC?
2. What sort of human resources activities need to be put in place reasonably quickly, and what human resources approaches need to be taken in the longer term to ensure ongoing strategic competitive advantage?

References

Appelbaum, S., Everard, A. and Hung, L. T. S. (1999) Strategic downsizing: critical success factors. *Management Decisions*, 37(7): 535–52.

Atkinson, J. (1984) Manpower strategies for flexible organisations. *Personnel Management*, (August): 28–31.

The Australian (2009) Others To Follow Bank's Executive Pay Cuts. Available from: http://www.theaustralian.com.au/business/news/bank-pay-cuts-set-trend/story-e6frg906-1225700359387 [accessed 21 April 2009].

The Australian (2009) Holden Trims Shifts To Avoid Layoffs. Available from: http://theage.drive.com.au/motor-news/holden-axes-600-jobs-in-adelaide-20070305-140fo.html [accessed 15 August 2011].

Australian Bureau of Statistics (2006) *Yearbook Australia 2006*. Cat. No. 1301.0. Canberra: Australian Bureau of Statistics.

Barney, J. B. and Wright, P. M. (1998) On becoming a strategic partner: the role of human resources in gaining competitive advantage. *Human Resource Management*, 37(1): 31–46.

Beechler, S. and Woodward, I. C. (2009) The global 'war for talent'. *Journal of International Management*, 15(3): 273–85.

Blyton, P. (1989) Working population and employment. In Bean, R. (ed.), *International Labour Statistics*. London: Routledge, pp. 18–51.

Boxall, P., Macky, K. and Rasmussen, E. (2003) Labour turnover and retention in New Zealand: the causes and consequences of leaving and staying with employers. *Asia Pacific Journal of Human Resources*, 41(2): 195–214.

Boyer, R. (1988) *The Search for Labour Market Flexibility: The European Economies in Transition*. Oxford: Clarendon Press.

Brannick, M. T., Levine, E. L. and Morgeson, F. P. (2007) *Job and Work Analysis: Methods, Research, and Applications for Human Resource Management* (2nd edn). Los Angeles: Sage.

Burgess, J. (1997) The flexible firm and growth of non-standard employment. *Labour and Industry*, 7(3): 85–102.

Buultjens, J. (2001) Casual employment: a problematic strategy for the registered clubs sector in New South Wales. *Journal of Industrial Relations*, 43(4): 470–7.

Campbell, I. and Burgess, J. (2001) Casual employment in Australia and temporary employment in Europe: developing a cross-national comparison. *Work, Employment & Society*, 15(1): 171–84.

Cascio, W. and Wynn, P. (2004) Managing a downsizing process. *Human Resource Management*, 43(4): 425–36.

Corporate Leadership Council (2008) *HR Quarterly Trends Report*, Q4 – 2008. Catalogue Number CLC2456755. Arlington, VA: CLC.

Domberger, S. (1994) Public sector contracting: does it work? *Australian Economic Review*, (Third quarter): 91–6.

Edgar, F. and Geare, A. (2005) Employee voice on human resource management. *Asia Pacific Journal of Human Resources*, 43(3): 361–80.

Farrell, D., Laboisseire, M., Pascal, R., Rosenfeld, J., de Segundo, C., Sturze, S. and Umezawa, F. (2005) The Emerging Global Labour Market. Available from: http://www.mckinsey.com/mgi/reports/pdfs/emerginggloballabormarket/Part1/MGI_packagedsoftware_demand_case.pdf [accessed 15 August 2011].

Farrell, M. and Mavondo, F. (2004) The effect of downsizing strategy and reorientation strategy on a learning orientation. *Personnel Review*, 33(4): 383–402.

Gandolfy, F. (2008) Learning from the past – downsizing lessons for managers. *Journal of Management Research*, 8(1): 3–17.

Ghosh, D., Willinger, G. L. and Ghosh, S. (2009) A firm's external environment and the hiring of a non-standard workforce: implications for organisations. *Human Resource Management Journal*, 19(4): 433–51.

Guest, D. (2002) Human resource management, corporate performance and employee wellbeing: building the worker into HRM. *Journal of Industrial Relations*, 44(3): 335–58.

Guest, D., Michie, J., Conway, N. and Sheehan, M. (2003) Human resource management and corporate performance in the UK. *British Journal of Industrial Relations*, 41(2): 291–314.

Hall, R. (2006) Temporary agency work and HRM in Australia: 'Cooperation, specialization and satisfaction for the good of all'? *Personnel Review*, 35(2): 158–74.

Hochschild, A. R. (1983) *The Managed Heart: Commercialization of Human Feeling*. Berkeley, CA: University of California Press.

Holland, P., Sheehan, C. and De Cieri, H. (2007) Attracting and retaining talent: exploring human resources development trends in Australia. *Human Resource Development International*, 10(3): 247–62.

Huselid, M. A. (1993) The impact of environmental volatility on human resource planning and strategic human resource management. *Human Resource Planning*, 16(3): 35–51.

Huselid, M. A. (1995) The impact of human resource management practices on turnover, productivity and corporate financial performance. *Academy of Management Journal*, 38: 635–72.

Iverson, R. D. and Zatzick, D. (2007) High commitment work practices and downsizing harshness in Australian Workplaces. *Industrial Relations*, 46(3): 456–80.

Jeanneret, P. R. and Strong, M. H. (2003) Linking O*NET job analysis information to job requirement predictors: an O*NET application. *Personnel Psychology*, 56: 465–92.

Kalleberg, A. (2000) Nonstandard employment relations: part-time, temporary and contract work. *Annual Review of Sociology*, 26: 341–65.

Kryger, T. (2004) Casual Employment: Trends and Characteristics. Research Note No. 53, 2003–4. Canberra: Statistics Section, Australian Parliamentary Library.

Kulik, C. & Bainbridge, H. T. J. (2006) HR and the line: the distribution of HR activities in Australian organisations. *Asia Pacific Journal of Human Resources*, 44(2): 240–56.

Lam, S. S. and Schaubroeck, J. (1998) Integrating HR planning and organisational strategy. *Human Resource Management Journal*, 8(3): 5–19.

Legge, K. (2005) *Human Resource Management: Rhetorics and Reality*. Basingstoke: Palgrave Macmillan.

Losey, M. (2005) Anticipating change: will there really be a labor shortage? In Losey, M., Meisinger, S. and Ulrich, D. (eds), *The Future of Human Resource Management*. Virginia: John Wiley & Sons, pp. 23–37.

Lowry, D. (2001) The casual management of casual work: casual workers' perceptions of HRM practices in the highly casualised firm. *Asia Pacific Journal of Human Resources*, 39(1): 42–62.

Macdonald, C. L. and Sirianni, C. (eds) (1996) *Working in the Service Society*. Philadelphia: Temple University Press.

Nash, B., Holland, P. J. and Pyman, A. (2004) The role and influence of stakeholders in offshoring: developing a framework for analysis. *International Employment Relations Review*, 10(2): 20–49.

O'Reilly, A. (1973) Skill requirements: supervisor–subordinate conflict. *Personnel Psychology*, 26: 75–80.

Pocock, B. (2005) Work–life 'balance' in Australia: limited progress, dim prospects. *Asia Pacific Journal of Human Resources*, 43(2): 198–209.

Pocock, B., Buchanan, J. and Campbell, I. (2004) Meeting the challenge of casual work in Australia: evidence, past treatment and future policy. *Australian Bulletin of Labour*, 30(1): 16–32.

Rimmer, M. and Zappala, J. (1988) Labour market flexibility and the second tier. *Australian Bulletin of Labour*, 14(4): 564–91.

Rothwell, S. (1995) Human resource planning. In Storey, J. (ed.), *Human Resource Management: A Critical Text*. London: Routledge, pp. 167–201.

Rudd, K., Swan, W., Smith, S. and Wong, P. (2007) *Skilling Australia for the Future: Election 2007 Policy Document*. Canberra: T. Gartrell.

Schneider, B. and Konz, A. M. (1989) Strategic job analysis. *Human Resource Management*, 28(1): 51–63.

Schneider, B., White, S. and Paul, M. (1998) Linking service climate and customer perceptions of service quality: test of a causal model. *Journal of Applied Psychology*, 8(2): 150–63.

Sheehan, C., Holland, P. and De Cieri, H. (2006) Current developments in HRM in Australian organisations. *Asia Pacific Journal of Human Resources*, 44(2): 2–22.

Shiu, K. (2004) Outsourcing: are you sure or offshore? Identifying legal risks in offshoring. *NSW Society for Computers and the Law*, 37(3): 56.

Smith, M. (2005) The incidence of new forms of employment in service activities. In Macdonald, C. and Sirianni, C. (eds), *Working in the Service Society*. Philadelphia: The University Press, pp. 54–73.

Stewart, G. L. and Carson, K. P. (1997) Moving beyond the mechanistic model: an alternative approach to staffing for contemporary organizations. *Human Resource Management Review*, 7(2): 157–84.

Ulrich, D. (1987) Strategic human resource planning: why and how? *Human Resource Planning*, 10(1): 37–56.

Ulrich, D. (2006) The talent trifecta. *Workforce Management*, (September), pp. 32–3.

Vaiman, V. and Vance, C. M. (eds) (2008) *Smart Talent Management*. Cheltenham: Edward Elgar.

Van Buren, H. J. III (2000) The bindingness of social and psychological contracts: toward a theory of social responsibility in downsizing. *Journal of Business Ethics*, 25(3): 205–19.

Van den Heuvel, A. and Wooden, M. (1997) Self-employed contractors and job satisfaction. *Journal of Small Business Management*, 35(3): 11–20.

Wright, P., McMahan, G. and McWilliams, A. (1994) Human resources as a source of sustained competitive advantage. *International Journal of Human Resource Management*, 5: 299–324.

Zatzick, C. and Iverson, R. D. (2006) High-involvement management and workforce reduction: competitive advantage or disadvantage? *Academy of Management Journal*, 49: 281–303.

Zula, K. J. and Chermack, T. J. (2007) Human capital planning: a review of literature and implications for human resource development. *Human Resource Development Review*, 6(3): 245–62.

Zyglidopoulos, S. C. (2003) The impact of downsizing on the corporate reputation for social performance. *Journal of Public Affairs*, 4(1): 11–25.

Zyglidopoulos, S. C. (2005) The impact of downsizing on corporate reputation. *British Academy of Management*, 16: 253–9.

CHAPTER 9
Recruiting and selecting employees

OUTLINE

- Introduction
- Recruitment and selection policies
- HRM in practice 9.1: Employer branding and the employment 'deal'
- Recruitment and attraction
- HRM as I see it: Tania Hummel, Macmillan Publishers
- Selection
- HRM in practice 9.2: Trapped in the 'marzipan layer'
- HRM and globalization: Unpacking the meaning of credentials
- Psychometric testing
- Case study: Watson and Hamilton Lawyers
- Summary, Vocab checklist for ESL students, Review questions and Further reading to improve your mark

OBJECTIVES

After studying this chapter, you should be able to:
- Understand the importance of recruitment and selection in the formation of the employment relationship
- Understand the key features of recruitment and selection policies
- Explain the nature of attraction in recruitment
- Explain the effectiveness of various selection methods

Introduction

'You're hired!' And with these words, on an annual basis, Lord Alan Sugar selects his latest recruit. Each year, a range of budding apprentices present themselves to

Lord Sugar and his panel as part of the BBC's flagship recruitment and selection programme. Although it is clearly a balance between human resources (HR) practice and entertainment, and is presented as the job interview from hell, *The Apprentice* also covers some of the key features of recruitment and selection, effective or otherwise. First, a position is made available, to which apparently several thousand people are attracted. Whereas it is not entirely clear what is in the job description or personnel specification, suffice it to say that there is a six-figure salary. Then, through a series of 'auditions' as well as interviews, around 70 applicants are selected for a second round, followed by psychological tests, from which the short list of 16 are presented to Lord Sugar. In the following weeks, through a series of tasks, aided by the assessment of trusted colleagues, choices are made about the applicants – usually resulting in the immortal line 'You're Fired!' – until an appointment is made in the final week of the programme.

It is often the case that those who make it to the final are strikingly different in terms of their education, experience and personality characteristics. These are, however, less relevant than the chance for Lord Sugar and his panel to base their assessments on what they see so that they can predict how a potential employee might behave in the future and fit into the organization. Of course, whether the winner's job with the organization meets their expectations as part of an evolving employment relationship and a positive psychological contract based on a mutual and reciprocal understanding is something that is left to our imagination.

> **reflective question**
>
> What are your expectations for employment? What attracts you to employment opportunities in the current economic climate?

Recruitment and selection policies

Recruitment and selection have always been critical processes for organizations. In earlier chapters, we discussed ethics in recruitment and selection practices and how such practices can change or reinforce a particular culture. After a period during which recruitment difficulties had been reported in many organizations, and employer branding in terms of recruitment and selection was needed to stand out as a 'good employer' (Chartered Institute of Personnel and Development [CIPD], 2005b), the recession in the late 2000s led to a significant reduction in the number of vacancies. According to CIPD's (2010c) survey of over 480 organizations, fewer organizations were experiencing recruitment problems, and some had even cut or reduced their graduate schemes, although for many these remained the same (at 42 per cent). In circumstances where many applicants chase fewer jobs, just like in *The Apprentice*, employers clearly have more power, and therefore many approaches to recruitment and selection emphasize this power. Traditional approaches to recruitment and selection attempt to attract a wide choice of candidates for vacancies before screening out those who do not match the criteria set in the job descriptions and personnel specifications. Figure 9.1 shows an overall view of the stages

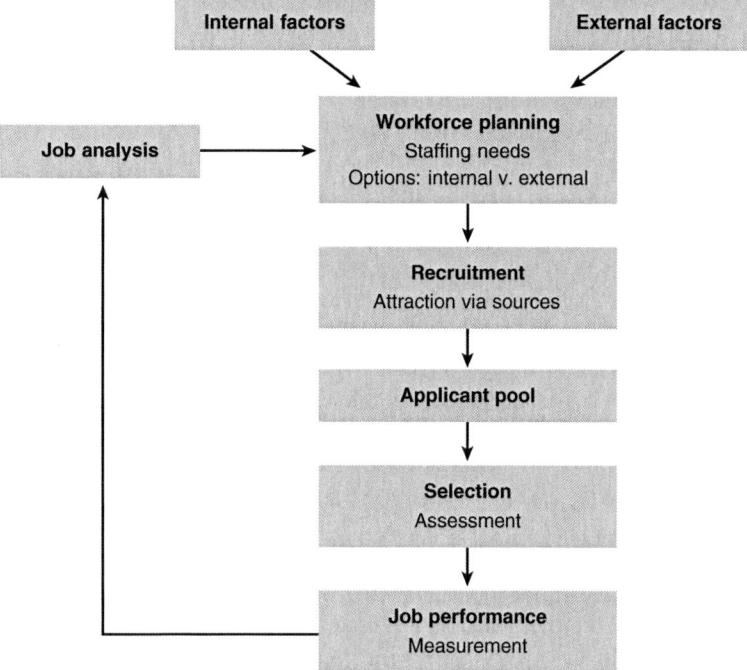

Figure 9.1 The stages of recruitment and selection

of recruitment and selection, and the connection of these processes to workforce planning.

There are wide variations in recruitment and selection policies and practices, reflecting an organization's strategy and its philosophy of people management. In large multinational organizations, for example, there is a distinction between policies to attract those destined for international careers and policies suited to local conditions (Sparrow, 2007). Where indicated by the workforce plan, an organization will seek ways of attracting a pool of applicants and then differentiating between them, avoiding the costs of hiring the 'wrong' ones (Newell, 2005, p. 115). In recent years, there has been interest in the idea of an employer brand (Knox and Freeman, 2006), based on the image the organization wishes to project to potential applicants in order to attract them. Many larger organizations use their websites for this purpose or employ recruitment agencies to help them (CIPD, 2010c).

Visit www.palgrave.com/business/bratton5 to read an HRM in practice feature on how Adidas attracts new staff.

The employer brand will also be reflected in the psychological and behavioural characteristics expected of employees, which are expressed through competency frameworks (Roberts, 1997); we will explore these below. Such frameworks have allowed organizations to adopt a range of sophisticated recruitment and selection

HRM in practice 9.1:   Employer branding and the employment 'deal'

Employer branding is now recognized as an important part of the HR 'toolkit', stimulated by a growing awareness of the application of marketing principles in attracting better applicants and leveraging employee engagement and retention. This places the spotlight on the employer's 'brand promise', which has been defined as the employee value proposition (EVP) or employment 'deal', initially promoted by recruitment consultancies since the 1990s as part of the 'war for talent'. This centres around promoting a positive image of the organization as a good place to work, as illustrated by Google's portrayal of the 'Top 10 Reasons' to work for the company, such as having fun, fulfilling work and a supportive workplace (Google, 2012).

Consultancy-driven recipes for 'employer of choice' strategies have become very popular, and employers are increasingly seeking more sophisticated means of linking their HR strategy and the corporate brand, beyond the aim of attracting job applicants. The challenge is to find a way of building employees' 'buy-in' to a new brand articulation in ways that enhances their engagement and performance, especially during periods of redundancy and cost-cutting. More active employee involvement is key, as shown by the Co-operative Group's attempts to reinvent its company brand during a time of declining performance. In the words of the Director for HR (MacLeod and Clarke, 2009, p. 45):

> *The engagement strategy was a catalyst for rebuilding trust and confidence between individuals, their line managers and the organisation. We asked people how they felt about working here, why they felt that way and what should be done to change things.*

Research into making and keeping an employer brand promise has been informed by exchange concepts, notably the idea of the psychological contract. This is commonly described in terms of a reciprocal relationship of inducements from employers in exchange for contributions from their employees – for example, meaningful work pay and benefits in return for the employees' initiative and discretionary effort.

Detractors have, however, pointed to the somewhat passive role accorded to employees in the current modelling of human resource management (HRM) and EVP, treating them essentially as *consumers* 'buying into' their employer's vision and brand, rather than as active *producers* of HR practices or employer brand. This is promoted by an over-reliance on statistical instruments concerned with the mechanistic cause-and-effect relationships between organizational 'drivers' and employees' performance. More research work needs to be done on how employers might reformulate the design process of EVPs in order to facilitate more authentic employee involvement and participation that are of mutual benefit to the stakeholders involved.

> **Stop!**   Academic debates about the emergent concepts of EVP and engagement have pointed to unrealistic *unitarist thinking* about the employment relationship, which assumes that what is good for the organization is always good for employees and vice versa. What is your view?

Sources and further information:

See MacLeod and Clarke's (2009) report to the government, *Engaging for Success,* and for further insight into employee engagement, see Balain and Sparrow (2009). An examination of how

→

linkages between social exchange, EVP and engagement can be applied in practice is contained in Francis and Reddington (2012).

Note: This feature was written by Professor Helen Francis and Dr Martin Reddington at Edinburgh Napier University.

Visit the companion website at www.palgrave.com/business/bratton5 for bonus HRM in practice features on how Adidas attracts new staff, and on the Co-op's internship scheme.

---

techniques in order to identify and admit the 'right' people. In this way, as 'organizationally defined critical qualities' (Iles and Salaman, 1995, p. 204), a competency framework augments an organization's power. For example, one tool of assessment we will consider is personality testing, and a survey by Piotrowski and Armstrong (2006) found that popular qualities for testing included integrity and potential for violence. Such information can be used to make judgements about who to admit. Crucially, however, such models need to work within the constraints of a legal context and policies for diversity management (Daniels and Macdonald, 2005).

> **reflective question**
>
> How would an employer prove to you that it was seeking to develop its employer brand based on a positive psychological contract? Go to BP Global Careers at www.bpfutures.com. How has BP's image and brand been affected by the Gulf Oil Disaster?

Recruitment and attraction

Recruitment is the process of attracting the interest of a pool of capable people who will apply for jobs within an organization. In this definition, we can highlight three crucial issues. First, there is a need to attract people's interest in applying for employment. This implies that people have a choice about which organizations they wish to work for, even though during times of recession such choices might be limited. Second, people may be capable of fulfilling a role in employment, but the extent to which this will be realized is not totally predictable. Third, how capability is understood is increasingly determined by an organization's approach to talent management. There are some choices to be made, especially in terms of whether there should be an exclusive or an inclusive focus (Lewis and Heckman, 2006).

Under different labour market conditions, power in the recruitment process will swing between the buyers or sellers of labour – the employers and employees, respectively. It is therefore important to understand that the dimension of power will always be present in recruitment and selection, even in organizations that purport to have a high-commitment HR strategy. Thus, in conditions of recession, employers are likely to reduce recruitment budgets and costs, giving more attention to developing the talent that has already been employed (CIPD, 2010c).

HRM as I see it

Tania Hummel
Group Human Resources Director, Macmillan Publishers
www.macmillan.com

Macmillan Publishers Ltd is one of the largest international publishing groups in the world, with 7000 staff operating in more than 80 countries. Macmillan publishes a variety of academic and scholarly, fiction and non-fiction books and online content, as well as STM (science, technical and medical) and social science journals, educational course materials and dictionaries, and higher education textbooks. Divisions of the company include NPG (Nature Publishing Group), Macmillan Education, Pan Macmillan, Picador and Palgrave Macmillan.

Tania Hummel joined Macmillan in 2006 as Personnel Manager for the London divisions, having spent many years in publishing, most notably with Rough Guides and Lonely Planet publications. She has an MSc in HRM, with a special interest in management development.

Visit www.palgrave.com/business/bratton5 to watch Tania talking about recruitment, diversity and the challenges faced by HR in the publishing industry, and then think about the following questions:

1. How does Tania describe the differences between personnel management and HRM?
2. What does she see as the role of HR in the business?
3. What issues are facing recruitment today? How do companies ensure diversity in the workplace?

Budgetary factors will also affect how recruitment channels are used, with more use of online recruitment, as we will consider below. Generally, there needs to be an intelligent use of recruitment channels in all circumstances. For example, the ageing profile of the workforce requires an adjustment of recruitment polices (Lyon and

Glover, 1998). Henkens et al. (2005) found that the use of the Internet and agencies for recruitment reflected a bias towards younger applicants, whereas older workers were more dependent on formal channels of recruitment such as newspapers and journals.

In addition, since the early 1990s, there have been more graduates entering the labour market, but the number of 'graduate' jobs has not kept pace, with a consequent reduction in the power of many new graduates to find employment on advantageous terms (Brannie, 2008). This means that many graduates will take longer to find employment that matches their skills and aspirations. It might also affect the perceptions of value to be gained from studying for a degree against the price of a degree. Among today's graduates are those referred to as Generation Y (those born between 1977 and 1994), who are said to be confident and thrive on challenging but flexible work, expecting quick feedback and reward while maintaining a balanced lifestyle (Broadbridge et al., 2009).

HRM web links

Go to www.ashridge.org.uk/Website/Content.nsf/wFARCRED/Generation+Y?opendocument to find out about Ashridge's Generation Y research project.

reflective question

Do you consider yourself as part of Generation Y? What are your expectations for working, and what do you expect in recruitment?

Fitting the person to the environment, organization and job

Effective recruitment depends on the extent to which the overall management philosophy supports and reinforces an approach to HRM that focuses on the utilization and development of new employees once they have joined an organization. Although HR policies will be designed to achieve particular organizational targets and goals, those policies will also provide an opportunity for individual needs to emerge and be satisfied. This view assumes that a fit between a person and the environment can be found so that their commitment and performance will be enhanced (Kristof, 1996). Some commentators doubt that such mutuality could ever occur on an equal basis, and believe that organizational needs, as determined by senior management, will always take precedence; however, individual needs may, through HRM activities, influence how the organization's needs are perceived. Recruitment and then selection processes will therefore aim to attract and admit those whom management view as the 'right' people for such an approach. In one sense, an organization already knows who the right people are for its vacancies since they are the very people who are already employed and are present in the company's talent pool. Such internal recruitment might be based on performance assessment and the decisions of senior managers, whose choices could be made on the basis of candidates' similarity to themselves (see Mäkelä et al., 2010).

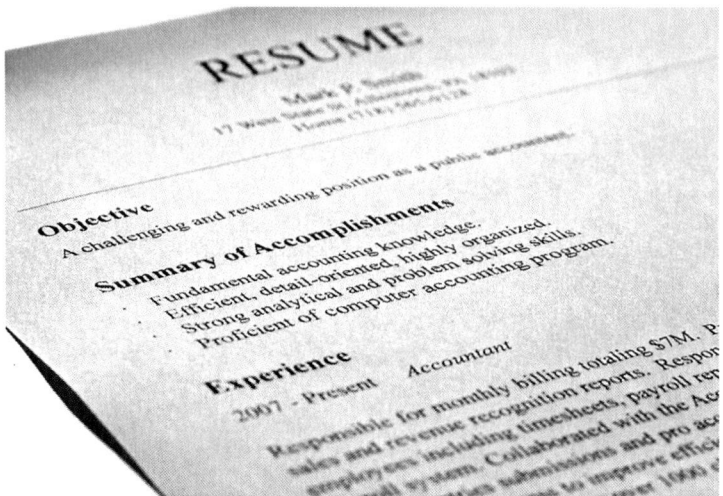

Recruitment is a process of attracting the right people to apply for the job
Source: ©istockphoto.com/Anatoly Vartanov.

Taking a strategic view of recruitment requirements starts with the strategic plan. Research by Tyson (1995) found that although there were many differences between organizations, HRM could help to shape the direction of change, influence culture and 'help bring about the mindset' that would decide which strategic issues were considered. HR considerations, including the results of a review of the quantity and quality of people, should thus be integrated into the plan. The goals, objectives and targets that then emerge set the parameters for performance in an organization and for how work is organized into roles and jobs. A key role for HR is to align performance within roles with the organization's strategy, so recruiting the right people for a role depends on how that role is defined in terms relating to the performance needed to achieve the strategy (Holbeche, 1999). Once a recruitment strategy has been formed, an organization might outsource its implementation, especially where there are a large number of staff to be recruited (Tulip, 2004), although recent moves to focus on the talent already employed might reduce this tendency (Ordanini and Silvestri, 2008).

Traditionally, creating a specification containing the requirements for a particular role has required the use of *job analysis techniques*; these may include a range of interviews, questionnaires and observation processes that provide information about work carried out, the environment in which it occurs and, vitally, the knowledge, skills and attitudes needed to perform the job well. In recent years, information derived from the analysis of work performance has been utilized to create a taxonomy or framework of either criterion-related behaviours or standards of performance referred to as *competencies*. Although most frameworks are developed within organizations and are based on the meanings of behaviour that exist within an organization, there are also frameworks that can be applied more generally or to specific groups in different organizations. According to the CIPD (2010d, p. 1), competencies are 'the behaviours that employees must have, or must acquire, to input into a situation in order to achieve high levels of performance'. (This definition, focusing on behaviour patterns, differs from the idea of competence used with Vocational Qualifications, which are related to performing activities within an occupation to a prescribed standard. You can read more about the development of Vocational Qualifications at www.qcda.gov.uk/qualifications/60.aspx.) Competency frameworks are concerned with behaviour that is relevant to the job and the effective or competent performance of that job, although factors such as equipment and the behaviour can also have an impact.

Competency frameworks are widely thought to help an organization to align its objectives with the various HR activities of recruitment and selection, appraisal, training and reward (Holbeche, 1999). In addition, competencies enhance a common understanding of effective behaviour at work and provide a basis for more consistency in assessment practices (Whiddett and Hollyforde, 2003).

HRM web links

SHL is one of the main suppliers of job assessment software that can be used to develop competencies. Details of its Universal Competency Framework can be found at www.shl.com/WhatWeDo/Competency/Pages/UniversalCompetencyFramework.aspx. SHL also provides a useful book on job analysis techniques, which you can download at www.shl.com/assets/resources/Best-Practice-Job-Analysis.pdf.

Table 9.1 shows how one large financial services organization in the UK sets out its competencies. Each competency is defined and described by a range of indicators that enables assessment and measurement. The competency of 'creating customer service' is, for example, indicated by:

- Anticipating emerging customer needs and planning accordingly
- Identifying the customers who will be of value to the company
- Recommending changes to current ways of working that will improve customer service
- Arranging the collection of customer satisfaction data and acting on them.

The analysis and definition of competencies should allow the identification and isolation of dimensions of behaviour that are distinct and are associated with competent or effective performance. Competencies can therefore be used to provide, at least from an organization's point of view, the behaviours needed at work to achieve the business strategy. On this assumption, the assessment of competencies is one means of selecting employees, as will be discussed below. Competencies will enable organizations to form a model of the kinds of employee they wish to attract through recruitment.

HRM web links

Competency frameworks are now widely established in all kinds of organization. Check how the British Medical Association advocates the use of its framework at www.bma.org.uk/about_bma/bma_jobs/HRCompetencies.jsp?page=1. Note how this framework is used in recruitment.

Table 9.1 Competencies in a financial services organization

Personal focus	Self-control
	Self-development
	Personal organization
	Positive approach
Customer focus	Creating customer service
	Delivering customer service
	Continuous improvement
Future focus	Delivering the vision
	Change and creativity
Business focus	Delivering results
	Providing solutions
	Systemic thinking
	Attention to detail
People focus	Developing people
	Working with others
	Influencing
	Leading

Whatever the model constructed, an organization's commitment to its HR processes will form part of its evolving value system and make it even more attractive to those seeking employment. Many organizations seek to express their values by statements of visions and missions. For example, the following can be found at www.morrisons.co.uk/Corporate/Corporate-responsibility-2011/Responsible-retailing/Our-values.

> Our values are at the heart of everything we do, defining what we expect of each other and what our customers can expect of us as we aim to deliver our vision of becoming the 'Food Specialist for Everyone'.
>
> CAN DO
>
> Can do is about making things happen. It's about getting the job done and delivering results. It's about being positive and rising to a challenge.
>
> ONE TEAM
>
> One team is about working together to reach a common goal. It's about keeping our promises, building trust and respect, and valuing each other's contribution.
>
> BRINGING THE BEST OUT OF OUR PEOPLE
>
> Bringing the best out of our people is about developing ourselves and those around us. It's about constantly learning so we can improve the way we work and the experience we give our customers.
>
> GREAT SELLING AND SERVICE
>
> Great selling and service is about delivering a great experience for our customers. It's about sharing our knowledge and know-how and always striving to do better.

RECRUITING AND SELECTING EMPLOYEES

GREAT SHOPKEEPING

Great shopkeeping is about setting high standards and taking care of every detail. It's about having pride in our work and making quality our top priority.

FRESH THINKING

Fresh thinking is about finding new and better ways of working. It's about greater awareness, asking questions and coming up with bright ideas that give us the edge.

Such statements form part of the image, or 'brand' in talent management terms, that is projected by the company. Projected images, values and information on espoused goals will be made sense of by people in external labour markets, including both those employed and those unemployed. This interaction will determine how attracted potential recruits feel to an organization.

> **reflective question**
>
> Think about an organization you would like to work for. What images, values and information related to that organization come into your mind? What is the brand of that organization?

The image projected by an organization and the response from potential employees provide the basis for a compatible person–organization (P–O) fit, a variant of the person–environment fit referred to earlier (in addition to P–O fit, person–vocation fit, person–job fit, person–preferences for culture fit, and person–team fit; see Barber, 1998; Wheeler et al., 2005.) Schneider (1987), using a theory of interactional psychology, proposed an attraction–selection–attrition framework to explain the workings of this process and the differences between organizations that are caused by the attraction of people to the organization's goals, their interaction with those goals

Source: Courtesy of Morrisons PLC.

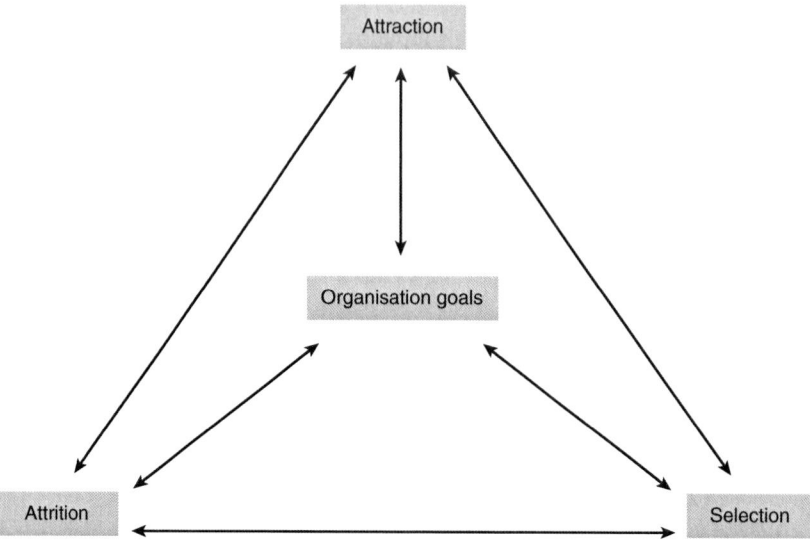

Figure 9.2 An attraction–selection–attrition framework
Source: Schneider (1987), p. 440. Reproduced with the permission of John Wiley & Sons, Inc.

and the fact that 'if they don't fit, they leave' (Schneider, 1987, p. 437). The proposed framework is shown in Figure 9.2. Schneider argued that people are attracted to an organization on the basis of their own interests and personality. Thus, people of a similar type will be attracted to the same place. Furthermore, the attraction of similar types will begin to determine the place. Following selection, people who do not fit, because of either an error or a misunderstanding of the reality of an organization, will leave, resulting in attrition from that organization.

At the heart of the framework lie organizational goals, originally stated by the founder and/or articulated by top managers, and out of these emerge the structures and processes that will form the basis of decisions related to attraction. This framework was supported by research conducted by Judge and Cable (1997), who found that applicants seek P–O fit, attempting to match their values with the reputation surrounding an organization's culture. Understanding the operation of P–O fit can prevent unnecessary and expensive attrition. One area that suffers from high staff turnover is call-centre work. McCulloch and Turban (2007) considered P–O fit related to selection in 14 call centres in the USA and Canada among over 200 staff who stayed and those who left, showing that taking P–O fit into account during selection can play a key role in preventing high attrition.

Furthermore, P–O fit can be enhanced by an attention to socialization processes once new employees have been selected (Cable and Parsons, 2001), and in recent years, there has been growing interest in retaining talent through *onboarding* programmes (Dai and de Meuse, 2007). For example, Google's onboarding programme for software engineers includes face-to-face, online and on-the-job training, mentoring, membership of a support community and practice-based learning, all deemed to be successful in creating a congruence between Google's values and the values of those seeking sustained employment in the company (Johnson and Senges, 2010).

In addition to P–O fit, there is also interest in the extent to which there is a match between an individual's skills, knowledge and abilities and the requirements of a job, referred to as the 'person–job' (P–J) fit. Research by Carless (2005) found that both P–O and P–J fit were positively linked to attraction – the perception that an organization was a desirable place to work. However, P–J fit becomes more important in relation to a candidate's intention to accept a job offer, suggesting that once applicants move toward job acceptance, they become more concerned with how they will use their abilities than with working in an organization that matches their values. There is also the issue of person–team fit (Hollenbeck, 2000), which considers how people can be matched to variations in organizational structure. For example, in a decentralized structure in which the focus is on self-managing teams, different characteristics might be required compared with more centralized or departmental structures.

This analysis of attraction, based on images and congruence of values, and then use of abilities, has been complicated by recent concerns about attracting a more diverse workforce. Recent changes in legislation have also set limits on the expression of values. For example, images used in advertisements for recruits need to take into consideration possible discrimination against older applicants.

Recruitment channels

The main means of attracting applicants can be summarised as follows:

- Walk-ins
- Employee referrals
- Advertising
- Websites
- Recruitment agencies
- Professional associations
- Educational associations.

Advertising and other recruitment literature comprise a common means by which the organization's values, ethos and desired image are made manifest, often in the form of glossy brochures. The utilitarian approach that focused on specifying job details, terms and conditions has been superseded by advertising that attempts to communicate a message about the company image, possibly over a long period of time through 'low-involvement' advertisements that seek to create awareness of an organization rather than generate recruits (Collins and Han, 2004). A good example might be the series of adverts for BT broadband, which clearly advertises a product but maintains ongoing awareness of BT as a brand and an organization. There has been a marked shift towards recruitment advertisements that are creative and reflect the skills normally used in product marketing. Recruitment advertising is now fully established within mainstream advertising.

HRM web links

Go to www.makeupyourownmind.co.uk/quality-scouts-home.html to find out about McDonald's Quality Scouts. What are the various methods used to attract applicants?

Over the last decade, there has been a rapid growth in online recruitment, e-recruitment having become another facet of the rapid progression of e-HRM. As a result, organizations are advised to consider the design of their websites and the terms that applicants might use to carry out job and vacancy searches (Jansen and Jansen, 2005). It has also been shown that the usability of a company's website affects an applicant's perception of a job (Cappelli, 2001), and that content features such as testimonials by current employees, pictures, policies and awards can affect perceptions of the organization's culture (Brady et al., 2009). Some companies use websites combined with 'smart phone' apps in recruitment.

According to the CIPD (2010c), 63 per cent of organizations regard their own website as their most effective method of attracting applications. The survey also found that 33 per cent make use of commercial job boards such as Monster (www.monster.co.uk) and StepStone (www.stepstone.com), although evidence from other surveys suggests that such sites can also attract unsuitable applicants (Parry and Tyson, 2008). Further research also found different attitudes towards commercial job boards in comparison to company websites, including the potential of reaching a wider pool of applicants and the convenience of the method (Parry and Wilson, 2009).

In many cases, especially at a time when there are more applicants than vacancies, online applications via websites can be a way of saving costs in recruitment and also allowing a faster response and turnaround. Although cost saving is clearly a major benefit, some companies see online recruitment more strategically. For example, when Whitbread faced the problem of recruiting managers for its 400-site Brewsters and Brewers Fayre restaurant business, it developed its own recruitment website. The site was searched over 100,000 times in the first 4 months, with 1300 applications. This enabled the company to build a database and maintain contact with potential candidates. Another benefit to the company was its ability to establish consistency in its brand to potential employees (Smethurst, 2004).

As online recruitment has developed, it has been accompanied by the use of tools for filtering applicants and tools for starting the selection process (Parry and Tyson, 2008), probably much valued by employers during a recession when the ratio of applications to positions available will be high. Pollitt (2008) reports the approach of the mobile phone company 3, who work with a commercial e-recruitment operator that provides five online 'gateways' for both external and internal recruitment. Applicants can view video clips of employees talking about working for 3, as well as upload their details and create e-mail alerts for jobs that become available. They can also monitor the progress of any application made and receive messages on their mobile phone.

HRM web links

Check the services provided by ActiveRecruiter at www.taleo.com/solutions/recruiting and Real Match at www.realmatch.com.

> **reflective question**
>
> Go to either the British Airways website at www.britishairwaysjobs.com/baweb1, or that of investment company Merrill Lynch at www.totalmerrill.com/publish/mkt/campaigns/careers/index.aspx. How do you think these websites filter out those who do and do not wish to work for British Airways or Merrill Lynch? Did you take the interactive challenges? Does online recruitment increase the power of employers in the graduate labour market?

In the late 2000s, social networking sites such as Facebook and LinkedIn, and social media such as Twitter, have grown in popularity, and all of these allow information about vacancies in organizations to be shared. While informal 'word of mouth' information about jobs has long been recognized for its accuracy and effectiveness in employee referrals (Iles and Salaman, 1995), employees can quickly, through Web 2.0 social networking, refer their friends or contacts towards vacancies – although how useful this will be to an organization will depend on the value of those people's social networks (Casella and Hanaki, 2008). It is, of course, also possible for organizations to explore the public pages of network sites to assess the extent and value of a person's links or to find other applicants within a network. Research in Belgium suggests there is some interest among recruiters in the use of social networking sites, especially LinkedIn, but also the possibility that such interest will lead to biased decisions on selection based on profile pictures and personality as indicated by the person's presence on a site (Caers and Castelyns, 2010).

Internships or placements

One method of attracting applicants is through internships or placements, which are often used by students for work-based research as part of their programmes (Hynie et al., 2011), but also provide an opportunity for students to gain experience and increase their marketability. If students then take up positions within the organization, the organization gains through the motivation of students to work and in terms of savings on training and induction. Research suggests that experience gained from internships increases employment prospects and starting salaries. Where internees perform well, employers place more value on such programmes (Gault et al., 2010). Because internships and placement offer employers an advanced opportunity to assess potential applicants, a selection process is increasingly used, involving some of the methods we will consider below.

> **HRM web links**
>
> Explore internship opportunities and the selection process at www.graduatesyorkshire.co.uk/internships.

> Visit www.palgrave.com/business/bratton5 to read an HRM in practice feature on the Co-op's internship scheme.

Job descriptions

A further manifestation of the image projected by an organization to which recruits will be attracted is a description of the actual work that potential employees will be required to do. The traditional way of providing such information is in the form of a *job description*, usually derived from a job analysis and a description of the tasks and responsibilities that make up the job. Against each job description, there is normally a specification of the standards of performance. A typical format for a job description is given in Figure 9.3.

In addition to a job description, there is, in the form of a *personnel or person specification*, some attempt to profile the 'ideal' person to fill the job. It is accepted that the ideal person for the job may not actually exist, and that the specification will be used only as a framework within which a number of candidates can be assessed. In the past, a format for a personnel specification has been the seven-point plan, based on the work of Rodger (1970) and shown in Figure 9.4. An alternative to the seven-point plan was Munro-Fraser's fivefold grading system (1971), as in Figure 9.5. In both forms of personnel specification, it was usual to indicate the importance of different requirements. Thus, certain requirements might be expressed as essential and others as desirable.

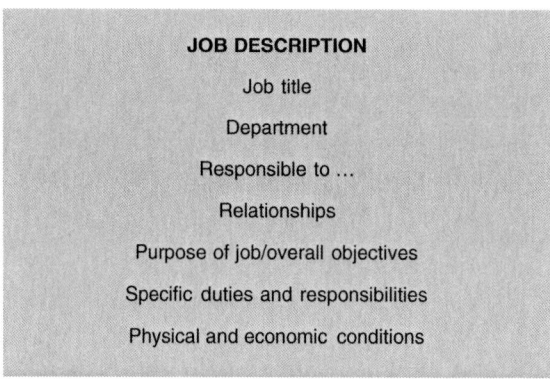

Figure 9.3 Job description format

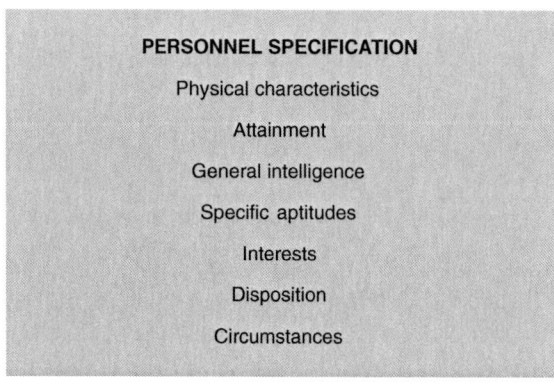

Figure 9.4 Rodger's seven-point plan

> **PERSONNEL SPECIFICATION**
>
> Impact on other people
>
> Qualification and experience
>
> Innate abilities
>
> Motivation
>
> Adjustment

Figure 9.5 Munro-Fraser's fivefold grading system

Both job descriptions and personnel specifications have been key elements in the traditional repertoire of HR managers. Over the years, various attempts have been made to develop and fine-tune techniques and practices. One such development has been the shift of emphasis in job descriptions away from specifying tasks and responsibilities towards the results to be achieved (Plachy, 1987). There has, however, been a growing awareness of the limitations and problems of such approaches. Watson (1994) noted that job analysis, used to produce job descriptions and person specifications, relied too much on the analyst's subjective judgement in identifying the key aspects of a job and deriving the qualities that related to successful performance. In addition, the use of frameworks such as the seven-point plan may provide a 'cloak for improper discrimination' (Watson, 1994, p. 189). Current legislation on discrimination needs to be carefully considered in job descriptions and person specifications. For example, criteria set for physical characteristics might discriminate against applicants with a disability who in fact have the ability to do the job.

HRM web links

In the UK, ACAS provides examples of job descriptions and personnel specifications at www.acas.org.uk/index.aspx?articleid=1393.

The move towards flexibility and changing work practices has seen the appearance of new forms of work description. It is argued that traditional job descriptions are too narrow and may restrict opportunities for development and growth within jobs (Pennell, 2010). Some organizations have replaced or complemented job descriptions with performance contracts. These contain details of what a job-holder agrees to accomplish over a period of time, summarising the purpose of a job, how that purpose will be met over the time specified and how the achievement of objectives will be assessed. This approach allows job requirements to be adjusted by agreement between the job-holder and his or her manager. It also allows a clear link to other HR processes. Performance contracts signal to new recruits the expectation that their jobs will change and that they cannot rely on a job description as the definitive account of their work. Adler (Adler, N. J., 2002) refers to this reorientation as performance-based recruitment and selection.

As we have already discussed, competencies are used to create a specification of the characteristics of those sought for particular positions (Industrial Relations Services, 2003a; Roberts, 1997). It has been argued (Feltham, 1992) that the use of competencies allows organizations to free themselves from traditional stereotypes in order to attract applicants from a variety of sources. Stereotypes of the ideal person may be contained within personnel specifications, and organizations may, despite warnings, be reinforcing the stereotype in their recruitment practices. Competencies appear to be more objective, have a variety of uses in attracting applicants and allow an organization to use more reliable and valid selection techniques.

The test of success of a recruitment process is whether it attracts a sufficient number of applicants of the desired quality within the budget set (Connerley et al., 2003). Traditionally, applications are made by a combination of letter, a completed application form and/or a CV. Increasingly, such forms can be submitted by email or completed online (Parry and Wilson, 2009). Recruiters might reasonably expect a number of applicants per position available, referred to as the recruitment ratio, thus allowing a choice to be made. Too many applicants may reduce the cost per applicant but add further costs in terms of the time taken to screen the applications. Too few applicants may be an indication of a tight labour market but may also be an indication that the values, ethos and image projected by the organization onto the market, including information on the work, as provided by job descriptions and specifications, are poor attractors. Recruiters need to monitor the effect of such factors on the recruitment process. If there are insufficient applicants from particular ethnic groups, too few men or women or disabled applicants, the recruitment process may indirectly discriminate and/or fail to meet legal requirements.

Selection

As we have seen, it is usual for an organization that wishes to recruit new employees to define criteria against which it can measure and assess applicants. Increasingly, such criteria are set in the form of competencies composed of behavioural characteristics and attitudes. Rather than trust to luck, organizations are using more sophisticated selection techniques. Organizations have become increasingly aware of making good selection decisions, since selection involves a number of costs:

- The cost of the selection process itself, including the use of various selection instruments
- The future costs of inducting and training new staff
- The cost of labour turnover if the selected staff are not retained.

The CIPD's research (2010c) on selection methods used in UK organizations showed that competency-based interviewing was the most common approach (78 per cent), followed by interviewing following the contents of the CV/application form (that is, biographical; 64 per cent), structured panel interviews (61 per cent) and telephone interviews (47 per cent). Other methods being used were references before interviews, group exercises and tests for specific skills, general abilities, literacy/numeracy, attitudes and personality; in addition, 42 per cent also used an assessment centre.

The configuration of selection techniques chosen will depend on a number of factors. As argued by Wilk and Cappelli (2003, p. 117), it is not simply a case of 'more is better'. Selection methods will depend on the characteristics of the work and the level of pay and training. It is also crucial to remember that decisions are being made by both employers and potential employees, even during a recession, and that the establishment of mutually agreed expectations during selection forms part of the psychological contract, which will strongly influence an employee's attitudes and feelings towards the organization (Herriot et al., 1997). According to Hausknecht et al. (2004), there are good reasons why organizations need to consider the reaction of applicants to selection methods:

- If selection is viewed as invasive, the attraction of the organization may be diminished.
- Candidates who have a negative experience can dissuade others.
- A negative selection experience can impact on job acceptance.
- Selection methods are covered by legislation and regulations relating to discrimination.
- Mistreatment during selection will put off future applications and may also stop applicants from buying the organization's products or using their services.

HRM in practice 9.2: Trapped in the 'marzipan layer'

The *Sex and Power 2011* report by the Equality and Human Rights Commission found that the rate of progress towards gender equality in senior management had remained extremely slow, and that the process had even reversed in some sectors. Despite women starting on their career ladder often better qualified than men, after some years women either drop out of management or remain trapped in 'the marzipan layer' below senior management, leaving the higher ranks to be dominated by men (as quoted in *Guardian*, August 17, 2011).

This phenomenon, often referred to as the 'glass ceiling', has been attributed to both continuing direct discrimination (which remains unlawful) and more subtle indirect discrimination such as an expectation to work long hours that clashes with family responsibilities (a clash still less likely to be experienced by men).

A good example of the way these pressures permeate a whole organizational culture is shown by Jacqueline Watts' examination of women civil engineers in the extremely male world of the construction industry (Watts, 2009). When newcomers who are different (in their gender or ethnicity) join an existing group, one response is what is called 'boundary heightening', in which the majority deliberately emphasize their group characteristics. Thus, when a woman enters predominantly male territory such as a building site, the amount of sexual innuendo and jokes or displayed pornography may actually increase. Similarly, in the setting of the boardroom, the pre-business conversation may be devoted to male sports interests, effectively excluding the sole woman present.

Watts' women engineers all remarked on the expectation that they would work long hours (the general feeling that 'hard working means long working') and on the predominantly male management style; this was seen by the women respondents as authoritarian and top-down compared with their own preferred style of more inclusive, participative management. When on site and faced with the boundary-heightening behaviour described

→

Source: ©istockphoto.com/Peter Close.

above, the women engineers felt compelled to defeminize their clothing and appearance (no make-up or heels) 'otherwise you'd never survive'. All, however, found the heightened visibility, sexual harassment and intimidation to be emotionally draining, and this had led one participant to leave the profession.

The chances of resisting these pressures were seen as slim to non-existent: to emphasize work–life balance in the face of the 'heroic narrative' of staying late would cast them as slackers and open them up to criticism. The women felt they had no option but to collude with the male style of management in choosing, for example, not to voice any concerns they might have over staff workloads in case they were seen as less committed.

Watts concludes that:

> Women managers experience challenges not faced by male counterparts because of the dominant masculinist ethos of corporate management culture that privileges men, ranks some men above others and places women on the periphery of the managerial class.

Stop! The continued exclusion of women from senior decision-making roles is clearly a huge waste of talent and expertise. How would you remedy this, given that the equality legislation has had relatively little effect on the cultural pressures indicated above?

Sources and further information:

See Watts (2009) for more information of her study of women in engineering.

Note: This feature was written by Chris Baldry at the University of Stirling.

> **reflective question**
>
> How would you react to a negative experience in a selection process?

An important factor is the perception of fair treatment, and this applies to both the methods used and the process as a whole, referred to as procedural justice or fairness (Gilliland, 1993). Bauer et al. (2001) have sought to measure the reactions of applications for jobs using a procedural justice scale relating to selection. Items in the scale include the job-relatedness of tests, the 'opportunity to perform', which is the chance to demonstrate knowledge, skills and abilities, the provision of feedback and treatment with warmth and respect. The scale could be used by organizations to evaluate the fairness of their selection procedures and the correction of problems. Positive reactions to selection can result in greater efforts to perform, which can in turn help organizations to identify the best candidates (Hausknecht et al., 2004).

Underlying the process of selection and the choice of techniques are two key principles:

- *Individual differences* – Attracting a wide choice of applicants will be of little use unless there is a way of measuring how people differ. People can vary in many ways, for example intelligence, attitudes, social skills, psychological and physical characteristics, experience and so on.
- *Prediction* – Recognition of the way in which people differ must be extended to a prediction of performance in the workplace.

Selection techniques will, to a varying degree, reflect these principles of measuring differences and predicting performance. Organizations may increasingly use a variety of techniques, and statistical theory is used to give credibility to those techniques which attempt to measure people's attitudes, attributes, abilities and overall personality. Some commentators would suggest that this credibility is 'pseudoscientific' and that many limitations remain with selection techniques. Iles and Salaman (1995), for example, claim that this 'psychometric' model appears to value:

- *Individualism* – in which individual characteristics are claimed to predict future performance
- *Managerialism* – in which top managers define the criteria for performance
- *Utility* – in which the costs and benefits, in monetary terms, of using different selection techniques are assessed.

> **reflective question**
>
> What do you think are the implications associated with individualist, managerialist and utilitarian values in the selection process?

We are once again reminded that power is an important consideration when making decisions about employing people. Selection instruments often seem to be neutral and objective, but the criteria built into such instruments that allow the selection and rejection of applicants make up a knowledge base that provides the organization and its agents with power.

Reliability and validity issues

Two statistical concepts – reliability and validity – are of particular importance in selection. *Reliability* refers to the extent to which a selection technique achieves consistency in what it is measuring over repeated use. If, for example, you were being interviewed by two managers for a job in two separate interviews, you would hope that the interview technique would provide data such that the interviewers agreed with each other about you as an individual. Alternatively, if a number of candidates were given the same selection test, you would want to have some confidence that the test would provide consistent results concerning the individual differences between candidates. The statistical analysis of selection techniques normally provides a reliability coefficient, and the higher the coefficient (that is, the closer it is to 1.0), the more dependable the technique.

Validity refers to the extent to which a selection technique actually measures what it sets out to measure. There are different forms of validity, but the most important in selection is criterion validity, which measures the results of a technique against set criteria; this may be the present success of existing employees (concurrent validity) or the future performance of new ones (predictive validity).

Validation is in practice a complex process, and studies involving a large number of candidates would be required in order to allow a correlation coefficient to be calculated – in testing with criteria, this is referred to as a *validity coefficient*. If the coefficient is less than 1.0, an imperfect relationship between the test and the criterion is indicated. Even if the coefficient indicates such a relationship, a selection technique may, however, still be worth using: that is, you would be better to use the instrument than not use it. In addition, different selection techniques can be assessed in relation to each other according to their validity coefficient results. One difficulty is that it usually takes a long time to conduct validity studies, and by the time such studies were completed, it would be highly likely that the work from which some of the criteria were derived would have changed. Validity is also related to the particular environment in which performance is carried out. Such problems have not, however, stopped many organizations using tests and other selection techniques that have been validated by the test designers in a range of organizations or situations. (Go to www.socialresearchmethods.net/kb/measure.php for more details on validity and reliability.)

CVs and biodata

For many positions, applicants will be asked to provide a CV (a curriculum vitae, called a résumé in the USA and Canada), which enables them to set out their experience, skills and achievements. Importantly, it also provides an early chance for the organization to screen the applicants before moving to the next stage of selection. There has been interest in how selectors make decisions on the basis of information contained in CVs, and whether such decisions are informed by the criteria set out in the job descriptions and specifications, or are subject to personal bias.

For example, would an applicant who attended a particular university be more likely to be selected on the basis of their CV? Proença and de Oliveira (2009) examined the assessment of CVs in selection and the reasoning used by selectors. They found some interesting contradictions between the use of objective knowledge and criteria, as set out in the formal documentation, and more implicit knowledge and emotion.

In addition to CVs, there is growing interest in information about a person's past experiences and behaviours in particular situations. This can be gathered by questionnaires including several multiple-choice questions and/or scenarios seeking data that can be verified as factual. Such information is referred to as *biodata*. Items can then be scored to predict against aspects of future behaviour such as job performance and absenteeism, results that have been shown to have relatively high validity (see Becton et al., 2009).

Selection interviewing

Of all the techniques used in selection, the interview is the oldest and most widely used, along with application forms and letters of reference, referred to by Cook (1994, p. 15) as 'the classic trio'. In recent years, with the advent of secure technology, interviews can also take place by video. Various attempts have been made to classify selection interviews, and it may be useful to point out some of the categories that have been developed:

- *Information elicited* – interviews have a specific focus and require information at different levels:
  - An interview may focus on facts. The style of the interview will be direct, based on a question and answer session.
  - An interview may focus on subjective information once the factual information has been obtained.
  - There may also be a focus on underlying attitudes, requiring intensive probing techniques and usually involving qualified psychologists.
- *Structure* – interviews may vary from the completely structured, based on planned questions and responses, to the unstructured, allowing complete spontaneity for the applicant and little control for the interviewer. A compromise between the two extremes is most likely, the interviewer maintaining control by the use of guided questions but allowing free expression on relevant topics.
- *Order and involvement* – the need to obtain different kinds of information may mean the involvement of more than one interviewer. Applicants may be interviewed serially or by a panel.

The selection interview has been the subject of much review and research over the past 60 years. During much of that time, overall results on the validity and reliability of interviews have been disappointing. In 1949, Wagner carried out the first comprehensive review of research associated with the employment interview. Wagner noted that, in the 174 sets of ratings that were reported, the reliability ranged from a correlation coefficient (r) of 0.23 to one of 0.97, with a median value of $r = 0.57$. Validity, from the 222 results obtained, ranged from $r = 0.09$ to $r = 0.94$, with a median of $r = 0.27$ (Wagner, 1949). Wagner considered such results to be unsatisfactory. This pattern of low-validity results continued in other research for the next four decades. In their review, for example, Ulrich and Trumbo (1965) agreed that the interview seemed to be deficient in terms of reliability and validity, and they were forced to conclude that judgements about overall suitability for employment should be made by other techniques.

There have been two lines of research to examine the reasons behind such poor results for the selection interview. The first focuses on how interviewers process information that leads to a decision on acceptance or rejection. The second focuses on the skills of effective interviewing. Table 9.2 outlines a summary of this research.

By 1982, Arvey and Campion (1982) were able to report less pessimism about reliability and validity when interviews were conducted by boards (panels) and based on job analysis and job information. In particular, reference was made to the success of *situational interviews* (Latham et al., 1980). In these, interview questions are derived from systematic job analysis based on a critical incident technique (see Flanagan, 1954). Questions focus on descriptions of what an applicant would do in a series of situations. Responses are judged against benchmark answers that identify poor, average or excellent employees.

In addition to situational interviews, Harris (1989) reported on other developments in interview format that relied on job analysis. These included *behaviour description interviews*, which assess past behaviour in various situations, and

Table 9.2 Reasons for poor results from selection interviewing

Processing of information	
Pre-interview	Use of application forms to reject the applicant on grounds of sex, academic standing or physical attractiveness
First impressions	Decisions made quickly lead to a search during the rest of the interview for information to support those decisions. Negative information will be heavily weighted if the decision is rejection, but a positive early decision may lead to warm interviewer behaviour
Stereotypes	Interviewers may hold stereotyped images of a 'good' worker against which applicants are judged. Such images may be personal to each interviewer and are potentially based on prejudice
Contrast	Interviewers are influenced by the order in which applicants are interviewed. An average applicant who follows below-average applicants may be rated as above average. Interviewers may compare applicants against each other rather than against objective criteria
Attraction	Interviewers may be biased towards applicants they 'like'. This attraction may develop where interviewers hold opinions and attitudes similar to those of the applicant
Skills of interviewing	
Structure	Variations in interview structure affect reliability, low scores being gained for unstructured interviews
Questions	Interviewers may use multiple, leading, embarrassing and provocative questions
Listening	Interviewers may talk more than listen, especially if they view the applicant favourably. Interviewers may not be 'trained' to listen effectively
Retention and interpretation	Interviewers may have a poor recall of information unless guides are used and notes made. Interviewers may have difficulty in interpreting the information

HRM AND GLOBALIZATION
Unpacking the meaning of credentials

In a fascinating new study of higher education in the USA, sociologist Ann Mullen writes 'we need to look not just at *who* goes to college, but at who goes *where* to college' (Mullen, 2010, p. 5). The main thrust of her argument is that even though more and more students are attending college and earning credentials, post-secondary education in the USA remains highly stratified. Even when students graduate with the same credential (the baccalaureate or bachelor's degree), its value and prestige will depend on the institution that awarded it.

Mullen's analysis alerts us to a challenge in employee recruitment. What do credentials stand for? At first glance, they appear to solve the problem of globalizing markets for educated labour. Employers seem justified in believing that knowledge and skill would be similar between similar credentials earned in different countries. But if the meaning of the same credential varies within a developed country such as the USA, as Mullen suggests, one must obviously proceed cautiously when attempting to evaluate the meaning of credentials earned in different countries.

As a starting point, it is helpful briefly to consider different theories of credentialism. Steven Brint provides an overview starting with a definition: 'By credentialism, I mean the monopolization of access to rewarding jobs and economic opportunities by the holders of educational degrees and certificates' (Brint, 2006, p. 166). He then proceeds to review various criticisms of credentialism. Many of these criticisms focus on the question of whether credentials are 'information-rich': does the possession of a credential tell us whether a person has the knowledge and skill that will enable them to perform the tasks and duties of a particular job? If the answer is 'yes', they are indeed information-rich.

But perhaps credentials are not information-rich in the way suggested above. Perhaps they just tell us that a person is trainable (or educable): the person has qualities of attentiveness and perseverance that will enable them to learn on the job. Or perhaps credentials are merely signals of a person's social background: an employer may believe that a particular university produces upper-class applicants who are a better 'fit' for the organization. Here, credentials are not information-rich, at least not in the sense that they tell employers specific things about job-related knowledge and skill.

The question of whether credentials are information-rich becomes even more challenging when we are referring to situations in which HR professionals from one country are responsible for hiring credentialled workers from another country. This situation, which is becoming more common all the time, forces us to think critically about what credentials mean and what they tell us about the person who has earned them. To answer this question satisfactorily, we must know something about the education system in the country where the credential was earned, and this knowledge is often not readily available.

Stop! The credentials demanded for access to particular occupations sometimes seem unjustified. Provide one example of a situation where demands for higher entry-level credentials are justified, and one example of where they are not. If such increased demands are not justified, why are they made?

You have been accused of discrimination for your criticisms of the credentials earned in a developing country. As an HR professional, how would you respond? What institutions have been created to evaluate the meaning and value of credentials?

Sources and further information:

See Brint (2006) and Mullen (2010) for more information on credentials.

Note: This feature was written by David MacLennan at Thompson Rivers University.

Source: ©istockphoto.com/ericsphotography.

comprehensive structured interviews, which contain different types of question, for example situational, job knowledge, job simulation and work requirements. Such developments have resulted in an enhanced effectiveness of the selection interview and improved scores for reliability and validity. To achieve the benefits of such improvements, organizations need to pay more attention to providing formal training on structured selection interviewing. This is, however, not always easy to achieve since untrained interviewers may believe they are doing a good job in predicting future performance (Chapman and Zweig, 2005).

The use of questions about past behaviour combined with competencies in selection interviews has enhanced effectiveness even further. Pulakos and Schmitt (1995) compared the validity results during the selection process for experience-based (or behavioural) questions and situational questions. The former are past-oriented questions and are based on the view that the best predictor of future performance is past performance in similar situations. Applicants are asked job-relevant questions about what they did in other situations. This contrasts with situational questions, in which applicants are asked what they would do in response to particular events in particular situations. Responses to both types of question can be scored on behaviour scales, but experience-based questions have shown better results with respect to predictions of job performance, that is, predictive validity.

These results can then be used by organizations with competency frameworks. An ICT company has, for example, a competency relating to 'managing meetings'. Interviewers could base their questions around an applicant's past behaviour in managing meetings by asking the applicant to explain what she or he did in managing a specific meeting. Follow-up questions can be used to reveal further features of the applicant's performance, which can then be assessed against the competency indicators. Research by Campion et al. (1997, p. 655) found that these were 'better questions' that enhanced the effectiveness of the interview.

Barclay (1999) found a rapid increase in the use of structured techniques as part of a more comprehensive approach to selection. In particular, it was found that behavioural interviewing was being used systematically, especially in combination with a competency framework. Further research by Barclay (2001) found that behavioural interviewing was referred to in a variety of ways in organizations, for example competency-based interviewing, criterion-based interviewing, skills-based interviewing, life questioning and behavioural event interviewing. It was claimed that, however it was referred to, behavioural interviewing had improved the selection process and decisions made, a finding supported by Huffcutt et al. (2001) in their study of the use of interviews for positions of high complexity.

However, these approaches to interviewing have not been without criticism. First, since behavioural or competency-based questions are based on past behaviour, there is an assumption that behaviour is consistent over time, allowing prediction into the future. This assumption can be challenged on the basis that people do learn from their mistakes and can learn new ways of behaving. Furthermore, it might be suggested that people also tend to behave according to contingent factors such as time, place and especially the presence of others. A second assumption is that the questions allow a fair comparison between different candidates. They might, however, disadvantage those candidates with more limited experience or a poor recall of their experience, even though they might possess attributes or ideas that are not revealed in an interview (Martin and Pope, 2008). Even though a structured approach provides a degree of control over the interview, it still might possible for applicants to prepare their answers in advance or distort their responses to create a desirable impression (Levashina and Campion, 2006).

It is interesting at this point to note that much of the progress in interviews as a selection technique has occurred where organizations have sought to identify behaviour and attitudes that match their models of employees to be selected. This has required an investment in more sophisticated techniques of analysis. It is agreed that traditional job analysis techniques allow the production of job models in terms of tasks and responsibilities; however, organizations faced with change and seeking to employ workers whose potential can be utilized and developed will increasingly turn to techniques of analysis producing inventories of the characteristics and behaviours, such as competencies, that are associated with effective performance in the present and the future.

One consequence of more structured approaches to interviewing, including the training of interviewers, is the impact on applicants' reactions. A review by Posthuma et al. (2002) reported growing research interest in such reactions, generally showing that applicants prefer interviews compared with other selection instruments – the interview had greater *face validity* – which concerns whether applicants judge selection techniques to be related to the job (Smither et al., 1993).

One interesting dilemma, however, emerges for organizations – should the interview focus on establishing a good relationship with an applicant to elicit a positive reaction from the candidate about the selection process, or should the interview be concerned with using good structure and sophisticated questions that have higher predictive validity? In their research, Chapman and Zweig (2005, p. 697) found that this tension exists, with some interviewers preferring less structure in favour of building a rapport that 'potentially contaminates an otherwise standardized procedure'. Organizations need to recognize that the interview is a source of anxiety for applicants, inevitably affecting their performance. The danger is that an anxiety-affected interview performance may mask an applicant's ability to perform the job (McCarthy and Goffin, 2004). In addition, applicants' self-evaluation can impact on their perception of fairness and reactions to interviews in selection. Applicants who evaluate themselves positively are more likely to view the interview as fair (Nikolaou and Judge, 2007).

> **HRM web links**
>
> Selection interviews can be quite daunting for candidates. For particular guidance on competency-based interviews, try www.allaboutmedicalsales.com/competency.html.

Psychometric testing

Selection based on competencies and attitudes has been one result of the increased attention given to identifying psychological factors through testing, and to how such factors predict job performance. Testing, it would seem, offers organizations a cost-effective process in their search for the right people to match the company's personality. For example, during the expansion of the coffee house chain Costa, 1800 new 'team' members were sought. The company worked with a testing house to develop a team-member personality questionnaire based on the company's values that measured particular qualities, such as a person's achievement orientation (Dawson, 2005).

We can make the following distinctions between different kinds of test:

- *Ability tests* – these focus on mental abilities such as verbal reasoning and numerical power, but also include physical skills testing such as keyboard speeds. In such tests, there may be right/wrong answers or measurements that allow applicants for a position to be placed in ranked order.
- *Inventories* – these are usually self-report questionnaires about personality, indicating traits, intelligence, values, interests, attitudes and preferences. There are no right/wrong answers but instead a range of choices between possible answers.

Taken together, tests of personality and ability are referred to as *psychometric tests* and have a good record of reliability and validity. Most people have some fears related to any test, and this has caused confusion over the meaning, use and value of psychometric tests. The 1990s saw a rapid growth in the number of organizations using such tests, which was the result of more people, especially HR practitioners, being trained to administer them (McHenry, 1997). The CIPD survey (2010c) indicated that 44 per cent of organizations used personality/attitude/psychometric questionnaires, 43 per cent used literacy and/or numeracy tests, and 27 per cent used general ability tests.

Both forms of test provide a set of norms, developed from the scores of a representative group of people (the 'norm' group) of a larger population, for example UK adult men or women in a sales role. Figures are then expressed in percentiles, which allows for standardization. Thus, a raw score of 120 on a personality test or a section of a test might be placed in the 60th percentile, indicating that the applicant's result is higher than that of 60 per cent of the norm group but less than the score obtained by 40 per cent of the group. If the test had good predictive validity, this would be a valuable indicator allowing a comparison to be made between different applicants. Inventories would also include some allowance for 'distortions' and 'fake' responses (Dalen et al., 2001) as personality tests are generally thought to be less reliable than ability tests. An important issue here is the extent to which a test might discriminate against particular groups of people, which can lead to legal challenges (Jackson, 1996).

> **reflective question**
>
> A personality questionnaire contains the item 'I think I would make a good leader.' This was answered 'true' by twice as many men as women, implying that men are twice as likely to become good leaders. What do you think of such an item and its implication?

Ability tests may be of a general kind, for example those relating to general mental ability or abilities such as verbal fluency and numerical ability. In addition, there are also tests for specific abilities, often referred to as aptitude tests, for example for manual dexterity and spatial ability. Furthermore, there are tests for specific jobs, such as computer aptitude and sales aptitude (Toplis et al., 2005).

For many years, there has been a great deal of interest in the extent to which general mental ability and cognitive abilities can be shown to be valid in terms of predicting performance and can be generalized across a range of occupations (see Schmidt, 2002). For example, Bertua et al. (2005) sought to examine whether general mental ability and cognitive ability tests were valid predictors of job performance and training success in UK organizations. They did this by completing a meta-analysis of 56 papers and books covering 283 samples of testing. The analysis showed that the tests were valid predictors of performance and training success across a range of occupations, including senior managers. This was also the case for changes in the composition of job roles. The authors claimed that the results provided 'unequivocal evidence for the continued and expanded use of general mental ability tests for employee selection in UK organizations' (Bertua et al., 2005, p. 403).

> **HRM web links**
>
> The Watson–Glaser test measures high-level verbal reasoning abilities and is often used in selecting managers and professionals. Go to www.talentlens.co.uk/select/watson-glaser-critical-thinking-appraisal.aspx#description for more details.

On the personality front, there has over the past 25 years been growing interest in what has been referred to as the five-factor model as an explanation of the factors that determine a person's personality (Wiggins, 1996). The five-factor model – sometimes called the 'big five' model of personality – proposes that differences between people can be measured in terms of degrees of:

- *Emotional stability (neuroticism)* – adjustment versus anxiety, level of emotional stability, dependence versus independence
- *Extroversion* – sociable versus misanthropic, outgoing versus introverted, confident versus timid
- *Openness to experience* – reflection of an enquiring intellect, flexibility versus conformity, rebelliousness versus subduedness
- *Agreeableness* – friendliness versus indifference to others, a docile versus a hostile nature, compliance versus hostile non-compliance
- *Conscientiousness* – the most ambiguous factor, seen as educational achievement, or as will or volition.

Salgado (1997) sought to explore the predictive validity of the five-factor model in relation to job performance through a meta-analysis of 36 studies that related validity measures to personality factors. It was found that conscientiousness and emotional stability showed most validity for job performance, and that openness to experience was valid for training proficiency.

There are, however, doubts about an over-reliance on personality tests with respect to their use in predicting future performance, especially in relation to complex tasks such as management. Within the five-factor model, for example, conscientiousness has been highlighted as a predictor of overall job performance. However, a study by Robertson et al. (2000) attempted to test the link between conscientiousness and the performance of 453 managers in five different companies. The results showed no overall statistical relationship, although there was a link with particular performance factors such as being organized and being quality-driven. It was also found that there might be an inverse relationship between conscientiousness and promotability. This result supports the view that suitability for complex work cannot be assessed on the basis of a narrow measurement of a psychological profile.

This situation also applies to the assessment of intelligence. Ceci and Williams (2000) suggest that the measurement of intelligence, although used in various ways by HR departments, does have drawbacks if such measurement is based on the assumption of intelligence as a fixed property of individuals. They argue that intelligent behaviour such as complex thinking is strongly connected to the setting, composed of the task, the location and the other people involved.

Limitations on the value of intelligence, as measured by intelligence quotient tests, as a predictor have led to a growing interest in the assessment of another kind of intelligence based on feelings, sensing others' feelings and the ability to perform at one's best in relationship with others. This is referred to as *emotional intelligence* (Dulewicz and Higgs, 2000), and there is mounting evidence that employers are attempting to utilize this view of intelligence in their competency frameworks (Miller et al., 2001). Emotional intelligence has been popularized by the work of Daniel Goleman (2006), who divides emotional intelligence into five emotional competencies:

- The ability to identify and name one's emotional states and to understand the link between emotions, thought and action
- The capacity to manage one's emotional states – to control emotions or to shift undesirable emotional states to more adequate ones
- The ability to enter into emotional states (at will) associated with a drive to achieve and be successful
- The capacity to read, be sensitive to and influence other people's emotions
- The ability to enter and sustain satisfactory interpersonal relationships.

Partly as consequence of the interest in emotional intelligence, efforts have been made to develop a test with valid and reliable psychometric properties. For example, Akerjordet and Severinsson (2009) describe the design of an Emotional Intelligence Scale and an Emotional Reactions and Thoughts Scale for use in maternity care. Interestingly, they suggested that self-reporting might pose difficulties.

HRM web links

Find out more about emotional intelligence tests at www.haygroup.com/ww/services/index.aspx?id=1566. You can try a test online at www.ivillage.co.uk/test-your-emotional-intelligence-eq/74101.

Self-reporting in the completion of tests is a key issue considered by Morgeson et al. (2007a), who provide a fascinating review of personality testing based on the author's considerable experience and expertise in the field. They conclude that, in view of the self-reporting process that most tests employ, faking should not only be expected, but could also actually be seen as an ability that could be useful in certain situations. They highlight the generally low validity figures for such tests, suggesting that measures which are more job-related carry greater face validity because the results can be explained more easily. They also suggest a need for an alternative to self-report measures.

An interesting finding about tests is that academics' debates on validity are not especially significant for practitioners, who tend to choose tests because they are well-known (Furnham, 2008). This means that the most popular tests are the:

- Myers–Briggs Type Indicator (www.myersbriggs.org/my-mbti-personality-type/mbti-basics)

- 16PF Questionnaire (www.ipat.com/about/16pf/Pages/default.aspx)
- Belbin Team Role (www.belbin.com/rte.asp?id=8)
- Occupational Personality Questionnaire (www.shl.com/assets/resources/OPQ-UK.pdf).

Online testing

Online testing is also being used for selection and other HR purposes, this being referred to as e-assessment. One feature of testing is to provide a filter for organizations in order to reduce the number of unsuitable candidates (Czerny, 2004), although such a process may also screen out good applicants. A CIPD (2010c) survey found that 32 per cent of organizations were using preapplication elimination/progression questions, and most of this would have occurred online. The banking organization Lloyds TSB, for example, has an online application form based on its competency framework; this acts as the first stage in filtering applicants. For the second stage, there is a 20-minute numerical reasoning test, also completed online (Pollitt, 2005). The results of this test are then scored electronically, and this feeds into the bank's recruitment management system.

It is claimed that online testing provides organizations with the ability to test at any time and any place in the world, with the added benefit of being able to process the applicants quickly (Lievens and Harris, 2003). Furthermore, as tests are taken, the results can be accumulated and used to improve the validity of the tests. There might even be a correlation between performance in online tests and successful learning at work. One difficulty, however, is that there is a loss of control over the administration of a test; thus, you can take a test at any time and in any place in the world – but also with anyone else to help. Toplis et al. (2005, p. 52) pose the question, 'How do you know who is responding to the test at the end of the line?' There is, however, interest in comparing Internet testing with traditional paper and

Online testing, or e-assessment, is a popular form of candidate selection, especially in the early stages of recruitment, when it can be used to filter out applicants
Source: ©istockphoto.com/webphotographeer.

pencil testing. One issue, for example, is whether a person has an understanding of computers, which can affect the perceptions of a test (Weichman and Ryan, 2003).

Potosky and Bobko (2004) compared the responses of 65 students to Internet and paper and pencil versions of untimed and timed tests. They also assessed the students' understanding of computers in advance of the process and their reactions at the end. One interesting finding was the issue of timing; that is, it was reported that time on the Internet (virtual time) was different from actual time. This affected the time to find and read the instructions or the time to download a test online. The appearance of a test is also affected online, with fewer items being seen compared with a full paper test. This may also affect the order in which items are responded to since it is easier to move around a paper test compared with its online counterpart. The results showed interesting differences in test performance between the Internet and paper and pencil versions on the timed test. For the untimed test, there was little difference.

Another issue is the perception of efficiency and user-friendliness of the website in taking tests online. For example, sites that are difficult to navigate will affect applicants' overall satisfaction , especially in the earlier stages of selection (Sylva and Mol, 2009).

reflective question

How do you feel about taking a test online?

Whatever developments occur in the use of e-assessment in recruitments, all tests need to conform to the requirements of discrimination laws. In the UK, tests should be endorsed by the British Psychological Society, which will check for any sexual and ethnic bias within the test. In addition to this endorsement, the impact of tests needs to be followed up and monitored to ensure that a test does not result in discrimination in practice against one sex or particular ethnic groups.

HRM web links

You can find many tests to take yourself – without applying for a job. Go to www.myskillsprofile.com/index.php?partnerid=2221. From there, for example, you can take an online emotional intelligence test at www.myskillsprofile.com/instructions/eiq16.

Assessment centres

In their examination of organizational selection practices, Wilk and Cappelli (2003) found that as the complexity and demands of work increased, there was a need for a variety of selection methods. The CIPD (2010c) found that 42 per cent of organizations used assessment centres during selections. Given the weakness of single measures, organizations can combine techniques and apply them together at an event referred to as an assessment centre. Such events may last for 1–3 days, during which a group of applicants for a post will undergo a variety of selection techniques. For example, in the case of Lloyds TSB referred to above (Pollitt, 2005), the last stage of the selection process is attendance at an assessment centre, lasting 24 hours (from 5 pm until 5 pm the following day). Candidates attend in groups of 12 or 24 and are observed by assessors as they complete an interview, a case study presentation, group exercises and a role play. They also complete a numerical reasoning test to verify the online test.

We can make a distinction here between development centres, which yield information to help identify development needs, and assessment centres, which are designed to yield information to help make decisions concerning suitability for a job. Assessment centres can also be used to select participants for training programmes, especially for leadership and management development, and to promote internal applicants to more senior positions (Thornton and Gibbons, 2009).

It is argued that it is the combination of techniques, providing a fuller picture of an applicant's strengths and weaknesses, that makes assessment centres so valuable. Woodruffe (2000) outlines four generalizations about assessment centres:

- Participants are observed by assessors who are trained in the use of measurement dimensions such as competencies.
- Assessment is by a combination of methods and includes simulations of the key elements of work.
- Information is brought together from all the methods, usually under competency headings.
- Participants can be assessed in groups.

Although there may be no such thing as a 'typical' assessment centre (Spychalski et al., 1997), the general methods used are group discussions, role plays and simulations, interviews and tests. The following activities were, for example, used in the assessment centre to select customer service assistants for European Passengers Services Ltd (Mannion and Whittaker, 1996, p. 14):

- Structured interview
- Perception exercise
- Communication exercise
- Personality inventory
- Customer service questionnaire
- Tests for clear thinking and numerical estimation.

The objectives for using these methods were to generate information about:

- The ability to work under pressure
- Characteristic behaviour when interacting with others
- Preferred work styles
- The ability to think quickly
- The ability to make quick and accurate numerical estimates
- Experience and aptitude for a customer service role.

The European Passengers Services assessment centre process was judged to be a success, underpinned by the objectives and standardized decision-making of the assessors. Candidates attending an assessment centre will be observed by assessors who should be trained to judge candidates' performance against criteria contained within the dimensions of the competency framework used.

There has been interest in assessment centres that measure dimensions of personality and/or behaviour, referred to as dimension-based assessment centres (Lance, 2008), based on the judgement of assessors while candidates complete the exercises. A common problem is that assessor ratings may be affected because there are too many people to assess at the same time during an exercise (Melchers et al., 2010), and this problem may become more difficult to solve when organizations attempt to save costs by reducing the number of assessors. One possibility is to focus more on interviews with higher validity possibilities that measure dimensions similar to those of an assessment centre, thus screening out applicants who score less well at the interview and reducing the number to measure at the assessment centre (Dayan et al., 2008). Another possibility is to use measurement dimensions that are more focused and specific to particular tasks, in contrast to measurements that are used across all exercises. This approach is a feature of task-based ACs, where attention is given to specific dimensions of behaviour for each task, which are observable in the outcomes of participating in that task (Jackson et al., 2010).

reflective question

Have any of your colleagues applying for graduate training programmes been put through an assessment centre? What was their reaction to this process?

If your colleagues were to relay negative reactions to you about their experience of selection techniques with one organization, this might affect your image of it. Again, the question of face validity is important – whether the applicants feel that the selection techniques are connected to the job. For example, in response to the problem that an assessment centre lacked realism and variety, the accountancy firm Ernst and Young ran its centre in real offices, having candidates answer emails and telephone calls. This apparently made the organization's expectations clearer (Trapp, 2005). Kolk et al. (2003) found no difference to the process in terms of validity when they made an assessment centre more transparent to candidates by revealing, prior to their attendance, the dimensions of assessment that would be observed and used to make judgements.

Pre-employment activities

During recruitment and selection, even in times of recession, both parties in the relationship are making decisions. It is therefore important for an organization to recognize that high-quality applicants, attracted by the organization's image, could be lost at an early stage unless they are supplied with realistic organization and work information. Applicants have expectations about how the organization will treat them, and recruitment and selection represent an opportunity to clarify these.

Realistic job previews (RJPs) provide a means of achieving this by offering 'accurate, favourable, and unfavourable job-related information to job candidates'

(Templer et al., 2006, p. 158). RJPs can take the form of case studies of employees and their work, the chance to 'shadow' someone at work, job sampling and videos, the aim being to enable applicants' expectations to become more realistic. One possibility therefore is that expectations about work and an organization can be lowered, allowing applicants to deselect themselves; however, for those who continue into employment, organizational commitment, job satisfaction, performance and job survival are likely to increase (Phillips, 1998; Premack and Wanous, 1985).

A key feature of RJPs is their promotion of accurate pre-employment expectations that serve to 'vaccinate' employees for when they are faced with job demands once employed. RJPs also serve to communicate an organization's honesty about such demands (Hom et al., 1999). For example, if the work is located overseas, there is a need for information about living in another country, referred to as a realistic living conditions preview (Templer et al., 2006). Research in Canada by Richardson et al. (2008) highlighted the importance of realistic living conditions previews in revealing non-work factors such as the well-being of the partners and children of those employees who live abroad.

What is clear is that recruitment and selection provide an arena for engagement between organizations and potential employees in which both parties develop an 'image' of each other. If managers fail to understand the mutuality of this process, they endanger the attractiveness of the organization and thereby threaten the organization's ability to recruit good applicants (Hausknecht et al., 2004). In combination with RJPs, organizations such as Siemens and DaimlerChrysler provide applicants with a link to current employees who act as mentors (Spitzmüller et al., 2008), and this can play a role in increasing attraction.

CASE STUDY

Watson and Hamilton Lawyers

Setting

In England and Wales, the provision of legal services has been slowly moving in the direction of increased competition between law firms, prompted by changes in the regulatory framework that seeks to remove restrictive barriers so that clients can benefit. Many law firms, especially those which operate in commercial law, have already sought to enhance their position in the market by embracing marketing expertise and placing more focus on the achievement of outcomes that satisfy client requirements.

Watson and Hamilton Lawyers (WHL) is a medium-sized firm of UK commercial lawyers, based in the Midlands. Within the firm, there are around 50 directors who have an equity stake in the firm, with a further 60 staff who are professionally qualified as lawyers, 50 staff who are qualified as legal executives and around 40 support staff including HR and marketing. WHL's strategy is to pursue a path of expansion and growth based on offering high-quality legal services to clients.

A key finding has been the recognition that around 80 per cent of fee income is generated from 20 per cent of clients, who are seen as crucial to the delivery of the firm's strategy in two ways: first, such clients need to be retained and, second, they also need to be the focus of the development of business relationships. Therefore, in a difficult market, the senior directors of the firm saw the retention of key clients and the development of opportunities for future business with clients as paramount. Following research, a number of crucial behaviours and actions that needed to be enacted were identified (see the table). Once such behaviours had been identified, it was recognized that they could be used in a variety of ways at WHL, such as:

- In selecting new staff
- In assessing the potential of lawyers for future development, including self-assessment and development
- For senior staff coaching and developing more junior staff
- In setting targets and goals for development
- In reviewing progress against targets
- As a common language for the firm to talk about performance.

Retaining clients	*Developing opportunities for future business*
1.1 Establishing contact	2.1 Working in partnership
1.2 Attending to needs and requirements	2.2 Delivering a quality service
1.3 Making the relationship work	2.3 Nurturing
1.4 Building value	2.4 Seeing the opportunities
1.5 Adding value	2.5 Exploiting those opportunities

It is vital for WHL that its employees develop and maintain good business relationships with their clients
Source: ©istockphoto.com/Alexander Raths.

The problem

Soon after the development of these behaviours, it became obvious that recruitment and selection procedures would need to change. The firm had a poor history relating to these areas, particularly in relation to professional staff, who were essential for fee-earning. Applicants were most commonly attracted through informal contacts, and decisions for employment were made on 'feel'. While the strategy and senior directors provided the parameters for decisions on recruitment and selection, managers were then 'given free rein', and most recent staff had been recruited on the basis of 'word of mouth' information obtained informally using 'field knowledge'.

Job descriptions (and personnel specifications) were not always produced, and evidence suggested that there was little involvement on the part of HR. There was no information on selection methods, questions used, criteria for assessing responses or judgements made on suitability. There was a 'perception of secrecy', with a strong possibility that decisions were biased towards the status quo and towards reinforcing the culture within a department.

There was apparent confusion over responsibility for determining vacancies for fee-earning staff and over how potential applicants were identified, especially with respect to the use of 'field knowledge'. Given the importance of behaviours relating to retaining clients and developing opportunities for future business, those involved in selection seemed to have little understanding of such requirements for fee-earners, nor were they using selection methods to make such assessments.

Assignment

Working in a group or on your own, prepare a report that argues for changes to the recruitment and selection policy incorporating the crucial behaviours of retaining clients and developing opportunities for future business. Explain how the 'perception of secrecy' can be tackled through a more effective assessment process based on these behaviours.

Note: This feature was written by Jeff Gold.

Visit the companion website at www.palgrave.com/business/bratton5 for guidelines on writing reports.

Summary

- This chapter has examined the nature of recruitment and selection in organizations.
- The attraction and subsequent retention of employees is crucial to an employment relationship, which is based on a mutual and reciprocal understanding of expectations. Employers have, however, significant power in recruitment and selection. The overall approach taken will reflect an organization's strategy and its philosophy towards people management.

- Recruitment and selection practices are bound by the law of the land, especially with respect to discrimination in terms of sex, race, disability, age and sexual orientation. In the UK, the Equality Act 2010 provides a simplification of discrimination legislation. Unless exempted by the provisions of occupational requirement, discrimination is against the law directly, indirectly or by harassment or victimization. The antidiscrimination legislation set forward over the past 35 years provides the foundation for a growing interest in diversity at work.

- It is essential that organizations see that, whatever the state of the labour market and their power within it, contact with potential recruits is made through the projection of an 'image' that will impact on and reinforce the expectations of potential recruits.

- Competency frameworks have been developed to link HR practices to the key requirements of an organization's strategy. Competencies can be used to form a model or 'image' of the kinds of employee that an organization is seeking to attract and recruit. The response to the image provides the basis for a compatible P–O fit. Images or the 'brand' will feature in recruitment literature and, increasingly, on the Internet via e-recruitment.

- There has been a growth in online recruitment as a form of e-recruitment, with recent surveys showing that 63 per cent of organizations regard their own website as the most effective method of attracting applications. Features on websites such as testimonials by current employees, pictures, policies and awards can affect perceptions of an organization's culture. Social networking sites now allow a sharing of information about vacancies and applicants.

- Key documents in recruitment and selection are job descriptions and personnel specifications, although there is a growing awareness of the limitations of traditional approaches to their construction. Some organizations have switched to performance contracts, which can be adjusted over time. In addition, personnel specifications may be stated as competencies, which appear more objective.

- Selection techniques seek to measure differences between applicants and provide a prediction of future performance at work. Techniques are chosen on the basis of their consistency in measurement over time – reliability – and the extent to which they measure what they are supposed to measure – validity. Applicants' experience of selection methods, especially perceptions of fair treatment, strongly influences feelings their towards the organization.

- There are a range of selection techniques, the most common of which is the interview, and this has been the subject of much research. Recent years have indicated that a structured approach and the use of behavioural interviewing based on competencies increase the effectiveness of interviews in selection. The use of competencies in selection is a reflection of the current interest in assessing personality and abilities by the use of psychometric tests. Techniques of selection may be combined in assessment centres to provide a fuller picture of an applicant's strengths and weaknesses.

- Online testing allows organizations to process applicants more quickly. This may, however, filter out good applicants as well as unsuitable ones.

- Applicants have expectations about how the organization will treat them, and the recruitment and selection process represents an opportunity to clarify these. The use of RJPs can increase commitment and job satisfaction by clarifying expectations and communicating an organization's honesty.

Vocab checklist for ESL students

- aptitude (n)
- assessment centre (n)
- attrition (n)
- coefficient (n)
- competencies (n), competent (adj)
- competing framework (n)
- curriculum vitae (CV) (n)
- discriminate (v), discrimination (n), discriminatory (adj)
- face validity (n)
- flagship (n)
- opportunity to perform (n)
- person–job (P–J) fit (n)
- personnel specification (n)
- person–organization (P–O) fit (n)
- pessimism (n), pessimist (n), pessimistic (adj)
- procedural justice (n)
- pseudoscientific (adj)
- realistic job preview (RJP) (n)
- realistic living conditions preview (n)
- recruitment ratio (n)
- reliability (n), reliable (adj)
- validity (n), validation (n), valid (adj)

Visit www.palgrave.com/business/bratton5 for a link to free definitions of these terms in the Macmillan Dictionary, as well as additional learning resources for ESL students.

Review questions

1. Who holds the power in recruitment and selection?
2. How can recruitment and selection support an organization's diversity strategy?
3. How can the predictive validity of the employment interview be improved?
4. Should job descriptions be abandoned in recruitment and selection?
5. 'Appeal to their guts instead of just their brains.' How far do you agree with this view of graduate recruitment?
6. Are assessment centres a fair and valid way of selecting employees?

Further reading to improve your mark

Reading these articles and chapters can help you gain a better understanding and potentially a higher grade for your HRM assignment.

- Selection techniques and methods have always been subject to criticism at a variety of levels, including measurement criteria, validity and reliability, decision-making and applicant reactions. For a broad-ranging review of the research in this area, see P. Sackett and F. Lievens (2008) Personnel selection. *Annual Review of Psychology*, **59**: 419–50.
- A key issue in selection is the perception of fairness of the methods used. A very interesting cross-national comparison of procedural justice can be found in N. Anderson and C. Witvliet (2008) Fairness reactions to personnel selection methods: an international comparison between the Netherlands, the United States, France, Spain, Portugal, and Singapore. *International Journal of Selection and Assessment*, **16**(1): 1–13.

- Diversity issues are increasingly important in recruitment and selection. M. Van den Brink, M. Brouns and D. Waslander, D. (2006), in their article Does excellence have a gender? *Employee Relations,* **28**(6): 523–39, consider the recruitment of professors in The Netherlands, finding gender differences in terms of selection and recruitment procedures.
- There is an interesting debate about the value of personality tests in selection. An argument in favour of tests is presented by D. S. Ones, S. Dilchert, C. Viswesvaran and T. A. Judge (2007) In support of personality assessment in organizational settings. *Personnel Psychology,* **60**: 995–1027. A response is provided by F. P. Morgeson, M. A. Campion, R. L. Dipboye, J. R. Hollenbeck, K. Murphy and N. Schmitt (2007b) Are we getting fooled again? Coming to terms with limitations in the use of personality tests for personnel selection. *Personnel Psychology,* **60**: 1029–49.

Visit www.palgrave.com/business/bratton5 for lots of extra resources to help you get to grips with this chapter, including study tips, HRM skills development guides, summary lecture notes, and more.

References

Adler, L. (2002) *Hire With Your Head.* Chichester: John Wiley & Sons.
Akerjordet, K. and Severinsson, E. (2009) Emotional intelligence. Part 1: The development of scales and psychometric testing. *Nursing and Health Sciences,* **11**: 58–63.
Arvey, R. D. and Campion, J. E. (1982) The employment interview: a summary and review of recent research. *Personnel Psychology,* **35**, 281–322.
Balain, S. and Sparrow, P. (2009) *Engaged to Perform: A New Perspective on Employee Engagement.* White Paper 09/04. Lancaster: Lancaster University Management School.
Barber, A. E. (1998) *Recruiting Employees: Individual and Organizational Perspectives.* Thousand Oaks, CA: Sage.
Barclay, J. (1999) Employee selection: a question of structure. *Personnel Review,* **28**(1/2): 134–51.
Barclay, J. (2001) Improving selection interviews with structure: organisations' use of 'behavioural' interviews. *Personnel Review,* **30**(1): 81–101.
Bauer, T. N., Truxillo, D. M., Sanchez, R. J., Craig, J. M., Ferrera, P. and Campion, M. A. (2001) Applicant reactions to selection: development of the selection procedural justice scale (SPJS). *Personnel Psychology,* **54**(2): 387–421.
Becton, J. B. and Field, H. S. (2009) Cultural differences in organizational citizenship behaviour: a comparison between Chinese and American employees. *International Journal of Human Resource Management,* **20**(8): 1651–69.
Bertua, C., Anderson, N. and Salgado, J. (2005) The predictive validity of cognitive ability tests: a UK meta-analysis. *Journal of Occupational and Organizational Psychology,* **78**, 387–409.
Brady, P. W., Meade, A. W., Michael, J. J. and Fleenor, J. W. (2009) Internet recruiting: effects of website content features on viewers' perceptions of organizational culture. *International Journal of Selection and Assessment,* **17**(1): 19–34.
Brannie, M. (2008) Graduate recruitment and selection in the UK. *Career Development International,* **13**(6): 497–513.
Brint, S. (2006) *Schools and Societies.* Stanford, CA: Stanford Social Sciences.
Broadbridge, A., Maxwell, G. A. and Ogden, S. M. (2009) Selling retailing to Generation Y graduates: recruitment challenges and opportunities. *International Review of Retail, Distribution and Consumer Research,* **19**(4): 405–20.
Cable, D. M. and Parsons, C. K. (2001) Socialization tactics and person–organization fit. *Personnel Psychology,* **54**(1): 1–23.
Caers, R. and Castelyns, V. (2010) LinkedIn and Facebook in Belgium: the influences and biases of social network sites in recruitment and selection procedures. *Social Science Computer Review,* **29**(4): 437–48.

Campion, M. A., Palmer, D. K. and Campion, J. E. (1997) A review of structure in the selection interview. *Personnel Psychology*, 50: 655–702.

Cappelli, P. (2001) Making the most of on-line recruiting. *Harvard Business Review*, 79, 139–46.

Carless, S. A. (2005) Person–job fit versus person–organization fit as predictors of organizational attraction and job acceptance intentions: a longitudinal study. *Journal of Occupational and Organizational Psychology*, 78: 411–29.

Casella, A. and Hanaki, N. (2008) Information channels in labor markets: on the resilience of referral hiring. *Journal of Economic Behavior and Organization*, 66, 492–513.

Ceci, S. and Williams, W. (2000) Smart bomb. *People Management*, 6(17): 32–6.

Chapman, D. and Zweig, D. (2005) Developing a nomological network for interview structure: antecedents and consequences of the structured selection interview. *Personnel Psychology*, 58: 673–702.

Chartered Institute of Personnel and Development (2005b) *Recruitment, Retention and Turnover*. London: CIPD.

Chartered Institute of Personnel and Development (2010c) *Resourcing and Talent Planning*. London: CIPD.

Chartered Institute of Personnel and Development (2010d) 'Competency and competency frameworks'. Available at: www.cipd.co.uk/subjects/perfmangmt/competnces/comptfrmwk.htm (accessed January 12, 2011).

Collins, C. and Han, J. (2004) Exploring applicant pool quantity and quality: the effects of early recruitment strategies, corporate advertising and firm reputation. *Personnel Psychology*, 57: 685–717.

Connerley, M. L., Carlson, K. D. and Mecham, R. L. (2003) Evidence of differences in applicant pool quality. *Personnel Review*, 32(1): 22–39.

Cook, M. (1994) *Personnel Selection and Productivity*. Chichester: John Wiley & Sons.

Czerny, A. (2004) Not so quick and easy. *People Management*, 26 February: 14–15.

Dai, G. and DeMeuse, K. P. (2007) *A review of on boarding research*. White Paper. Los Angeles, CA: Korn/Ferry International.

Dalen, L. H., Stanton, N. A. and Roberts, A. D. (2001) Faking personality questionnaires in personnel selection. *Journal of Management Development*, 20(8): 729–41.

Daniels, K. and Macdonald, L. (2005) *Equality, Diversity and Discrimination*. London: Chartered Institute of Personnel and Development.

Dawson, M. (2005) Costa's 'filter' gets the right employees. *Human Resource Management International Digest*, 13(4): 21–2.

Dayan, K., Fox, S. and Kasten, R. (2008) The preliminary employment interview as a predictor of assessment center outcomes. *International Journal of Selection and Assessment*, 16(2): 102–11.

Dulewicz, V. and Higgs, M. (2000) Emotional intelligence: a review and evaluation. *Journal of Managerial Psychology*, 15(4): 341–72.

Feltham, R. (1992) Using competencies in selection and recruitment. In S. Boam and P. Sparrow (eds) *Designing and Achieving Competency*. (pp. 89–103). Maidenhead: McGraw-Hill.

Flanagan, J. C. (1954) The critical incident technique. *Psychological Bulletin*, 51(4): 327–59.

Francis, H. and Reddington (2012) Employer branding and organisational effectiveness. In Francis, H., Holbeche, L. and Reddington, R. (eds) *People and Organisational Development: A New Agenda for Organisational Effectiveness*. London: Chartered Institute of Personnel and Development.

Furnham, A. (2008) HR professionals' beliefs about, and knowledge of, assessment techniques and psychometric tests. *International Journal of Selection and Assessment*, 16(3): 300–5.

Gault, J., Leach, E. and Duey, M. (2010) Effects of business internships on job marketability: the employers' perspective. *Education and Training*, 52(1): 76–88.

Gilliland, S. W. (1993) The perceived fairness of selection systems: An organizational justice perspective, *Academy of Management Review*, 18: 694–734.

Goleman, D. (2006) *Emotional Intelligence* (10th anniversary edition). London: Bantam.

Google (2012) 'Top 10 reasons to work at Google'. Available at: www.google.co.uk/jobs/reasons.html.

Harris, M. M. (1989) Reconsidering the employment interview: a review of recent literature and suggestions for future research. *Personnel Psychology*, **42**: 691–726.

Hausknecht, J., Day, D. and Thomas, S. (2004) Applicant reactions to selection procedures: an updated model and meta-analysis. *Personnel Psychology*, **57**: 639–83.

Henkens, K., Remery, C. and Schippers, J. (2005) Recruiting personnel in a tight labour market: an analysis of employers' behaviour. *International Journal of Manpower*, **26**(5): 421–33.

Herriot, P., Manning, W. E. G. and Kidd, J. M. (1997) The content of the psychological contract. *British Journal of Management*, **8**(2): 151–62.

Holbeche, L. (1999) *Aligning Human Resources and Business Strategy*. Oxford: Butterworth Heinemann.

Hollenbeck, J. (2000) A structural approach to external and internal person–team fit. *Applied Psychology: An International Review*, **49**(3): 534–49.

Hom, P. W., Griffeth, R. W., Palich, L. E. and Bracker, J. S. (1999) Revisiting met expectations as a reason why realistic job previews work. *Personnel Psychology*, **52**(1): 1–16.

Huffcutt, A. I., Weekly, J. A., Wiesner, W. H., DeGrout, T. G. and Jones, C. (2001) Comparison of situational and behavior description interview questions for higher-level positions. *Personnel Psychology*, **54**(3): 619–44.

Hynie, M., Jensen, K., Johnny, M., Wedlock, J. and Phipps, D. (2011) Student internships bridge research to real world problems. *Education and Training*, **53**(1): 45–56.

Iles, P. and Salaman, G. (1995) Recruitment, selection and assessment. In Storey, J. (ed.) *Human Resource Management* (pp. 203–33). London: Routledge.

Industrial Relations Services (2003a) Sharpening up recruitment and selection with competencies. *IRS Employment Review*, **782**: 42–9.

Jackson, C. (1996) *Understanding Psychological Testing*. Leicester: BPS Books.

Jackson, D. J. R., Stillman, J. A. and Englert, P. (2010) Task-based assessment centers: empirical support for a systems model. *International Journal of Selection and Assessment*, **18**(2): 141–54.

Jansen, B. and Jansen, K. (2005) Using the web to look for work. *Internet Research*, **15**(1): 49–66.

Johnson, M. and Senges, M. (2010) Learning to be a programmer in a complex organization. *Journal of Workplace Learning*, **22**(3): 180–94.

Judge, T. A. and Cable, D. M. (1997) Applicant personality, organizational culture and organization attraction. *Personnel Psychology*, **50**: 359–94.

Knox, S. and Freeman, C. (2006) Measuring and managing employer brand image in the service industry. *Journal of Marketing Management*, **22**(7–8): 695–717.

Kolk, N., Born, M. and van den Flier, H. (2003) The transparent assessment centre: the effects of revealing dimensions to candidates. *Applied Psychology: An International Review*, **52**(4): 648–68.

Lance, C.E. (2008). Why assessment centers do not work the way they are supposed to. *Industrial and Organizational Psychology: Perspectives on Science and Practice*, **1**: 84–97.

Latham, G. P., Saari, L. M., Pursell, E. D. and Campion, M. A. (1980) The situational interview. *Journal of Applied Psychology*, **65**: 422–7.

Levashina, J. and Campion, M. A. (2006) A model of faking likelihood in the employment interview. *International Journal of Selection and Assessment*, **14**: 299–316.

Lewis, R. E. and Heckman, R. J. (2006) Talent management: a critical review. *Human Resource Management Review*, **16**(2): 139–54.

Lievens, F. and Harris, M. M. (2003) Research on internet recruiting and testing: current status and future directions. In C. L. Cooper and I. T. Robertson (eds) *International Review of Industrial and Organizational Psychology*, **16**: 131–65.

Lyon, P. and Glover, I. (1998) Divestment or investment? The contradictions of HRM in relation to older employees. *Human Resource Management Journal*, **8**(1): 56–68.

McCarthy, J. and Goffin, R. (2004) Measuring job interview anxiety: beyond weak knees and sweaty palms. *Personnel Psychology*, **57**: 607–37.

McCulloch, M. and Turban, D. (2007) Using person–organization fit to select employees for high-turnover jobs. *International Journal of Selection and Assessment*, **15**(1): 63–71.

McHenry, R. (1997) Tried and tested. *People Management*, January 23: 32–7.

Macleod, D. and Clarke, N. (2009) *Engaging for Success: Enhancing Performance Through Engagement*. London: Department of Business.

Mäkelä, K., Björkman, I. and Ehrnrooth, M. (2010) How do MNCs establish their talent pools? Influences on individuals' likelihood of being labeled as talent. *Journal of World Business*, **45**(2): 134–42.

Mannion, E. and Whittaker, P. (1996) European Passenger Services Ltd – assessment centres for recruitment and development. *Career Development International*, **1**(6): 12–16.

Martin, P. and Pope, J. (2008) Competency-based interviewing – has it gone too far? *Industrial and Commercial Training*, **40**(2): 81–6.

Melchers, K. G., Kleinmann, M. and Prinz, M. A. (2010) Do assessors have too much on their plates? The effects of simultaneously rating multiple assessment center candidates on rating quality. *International Journal of Selection and Assessment*, **18**(3): 329–41.

Miller, L., Rankin, N. and Neathey, F. (2001) *Competency Frameworks in UK Organizations*. London: Chartered Institute of Personnel and Development.

Morgeson, F. P., Campion, M. A, Dipboye, R. L., Hollenbeck, J. R., Murphy, K. and Schmitt, N. (2007a) Reconsidering the use of personality tests in personnel selection contexts. *Personnel Psychology*, **60**, 683–729.

Mullen, A. (2010) *Degrees of Inequality: Culture, Class and Gender in American Higher Education*. Baltimore, MD: Johns Hopkins University Press.

Munro-Fraser, J. (1971) *Psychology: General, Industrial, Social*. London: Pitman.

Newell, S. (2005) Recruitment and selection. In S. Bach (ed.) *Managing Human Resources* (pp. 115–47). Oxford: Blackwell.

Nikolaou, I. and Judge, T. (2007) Fairness reactions to personnel selection techniques in Greece: the role of core self-evaluations. *International Journal of Selection and Assessment*, **15**(2): 206–19.

Ordanini, A. and Silvestri, G. (2008) Recruitment and selection services: efficiency and competitive reasons in the outsourcing of HR practices. *International Journal of Human Resource Management*, **19**(2): 372–91.

Parry, E. and Tyson, S. (2008) An analysis of the use and success of online recruitment methods in the UK. *Human Resource Management Journal*, **18**(3): 257–74.

Parry, E. and Wilson, H. (2009) Factors influencing the adoption of online recruitment. *Personnel Review*, **38**(6): 655–73.

Pennell, K. (2010) The role of flexible job descriptions in succession management. *Library Management*, **31**(4/5): 279–90.

Phillips, J. M. (1998) Effects of realistic job previews on multiple organizational outcomes: a meta-analysis. *Academy of Management Journal*, **41**(6): 673–90.

Piotrowski, C. and Armstrong, T. (2006) Current recruitment and selection practices: a national survey of Fortune 1000 firms. *North American Journal of Psychology*, December: 488–93.

Plachy, R. J. (1987) Writing job descriptions that get results. *Personnel*, October: 56–63.

Pollitt, D. (2005) E-recruitment gets the Nike tick of approval. *Human Resource Management International Digest*, **13**(2): 33–5.

Pollitt, D. (2008) Online recruitment connects 3 with top talent. *Human Resource Management International Digest*, **16**(4): 25–6.

Posthuma, R., Morgeson, F. and Campion, M. (2002) Beyond employment interview validity: a comprehensive narrative review of recent research and trends over time. *Personnel Psychology*, **55**: 1–82.

Potosky, D. and Bobko, P. (2004) Selection testing via the internet: practical considerations and exploratory empirical findings. *Personnel Psychology*, **57**: 1003–34.

Premack, S. L. and Wanous, J. P. (1985) A meta-analysis of realistic job preview experiments. *Journal of Applied Psychology*, **70**(4): 706–19.

Proença, M. T. and de Oliveira, E. T. (2009) From normative to tacit knowledge: CVs analysis in personnel selection. *Employee Relations*, **31**(4): 427–47.

Pulakos, E. D. and Schmitt, N. (1995) Experienced based and situational questions: studies of validity. *Personnel Psychology*, **48**: 289–309.

Richardson, J., McBey, K. and McKenna, S. (2008) Integrating realistic job previews and realistic living conditions previews. *Personnel Review*, **37**(5): 490–508.

Roberts, G. (1997) *Recuitment and Selection*. London: Institute of Personnel and Development.

Robertson, I. T., Baron, H., Gibbons, P., MacIver, R. and Nyfield, G. (2000) Conscientiousness and managerial performance. *Journal of Occupational and Organizational Psychology*, **73**(2): 171–81.

Rodger, A. (1970) *The Seven Point Plan* (3rd edn). London: NFER.

Salgado, J. F. (1997) The five factor model of personality and job performance in the European Community. *Journal of Applied Psychology*, **82**(1): 30–43.

Schmidt, F. L. (2002) The role of general cognitive ability and job performance: why there cannot be a debate. *Human Performance*, **15**: 187–210.

Schneider, B. (1987) The people make the place. *Personnel Psychology*, **40**: 437–53.

Smethurst, S. (2004) The allure of online. *People Management*, 29 July: 38–40.

Smither, J., Reilly, R., Millsap, R., Pearlman, K. and Stoffey, R. (1993) Applicant reactions to selection procedures. *Personnel Psychology*, **46**: 49–76.

Sparrow, P. (2007) Globalization of HR at function level: four UK-based case studies of the international recruitment and selection process. *International Journal of Human Resource Management*, **18**(5): 845–67.

Spitzmüller, C., Neumann, E., Spitzmüller, M., Rubino, C., Keeton, K., Sutton, M. T. and Manzey, D. (2008) Assessing the influence of psychosocial and career mentoring on organizational attractiveness. *International Journal of Selection and Assessment*, **16**(4): 403–15.

Spychalski, A. C., Quiñones, M. A., Gaugler, B. B. and Pohley, K. (1997) A survey of assessment center practices in the United States. *Personnel Psychology*, **50**, 71–90.

Sylva, H. and Mol, S. (2009) E-Recruitment: a study into applicant perceptions of an online application system. *International Journal of Selection and Assessment*, **17**(3): 311–22.

Templer, K. J., Tay, C. and Chandrasekar, N. A. (2006) Motivational cultural intelligence, realistic job preview, realistic living conditions preview, and cross-cultural adjustment. *Group and Organization Management*, **31**(1): 154–73.

Thornton, G. and Gibbons, A. (2009) Validity of assessment centers for personnel selection. *Human Resource Management Review*, **19**(3): 69–187.

Toplis, J., Dulvicz, V. and Fletcher, C. (2005) *Psychological Testing* (4th edn). London: Chartered Institute of Personnel and Development.

Trapp, R. (2005) The mirror has two faces. *People Management*, 19 May: 40–2.

Tulip, S. (2004) Hired education. *People Management*, September 30: 46–9.

Tyson, S. (1995) *Human Resource Strategy*. London: Pitman.

Ulrich, L. and Trumbo, D. (1965) The selection interview since 1949. *Psychological Bulletin*, **63**: 100–16.

Wagner, R. F. (1949) The employment interview: a critical summary. *Personnel Psychology*, **2**: 17–46.

Watson, T. (1994) Recruitment and selection. In Sisson, K. (ed.) *Personnel Management* (pp. 185–252). Oxford: Blackwell.

Watts, J. J. (2009) Leaders of men: women 'managing' in construction. *Work Employment and Society*, **23**(3): 512–30.

Weichman, D. and Ryan, A. (2003) Reactions to computerized testing in selection contexts. *International Journal of Selection and Assessment*, **11**: 215–29.

Wheeler, A. R., Buckley, M. R., Halbesleben, J. R., Brouer, B. and Ferris, G. R. (2005) The elusive criterion of fit revisited: toward an integrative theory of multidimensional fit. *Research in Personnel and Human Resources Management*, **24**: 265–304.

Whiddett, S. and Hollyforde, K. (2003) *A Practical Guide to Competencies*. London: Chartered Institute of Personnel and Development.

Wiggins, J. S. (ed.) (1996) *The Five-factor Model of Personality*. New York: Guildford Publications.

Wilk, S. and Cappelli, P. (2003) Understanding the determinants of employer use of selection methods. *Personnel Psychology*, **57**: 103–24.

Woodruffe, C. (2000) *Development and Assessment Centres* (3rd edn). London: Chartered Institute of Personnel and Development.

CHAPTER 10
Recruitment and selection
Olivia Kyriakidou

- Introduction
- Stages of recruitment and selection
- Critical analysis and discussion
- Benefits of studying HRM from a critical perspective
- Conclusion
- For discussion and revision
- Further reading
- Case study: The design of a new multinational personnel selection system at MobilCom
- References

After reading this chapter, you should be able to:
- Describe the personnel selection system and its component parts
- Understand the role played by the rational and objective staffing technologies, including job analysis and recruitment and selection methods
- Critically assess the concern with the selection–performance relationship that underlines the personnel staffing agenda
- Come to terms with the fact that employees are not simple 'human resources' that can be selected, recruited, controlled and processed, but are human beings characterized by agency, subjectivity and reflexivity
- Consider the international implications of recruitment and selection, analyse the different selection methods for expatriates and develop effective methods for selecting expatriate managers

- Understand the necessity of studying recruitment and selection from a critical perspective, exploring, in particular, the ethical dimensions
- Identify future theoretical and practical challenges in the field of research into recruitment and selection

Introduction

Recruitment and selection are seminal topics within human resource management (HRM), ensuring that organizations have the necessary human skills, knowledge and capabilities to enable the organization to continue into the future. Recent recognition of the strategic potential of recruitment and selection to enhance organizational performance has placed great emphasis on getting the 'right person' for a post. Selecting the 'right person' means that the personnel recruitment and selection agenda should be dominated by a concern with formalization, enshrined in its language of 'objectivity', 'reliability' and 'validity', with a technology and method that attempt to maximize 'decision-making accuracy', and with the selection–performance relationship.

In most HRM practice, performance is conceptualized in strict economic terms, excluding any consideration of issues of fairness and acceptability for whichever individuals, groups or authorities might take an interest in the selection decisions. Moreover, formalization refers to the use of formal methods that are supposed to aid an objective, fair and rational selection decision, guarding at the same time against inefficiency and discrimination through the use of scientifically validated techniques. This agenda prescribes practices that, if followed properly, should guarantee the 'truth' of selection decisions, producing a better match between the individual and the organization at the point of selection. These practices should also remove any ethical uneasiness from personnel decision-making.

Underpinning this assumption is the idea that the information identified as being central or critical to good selection decisions can be understood as being relatively neutral. 'Neutral' means here that the content of knowledge, skills and ability profiles is treated as largely reflecting the reality of the person's role. However, there is a considerable danger of managers having too much faith in the neutrality and predictive powers of selection techniques and procedures that tend to ignore the amount of human interpretation and intuition involved in all staffing activities. A more critical way of thinking indicates that selection processes should not exclude the broader moral, social and political considerations (Janssens and Steyaert, 2009) that are embedded in a pluralist approach – an approach that stresses the existence of divergent interests within organizations – or the roles of the following in enacting certain types of personnel selection technology:

- *human agency* – in other words, employees' capacity to make choices and to impose those choices on their world of work;
- *subjectivity* – defined as the ability of the employees to have consciousness and relationships with other entities;

- *reflexivity* – the capacity of employees to recognize the impact of forces of organizational socialization on them, and to alter their places in the organization's social structure.

Such a critical way of thinking is further strengthened by research studies exploring the international dimensions of personnel selection. For instance, it has been reported that, consistent with the national culture, organizations in the USA typically have cultures that emphasize individual achievement, competition and rationality (Stone and Stone-Romero, 2004). As a result, the ideal job applicant is one who is individualistic and achievement-oriented (Syed, 2008). In such situations, individuals who come from collectivist societies could be disadvantaged during the processes of recruitment and selection. Similarly, Bevelander (1999) highlights the fact that, in many countries, many monotonous jobs that used to involve low or unskilled labour are increasingly being replaced by jobs that require higher communicative and social abilities, as well as culture-specific social competence and language skills. Such an orientation towards specific social skills that are mainly possessed by those who are native-born may, however, lead to personnel recruitment and selection practices that are not sensitive to the cultural diversity of the labour force.

The structure of this chapter is as follows. In the first section, we will explore the classical theories and current research that underpin the three basic elements of a personnel selection system:

- studying the job to be performed;
- recruiting a pool of applicants for the job;
- selecting the 'best' from the applicant pool.

Such an exploration will be enriched by international considerations and implications for recruitment and selection, with a special focus on expatriate managers.

Finally, we will adopt a critical perspective that tries to reveal the ethical issues underpinning personnel staffing and problematize the currently strong relationship between selection practices and performance.

Stages of recruitment and selection

Most recruitment and selection procedures involve several stages that occur over a period of time. The process usually first includes a job analysis that results in a job description and personnel specification in order to uncover all the qualities that are necessary to perform the job successfully. This analysis also incorporates an initial recognition of the need for new staff and recruitment advertising, followed by pre-screening applicants, and finally the selection decisions and induction of new employees into the organization. This systems view is generally based on the traditional 'predictivist' perspective on selection, which views the job as a given and stable entity into which the most suitable candidate needs to be recruited. Person–job fit is therefore of primary importance. Figure 10.1 illustrates the process and is reasonably self-explanatory in terms of the critical objectives and key activities that are involved at each phase.

HRM / HRD IN ITS CONTEMPORARY CONTEXT

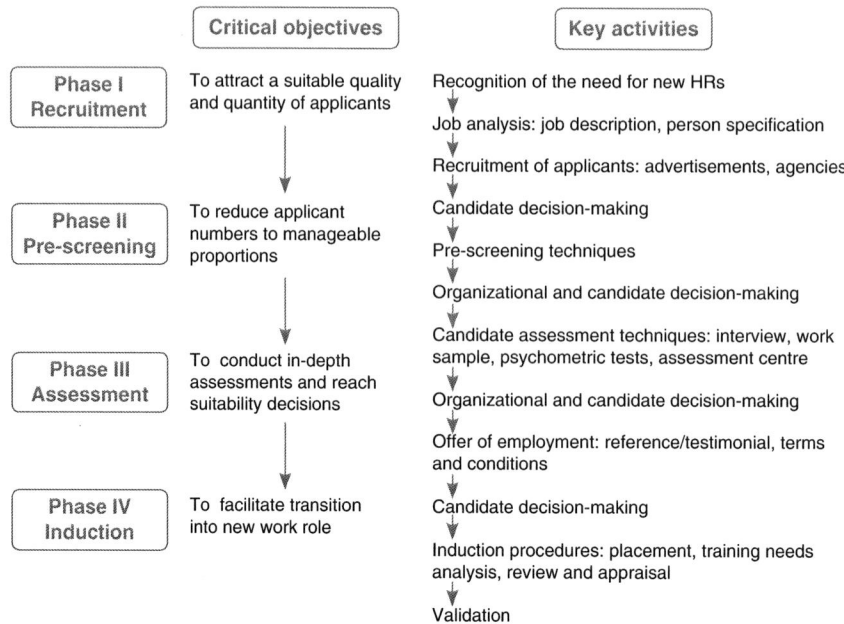

Figure 10.1 The recruitment and selection process

The advantage of taking such a 'systems view' of selection is that it provides a holistic overview of the entire process underlying two pertinent issues: bilateral decision-making and validation feedback loops. First, decisions are made by both the recruiter and the candidate at several points in the process, supporting the constructivist perspective that both parties consider possible employment options and make decisions over whether to accept a working relationship with each other. Selection therefore serves as an opportunity to exchange information and develop mutual expectations and obligations. Hence, from this perspective, selection aims to ensure not only a person–job fit, but also a person–organization fit (that is, a fit between the applicant's values and organizational culture) and a person–team fit (that is, a fit between the applicant's skills and attitudes and the climate of the immediate working group).

Second, the systems view highlights the importance of the validation feedback loop. In larger scale selection processes, where numerous recruitment decisions are reached over a period of time, the crucial question from the organization's perspective is: 'How accurate are these decisions in selecting individuals who subsequently turn out to be effective job performers?' This question has driven much of the research from the psychometric perspective. Validation feedback loops recycle information on the effectiveness of selection decisions into the selection process at different stages in order to modify and improve the procedure.

Job analysis

The traditional role of job analysis is to provide a fixed starting point for all subsequent steps in the selection process. Job analysis refers to one or more procedures designed to collect information about the tasks people perform and the skills they require to do those jobs effectively. It is a process for describing what is done in any job – not the best way to do it, nor what it is worth to have the job done. Job analysis traditionally seeks the information on the following:

- work activities, including both individual behaviours and job outcomes;
- the machines, tools, equipment and work aids used;
- job-related tangibles and intangibles, such as materials processed and knowledge applied, respectively;
- standards of work performance;
- job context;
- personnel requirements, such as education, experience, aptitudes and so forth.

The end product of job analysis is often a job description, which is a factual statement of the tasks, responsibilities and working conditions involved in a particular job. Box 10.1 presents an example of a job description for a first-level supervisor post. The job description should also include elements of contextual performance as

---

Box 10.1 Job analysis: First-Level Supervisor – Department of Operations

Performance dimensions and task statements:
Organizing work; assigning work; monitoring work; managing consequences; counselling, efficiency review, and discipline; setting an example; employee development.

Knowledge, skills, abilities and other characteristics (KSAOs) and definitions:
Organizing; analysis and decision-making; planning; communication (oral and written; delegation; work habits; carefulness; interpersonal skill; job knowledge; organizational knowledge; toughness; integrity; development of others; listening.

Predictor measures

- Multiple-choice in-basket exercise
  (assume the role of the new supervisor and work through the in-basket on the desk)
- Structured panel interview
  (predetermined questions about past experiences relevant to the KSAOs)
- Presentation exercise
  (make a presentation to a simulated work group about a change in their working hours)
- Writing sample
  (prepare a written reprimand for a fictitious employee)
- Training and experience evaluation exercise
  (give examples of training and work achievements relevant to certain KSAOs)

there is still a tendency to focus upon specific, discrete tasks and ignore contextual aspects such as maintaining morale, courtesy and other citizenship behaviours (Viswesvaran and Ones, 2000). There may also be a person specification, which details the knowledge, skills, abilities, experiences and attributes or attitudes required to perform the job effectively.

However, Hough and Oswald (2000) indicate that, in recognition of the increasingly rapid changes that are taking place in the workplace, job analysis should focus on tasks and on the cross-functional skills of workers, including information on personality, cognitive, behavioural and situational variables, rather than on more static aspects of jobs. Moreover, in many selection situations, the need to understand the job is made particularly complex and difficult because the job in question is likely to be radically different, in ways that are very difficult to predict, within as little as 5 or maybe 10 years. Finally, at the managerial/professional level, someone may be employed to fulfil objectives or agendas as opposed to specific tasks. In such instances, Cascio (1995) says that what can often remain is something more 'person-like' than 'job-like' insofar as the job (as a set of objectives or agendas) is defined and enacted in a highly individualized manner.

The recruitment process

In most reviews of recruitment research, authors have offered organizing models of the recruitment process (see, for example, Rynes and Cable, 2003). Figure 10.2 presents a model developed by Breaugh et al. (2008). Given the detailed nature of the model, we will not provide a thorough discussion of all of its contents. However, a key part of Figure 10.2, the box labelled 'Intervening job applicant variables', does merit elaboration. Although some of these variables (for example, what makes a position attractive) have received attention, many other variables (such as attracting applicants' attention and applicant self-insight) have received almost no attention from recruitment researchers (Breaugh et al., 2008).

A consideration of the job applicant variables portrayed in Figure 10.2 should play a central role in how an employer plans its recruitment process. For example, if an employer is interested in attracting the attention of individuals who are not currently looking for jobs, many commonly used (and commonly studied) recruitment methods (for example, newspaper advertisements or job fairs) may not be particularly effective. Similarly, if an organization hopes to improve person–job/organization fit by providing realistic information during the recruitment process, applicant self-insight is important to consider – even having received the information, applicants without such insight may not be able to evaluate whether the position described represents a good fit for them. Research (see Rynes and Cable, 2003; Breaugh et al., 2008) has found that many job applicants:

- have an incomplete and/or inaccurate understanding of what a job opening involves;
- are not sure what they want from a position;
- do not have a self-insight with regard to their knowledge, skills and abilities;
- cannot accurately predict how they will react to the demands of a new position.

RECRUITMENT AND SELECTION

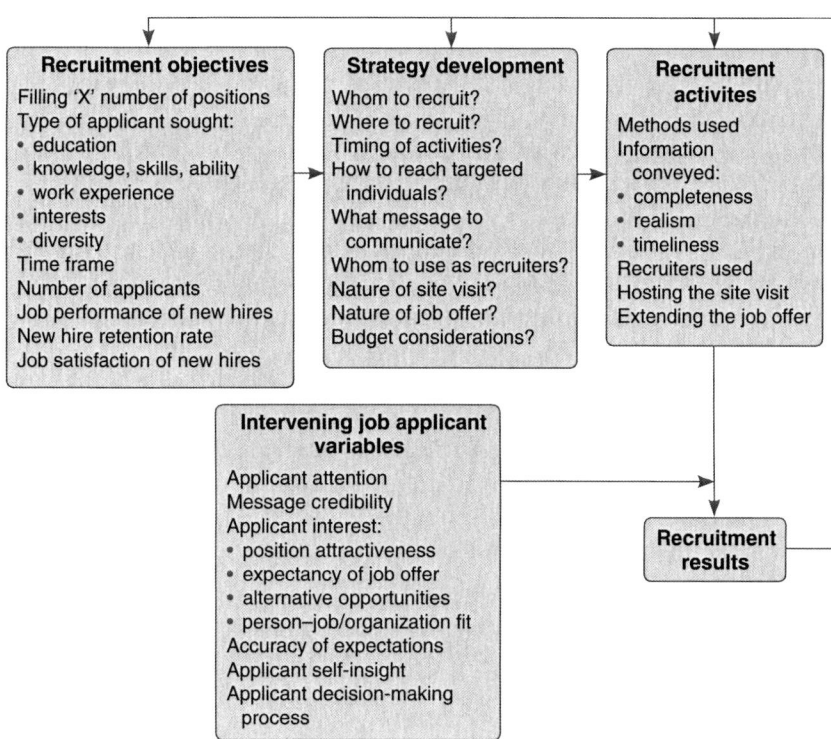

Figure 10.2 A model of the recruitment process

Recruiting methods

External recruitment

Having done a thorough job analysis and produced an accurate job description, including a realistic person specification, the organization is now ready to start recruiting potential applicants. With regard to the term 'external recruitment', this could be defined as encompassing an employer's actions that are intended to:

- bring a job opening to the attention of potential job candidates who do not currently work for the organization;
- influence whether these individuals apply for the opening;
- affect whether they maintain interest in the position until a job offer is extended;
- influence whether a job offer is accepted.

External recruitment sources The types of recruitment method (Table 10.1) that an employer uses may make a difference to the process here. The two most common explanations for why this might happen (Zottoli and Wanous, 2000) have been labelled the *realistic information hypothesis* and the *individual difference hypothesis*. Simply stated, the realistic information hypothesis suggests that individuals recruited via certain methods such as employee referrals have a more accurate

Table 10.1 External recruitment sources

Employee referrals	Advantages: low-cost, high-quality hires, decreased hiring time, opportunities to strengthen the bond with current employees
	Employees carefully pre-screen applicants due to the activation of a mechanism to protect their reputation: they provide difficult-to-obtain information and coaching, and press their referrals to perform
Job advertisements	Advertisements with more information result in job openings being viewed as more attractive and more credible, increasing applicants' interest and resulting in a better person–organization fit. The inclusion of pictures of minority groups seems to increase the attraction of diverse applicants to the organization
Internet/employer's website	These sources generate a large number of applicants at a relatively low cost; the effectiveness of these sources depends upon the employer's visibility and reputation, as well as the aesthetics, content and function of the website
	A potential limitation is that a firm may be inundated with applications from individuals who are not good candidates for the positions. As a way to address this issue and given its interactive capability, a website could provide potential applicants with feedback concerning person–job/organizational fit
Universities, colleges and placement offices	These are a source of people with specialized skills for professional positions. The choice of colleges and universities might depend on past experiences with students at the school, the quality of recent hires, offer acceptance rates and skills, experience and training in the desired areas, ranking of school quality and the costs of recruiting at a particular school
Cooperatives, internships and job fairs	These are part-time working arrangements that allow the organization to obtain services from a part-time employee for a short period of time; they also give the organization an opportunity to assess the person for a full-time position after graduation
Employment agencies and executive search firms	One source of lower level, non-managerial employees is employment agencies. For higher level positions, executive search firms, or 'headhunters', may be used. Care must be exercised in selecting an employment agency for two reasons. First, many agencies might flood the organization with CVs without careful screening. Second, they may misrepresent the organization to the candidate and the candidate to the organization if they are concerned only with a quick placement and pay no regard to the costs of poor future relationships with clients

understanding of what a position involves. The individual difference hypothesis posits that different recruitment methods may bring a job opening to the attention of different types of individual who vary in terms of important attributes (for example, their ability or work ethic).

Recruiter effect Chapman et al. (2005) found that individuals who viewed a recruiter as having been personable, trustworthy, informative and/or competent were more attracted to a position with the recruiter's organization. Recruiters' behaviour can be very important as the way they treat an applicant may be viewed as a signal of how the person would be treated if hired.

Rynes et al. (1991: 59) have found that recruiters were:

> associated with changes in many job seekers' assessment of fit over time – 16 of 41 individuals mentioned recruiters or other corporate representatives as reasons

for deciding that an initially favored company was no longer a good fit, whereas an identical number mentioned recruiters as a reason for changing an initial impression of poor fit into a positive one.

Breaugh et al. (2008) underline the importance of different types of recruiters because:

- they vary in the amount of job-related information they possess;
- they differ in terms of their credibility in the eyes of recruits;
- they signal different things to job candidates.

Finally, with regard to the relative importance of recruitment with respect to characteristics associated with the position being offered, conventional wisdom is that position attributes such as pay, job tasks and working hours are more important to job applicants than such recruitment variables as the content of a job advertisement, the design of a company's employment website or a recruiter's behaviour. Comparisons of the relative impact of recruitment variables and position attributes have resulted in some individuals questioning whether the manner in which an employer recruits is important.

In this context, two factors should be considered. First, if an employer does a poor job of recruiting, it may not bring job openings to the attention of the types of people it is seeking to recruit. Second, even if a position is brought to the attention of targeted individuals, poor treatment during the recruitment process may result in individuals withdrawing as job candidates before an employer has even had a chance to present a job offer (Boswell et al., 2003).

Internal recruitment

The objective of the internal recruitment process is to identify and attract applicants from among individuals already holding jobs within the organization (Table 10.2). Many organizations have recognized that careful management of their existing employee base may be a cost-effective way to fill upper-level managerial and professional vacancies.

Realistic job previews

A realistic job preview (RJP; which is provided through work simulations and work tours among other things) requires that employers should provide recruits with candid information concerning the pleasant, and also the unpleasant, aspects of the job as a way to address inaccurate job expectations and decrease turnover.

Three important job applicant-related variables – anchoring and adjustment, the inability to predict how one will react to events in the future, and a lack of self-insight – need to be highlighted in the context of RJPs. Concerning anchoring and adjustment, research in social psychology (Kruglanski and Sleeth-Keppler, 2007) has found that, having formed an initial attitude concerning a topic, individuals typically do not adjust this attitude sufficiently after receiving additional relevant

Table 10.2 Internal recruitment sources

Job postings	These spell out the duties and requirements of the job and show how applicants can apply. Their content should be based on the job description and should clearly define the knowledge, skills, abilities and other characteristics (KSAOs) needed to perform the job. The main characteristics that lead to high satisfaction on the part of users include the adequacy of job descriptions and job notification procedures, the treatment received during the interview, the helpfulness of counselling and the provision of constructive feedback, and the fairness of the job-posting system
Intranet and intraplacement	These informs employees quickly about job postings and prospects inside the organization. Some companies include an online career centre where employees can also gain access to information about the KSAOs needed for positions that might interest them
Talent management system	This monitors and tracks the utilization of employees' skills and abilities throughout the organization
Career development centres	These provide employees with opportunities to take interest inventories – self-assessment tools that assess employees' likes and dislikes related to a variety of activities, objects and types of person – assess their personal career goals and have discussions with representatives across the organization. In this way, employees learn about themselves, have a chance to hear about the career options within the organization, and develop methods to structure internal career paths that match their interests
Replacement and succession plans	Succession plans are organized by position and list the skills needed for the prospective position

information. This suggests that providing an RJP to an applicant who already has an opinion of what a position with an employer involves may not result in an adequate adjustment of their initial opinion.

Moreover, Dunning (2007) has shown that people who are asked to predict how they will react to a future state of events they have little experience of are typically unable to make accurate predictions. This inability to predict one's reactions means that, even if an organization provides descriptive information about what a job involves, the recipient of an RJP may have difficulty anticipating how he or she will react to various aspects of the new job. This inability to predict one's reactions can be at least partially overcome if an RJP includes information that is both descriptive (that is, factual) and judgemental (that is, addresses the reactions other employees have to the job attributes) (Breaugh et al., 2008).

The effectiveness of an RJP can also be limited by a lack of self-insight on the part of applicants concerning their abilities or what they want in a job. Schmeichel and Vohs (2009) indicate that individuals frequently lack self-insight and typically have an inflated view of their abilities.

Finally, RJPs could be used not only for entry-level hiring, but also for internal recruitment. For example, a study by Caligiuri and Phillips (2003) described how one employer successfully used an RJP to help its current employees make decisions concerning overseas assignments. Templer et al. (2006) also documented the effectiveness of an RJP in facilitating the crosscultural adjustment of employees transferred to non-US assignments.

Personnel selection methods

Application forms, CVs and references

CVs and application forms are used as a straightforward way of giving a standardized synopsis of the applicant's history in order to pre-screen applicants and generate a shortlist of candidates to be invited to the next stage. To facilitate effective pre-screening decision-making, an application form should ideally be designed according to the selection criteria, and a systematic screening process should be adhered to. However, research into graduate recruitment suggests that the typical process is far from systematic (Knights and Raffo, 1990), and this can clearly impact negatively on the selection process in the longer term. Moreover, there is evidence suggesting that the inclusion of competency statements in CVs (for example, 'I am highly motivated with a proven track record in achieving goals and targets') increases the probability of producing an invitation to an interview (Earl et al., 1998). Although application forms are very popular in the UK, there are cultural differences across Europe, with standard application documents being more popular in Germany and CVs being more widely used in Denmark (Shackleton and Newell, 1997).

References involve the assessment of an individual by a third party, for example the applicant's previous employer. The use of references is more common in the UK, Ireland and Belgium than in France, Sweden, The Netherlands and Portugal (Shackleton and Newell, 1997). References may involve either an open-ended format or a structured format with questions developed from selection criteria. References may serve at least two purposes: first, to confirm the accuracy of information provided by the applicant, and second, to obtain information on the applicant's previous work experience and performance.

However, references suffer from problems of restriction of range (as they may provide limited information regarding the areas of interest), low predictive validity, low interrater reliability, low criterion-relatedness (as they are not linked to specific performance areas) and leniency (a bias that occurs when a manager rates an employee too positively), with few applicants being given negative evaluations; this suggests that not too much reliance should be placed upon their content (Shackleton and Newell, 1997). Their validity can be improved when references are sought on a criterion-specific basis (Smith and George, 1992) or by structuring references in the form of systematic ratings of 'personality' (Mount et al., 1994). References are therefore rarely used in the decision-making process, being more likely to be used merely as a final check before any job offer is made.

Selection interviews

The use of interviews as selection technique continues unabated. In organizations around the world, selection interviews continue to be one of the most frequently used methods to assess candidates for employment (Wilk and Cappelli, 2003). McDaniel et al. (1994: 599) define the interview as a 'procedure designed to predict future job performance on the basis of applicants' oral responses to oral enquiries'. Guion (1998), however, cautions against this generic definition because it assumes that interviews are monolithic entities, like tests. Beyond everything else, we should keep in mind that the selection interview is a social interaction where the interviewer and applicant exchange and process information gathered from each other.

The clearest boundary can be drawn between the traditional unstructured (measuring, for example, social skills and aspects of personality) and more structured forms of interview (measuring, for example, cognitive ability and tacit or job knowledge). Traditionally, interviews are used merely to form a global impression about applicants' job suitability, including whether they would 'fit in', rather than asking them job-related questions. By contrast, structured interviews involve a series of job-related questions with predetermined answers consistently applied across all interviews for a particular job (that is, there is a standardization of questions, question sequence, interview length, evaluation and so on). Probably the most consistent finding in interview research is that interviewers' judgements are more predictive of job performance when based on structured rather than unstructured interviews (Dipboye et al., 2004).

The two main ways of structuring interviews are situational interviewing and behaviour description interviewing. The *situational interview* (Latham and Saari, 1984), which assumes that intentions and behaviours are related, tries to elicit from candidates how they would respond to particular work situations. The situational questions can be developed using the critical incident technique of job analysis, which tries to identify the behaviours critical to effective performance on the job. This is then translated into a question about a hypothetical but job-relevant situation. A scoring guide is developed for evaluating an interviewee's response to each question by providing examples of behavioural responses to that question. One such example of a situational interview taken from Latham and Saari (1984) is shown in Box 10.2.

The *behavioural description interview* is a variant of the situational interview (Janz, 1982). But where the situational interview invites applicants to respond to questions in light of how they might behave, the behavioural interview requires an examination of how the applicant has actually behaved in the past when encountering similar incidents (with the assumption that past behaviour predicts future behaviour).

Interestingly, *panel interviews*, also referred to as board interviews or team interviews, involving multiple raters for the same set of applicants, are another means

---

Box 10.2 Example of a situational interview

For the past week you have been consistently getting the jobs that are the most time-consuming (for example, poor handwriting, complex statistical work). You know it's nobody's fault because you have been taking the jobs in priority order. You have just picked your fourth job of the day and it's another 'loser'. What would you do?

Interviewees offer unstructured responses that are then scored against benchmark answers. The benchmark answers for the example question are 1 = Thumb through the pile and take another job (poor); 3 = Complain but do the job anyway (average); 5 = Take the job without complaining and do it (good).

Source: Adapted from Latham and Saari (1984: 571).

of adding structure. Despite their considerably higher administrative costs, they are expected to result in increased reliability and validity over comparably structured one-to-one interviews (Conway et al., 1995). However, the relational demography, which refers to similarity in terms of demographic attributes, and the racial composition of the interview panel may affect judgements in ways that are consistent with similarity–attraction and social identity theories showing same-race biases (McFarland et al., 2004; Buckley et al., 2007). Moreover, Herriott (2003) has suggested that the process of discussion among individual raters can substantially distort the consensual score through conformity and polarization effects, implying that it is perhaps better to obtain individual ratings from panel members before they have a chance to discuss them.

Despite the evidence showing that interviews containing high levels of structure can be valid predictors, surveys show that managers, human resources professionals and organizations use them only infrequently. Most human resources professionals report using interviews with a moderate degree of structure as this affords them more autonomy and ownership over the process (Lievens and De Paepe, 2004). The use of less structured interviews is related to interviewers' concerns about:

- having discretion in terms of how the interview is conducted;
- losing informal, personal contact with the applicant;
- the time demands of developing structured interviews (Lievens and De Paepe, 2004).

There is also a tendency for operational and human resources personnel to use 'satisficing' as opposed to maximizing selection practices. This means that human resources personnel mainly ask themselves 'What must I do at the very minimum to get the best applicants?' instead of asking 'What can I do to most maximize the possibility of getting the best applicants?' Finally, when interviewers are required to justify the procedures they followed in making their ratings – procedure accountability – they are more likely to use structured interview procedures and make better judgements (Brtek and Motowidlo, 2002).

In practice, there is tension between increasing the structure of the interview (to enhance its validity) and avoiding adverse reactions on the part of the applicant. Although the unstructured interview may be charged with being overly personal, the highly structured interview may create an adverse reaction because it is perceived as 'depersonalizing'. Overall, applicants demonstrate a distinct preference for unstructured over structured interviews (Hough and Oswald, 2000). Also, the less structured the interview, the more symbolic opportunity there is for the applicant to get a feel for the organization and its culture (via the interviewer), enabling a more realistic decision to be made on whether to accept any job offer (Anderson, 2001). Mini Case Study 10.1 highlights the dilemmas behind the use of highly structured interview formats.

Applicant factors and characteristics   Recent research has found evidence for the existence of subtle discrimination in interviews. Frazer and Wiersma (2001) found that, 1 week after conducting interviews, interviewers recalled African-American applicants as having given less intelligent answers compared with white applicants.

Similarly, Purkiss et al. (2006) observed that those applicants with both an ethnic name and a corresponding accent received the least favourable interviewer ratings, whereas applicants with a Hispanic name but no accent were evaluated most favourably. This result provides support for 'expectancy violation theory' (Jussim et al., 1987): the applicants with Hispanic names were likely to be expected to speak with an accent; when they did not, thus violating expectations, they were viewed more positively.

Finally, there is evidence suggesting an existence of selection bias against overweight applicants, especially when the interviewers perceive the applicants' obesity as being controllable (Kutcher and Bragger, 2004). In addition, Bragger et al. (2002) indicate that pregnancy discrimination claims are the fastest growing type of employment discrimination charge.

Mini Case Study 10.1

Does your company need a highly structured interview format?

David Hill was getting tired. Having sat on Speed's interview panel conducting graduate 'milk round' interviews over the past 5 days at the company's Athens offices, he had become so accustomed to the structured format that he could completely recite the standardized questions asked of all candidates – in reverse order if needs be.

More to the point, his two line management colleagues on the interview panel had needed strict chairing throughout the interviewing process, as both had pronounced tendencies to stray away from the structured format. One in particular, John Oliver, the Director of Speed Production, could not on occasions resist the temptation of asking candidates questions on their personal and family circumstances. This was especially unfortunate, David Hill felt, given that the company had paid a firm of HRM consultants a considerable sum to introduce a highly structured interview format. Still, he mused to himself, only one more candidate to see today and they would be finished. He glanced at the clock – 5.00 pm – settled back into his chair, composed himself and enquired of his fellow panel members whether they were ready for the last interviewee.

Questions:

1. Was David Hill correct to commission a firm of HRM consultants to develop a highly structured interview format?
2. If structure is a 'good thing' in terms of improving the validity and reliability of interviews, could there be situations in which structure would be disadvantageous?
3. How should the chair of an interview panel deal with maverick interviewers who either:
   - deviate from the standardised format; or
   - ask personal or intrusive questions?

Biodata

The use of biodata for employee selection has a long history, and many researchers (for example, Ployhart et al., 2006) have concluded that biodata are one of the best selection devices for predicting employees' performance and turnover.

Biodata forms typically assess factual and sometimes also attitudinal factors that seek biographical information or assess descriptions of individuals' life histories using a retrospective, quasi-longitudinal, self-report format; they should be defined only in terms of an applicant's past behaviour and experience (Mael, 1991). These past behaviours and experiences can reflect events that have occurred in various contexts:

- a work setting (for example, quitting a job without giving notice);
- an educational setting (for example, graduating from college);
- a family environment (for example, travelling widely while growing up);
- community activities (for example, volunteering for a not-for-profit organization);
- other domains (for example, activity in local politics and religious activities, or whether the applicant knows people who work for the organization).

Biodata items are often referred to as 'hard' and 'soft' items respectively, in that the former are potentially verifiable whereas the latter are not. Finally, research suggests that biodata scales can be developed so as to be useful in different organizations since the biodata items are relevant to a given job (for example, insurance agent or supervisor) regardless of the organization. Indeed, Dalessio et al. (1996) argue that a biodata scale that has been found to be valid in one country will have value if used in other countries.

A concern that has been raised with using biodata is their adverse impact on members of protected groups (see, for example, Sharf, 1994). Drakeley (1989) also criticizes the model for being derived from work primarily involving a 'classification' of North American university students and thus not being generalizable to other populations. Given some of the items that have been used (for example, age and educational level), this concern seems appropriate. In particular, biodata items that reflect cognitive ability (such as college grade point average) are likely to result in a negative effect. As there is not a lot of research regarding adverse impact, it seems prudent for an organization to examine each biodata item it is considering using. Applicants might also be likely to react negatively to items that are perceived as lacking job-relatedness, are perceived as fakable and are perceived as overly personal in nature.

Psychometric tests

A test can be defined as a standardized measure of aptitude, knowledge, ability or performance that is administered and scored using fixed rules – most of them statistical – and procedures. All psychometric tests are scaled using a finely graded numerical system and a set of statistical formulae to ensure their reliability and validity. Most psychometric tests are also norm-referenced such that the range and distribution of scores obtained from many different types of sample provide group-specific norms against which to compare an individual's score. The scores for a managerial applicant, for example, will be examined with reference to the most closely matching set of norms (that is, managerial).

Reference to norms can also demonstrate whether the test is 'transportable' from one context to another. For example, it has only been fairly recently that UK norms for the well-known and much-used US-developed 16 Personality Factors Test (16PF) have become available. Finally, there is a variation across Europe in relation to the use of psychometrics, with Britain, Belgium and Portugal making more substantial use of the technique than Germany or Italy (Shackleton and Newell, 1997). Psychometric tests can be divided into two main categories: cognitive ability tests (CATs) and personality tests.

Cognitive ability tests Since the very earliest research on personnel selection, cognitive ability has been one of the major methods used to attempt to discriminate between candidates and to predict their subsequent performance. CATs can be classified somewhat arbitrarily into:

- achievement tests
- specific aptitude tests
- general mental ability (GMA) tests.

Achievement tests measure skills that have already been acquired and tap current knowledge or ability in a particular ability domain, usually as a function of education or training. *Aptitude tests* look at what one is capable of doing in the future, usually in specific domains such as mechanical aptitude, spatial and perceptual ability, verbal and numerical aptitude and psychomotor ability. *GMA tests* are designed to give an overview of mental capacity indicative of the individual's overall capability for acquiring and using knowledge, passing examinations and succeeding at work.

A variety of questions are included in such tests, including ones relating to vocabulary, analogies, similarities, opposites, arithmetic, number extension and general information. Many meta-analytic studies (see, for example, Schmidt and Hunter, 1998; Salgado et al., 2003) have produced conclusive results not only concerning the validity of cognitive validity, but also showing that the core dimension of cognitive ability (GMA, or 'g') is the key component in providing predictions of subsequent job performance.

The idea of using only an ability test score to select someone is nonetheless highly controversial, underpinned by moral as well as legal debate. For years, it has been consistently argued that ability-testing does not produce differentially unfair predictions for different groups of people. Recently, however, there have been findings suggesting that ability-testing is unfair to minority groups, with over 60 per cent of black individuals likely to be incorrectly rejected for a job (Chung-Yan and Cranshaw, 2002). This finding is set to cast the legal and moral debate into a completely different landscape and has prompted some to develop latent intelligence tests presented as work samples (Klingner and Schuler, 2004). These are, however, potentially costly to develop because they 'sample' work pertinent to particular occupational groups or job, but they may signal one constructive way forward on the issue of how to balance efficiency needs against legal imperatives and psychological concerns.

Moreover, some maintain that many jobs, especially managerial jobs, presuppose 'tacit' knowledge or action-oriented 'know how' rather than ability per se (Sternberg and Wagner, 1995), 'emotional intelligence' (the ability to perceive, understand and manage emotion; Goleman, 1996) and at least some level of commitment (Meyer and Allen, 1997). Reviews, however, show that tests of tacit knowledge, emotional intelligence and 'practical' intelligence do not produce better predictive or incremental validities than CATs (Salgado, 1999), indicating that they are just different ways of referring to 'job knowledge' (Schmidt and Hunter, 1993). Finally, the increased cognitive demands of today's technologically complex, fast-paced, consumer-oriented economic environment underline the fact that GMA might seriously matter to performance.

Personality inventories   Personality measures are increasingly being used by managers and human resource professionals to evaluate the suitability of job applicants for positions across many levels in an organization. There are many different types of personality measure, each assuming a certain number of traits and trait structures. Cattell's (1965) work led to the development of the now-renowned 16PF, one of the most widely used measure of personality in the occupational context. A contrary view is provided by the Eysenck Personality Questionnaire (Eysenck, 1982), which assumes a three-factor personality model: extroversion/introversion, neuroticism/stability and psychoticism.

The contemporary view is that there are five superordinate trait dimensions (the so-called 'big five', or FFM) by which all people can be described (Costa and McCrae, 1990):

- *Extroversion:* the degree to which someone is talkative, sociable, active, aggressive and excitable.
- *Agreeableness:* the degree to which someone is trusting, amiable, generous, tolerant, honest, cooperative and flexible.
- *Conscientiousness:* the degree to which someone is dependable and organized, and conforms and perseveres on tasks.
- *Emotional stability:* the degree to which someone is secure, calm, independent and autonomous.
- *Openness to experience:* the degree to which someone is intellectual, philosophical, insightful, creative, artistic and curious.

Box 10.3 provides some sample items from a personality characteristics inventory.

Until quite recently, personality was not a popular method on which to base the selection of personnel. Schmitt et al. (1984) reported very low validities for the relationship between personality and job performance, and Blinkhorn and Johnson (1990) have argued that using personality tests can delude people into assuming that these offer a comprehensive picture of a person, as well as 'overly objectifying' the person. Moreover, few would dispute the conclusion that non-work-related selection tools are relatively poor predictors of job success relative to structured interviews and ability tests and should thus be treated with caution (Robertson and Smith, 2001). However, renewed interest in personality testing and the acceptance of the FFM personality structure has led to a widespread belief and confidence that personality can play a significant role in effective personnel selection.

> **Box 10.3 Sample items from a personality characteristics inventory**
>
> *Conscientiousness*
> I can always be counted on to get the job done
> I am a very persistent worker
> I almost always plan things in advance of work
>
> *Extraversion*
> Meeting new people is enjoyable to me
> I like to stir up excitement if things get boring
> I am a 'take-charge' type of person
>
> *Agreeableness*
> I like to help others who are down on their luck
> I usually see the good side of people
> I forgive others easily
>
> *Emotional stability*
> I can become annoyed at people quite easily (reverse-scored)
> At times, I don't care about much of anything (reverse-scored)
> My feelings tend to be easily hurt (reverse-scored)
>
> *Openness to experience*
> I like to work with difficult concepts and ideas
> I enjoy trying new and different things
> I tend to enjoy art, music, or literature
>
> *Source*: Adapted from Mount and Barrick (1995: 43).

Conscientiousness is considered to be the best predictor of job performance across various performance criteria such as team performance, leadership emergence, task role behaviour, and occupational groups (Schmidt and Hunter, 1998). Ones and Viswesvaran (1998) argue that this finding is not surprising really in that a conscientious person is more likely to spend time on assigned tasks, acquire greater job knowledge, set goals autonomously and persist in achieving them, go beyond role requirements and avoid being counterproductive; however, they advocate the use of some kind of 'social desirability' screening measure in order to minimize the likelihood of distortion.

Apart from conscientiousness, the other FFM dimensions vary in their predictive effects depending on the nature of the performance criterion and the occupational group. For example, agreeableness and openness to experience are related to performance involving interpersonal skills (Nikolaou, 2003), whereas conscientiousness and extraversion predict managerial performance significantly better in jobs categorized as being high in autonomy (Barrick and Mount, 1993). Witt (2002) reported that extraversion was related to job performance when employees were also high in conscientiousness, but with employees low in conscientiousness, extraversion was negatively related to performance. Mol et al. (2005) investigated the relations between expatriate job performance and the FFM personality dimensions, and found that extraversion, emotional stability, agreeableness, and conscientiousness predicted job performance.

Finally, regarding the relationship between FFM and non-standard performance criteria, Williams (2004) found that openness to experience was significantly related to individual creativity, whereas O'Connell et al. (2001) reported a significant correlation between conscientiousness and organizational citizenship behaviours. Lin et al. (2001), investigating the relation between the FFM and customers' ratings of service quality, reported significant relationships between openness to experience and assurance behaviours, conscientiousness and reliability, extraversion and responsiveness, and agreeableness and both empathy and assurance behaviours. In addition, LePine and Van Dyne (2001) found that conscientiousness, extraversion and agreeableness were related more strongly to change-oriented communications and cooperative behaviour than to task performance. Finally, Lievens et al. (2003) found that openness to experience was significantly related to performance during crosscultural training in a sample of European expatriate managers.

The study of the impact of personality on team behaviour and performance is another area that has seen renewed activity in recent years. Overall, extraversion appears to be the best predictor of team performance (Morgeson et al., 2005), group interaction styles (Balthazard et al., 2004), oral communication (Mohammed and Angell, 2003), emerging leadership behaviour (Kickul and Neuman, 2000), task role behaviour (Stewart et al., 2005) and performance in leadership tasks (Mohammed et al., 2002). Moreover, conscientiousness and emotional stability are the two other FFM constructs found to be generally good predictors of team-related behaviour and performance (Halfhill et al., 2005).

Faking and personality assessment The most pervasive concern that human resources practitioners have regarding the use of personality testing in personnel selection is that applicants may strategically 'fake' their responses and thereby gravely reduce the usefulness of the personality scores. However, most of the research concerning the effects of impression management or intentional or unintentional distortion on the validity of personality assessment has provided results indicating that, in practical terms, there are relatively few problems (see, for example, Barrick and Mount, 1996). Intentional distortion could be minimized if applicants were warned of the consequences of such distortion. Moreover, human resources professionals should also consider incorporating the 'threat of verification' into the faking warning, as applicants may respond more honestly when they believe that their responses will be subject to verification. The threat of verification becomes even more real when accompanied by carefully developed letters of reference that may provide a valid assessment of the applicant's personality.

Finally, it may still be valuable to include 'social desirability' scales in personality instruments, even though there is now considerable evidence that they generally do not improve validity and that elevated scores on typical social desirability scales may be more a function of valid personality differences than of the motivation to fake the results (Ellingson et al., 1999).

Assessment centres

Assessment centres have recently become popular in the business sector for assessing suitability across a whole range of jobs; they mainly measure general intelligence, motivation to achieve, social competence, self-confidence and dominance. In this sense, the primary construct measured relates to the person's GMA. Assessment centres are meant to simulate the job realistically, employ a variety of techniques for eliciting evidence, assess several applicants at once on several criteria and involve several trained assessors. The rationale behind the use of an assessment centre is that an applicant who can perform a sample of the job satisfactorily can probably perform the job itself. How true this is, though, depends on the extent to which the job sample reflects the whole job.

The assessment centre is organized around behavioural dimensions identified through job analysis, and activities are chosen according to their capacity for creating a situation in which these dimensions can be demonstrated. Across Europe, there are wide differences in the use of assessment centres for selection: they are more common, particularly in large organizations, in the UK, Belgium, Denmark and Germany, and less common in France, Switzerland, Spain and Italy (Shackleton and Newell, 1997).

The types of activity involved vary considerably from one assessment centre to another. Individual activities may include psychological tests, biodata inventories and personality tests. Candidates may be asked to perform written and oral communication exercises (such as preparing written and oral reports) and undertake an in-basket exercise. An in-basket exercise requires the candidate to deal with the kind of correspondence that usually accumulates while an executive is on vacation. It contains requests, questions, directives and various pieces of information that must be handled within a specified period of time. Dyadic activities include role-playing exercises, such as how to deal with a troublesome employee or how to interview an applicant for a job, as well as group exercises including the leaderless group discussion, in which candidates work together without any assigned roles on some organizational problem.

However, Zedeck and Cascio (1984) suggest that we should question the assessment centre as a valid selection procedure as many questions have arisen over the validity and reliability of assessing specific competencies. In addition, Lievens and Klimoski (2001) argue for a need to establish the utility and cost-effectiveness of assessment centres. Finally, assessment centres may operate to maintain the status quo in managerial jobs. Individuals who might be successful on the job, yet do not resemble the present employees, can be neglected. Organizational policies and traditions in hiring and promotion may influence who is successful in the organization. If this is the case, basing assessment centres on current employees will amplify these effects.

Work samples

Work samples are said to be one of the most appropriate means of selection because of the 'point-to-point correspondence' between the job and the assessment scenario (Smith and George, 1992). It is an analogous test (as opposed to an analytical test) designed to replicate the key activities of a job. Work samples are relatively easy to construct for manual jobs, clerical jobs (for example, typing) or those involving contact with clients (for example, role-play dealing with a complaint). For more managerial/intellectual jobs, work samples may be built around specific and identifiable concrete tasks (such as writing a report or dealing with the in-basket). These can then be used to assess both performance and 'trainability' potential.

A prime example of a work sample test is the 'in-basket' exercise. One potential problem with the use of in-basket exercises, however, is the organizations' heavy reliance on 'off-the-self' packages. Moreover, just like any other test, a work sample needs to be carefully constructed and validated. The most valid work samples not only correspond with a particular task, but also capture some of its contextual features (Robertson and Kandola, 1982). A basic rule of thumb is to ensure that the work sample is as 'complex' and 'ambiguous' as the task itself; however, the downside here is that the 'sample' cannot be 'transferred' across jobs (unless jobs are similar). On the other hand, the approach provides a good source of RJP for the applicant. Porteous (1997) says that because reliable and valid work samples are time-consuming and costly to construct, administer and score, they are of most value when used in the final stages of a selection process.

Integrity and honesty tests

Integrity and honesty tests are used to predict the likelihood that the individual will engage in counterproductive behaviour such as theft, violence, excessive absenteeism and dishonesty (Hogan and Brinkmeyer, 1997). Integrity tests are more popular in the USA than in most European countries, although both US and French applicants have been found to react somewhat negatively to these tests (Steiner and Gilliland, 1996). There are three types of integrity testing:

- overt measures of integrity dealing with attitudes towards theft and other forms of dishonesty, including admissions of theft and other illegal activity;
- personality-oriented methods, which include questions on various dimensions, such as dependability, conscientiousness and social conformity;
- clinical measures such as the 'galvanic skin response', an indicator of increased physiological arousal.

There are many disagreements about the value of integrity testing, as well as about its ethical status since the construct of integrity is vague and ill-defined, and there is no compelling evidence for its criterion-related validity (Camara and Schneider, 1995). Other concerns include misclassification, high selection thresholds and the adverse impact on applicants screened out by integrity test results, coupled with the fact that anyone can use them. By contrast, Ones et al. (1995) point to good construct and criterion validities suggesting that promising results that should not be ignored.

Recruiting and selecting expatriate managers

For effective performance in overseas work assignments, many researchers have concentrated on how to prepare potential expatriates for overseas transfer. For instance, Lanier (1979) recommends seven steps to be taken in preparing personnel:

1. A well-planned, realistic pre-visit to the site (country) involved.
2. Early language training prior to departure.

3. Intensive study on issues such as history, culture and etiquette.
4. The provision of country-specific handbooks, including useful facts.
5. The efficient, explicit provision of intercompany counselling facilities.
6. Meetings with returnees to hear 'old hand' tips.
7. Notification of the personnel office and spouses' committee on arrival.

Sieveking et al. (1981) stress the importance of orientation programmes prior to expatriation, which aim to do such things as:

- develop an understanding of personal and family values so that employees can anticipate and cope with the inevitably unsettling emotions that accompany culture shock;
- develop an appreciation of the important ways in which the host culture will differ from the employee's own culture, so that the employee can guide his or her behaviour accordingly;
- show the expatriate how he or she can be rewarded in ways in addition to income and travel, such as novelty, challenge and the opportunity to learn new skills;
- help expatriates to anticipate and begin to plan for hardships, delays, frustrations, material inconveniences and the consequences of close living and working with others;
- help expatriates to anticipate that, although they may have been superior employees in their own culture, they may need to gain greater satisfaction from experiences other than those which are work-related.

In a more considered and thoughtful paper on the selection of personnel for overseas, Tung (1981) outlines a contingency approach and notes four types of factor crucial to success in foreign assignments: (1) technical competence on the job; (2) relational abilities (social skills); (3) an ability to deal with environmental constraints (government, labor issues); (4) and family situation.

Tung offers a contingency approach of coping with the process based on a sensitive selection process. A contingency framework states that there is in practice no one criterion that could be used in all situations. Rather, each assignment should be viewed on its own. In each instance, the selection of the 'right person' to fill the position should be made only after a careful analysis of:

- the task (in terms of interaction with the social community);
- the country of assignment (in terms of the degree to which it is similar or dissimilar to that of the individual's home country);
- the candidate's personality characteristics (in terms of both the candidate's and the spouse's ability to live and work in a different cultural environment) (Tung, 1981).

Mendenhall et al. (1987) indicate that that a number of authors have identified criteria that predict acculturation and productivity in overseas assignments; these can be summarised as self-orientation, others-orientation and perceptual orientation. Mendenhall et al. suggest that *self-orientation* includes factors such as stress reduction, technical competence, dealing with isolation and alienation. *Others-orientation* includes factors such as relationship skills, willingness to communicate, respect and empathy for others. *Perceptual orientation* includes factors such as flexible attributions, high tolerance for ambiguity and being open-minded and non-judgemental.

Underscoring the importance of personal characteristics, Hailey indicates that the personality and attitude of expatriates is the key to their success, suggesting that:

> those who are outgoing, relaxed, and prepared to work within the local management style are perceived to adapt more successfully, while unsurprisingly those who are inflexible, arrogant, or straight jacketed fail to adapt to the local culture. (1996: 265)

Exercise

The company in this exercise is one of the leading pharmaceutical manufacturers in the UK. Because of the intense competition in the industry and the heightened competition for highly skilled personnel, the company believes that quality of work–life balance is a key factor in achieving competitive advantage. In support of this belief, the company is considering adopting a telecommuting work arrangement for selected jobs.

The job of Public Relations (PR) Specialist has been identified as an appropriate job for telecommuting owing to the fact that its responsibilities are mostly information-related activities that require independent mental effort with no supervisory responsibilities. The current job description for the PR Specialist is shown below; this reflects the primary job activities and qualifications for a full-time, in-office PR Specialist. There is currently only one job incumbent, and that person has just resigned. You have been asked to develop a plan for recruiting and hiring a replacement who will telecommute from home.

- What method of job analysis would you recommend to determine the job requirements and job specifications for a telecommuting job? Is the method you are recommending different from the method you would use if the job were being performed in a traditional office environment?
- What procedures do you recommend for recruiting and hiring a telecommuter? Are the procedures you are recommending different from the procedures you would use if the job were being performed in a traditional office environment?
- What changes would you make to the job description below in order to reflect the telecommuting nature of the job?
- What other recommendations would you make in order to ensure the successful implementation of a telecommuting work arrangement?

Job description

Job title: Public Relations Specialist
Department: Public Relations
Reports to: Director of Public Relations
General summary: Serves as a writer on numerous publications for the firm; coordinates materials; writes, edits and proofs articles, public relations publications and advertising copy using WordPerfect software.

> *Essential job functions:*
> 1. Writes, edits and proofs public relations articles, newspaper copy and human interest stories.
> 2. Writes advertising copy in conjunction with the marketing department.
> 3. Writes, edits and coordinates the printing and layout of the company newsletter.
> 4. Meets with executives to determine PR needs.
> 5. Meets with media officials and the public to publicise the firm's accomplishments.
> 6. Attends information meetings at the main office on an as-needed basis.
> 7. Gives presentations at meetings and other public events.
> 8. Performs other related duties as assigned by management.
>
> *Education and experience required*: Degree in Art/Graphic Design; demonstrated ability to use Windows computer hardware/software; some experience in television or public speaking; considerable knowledge of journalism principles, English grammar and usage; demonstrated ability to write newspaper, news and human interest articles, reports, brochures and advertising copy; demonstrated ability to work and communicate effectively with others.

Critical summary of theories

The above literature review shows an increasing homogenization in the approaches employed to account for the phenomena currently seen in personnel recruitment and selection; these are mainly dominated by a generic focus on improving the efficiency, effectiveness and fairness of personnel management practice and by a concern with the selection–performance relationship. Performance is conceptualized in strict economic terms, thus excluding any broader moral, social and political considerations of selection practice and policy.

Moreover, such approaches (for example, the ones that try to achieve a person–organization fit) assume that all members of an organization have mutual interests and are assimilated into the prevailing socioeconomic order of capitalism. This means that organizations will try to govern the souls of employees and regulate their social behaviour by attempting to persuade them to identify with managerial objectives and the philosophy of individualism as a fundamental way of thinking and behaving in the social and organizational world. The unreflecting adoption of the scientific and rational discourse of 'objectivity', 'validity' and 'reliability' that characterizes recruitment and selection practices reinforces the use of scientific discourse and plays a decisive role in the effective management of employees' performance by persuading them of the objective and rational character of these practices. Such an approach, however, mainly ignores the fact that personnel practices are the outcome of human interpretations, conflicts and generalizations (Watson, 2004), and that employee agency, subjectivity and reflexivity lead employees to many different types of engagement with HRM practices (Zanoni and Janssens, 2007).

Finally, there has been a standardization of employee selection practices and a treatment of certain individual competencies and job characteristics as neutral (that is, as reflecting the reality of the person or the role) rather than as socially constructed or situated. Instead of limiting inequalities, this has paradoxically legitimized gendered employment practices by cloaking them in false objectivity (Özbilgin and Woodward, 2004).

Personnel selection and ethics

Karen Legge (2007) has argued that we need to consider 'moral economy', that is, what moral norms concerning the good and the just should be embodied in and guide choices and action in organizations. Moral economy implies that, instead of being preoccupied with issues of efficiency and performance in strict economic terms, we should include broader moral, social and political considerations related to the practice and policy of recruitment and selection.

First of all, personnel selection should refocus its attention on the employees themselves by considering not only individual variables such as abilities, skills and competencies, but also the political nature of the employment relationship (Janssens and Steyaert, 2009), adopting a pluralist approach to managing the employment relationship. Such an approach criticizes the belief that staffing techniques that lead to high performance are beneficial for employees and for unions that accept them, draws attention to the negative effects of such techniques (such as work intensification) and highlights the existence of continued discrimination against marginalized groups (Knights and McCabe, 1998). Moreover, the complexity of the employment relationship demands an exploration of the impact of a number of issues, such as fear of lay-offs, perceptions of job opportunities, unemployment and labour market positions, on personnel recruitment and selection; however, the interests and perspectives of multiple stakeholders (including employees) must not be ignored.

Furthermore, the quantitative techniques involved in recruitment and selection procedures are methods that create a technical-scientific order in which the technical is superimposed on the moral and constructs a rational, goal-directed image of organizational effectiveness. Consequently, the management of personnel staffing concerns itself with the technical application of techniques even where circumstances may indicate that these might not be the most appropriate responses.

Finally, we need to ensure that the voices of those who tend to be excluded from mainstream analyses are better represented in the theory and practice of recruitment and selection. This includes, but is not limited to, those in non-standard forms of employment, minority workers and those working outside Western industrialized economies.

Critical analysis and discussion

The formalization part of the personnel selection agenda reinforces an image of the work organization as a black-box system that functions more or less well in performance terms according to the neutral, scientific and formal, rational procedures that convert human resource 'inputs' into outputs. Consequently, the objectives pursued by the implementation of such procedures (that is, a maximization of efficiency and effectiveness) should be of benefit to all concerned – managers, employees, government and 'the public' alike. However, it is rare for such 'best practices' to be subjected to any critical analysis of the potential 'operating' costs, the 'unintended consequences' or – more graphically – the 'collateral damage' resulting from their introduction. What is 'good' for business is not necessarily 'best practice' for employees. In this respect, it is important to note that such procedures are never neutral: they always implicate and privilege particular social values, if not also specific socioeconomic interests.

Moreover, the mainstream analysis of personnel selection processes and procedures is based on a unitarist approach – one in which all members of an organization are assumed to have mutual interests. In practice, however, recruitment and selection practices seem to be enacted by both candidates and selectors within organizations. If we take into account concepts such as agency and subjectivity, and recognize employees as human beings capable of reflexive thought and action (Giddens, 1993), there is a possibility that different employees actively engage in different ways with recruitment and selection practices, undermining, delaying or supporting their implementation. On the other hand, selectors do not simply adopt the 'scientific' and rational principles of the practices, but appear to manipulate them according to pre-existing local power relations, since the design of such practices is 'mediated' by managerial interpretation and political manoeuvring (Watson, 2004). One should not ignore the fact that human resources strategies are the outcomes of human interpretations, conflicts, guesses and rationalizations, albeit those of human agency operating within a context of social and political-economic circumstances.

Finally, a significant consequence of the ever-increasing emphasis on the human resources–performance link has been the progressive exclusion of more and more alternative voices, as well as practices that do not necessary promote high commitment and high performance (MacDuffie, 1995). Hence, the problems and issues of personnel selection have largely been ignored in small and medium-sized organizations (see, for example, Taylor, 2004), in various forms of subcontracting designed to increase 'flexibility' through the creation of 'dependent self-employment' (Muehlberger, 2007); there is little specific reference to unionized workplaces or to the increasing problems associated with (and for) immigrant labour, as well as employees in non-Western and so-called developing economies. Similarly, the increasing resort to outsourcing work to countries where labour is cheaper is excluded from the mainstream 'recruitment and selection agenda'. The irony here, of course, is that most of these social practices can be seen as reflecting the 'success' of the globalization project as they can all be seen to be symptoms of the successful deregulation of labour markets, which is a central element of the neo-liberal policy agenda.

Benefits of studying HRM from a critical perspective

A critical perspective is advanced here in order for personnel recruitment and selection practices to be better contextualized within the prevailing socioeconomic, political and cultural factors that shape those practices. In addition, the aim is that the scientific, objective and rational assumptions and language of recruitment and selection may be challenged, and that voices excluded from mainstream personnel selection may be heard. The adoption of a pluralist frame of reference, in which the employment relationship is understood to involve and articulate different interests, has the potential to reintroduce the possible contribution of those 'external' to the organization, such as the state or trade unions, as significant actors in devising selection policies and practices. Such an approach will force selection specialists to consider possible ways of managing the endemic potential conflicts associated with such differential interests.

Moreover, the deconstruction of the natural and neutral language of science, rationality and objectivity that is used to legitimize 'reliable' and 'valid' recruitment and selection procedures might expose the institutionalized power inequalities, as well as the local power relations within organizations that reinforce, but also impede, the implementation of these procedures in practice. A critical perspective directs us towards an analysis of the contextual circumstances in which certain practices are, or are not, adopted by management.

This is perhaps most clearly evident in another aspect of denaturalization: the concern of critical approaches to reveal how the content of knowledge and the individual skills and ability profiles identified as being central or critical to making good selection decisions are understood as relatively neutral and are treated as largely reflecting the reality of the role or the person. Viewing competencies as individual-level attributes deflects attention away from how their meaning is socially constructed in specific contexts. By treating individual skills and job characteristics as neutral rather than as socially constructed or situated, we are in danger of either privileging certain modes of performance or reproducing the idea that different groups are naturally suited to some roles rather than others; this then undermines the chances of achieving equal opportunities. Consequently, recruitment and selection would benefit from the adoption of a critical perspective as it can offer additional insights into how roles, identities and individual competencies are socially constructed and identify the implications of these processes for selection and recruitment.

Finally, a critical perspective will provide a voice for all those marginalized from mainstream personnel recruitment and from research into and the practice of selection. These include, for example, employees of the following: large multinational corporations, non-Western and so-called developing economies, small and medium-sized enterprises, public and third-sector organizations, alternative forms of organization (for example, cooperatives) and non-standard forms of employment. It will also encompass those who are self-employed, subcontractors, part-time and agency workers, and immigrant labour, among others. Such a focus will enhance our understanding of what is happening to employment regulation outside large and multinational corporations.

In short, Boxall et al. (2007) argue that a critical perspective on HRM should be concerned with why management does what it does; with how contextualized processes of HRM work in practice; and with questions of 'for whom and how well' when assessing the outcomes of HRM, taking account of both employee and managerial interests, and laying a basis for theories of wider social consequence.

Conclusion

Employee staffing decisions involving the recruitment and selection of individuals are made every day in work organizations. There has been a tendency for a rational and scientific technology to be applied to these personnel choices. This involves strongly formalized procedures and the heavy use of such devices as psychological tests. Such technology is intended to help select individuals in a way that will be deemed efficient, acceptable and fair.

However, this approach tends to become restrictive and counterproductive. Its use can be associated with a controlling way of thinking about work organizations and people. A more realistic and critical way of thinking indicates that selection processes are highly ambiguous and are dependent on basic human processes of judgement, guesswork, chance-taking, debate and negotiation. Selection processes in general are better seen as parts of broader and more continuous processes of bargaining and adjustment in which both organizational arrangements and human beings themselves change and adapt within the ongoing negotiated order of the organization.

FOR DISCUSSION AND REVISION

1. If you had entered into a joint venture with a foreign company but knew that women were not treated fairly in that culture, would you consider sending a female expatriate to handle the start-up? Why or why not?
2. Evaluation hiring is a procedure in which a job candidate is hired by a staffing company but put to work at another company. After a set period of time (usually 90 days), the company decides whether to hire the person as a permanent employee. Analyse the benefits for the company that arise from using such a procedure. What ethical issues are involved in evaluation hiring?
3. Should applicants be selected primarily on the basis of their ability or on personality/fit? How can fit be assessed?
4. You work for a medium-sized, high-tech firm that faces intense competition on a daily basis. Change seems to be the only constant in your workplace, and each worker's responsibilities shift from project to project. Suppose you have the major responsibility for filling the job openings at your company. How would you go about recruiting and selecting the best people? How would you identify the best people to work in this environment?
5. In many organizations that have worked to a team structure, the team is the principal unit where the work gets done. However, most organizations recruit and hire as though there were one job description and the team did not exist. If there are distinct roles to be played within a team, how would you go about recruiting and hiring for them? The characteristics needed by individual team members depend on the team and the strengths and weaknesses of other team members. How could you include this dynamic and interactive nature in the recruitment and hiring process?

6. One of the strategic staffing choices is whether to pursue workforce diversity actively or passively. First suggest some ethical reasons for an active pursuit of diversity, and then suggest some ethical reasons for a more passive approach. Assume that the type of diversity in question is an increasing representation of women and ethnic minorities in the workforce.
7. Why is it important for the organization to view all components of staffing from the perspective of the job applicant?
8. Assume that the organization you work for practises strict adherence to the rules of objective, scientific and rational recruitment and selection. But beyond that, it seems that 'anything goes' in terms of tolerated staffing practices. What is your assessment of this approach?
9. Do you think that targeted recruitment systems, for example those targeting older workers, women, minority groups or people with the desired skills, are fair? Why or why not?
10. Cognitive ability tests are one of the best predictors of job performance, yet they have a substantial adverse impact on minority groups. Do you think it is fair to use such tests? Why or why not?
11. Do you think it is ethical for employers to select applicants on the basis of questions such as 'Dislike loud music' and 'Enjoy travelling around the world with a backpack' even if the scales that such items measure have been shown to predict job performance? Explain your answer.
12. Given recent changes in the nature of work, especially during the period of economic turbulence, discuss the relative effectiveness of job analysis techniques and suggest how they might be improved.
13. Suppose that you are asked to write a recommendation letter for a friend you like but consider unreliable. Would it be ethical for you to write a positive reference even though you anticipate that your friend will not be a good employee? If not, would it be ethical for you to agree to write the letter knowing that you will not be very positive in your assessment of your friend's abilities?

Further reading

Books

Bolton, S. C. and Houlihan, M. (2007) *Searching for the Human in Human Resource Management*. London: Palgrave Macmillan.

Boxall, P., Purcell, J. and Wright, P. (2007) *The Oxford Handbook of Human Resource Management*. Oxford: Oxford University Press.

Grey, C. and Willmott, H. (2005) *Critical Management Studies: A Reader*. Oxford: Oxford University Press.

Legge, K. (1995) *Human Resource Management: Rhetorics and Realities*. London: Palgrave Macmillan.

Leopold, J., Harris, L. and Watson, T. J. (2005) *The Strategic Management of Human Resources*. London: FT Prentice Hall.

Pinnington, A., Macklin, R. and Campbell, T. (2007) *Human Resource Management: Ethics and Employment*. Oxford: Oxford University Press.

CASE STUDY

The design of a new multinational personnel selection system at MobilCom

On Monday morning at 7.30 am, Dr Hans was leaving his apartment, one specifically rented to expatriates, and was heading towards his office in Kuala Lumpur's central business district. On the way, he listened to the voice messages on his mobile phone, one of which was from the assistant of the firm's owner, Frank. The message stated that Hans was expected to call back before his meeting with the human resources (HR) team that he was leading. The team meeting was scheduled in order to bring together Hans and Chinese HR experts to form a crossfunctional project team responsible for the development and implementation of a new personnel process within the context of global restructuring, in order to fill 25 middle management positions in the Australasia region.

According to the in-house global localization policy of the company, MobilCom, 90 per cent of the new management positions were to be filled by individuals originating from the country they would be working in. The affected areas included sales and marketing, purchasing, supply chain management, and finance and accounting, at locations in Hong Kong, Kuala Lumpur, Bangkok, Jakarta, Singapore, Sydney, Oakland and Port Moresby (Papua New Guinea). The new personnel selection system was part of the company's new objective to standardize all HR instruments for selection purposes around the globe. This new personnel selection system had to be developed internally.

When Hans first heard about the above changes, it immediately occurred to him that this would not be easy as personnel selection procedures varied significantly between countries. He also knew that the existing selection instruments were by no means flawless in any specific country. After the application documents had been analysed, structured interviews with the candidates were conducted by a department representative and an HR specialist. If both interviewers came to a positive conclusion on the candidate's qualifications, the top candidates were sent to an individual assessment centre in order to highlight their interpersonal competencies rather than their professional competencies. The approach of the individual assessment centres consisted of biographical questions, case studies on leadership in an international context and participation in a leaderless group discussion. Ultimately, additional references were obtained for each candidate, although different procedures existed in different countries. After the reference checks had been completed, each candidate received written feedback, and a report was generated and added to the successful candidate's personnel file.

For several years now, Hans had been finding faults in the design of the procedures used at the individual assessment centres, but he could not influence possible modifications because the individual assessment centres were run by external consulting firms. In addition, he had been questioning the validity of the information obtained from the centres, as well as the selection system as a whole. He felt there was a need to improve the contents of the structured interviews that were based on the candidate's current situation, as opposed to the candidate's previous work experience. Overall, efforts to improve the current selection systems had only rarely been undertaken owing to limited time and a limit budget allotted for personnel affairs – a fact that Hans had already pointed out to management several times.

The development of a new multinational personnel selection system now posed a huge challenge for Hans and his project team. His team, comprising Australian and

Chinese members with HR knowledge as well as HR managers from headquarters, had already been working on the development of the new personnel selection system for 4 months. Over the past few weeks, numerous meetings had been held, yet no significant progress had been made. One reason could be the fact that there was obvious heterogeneity between the opinions of the Australian and Asian team members regarding the new personnel selection system. This created a tense atmosphere and dissent with respect to sharing the workload. The goal of today's meeting was to come to a consensus on several important issues:

- what individual modules the new personnel selection system should contain;
- whether country-specific adaptations were necessary and feasible for each module;
- the implementation process of the new personnel instrument at each location.

When Hans arrived at his office, one of the three Chinese secretaries reminded him that Frank was waiting for him to return his call. She avoided eye contact by looking down to the floor, but with a big smile and gestures that appeared submissive as she perpetually nodded her head. Hans rang Frank, and Frank began speaking:

> Dr Hans, you know how much I appreciate your dedication to the company, but I have concerns about the current international selection procedures. We need something that is going to work, and work immediately! And don't you dare try to offer me this empirical or validity stuff. I don't give a damn. You have a whole department with highly qualified people. I assume you are capable of filling these vacant management positions. We also need a selection system that works everywhere. We cannot afford to apply different procedures in every country. What we need are consistent procedures, something applicable crossnationally and cross-regionally. You, as a cosmopolitan man, should know exactly what I mean. I also expect everything to be documented in complete detail.

Although Hans shared Frank's enthusiasm for an improved personnel selection system, there were many complications that could arise; Frank seemed completely unaware of these, and Hans tried to inform him about the possible problems. Hans argued that although a multinational selection system would have its advantages, these advantages might become costly if they could not easily be implemented in each region. Each country has its own unique economic and education situations, which would undoubtedly cause difficulties when creating a universal personnel selection system. With respect to cultural difference, he argued that a standardized personnel selection system would also ignore cultural differences and culture-specific circumstances. This would affect not only individual modules in the system, but also the basic job requirements, the adaptation of modules to specific countries, and the use of specific selection methods. Hans also expressed his concern with Frank's lack of interest in testing the validity of the new selection procedures.

Of course, that wasn't exactly what Frank wanted to hear:

> Don't tell me about problems; I want solutions. And you should not forget that this is what I pay you and your team to do. You have until the end of this week to deliver the final and written conclusions on this matter. If not, I will reduce your team in

Kuala Lumpur by half, and I will delegate the development of this new system to global headquarters. Either you come up with something useful by the end of this week, or central headquarters will do the job. End of discussion.

The team meeting

At the meeting, Hans informed everyone about the current situation with Frank, set the objectives of the meeting and asked for the detailed recording of everything they discussed. The Chinese colleagues agreed by nodding their heads uniformly, a behaviour that was always expected when there was an order from a member with higher hierarchical status, whereas the Australian colleagues openly disapproved the detailed recording of the discussions.

During the meeting, there was an apparent disagreement between a Chinese HR employee and the Australian economist regarding the definitions of the job requirements and their profiles. Yu wanted to include 15 dimensions – five components that tested the candidate's professional competencies and 10 dimensions that evaluated social competencies. However, Andreas openly disagreed with this proposition, stating: 'I have told you many times that the acquisition of 15 dimensions is simply impossible. It is important to define clearly distinguishable job requirements that are measurable, describable and equally relevant in all countries in the region'.

Yu, intimidated by her Australian colleague's manner, blushed and looked down towards the floor, signalling that she did not dare to say anything further. She often found it difficult to cope with negative feedback, particularly when it occurred in front of her colleagues. There had been several times already when she had not been able to stand up to Andreas, which seemed to affect her more and more each time. She had once spoken to Hans about her difficulties communicating with Andreas; however, Hans was quickly irritated by the complaint and asked her to wait and hope for an improvement in the situation. Yu never discussed the situation with Hans again.

The German in-house psychologist intervened in the discussion and proposed the inclusion of six competencies – technical and vocational skills, social competencies, leadership competencies, communicative competencies, flexibility, and adaptability – that showed great validity and reliability. There was disagreement from some Chinese members, who proposed the inclusion of several more and different competencies, which ended with them feeling irritated and intimidated. Andreas proposed that, due to the time pressure, they should bring a majority vote with respect to the skills, but the Chinese HR member argued: 'No, a majority vote is not the solution. It may lead to good decisions not succeeding because certain team members follow the uniform opinion of the majority. We should try to reach a consensus on this issue.' The dispute was solved by Hans, who decided which would be the final job requirements for selecting the managers, and who adopted the six dimensions proposed by the German team members.

The next important issue on the agenda was to define the modules and the job requirements for each module. For this issue, there was agreement that a multinational selection system should be two-tiered. The first tier would consist of three modules: viewing the candidates' application documents, a telephone conference with the applicants that should be conducted in an unstructured manner, and obtaining three references from former employers. Unlike the current procedures, references should not only be used to verify the past employment and duration of employment, but also include a statement regarding the candidate's personality. Four modules would follow in the second tier – a panel interview, a biography-oriented in-depth interview, a simulated group exercise and testing procedures. All the modules were described in great detail, and emphasis was placed on including standardized tests in order to increase the validity of the entire process, even though there is evidence that intelligence and personality tests are not generally highly accepted and that cultural problems exist.

Towards the end of the long and detailed presentation of the modules, Hans's colleague Anne, who held a MBA degree from one of the major Australian business schools, interrupted: 'I don't want to be rude, but isn't it important to take the candidate's perspective into consideration, as well?' But Andreas countered: 'Unfortunately, nobody cares about the candidate's perspective. We are interested in choosing the right person, certainly not in satisfying the applicants – these never-ending discussions on fairness and acceptance. Reality differs significantly from the ideal procedures we are taught in university.'

Now, Angela jumped into the discussion:

> But let's not forget that management is not just a technical matter, and sometimes, if you find someone generally useful, then you could adapt the job to fit the person. The selection process is always a sort of negotiation between the potential employee and the potential employer. We, as recruiters, cannot really know what any of these people are really going to be like if you take them on. Therefore, we need to deploy the basic human skills of eliciting helpful responses from people and judging the likelihood of one person being a better bet for the organization than another. In this sense, there is no 'right person', there is only 'the better bet'. Some of the most important determinants of how well someone does the job are ones that arise after the appointment of the individual.

Hans could not stand any further disputes at the time and took the initiative to terminate the long meeting, which had at least achieved the first step towards specifying the modules in terms of content and procedures. However, they had not been able to specify the adaptations for each target country and the ways of implementing those modules. Hans thought that he should make the decisions himself and then include them in the report to be handed to Frank.

Right after the meeting, Hans went straight to his office and did not come out again for the rest of the afternoon. As soon as he had received the minutes of the meeting, he wrote his final report for Frank. He later received a short notice sent by Frank, informing him that important basic conditions and necessary adaptations had not sufficiently been taken into consideration in the new multinational personnel selection system; therefore, he had handed the case over to global headquarters. Finally, he stated that there would be staff-related consequences for Hans's department in Kuala Lumpur.

Questions

1. Describe in detail all the modules included in the two-tiered selection system proposed by the team.
2. What is the critical analysis of the case study?

References

Anderson, N. (2001) Towards a theory of socialization impact: selection as pre-entry socialization. *International Journal of Selection and Assessment*, 9(1/2): 84–91.

Balthazard, P., Potter, R. E. and Warren, J. (2004) Expertise, extraversion and group interaction styles as performance indicators in virtual teams. *Database for Advances in Information Systems*, 35(1): 41–64.

Barrick, M. R. and Mount, M. K. (1993) Autonomy as a moderator of the relationship between the Big Five personality dimensions and job performance. *Journal of Applied Psychology*, 78(1): 111–18.

Barrick, M. R. and Mount, M. K. (1996) Effects of impression management and self-deception on the predictive validity of personality constructs. *Journal of Applied Psychology*, 81: 261–72.

Bevelander, P. (1999) The employment integration of migrants in Sweden. *Journal of Ethnic and Migration Studies*, 25(3): 445–68.

Blinkhorn, S. and Johnson, C. (1990) The insignificance of personality testing. *Nature*, 348: 671–2.

Boswell, W. R., Roehling, M. V., LePine, M. A. and Moynihan, L. M. (2003) Individual job-choice decisions and the impact of job attributes and recruitment practices: a longitudinal field study. *Human Resource Management*, 42: 23–37.

Boxall, P., Purcell, J. and Wright, P. (2007) Human resource management: scope, analysis, and significance. In Boxall, P., Purcell, J. and Wright, P. (eds), *The Oxford Handbook of Human Resource Management*. Oxford: Oxford University Press, pp. 1–16.

Bragger, J. D., Kutcher, E., Morgan, J. and Firth, P. (2002) The effects of the structured interview on reducing biases against pregnant job applicants. *Sex Roles*, 46: 215–26.

Breaugh, J. A., Macan, T. H. and Grambow, D. M. (2008) Employee recruitment: current knowledge and directions for future research. In Hodgkinson, G. P. and Ford, J. K. (eds), *International Review of Industrial and Organizational Psychology*, Vol. 23. New York: John Wiley & Sons, pp. 45–82.

Brtek, M. D. and Motowidlo, S. J. (2002) Effects of procedure and outcome accountability on interview validity. *Journal of Applied Psychology*, 87(1): 185–91.

Buckley, M. R., Jackson, K. A., Bolino, M. C., Veres, J. G. III and Field, H. S. (2007) The influence of relational demography on panel interview ratings: a field experiment. *Personnel Psychology*, 60: 627–46.

Caligiuri, P. M. and Phillips, J. M. (2003) An application of self-assessment realistic job previews to expatriate assignments. *International Journal of Human Resource Management*, 14: 1102–16.

Camara, W. J. and Schneider, D. L. (1995) Questions of construct breadth and openness of research in integrity testing. *American Psychologist*, 50: 459–60.

Cascio, W. F. (1995) Whither industrial and organizational psychology in a changing world of work. *American Psychologist*, 50(11): 928–39.

Cattell, R. B. (1965) *The Scientific Analysis of Personality*. Harmondsworth: Penguin.

Chapman, D. S., Uggerslev, K. L., Carroll, S. A., Piasentin, K. A. and Jones, D. A. (2005) Applicant attraction to organizations and job choice: a meta-analytic review of the correlates of recruiting outcomes. *Journal of Applied Psychology*, 90: 928–44.

Chung-Yan, G. A. and Cranshaw, S. F. (2002) A critical re-examination and analysis of cognitive ability tests using the Thorndike model of fairness. *Journal of Occupational and Organisational Psychology*, 75(4): 489–509.

Conway, J. M., Jako, R. A. and Goodman, D. F. (1995) A meta-analysis of interrater and internal consistency reliability of selection interviews. *Journal of Applied Psychology*, 80: 565–79.

Costa, P. T. Jr and McCrae, R. R. (1990) *The NEO Personality Inventory Manual*. Odessa, FL: Psychological Assessment Resources.

Dalessio, A. T., Crosby, M. and McManus, M. A. (1996) Stability of biodata keys and dimensions across English-speaking countries: a test of the cross-situational hypothesis. *Journal of Business and Psychology*, 10: 289–96.

Dipboye, R. L., Wooten, K. and Halverson, S. K. (2004) Behavioral and situational interviews. In Thomas, J. C. (ed.), *Comprehensive Handbook of Psychological Assessment*, Vol. 4, *Industrial and Organizational Assessment*. Hoboken, NJ: John Wiley & Sons, pp. 297–316.

Drakeley, R. J. (1989) Biographical data. In Herriot, P. (ed.) *Handbook of Assessment in Organizations*. Chichester: Wiley, pp. 439–53.

Dunning, D. (2007) Prediction: the inside view. In Kruglanski, A. W. and Higgings, E. T. (eds), *Social Psychology: A Handbook of Basic Principles*. New York: Guilford Press, pp. 69–90.

Earl, J., Bright, J. E. and Adams, A. (1998) 'In my opinion': what gets graduates resumes short-listed? *Australian Journal of Career Development*, 7: 15–19.

Ellingson, J. E., Sackett, P. R. and Hough, L. M. (1999) Social desirability corrections in personality measurement: issues of applicant comparison and construct validity. *Journal of Applied Psychology*, 84: 155–66.

Eysenck, M. W. (1982) *Attention and Arousal*. New York: Springer-Verlag.

Frazer, R. A. and Wiersma, U. J. (2001) Prejudice versus discrimination in the employment interview: we may hire equally, but our memories harbour prejudices. *Human Relations*, 54: 173–91.

Giddens, A. (1993) *The Constitution of Society: Outline of the Theory of Structuration*. Cambridge: Polity Press.

Goleman, D. (1996) *Emotional Intelligence*. New York: Bantam Books.

Guion, R. M. (1998) *Assessment, Measurement and Prediction for Personnel Decisions*. Mahwah, NJ: Lawrence Erlbaum.

Hailey, J. (1996) The expatriate myth: cross-cultural perceptions of expatriate managers. *International Executive*, 38(2): 255–71.

Halfhill, T., Nielsen, T. M., Sundstrom, E. and Weilbaecher, A. (2005) Group personality composition and performance in military service teams. *Military Psychology*, 17(1): 41–54.

Herriott, P. (2003) Assessment by groups: can value be added? *European Journal of Work and Organizational Psychology*, 12(2): 131–45.

Hogan, J. and Brinkmeyer, K. (1997) Bridging the gap between overt and personality-based integrity tests. *Personnel Psychology*, 50: 587–600.

Hough, L. A. and Oswald, F. L. (2000) Personnel selection: looking toward the future – remembering the past. *Annual Review of Psychology*, 51: 631–64.

Janssens, M. and Steyaert, C. (2009) HRM and performance: a plea for reflexivity in HRM studies. *Journal of Management Studies*, 46(1): 143–55.

Janz, T. (1982) Initial comparisons of patterned behaviour description interviews versus unstructured interviews. *Journal of Applied Psychology*, 67: 577–80.

Jussim, L., Coleman, L. M. and Learch, L. (1987) The nature of stereotypes: a comparison and integration of three theories. *Journal of Personality and Social Psychology*, 52: 536–46.

Kickul, J. and Neuman, G. (2000) Emergent leadership behaviors: the function of personality and cognitive ability in determining teamwork performance and KSAs. *Journal of Business and Psychology*, 15(1): 27–51.

Klingner, Y. and Schuler, H. (2004) Improving participants' evaluations while maintaining validity by a work sample-intelligence test hybrid. *International Journal of Selection and Assessment*, 12(1–2): 120–34.

Knights, D. and McCabe, D. (1998) The times they are a changin'? Transformative organizational innovations in financial services in the UK. *International Journal of Human Resource Management*, 9: 168–84.

Knights, D. and Raffo, C. (1990) Milk round professionalism in personnel recruitment: myth or reality? *Personnel Review*, 19: 28–37.

Kruglanski, A. W. and Sleeth-Keppler, D. (2007) The principles of social judgment. In Kruglanski, A. W. and Higgings, E. T. (eds), *Social Psychology: A Handbook of Basic Principles*. New York: Guilford Press, pp. 116–37.

Kutcher, E. J. and Bragger, J. D. (2004) Selection interviews of overweight job applicants: can structure reduce the bias? *Journal of Applied Social Psychology*, 34: 1993–2022.

Lanier, A. R. (1979) Selecting and preparing personnel for overseas transfer. *Personnel Journal*, 58: 160–3.

Latham, G. P. and Saari, L. M. (1984) Do people do what they say? Further studies on the situational interview. *Journal of Applied Psychology*, 69: 569–73.

Legge, K. (2007) Putting the missing H into HRM: the case of the flexible organisation. In Bolton, S. C. and Houlihan, M. (eds), *Searching for the Human in Human Resource Management*. London: Palgrave Macmillan, pp 115–36.

LePine, J. A. and Van Dyne, L. (2001) Voice and cooperative behavior as contrasting forms of contextual performance: evidence of differential relationships with big five personality characteristics and cognitive ability. *Journal of Applied Psychology*, 86(2): 326–36.

Lievens, F. and De Paepe, A. (2004) An empirical investigation of interviewer-related factors that discourage the use of high structure interviews. *Journal of Organizational Behavior*, 25: 29–46.

Lievens, F. and Klimoski, R. J. (2001) Understanding the assessment centre process: where are we now? *International Review of Industrial and Organizational Psychology*, 16: 245–86.

Lievens, F., Harris, M. M., Van Keer, E. and Bisqueret, C. (2003) Predicting cross-cultural training performance: the validity of personality, cognitive ability, and dimensions measured by an assessment center and a behavior description interview. *Journal of Applied Psychology*, 88(3): 476–86.

Lin, N.-P., Chiu, H.-C. and Hsieh, Y.-C. (2001) Investigating the relationship between service providers' personality and customers' perceptions of service quality across gender. *Total Quality Management*, 12(1): 57–67.

McDaniel, M. A., Whetzel, D. L., Schmidt, F. L. and Maurer, S. (1994) The validity of employment interviews: a comprehensive review and meta-analysis. *Journal of Applied Psychology*, 79: 599–616.

MacDuffie, J. P. (1995) Human resource bundles and manufacturing performance: organizational logic and flexible production systems in the world auto industry. *Industrial and Labor Relations Review*, 48(2): 197–221.

McFarland, L. A., Ryan, A. M., Sacco, J. M. and Krista, S. D. (2004) Examination of structured interview ratings across time: the effects of applicant race, rater race, and panel composition. *Journal of Management*, 30: 435–52.

Mael, F. A. (1991) A conceptual rationale for the domain and attributes of biodata items. *Personnel Psychology*, 44: 763–92.

Mendenhall, M., Dunbar, E. and Oddu, G. (1987) Expatriate selection, training and career pathing: a review critique. *Human Resource Management*, 26(3): 331–45.

Meyer, J. P. and Allen, N. J. (1997) *Commitment in the Workplace: Theory, Research and Application*. Thousand Oaks, CA: Sage.

Mohammed, S. and Angell, L. C. (2003) Personality heterogeneity in teams: which differences make a difference for team performance? *Small Group Research*, 34(6): 651–77.

Mohammed, S., Mathieu, J. E. and Bartlett, A. L. (2002) Technical–administrative task performance, leadership task performance, and contextual performance: considering the influence of team- and task-related composition variables. *Journal of Organizational Behavior*, 23(7): 795–814.

Mol, S. T., Born, M. P., Willemsen, M. E. and Van Der Molen, H. T. (2005) Predicting expatriate job performance for selection purposes: a quantitative review. *Journal of Cross-Cultural Psychology*, 36(5): 590–620.

Morgeson, F. P., Reider, M. H. and Campion, M. A. (2005) Selecting individuals in team settings: the importance of social skills, personality characteristics, and team work knowledge. *Personnel Psychology*, 58(3): 583–611.

Mount, M. K. and Barrick, M. R. (1995) *Manual for Personal Characteristics Inventory*. Livertyvill: Wonderlic Personnel Test.

Mount, M. K., Barrick, M. R. and Strauss, J. P. (1994) The joint relationship of conscientiousness and ability with performance: test of the interaction hypothesis. *Journal of Management*, 25: 707–21.

Muehlberger, U. (2007) *Dependent Self-employment: Workers on the Border Between Employment and Self-employment*. Basingstoke: Palgrave Macmillan.

Nikolaou, I. (2003) Fitting the person to the organisation: examining the personality – job performance relationship from a new perspective. *Journal of Managerial Psychology*, 18(7/8): 639–48.

O'Connell, M. S., Doverspike, D., Norris-Watts, C. and Hattrup, K. (2001) Predictors of organizational citizenship behavior among Mexican retail salespeople. *International Journal of Organizational Analysis*, 9(3): 272–80.

Ones, D. S. and Viswesvaran, C. (1998) The effects of social desirability and faking on personality and integrity assessment for personnel selection. *Human Performance*, 11: 245–69.

Ones, D. S., Viswesvaran, C. and Schmidt, F. L. (1995) Integrity tests: overlooked facts, resolved issues, and remaining questions. *American Psychologist*, 50(6): 456–57.

Özbilgin, M. and Woodward, D. (2004) Belonging and otherness: sex equality in banking in Turkey and Britain. *Gender, Work and Organization*, 11(6): 668–88.

Ployhart, R. E., Schneider, B. and Schmitt, N. (2006) *Staffing Organizations: Contemporary Practice and Theory* (3rd edn). Mahwah, NJ: Lawrence Erlbaum.

Porteous, M. (1997) *Occupational Psychology*. London: Prentice Hall.

Purkiss, S. L., Segrest, W. L., Perrewe, P. L., Gillespie, T. L., Mayes, B. T. and Ferris, G. R. (2006) Implicit sources of bias in employment interview judgments and decisions. *Organizational Behavior and Human Decision Processes*, 101: 152–67.

Robertson, I. T. and Kandola, R. S. (1982). Work sample tests: validity, adverse impact, and applicant reaction. *Journal of Occupational Psychology*, 55: 171–83.

Robertson, I. T. and Smith, M. (2001) Personnel selection. *Journal of Occupational and Organizational Psychology*, 74: 441–72.

Rynes, S. L. and Cable, D. M. (2003) Recruitment research in the twenty-first century. In Borman, W. C., Ilgen, D. R. and Klimoski, R. J. (eds), *Handbook of Psychology: Industrial and Organizational Psychology*, Vol. 12. Hoboken, NJ: John Wiley & Sons, pp. 55–76.

Rynes, S. L., Bretz, R. D. Jr and Gerhart, B. (1991) The importance of recruitment in job choice: a different way of looking. *Personnel Psychology*, 44: 487–521.

Salgado, J. F. (1999) Personnel selection methods. In Cooper, C. L. and Robertson, I. T. (eds), *International Review of Industrial and Organizational Psychology*, Vol. 14. Chichester: Wiley, pp. 1–54.

Salgado, J. F., Anderson, N., Moscoso, S., Bertua, C., De Fruyt, F. and Rolland, J. P. (2003) A meta-analytic study of general mental ability validity for different occupations in the European Community. *Journal of Applied Psychology*, 88(6): 176–84.

Schmeichel, B. J. and Vohs, K. D. (2009) Self-affirmation and self-control: affirming core values counteracts ego depletion. *Journal of Personality and Social Psychology*, 96(4): 770–82.

Schmidt, F. L. and Hunter, J. E. (1993) Development of causal models of processes determining job performance. *Current Directions in Psychological Science*, 1: 89–92.

Schmidt, F. L. and Hunter, J. E. (1998) The validity and utility of selection methods in personnel psychology: practice and theoretical implications of 85 years of research findings. *Psychological Bulletin*, 124(2): 262–74.

Schmitt, N., Gooding, R. Z., Noe, R. A. and Kirsch, M. (1984) Meta-analyses of validity studies. *Journal of Applied Psychology*, 70: 280–9.

Shackleton, V. and Newell, S. (1997) International assessment and selection. In Anderson, N. and Herriot, P. (eds), *International Handbook of Selection and Assessment*. Chichester: Wiley, pp. 81–95.

Sharf, J. C. (1994) The impact of legal and equal employment opportunity issues on personal history inquiries. In Stokes, G. A., Mumford, M. D. and Owens, W. A. (eds), *Biodata Handbook*. Palo Alto, CA: Consulting Psychologists Press, pp. 351–90.

Sieveking, N., Anchor, B. and Marston, R. (1981) Selecting and preparing expatriate employees. *Personnel Journal*, 18: 197–202.

Smith, M. and George, D. (1992) Selection methods. In Cooper, C. L. and Robertson, I. T. (eds), *International Review of Industrial and Organizational Psychology*, Vol. 7. Chichester: Wiley, pp. 55–97.

Steiner, D. D. and Gilliland, S. W. (1996) Fairness reactions to personnel selection techniques in France and the United States. *Journal of Applied Psychology*, 81: 134–41.

Sternberg, R. J. and Wagner, R. K. (1995) *Practical Intelligence in Everyday Life*. Cambridge: Cambridge University Press.

Stewart, G. L., Fulmer, I. S. and Barrick, M. R. (2005) An exploration of member roles as a multilevel linking mechanism for individual traits and team outcomes. *Personnel Psychology*, 58(2): 343–65.

Stone, D. L. and Stone-Romero, E. F. (2004) The influence of culture on role-taking in culturally diverse organizations. In Stockdale, M. S. and Crosby, F. J. (eds), *The Psychology and Management of Workplace Diversity*. Malden, MA: Blackwell Publishing, pp. 78–99.

Syed, J. (2008) Employment prospects for skilled immigrants: a relational perspective. *Human Resource Management Review*, 18: 28–45.

Taylor, S. (2004) Hunting the snark: a critical analysis of human resource management discourses in relation to managing labour in smaller organizations. In Marlow, S., Patton, D. and Ram, M. (eds), *Managing Labour in Small Firms*. London: Routledge, pp. 18–42.

Templer, K. J., Tay, C. and Chandrasekar, N. A. (2006) Motivational cultural intelligence, realistic job preview, realistic living condition preview, and cross-cultural adjustment. *Group and Organization Management*, 31: 154–73.

Tung, R. L. (1981) Selection and training of personnel for overseas assignments. *Columbia Journal of World Business*, 16(1): 68–78.

Viswesvaran, C. and Ones, D. S. (2000) Perspectives of models of job performance. *International Journal of Selection and Assessment*, 8: 216–25.

Watson, T. (2004) HRM and critical social science analysis. *Journal of Management Studies*, 41: 447–67.

Wilk, S. L. and Cappelli, P. (2003) Understanding the determinants of employer use of selection methods. *Personnel Psychology*, 56: 103–24.

Williams, S. D. (2004) Personality, attitude, and leader influences on divergent thinking and creativity in organizations. *European Journal of Innovation Management*, 7(3): 187–204.

Witt, L. A. (2002) The interactive effects of extraversion and conscientiousness on performance. *Journal of Management*, 28(6): 835–51.

Zanoni, P. and Janssens, M. (2007) Minority employees engaging with (diversity) management: an analysis of control, agency and micro-emancipation. *Journal of Management Studies*, 44: 1371–97.

Zedeck, S. and Cascio, W. F. (1984) Psychological issues in personnel decisions. *Annual Review of Psychology*, 35: 461–518.

Zottoli, M. A. and Wanous, J. P. (2000) Recruitment source research: current status and future directions. *Human Resource Management Review*, 10: 353–83.

CHAPTER 11
Performance management
Jane Maley

- Introduction
- The strategic importance of performance management in a global context
- Characteristics of performance management
- The criteria of an effective performance management system
- Ethics in performance management
- Main approaches to performance appraisal
- Multisource feedback
- Identifying strategies to improve international performance
- Performance management in an international context
- Conclusion
- For discussion and revision
- Further reading
- Case study: Performance appraisals in the not-for-profit sector
- References

After reading this chapter, you should be able to:
- Understand the strategic importance of a performance management system in a global context
- Explain the purpose, criteria and ethics of an effective global performance management system
- Identify the main approaches to performance appraisal
- Critically reflect on the most effective sources for performance management
- Recognize strategies to improve performance

Introduction

This chapter looks at one of the most critical procedures within a multinational corporation (MNC) – the international performance management system. Performance management is the process by which organizations set goals, determine standards, assign and evaluate work, and distribute rewards. These systems are now widely and routinely used for many employees. Their use increased through the 1990s as a result of the pressures of globalization, increased competition and a greater analysis of all the characteristics of employee performance (Varma et al., 2008). Performance management systems were originally used for managers, professionals and technical employees, but today they are frequently used to appraise staff at all levels in many parts of the world.

Measuring the performance of individuals and teams has become an important tool to ensure good organizational performance, and is critical to identifying possible gaps between job expectations and the organization's strategic intent. Hence performance management is considered to be a central element of strategic human resource management (HRM), and it is argued that a successful performance management system is vital if an organization wants to implement strategy into employee action. If the process is conducted appropriately, it can provide a huge benefit for a firm, its supervisors and its employees. An effective performance management system can help to create a sustainable competitive advantage for the firm that is not easy for others to replicate (Hanson et al., 2005).

Nonetheless, performance management is viewed by many managers around the world as a pointless annual ritual, and the use of, and satisfaction with, performance appraisal systems has a history of being problematic (Nankervis and Compton, 2006). As with everything else in the global arena, managing performance in an international context is a lot more complex than is the case with a one-dimensional national structure.

There are a number of reasons for the complications arising in the cross-border context. First, culture profoundly influences management practices. For example, the purpose of performance management, employees' acceptance of the system, and the cultural value dimensions that affect performance management vary immensely across borders (Claus and Briscoe, 2009). The unique norms, values and beliefs inherent in different cultures affect the way employees are controlled as well as their perceptions of equity, expectations and justice. Consequently, a performance management system developed in one country may not be suitable in another (Chiang and Birtch, 2010).

Second, organizations must be cognizant of the potential influence of other institutional and economic factors that may influence performance management (Chiang and Birtch, 2010). Third, international human resources managers in MNCs face a major dilemma in terms of reconciling whether performance management should be a single, standard practice throughout the organization, or a divergent system that can be used to reflect local culture and local management practices.

Finally, the performance management of international employees presents particular challenges. In addition to the special case of the expatriate manager, who has been the focus of much research over the past two decades, other international employees need attention too. For instance, employees in an MNC's subsidiary who are nationals of the country in which they are working have been found to be neglected in international performance management studies (Dowling et al., 2008). For example, the manager of the subsidiary has been found to require particular consideration. These managers are usually isolated from their supervisor, and it has been found (Maley and Kramar, 2007) that they may experience difficulties in the conduct of their own performance appraisal.

In other words, the dilemma of both geographical distance and cultural distance must be considered when a company operates across different countries and continents (Harzing and Noordhaven, 2005). The performance management system cannot be one-dimensional, and human resources managers need systems that can be applied to a range of cultural values.

The structure of this chapter is as follows. It begins with a review of the strategic importance of the performance management system in a global context. This is followed by an examination of the various characteristics that underpin a performance management system, which includes the purpose, criteria and ethics of performance management. Subsequently, the key approaches and the value of multiple sources in a crosscultural setting are considered. This section includes various suggestions to help improve the performance management process. Next there is an overview of performance management in an international context. Finally, there is a summary of the chapter that incorporates a critical evaluation and the future direction of performance management, and outlines the benefits of studying performance management from a critical perspective.

The strategic importance of performance management in a global context

In order to understand the strategic significance of performance management in a global setting, it is important to recognize that the purpose and approach of performance management changes as the MNC expands and subsidiaries develop. These changes have been attributed to the staffing structures and strategies of human resources (Birkinshaw and Morrison, 1995). Evidence suggests that it is these structures and strategies that determine the types of employee who will be employed in an international setting (Dowling et al., 2008), as well as the importance placed on the purpose and approach of performance management (Maley, 2011).

Three key types of international employee have been identified:

- Parent country nationals (PCNs). These employees are from the parent country; expatriates are always PCNs.
- Host country national (HCNs). These employees work in their host subsidiary.
- Third country nationals (TCNs). These employees are not from the parent office and do not work in their host country.

For example, the US MNC General Electric employs Australian citizens in its Australian operations (HCNs), often sends US citizens (PCNs) to Asia-Pacific countries on assignment, and may send some of its UK employees on an assignment to its Japanese subsidiary (TCNs). The nationality of the employee has been found to be a major factor in determining the person's category.

The employees in its subsidiaries (HCNs, TCNs) become increasingly more important to the success of the MNC as the globalization strategy advances and the subsidiary takes a central role in the success of the MNC. For that reason, the international performance management process must consider not only the employees from the parent country (HCNs), but also these new forms of employee (Milliman et al., 2002). The concept of the 'global professional' was introduced. In this chapter, this idea will be extended to illustrate three distinct category of global employee. What is more, as the MNC continues to expand, there will be an increasingly larger percentage of the organization that is both geographically and culturally distant from the parent MNC (Harzing and Noordhaven, 2005). This widening cultural distance has been found to have a major effect on the purpose, criteria, acceptance and ethics of performance management (Fenwick, 2005). Consequently, the international performance management process needs to adopt a broader cultural perspective with an appreciation of cultural diversity.

Characteristics of performance management

Performance management and performance appraisal

'Performance management' is the general term for a number of human resources functions that are concerned with managing performance. It is the systematic process that involves employees, as individuals and members of a group, in improving organizational effectiveness to accomplish the firm's mission and goals. Employee performance management (Figure 11.1) includes:

- planning work and setting expectations;
- continually monitoring performance;
- developing the capacity to perform;
- periodically appraising performance;
- rewarding good performance.

It is important to reiterate here that these numerous functions are much more complex to administer in an international setting.

The aspects of the performance management cycle are magnified and become more complex when a firm globalizes. When a company internationalizes its operations, the human resources manager needs to become familiar with the aspects of performance management that may be influenced by the political, economic, legal and cultural feature of the countries in which the MNC is operating. In addition, the human resources manager must be aware of the various stages of evolution of the subsidiary and how these stages may impact on the individual functions of the performance management system. The appraisal is therefore just one component of the performance management system, albeit a major component. Along with the other important functions, it forms part of the umbrella of performance management. The cycle can form a structure for the design of a performance management

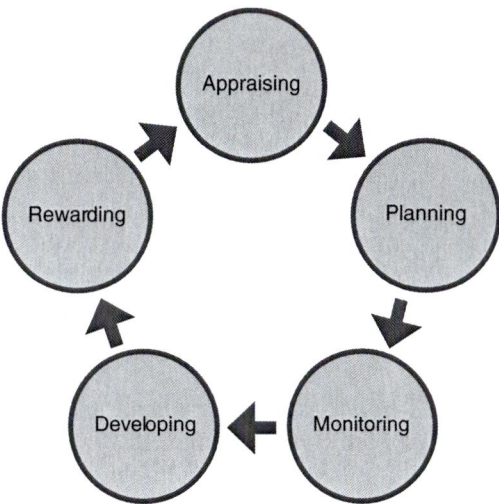

Figure 11.1 The performance management cycle

system in diverse cultures; its particular form and method of implementation may, however, vary between different cultures.

The purpose

The purpose of the international performance management system, in particular the performance appraisal, has been the focus of recent debate and discussion by academic scholars and practitioners; this has indicated that employees often have little idea why their supervisor is conducting a performance appraisal (Chiang and Birtch, 2010). Because its purposes are not always well understood, the performance management systems tend to be poorly implemented in many countries (Claus and Briscoe, 2009). Three key aspects of purpose in the global context will be considered in this chapter – first, what influences the purpose; second, the implications of the purpose; and third, the purposes themselves – and these elements will now be considered in turn.

What influences the purpose?

The strategic human resources literature (Wright and McMahan, 1992; Delery and Doty, 1996; Ulrich, 1997) and international HRM literature (De Cieri and Dowling, 1998; Ghoshal and Bartlett, 1998; Harvey et al., 2002) have established that strategic alignment and internationalization have an enormous influence on the purpose of performance management. Claus and Briscoe (2009) argue that context-specific issues need to be taken into account when executing performance management activities, and that multiple contextual elements are critical to understanding the universality and purpose of performance management practices. Similarly, Milliman et al. (2002) propose that contextual factors direct the purpose of the performance appraisal: for example, the firm's strategy, structure, industry, culture (both national

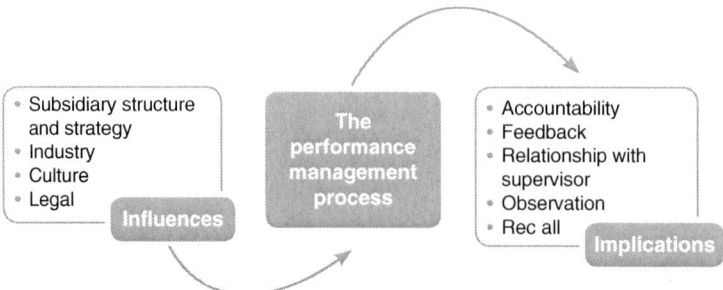

Figure 11.2 The purpose of performance management: the influences and implications

and organizational) and local regulations may influence the type and selection of performance management purposes (Figure 11.2).

Implications of the purpose

In turn, the purpose of the performance management has been found to affect the associated level of accountability (Harris et al., 1995; Mero and Motowildo, 1995), the feedback (Aguinis, 2008), the relationship with the supervisor (Maley and Kramar, 2007), and the level and accuracy of observation and recall (Cleveland and Murphy, 1992; Farr and Jacobs, 2006).

The purpose of performance management in MNCs

Milliman et al. (2002) contend that the purpose of performance management is based on a similar fundamental premise in most countries – to control individuals in firms to maximize the MNC's financial performance. This view is shared by Cardy and Dobbins (1994) and Ouchi (1982). Milliman et al. (2002) add that although performance management is based on similar fundamental ideas in many countries, its specific purpose and practice may vary slightly between nations. Performance management is also seen as an important way to identify employee strengths and weaknesses, evaluate training needs, set plans for further development and provide motivation by ascertaining rewards and career advancement (Cardy and Dobbins, 1994). Lansbury and Quince (1988) proposed that one of the first steps in establishing a performance management scheme should be to determine what the scheme is supposed to achieve.

A pragmatic depiction of performance management purpose is offered by De Cieri and Kramar (2010), who describe the purpose as threefold:

- as a strategic link to the firm's goals;
- to supply data for administrative use;
- for developmental purposes.

Milliman et al. (2002) expand this viewpoint by describing five main purposes: documentation, development, administrative purposes involving pay and promotion, and subordinate expression.

> **Box 11.1 The cultural context of performance appraisal**
>
> Chiang and Birtch (2010) recently investigated the effects of culture on the purposes of performance appraisal in the banking industry in seven countries across Europe, Asia and North America. They found that the effects of power distance, collectivism, masculinity and uncertainty avoidance (see Hofstede, 1980) should not be understated, nor are they straightforward. Multinational organizations must be cognizant of the potential influence that a range of other organizational, institutional and economic factors may wield on appraisal.
>
> These findings hold significant implications for the theoretical underpinnings of appraisal, a management tool largely rooted in the values and traditions of US equity, expectancy and procedural justice (see below). Chiang and Birtch conclude that not only is the transferability of appraisal and its operationalization affected by interactions with divergent cultures and contextual settings, but new hybrid appraisal architectures are also emerging that demand further research.

Moreover, subordinate expression is an important addition and highlights the significance of feedback in the appraisal (Cardy and Dobbins, 1994; Cascio, 2000, 2003; DeNisi and Pritchard, 2006). Milliman et al. (2002) found that cultures characterized by high individualism (Hofstede, 1980), in particular that of Australia, place an enormous emphasis on subordinate expression and feedback, and view this as a crucial part of the appraisal purpose.

It appears that the purpose of the performance appraisal may vary between cultures and change as the subsidiary evolves through various structures and strategies. Murphy and Cleveland (1995) claim that whereas over 85 per cent of US MNCs use appraisals for administrative purposes, in particular salary decisions, performance management is less frequently used for training and development purposes. They also expressed a key concern that information from performance appraisals is used by raters, ratees and firms for many purposes, and that the goals pursued by the rater and ratees are not necessarily the same as those pursued by the firm.

However, Murphy and Cleveland (1991) suggested in an earlier study that too many purposes could be conflicting, and that one or two purposes tend to dominate and cancel out the others. This argument was also advanced by Milliman et al. (2002), who proposed that expectations might be high in relation to what could be realistically achieved, and that firms needed to devote more time and effort to the appraisal process. Furthermore, they concluded that the purpose of appraisal had fallen short not only in the USA, but also in 10 other countries they sampled. A simple definition of the purpose of performance management has been proposed by DeNisi and Pritchard (2006). They propose that the purpose is to accurately diagnose individual and group performance in order to be able to reward good performance and remedy poor performance so that, in the aggregate, overall organizational performance will be enhanced.

In sum, the evidence in the literature points to the fact that an MNC's purpose in conducting appraisals will be shaped by several contextual factors (see also Box 11.1). In addition, the purpose may influence various aspects of the appraisal process and outcome. It is for these reasons that the purpose needs to be clearly communicated by the firm or at least understood by all its international employees. In other words, not only should the subordinate and supervisor's expectations be aligned, but both also need to be congruent with the MNC's rationale for using a performance management system (Milliman et al., 2002). The literature on the purpose of performance management indicates that the purpose is vitally important, having widespread and pervasive implications that impinge on many aspects of the MNC's operations.

The criteria of an effective performance management system

Just as it is important to have a clearly defined purpose for conducting the performance management process, particularly in an international context, it is also fundamental to have a set of clear criteria by which to measure employees' performance. All too often, employees do not fully understand the particular criteria according to which they are being measured.

Research has focused on whether culture affects the performance criteria used in performance appraisal. Lam et al. (1999) found that criteria were treated differently across different cultures, indicating that there are emic (culturally specific) and etic (universal) dimensions in the perception of performance criteria. In additional, national differences in power distance also played an important role in defining the criteria (Lam et al., 1999). Another study found that there were culturally related and culturally neutral performance dimensions for retail managers in Singapore and Australia, and that the importance attached to the criteria varied significantly, showing the mediating effect of culture (Campbell and Zarkada-Fraser, 2000).

An effective international performance management system needs in particular to identify performance criteria that are important to the MNC and related to the job at hand (Arvey and Murphy, 1998). There are several different opinions on which external criteria should be used to evaluate performance. A recent standpoint (Kramar and Bartram, 2010) advocates five clear criteria: strategic alignment, validity, reliability, specificity and acceptability. These recommendations are unequivocal and, importantly, encompass all the important areas, including acceptability and strategic congruence – the latter being the term used to define the alignment of HRM strategy with the overall business strategy. Each criterion will now be discussed in relation to the performance appraisal.

Strategic alignment

Strategic alignment is the degree to which the employee's individual performance management system matches or fits with the organization's global business plan. In other words, the employee's performance objectives should be aligned with those of the supervisor, and the supervisor's plan should be aligned with the manager's performance objectives, and so forth up to the objectives of the CEO and the board of directors. It has been proposed that performance criteria include the individual's aspirations, and that the individual's best possible performance criteria need to be identified and fitted with the firm's conceptual criteria (Borman, 1994). More recently, the system of the balanced scorecard (BSC), developed by Kaplan and Norton (1992), has become a popular method of developing strategic congruence by linking the firm's long-term goals to its employees' short-term actions.

Validity

Validity and reliability are statistical terms (and concepts) that lie at the centre of most research into the various aspects of performance appraisal. They get to the heart of concerns over biases inherent in the performance appraisal process – reducing these biases increases the effectiveness of the performance management system.

Validity refers to fact that people are being measured on areas that are truly important to the firm's objectives, and refers to the extent to which a performance measure assesses all the relevant aspects of the job (De Cieri and Kramar, 2010). If a performance management process lacks validity, it does not measure all aspects of the employee's performance.

Failure of validity is a very common phenomenon in performance management. A recent study of the performance management systems of national managers from MNCs of British, European and USA origin found that 80 per cent of performance appraisal lacked validity and did not measure important aspects of the national manager's job (Maley and Kramar, 2007). Validity has been found to be particularly important to many employees, and has been found to be a major contributor of poor employee acceptability of the system. Both validity and reliability are also important in recruitment and selection, and it is therefore well worth understanding these scientific terms and their relevance in international HRM.

Reliability

Reliability refers to uniformity of performance and to freedom from random error. There are several types of reliability that are pertinent to the performance appraisal. The most important is *interrater reliability*; this refers to the level of consistency among the supervisors who are appraising the employees. Evidence indicates that many supervisors are subjective, and therefore their appraisal of employees will be low in reliability.

Another important and relevant form of reliability in performance measurement is the reliability and constancy of measures over time. This is particularly important in a seasonal business. Take, for example, sales people who work in real estate. The real estate market in most Western countries typically picks up in late winter and reaches a peak in late summer. Louis Evangelidis, a real estate proprietor in Sydney, Australia, has stated that, in order to accurately assess a new salesperson, their sales performance needs to be assessed over a complete year. If, for example, a salesperson starts with the firm in early autumn and is first reviewed at the end of their first 6 months in late winter, their sales will be evaluated over a period where sales are predictably slow. This will most likely compare unfavourably with the results of another salesperson who has worked and been assessed over the previous 6 months (the high season). Many businesses exhibit such seasonal fluctuations, and these must be considered in order to improve appraisal reliability.

It is extremely challenging in the workplace to obtain good reliability in performance appraisal, but it is a challenge that human resources managers and supervisors must strive to meet. Scholars have researched and written copious amounts of data on the reliability of performance appraisal, but there is little evidence of a quick fix. The whole culture of a firm often needs to change in order to achieve high reliability in performance appraisals.

Acceptability

The behavioural criterion of acceptability of the performance appraisal is a fairly recent addition to the field, and research literature on acceptability from the perspective of the employee is limited. An exception is a recent study conducted in China (Taormina and Goa, 2009) that found acceptability of performance appraisal to be paramount and to relate to the way in which the performance appraisal process was executed. In the same way, acceptability of ratee appraisal in an international context has been found to increase when the ratee has regular communication and a positive relationship with the rater (Milliman et al., 2002).

From the perspective of the appraisees, acceptability is more likely to occur when they perceive the appraisal to be fair (Taylor et al., 1998; Bradley and Ashkanasy, 2001) and when the feedback they receive from the appraiser is timely and accurate (Milliman et al., 2000; Sully De Luque and Sommer, 2007). Moreover, where a subordinate and a supervisor are geographically distant, regular feedback has been found to be particularly important (Cascio, 2000; Milliman et al., 2002; Harzing and Noordhaven, 2005; Sully De Luque and Sommer, 2007). Hedge and Teachout (2000) have claimed that acceptability may be the critical criterion for determining the success of the performance management process.

In the international setting, a vital aspect of the acceptability of the performance appraisal process on the part of both the supervisor and the employee has been found to be attributed back to how clear the purpose of the appraisal is (Lindholm et al., 1999; Milliman et al., 2002; Maley, 2009). The acceptability and purpose of performance management emerge from the literature as both paramount and interdependent. Evidence suggests that, from an employee's perspective, the performance management process needs to have a clear purpose in order for it to be acceptable, and that purpose also has to be acceptable.

The relationship between purpose and acceptability reinforces the need for the performance appraisal to be embedded in a performance management system rather than to stand alone as a human resources event. For example, if appraisal is part of a fully fledged performance management system, it is more likely that the appraisal will be linked to the organization's strategy, and that both compensation and training and development needs will be achieved. Under these conditions, the appraisal is more likely to be acceptable to the ratee.

Construct theories and acceptability

Construct theories may help to explain the phenomenon of the acceptability of performance management. For example, a psychological explanation for people's resistance to performance evaluation could be that a negative evaluation can represent a threat to one's self-efficacy. Consequently, it might be expected that these feelings could be to some extent reduced if the appraisal criteria were acceptable and the purpose was clear to the person receiving the appraisal. The threat to self-efficacy that may occur in a dysfunctional appraisal could have a knock-on effect on many psychological aspects of the employee–employer relationship.

Cognitive dissonance theory (Festinger, 1957) is a theory on the basis of which aspects of performance appraisal may be interpreted. From the perspective of cognitive dissonance theory, a negative evaluation from another person would be inconsistent with the individual's generally upbeat perception of him- or herself as a capable person. Such conflicting cognitions would possibly affect the spirit of the individual's relationship with the MNC, that is the psychological contract with the organization.

Organizational justice (Colquitt et al., 2001) is another theoretical construct with which performance appraisal acceptability may be viewed. A dysfunctional performance appraisal system may affect the employee's perception of organizational justice. This construct may help to explain employees' attitudinal and behavioural reactions to both performance appraisal and organizational commitment (Masterson et al., 2000).

Because the appraisal has implications for individual reward, employees' perceptions of justice are especially significant. Erdogan (2002) claims that organizational justice has two subjective perceptions: *procedural justice* (fairness of procedures) and *distributive justice* (fairness of outcome). For example, when employees feel unfairly treated in their appraisal, they are likely to react negatively. Distributive justice is concerned with the perceived fairness of the outcomes or allocations received. In appraisal, in order to reach a perception of distributive justice, individuals compare their efforts with the rating they receive and the fairness of that rating (Erdogan, 2002).

On the basis of the two construct theories described above, an appraisal is unlikely to be perceived as acceptable unless those involved in the process perceive it to be unbiased (that is, from the perspective of cognitive dissonance theory) and fair (that is, from the perspective of MNC justice theory). It is reasonable to expect that, if employees believe they are being treated unfairly by the organization, this will in turn impact on their perception of their relationship with the organization. Thus, cognitive dissonance theory and organizational justice theory assist in understanding the acceptability of the performance management process.

The important point here is that the additional complexity of geographical distance and cultural distance in the global setting makes achieving the criterion of acceptability of the performance management system increasingly challenging to achieve. It is therefore essential that international human resources managers be mindful of the various contrasts influencing the acceptability of a performance management system within the MNC.

Ethics in performance management

For a performance appraisal to be acceptable, it must be ethical. One of the key intentions of an ethical performance appraisal should be to provide an honest assessment of performance. Although some supervisors are competent and lawful in reviewing an employee's performance, evidence suggests that there is an inconsistency in the approach to the ethics of performance management when a firm goes global, one which may cause employees to become frustrated, cynical, and withdrawn (Murphy, 1993).

Survey results in one large study (Aydinlik et al., 2008), examined the ways in which the largest private sector organizations in Sweden and Turkey communicated the intent of their codes of ethics to their employees. The research identified some interesting findings showing that the small group of companies in Turkey that have a code may appear to be more 'advanced' in their handling of ethics than Sweden. Such a conclusion is counterintuitive as one would have expected a developed nation like Sweden to be more advanced in these measures than a developing nation such as Turkey. Culture may play a large role in the implementation of ethics in corporations and could be a major reason for this difference. Moreover, it has been reported that, in performance appraisals, factors not related to performance (for example, race) are one of the top 10 serious ethical considerations for human resources managers in MNCs. It is, therefore, paramount that firms ensure that their performance management processes are conducted to a high ethical standard.

The climate in some organizations does not encourage people to think through ethical considerations because of an overwhelming focus on the bottom line (Maley and Kramar, 2007). The pressure from the parent company to meet unrealistic performance objectives may encourage managers to cut corners or act in an unethical manner. A case in point can be found in the history of Enron (see Mini Case Study 11.1): managers at Enron were given unrealistic performance objectives that resulted in dysfunctional and unethical behaviour.

Mini Case Study 11.1

Ethics: performance appraisal at Travelscence

In 2004, Keith Gavin became financial controller and a member of the executive committee of Travelscence, a medium-sized, family-owned travel agency in the Hunter valley, 2 hours' drive north of Sydney, Australia. Keith sold his home in Sydney and relocated to the Hunter valley with his wife and two young children aged 8 and 10 to take up the position. He was the first person from outside the family running the company to hold a senior position in it or to be included on the executive committee, and he took the job despite sensing that some members of the family were concerned about his ability to fit in with the company culture.

One year after Keith had commenced work at Travelscence, the company decided to downsize. This was a response to huge changes never before seen in the travel business industry. Keith, who had been through this before when he was a financial controller in the healthcare industry, agreed this was good for the long-term health of the 35-year-old company. He decided not to be anxious that the dynasty members of Travelscence seemed more concerned about short-term profits.

The MD, Max Murphy, was relying on Keith to help him determine how to downsize in an ethical manner – Max said he trusted Keith more on this than he did Sonia Foley, the human resources manager. On Keith's recommendation, the company decided to make its lay-off decisions based on the annual performance appraisal ratings of the employees. Each department manager would submit a list of employees ranked by the average score of their last three appraisals. At some point, Keith and the executive committee would decide who would be made redundant. This decision would be based on the employees with the poorest performance.

When Keith received the evaluations, he was confused. Six employees did not appear to have been appraised. However, their names were highlighted for redundancy. When he asked the relevant managers to explain, they told him that these employees had been with the company for many years. When performance appraisals had been introduced 10 years earlier, Max had agreed to a request from this group of loyal employees that they would not have to endure formal performance appraisal, which they felt was unnecessary. The managers told Keith they had questioned this decision, and Max reassured them that it would only be temporary and that in the interim he would evaluate them himself.

When Keith discussed this matter with the Max, he said that he had never had the time to conduct the appraisals. He also said that it was less important because these particular six employees were all very near retirement age. He added that the firm had been good to them and that they had received more than enough retirement superannuation. In addition, Australian legislation required Travelscence to pay them a generous redundancy package. Max believed that the right thing to do was to keep the jobs for the younger guys, the breadwinners with families. Max reassured Keith that the six employees would never dream of causing a disruption or taking Travelscence to court. Keith enquired whether they were actually performing satisfactorily, and Max said he was uncertain.

As Keith left the office, Max told him that he was doing a tremendous job and that he had made a big impact on the executive committee. Max confirmed that Keith was right to let the six old-timers go, and added that although Travelscence was a caring company, that they could not keep 'dead wood' for ever. Keith left Max's office knowing that he had some principled and ethical decisions to make.

Questions

1. How would you describe the management of the human resources function at Travelscence?
2. What are the ethical issues in this case?
3. What are the personal and professional dilemmas for Keith Gavin, and what do you believe is the right action for him to take?

Source: Case based on a personal interview with the informant, June 2009.

In a crosscultural setting, supervisors must take extra precautions to ensure that the performance management process maintains equality, equity and justice. Stakeholder theory states that 'the MNC and its managers are responsible for the effects of activities on others' and that 'the MNC should be managed for the benefit of the stakeholders'. This theory supports utilitarian ethics. In performance management, this relates to equity, procedural and distributive justice, autonomy, respect and safety in the workplace. As a rule, these principles are to some degree understood by many cultures.

Notwithstanding, basic rights in a performance management process also include principles that are not easily translated across all cultures. These principles include feedback, openness and consultation, which are not usual traits of collectivist, high-power-distance cultures. The international human resources manager must be alert to the sensitivities of the ideals of these cultures within the four key dimensions of cultures (Hofstede, 1980). International research evidence indicates that, if the firm's purpose for doing the performance appraisal is clearly communicated throughout the organization, and the criteria of strategic congruence, validity, reliability and acceptability are upheld to a high ethical standard, the performance management process is more likely to be successful.

Main approaches to performance appraisal

Informal

Performance appraisal may be either informal or formal. An informal approach to performance appraisal was once commonplace and still occurs in some small to medium-sized organizations. An informal approach usually involves giving an employee some degree of guidance and feedback. Bernadette Harris, for example, is the owner and manager of a small estate agency in North Yorkshire, UK, and manages her employees with an informal performance appraisal process. Bernadette has five staff members – three salespeople, a receptionist and a customer service assistant; she considers that she gives her staff regular feedback and guidance, but she does not formally document the process. Bernadette believes that her company is small enough to manage with an informal performance appraisal system.

Although this method may be satisfactory for small businesses, it can become cumbersome and unmanageable in larger organizations. Once a firm has more than about a dozen employees, it is recommended that a more formal system be introduced. According to Chiang and Birtch (2010), informal performance appraisal is more commonly found in individualistic cultures.

Formal

A formal system of performance appraisal involves a formal documented interview with the employee and is the process typically employed in MNCs. There are several types of formal appraisal system. When choosing the type of performance appraisal system that the company should use, the human resources manager needs to consider the compatibility of the system with the strategic business objectives of the organization, as well as specific purposes of the performance evaluation. The major types of appraisal methods will now be reviewed.

Major types of performance appraisal systems

In this section, we will explore the various approaches to measuring and managing performance. Today, most firms, certainly most MNCs, use a behavioural type of performance appraisal combined with an objective goal-based method such as management by objectives (MBO) or key performance indicators. Essays and critical incidents are rarely used these days, except perhaps in a very small number of small to medium-sized enterprises. In the past, some firms conducted closed or blind performance appraisal systems. In a closed system, the employee did not participate in the process and was unaware what was written about them (see Box 11.2).

Box 11.2   Appraisals at Atomic Energy

The former UK Atomic Energy Authority was one of the first government agencies to be privatized by then British Prime Minister Margaret Thatcher in 1981. The newly formed company was named Amersham International. This new organization continued with the old system of performance appraisal, which utilized a closed appraisal method for all employees. Not surprisingly, this process resulted in a degree of mistrust between the management and employees. A more transparent process that involved employee participation was introduced in the mid-1980s. Following the introduction of an open, transparent performance management system, the company's profits started to increased dramatically after a 5-year decline.

Source: Interview with the Chief Operating Officer, Amersham International, May 2000.

Major types of performance appraisal are outlined in Table 11.1 and will now be discussed.

Ranking

Ranking compares each person's performance, with the manager ranking all subordinates from 'best' to 'worst'. Typically, 10 per cent of ratings are required to be poor or excellent. Ranking forces the rater to distribute the ratings evenly across a broader range of results. This is similar to scaling requirements in university examinations. Ranking can occur independently without any other system being involved, but this raw ranking method is rarely used nowadays.

The General Electric Company, however, gave forced ranking a degree of respectability. It is argued that forced ranking avoids problems of manager bias and, in particular, leniency. On the other hand, forced ranking was believed to be one of the major factors contributing to the dysfunctional behavior of employees that triggered the downfall of Enron.

Table 11.1 Summary of performance appraisal approaches

Method	Description	Positive features	Drawbacks
Ranking	Employees ranked from best to worst	Reduces bias	Disliked by both individualistic and collectivist cultures
Behaviour observation scales	Use critical incidents to develop a list of the desired behaviours	High acceptability Reliable Valid	Can be complicated and costly to set up, particularly for global operations
Management of objectives/key performance indicators	Manager and employee set goals	High acceptability	May not fit a collective culture Destroys teamwork Lacks comparability

Behaviour observation scales

Behaviour observation scales (BOSs) use critical incidents to develop a list of the desired behaviours needed to perform a specific job successfully. This method has recently gained in popularity and is used by many large MNCs.

Medtronic Incorporated is a Fortune 500 company that makes medical and surgical devices. Its US headquarters is in Minneapolis, but the company operates in 120 countries around the world. Medtronic uses a BOS appraisal-based system for its 38,000 employees. Tziner and Kopelman (2002) collated the results of four separate studies with samples in two nations (Israel and Canada) and lent support to the proposition that performance appraisal and review based on BOSs may be superior to other appraisal methods as it may yield more favourable attitudinal effects.

Goal setting

Employee motivation and performance are improved if employees clearly understand and are challenged by what is to be achieved. If performance management is to have a developmental purpose, it ought to focus on the process of getting results, and that process must be considered in terms of the job-related behaviours over which the individual employee has control.

There has been much support for MBO among HRM scholars. For example, Wright and Snell (1998) believe that MBO is a flexible process and that this flexibility means that it can be used across a large range of jobs. Although MBO was originally intended for use as a stand-alone process, it has in practice been found to be used alongside traditional methods of appraisal such as behavioural methods, in a belt-and-braces style of approach. MBO has been found to be acceptable method of appraisal in individualistic cultures. This could be because of its emphasis on goals and measurement, as well as employees' involvement and collaborative efforts, which are integrated into the MBO philosophy. Dinesh and Palmer (1998) argue that performance management systems incorporating MBO appear to offer significant advantages, such as good validity, reliability, strong specificity in terms of results, high acceptability and a very good opportunity for strategic congruence.

In contrast, however, some scholars are not in favour of MBO. For example, it has been argued that MBO may destroy teamwork (Deming, 1982), and there may be conflict with total quality management initiatives (Levinson, 1991; Castellano and Harper, 2001). Furthermore, MBO can lack comparability and therefore have limitations with regards to their administration, particularly if the administration requires valid comparisons, such as promotion and salary awards (Bernardin and Beatty, 1984; Wood and Marshall, 1993). Importantly, the concept of individual objectives does not fit with the ideals of teamwork found in a collectivist society (Hofstede and Hofstede, 2005), and therefore MBO-type objectives may have cross-cultural limitations.

The BSC is a performance management framework that became popular during the early 1990s. Kaplan and Norton (1992) presented the BSC as an integrative device that would encourage and facilitate the use of non-financial information by senior managers in organizations, with the choice of non-financial measure being driven primarily by 'strategic' considerations. They argued that, when equipped with this better information, managers would be able to deliver improved strategic performance. As a consequence, BSC has attracted considerable interest among organizations seeking to improve the implementation of their strategies (Lawrie, 2004).

On the other hand, Othmana et al. (2006) raise questions about the effectiveness of BSCs and argue that their effective implementation may be more difficult to develop in Malaysian organizations. Other researchers argue that there are inherent weaknesses in the concept of the BSC itself, and that these weaknesses will limit its usefulness.

Multisource feedback

The supervisor as a source

So far, this chapter has assumed that the sole arbiter of performance is the supervisor, and that information from other sources is indirect and filtered through him or her. In many MNCs, this is the case, but there is evidence that this may not always be the best practice. It is apparent from human resources research that one of the key problems for the supervisor in evaluating subordinates' performance is that it is extremely difficult to observe employees' behaviour directly. Supervisors often complain that they do not always have time to fully observe the performance of their employees.

This is particularly evident in MNCs where supervisors may be managing employees across national borders. Murphy and Cleveland (1995) argue that supervisors are one of the groups least able to assess behaviour, and contend that much of what the supervisor knows about employees is probably the result of secondary data or indirect data rather than direct observation. For this reason, people other than the supervisor may be better placed to evaluate employees' performance, as they may have more opportunity to directly observe them. As a result, direct supervisors, peers, customers and employees themselves can all provide information on the employee's performance.

Moreover, the requirement for superior objectivity, the increased use of teams and the accent on customer service and quality have created awareness in using multiple sources to evaluate employees' performance (Eichinger and Lombardo,

2003; Levy and Williams, 2004; see also Box 11.3). A study conducted by the Corporate Leadership Council (2006) revealed that 90 per cent of Fortune 1000 firms had implemented some degree of multisource feedback. The same study revealed that the presence of multisource feedback increased individual performance by 8.1 per cent.

Box 11.3   Multisource assessment at Peace Corps

The Peace Corps, a government initiative created by President John F. Kennedy, implemented the use of self-appraisal tests, based on the premise that individuals would adapt better to cultural change if they had a better understanding of themselves.

In 1970, Robert Dorn, who worked in Peace Corps leadership training, joined the Center for Creative Leadership and introduced the practice of self-appraisal. Years later, Robert Bailey, an economist who had worked for Dorn, had the idea of including others in the assessment process and initiated the multisource assessment process.

Source: Justo (2009).

Subordinates as sources

Murphy and Cleveland (1995) argue that subordinates may be a strong source of information for the employee, especially in relation to interpersonal behaviours and results. The subordinate may not fully understand all aspects of the manager's job, but he or she will directly witness interpersonal behaviours that the supervisor or peer assessor may miss. The subordinate usually has day-to-day contact with the employee and would therefore usually have a reasonable view of his or her behaviours. Feedback from a subordinate is a valuable resource for the employee, as one of the keys to effective performance as a manager is the ability to get good work from one's subordinates (Mintzberg, 1973; Ilgen and Feldman, 1990).

Even though subordinates may be the optimal source for behavioural information, they cannot usually assess all tasks or technical skills (Murphy and Cleveland, 1995), and subordinate assessment, which turns the normal hierarchy on its head, may be uncomfortable for both the subordinate and the boss (Carroll and Schneier, 1982). This has been suggested as the principle reason that not all MNCs have adopted this system, despite the merits it has to offer for assessing behaviours (Eichinger and Lombardo, 2003). The idea of reversing the hierarchy does not translate well into a collectivist society with a low individuality or a high power-distance dimension. These cultures acknowledge a leader's power and do not like to reveal or ask too much personal information.

Self as source

Self-assessment – the facility of employees to assess their own performance – has become routine over the past decade. Ashford et al. (2003) found that self-assessment offered the qualities of self-trust, reliability, availability and trustworthiness. She found that, in order to perform self-assessment, an individual must perform three tasks: establish a standard, decide which feedback cues to use, and correctly interpret those cues. She also stressed that decoding cues was the most vital aspect but the most neglected. Many of the employee's cues from supervisors may come indirectly by e-mail, or by telephone, and, according to Cascio (2000), these indirect cues could be more susceptible to encoding problems. According to Ashford et al. (2003), when decoding cues, the individual needs to maintain self-preservation as a self-confident performer.

There is evidence from the USA that self-rating is more lenient than ratings obtained from supervisors (Eichinger and Lombardo, 2003). In contrast, self-ratings were examined in China by Yu and Murphy (1993), showing that Chinese workers would self-rate themselves lower than their peers or supervisors. This is not surprising considering that China is a high-power-distance, collectivist society where modesty and humility are highly respected.

Evidence, therefore, points to self-appraisal offering a degree of reliability, validity and acceptability to the employee. Moreover, in turbulent times, when such events as mergers and restructuring occur with increasing frequency, the pressing reality of having to survive in such a setting makes the self-assessment process an important area of inquiry for the employee.

Peers as sources

It has been argued that peers are in closer proximity to ratees than supervisors, and are therefore more able to give accurate assessments (Borman, 1994). This is particularly evident in teams. However, research indicates that effective peer appraisals require a great degree of trust among team workers, a non-competitive reward system, and frequent opportunities for colleagues to observe each other. There is evidence, however, that peers tend to give harsh evaluations (Saavedra and Kwun, 1993). Peer evaluations are often not acceptable in collectivist cultures and have been found to be unacceptable in China, Korea and Japan (Gillespie, 2006).

Multisource feedback (360-degree appraisal)

The process of multisource feedback (360-degree appraisal) involves obtaining feedback from subordinates, peers, supervisor, self and customers. This gives everyone more information about a ratee's behaviours, thus enhancing the potential for improvement. In recent years, multisource feedback has received a deal of research and management attention, the general findings suggesting that multisource feedback results in more accurate ratings (Palmer and Loveland, 2008). There is sometimes disagreement among the various sources used (Eichinger and Lombardo, 2003), yet if all the ratings produced the same findings, there would probably be little value in obtaining information from all sources – each of the rating sources appears to have its own inherent advantages and disadvantages.

On the one hand, experienced supervisors usually have good norms because they have seen several employees working on the job; this can result in well-calibrated views of different performance levels, and supervisor rating is acceptable across most cultures. Peers are often in closer proximity to the work being done.

Self-ratings, however, have the advantage that there is a large amount of information conveniently available. In addition, other forms of feedback have been found to be invaluable when managing employees who are geographically distant and whose supervisor may not be there to witness the majority of their behaviours. Moreover, it is argued (Kaplan and Palus, 1994) that all sources should be used if an accurate and comprehensive assessment is to be achieved. On the other hand, peers and subordinates are often inexperienced in making rater and task judgements, and may be aware of only a small portion of a manager's performance; self-ratings can be distorted because of an inflated perception of one's own performance.

In an international context, multisource feedback has been found to be particularly challenging, and recent evidence suggests that multisource feedback is not transferable across all cultures. For example, Varela and Premeaux (2008) investigated the effect of crosscultural values on multisource feedback with managers from Venezuela and Colombia, two collectivistic and high-power-distance countries. The results of their study indicated that cultural values distort the evaluations involved in multisource systems. Specifically, unlike reports of studies conducted in individualistic and low-power-distance environments, Varela and Premeaux found that peers were the least discrepant source of information, that subordinates tended to provide the highest evaluations across all the feedback sources, and that there was an excessive emphasis on people-oriented behaviours. Likewise, Gillespie (2006) addressed whether multisource feedback ratings made by subordinates were equivalent across national cultures in Great Britain, Hong Kong, Japan and the USA. These results emphasize the need for MNCs to use caution when transporting multisource feedback to international locations.

Identifying strategies to improve international performance

In many cases, the appraisal interview will provide the foundation for noting inadequacies in employees' performance and for making improvements – unless these inadequacies are brought to the employee's notice, they are likely to become critical. Poor employee performance is most likely to be due to one or more of three conditions. For example, if an employee's performance is not up to standard, it could be caused by either:

- a lack of skill;
- a lack of knowledge;
- a lack of motivation.

For satisfactory performance to occur, an employee usually requires certain skills, knowledge and motivation suited to the job. In addition, the supervisor needs to be able to detect these three important traits, which can be challenging when the supervisor and employee are from different cultures.

The first step in managing unsatisfactory performance is to detect and determine the reason behind it. This almost certainly requires the supervisor to be trained to conduct a professional performance appraisal interview. Once the source of the problem is known, a course of action can be planned. For instance, if the performance issues are due to a lack of skills or knowledge, the solution may lie in providing training and development in an effort to improve the employee's deficiency of skills and knowledge. Poor motivation may have a devastating effect on performance, but it is often difficult to diagnose and is frequently a multifaceted, complex matter; this may be particularly difficult to detect in another culture. Nonetheless, it is essential that employees with low levels of motivation are identified during the appraisal interview. These employees in particular need to be given enough time to express their views through an adequate feedback session.

Politics

It has also been found that politics, combined with power, plays a fundamental role in the appraisal process. Longnecker (1994) found that increased power on the part of the rater may make the rater more critical and more likely to rate the employee harshly. It is therefore necessary for the human resources manager to carefully monitor the performance appraisal process and ensure that the appraisal system is fair, and that politics are kept to a minimum.

Trust

A low level of trust between either the employee and the company, or the employee and the supervisor, has been found to have a detrimental effect on the outcome of the appraisal. Murphy and Cleveland (1995) noted that trust between an individual and the organization reduces the need for appraisal to be used as a control mechanism. In addition, they reported that as trust increases, it is likely that the appraisal will be future-oriented, focused on developmental processes generally used in a productive manner and, above all, fair. It is essential, therefore, that the supervisor and employee meet regularly in an attempt to build trust.

Fairness

The employee's perception of the supervisor's trustworthiness has been found to be related to the interpersonal atmosphere, helpfulness and perceived fairness of the session (Bradley and Ashkanasy, 2001). Kramar and Bartam (2010) contend that, for a performance appraisal system to be fair, several criteria must be met:

- the employee must have adequate notice;
- the employee must fully understand the purpose, criteria and standards of the system;
- the employee must be given a fair hearing;
- the rater must apply performance standards with consistency across all employees.

A fair appraisal system has been found to increase the level of trust and acceptability (Juncaj, 2002), which makes fairness a crucial component of the appraisal system.

Feedback

Feedback has been identified as essential for a satisfactory performance appraisal. In spite of this, most employees do not get adequate feedback from their supervisors (Longnecker and Gioia, 1988; Juncaj, 2002; Milliman et al., 2002; Cascio, 2003; Maley, 2009). It is necessary, therefore, for the supervisor to ensure that there is adequate time during the appraisal interview for feedback and employee expression. Gosselin et al. (1997) established that employees preferred receiving formal appraisals at least twice per year, with ongoing informal feedback throughout the year. A study conducted by the Corporate Leadership Council (2006) revealed that feedback and that fairness and accuracy of informal feedback increased staff performance by 39.1 per cent.

Performance management in an international context

Performance management has been shown to be susceptible to many problems when a firm globalizes its operations. All HRM processes have been identified as becoming more complex due to the geographical and cultural distance between the subsidiary and the head office (Shen, 2004; Harzing and Noordhaven, 2005; Sully De Luque and Sommer, 2007; Taormina and Goa, 2009). The end result is that international employees are often found to be predominantly despondent about their performance management (Fenwick, 2004; Maley and Kramar, 2007; Taormina and Goa, 2009).

The cultural impact of performance management

Performance appraisal is an area that experiences a great deal of difficulty when translated into different cultural environments (Hempel, 2001; Shen, 2004). For example, ratee bias (Tziner et al., 1998), work practice (Dowling et al., 1999), productivity (Harvey et al., 2002; Milliman et al., 2002), interpretation (Milliman et al., 2000), perception of status (Chong, 2008) and the need for feedback and acceptance of the appraisal system (Bradley and Ashkanasy, 2001, Chong, 2008; Milliman et al., 2002) have all been found to be influenced and shaped by culture.

Tziner et al. (1998) found that, although there was some consistency in appraisals across cultural settings, cultural attitudes and beliefs could influence ratee discrimination. They found that confidence in the international performance appraisal was strongly influenced by culture. For example, they argued that raters in international settings were more susceptible than domestic raters to distorting and inflating their subordinate's performance appraisal ratings.

Dowling et al. (2008) state that culture is one of the most significant constraints that must be considered when evaluating employees in a foreign subsidiary. They argue that variations in work practices between the parent MNC and the subsidiary need to be recognized. For example, one does not fire a Mexican manager just because worker productivity in Mexico is half the US average. In Mexico, this would mean that a manager working to US criteria would be working three or four times harder than the average Mexican manager. Dowling et al. argue that international appraisals require relevant comparative data rather than absolute numbers; the

> **Mini Case Study 11.2**
>
> **Point of view: unfair performance management in schools in England**
>
> Tom O'Malley, a geography teacher in southern England, has this to say about performance management:
>
> > When performance management first came in, it was seen as an initiative aimed at tightening control on the profession. Performance management would ensure teachers set annual targets that were deemed appropriate by the establishment, agreed by the schools and overseen by local authority inspectors and OFSTED (the Office for Standards in Education). Targets were to be agreed between the individual being assessed and an assigned performance management mentor. Targets were usually, although not always, at least in part tied closely to measurable academic standards. Teachers who were deemed to have successfully completed the set targets by their line managers and performance management mentors, as well as by the head teacher, were often eligible for rewards in the way of promotion and salary increase.
> >
> > The whole system is hampered by the practical difficulties of finding the time for meetings between key staff to complete the process, and for verification of progress through lesson observation, etc., not to mention agreeing recorded outcomes. Establishing what constitutes 'progress' in the world of education and understanding what this looks like for any given child or class or cohort, and then agreeing how best this can be measured, is fraught with difficulty. In practice, successful annual performance management depends as much or more on a positive relationship with a teacher's assessor than on any real 'progress' in relation to the actual or perceived needs and progress of the children being educated. Consequently, performance management is becoming increasingly viewed as an unfair game one needs to play and, in terms of improving schools, is gradually diminishing.
>
> **Question**
>
> 1. Is this another disgruntled teacher, or is there evidence of more widespread performance management problems in the British school system?

harassed Mexican manager in the above example has to live within Mexican constraints, not European or North American ones, which can be very different. Additionally, Harvey et al. (2002) and Milliman et al. (2002) found that the way MNCs measure worker productivity is often similar, but the results appear different because of cultural nuances.

Interpretation of the performance appraisal incorporates the issue of cultural applicability (Milliman et al., 2000). In different cultures, for example, the performance appraisal can be interpreted as a signal of distrust or even as an insult. In Japan, for instance, it is important to enable one to 'save face' by avoiding direct confrontation and, according to Dowling et al. (1999), this influences the way in which performance appraisal is conducted. A Japanese manager cannot point out a work-related problem or error committed by a subordinate. He would explain the consequences of a mistake without pointing out the actual mistake.

A study involving 10 leading Chinese MNCs (Shen, 2004) found that there were commonalities in the procedures and criteria of international performance appraisal between Chinese and Western MNCs. However, Shen (2004) found that the purpose of performance appraisal in Chinese MNCs was largely to decide how much to pay rather than for the organizational development, as it was more concerned with short-term business achievement. He also found performance appraisals in Chinese MNCs to be low in feedback and less transparent. In addition, it has been established that different forms of multisource assessment other than the traditional supervisory appraisal are virtually non-existent in China and Hong Kong (Entrekin and Chung, 2001; Shen, 2004). Research from Hong Kong (Snape et al., 1998) revealed that Hong Kong respondents had a preference for group-based appraisal, and that appraisals were more directive and less participative. The appraisals in Hong Kong companies were found to have been modified to suit the cultural collectivist characteristics of the society

In Indian firms, Varma et al. (2005) found that interpersonal relations and performance levels had an effect, and that performance level had a significant effect, on performance ratings, and that supervisors inflated the ratings of low performers, suggesting local that cultural norms might be operating as a moderator.

Acceptance of the performance appraisal by both the rater and the ratee has been argued to be essential for a successful appraisal (Bradley and Ashkanasy, 2001). In the international setting, acceptance of performance appraisal has been found to vary widely across different cultures (Milliman et al., 2002; see also Box 11.4). For instance, Japanese employees have been found to be less accepting of the appraisal process than USA employees.

Box 11.4 Performance appraisals at Chinese multinationals

In a recent large study (Shen, 2004), Chinese multinationals were found to adopt different approaches towards different groups, particularly different nationalities and those of managerial status. The Chinese international performance appraisals were found to be a mix of home and local appraisal systems, and of traditional Chinese personnel management and modern Western human resources concepts. Moreover, Chinese international performance appraisal policies and practices were found to be affected by various host-contextual and firm-specific factors, and there was also an interplay between international performance and other international HRM activities.

The divergence–convergence question

One of the most perplexing questions on the cultural impact of appraisal concerns whether performance appraisal systems designed in parent MNCs should be transferred to other countries (Harvey, 1997). On the one hand, Dowling et al. (2008) hold that this is possible providing the manager conducting the performance appraisal is sensitive to foreign values. On the other hand, Hempel (2001) and Vance (2006) argue that it is doubtful that traditional principles guiding the design and management of appraisal in Western countries can be successfully transferred to other countries. Vance (2006) found that cultural management styles may translate into distinct differences in the optimal management of performance, raising important doubts about how traditional performance appraisal principles can be transferred across boundaries. Hempel (2001) presented both theoretical arguments and exploratory results suggesting that Western-style performance appraisals need to be extensively modified in order to work with Chinese employees. He argues that until more is known in this area, there should be strong reservations about the direct applicability of the performance appraisal practices typically implemented by US and European MNCs.

International legislation

It is important for the international human resources manager to understand that industrial relations governing performance management will most likely differ across national boundaries (Harzing and Ruysseveldt, 2005). It is essential to acknowledge that, in the industrial relations field, no industrial relations system can be understood without appreciating the way in which rules are established and implemented, and decisions are made, in the society concerned. It is usually necessary to have some appreciation of the historical origin of the country's performance appraisal legislation.

Conclusion

This chapter has addressed the crucial issue of performance evaluation. It has discussed the contentious nature of performance management and its implications for the organization and its employees. Recommendations to improve performance management are nothing new. Improvements to the system have been recommended since the inception of performance appraisal over 50 years ago. There has been a plethora of ideas to improve the basic concept of managing employee performance. Fifty years later, this area still arouses controversy, and if we make predictions on the future based on the past, we can expect even more change.

The further use and refinement of behavioural methods (BOS) will be a major step in the development of performance appraisal systems. Behavioural methods possess good validity and reliability and are presently widely used in MNCs. BOSs will soon become cost-effective and accessible for smaller and medium-sized enterprises.

A weakness in many performance appraisal programmes is that managers and supervisors are not trained to give appraisals. This means that these managers may give inadequate appraisals; they particularly make rater errors and are less likely to give sufficient feedback to their subordinates. Arvey and Murphy (1998) proposed that rater training showed some promise in improving the effectiveness of performance ratings and that the systematic errors, particularly leniency and the halo effect – a classic finding in social psychology in which initial evaluations of a person carry over into judgements about their specific traits – were found to be reduced with rater training. It is envisaged that there will be more emphasis on training managers to give effective performance appraisal and manage the overall performance management process.

The area of culture in the MNC presents many challenges, and firms will need to consider the acceptability of performance appraisal and performance management in different cultures, and recognize that 'one performance management system may not fit' (Chong, 2008). Research has revealed that only scant attention has been paid to the performance management of international employees (Harvey, 1997; Maley and Kramar, 2007; Claus and Briscoe, 2009). MNCs, therefore, should consider their international employees and need to think about tailoring the performance management system to fit the norms and beliefs of the various national cultures they work with.

The virtual office presents difficulties for performance management. Online performance management systems are now widespread. Unfortunately, firms often introduce elaborate and expensive performance management systems but fail to ensure that employees know how to use them adequately. It has even been suggested that managers tend to give more negative ratings using online appraisals compared with those given on an old-fashioned paper form (Kurzberg et al., 2005). There is little doubt that technology has impacted the way in which firms manage performance management, and this is an area that will continue to witness enormous change. For example, the impact of the speed of communication and social network sites could have a major influence on the politics of performance management.

Performance management is a human relations process and needs trust between the supervisor and the employee in order to work well. Although progressive contemporary technology has removed the burden of many tedious administrative tasks in the office, it must be considered that, for a performance management process to work effectively across a diversity of cultures, there need to be three vital activities between the supervisor and the subordinate that cannot be substituted by a computer:

- regular face-to-face contact;
- repeated opportunity for feedback;
- follow-up of performance appraisal.

In other words, looking towards the future, the MNC's performance appraisal must be embedded in a performance management system that transcends all cultures.

Benefits of studying performance management from a critical perspective

Studying performance management in organizations from a critical outlook permits future international managers to acquire a better perception of the numerous perspectives of their different employees. This involves understanding cultural divergence and the structural and strategic inconsistency of human resources. Interpreting both cultural and structural differences and their effect on performance management will allow future international managers to weigh up situations, identify problems and determine suitable solutions to the multifaceted issue of international performance management.

International performance management, although not new, has not yet matured. Some significant studies have been carried out, but they have provided conflicting results, and a complete body of knowledge is some time away. Nevertheless, there is little doubt that, in some form, performance management and its main activity – performance appraisal – are preferred to the alternative of doing nothing. It is therefore critical that we not only continue to refine and perfect the process, but also gain a better insight into the process in an international context. It is only by studying the process that we will be able to redefine and improve it.

Finally, international performance management research will be substantially strengthened by an effective collaboration between university scholars and industry practitioners (Perkmann and Walsh, 2007). As the complexity of international management issues and the velocity of change in international business increases, such collaborations may become essential if research is to make any real difference to an academic understanding of the issues surrounding international performance management.

FOR DISCUSSION AND REVISION

Questions

1. How has globalization changed the nature of the performance appraisal?
2. How does performance appraisal differ from performance feedback?
3. What are the challenges involved in giving feedback to employees from a different culture?
4. How can leaders influence the creation of a performance-based culture in a MNC?

Exercise

1. Go to the University of Massachusetts (UMASS) website at http://www.umass.edu/humres/library/PMPGuide.pdf and review the information on the performance management process for academic staff.

   - Assess the procedure and criteria used at UMASS and suggest the strengths and weaknesses of the system.
   - Compare and contrast performance management at UMASS with that of the multinational healthcare company Medtronic after looking at their website: http://www.medtronic.com/2010CitizenshipReport/total-employee/global-learning.html

---

Further reading

Books

Brewster, C., Carey, L., Dowling, P., Grobbler, P., Holland, P. and Warnich, S. (2007) *Contemporary Issues in Human Resource Management* (2nd edn). Cape Town: Oxford University Press Southern Africa.

Briscoe, D., Randall, S. and Clauss, L. (2009) *International Human Resource Management: Policies and Practice for Multinational Enterprises* (3rd edn). London: Routledge.

Casio, W. (2006) Global performance management systems. In Stahl, G. K. and Bjorkman, J. (eds) *Handbook of Research in International Human Resource Management*. Cheltenham: Edward Elgar, pp. 176–96.

Dowling, P., Festing, M. and Engle, S. (2008) *International Human Resource Management*. Melbourne: Cengage Learning.

Harzing, A. W. and Van Ruysseveldt, J. (2005) *International Human Resource Management*. London: Sage.

Kramar, R. and Bartam, T. (2010) *Human Resource Management in Australia: Strategy, People and Performance* (5th edn). Sidney: McGraw-Hill.

Nankervis, A., Comptom, R. and Baird, M. (2007) *Strategic Human Resource Management* (6th edn). Melbourne: Cengage Learning.

Stone, R. J. (2008) *Human Resource Management* (6th edn). Milton, Queensland: John Wiley.

CASE STUDY

Performance appraisals in the not-for-profit sector

The Foundation, founded in the USA in 1960, is an international evangelical relief and development organization whose stated goal is 'to work with the poor and oppressed to promote human transformation, seek justice and bear witness to the good news of the Kingdom of God'. Working on six continents, The Foundation is a large relief and development organization that in 2009 had a $1.5 billion budget. In that same year, the group's total revenue, including grants, products and foreign donations, was $2.6 billion.

William Webster was a senior aid manager for The Foundation. William, a US citizen, had joined The Foundation's Boston office with excellent references following 10 years of global experience in international aid management, including working in Haiti, Mexico and India. Thirty-five-year-old William had an accounting degree from the University of New York and an International MBA from Columbia Business School. He had been working for The Foundation for 2 years when he gave the following account of his performance management experience there:

'Originally I was hired as the senior program manager for all of The Foundation's programmes worldwide. When I arrived for duty, the position had been split between me and a woman who had been at The Foundation for 5 years. She insisted on keeping India and Pakistan and would not cooperate in my redesign of the regional offices. This came as a great shock. I felt this was crazy as I had actually been on the ground in India for 2 years and felt I had a good understanding of the culture and people.

'This woman appeared to me to be very close to the director. They shared a love of the theatre and, as far as I can gather, were really good friends and frequently visited the theatre, opera and ballet together. This part of the arts is, I'm afraid, something I know very little about. While I enjoy a West End production, I am more a ball game kind of guy. To cut to the chase, in the end she and I didn't get along very well. After 2 years, the tsunami hit Asia and I told the chief operating officer (whom I reported to) that I would rather work on a special project, such as the tsunami-affected areas, and start a new programme in Indonesia. The chief operating officer took over my responsibilities. I told him that we needed one person in the role of senior program manager.

'After a few months, they hired a very capable Vice President of Programs, and I reported to her. We went out for lunch, and the topic of the Myers–Briggs personality test came up. She told me that she was an ENTJ (I am an INFP – the direct opposite). I went back to the office after lunch and looked up ENTJ. One of the famous quotes of a typical ENTJ is, 'I'm so sorry you have to die', so I knew I was in trouble. She came into the company like a bulldozer and ruffled a lot of feathers.

'I had been trying to raise funds for the tsunami and had $1 million to work with. I put together several proposals and started the programme in Indonesia. My assistant was a very power-hungry, ambitious recent graduate from graduate school, and her room-mate was best friends with the new VP of Programs. I assured her that we would raise the funds, but it took longer than I expected. Part of the problem was that there were no clear objectives for me and I had the office politics stacked against me.

'One Friday afternoon, a meeting was scheduled for my assistant Mary and me to meet with the VP of Programs. The VP then said that there was no need for Mary to join the meeting. I walked into the conference room and found the head of human resources and the chief operating officer in the room. The human resources manager proceeded to tell me that they were going to let me go but gave no reason. One of the most surprising things was that I had been given a very good performance appraisal a month earlier. Nothing negative had been raised, and all the top boxes had been ticked. The human resources manager, whom I had only met briefly once or twice before, asked me if I had anything to say. I told her I didn't know what to say. The three of them got up and left the room and closed the door. I remember sitting there crying alone.

'A week after I was let go, the American Red Cross granted the Foundation a $10 million grant for the tsunami programme – the proposal I had written and submitted. The chief operating officer resigned from his post a month later, and the VP resigned from hers within a year.'

Questions

1. Describe the major HRM issues at The Foundation?
2. If you were the head of human resources at The Foundation, how would you have handled this situation?
3. Describe the role of objectives and feedback in this case.
4. Discuss the process you might implement to strengthen the performance management process at The Foundation.

Source: This case is based on a personal interview with the informant. The name of the organization and employee have been changed for confidentiality.

References

Aguinis, H. (2008) Enhancing the relevance of organizational behaviour by embracing performance management research. *Journal of Organizational Behavior*, 9: 139–45.

Arvey, R. and Murphy, K. (1998). Performance evaluations in work settings. *Annual Review of Psychology*, 49: 141–68.

Ashford, S. J., Blatt, R. and Vande Walle, D. (2003) Reflections on the looking glass: a review of search on feedback-seeking behavior in organizations. *Journal of Management*, 29(6): 773–90.

Aydinlik, D., Arzu, D. and Ulgen, G. (2008) Communicating the ethos of codes of ethics within the organization: a comparison of the largest private sector organizations in Sweden and Turkey. *Journal of Management Development*, 27(7): 778–95.

Bernardin, H. and Beatty, R. (1984) *Performance Appraisal: Assessing Human Behaviour at Work*. Boston: Kent.

Birkinshaw, J. and Morrison, A. (1995) Configurations of strategy and structure in subsidiaries of MNCs. *International Business Studies*, 26(4): 729–40.

Borman, W. C. (1994) *Performance Evaluation in Organisations*: Farnham, Surrey: International Library of Management.

Bradley, L. and Ashkanasy, N. (2001) Performance appraisal interview: can they really be objective and are they useful anyway? *Asian Pacific Journal of Human Resources*, 39(2): 83–97.

Campbell, F. and Zarkada-Fraser, A. (2000) Measuring the performance of retail managers in Australia and Singapore. *International Journal of Retail and Distribution Management*, 28(6): 228–43.

Cardy, R. L. and Dobbins, G. H. (1994) *PA: Alternative Perspectives*. Cincinnati, OH: South-Western College Publishing.

Carroll, S. and Schneier, C. E. (1982) *Performance Appraisal and Review Systems: The Identification, Measurement and Development of Performance in Organisations*. Glenview, IL: Scott, Foresman.

Cascio, W. F. (2000) Managing a virtual work place. *Academy of Management Executive*, 12(3): 81–91.

Cascio, W. F. (2003) *Managing Human Resources: Productivity, Quality of Work Life, Profits* (8th edn). New York: McGraw-Hill.

Castellano, J. and Harper, R. (2001) The problems with MBO. *Quality Process*, 34(3): 39–49.

Chiang, F. T. and Birtch, T. (2010) Appraising performance across borders: an empirical examination of the purpose and practices of performance appraisal in a multi-country context. *Journal of Management Studies*, 47(7): 1365–92.

Chong, E. (2008) Managerial competency appraisal: a cross-cultural study of American and East Asian Managers. *Journal of Business Research*, 61(3): 191–200.

Claus, L. and Briscoe, D. (2009) Employee performance management across borders: a review of the relevant literature. *International Journal of Management Reviews*, 11(2): 175–96.

Cleveland, J. and Murphy, K. (1992) Analysing performance appraisal as goal-directed behaviour. In Ferris, G., Rowland, K. R. (eds) *Research in Personnel and Human Resource Management* (Vol. 10). Greenwich, CT: JAI Press, pp. 121–85.

Colquitt, J. A., Kossek, E. E. and Raymond, A. (2001) Care giving decisions, well-beings, and performance: the effects of place and provider as a function of dependent type and work-family climates. *Academy of Management Journal*, 44(1): 29–44.

Corporate Leadership Council (2006) *Considerations for Implementing 360-Degree Reviews: Secondary Research Findings*. Washington, DC: Corporate Executive Board.

De Cieri, H. and Dowling, P. (1998) *The Tortuous Evolution of Strategic Human Resources in Multinational Enterprises*. Department of Management, Working Paper in Human Resource Management and Industrial Relations No. 5. Melbourne: University of Melbourne.

De Cieri, H. and Kramar, R. (2010) *Human Resource Management in Australia* (3rd edn). North Ryde, NSW: McGraw-Hill.

Delery, J. and Doty, D. H. (1996) Modes of theorising in strategic human resource management: tests of universalistic, contingency and configurational performance predictions. *Academy of Management Journal*, 39(4): 802–22.

Deming, W. E. (1982) *Quality Productivity and Competitive Position*. Cambridge, MA: Massachusetts Institute of Technology Press.

DeNisi, A. S. and Pritchard, R. D. (2006) Performance appraisal, performance management and improving individual performance: a motivational framework. *Management and Organization Review*, 2: 253–77.

Dinesh, D. and Palmer, E. (1998) MBO and the balanced scorecard: will Rome fall again? *Management Decisions*, 36(6): 363–9.

Dowling, P., Welch, D. and Schuler, R. (1999) *International Dimensions of Human Resources*. Cincinnati, OH: South-Western College Publishing.

Dowling, P., Festing, M. and Engle, S. (2008) *International Human Resource Management* (5th edn). Melbourne: Cengage Learning.

Eichinger, R. and Lombardo, M. (2003) Knowledge 360-degree theory. *Human Resource Planning*, 26(4): 34–45.

Entrekin, L. V. and Chung, J. K. (2001) The attitudes toward different sources of executive appraisal: a comparison of Hong Kong Chinese and American managers in Hong Kong. *International Journal of Human Resource Management*, 12(6): 965–87.

Erdogan, B. (2002) Antecedents and consequences of justice perceptions in performance appraisals. *Human Resource Management Review*, (12): 555–78.

Farr, J. and Jacobs, R. (2006) The criterion problem today and into the 21st century. In Bennett, W., Lance, C. E. and Woehr, D. J. (eds) *Performance Measurement: Current Perspectives and Future Challenges*. Mahwah, NJ: Lawrence Erlbaum, pp. 321–38.

Fenwick, M. (2004) International assignments and expatriation. *Asian Pacific Journal of Human Resources*, 42(3): 365–77.

Fenwick, M. (2005) International compensation and performance management. In Harzing, A. W. and Ruysseveldt, J. (eds) *International human resource management*. London: Sage, Chapter 12.

Festinger, L. (1957) *A Theory of Cognitive Dissonance*. Stanford, CA: Stanford University Press.

Ghoshal, S. and Bartlett, C. (1998) *Managing Across Borders: The Transnational Solution*. London: Random House Business.

Gillespie, T. (2006) Internationalizing 360-degree feedback: are subordinate ratings comparable? *Journal of Business and Psychology*, 19(3): 361–82.

Gosselin, A., Werner, J. M. and Halle, N. (1997) Ratee preference and appraisal. *Human Resource Development Quarterly*, 8(4): 315–33.

Hanson, D., Dowling, P. J., Hitt, M. A., Ireland, D. R. and Hoskisson, R. E. (2005) *Strategic Management: Competitiveness and Globalisation* (2nd edn). Victoria, Australia: Thomson Learning Australia.

Harris, R., Smith, D. E. and Champagne, D. (1995) A field study of PA purpose research vs administrative based ratings. *Personnel Psychology*, 48(1): 151–60.

Harvey, M. (1997) Focusing on international performance appraisal process. *Human Resources Development*, 8(1): 41–62.

Harvey, M., Speier, C. and Novicevic, M. (2002) The evolution of SHRM systems and their application in a foreign subsidiary context. *Asian Pacific Journal of Human Resources*, 40(3): 284–300.

Harzing, A.W. and Noordhaven, N. (2005) Geographical distance and the role of management of the subsidiaries: the case of subsidiaries down under. *Asian Pacific Journal of Management*, 23: 167–85.

Harzing, A.W. and Ruysseveldt, J. (2005) *International Human Resource Management*. London: Sage.

Hedge, J. W. and Teachout, M. S. (2000) Exploring the concepts of acceptability as a criterion for evaluating performance measures. *Group and Organisation Management*, 25(1): 22–44.

Hempel, P. (2001) Differences between Chinese and Western managerial views of performance. *Personnel Review*, 30(2): 203–26.

Hofstede, G. (1980) *Culture's Consequences: International Differences in Work Related Values*. Beverly Hills, CA: Sage.

Hofstede, G. and Hofstede, G. J. (2005) *Cultures and Organisations: Software of the Mind*. London: McGraw-Hill.

Ilgen, D. and Feldman, J. M. (1990) Performance appraisal: a process focus. In Cummings, L. and Staw, B. (eds) *Evaluation and Employment in Organisations*. Greenwich, CT: JAI Press.

Juncaj, T. (2002) Do performance appraisals work? *Quality Progress*, 35(11): 45–9.

Justo, A. (2009) The Effective Implementation of Multi-source Feedback Processes. Available from: http://armandojusto.blogspot.com/2009/09/effective-implementation-of-multi.html [accessed 14 October 2011].

Kaplan, R. S. and Norton, P. (1992) The balanced scorecard – measures that drive performance. *Harvard Business Review*, 70(1): 71–5.
Kaplan, R. and Palus, C. J. (1994) *Enhancing 360-Degree Feedback for Senior Executives*. Greensboro, NC: Center for Creative Leadership.
Kramar, R. and Bartram, T. (2010) *Human Resource Management in Australia*. Australia: McGraw-Hill.
Kurzberg, T., Naquin, C. and Belkin, Y. (2005) The effects of email communication on peer ratings in actual and simulated environments. *Organizational Behavior and Human Decision Processes*, 98(2): 216–226.
Lam, S., Hui C. and Law, K. (1999) Job-analysis; organizational-behavior; supervision-of-employees; cultural-differences. *Journal of Applied Psychology*, 84(4): 594–601.
Lansbury, R. D. and Quince, A. (1988) Performance appraisal: a critical review of its role in HRM. In Palmer, G (ed.) *Australian Personnel Management: A Reader*. Melbourne: Macmillan.
Lawrie, G. (2004) Third-generation balanced scorecard: evolution of an effective strategic control tool. *International Journal of Productivity and Performance Management*, 53(7): 611–30.
Levinson, H. (1991) Management by whose objectives. *Harvard Business Review*, 69(92): 176–90.
Levy, P. and Williams, J. (2004) The social context of performance appraisal: a review and framework for the future. *Journal of International Management*, 30(6): 881–905.
Lindholm, N., Tahvanainen, M. and Bjorkman, I. (1999) Performance appraisal of host country employees: Western MNEs in China. In Brewster, C. and Harris, H. (eds) *International HRM: Contemporary Issues in Europe*. London: Routledge, pp. 143–59.
Longnecker, C. O. (1994) The paradoxes of political appraisal: tales from the dark side. Paper presented at the Society for Organisational and Industrial Psychology Conference, September 1994, Nashville, TN, USA.
Longnecker, C. O. and Gioia, D. A. (1988) Neglected at the top: executives talk about appraisals. *Sloan Management Review*, 21: 183–93.
Maley, J. (2009) The impact of the performance appraisal on the psychological contract of the remote subsidiary manager. *South African Journal of Human Resource Management*, (2): 63–73.
Maley, J. (2011) The influence of various human resource management strategies on the performance management of subsidiary managers. *Asia Pacific Journal of Business*, 3(1): 2.
Maley, J. and Kramar, R. (2007) International performance appraisal: policies, practices and processes in Australian subsidiaries of healthcare MNCs. *Research and Practice in Human Resource Management*, 15(2): 21–41.
Masterson, S., Lewis, K., Goldman, B. and Taylor, M. (2000) Integrating justice and social exchange: the differing effects of fair procedures and treatment on work relationships. *Academy of Management Journal*, 43: 738–48.
Mero, N. P. and Motowidlo, S. J. (1995) Effects of rater accountability on the accuracy and the favourability of performance ratings. *Journal of Applied Psychology*, 80(4): 517–24.
Milliman, J., Taylor, S. and Czaplewski, A. (2000) Performance feedback in MNC: opportunities for organizational learning. *Human Resource Planning*, 25(3): 29–44.
Milliman, J., Nason, S., Zhu, C. and De Cieri, H. (2002) An exploratory assessment of the purpose of PA in North and Central America and the Pacific Rim. *Asian Pacific Journal of Human Resources*, 40(1): 78–101.
Mintzberg, H. (1973) *The Nature of Managerial Work*. New York: Harper & Row.
Murphy, K. (1993) *Honesty in the Workplace*. Belmont, CA: Wadsworth.
Murphy, K. and Cleveland, J. (1991) *Performance Appraisal: An Organisational Perspective*. Boston: Allyn & Bacon.
Murphy, K. and Cleveland, J. (1995) *Understanding Performance Appraisal*. London: Sage.
Nankervis, A. and Compton, R. (2006) Performance management: theory in practice. *Asian Pacific Journal of Human Resources*, 44(1): 83–101.
Othmana, R., Domil, A., Senik, Z., Abdullah, A. and Hamzah, H. (2006) A case study of balanced scorecard implementation in a Malaysian company. *Journal of Asia-Pacific Business*, 7(2): 55–72.
Ouchi, W. (1982) *Theory Z*. New York: Addison-Wesley.

Palmer, J. and Loveland, J. (2008) The influence of group discussion on performance judgment accuracy, contrast effects and halo. *Journal of Psychology: Interdisciplinary and Applied*, 142(2): 117–30.

Perkmann, M. and Walsh, K. (2007) University–industry relationships and open innovation: towards a research agenda. *International Journal of Management Reviews*, 9(4): 259–80.

Saavedra, R. and Kwun, S. K. (1993) Peer evaluation in self-managing work groups. *Journal of Applied Psychology*, 78(3): 450–62.

Shen, J. (2004) International performance appraisals: policies, practices and determinants in the case of Chinese multinational companies. *International Journal of Management*, 25(6): 547–63.

Snape, E., Thompson, D., Yan, F. and Redman, T. (1998) Performance appraisal and culture: practice and attitudes in Hong Kong and Great Britain. *International Journal of Human Resource Management*, (5): 842–61.

Sully De Luque, M. and Sommer, S. (2007) The impact of culture on feedback seeking behaviour: an integrated model and propositions. *Academy of Management Review*, 25(4): 829–49.

Taormina, R. and Gao, J. (2009) Identifying acceptable performance appraisal criteria: an international perspective. *Asia Pacific Journal of Human Resource Management*, 47(1): 102–24.

Taylor, S., Masterson, S., Renard, M. and Tracy, K. (1998) Managers reactions to procedurally just management systems. *Academy of Management Journal*, 41(5): 568–79.

Tziner, A. and. Kopelman, R. (2002) Is there a preferred performance rating format? A non-psychometric perspective. *Applied Psychology*, 51: 479–503.

Tziner, A., Murphy, K. and Cleveland, J. (1998) Relationships between attitudes towards organisations and performance appraisal systems and rating behaviour: a multinational study. Paper presented at the 24th International Congress of Applied Psychology, May 1988, San Francisco, USA.

Ulrich, D. (1997) *Human Resource Champions*. Boston: Harvard Business School Press.

Vance, C. M. (2006) Strategic upstream and downstream considerations for effective global performance management. *International Journal of Cross Cultural Management*, 6(1): 37–56.

Varela, O. and Premeaux, S. (2008) Cross-cultural values affect multisource feedback dynamics? The case of high power distance and collectivism in two Latin American countries. *International Journal of Selection and Assessment*, 16(2): 134–42.

Varma, A., Pichler, S. and Srinivas, E. (2005) The role of interpersonal affect in performance appraisal: evidence from two samples – the US and India. *International Journal of Human Resource Management*, 16(11): 2030–43.

Varma, A., Budhwar, P. and De Nisi, A. (2008) *Performance Management Systems: A Global Perspective*. New York: Routledge.

Wood, R. and Marshall, V. (1993) Performance appraisal: practice, problems and issues. Paper presented at the Private Pay for Public Work conference, May 1993, Paris, France.

Wright, P. M. and McMahan, G. C. (1992) Theoretical perspectives for strategic human resource management. *Journal of Management*, 18: 295–320.

Wright, P. and Snell, S. (1998) Toward a unifying framework for exploring fit and flexibility in strategic human resource management. *Academy of Management Review*, 23(4): 756–72.

Yu, J. and Murphy, K. (1993) Modesty bias in self-ratings of performance: a test of the cultural relativity hypothesis. *Personnel Psychology*, (46): 357–63.

CHAPTER 12
Reward management
John Shields

- Introduction
- Employee rewards: nature and purpose
- Intrinsic versus extrinsic rewards: which are more motivating?
- Taking a critical perspective on reward management
- Base pay
- Benefits plans
- Performance-related reward plans
- Reward communication
- Employment relations and reward management
- International reward management
- Conclusion
- For discussion and revision
- Further reading
- Case study: The strategy and practice of rewards in Chinese MNCs
- References

After reading this chapter, you should be able to:
- Appreciate the value of a constructively critical (pluralist) approach to understanding the theory and practice of reward management, particularly taking an employee-centred perspective
- Understand how reward strategies, programmes and policies are structured in both domestic and international contexts
- Demonstrate a detailed awareness of the variety of financial and non-financial reward practices and of the different motivational and behavioural assumptions associated with particular types of reward
- Recognize the concepts, methods and techniques associated with managing employee reward in both domestic and international contexts

- Demonstrate a detailed understanding of the differences and complementarities between each of the three main components of monetary reward for employees: base pay, benefits and performance pay
- Understand the options and challenges involved in the application of theories, concepts and practices related to reward
- Appreciate how social and cultural factors affect employees' perceptions of pay fairness, and how these perceptions affect the design and effectiveness of pay programmes
- Formulate practical solutions to the challenges of designing and implementing reward strategies, programmes and policies that will support the organization's needs to attract, retain, motivate and develop domestic and international employees

Introduction

Reward management is one of the most important yet most problematic of all human resource management (HRM) functions. Reward management is not only one of the most technically demanding facets of HRM, but also one of the most complex and controversial in terms of the assumptions and debates surrounding the drivers of human motivation and work behaviour. Rewards are a 'red button' issue in the domain of people management.

As experienced human resources professionals know, reward management is very easy to do badly – but difficult to do well. An effective reward system has to be not only soundly designed and integrated, but also carefully implemented, communicated and monitored. The telltale signs of reward mismanagement include perceived reward inequity (or unfairness), low motivation and effort on the part of employees, low job satisfaction, reduced commitment to the organization, higher intention to leave and increased staff turnover: in short, poor 'engagement' of employees with their job, their managers, their peers, their organization and its customers.

This chapter presents an overview of the controversies, concepts and practices associated with the reward management function. In doing this, it offers a constructively critical perspective on the main theories, tools and techniques for configuring effective reward systems for both domestic and international employees. First, we will consider the basic nature and purpose of remuneration and other rewards. We then proceed to explore one of the central debates in the field – that surrounding the relative merits of extrinsic and intrinsic rewards. Next, we will consider the value of seeking to understand reward management from a constructively critical (pluralist) perspective, particularly in relation to acknowledging that employees are not simply 'resource' objects but, rather, are organizational stakeholders with their own distinct needs, expectations and rights, as well as their own responsibilities and contractual obligations to their employer.

Attention then turns to the three main elements of monetary reward or remuneration – base pay, benefits and performance-related rewards – and the types of pay plan associated with each of these. We will consider the general strengths and weaknesses of each major pay plan type, along with debates concerning both the effectiveness and the fairness of incentive plans and other performance-related reward practices.

As reward effectiveness is not simply a matter of system design, but also a function of how clearly and consistently the system's principles and practices are communicated to the employees concerned, the penultimate section of the chapter will examine both reward communications and the cognate and highly controversial matter of reward secrecy and transparency.

Finally, we will explore the special challenges associate with managing employee rewards in international contexts, noting the differences between 'home', 'host' and 'regional' approaches to reward configuration. This section also sets the stage for the chapter's major case study, which describes the additional challenges and options associated with the management of reward systems in an international context. Specifically, this case study of the reward strategies and practices of Chinese multinational corporations (MNCs) invites us to reflect on the complexities of reward management for line employees and expatriate reward management in host country contexts. As we shall see, the case highlights the dual approach to international reward practice favoured by firms headquartered in this rapidly emerging economic superpower.

However, before immersing ourselves in the details of domestic and international reward practice, it is important that we address the nature and purpose of rewards in general.

Employee rewards: nature and purpose

A reward may be anything tangible (for example, pay) or intangible (for example, praise) that an organization offers to its employees in exchange for their belonging to the organization and for contributing work behaviours and results of the type that the organization needs from its people in order to meet its strategic objectives, however these might be defined.

A reward system has four primary objectives:

- To attract (or 'buy') the right people at the right time for the right jobs, tasks or roles.
- To retain the best people by satisfying their work-related needs and aspirations, and recognizing and rewarding their contribution.
- To develop (or 'build') the required workforce capabilities by recognizing and rewarding employees' actions to enhance their knowledge, skill and ability.
- To motivate employees to contribute to the best of their capability by recognizing and rewarding high individual and group contributions towards meeting the organization's strategic objectives.

At the same time, a well-designed and administered reward system has a number of important secondary objectives. In particular, it should seek to be the following:

- *Needs-fulfilling*: the rewards should be of value to employees in satisfying their relevant human needs.

- *Equitable or 'felt-fair'*: reward levels should be seen to be both commensurate with individual contributions and appropriate in comparison with the reward levels received by others.
- *Legal*: rewards should comply with relevant legal requirements regarding employees' rights and entitlements, including standards for mandatory minimum pay and benefits.
- *Affordable*: the rewards allocated, and any associated on-costs, should fall within the organization's financial means.
- *Cost-effective*: there should be an appropriate 'return on investment' from total reward outlays.
- *Strategically aligned*: the reward system should be configured so as to support the organization's strategic objectives.

There is, however, considerable potential for conflict between these objectives. For instance, tensions may arise between the goals of cost-containment and of offering rewards that are sufficient to attract and retain the right type and number of employees. From an organizational perspective, the optimal approach is not necessarily the cheapest. Rather, the optimal approach is the one that will maximize the returns to the organization in comparison with the outlay made – and this takes us back to the vital matter of strategic reward management.

Exercise

- What would you say are the three most important functions of any system of employee reward, and why do you think these are the most important overall?

Intrinsic versus extrinsic rewards: which are more motivating?

Rewards can be divided into two broad categories: 'extrinsic' and 'intrinsic'.

Extrinsic rewards arise from factors associated with but external to the job that the employee does, that is, from the job context. Extrinsic rewards are of three main types:

- financial rewards
- developmental rewards
- social rewards.

Financial rewards – also referred to as 'pay', 'remuneration' or 'compensation' – are also of three main types:

- base pay (the fixed component of the total remuneration);
- benefits, such as the employer's contributions to superannuation and personal health insurance;
- performance-related pay plans, including 'incentives', which vary with the performance measured.

Although pay may be the most obvious form of extrinsic reward, it is not the only form of reward, nor is it necessarily the most important in terms of influencing employees' attitudes, behaviour and effort. *Developmental rewards* cover those rewards associated with personal learning, development and career growth, such as skills training and performance and leadership coaching. *Social rewards* are those associated with seniority and other forms of social esteem or status, a positive organizational climate, support for performance, quality of supervision, work-group affinity, and opportunities for enhanced work–life balance, such as flexible working time arrangements, staff sabbaticals, fitness and wellness programmes, and so on. In some cultures, developmental and social rewards may be more highly prized than rewards of a monetary nature. As the example in Box 12.1 suggests, employees in India may respond much more positively to having access to a clear career pathway than to being offered performance-related pay.

Intrinsic rewards arise from the content of the job itself, including the interest and challenge that it provides, task variety and autonomy, the degree of feedback, and the meaning and significance attributed to the job. One of the most important determinants of the level of intrinsic rewards in any organization is thus the way

---

Box 12.1 For Indian employees, money isn't everything

Globe Ground India (GGI), a subsidiary of the German airline Lufthansa, operates passenger and cargo handling for Lufthansa, as well as ground and ramp activities in Delhi, Mumbai and a number of other Indian cities. In 2006, facing serious staff turnover and motivation problems, GGI conducted focus interviews with staff with a view to identifying ways in which the firm's reward system could be strengthened to improve staff retention and motivation.

The initial plan was to use the information gathered to develop a long-term incentive plan on top of the yearly bonus. However, one of the interview questions asked staff to nominate the 'highest incentive for you to increase your motivation', and the results were both unexpected and revealing. Staff rated 'money/higher wages' as third behind 'career/status' and 'job pleasure/enjoyment'. Clearly, intrinsic rewards and developmental opportunities were most salient for GGI's staff. Other studies confirm that career management, job design, benefits entitlements and consistent salary adjustment are particularly important to employees in India.

After analysing the results, GGI developed and introduced a new 'total rewards' approach focusing not on long-term incentives but on meeting employees' developmental and job interest needs, and on offering career pathways and prospects. This approach was then set out clearly and comprehensively in a new human resources manual.

This is not to suggest that money does not matter at all. As employees often queried the prior mode of salary adjustment and argued for seniority-based adjustment, the manual explains that salary increases are based on individual contribution and not on time of service alone.

Source: Adapted from Lang (2008).

in which its jobs are designed. One of the longstanding and animated debates in contemporary theory and practice in reward management concerns the relative merits of intrinsic and extrinsic rewards. Many commentators contend that extrinsic rewards in general, and performance-related pay in particular, are the most powerful motivators (see, for example, Deci and Ryan, 1985; Kohn, 1993a, 1993b). Others argue that intrinsic rewards provide the best basis for superior motivation and performance (see, for example, Gupta and Mitra, 1998; Gerhart et al., 2009).

Arguments that support incentive-based rewards derive either explicitly or implicitly from one or other of the main 'process' theories of work motivation. These theories, which include agency theory, reinforcement theory, expectancy theory, goal-setting theory and equity theory, all emphasize the centrality of employees' cognitive processes in understanding and managing the relationship between rewards and task motivation (Shields, 2007):

- *Agency theory*, which assumes a potential conflict of interest between 'principals' (that is, owners) and self-seeking 'agents' (that is, hired employees), holds that performance-contingent pay is the most effective means of aligning employees' economic interests with those of employers/owners.
- *Reinforcement theory* posits that a timely reward for a given desired action will motivate employees to repeat the rewarded action, whereas punishment in the form of non-reward will extinguish any misbehaviour.
- *Expectancy theory* holds that an incentive is likely to motivate higher work effort if: (1) employees see the promised reward as personally valuable; (2) they expect that they can achieve the required level of performance; and (3) they trust the employer to deliver the reward in exchange for the achieved performance.
- *Goal-setting theory* suggests that employees will be motivated more strongly by performance targets that are specific, agreed and challenging, and by feedback that is precise and instantaneous.

A further common rationale for performance-related rewards is that they operationalize the 'equity' norm of distributive justice. *Equity theory* proposes, in part, that reward satisfaction stems from making employee reward outcomes (including pay level) commensurate with employees' individual inputs (Shields, 2007). In short, high performers should be paid more than low performers, with the inequality of the reward being proportional to the difference in individual performance. This is a common justification for performance-related pay. However, some motivation theorists question the claimed efficacy of extrinsic rewards and propose that rewards that are intrinsic to the job are the only true motivators.

Exponents of cognitive evaluation theory go further still, contending that the use of extrinsic rewards (and punishments) may destroy the intrinsic motivation that flows from inherent interest in the job. Also known as intrinsic motivation theory, *cognitive evaluation theory* posits that people are much more likely to act first and only evaluate, rationalize and ascribe meaning and motive to what they have done after the event. The tendency is to confer motivational meaning on the behaviour – that is, to attribute meaning and purpose to it – only in retrospect. People are more likely to ask, 'Why *have* I done this?' than 'Why *should* I do this?' Cognitive evaluation theory suggests that individuals who have been deriving

> **Box 12.2 Intrinsic versus extrinsic rewards – which are best?**
>
> The assumption that extrinsic and intrinsic factors are dichotomous rather than complementary is open to challenge. Some research suggests that extrinsic and intrinsic rewards can make a joint contribution to job satisfaction and other desired work attitudes and behaviour. Cameron and Pierce (1997) used a meta-analysis of a hundred studies of reward–performance effects to argue that intrinsic and extrinsic motivation combine in an additive way to produce an overall motivational force. They found that people generally enjoyed performing a task more rather than less when they received an extrinsic verbal or tangible reward. In particular, Cameron and Pierce highlighted that praise led to greater task interest and performance. The negative effects of extrinsic rewards, they suggested, were limited and easily prevented.
>
> Exponents of the intrinsic rewards approach assume that it is possible to enrich all jobs when, in reality, this is not always so. For better or worse, many manufacturing and service organizations succeed quite effectively with job assignments that have limited skill content, a narrow task range and low autonomy.

high intrinsic rewards for their work tasks may radically revise their self-attributed motives for doing the work once a financial incentive is offered to them.

The point here is that the initial motivation to do something is likely to be implicit and intrinsic rather than premeditated and driven by the pursuit of some extrinsic reward. For this reason, Deci and Ryan (1985) argue that extrinsic rewards should not be applied to task performance because these may very well dissipate the intrinsic motivation that may initially have driven the employee's performance. The perception of being 'controlled' extrinsically is assumed to be demotivating, a point embraced with some passion by several prominent opponents of performance incentives (Kohn, 1993a).

Nevertheless, cognitive evaluation theory is also open to challenge. As suggested in Box 12.2, it is by no means clear that intrinsic and extrinsic motivation are opposites; indeed, as critics suggest, the weight of evidence indicates that the two are, if anything, mutually reinforcing (Rynes et al., 2005). Furthermore, it is questionable whether most work behaviour is impulsive rather than premeditated, experience suggesting that both play a part in work behaviour. On the practical side, although cognitive evaluation theory may be quite appropriate for jobs and roles that are intrinsically motivating in the first instance, not all jobs will be intrinsically rewarding. In such cases, it will be necessary either to enrich the job content or to offer more in the way of pay or other extrinsic rewards.

Taking a critical perspective on reward management

The debate over the relative influence of intrinsic and extrinsic motivational drivers and rewards also illustrates the value of adopting a constructively critical approach to the theory and practice of reward management. An ill-conceived reward system may not only fail to elicit the desired behaviour, but may instead also encourage behaviour that is dysfunctional, deceptive or even destructive; that is, it may give rise to endemic organizational misbehaviour. A critical approach to reward management may help to avert such problems.

A critical approach to reward management requires us to both question our assumptions about what employees may find rewarding and motivating, and also to seek to interpret reward management from a multi-stakeholder (or 'pluralist') perspective – one acknowledging that employees have rights, interests and expectations that are not wholly congruent with those of the employing organization. As such, a critical approach moves away from the 'unitarist' or 'managerialist' assumption that the only relevant stakeholder interest is that of the employer, and that employees are merely 'human resource' objects serving employer-determined ends (Watson, 2004). It also reminds us of the ethical importance and analytical value of adopting an employee-centred approach to understanding the nature and impact of reward management practice (Grant and Shields, 2006). What is a cost to the employer is income and economic security for employees and their dependents; what is a competitive level of pay to the employer may be seen as inequitable by the employee.

Building on these points, a critical pluralist approach also requires consideration to be given to the nature and significance of employees' 'voice', 'say' or 'representation' in determining rewards. How much influence do employees have, either collectively or individually, over the processes by which their monetary rewards are determined? In developed economies, trade unions have traditionally been seen as the chief vehicles of the collective voice in determining pay and conditions of employment, particularly by means of collective bargaining at industry or enterprise level. In 'coordinated' market economies of the type typical of the northern and western Member States of the European Union, the unions' influence in setting pay has traditionally been paralleled by government intervention and regulation designed both to protect low-paid workers and moderate pay increases for employees with greater bargaining power.

However, in developed economies, recent decades have witnessed a decline in union membership and union influence via collective bargaining, particularly in the private sector, along with a retreat from direct government intervention in pay regulation, and this has been accompanied by significant changes in employee voice. Such changes are sometimes taken as signifying the erosion of the employee's voice and a strengthening of 'managerial prerogative' in pay determination.

An alternative interpretation is that employee 'say in pay' has assumed new forms rather than necessarily diminishing. According to Lindrop (2009), new outlets for collective and individual employee voice have emerged. In countries such as the UK and Australia, the vacuum created by the decline in union collective bargaining has been filled, in part, by the rise of new institutions to determine pay, including occupational pay review bodies and tribunals changed with determining 'fair pay' standards for low-paid workers.

At an organizational level, suggests Lindrop (2009), the new voice mechanisms include collective mechanisms such as joint management–employee consultative committees and individually focused direct communication practices, for example direct employee attitude surveys; these are designed in part to inform improvements in reward system design and hence to strengthen employees' satisfaction with rewards, as well as their motivation and commitment to the organization. As we shall see, various forms of 'financial participation' on the part of employees, such as employee share ownership and profit-sharing, may also be vehicles for employee voice and involvement. Yet the extent to which these new mechanisms do in fact support a genuine voice and influence, and a critical pluralist perspective, requires their consequences to be examined from the employees' frame of reference rather than simply from that of the employing organization.

A critical approach also reminds us that the language of reward management – the 'discourse' or 'talk and text' – serves to influence ('construct') employees' and management's perceptions of themselves, each other, the nature of the employment relationship, organizational power inequalities and, indeed, organizational 'reality' itself.

Drawing on the work of French philosopher and historian, Michel Foucault, Barbara Townley (1993a, 1993b, 1994, 1998, 1999) argues that managers simultaneously empower themselves and subjugate those whom they are managing. They do this by means of discourses and practices that individualize, objectify and discipline workers and shape their subjectivity and concept of self and work reality by means of complex regimes of classification, ordering and measurement. As such, the language associated with reward practices such as job evaluation, performance-related pay and competency-based pay can be understood as serving to shape employees' perceptions that differences in reward levels are natural, appropriate and objectively determined.

For our purposes, the key point here is that reward management is concerned with shaping employees' identities, attitudes and behaviour through both language and practice. From a critical perspective, then, it is important that we appreciate the centrality of reward concepts, how these are communicated to employees by managers, and the meanings that employees attribute to these discursive concepts (Grant and Shields, 2006).

Base pay

Base pay is the foundational or 'fixed' component of remuneration and, for most employees, typically comprises the largest single component of total remuneration, with benefits and performance pay making up the remainder. In many countries, legislatures or tribunals have prescribed the payment of guaranteed minimum wage or salary levels. Base pay is generally regarded as the pay type best suited to addressing the objectives of attracting and retaining staff. Providing each employee with a guaranteed level of base pay demonstrates the employer's commitment to the employee, which in turn means that the employee is more likely to reciprocate. Base pay is also the pay component most closely involved in the setting and enforcement of minimum pay standards.

Although base pay systems can be very diverse, there are two broad approaches to building base pay:

- job-based pay;
- person-based pay.

As well as making different assumptions about what base pay can contribute to an organization and how it can do so, these two approaches to configuring base pay entail distinct types of pay structure (that is, the formal 'architecture' of the base pay system) as well as different modes of evaluation (that is, the pricing of jobs and/or job-holders) and distinct modes of pay progression (that is, the 'rules' determining how each person's base pay level adjusts over time). Table 12.1 highlights the main points of difference between the job-based and person-based approaches, while Table 12.2 summarises the two main base pay options, including the structures, evaluation techniques and modes of progression associated with each.

Job-based base pay

The traditional practice has been to fix base pay according to the 'size' or 'value' of the *job* or *position* occupied. Jobs of larger 'size' – that is, with a greater content of tasks, duties and responsibilities – attract higher levels of base pay, and employees can increase their base pay chiefly by ascending a hierarchy of job-related pay steps incorporated into either a ladder-like pay scale or a stairway of narrow job grades.

A pay scale typically consists of a hierarchy of position-specific pay levels, each comprising a sequence of flat pay rates, steps or points. Traditionally, stepwise pay increments within each level were based on seniority or service, with the increase occurring automatically after each year of service.

Table 12.1 Job-based versus person-based base pay

Job-based base pay	Person-based base pay
Jobs add value	Individuals add value
Pay for job's worth	Pay for individual's worth
Pay for the 'size' of the job occupied	Pay for each individual's capacity to perform (that is, their KSAs)
Standard rate for the job, irrespective of KSA differences between job-holders	Different rates of pay depending on assessed capacity (KSAs)
Time-based payment according to time on the job	Time-based payment according to KSA levels
Direct external market pricing	Indirect external market pricing (disaggregated job pay rates)
Evaluation method: job evaluation	Evaluation methods: skill and/or competency assessment
Pay progression and promotion are based on seniority or merit	Pay progression is based on KSA development
Reinforces the promotional hierarchy	Reinforces KSA development

KSA, knowledge, skill and ability.

Table 12.2 Options for base pay

	Structures	Evaluation techniques	Modes of pay progression
Job-based pay	Pay ladders Narrow grades	Market surveys and/or job evaluation	Seniority and/or 'merit'-based increments and promotion
Person-base pay	Broad grades or job families Broadband systems	Skill assessment Competency assessment	Skill sets Competency zones or levels

A narrow grade (also known as a 'job grade') houses a group of jobs of similar size/value to the organization, and specifies a pay range for these jobs rather than a scale step or spot rate. Each grade will cover a group of jobs regarded as being of similar value to the organization and therefore worthy of roughly the same range of base pay. Unlike simple pay scales, each grade allows for some variance in pay level based on the 'merit' of the individual job holder, but the range over which pay can vary is usually quite narrow, typically no more than 30 per cent, with the midpoint of the range serving as the pay rate for acceptable proficiency in the job (Shields, 2007; Perkins and White, 2008).

In job-based systems, there are two main techniques for pricing each job or position: market surveys and job evaluation.

Market surveys involve setting pay rates for particular jobs according to what other employers are paying for the same or similar jobs in external labour markets. Regular market surveys also allow organizations to monitor changes in market rates and adjust their own pay rates accordingly. As such, the approach emphasizes 'external competitiveness' in determining the rate for the job. The organization ascertains the range of amounts that other organizations are paying for jobs similar to its own, and then makes a strategic choice about where it will position itself relative to its competitors. For this purpose, the market range for each position is commonly expressed as either percentile or quartile means (Shields, 2007). Rather than undertaking the data-gathering themselves, many organizations use the market data provided by consulting firms specializing in remuneration.

Job evaluation, which is frequently seen as an alternative to reliance on market data, involves determining relative pay rates by relating them to the importance or relative value of the job to the organization. This is achieved by comparing jobs on a number of factors thought to be important in determining job value, such as skill, effort, responsibility or working conditions. The end result of job evaluation is a hierarchy of jobs in which all jobs of similar value to the organization, no matter how different they might be in other respects, are placed at the same level in the job-based pay hierarchy. As such, job evaluation emphasizes 'internal equity' in setting job-based pay rates rather than 'external competitiveness' per se (Shields, 2007; Perkins and White, 2008).

Job evaluation is thus a means of establishing and maintaining equitable differences in base pay between jobs within the organization, particularly between jobs at different organizational levels. The degree of difference in pay level between jobs at the top and the bottom of an organizational hierarchy is also known as 'vertical pay dispersion', and there is considerable debate over whether a high degree of dispersion is preferable to a low degree of dispersion or vice versa. Critical Thinking 12.1 challenges you to frame your views about this important aspect of base pay structure.

The most widely used approach to systematic job evaluation is the points factor method. A points factor system typically has four main elements:

1. *'Compensable' factors*: job inputs (such as skill, knowledge, education, training and experience), job reqirements (such as mental effort, physical effort, decision-making and supervision), job outputs (such as product accuracy, consequences of error, and responsibility for cash and assets) and job conditions (work environment, hazards, and so on).

> **Critical Thinking 12.1**
>
> **Pay dispersion**
>
> The term 'pay dispersion' refers to the degree of inequality in pay levels between jobs at the same organizational level (also called 'horizontal pay dispersion') and between jobs at different levels in the organization (also known a 'vertical pay dispersion') (Gerhart and Rynes, 2003).
>
> **Questions**
>
> 1. Is it better for an organization to have a high degree of vertical pay dispersion or a low degree of vertical dispersion?
> 2. How might the appropriateness of high variability differ according to the company's social and cultural context?

2. *Points-based rating scales* for these factors based how much of each factor is present.
3. *Factor weightings* reflecting the 'value-adding' importance of each factor for the organization.
4. Assigning a monetary value to the total number of points assigned to each job.

As a means of valuing jobs and developing job-based pay structures, the points factor approach has much to commend it. It can introduce order, rationality, strategic focus and consistency into potentially arbitrary pay structures by using transparent and clearly defined measures of job size, and by offering a consistent means of measuring the relative size or value of the jobs involved. Furthermore, the points factor approach can also help to identify and eliminate inequities in the existing pay structure, as well as provide a rational basis for setting pay rates for new or changed jobs.

However, the points factor approach also has some weaknesses and drawbacks. In focusing on relative comparisons of job contents and on generic job content factors, it may downplay or even ignore critical strategic success factors related to the market, a point actually conceded by commentators who assert the continuing relevance of the approach to contemporary reward practice. According to Lawler (1988, 1990), points factor methods highlight job size over job-holder contribution, emphasize internal equity over external competitiveness, and reinforce bureaucracy and hierarchy. In practice, a well-managed system of job-based pay requires simultaneous attention to both internal equity and external competitiveness (Heneman and LeBlanc, 2002).

Job evaluation is sometimes seen as a means of correcting the gender-based pay inequality and distributive injustice (that is, unfairness in terms of reward outcome) evident in the wider labour market. Yet whether organizationally specific job evaluation can do much to further pay equity is a moot point. Indeed, some have argued that badly designed and badly implemented job evaluation may be a cause of continuing gender pay inequality rather than a reliable remedy (England and Kilbourne, 1991; Gupta and Jenkins, 1991).

> **Exercise**
>
> - When it comes to pricing jobs, what are the three main advantages of focusing on 'internal equity' considerations via the use of job evaluation?
> - What are the three main disadvantages of such an approach to job pricing?

Person-based base pay

More recently, the trend has been to configure base pay around the skills and competencies of the person rather than the 'size' of the job occupied, and to couple this to very different base pay structures. Person-based pay can be configured according to the ('hard') technical knowledge and skills possessed by the individual employee, according to underlying ('soft') personal abilities or competencies, or in terms of a combination of both 'hard' and 'soft' attributes.

By recognizing and rewarding the acquisition of technical skills and job-related knowledge, skill-based pay is said to facilitate functional flexibility through multi-skilling and teamworking. Multiskilling allows employees to be redeployed quickly without delays for retraining and minimizes the downtime arising from a lack of the required skills. By breaking down rigid job demarcations, it can in addition enable a more flexible utilization of the workforce as employees acquire a breadth and depth of relevant skills. Skill-based pay also lends itself to employees' involvement in system design and administration (Barrett, 1991; Ledford, 1991a, 1991b; Ledford and Heneman, 1999; Shields, 2007).

The basic building block for a skill-based system is the *skill set*. A skill set consists of a bundle of related tasks and activities – or 'skill elements' – the mastery of which constitutes a finite and verifiable unit of learning that can be used to develop and deliver training. Each skill set becomes a training module that must be completed successfully in order to warrant a further increase in the amount of base pay. In order to determine pay, associated skill sets are commonly housed in structures known as 'broad grades'. The pay range for each broad grade is typically 40–60 per cent, that is, some two to three times that of a narrow grade. Monetary values are attached to each skill set according to the estimated learning time required (Ledford, 1991b; Shields, 2007).

The combination of broad grades and skill-based pay is especially appropriate for roles with significant technical knowledge and skill requirements, such as process work, technical or paraprofessional roles, maintenance work and administration. In such roles, technical skills are relatively easy to identify, impart, assess and reward.

Some commentators suggest that a better means of configuring person-based base pay is to focus on assessing and rewarding deeply embedded abilities or 'competencies' such as leadership ability, motivation to achieve goals, persistence, composure, problem-solving ability, and so on. The appeal of the competencies approach lies chiefly in its focus on those personal attributes that are seen to be the most important and reliable drivers of high individual performance. As such, the suggestion that competency assessment should apply not only to performance management and development, but also to employee reward has intuitive appeal. Likewise, the competencies model is applicable to staff at all levels of the organization and not just to skilled manual workers (Armstrong and Brown, 1998; Shields, 2007).

The defining features of competency-based pay are:

- a system of competency assessment;
- a 'broadbanded' pay structure.

Broadbanding (also known as 'career banding') involves doing away with a large number of narrow jobs arranged in a steep hierarchy in favour of a much smaller number of job bands. Pay ranges are substantially wider – frequently 100–300 per cent – and the mode of pay progression is linked to either competency assessment or a combination of competency development and performance outcomes. A typical broadbanded structure will have between five and 10 bands.

Progression within a given broadband may be linked either to competency assessment alone (that is, competency-*based* broadbanding) or to a combination of competency assessment and individual performance outcomes (that is, competency-*related* broadbanding). The latter approach is also known as 'contribution-related pay'. In purely competency-based systems, each broadband is divided into a small number of competency 'zones', each representing a successively deeper level of competency development. Pay increments are not automatic, and progression to the upper zones is not guaranteed. In fact, both in-zone and between-zone progression becomes increasingly difficult as competency requirements become more demanding (Rosen and Turetsky, 2002; Shields, 2007; Perkins and White, 2008).

Competency-based broadbanding promises employers an unprecedented degree of flexibility in determining individual base pay levels. Broadbanding has many potential advantages over traditional graded structures. By flattening job hierarchies, it can redirect employees' attention away from competition for jobs and promotion, and towards individual and group contributions to organizational success. Uncoupling promotion from individual career development and base pay progression redefines career 'success' from a vertical to a horizontal trajectory. This means that individuals no longer have to aspire to a managerial role in order to further their careers and base pay. By linking career development and pay progression to capability and achievement in terms of individual performance, broadbanding also supports a more strategic approach to reward management. For these reasons, the competencies model is also especially applicable to high-performance knowledge work, managerial and executive roles. It is also applicable to service work roles (Shields, 2007).

Despite their promise, person-based approaches have a number of potential drawbacks (Murray and Gerhart, 2000; Shields, 2007; Canavan, 2008; Ledford, 2008):

- Paying for skills and competencies does not guarantee that the employee will apply them effectively.
- Skill and competency assessment is administratively complex and costly.
- Labour market values are still determined mainly by job 'size' rather than by the skills and competencies of individual job holders, so valuation remains problematic.

- 'Topping out': once employees have acquired all the skills or demonstrated all of the required competencies, their base pay will plateau. They may therefore lose task motivation and organizational commitment unless additional rewards, such as performance incentives, are made available.
- Obsolescence of skills and competencies: employees whose skills or competencies are no longer needed, for example because of changes to the product range or in terms of technology, may be exposed to a pay reduction or even redundancy.
- The wider pay ranges characteristic of person-based systems may create unrealistic expectations of opportunities for pay rises, and this can cause feelings of pay inequity, especially if these expectations remain unfulfilled.

For these reasons, the enthusiasm initially associated with skills- and competency-related pay has, in recent years, been replaced by a healthy degree of caution (Hofrichter and McGovern, 2001; Heneman and LeBlanc, 2003).

Benefits plans

Employee benefits are financial rewards that directly supplement the cash base pay and are generally focused on addressing the well-being and long-term security needs of employees and their dependants. As such, benefits are an increasingly heterogeneous phenomenon, ranging from employers' contributions to employee superannuation (that is, retirement savings) planning, health and medical insurance and paid holiday leave, to various work-related 'fringe benefits' such as employer-funded mobile technology and travel.

Voluntary benefits

Although employers in most countries are obliged by law to make certain benefits available to employees (that is, 'mandatory benefits'), it is also open to employers to offer employees additional benefits as part of a strategic approach to reward management (that is, 'voluntary benefits'). In many developed countries, benefits comprise a growing proportion of total remuneration costs (Shields, 2007; Wright, 2009). Depending on the country involved, mandatory benefits may include employer-funded superannuation savings, life, health and disability insurance, worker compensation, various forms of paid leave (for example, annual, long-service, sickness, parental or carer leave) and severance pay.

Voluntary benefits can enhance the organization's ability to attract and retain high-value employees and enable it to offer employees a more appealing 'value proposition'. As the workforce becomes more diverse and as the employees' level of education and expectation of reward rises, voluntary benefits are likely to assume an increasingly critical role in the ability of the reward management system to attract, retain and motivate high-potential and high-performing employees.

Voluntary benefits include a wide range of rewards known collectively as 'fringe benefits', such as discount company loans, housing or mortgage subsidies, product or service discounts, company cars and/or free parking, self-education expenses, and the like. In addition to fringe benefits of a financial nature, many organizations now offer a range of voluntary non-monetary benefits carefully targeted at enhancing employees' work–life balance and well-being. These benefits include, among others, wellness programmes of various types. Examples include free medical check-ups, in-house gyms or subsidised gym membership, personal trainers, aerobics, yoga, pilates and t'ai chi classes, in-office massages, stress reduction and relaxation sessions, ergonomic consultations, meditation rooms, staff health food canteens, nutrition seminars, weight control programmes and quit smoking programmes. As well as being inherently beneficial to employees themselves, health and fitness initiatives such as these can make a significant contribution to reducing absenteeism and raising productivity (Shields, 2007). In part, these non-monetary plans are also targeted at reducing the costs associated with compulsory financial benefits, including statutory sick leave and stress leave entitlements.

Flexible benefits

The content of benefits packages may be either 'fixed' or 'flexible.' They may have a standard content, with the composition being determined by legal requirements and employer choice. Alternatively, they may be flexible in content, with employees having a degree of choice in how best to configure their package within a range of options made available voluntarily by the employer. The latter are also known as 'flexible' or 'cafeteria' benefits plans. The logic of flexible packages is that one size does not fit all. Differences in age, family responsibilities, financial circumstances and lifestyle preferences mean that different employees will have different benefit needs, and the needs of any one employee will change considerably over time (Long, 2006; Shields, 2007).

Exercise

- Why do the reward systems of some organizations place such a strong emphasis on voluntary benefits?

Performance-related reward plans

Performance-related reward plans, including incentives, cover rewards given on the basis of performance (that is, desired behaviour or results) delivered by employees either individually or collectively. An 'incentive' is a payment made on the basis of past performance in order to reinforce and enhance future performance. Performance pay is usually an overlay to base pay, and it varies according to the level of measured or assessed performance. In short, performance pay is contingent or 'at risk', rather than fixed or guaranteed.

Although there are many types of performance-related rewards, these can be classified according to four key variables: the *performance unit* involved (individual, work group or whole organization); the *performance criteria* used (behaviour, results or both); the *time frame* over which performance is measured (short term or long term); and the *form of reward* (monetary, non-monetary or company share equity) (Shields, 2007). Using these dimensions, we can identify three main categories of performance-related rewards:

- individual performance-related reward plans;
- collective short-term cash incentive plans;
- collective long-term equity-based incentive plans.

Table 12.3 summarises the specific reward practices within each of these three broad categories, and each of these practices will be examined in more detail below.

Individual performance plans

Schemes that reward individuals on the basis of formal performance appraisal scores are known generically as *merit pay* plans. In traditional merit pay plans, payments take the form of cumulative additions to base pay. These additions are termed 'merit raises' or 'merit increments.' These reward employees for appraised performance in a previous time period – typically 1 year – by raising their base pay to a higher level in the relevant job-based pay range.

From an organizational perspective, merit increments have a number of potential advantages. Since pay increments are linked to the individual performance achieved, the risk of the employer receiving no return on a pay increase is less than would be the case where pay is not directly performance-related, as in a traditional structure involving seniority-based pay scales. Because they are a permanent addition to base pay, merit increments can also reinforce the attraction and retention of staff.

On the other hand, because merit increments combine performance pay and base pay, employees may fail to see a clear and objective 'line of sight' between performance and pay outcomes. Since each merit increment is a permanent

Table 12.3 Performance-related reward options

Who? (= performance entity or unit) and when (= time frame for payout)	How? (= behaviour)	How much? (= results)
Individual performance reward plans	Merit raises or increments Merit bonuses Discretionary bonuses Individual non-cash recognition awards	Piece rates Sales commissions Goal-based bonuses
Collective/group short-term incentives		Profit-sharing Gain-sharing Goal-sharing Team incentives Team non-cash recognition awards
Organization-wide long-term incentives		Share grant plans Share purchase plans Share option plans Executive long-term incentive plans

addition to base pay, the resulting compound increase in base pay can over time compromise the cost-effectiveness of the pay system. The emphasis on individualism may also be problematic in national cultural contexts that place a high value on collectivism, as is the case throughout much of South-East Asia and Latin America.

An alternative approach is the *merit bonus* method, in which the appraisal-based payment does not roll into base pay but instead stands apart from it and does not become an ongoing entitlement (Shields, 2007). The critical difference between this approach and traditional merit increments is that the payments made are conditional rather than cumulative. To be retained, the bonus must be must be re-earned. Motivation is driven by both the prospect of a higher bonus and the risk of loss of the bonus. Although this may be appropriate in many Western contexts, at-risk bonuses may be quite incompatible with cultures high on 'uncertainty avoidance', such as those in Latin America, Eastern Europe and Japan (Hofstede, 1984).

A simpler form of cash recognition is the discretionary bonus. These are irregular 'lump sum' awards for outstanding performance made at the discretion of the supervisor and/or senior management. Discretionary lump sum payments, being highly visible, can communicate a strong performance message. By the same token, the absence of formal performance assessment means that award allocation may be seen as being arbitrary and as having little clear link between performance and reward.

Incentives geared to measured individual results, or individual 'payment-by-results' plans, are among the oldest and most enduring of all performance pay plans. A major attraction of results-based plans for employers is that they offer greater certainty, immediacy and objectivity in the pay–performance relationship than are offered by other pay plans. Included in this category are piece rates, sales commissions and bonus payments to individuals for goal achievement.

Piece rates were developed primarily for labour-intensive manufacturing jobs and had their heyday in the early to mid-20th century, when they lay at the forefront of innovation in reward theory and practice in industrialized economies. However, interest in individual output-based incentives of this type has waned with the relative decline in manufacturing activity in Western economies. Instead, sales commissions remain widely used in such sectors as consumer retailing, finance, insurance and real estate, and goal-based individual reward plans have become an increasingly important feature of white-collar professional and managerial work. For these reasons, we shall focus here on commissions and goal-based bonuses.

In general, *commissions* have the attraction of being simple to set and measure. They institute automatic task clarity and provide instant feedback and reinforcement. However, they may also encourage aggressive, deceptive or negligent selling practices, foster excessive competition among sales workers working for the same firm, and encourage sales staff to neglect important tasks, such as good record-keeping, after-sales follow-up and the training of new sales workers (Shields, 2007). Clearly, commissions are only applicable in sales roles.

Goal-based bonus plans, however, are capable of being adapted to virtually any role. In essence, these plans entail annual or quarterly bonus payments linked directly to individual goal setting. If the goals are financial in nature, such plans are self-funding, which means that they avoid one of the major shortcomings of traditional merit pay plans – budget underfunding. Even so, goal setting can be problematic. Where goals are either too loose/easy or too tight/hard, too few or too many, a goal-based bonus plan is unlikely to be effective. Rewarding only the hard, measurable results may encourage employees to ignore equally important but less quantifiable aspects of the job or role. For these reasons, individual results-based incentive plans tend to be of measure a range of parameters and often built around a 'balanced scorecard' of weighted indicators and goals (Shields, 2007).

Many organizations now use recognition of a non-monetary nature to reward individual performance. Non-cash rewards range from merchandise, shopping vouchers and retailer-specific debit cards to symbolic awards in the form of plaques, 'thank you' notes, pins, watches, pens and desk-sets, and the like. Such rewards are said to have the advantage of being personalized, immediate and more enduring than cash (Nelson, 1994; McAdams, 1999). McAdams (1999: 245–51) asserts: 'It is easier and more effective to promote the excitement of a non-cash award than its cash equivalent. Non-cash awards have built-in excitement and recognition factors that cash simply doesn't have.' They are also likely to be less costly than cash. Conversely, non-cash recognition plans may create an atmosphere of 'winners' and 'losers' (when the same few employees repeatedly get the award) or, alternatively, of 'everyone a winner' (where everyone takes a turn at receiving recognition). They may also be demotivating where employees feel that the reward is tokenistic (Shields, 2007).

Exercise

- When it comes to recognizing and rewarding individual performance, what are the three main advantages and three chief disadvantages of using non-cash recognition plans?

Collective performance plans

In certain contexts, rewarding group results may have decided advantages over individual performance rewards. The latter may be quite dysfunctional in organizations where work is organized on interdependent and cross-functional lines and where results are founded on a high degree of interemployee cooperation. Interdependence of this type is one of the hallmarks of teamworking and high-involvement management.

In such organizations, it may be neither possible nor logical to attribute performance to specific individuals, since what counts is collective effort and contribution. Collective incentives may encourage employees to work collaboratively to achieve goals that require teamwork and cooperation. Accordingly, collective incentive schemes are more likely to elicit a greater degree of organizational citizenship behaviour than are schemes of an individual nature. Collective incentives may also be more appropriate in national cultural contexts where collectivism is valued above individualism, such as in most Asian countries and in Latin America (Hofstede, 1984). Workplace-wide collective plans are also likely to encounter less opposition from trade unions than are individual incentive plans. Table 12.4 summarises the main advantages and disadvantages of collective incentives generally.

Table 12.4 Collective incentives – pros and cons

Advantages	Disadvantages
Provide an incentive for improving group performance	Employees may feel that group reward undervalues individual contributions
Self-funding; total labour costs vary with organizational 'capacity to pay'	The bigger the group, the weaker the 'line of sight'
Can increase employees' understanding of the business	'Free-riding'/'social loafing'
	Conflict over peer surveillance and peer pressure
Self-monitoring reduces supervision costs	Perverse sorting: everyone will want to belong to the group that gets the highest rewards
Peer pressure on underperformers	
Encourage organizational commitment and citizenship behaviour	May encounter resistance from middle managers

This is not to suggest that collective incentive plans are necessarily incompatible with individual performance pay plans. With careful planning, it is possible to combine the two approaches in such a way that they are mutually reinforcing. For instance, while the funding of a performance pay pool might be based on measures of an improvement in collective results, the distribution of payments from the pool could be based on an assessment of individual contribution (Heneman and Von Hipple, 1995; Merriman, 2009).

Most collective incentive plans fall into one or other of three plan types:

- profit-sharing
- gain-sharing
- goal-sharing.

Profit-sharing

A profit-sharing plan typically involves a formal arrangement under which bonus payments are made to eligible employees on a regular (usually annual) basis, based on a formula that links the size of the total bonus pool to an accounting measure of periodic (typically annual) profit, such as net profit (total income less operating costs) or net profit after tax. By allowing overall labour costs to be varied automatically according to the employer's 'capacity to pay', profit-sharing is seen as providing a form of organizational insurance against external contingencies, particularly fluctuations in demand and prices in the product market. As such, profit-sharing is wholly self-funding. It may also increase employees' identification with and understanding of the organization's financial circumstances, enhance citizenship behaviour and reduce industrial conflict.

Conversely, because profitability is influenced by many variables that are beyond the employees' collective control, the line of sight between individual performance and reward is likely to be weak; that is, the 'instrumentality' (cause-and-effect) link between effort and reward, as prescribed by expectancy theory (see above), is at best very weak. For the same reason, profit-sharing may give rise to 'free-riding' or 'social loafing', especially where payments are allocated on an equal basis irrespective of individual contribution (Shields, 2007).

Gain-sharing

Gain-sharing is a form of collective performance-related pay in which management shares with all its employees in a particular production plant or business unit the financial gains associated with specific measures of improvement in the results achieved by that work group, as measured against a historical benchmark of the group's performance. Traditional gain-share plans emphasize 'hard' single-factor performance measures such as reductions in labour cost or improvement in labour productivity.

Like profit-sharing, such plans are self-funding, but gain-sharing also has a number of advantages over profit-sharing. Such schemes can be targeted to particular plants, departments or divisions, or to discrete business units in the wider organization. This compares with profit-sharing, which is generally organization-wide. Unlike profit-sharing, this approach can be applied in public sector and other non-profit organizations. It also seeks to reward only those results that are within the group's control. It can support a high-involvement culture through employee involvement programmes and devolution of decision-making. In addition, it is compatible with a unionized workforce and collective bargaining (Kim and Voos, 1997; Dalton, 1998).

The emphasis on continuous improvement means that gain-sharing is well suited to competitive strategies emphasizing either cost containment, quality improvement or both. However, traditional gain-share plans are a poor fit for highly dynamic contexts since each change in technology, work organization and product type will require a recalibration of historical performance benchmarks. Cost-focused plans also ignore non-financial or 'soft' aspects of group performance, such as work-site safety, environmental compliance and customer satisfaction (Shields, 2007).

Goal-sharing

Goal-sharing is the collective equivalent of individual goal-based bonuses (discussed above) and, like the latter, draws on the technique of goal setting. While goal-sharing resembles gain-sharing, it has several major differences. Goal-sharing is future-oriented, whereas gain-sharing is tied to retrospective performance benchmarks. This makes goal-sharing simpler to develop and more flexible, as well as wider in application and better placed to accommodate rapid changes in technology and product or service type. Goal-sharing generally includes both 'soft' performance factors, such as customer satisfaction and product quality, and financial targets. However, this means that goal-sharing is generally not self-funding, which in turn gives rise to the possibility of underfunding and of bonus payments that may not be seen as being commensurate with the group's achievements (Shields, 2007).

Employee share plans

Organization-wide, long-term incentive plans – more commonly known as employee share (or 'stock' or 'equity') plans, or ESOPs – allow eligible employees access to share ownership in the organization that employs them and reward employees for improvements over time in the employing firm's share market performance (via an appreciation in share price) and operating performance (via share dividends and special bonus share issues).

As such, share plans are seen as having a long-term benefit by reinforcing employees' commitment to the success of the organization. Because they stand to foster an 'ownership' mentality among employees, broadly based share plans (that is, plans in which many or most employees are eligible to participate) are particularly appropriate for organizations that embrace a high degree of employee involvement and participation (Kaarsemaker and Poutsma, 2006). Depending on how they are configured, share plans may also give employee-owners a genuine voice in management of the business and perhaps in managing other elements of the firm's reward system. However, the precise attitudinal and behavioural outcomes will depend on, among other things, the extent of employee eligibility and take-up, and on the particular plan or plans involved.

Although share employee plans come in a wide variety of forms, most fall into one of three main types:

- share grant plans
- share purchase plans
- option plans.

Share grant plans

With share grant plans, employees receive a gift of fully paid shares in the firm. In some cases, the shares granted can be traded immediately, which means that the grant is technically 'unrestricted'. However, it has become increasingly common for share grants to have certain limitations attached, which generally means that ownership does not transfer ('vest') immediately and/or that the shares cannot be tradable immediately in the same way as 'common stock' (that is, ordinary shares held by external investors). Conditional share grants of this type are known as 'restricted' share plans: while employees are not required to outlay any of their own money, they usually cannot sell their shares until a specified minimum period has elapsed. For the company, share grants may encourage long-term employee commitment and membership behaviour, particularly where restricted shares and trust arrangements are involved.

From the employee's perspective, regular share grants can serve as a convenient means for employees to supplement their retirement savings, although employee shareholders may well have a far higher risk exposure than external shareholders since the latter are more likely to have a diversified share portfolio covering a range of sectors, industries and firms (Shields, 2007).

Share purchase plans

With share purchase plans, employees have the opportunity to purchase part or all of a specified quota of shares in the company. Employees typically pay a small deposit on the full share purchase price, with the balance of the purchase price repayable over a specified term. The plan typically includes favourable purchase terms, such as a purchase price that is set below the prevailing market value and/or a low- or zero-interest loan from the company to fund the purchase. Some schemes allow the share purchase loan to be repaid from dividends so that the repayment period is open-ended and there is no employee outlay from personal savings. Other schemes allow employees to fund their acquisition in a tax-effective way by means of a 'salary sacrifice', which allows the employees to quarantine the outlay from their taxable income. Some schemes involve employee savings plans and pay deductions to fund the purchase. Legal ownership of the shares vests to the employee over time as the loan is paid off.

As share purchases funded by a company loan mean that employees are indebted to the company for the duration of the loan, employees may thus be more accommodating of management initiatives. Also, where employees have had to pay for the shares, their motivation in terms of 'ownership' is likely to be considerably stronger and more enduring than would be the case where shares have been received as a gift. This helps to explain why organizations in countries such as Australia tend to favour share purchase plans over share grant plans, a preference highlighted by the examples provided Box 12.3.

Box 12.3 Varieties of equity ownership in Australian firms

While only around 6 per cent of Australian employees receive shares as an employment benefit, some of the country's largest companies have broadly based share plans in place, and these come in a wide variety of forms.

At property development firm Lean Lease, employees own almost 8 per cent of the company. At communications giant Telstra, the employee share scheme is run by a trustee subsidiary, employees are offered interest free loans to acquire shares, and some employees are also eligible for extra shares and loyalty shares as a result of participating in the plan.

OneSteel offers tax-deferred and tax-exempt plans enabling employees to buy shares each month by means of salary sacrifice contributions, with those participating in the tax-exempt plan receiving fully paid shares to the value of $125 per year. Under this plan, shares must be held for a minimum of 3 years while the employee remains with the firm.

Furniture retailer Fantastic Holdings offers employees 11 matching shares for every 100 shares they purchase, with one in four employees participating in the plan.

At listed metals miner Perilya, employees own around 2 per cent of the firm through a share purchase plan, with 60 per cent of employees participating by means of salary sacrifice. The scheme grants shares to the value of 10 per cent of the employee's salary and then matches dollar for dollar any further contributions made.

Share plans are also used by private (that is, unlisted) companies. For example, food and energy firm Gardner Smith operates four schemes for its workforce in Australia and New Zealand. Employees with more than 12 months' service are eligible to participate, and just under 10 per cent of the firm's issues capital is targeted for employee ownership.

At advertising agency Clemenger, the employees own 53 per cent of the firm, with around one-third of its local employees participating.

Source: Adapted from Gettler (2010: 30–2).

By the same token, share purchase plans entail a greater risk all round than is the case with share grants. In particular, by their very nature, share purchase plans expose employees to greater financial risk. Employees committed to repaying the principal on a company loan at a fixed purchase price will experience severe financial difficulties if the share price collapses and the debt is not renegotiated or forgiven (Shields, 2007).

Employee option plans

A third type of share plan – employee option plans – gives employees the option of acquiring a specified quantity of company shares at a particular price on or after a designated future date. An option plan is a variant of share purchase in which the earliest date of purchase is set some time in the future. Such plans give the employee the right to buy a specified number of company shares at a predetermined price on a specified future date, such as the third anniversary of the option grant date. The price payable to exercise the option to acquire some or all of the shares – the 'strike price' – is commonly set at or below the market value of the shares at the time the option is granted.

Since the granting of an option does not confer an immediate ownership of equity, there will be no 'ownership' effect on motivation unless and until the option has been exercised. Until the options are exercisable, the main behavioural effects will be twofold. First, the restriction on exercising the options will reinforce staff retention, since the options are likely to be forfeited if the option-holder leaves the company. Second, during the holding period, the incentive effect will be largely extrinsic; that is, the holder will be motivated to improve the company's performance in order to strengthen market perceptions and increase the market share price, with a view to maximizing any capital gain when it becomes possible for the employee to exercise the option to buy and sell the shares involved.

However, with option plans, the line of sight between the employee's effort and the financial reward is even more remote than is the case with share bonus and purchase plans, since there is a significant delay in realizing any market-related rewards. In 'bull' share market conditions, in which most companies are experiencing share price appreciation, options may confer unearned ('windfall') gains on some option-holders. As with all equity plans, options are 'fair-weather' reward instruments: they may work well in times of share price growth, but can also compound a firm's problems if the share price falls, say in a declining ('bear') share market, and the market price falls below the option strike price. Option plans may also encourage a speculative outlook among employees rather than an ownership mentality (Shields, 2007).

Criticisms of performance-related rewards

Performance-related rewards are among the most controversial facets of contemporary HRM practice, with some critics contending that they are doomed to fail because they rest on invalid assumptions about employee motivation. Others similarly argue that they are inherently unfair.

Those who argue that performance pay is dysfunctional tend to base their case on the premises underlying cognitive evaluation theory, discussed above, that extrinsic performance-related rewards are inimical to intrinsic motivation. One proponent of this view, US social psychologist Alfie Kohn (1993a, 1993b), asserts that incentive pay plans fail because they:

- undermine intrinsic interest in the job;
- motivate people to pursue the reward rather than do a good job;
- are instruments of behavioural manipulation and punishment;
- rupture cooperative work relationships;
- ignore or mask the reasons underlying work problems;
- discourage sensible risk-taking.

Although well-publicised instances of failing incentive plans lend support to such arguments (see, for example, Beer and Cannon, 2004), these criticisms are themselves open to challenge on both theoretical and empirical grounds (see, for instance, Gupta and Mitra, 1998; Gupta and Shaw, 1998). Research shows that, under certain conditions (such as those prescribed by expectancy theory), incentives can exert a positive influence on performance, at least in certain organizational and cultural contexts (Gerhart and Rynes, 2003; Gerhart et al., 2009).

As we have seen, the assumption that extrinsic and intrinsic factors are dichotomous rather than complementary is also open to empirical challenge (see, for example, Cameron and Pierce, 1997). Overall, the evidence for a positive incentive effect is stronger for results-based plans than for plans based on behavioural assessment. Citing US examples, Gerhart and Rynes (2003: 170–1, 175) note that there are 'compelling examples of the effectiveness of results-oriented plans' and that there is 'ample evidence that results-based incentive plans can greatly increase performance'. Furthermore, they suggest (2003: 195) that strong individual results-based incentives have not only a positive incentive effect, but also a potentially powerful 'job-sorting' effect, whereby poor performers are actively 'managed out' while high performing individuals actively seek out positions that offer high reward for high effort.

A further criticism of Kohn's case is that he underplays the distinction between individual and collective incentives (Bennett Stewart et al., 1993; Cumming, 1994; Evans et al., 1995). Kohn overlooks that fact that group incentives are consciously directed towards encouraging the very attitudinal, behavioural and cultural characteristics that Kohn himself appears to endorse: teamwork, cooperation, shared effort and employee participation. Again, there is some evidence that appropriately designed group incentives can work (Gerhart et al., 2009) – what remains at issue empirically is the magnitude of the relationship.

So far we have only considered the arguments and evidence relating to the effectiveness of performance-related rewards in delivering the results and behaviours desired by the organization, that is, to whether such plans can and do 'work'. From the employees' perspective, however, an equally important – if not more important – consideration is whether such plans are fair.

One of the most common rationales for performance-related pay is that it operationalizes the 'equity' norm of distributive justice. To reiterate: equity theory proposes, in part, that reward satisfaction stems from establishing a good fit between an employee's inputs and outcomes. Reward relative to contribution – what could possibly be fairer? Yet there are those who argue that performance-related rewards can violate both distributive and procedural justice requirements. For instance, Heery (1996) argues that performance-related pay poses a threat to employee well-being because it contradicts employees' need for a stable and secure income, a need that is both economic and psychological. Without some level of guaranteed income, workers are likely to overwork and experience work-related stress and anxiety. Heery also suggests that performance-related pay tends to expose employees' pay to disproportionate risks. Shareholders may take calculated risks to reap a return, but employees have very different stakeholder needs, motives and expectations (Heery, 1996).

Critics also suggest that performance pay may also be procedurally unjust. According to Heery, such plans typically leave little scope for any independent representation of employees' interests, or 'voice'. Performance pay has also been questioned on the grounds that it may be especially disadvantageous to women employees. For instance, Rubery (1995) argues that women are likely to be worse off under performance-related pay, particularly where it takes the form of individual merit pay. In the context of the greater discretion available to line managers, the subjectivity inherent in behavioural assessment is likely to disadvantage women relative to men, especially in service work, where supervisory positions tend to be male-dominated. Furthermore, where individual incentives apply, the individualization of the employment relationship stands to weaken women's bargaining power further still. At least with job-based pay and job evaluation, the prospects for evening up the gender gap in pay and earnings are somewhat greater, partly because the process of pay determination is relatively open, transparent and amenable to collective bargaining (Rubery, 1995).

So the question remains: 'What proportion of an employee's total pay should be "at risk" against – or vary with – the performance?' Critical Thinking 12.2 invites you to formulate a considered position on the issue of 'pay variability'.

Perhaps the most meaningful conclusion to draw from these debates on the efficacy and fairness of performance pay is that such plans may have the potential to improve individual and group performance, but that the effectiveness and felt-fairness of any such plan will be contingent on several factors: the mode of application, particularly the manner in which the pay–performance linkage is configured;

Critical Thinking 12.2

Pay variability

The term 'pay variability' refers to the degree to which pay outcomes for any given job or any given set of job-holders will vary by performance rather than being fixed or guaranteed (Gerhart and Rynes, 2003).

Questions

1. Is it better for an organization to have a high or a low level of pay variability?
2. How might the appropriateness of high variability differ according to the social and cultural context?

how effectively this linkage is communicated and accepted; and how appropriate it is for the organizational context involved. In this respect, differences in social and cultural values are likely to be highly salient.

Reward communication

Creating and maintaining employees' understanding and acceptance of the way in which they are rewarded is one of the most challenging yet important aspects of contemporary organizational communication. In a recent survey of UK reward professionals (Cotton and Chapman, 2010), poor rewards communication was ranked as the single greatest risk to the effectiveness of a reward system. Evidence suggests that reward communications practice looms as a potentially powerful but underutilized human resource tool (Shields et al., 2009). Even the most elegantly designed and contextually appropriate reward system will fail to attract, retain and motivate employees unless it is understood and accepted by the managers and employees affected.

Clear communication of the philosophy and details underlying the reward system stands to increase employees' acceptance of the composition, structure and level of the rewards, as well as to sharpen employees' line of sight between what they contribute and how they are rewarded. Two-way communication also has great potential here. Given the centrality of reward practice to achieving strong employee engagement, giving employees a say in how they are rewarded may be an effective outlet for both the individual and the collective voice. Regular attitude surveys are one way in which employees can be given a 'say in pay'. Other possibilities here include focus groups and employee participation in job evaluation teams.

The other key stakeholder group in this respect comprises line managers. Without their 'buy-in', the line of communication between reward professionals and ordinary employees will be weak and unreliable. Given that such managers will also be pivotal to the administration and maintenance of the system, it is advisable that they are involved in the designing the reward process (Brown and Purcell, 2007).

However, reward communication does not necessarily equate with reward openness. The amount of pay information that should be shared with employees is a matter of longstanding debate, and a range of competing arguments have been advanced for both pay transparency and pay secrecy. The case for transparency rests on the proposition that unless employees understand the pay system and how their individual rewards are determined, the system cannot contribute to the strategic goals of the firm or gain the trust of employees. Conversely, opponents argue that employee privacy must be respected since a knowledge of how others are being paid can foster jealousy, cause performance problems and engender a cycle of 'catch-up' claims.

In determining the policy and practice of rewards communication, what, then, is the appropriate balance between disclosure and secrecy? Certainly, a policy of high transparency and regular employee attitude surveys would be more appropriate where a high-involvement management approach applied. Even here, though, it may be best to focus communication on the reward system 'rules' rather than on the details of pay outcomes for individual employees. Try your hand at addressing the issue of reward openness/secrecy by formulating responses to the questions posed in Critical Thinking 12.3.

> **Critical Thinking 12.3**
>
> **Reward secrecy and transparency**
>
> One approach to reward communication suggests that withholding from each employee details of the pay received by their fellow employees may restrain their demands for pay increases. In other words, revealing all may just encourage pay 'racheting', that is, employees in the same job or role demanding the same level of pay as that received by the highest paid employees in that role. The alternative approach proposes that pay secrecy of this type stands to violate the right of the employee to be treated with dignity and respect. Moreover, revealing more detail on reward levels, it is suggested, stands to reduce potentially counterproductive rumour and speculation about who has received what and why this might be so.
>
> **Questions**
>
> 1. In what circumstances might pay secrecy be appropriate or justified?
> 2. Can an organization have too much pay transparency?
> 3. When and how should reward information be communicated to employees?

Employment relations and reward management

Although the main focus of decisions relating to reward system configuration may be the individual organization or its constituent business units, determination of reward in general, and pay structure and level in particular, is also influenced by the context or contexts within which the organization operates. These contextual factors include:

- the nature of the relevant product and labour markets;
- sociocultural norms and standards;
- the nature of government intervention and regulation;
- the contours of the prevailing employment relations system.

Key elements of the employment relations system include the nature of organization and institutional power of the union and employer, the mode of industry-, regional- and national-level bargaining, and the nature and extent of the government's regulation of pay and conditions of employment. As noted earlier in the chapter, the employment relations context also shapes the opportunities for and mechanisms of employee voice in the process of reward determination. Likewise, it can widen or constrain management choices regarding organizational pay structure and level.

Governments can have a major influence on reward processes and outcomes via a direct regulation of pay levels, equal pay legislation, industrial tribunals, pay review bodies, fair/minimum/low-pay bodies, centralized wage indexation, mandatory provision for works councils, and the like. However, the degree of government influence over setting pay varies significantly over time and between countries and sectors.

The nature of national- and industry-level bargaining systems may also exert a strong influence on reward practice at the organizational level. Traditionally, the mode and level of pay have been central issues in unions' collective bargaining at all levels: national, industry, occupational, and organizational. As we have seen, trade unions generally prefer some types of pay plan over others – job-based pay over person-based pay, fixed pay over variable pay, group incentives over individual incentives, for example (Long and Shields, 2009). The general decline of union influence in developed economies has undoubtedly influenced pay practices and levels. However, according to Katz and Darbishire (2000, cited in Perkins and Vartiainen, 2010: 179), the pattern of change in the European context has been non-uniform: within both the union and non-union sectors, the degree of variation in pay levels and practices has increased in recent decades.

The impact of changes in the level of government intervention and collective bargaining within the European Union is illustrative of these wider contextual influences on determining reward. As noted by Perkins and Vartiainen (2010: 178):

Across much of the European continent – and featuring explicitly in the taxonomy adopted by the European Union – an attempt has been made to socialize employment relations using the existence of intermediaries between employers and employees to act as a mechanism for regulating the pay issue and to attempt to codify working practices that employers may be able to adopt to secure a return on the payments that agree to make to employees, as laid down in statutory provisions resulting from collective bargaining.

This regime of 'social partnership' and reward regulation dates back many decades and includes a wide range of mandatory provisions. The Equal Pay Directive of 1975 required member countries of the then European Economic Community to adhere to and enforce the principle of 'equal pay for work of equal value', a requirement reiterated under the Treaty of Amsterdam, effective from 1999. In practice, this has been taken to mean that job evaluation systems should be free from discrimination.

Wage indexation is another characteristic feature of European employment relations systems. Indexation aims to preserve the real value of wages by adjusting them automatically for price inflation. Works councils and joint consultative committees, coupled with multi-employer collective bargaining, have also been prominent features of the European approach to pay determination. In addition, there have been a number of initiatives at the level of the European Union to encourage employee share ownership and other forms of financial participation such as profit-sharing. In the late 1990s, the proportion of business units with 200 or more employees that had broad-based share plans averaged 16 per cent, and in the decade that followed, Belgium, France, Germany, The Netherlands and the UK all legislated to encourage greater share ownership on the part of employees (Pendleton, 2009).

However, there are now clear signs that these pillars of the model of the European 'coordinated' market economy are beginning to fragment. Although several countries still use indexation, a number (Denmark, France, Italy, The Netherlands and Spain) have now abandoned this form of pay regulation out of a fear that indexation will actually fuel inflation (Robinson and Winning, 2011).

Pre-existing pay disparities between Eastern European countries and European Union countries also poses a pay equity dilemma for the European Commission itself. With workers from Poland and the Baltic States flocking to take up more highly paid administrative jobs in the Commission's headquarters in Brussels, the earnings of these employees far exceeds the pay levels available to even the most senior office-holders in their countries of origin. The Commission has come under pressure to peg salaries to the pay structure in these countries. However, doing so would mean that some Commission employees would be doing the same work as fellow workers but for vastly different rates of pay (Castle, 2011).

Trade liberalization and exposure to international markets are also beginning to erode multi-employer collective bargaining within even the strongest coordinated economies in the European Union. The recent global crisis has impacted no less severely on the German employment model – until recently the exemplar of a 'coordinated market economy' and social partnership – than on those of less coordinated economies. Outcomes have included outsourcing, the rise of precarious employment, a growing low-wage sector, and the emergence of two-tier wage agreements under which unions agree to accept lower pay rates for non-union workers in exchange for the prospect of organizing the latter and coopting them onto works councils (Lehndorff et al., 2009; Haipeter, 2011).

In sum, as the European Union experience demonstrates, the changing nature of employment relations institutions and bargaining processes can exercise a powerful sway over pay structure and pay levels at the level of the individual organization.

International reward management

Most of the reward concepts and tools that we have discussed so far have emerged in Western business contexts and are thus informed by Western assumptions about the nature of the employment 'deal'. Yet whether they are engaged in international joint venture operations with host country partners, or in direct investment in subsidiaries in one or more host countries, firms with an international or multinational business focus – that is, MNCs – have to meet reward challenges that are often very different from those applicable to domestic employees.

These cross-border differences are relevant to three main groups of employee:

- host country nationals (HCNs) hired to work in the MNC's operations in the host country;
- home country employees sent abroad (that is, 'expatriated') for periods of time to manage or work in operations in host countries;
- employees from other countries – third country nationals (TCNs) – hired to work in either the home or host country operations.

Given the particular social, cultural, legal-institutional, economic and political context within which they live and their boundaries, HCN employees may have very different reward expectations from those in the firm's home base, as well as from expatriates and TCNs. For instance, in some countries such as India and Indonesia, employees have a strong cultural respect for hierarchy and equally strong attachments to a stable, long-term employment relationship and to customary allowances and benefits. Managing base pay and benefits for HCN employees thus requires that the conditions and traditions of the host country be carefully taken into account.

In order to maintain reward consistency, some MNCs export the main elements of their home country reward practice to their subsidiary operations in other countries (an 'exporter' or 'ethnocentric' approach). Others seek to adapt to local or regional conditions (an 'adaptor' or 'polycentric' approach), while still others apply a blend of home and host practices at either a national level (a 'geocentric approach') or a regional level (a 'regiocentric' approach). This means not only being aware of the reward expectations and entitlements of HCNs, but also having to make careful choices about how to reward local employees in order to establish and maintain a positive employment relationship (Bloom et al., 2003; Dowling et al., 2008).

Likewise, in configuring reward packages for expatriates, the MNC must decide whether it wishes to benchmark the level and mix of its rewards against parent country standards, host country standards or a blend of home and host or home and regional standards.

On this basis, we can identify three broad approaches towards configuring expatriate rewards:

- the home-based or 'balance sheet' approach;
- the host-based or 'going rate' approach;
- the region-based approach.

Home-based approach

This approach, which remains the preferred approach in Western MNCs, aims to maintain a relativity of rewards against those of home country employees while providing a beneficial inducement to compensate for the employee's foreign assignment. In essence, the approach links the expatriate reward level to the home country pay structure and seeks to preserve home country purchasing power and living standards by means of a 'balance sheet' of compensatory financial adjustments.

The approach typically covers four main reward components:

- *Base salary*: the main component that serves as a benchmark for other components.
- *A foreign service inducement, relocation or 'hardship' premium*: to attract home country employees to accept an expatriate assignment, or to compensate them for any hardship associated with a foreign assignment.
- *Allowances*: to compensate for any potential diminution in living standards relative to home standards, including cost of goods and services, housing expenses and differences in income tax liabilities.
- *Benefits*: including pension/superannuation contributions, health and medical insurance, social security, education expenses and paid leave entitlements (Dowling et al., 2008).

While the balance sheet approach preserves an equitable relationship between expatriate reward levels and those remaining in the parent entity, the approach may create a considerable pay discrepancy between expatriates and HCNs performing similar roles. In low-pay countries, such as India and China, this may trigger internal perceptions of inequity/distributive injustice among HCNs (Watson and Singh, 2005; Dowling et al., 2008).

Host-based approach

Here, the base salary is linked to salary levels in the host country, partly with a view to maintaining an equitable relationship in reward levels between the parent firm and HCNs. In general, if prevailing pay rates in the host country are high by international standards, the firm may have little choice but to match the local market. Conversely, if local pay levels are low by international standards, as is the case in most developing countries, the firm will typically augment its employees' base pay with additional allowances and benefits in order to attract home country and third country expatriates (Dowling et al., 2008).

The 'going rate approach' is relatively uncomplicated, sets a common standard for expatriates from both the parent country and third countries, reinforces expatriates' identification with the host country, and institutes a degree of equality with HCN salaries. Conversely, a strict adherence to the going rate approach will make it difficult to attract expatriates to low-pay locations, while the prospect of major variations in pay level from one posting to the next may be equally damaging.

Region-based approach

In essence, this is the remuneration approach typical of a geocentric staffing strategy and is especially well suited to a staffing strategy emphasizing labour mobility on a regional or a global scale, and selection of the best person for the position, irrespective of nationality. With such an approach, remuneration levels will need to be expressed in a major global currency, such as the US dollar, or a regional currency such as the Euro. The global approach also relies on the MNC developing a set of reward principles, policies and practices that fit its global strategy, structure and culture. The chief tenet of this approach is the marriage of competitiveness and flexibility of rewards at the local or regional scale, especially by allowing subsidiary managers the autonomy to configure the base pay, benefits and incentives in line with local standards. There must also be consistency in the worldwide application of a set of 'core' reward principles, including, for instance, performance-based recognition and reward differentiation (Bloom et al., 2003; Watson and Singh, 2005).

> **Exercise**
>
> - What are the three main differences between an 'exporter' and an 'adaptor' approach to managing the rewards of host country employees?

Conclusion

For many organizations operating within and between countries, employee rewards constitute the single largest operating expense. How – and how well – an employee reward system is designed, implemented, communicated and maintained can make the difference between the success and failure of the organization. Reward management is difficult to do well and easy to mismanage. The efficacy and fairness of reward practice is also the subject of an ongoing and robust debate.

This chapter has explored employee reward management from three perspectives: the critical, the applied and the international. Each perspective invokes different assumptions regarding the role of rewards in the employment relationship; each also carries different implications regarding the efficacy and fairness of rewards.

The *critical approach* alerts us to the dangers of 'unitarist' assumptions about the nature, meaning and influence of employee rewards. In essence, we have argued for a pluralist, or multi-stakeholder, framework for both understanding and 'managing' rewards. What is a cost to the organization is income and economic security to the employee, and what is valued by the organization may have little meaning or value for its employees.

In this sense, our exploration of the debate on the relative merits of extrinsic and intrinsic rewards serves to highlight the indeterminate nature of the relationship between the rewards on offer and the employees' reactions. Just as it is unsafe to assume that monetary rewards are invariably the primary motivator, so is it problematic to suppose that every employee is galvanized by the prospect of work that is inherently challenging and task-diverse. The key point here is that employees are not simply 'resource' objects but, rather, are organizational stakeholders with their own distinct needs, expectations and rights, as well as responsibilities and contractual obligations to their employer.

A critical pluralist perspective also alerts us to the changing nature and significance of the employees' voice in how rewards are determined. As we have seen, this 'say in pay' may take various forms: individual or collective; union or non-union; formal or informal; direct or indirect. Indeed, it is erroneous to think of the structure, type and level of rewards as being free of employee influence – that is, as being an artefact of unconstrained managerial discretion. Employee voice and agency continue to have an important bearing on setting pay, whether directly and collectively via the unions' collective bargaining activity, indirectly via minimum pay bodies and industrial tribunals, or by means of individual employees' choices about the worth and equity of the rewards on offer.

The *applied approach* draws attention to the vast variety of reward practices – and to the factors that should be taken into account in choosing between them. Here we have focused on the distinction between job- and person-based base pay, between fixed and flexible benefits plans, between individual and group performance pay plans, and between cash, non-cash and equity-based plans. We have also considered the general strengths and weaknesses of each major pay plan type, as well as examining debates on both the effectiveness and fairness of incentive plans and other performance-related reward practices. In essence, the chapter argues for an applied approach to reward management that favours 'best fit' over 'best practice'. In other words, the choice of plan type and structure of rewards, including horizontal and vertical pay dispersion and pay variability, should reflect the organization's particular strategy, structure and environmental circumstances rather than any supposed 'one best way' to configure the reward system.

The *international approach* draws attention to the wider context and the additional challenges and options associated with the management of reward systems in cross-border contexts. What works well in one country may be highly problematic in another country and national culture. Equally, however, this itself poses a major strategic challenge to MNCs based in home countries with strong national cultures: should their approach to international reward management simply reflect the home country practice, or should they seek to adapt to the practices of the host country and culture? Like the USA and Japan before it, China is now the archetypal instance of a strong home country culture. The end-of-chapter case study on the reward strategies and practices of Chinese MNCs accentuates the complexities of reward management for managing line employees' and expatriates' rewards in host country contexts that vary markedly from that of the parent entity's home country.

In sum, managing pay and other forms of reward is one of the most challenging and sensitive facets of contemporary HRM, while reward management itself is one of the most controversial areas of human resource practice. Perhaps more than with any other human resources process, it also allows human resources strategists to demonstrate their worth in terms of organizational effectiveness. Equally, effective reward management demands high-order competencies in organizational and behavioural analysis, as well as solid abilities in strategic decision-making, communication and human resource leadership. For these reasons, it can also be immensely rewarding in its own right.

FOR DISCUSSION AND REVISION

Questions

1. Why should a firm use base pay at all?
2. Why does the gender pay gap persist, who is responsible for it, and what (if anything) can be done about it?
3. What makes for an effective employee share plan?
4. What are the telltale signs of failure of a performance and reward system?

Exercise

1. Break the class into pairs and allocate the following pay practices to a specific pair of students. Have each pair consider the pros and cons of their assigned pay practice as a means of furthering pay equity between the genders, and then have each pair report back to the full group. The practices are:

   - points factor job evaluation
   - skill-based pay
   - competency-based broadbanding
   - flexible benefits

- merit raises
- discretionary bonuses.

2. As the human resources director of an MNC with a subsidiary operation in Indonesia, you have been asked to design a comprehensive reward system for the subsidiary's HCNs. What reward practices would you use?
3. Your UK-based organization is planning to open a major facility (eventually employing 5,000 people) in Thailand, for which your team will be responsible. Senior management has asked you to assess the impact that cultural values will have on using traditional UK reward practices for the HCNs there, and to propose a comprehensive reward system for the new facility. Specifically, you are required to address the following issues:

- the pros and cons of replicating in the Thai context the large pay differences between more senior executives, mid-level managers and the hourly workforce that apply in the UK context;
- the possibility of using incentive pay programmes driven by individual performance;
- identification of the benefits that employees will place a high value on, and those they will place a low value on;
- identification of work rules or traditions that may be different from those in the UK.

In making your assessment, you should refer to Hofstede's cultural dimension scores for the parent and host countries, which are available at: http://www.geert-hofstede.com/hofstede_dimensions.php

Further reading

Books

Armstrong, M. and Brown, D. (2006) *Strategic Reward. How Organisations Add Value Through Reward*. London: Kogan Page.
  A UK text with an applied focus and practical examples of innovative reward practices.
Armstrong, M. and Murlis, H. (2007) *Reward Management. A Handbook of Remuneration Strategy and Practice* (revd 5th edn). London: Kogan Page & Hay Group.
  The standard UK practitioner text in the rewards field, taking an applied rather than critical focus.
Gerhart, B. and Rynes, S. (2003) *Compensation. Theory, Evidence, and Strategic Implications*. London: Sage.
  A US text offering an excellent coverage of research and concepts related to reward management.
Gomez-Mejia, L. R. and Werner, S. (eds) (2008) *Global Compensation. Foundations and Perspectives*. London: Routledge.
  Contains several solid chapters on the theory and practice of international rewards.
Greene, R. J. (2010) *Rewarding Performance. Guiding Principles; Custom Strategies*. New York: Routledge.
  Provides an insightful and practical coverage of performance pay practices.
Guthrie, J. P. (2007) Remuneration: pay effects at work. In Boxall, P., Purcell, J. and Wright, P. (eds) *The Oxford Handbook of Human Resource Management*. Oxford: Oxford University Press, pp. 344–69.

An illuminating overview of theories and evidence on the effects of reward plans.

Henderson, R. I. (2006) *Compensation Management in a Knowledge-based World* (10th edn). Upper Saddle River, NJ: Prentice Hall.
A US text offering a solid coverage of applied aspects of reward management.

Long, R. (2006) *Strategic Compensation in Canada* (3rd edn). Toronto: Thomson Nelson.
Provides both a solid coverage of Canadian reward practice and a clear and persuasive discussion of the relationship between reward practices and organizational strategy, structure and management culture.

Martocchio, J. J. (2009) *Strategic Compensation: A Human Resource Management Approach* (5th edn). Upper Saddle River, NJ: Pearson/Prentice Hall.
A US text offering a solid coverage of applied aspects of reward management.

Milkovich, G. and Newman, J. (2007) *Compensation* (9th edn). New York: McGraw-Hill Irwin.
A leading US text in the rewards management field.

Perkins, S. and White, G. (2008) *Employee Reward. Alternatives, Consequences and Contexts.* London: Chartered Institute for Personnel and Development.
Offers a fresh and an insightful treatment of reward theory and practice from a UK perspective.

Rynes, S. L. and Gerhart, B. (eds) (2000) *Compensation in Organisations. Current Research and Practice.* San Francisco: Jossey Bass.
A multiauthor text offering a detailed and sophisticated coverage of the strategic and psychological dimensions of employee rewards. Retains value despite its publication date.

Shields, J. (2007) *Managing Employee Performance and Reward: Concepts, Practices, Strategies.* Melbourne: Cambridge University Press.
Offers an integrated coverage of performance and reward management from a 'best fit' perspective.

White, G. and Drucker, J. (eds) (2009) *Reward Management. A Critical Text* (2nd edn). London: Routledge.
The second edition of a multiauthor text with chapters covering all key aspects of reward practice from various critical perspectives.

WorldatWork (2007) *The WorldatWork Handbook of Compensation, Benefits and Total Rewards.* New York: Wiley.
Offers an encyclopaedic coverage of rewards practices for line employees and executives. The text is informed by a unitarist rather than a critical perspective. WorldatWork is the leading US body representing reward professionals.

Wright, A. (2004) *Reward Management in Context.* London: Chartered Institute of Personnel and Development.
Another useful UK text.

Journals

Gerhart, B., Rynes, S. and Fulmer, I. (2009) Pay and performance: individuals, groups, and executives. *Academy of Management Annals*, 3(1): 251–315.
Provides a provocative but circumspect and evidence-based argument in support of incentive plans for executives and line employees.

Werner, S. and Ward, S. (2004) Recent compensation research: an eclectic review. *Human Resource Management Review*, 14: 201–27.
A meticulous and high-level survey of rewards research and conceptual models for explaining the configuration and influence of reward systems. Particularly useful for framing research topics and models in the rewards field.

Other resources

Chartered Institute for Personnel and Development. Reward Management. Available from: http://www.cipd.co.uk/subjects/pay/default.htm

A UK professional body website carrying information on rewards practices and strategies, including survey data.

E-Reward UK. About e-reward. Available from: http://www.e-reward.co.uk/about.asp

A UK proprietary research organization website providing information on reward practices, strategies and case studies.

WorldatWork. Available from: http://www.worldatwork.org/waw/home/html/home.jsp

A US professional body website carrying information on rewards practices and strategies, including survey data.

CASE STUDY

The strategy and practice of rewards in Chinese MNCs

The People's Republic of China now plays a central role in global economic growth and development, and Chinese state-owned enterprises and private firms are rapidly internationalizing their operations in both developed and developing economies. China is a global economic power and yet a country that is still 'developing' rather than 'developed'.

Transition in Chinese domestic reward practices

Under China's old planned economy, Chinese domestic employment practices were based on long-term job security, lifelong social security, pay structures characterized by low dispersion/egalitarianism and group-based rather than individual incentives. The principal pay system was the national wage scales, which were determined by central legislation and regional government agencies and were configured differently for blue- and white-collar employees. Pay differences between low-skilled workers, skilled workers and managers were minimal, and wage increases were infrequent and primarily took the form of nationwide grade promotions for all employees (Dowling et al., 2008). The combination of egalitarian pay structures and the 'iron rice bowl' model, which addressed workers' basic needs through free housing, schooling and medical care, gave employees few extrinsic incentives to improve their performance or pursue promotion.

Since the 1980s, however, government controls have eased and firms have been given more autonomy to configure their own reward systems, albeit still within government guidelines. Job size has replaced age/seniority as the main determinant of reward level, and rising education levels have begun to influence pay differences. A performance-related reward approach in the form of an efficiency-based bonus has also been introduced to replace the grade-based system. Despite these changes, seniority and egalitarianism remain key characteristics of Chinese domestic reward practice, pay dispersion remains low, and enterprises tend to favour group bonuses over those of an individual nature.

International reward management in Chinese MNCs: a 10-company case study

How, then, do Chinese MNCs approach international reward management? Do they seek to export domestic practices or are they more adaptive and innovative in their cross-border approach? Does their approach emulate that of Western MNCs or do they take a different and perhaps uniquely Chinese path?

One of the few studies to date to have examined the reward practices of Chinese MNCs, that by Shen (2004), provided revealing evidence on these and related questions. Shen's study used a semi-structured, interview-based survey to collect data from 10 Chinese MNCs with subsidiaries in the UK. Of these case study companies, seven were state-owned enterprises covering a variety of industries – from banking and technology importing to airlines and shipping – while the remaining three were share-issuing companies in the electronics and health products fields.

Shen's study found that the pattern of reward practice in the case organizations was company-specific rather than simply being a reflection of national or industry factors. On the basis of the evidence generated, Shen identified four different approaches to international reward management in the companies studied:

- host-based;
- home salary plus host-based;
- contract-based;
- diplomat-based.

Rewards for host country nationals

All 10 companies used the host-based approach for non-executive HCNs and a contract-based approach for HCN executives, with pay levels for HCNs commonly set quite high by UK standards. For HCN non-executives, the pay package generally included a fixed salary contract plus an individual merit bonus, typically of 2–3 months' additional salary based on an individual performance appraisal. The contract-based system applied to HCN executives differed from both home- and host-based practices in that the pay package was negotiated directly between the individual manager and the firm's headquarters, with payment based on a combination of individual capability, project importance and divisional performance.

Expatriate rewards

For Chinese employees expatriated to a UK subsidiary, Shen's study identified three distinct reward approaches. In two firms, expatriates received a host-based salary plus their old home salary. One company adopted a negotiable contact-based approach identical to that applied to HCN executives; this emphasized individual capability, how important the project was and the assignment location.

The other seven companies used a post-based approach for their expatriates, with the pay package including a fixed position-based salary, a post-based individual performance bonus and a range of additional payments. The fixed component was much higher than for home-based employees. Bonuses were linked to divisional or departmental performance or to the status of the managerial post. This post-based approach, which accentuates hierarchy, originally used by the Chinese Foreign Ministry for international postings and now widely used by Chinese MNCs, is also commonly known as the 'diplomat-based' approach. In all cases, a uniform approach was applied to expatriate reward throughout all divisions within the subsidiary.

The Chinese dual model: the best of both worlds?

This heterogeneity is very different from the situation with domestic operations in Chinese enterprises, where companies tend to adopt a uniform approach to reward management. The contract and home-plus-host approaches are negotiable and based chiefly on individual capability and performance, compared with domestic reward practice under which pay is position-based and essentially non-negotiable. On this basis, Shen concluded that 'Chinese [international HRM] is more progressive than domestic HRM in adopting modern Western HRM concepts' (Shen, 2004: 23).

However, Shen's study showed in addition that this process of adaption also had uniquely Chinese characteristics, such that the firms involved could be seen as pursuing a 'dual' approach to international reward management. Even though the approaches taken were noticeably different from home-based reward practices, they also differed from the three standard approaches typically specified in the Western literature – host-based, home-based and region-based. The firms involved adopted a 'best fit' approach that took account of both firm- and employee-specific factors, with reward practices tailored to employees' nationalities and their position in the organizational hierarchy. Under the dual model, HCN reward was either host-based or contract-based, whereas expatriate reward varied substantially from firm to firm. According to Shen (2004), the dual model reflected the 'dilemma' of Chinese MNCs wanting both to embrace international practices, in order to encourage an international transfer of talent, while at the same time maintaining close control over reward practices in their subsidiaries so as to limit the discrepancy between domestic practices and expatriate experience.

Factors influencing reward strategy and practice in Chinese MNCs

The study also showed that the reward strategies and practices adopted were influenced more strongly by some firm-level and contextual factors than by others. Reward strategies were shaped chiefly by the firm's international competitive strategy, its degree of reliance on international markets, and senior management's perception of the efficacy and appropriateness of the Chinese domestic reward system. However, interfirm differences in actual reward practices, including reward structures and levels, were determined by a combination of three main contextual factors – legal, economic and sociocultural – and by several firm-specific factors, most notably the industry in which the firm is involved.

Turning first to contextual factors, pay levels were generous by both Chinese and UK standards in order to attract high-quality home and host country managers and professionals. The firms studied also placed much weight on conformity to host country mandatory requirements, including minimum pay rates and paid leave entitlements. In a significant departure from home country practice, all companies also offered expatriates paid holiday leave, although, as Shen suggests (2004), the relatively high levels of base pay and benefits for HNCs need to be weighed against the fact that the firms studied offered HCNs almost no opportunity for development, promotion or transfer to the parent entity.

The dual approach to host- and home-sourced employees also reflected the cultural differences between China and the UK. Chinese practice is that the salary is non-negotiable, set according to position, level, seniority and the firm's overall performance, and not specified in the employment contract. However, with UK HNCs, the need to negotiate pay packages that would attract, retain and motivate local talent meant that this dual approach was embraced uniformly by all of the case companies, as was the use of individual performance bonuses. This host-based approach was also applied selectively to some expatriates, although egalitarianism remained the dominant consideration in relation to this group.

The study also highlighted the influence of a number of firm-specific factors. Regarding the impact of international HRM strategy generally, while two companies embraced a universal host-based approach to rewarding both HCN and expatriate employees, the majority of companies sought to retain control over expatriate reward expectations by means of diplomat- and contract-based approaches. Companies pursuing a polycentric approach to staffing were more likely to favour host-based reward practices, whereas those favouring ethnocentric staffing tended to adopt the diplomat-based approach.

The attitudes of senior management to home and host reward models were also influential. All firms judged the Chinese model to be unsuitable for HCN employees. However, there were differences in perceptions of the transferability of the Chinese model to expatriates, with some companies opting for a host-plus-home-based approach, and others preferring a more cautious contract-based solution. The nature of the industry itself also had an impact, with individual performance pay more likely to be applied to employees in trading enterprises and sales offices than elsewhere. In addition, reliance on and exposure to international markets was an important factor: firms with a relatively low reliance on international markets were more likely to prioritize egalitarianism over pay competitiveness, chiefly via the diplomat-based approach. Conversely, firms with a high reliance on international markets were more inclined to favour host-based standards.

Interestingly, Shen's study suggests that a range of firm-specific factors commonly assumed to influence reward practices – factors such as organizational structure, organizational culture, international experience and the size of international operations – appeared to have little impact in this sample of firms.

In sum, Shen's 10-firm case study highlights the dual approach to international reward management taken by these Chinese firms, the characteristically Chinese approach to the adaptor or 'host' strategy, the tension between the objectives of egalitarianism and competitiveness in reward practice, and the complex array of home country, host country and firm-specific factors that serve to shape strategies and practices related to international rewards. Although it remains to be seen whether further internationalization will weaken the preference of Chinese MNC for a dual approach to international reward management, it is very likely that China's rapidly rising importance in the global economy will mean that Chinese firms will exercise far greater influence over global rewards in the decades to come.

Questions

1. Do you think that the 'dual' approach to international reward management preferred by Chinese MNCs is sustainable over the longer term as Chinese firms become progressively more integrated into the global economy?
2. If Chinese MNCs are to make greater use of HCNs in their staffing, how might they best modify their reward practices to support this change?
3. As China consolidates its position as an economic superpower, how might the reward practices preferred by Chinese MNCs influence trends in international reward management?

References

Armstrong, M. and Brown, D. (1998) Relating competencies to pay: the UK experience. *Compensation and Benefits Review*, (May–June): 28–39.

Barrett, G. V. (1991) Comparison of skill-based pay with traditional job evaluation techniques. *Human Resource Management Review*, 1: 97–105.

Beer, M. and Cannon, M. D. (2004) Promise and peril in implementing pay-for-performance. *Human Resource Management*, 43(1): 3–20; critical commentaries 21–50.

Bennett Stewart, G. III, Applebaum, E., Beer, M., Lebby, A. M., Amabile, T. M., McAdams, J., Kozlowski, L. D., Baker, G. P. III and Wolters, D. S. (1993) Rethinking rewards. *Harvard Business Review*, 71(6): 37–49.

Bloom, M., Milkovich, G. and Mitra, A. (2003) International compensation: learning from how managers respond to variations in local host contexts. *International Journal of Human Resource Management*, (December): 1350–67.

Brown, D. and Purcell, J. (2007) Reward management: on the line. *Compensation and Benefits Review*, 39(3): 28–34.

Cameron, J. and Pierce, D. (1997) Rewards, interest and performance: an evaluation of experimental findings. *ACA Journal/WorldatWork Journal*, 6(4): 6–15.

Canavan, J. (2008) Overcoming the challenge of aligning skill-based pay levels to the external market. *WorldatWork Journal*, 17(1): 18–25.

Castle, S. (2011) European Union salaries a haven for Eastern Europeans. *New York Times*, 8 March. Available from: http://www.nytimes.com/2011/03/09/world/europe/09latvia.html?_r=1 [accessed 20 March 2011].

Cotton, C. and Chapman, J. (2010) Rewards in the U.K. top 10 risks. *Workspan*, 53(1): 53–7.

Cumming, C. (1994) Incentives that really do motivate. *Compensation and Benefits Review*, (May–June): 38–40.

Dalton, G. (1998) The glass wall: shattering the myth that alternative rewards won't work with unions. *Compensation and Benefits Review*, 30(6): 38–45.

Deci, E. L. and Ryan, R. M. (1985) *Intrinsic Motivation and Self-determination in Human Behavior*. New York: Plenum Press.

Dowling, P. J., Welch, D. E. and Schuler, R. S. (2008) *International Human Resource Management: Managing People in a Multinational Context* (5th edn). Melbourne: Cengage Learning.

England, P. and Kilbourne, B. (1991) Using job evaluation to achieve pay equity. *International Journal of Public Administration*, 14(5): 823–43.

Evans, E., Hillins, J. F., McNally, K. A., Zingheim, P. K., Bahner, R. R. and Wilson, T. B. (1995) A series of essays about how rewards can succeed. *ACA Journal*, 4(2): 20–35.

Gerhart, B. and Rynes, S. (2003) *Compensation. Theory, Evidence, and Strategic Implications*. Thousand Oaks, CA: Sage.

Gerhart, B., Rynes, S. and Fulmer, I. S. (2009) Pay and performance: individuals, groups, and executives. *Academy of Management Annals*, 3(1): 251–315.

Gettler, L. (2010) Shares and share alike. *HR Monthly*, (March): 29–33.

Grant, D. and Shields, J. (2006) Identifying the subject: worker identity as discursively contested terrain. In Hearn, M. and Michelson, G. (eds) *Rethinking Work: Time, Space and Discourse*. Melbourne: Cambridge University Press, pp. 285–307.

Gupta, N. and Jenkins, G. D. (1991) Practical problems in using job evaluation systems to determine compensation. *Human Resource Management Review*, 1(2): 133–44.

Gupta, N. and Mitra, A. (1998) The value of financial incentives: myths and empirical realities. *ACA Journal/WorldatWork Journal*, 7(3): 58–66.

Gupta, N. and Shaw J. (1998) Let the evidence speak: financial incentives are effective!! *Compensation and Benefits Review*, 30(2): 26, 28–32.

Haipeter, T. (2011) Works councils as actors in collective bargaining: derogations and the development of codetermination in the German chemical and metalworking industries. *Economic and Industrial Democracy*. epub 22 February 2011, doi: 10.1177/0143831X10393039.

Heery, E. (1996) Risk, representation and the 'new pay'. *Personnel Review*, 25(6): 54–65.

Heneman, R. L. and LeBlanc, P. (2002) Developing a more relevant and competitive approach for valuing knowledge work. *Compensation and Benefits Review*, 34(4): 43–7.

Heneman, R. L. and LeBlanc P. (2003) Work valuation addresses shortcomings of both job evaluation and market pricing. *Compensation and Benefits Review*, 35(1): 7–11.

Heneman, R. L. and Von Hipple, C. (1995) Balancing group and individual rewards: rewarding individual contributions to the team. *Compensation and Benefits Review*, 27(4): 63–8.

Hofrichter, D. and McGovern, T. (2001) People, competencies and performance: clarifying means and ends. *Compensation and Benefits Review*, 33(4): 34–8.

Hofstede, G. (1984) *Culture's Consequences*. London: Sage.

Kaarsemaker, E. and Poutsma, E. (2006) The fit of employee ownership with other human resource management practices: theoretical and empirical suggestions regarding the existence of an ownership high-performance work system. *Economic and Industrial Democracy*, 27(4): 669–85.

Kim, D.-O. and Voos, P. (1997) Unionization, union involvement, and the performance of gainsharing programs. *Industrial Relations/Relations Industrielles*, 52(2): 304–32.

Kohn, A. (1993a) *Punished by Rewards*. Boston: Houghton Mifflin.

Kohn, A. (1993b) Why incentive plans cannot work. *Harvard Business Review*, 71(5): 54–63.

Lang, J. M. (2008) Human resources in India: retaining and motivating staff in a Lufthansa subsidiary. *Compensation and Benefits Review*, 40: 56–62.

Lawler, E. E. (1988) What's wrong with pointfactor job evaluation. *Compensation and Benefits Review*, 18(2): 20–8.

Lawler, E. E. (1990) *Strategic Pay: Aligning Organizational Strategies and Pay Systems*. San Francisco: Jossey-Bass.

Ledford, G. E. (1991a) Three case studies on skill-based pay: an overview. *Compensation and Benefits Review*, 23(2): 11–23.

Ledford, G. E. (1991b) The design of skill-based pay plans. In Rock, M. and Berger, L. (eds) *The Compensation Handbook: A State of the Art Guide to Compensation Strategy and Design* (3rd edn). New York: McGraw-Hill, pp. 199–217.

Ledford, G. E. (2008) Factors affecting the long-term success of skill-based pay. *WorldatWork Journal*, 17(1): 6–17.

Ledford, G. E. and Heneman, R. L. (1999). Pay for skills, knowledge and competencies. In Berger, L. A. and Berger, D. R. (eds) *The Compensation Handbook. A State-of-the-Art Guide to Compensation Strategy and Design* (4th edn). McGraw-Hill, pp. 143–56.

Lehndorff, S., Bosch, G., Haipeter, T. and Latniak, E. (2009) The vulnerability of an export champion: upheaval in the German employment model. Paper presented at the Annual Congress of the International Industrial Relations Association (IIRA), Sydney, Australia, August.

Lindrop, E. (2009) Employee voice in pay determination. In White, G. and Drucker, J. (eds) *Reward Management. A Critical Text* (2nd edn). London: Routledge, pp. 41–5.

Long, R. (2006) *Strategic Compensation in Canada* (3rd edn). Scarborough, ON: Thomson Nelson, pp. 187–213.

Long, R. and Shields, J. (2009) Do unions affect pay methods of Canadian firms? A longitudinal study. *Relations Industrielles/Industrial Relations*, 64(3): 442–65.

McAdams, J. L. (1999) Non-monetary rewards: cash equivalents and tangible awards. In Berger, L. A. and Berger, D. R. (eds) *The Compensation Handbook: A State-of-the-Art Guide to Compensation Strategy and Design* (4th edn). New York: McGraw-Hill, pp. 241–60.

Merriman, K. K. (2009) On the folly of rewarding team performance, while hoping for teamwork. *Compensation and Benefits Review*, 41(1): 61–6.

Murray, B. and Gerhart, B. (2000) Skill-based pay and skill seeking. *Human Resource Management Review*, 10(3): 271–87.

Nelson, B. (1994) *1001 Ways to Reward Employees*. New York: Workman Publishing.

Pendleton, A. (2009) Employee share ownership in Europe. In White, G. and Drucker, J. (eds) *Reward Management. A Critical Text* (2nd edn). London: Routledge, pp. 224–44.

Perkins, S. J. and Vartiainen, M. (2010) European reward management? Introducing the special issue. *Thunderbird International Business Review*, 52(3): 175–87.

Perkins, S. J. and White, G. (2008) *Employee Reward. Alternatives, Consequences and Contexts.* London: Chartered Institute of Personnel and Development.

Robinson, F. and Winning, N. (2011) EU nations may only get stay of execution on indexation. *Wall Street Journal* (7 March). Available from: http://online.wsj.com/article/BT-CO-20110307-710793.html [accessed 20 March 2011].

Rosen, A. S. and Turetsky, D. (2002) Broadbanding: the construction of a career management framework. *WorldatWork Journal*, 11(4): 45–55.

Rubery, J. (1995) Performance-related pay and the prospects for gender pay equity. *Journal of Management Studies*, 32(5): 637–53.

Rynes, S. L., Gerhart B. and Park, L. (2005) Personnel psychology: performance evaluation and pay for performance. *Annual Review of Psychology*, 56: 571–600.

Shen, J. (2004) Compensation in Chinese multinationals. *Compensation and Benefits Review*, 36: 15–25.

Shields, J. (2007) *Managing Employee Performance and Reward: Concepts, Practices, Strategies.* Melbourne: Cambridge University Press.

Shields, J., Scott, D., Sperling, R. and Higgins, T. (2009) Rewards communication in Australia: a survey of policies and programs. *Compensation and Benefits Review*, 41(6): 14–26.

Townley, B. (1993a) Foucault, power/knowledge, and its relevance for human resource management. *Academy of Management Review*, 18(3): 518–45.

Townley, B. (1993b) Performance appraisal and the emergence of management. *Journal of Management Studies*, 31(2): 221–38.

Townley, B. (1994) *Reframing Human Resource Management. Power, Ethics and the Subject at Work.* London: Sage.

Townley, B. (1998) Beyond good and evil: depth and division in the management of human resources. In McKinlay, A. and Starkey, K. (eds) *Foucault, Management and Organization Theory*. London: Sage, pp. 191–210.

Townley, B. (1999) Nietzsche, competencies and Übermensch: reflections on human and inhuman resource management. *Organization*, 6(2): 285–306.

Watson, T. (2004) HRM and critical social science analysis. *Journal of Management Studies*, 41(3): 447–67.

Watson, B. W. and Singh, G. (2005) Global pay systems: compensation in support of a multinational strategy. *Compensation and Benefits Review*, (January/February): 33–6.

Wright, A. (2009) Benefits. In White, G. and Druker, J. (eds) *Reward Management. A Critical Text* (2nd edn). London: Routledge, pp. 174–91.

PART THREE

CHAPTER 13
The Nature and Scope of HRD

Jim Stewart, Jeff Gold, Paul Iles, Rick Holden and Julie Beardwell

CHAPTER LEARNING OUTCOMES

After studying this chapter, you should be able to:
- Describe the history and origins of HRD
- Debate the meanings associated with HRD theory and practice
- Evaluate the arguments provided in support of current debates
- Apply a range of concepts in critically assessing HRD practice

CHAPTER OUTLINE

- Introduction
- History and origins of HRD
- Academic disciplines
- Contexts of practice
- Key debates and emerging themes
- Summary

Introduction

This book examines the idea of Human Resource Development (HRD). A general approach throughout the book is to focus on theoretical and conceptual understanding as well as the application of that understanding in practice. HRD is an area of professional practice as well as a subject of academic enquiry. The purpose of this first chapter is to look at the foundations of both. In other words, we will be concerned with discussing the results of academic theorizing and the results of research into professional practice. To achieve this purpose, we will provide a brief overview of the history and origins of the idea, identify the academic disciplines that have been drawn on to develop associated concepts and theories utilized within HRD, describe the various contexts in which HRD is argued to be practised and finally examine the current debates and emerging themes in HRD research.

Human Resource Development (HRD) takes capital letters for a reason. This reason is mostly associated with the interests of academics in universities (McGoldrick and Stewart, 1996). The capital letters denote a name and a proper noun that are used in academic titles of, for example, departments and personal titles such as Professor of Human Resource Development in universities. It is less common to see the term used in professional practice (Sambrook and Stewart, 2005). The words 'training' and 'development', used as both nouns and verbs, are more common in that context and sometimes are combined with the word 'learning', especially in personal and job titles. In fact, the Chartered Institute of Personnel and Development (CIPD), the professional body in the UK, use the words 'Learning and Development' rather than HRD in the title of its professional standards specifying the knowledge and skill requirements of professional practitioners (Harrison, 2005). It also titles its web pages as 'Learning, Training and Development'. So we can see here an immediate difference and distinction between HRD as a subject of academic enquiry and an area of professional practice. It is simply that HRD is more commonly used in academic contexts than it is in those of professional practice.

This simple difference also allows us to make a more important point. This is that HRD is a human construct. It does not have an objective or independent existence. In fact, 'it' is not even an 'it', at least not in the same sense that we say a chair is an 'it', as in 'it (the chair) has four legs and is used to sit on'. That being the case, we cannot describe and review the meaning and history of HRD as easily or in the same way as we might that of a chair. It is also the case that as a human construct, HRD does not have a settled and accepted meaning. Different people for different reasons argue different positions in relation to the meaning of HRD, and it is no easy or straightforward matter to determine whose argument might be right and whose might be wrong. In the end, there may be no definitive basis for making that judgement. Our own view is that this is the case, so in the end personal judgement has to be exercised in the face of ambiguity and uncertainty. The meaning of HRD is contested and subject to debate and argument. There is no definitive basis for deciding between the various arguments and positions. So, personal judgement, based on the best available evidence and a critical evaluation of and arguments built on that evidence, is the final determinant of a position on HRD. We will be using the term HRD as if it is indeed an 'it'. This is for the sake of brevity and ease of reading and should not be taken to negate our argument here.

ACTIVITY

Visit the CIPD's website – www.cipd.co.uk/subjects/lrnanddev/.

Contrast the CIPD's website with those of the University Forum for HRD – www.ufhrd.co.uk/wordpress/ and the Academy of HRD – www.ahrd.org.

The arguments made so far will be developed and expanded as this opening chapter proceeds. What is important at this point is that you are alerted to this overall uncertainty as you read what follows. We want you to exercise your personal judgement throughout this chapter and indeed throughout the book. It is best then to direct you on that path from the start. The Reflective questions below, as with others in the book, are designed to help you to achieve the objectives set for the chapter. These questions support the application and exercise of personal judgement. You will need to engage with others for this activity, which can be a group of colleagues or a seminar/tutorial group of students.

reflective questions

1. What reasons can you think of for the greater use of HRD in academic contexts compared to professional practice contexts?
2. What implications other than ambiguity and uncertainty arise from HRD being a contested term?
3. What criteria might you use in judging the validity of evidence and the logic of arguments on the meaning of HRD?

History and origins of HRD

As with its meaning, there is also debate over the origins of the term HRD. Some argue that it can be traced to what is known as 'Organization Development' (OD), which began in the USA sometime in the 1940s (Blake, 1995) without, as it were, catching on. Others, including Blake, attribute the first specific formulation to the American writer Leonard Nadler (1970). The definition offered by Nadler of this then new term is instructive:

> HRD is organized learning experiences provided by employers, within a specified period of time, to bring about the possibility of performance improvement and/or personal growth (quoted in Nadler and Nadler, 1989, p. 4)

This definition is interesting for reasons that will become clear soon and so it will be useful to bear it in mind. It is also an important definition because it shaped debates and controversies that continue now. For example, there seem to be two purposes attached to HRD in the definition. One is the possibility of 'improving performance'. However, it also suggests a purpose of bringing about 'personal growth'. It might be worth asking whether there is no connection between these two possible outcomes but the definition certainly seems to imply this is the case. These two possible purposes are, however, the focus of disagreement between those who adopt what is known as a 'performative' focus for HRD and those who adopt what is known as a 'learning' focus (Rigg et al., 2007). We do not need to examine these debates here but for now just note that the term 'HRD' is American in origin and emerged in common usage there sometime in the 1970s.

Debate centred on a number of factors in the years that followed. One significant piece of work to attempt to settle that debate was commissioned by the American Society of Training and Development and conducted by Pat McLagan (1989). This produced a specification of the key activities of HRD professionals in their practice, which were argued to encompass all levels and foci of development in work organizations, for example career and organization as well as personal and professional development. Rather than settle matters, McLagan's work merely stimulated new avenues of research and debate. Notable among these have been the contributions of McLean (2004) and Swanson (2001), in their debates on the foundations and theories of HRD, and Lynham (2000) and others on theory building in HRD. Other writers have focused on the basic philosophy of HRD, for example Holton and Kuchinke (see McGoldrick et al., 2004, for a summary).

Adoption of the term HRD came later to Europe and the UK, where it did not really prove popular until the late 1980s and more particularly the 1990s. Two early UK references were in Mumford (1986) and Stewart (1989). A simpler debate than that seen in the USA occurred in the UK between Oxtoby and Coster (1992), later contributed to by Stewart (1992), and published in the professional journal *Training and Development*. This debate centred on the values inherent in referring to 'employees', and thus people, as 'resources' and so debated the validity and utility of the term 'HRD'. Themes similar to those raised by Oxtoby and Coster are still subject to scrutiny (see, for example, Kuchinke and Han, 2005). More sophisticated debates have since grown in the UK, including that of Lee (2004), who argues against any attempt to define HRD on the basis that, in uncertain and unpredictable times, this would give 'the appearance of being in control' and 'serve the political and social needs of the minute' (p. 38). An additional continuing theme in HRD debates is that of the relationship of the term to longer established concepts such as Human Resource Management (HRM). This is a theme addressed early by Stewart and McGoldrick (1996) and in their later work with Watson (McGoldrick et al., 2004). The term 'HRM' had become prominent in the UK from the late 1980s as a particular approach to managing people, again after earlier work in the USA. HRM is argued to be more strategic in its outlook than personnel management as a necessary response to globalization and the internationalization of technology through gaining the commitment of workers as a source of competitive advantage and increasing productivity (Bratton and Gold, 2007). HRD could be seen as a subset of the HRM movement, although we will argue it has become increasingly a movement in its own right.

Another continuing theme on both sides of the Atlantic is the relationship of HRD with education, training and development. Part of that theme is to define each of the concepts so that each can be distinguished from the others. Stewart (1999) is not alone in suggesting that it is a futile debate but it does continue to fascinate some. A final continuing theme is differentiating HRD from Strategic HRD (SHRD). This too might be argued to be futile, especially since some writers distinguish HRD from training on the basis that HRD is strategic while training is operational (Stewart and McGoldrick, 1996). Others insist on a difference between HRD and SHRD, for example Walton (1999).

Many of the debates referred to above concern and are informed by different views on the way HRD theory and practice draws on established academic disciplines, so we will examine those possibilities in the next section. Before moving on, the following Activity will be useful in furthering understanding of the debates that have led to the current views on HRD.

> **ACTIVITY**
>
> Access two articles from the journals below, which will help to answer the following questions:
>
> 1. What is meant by the notion of 'performative' perspectives of HRD?
> 2. What is meant by the notion of 'learning' perspectives of HRD?
> 3. What are the key differences between the two perspectives?
> 4. What in your view are the main arguments in favour of and against each perspective?
>
> *Human Resource Development International* – www.tandf.co.uk/journals/routledge/13678868.html
>
> *Human Resource Development Quarterly* – www.josseybass.com/WileyCDA/WileyTitle/productCd-HRDQ.html
>
> *Human Resource Development Review* – http://hrd.sagepub.com/

Academic disciplines

It might seem a subject of little dispute to determine which academic disciplines underpin and inform HRD. That is part of the debate, however, at least as to which are the most significant and influential (see McGoldrick et al., 2004). What can be said with some confidence is that HRD is concerned with human behaviour, so disciplines concerned with understanding and explaining that behaviour are of some potential relevance to HRD (Stewart, 2007). These disciplines are referred to as the 'social sciences'. This generic heading is generally taken to include economics, politics, geography, sociology, social psychology, psychology and anthropology. Each of these can be and is argued to have informed and influenced the development of theory and understanding of HRD.

Psychology and its variants such as social psychology are probably not disputed as being central to the development of HRD. This is because the latter is focused on changing behaviour through learning, and psychology has been central in the development of learning theories. It is rare to find a textbook on HRD that does not include some discussion of learning theory. Human behaviour, while in some senses always a phenomenon of individuals, occurs in social contexts. Individuals behave in the context of, in relation and response to and, mostly, in the company of other individuals. This raises the possibility that learning is as much a social process as an individual process, so even within the limited context of learning theories, those developed in psychology may not tell the whole story. This point aside, we know that as social beings humans congregate in groups of varying types and sizes, for example families, tribes, organizations and nations. Thus, social sciences such as social psychology, sociology and anthropology are also drawn on because of their contributions to understanding human behaviour in the context of human collectives. A specific example of recent and current topicality is the application of the concept of 'culture' in organization studies. This concept was originally developed in anthropology in the study of tribes, communities and societies (Stewart and McGoldrick, 1996). Its relevance and application within HRD is because of interest in applying the concept of 'culture' to the study of work organizations and the association of HRD with such organizations, as suggested by Nadler's definition, given above. There are those who argue that HRD is primarily if not exclusively concerned with human behaviour in the context of work organization. We will examine this in more detail in the next section. For now though, this argument in part supports the view that economics and to a lesser extent politics are also essential disciplines informing HRD theory and practice (McLean, 2004). An example of the application of economic theory is the notion of 'human capital', which seeks to explain investment in education and training as well as being used to justify such investment (see Becker, 1964). A related economic concept is that of 'return on investment', which is often argued to be the 'gold standard' of evaluating HRD activity. Politics is argued to be of relevance because of its central concern with the notion of power and how power is and can be exercised in human groups. Power is a key concept in OD and, as we saw earlier, OD is held to be a component of HRD. This is not the only reason though, as it is an axiom of organizations that power is essential to influence decision making, especially in relation to resource allocation, so HRD practitioners need to understand these processes if they are to secure resources to support their work (Harrison, 2005). Geography may seem the least likely social science to have relevance to HRD, and it certainly has not been as significant as the others discussed. However, with the theme of globalization now prominent, along with the economic and social problems facing groups, communities, regions, cities and nations, it would seem that geography is bound to become another source of understanding for those in HRD in future years (Marquardt et al., 2004).

This brief summary of academic disciplines suggests that HRD is not itself subject to independent theorizing or theory development. This view is not necessarily widely shared (Mankin, 2001) but it does have some support (Stewart, 2007). The summary also suggests that only the social sciences are of interest to HRD. This view is also open to challenge, since at least some of the natural sciences also have useful and relevant contributions to understanding human behaviour. This is perhaps most obviously the case with the natural sciences concerned with the development and application of evolutionary theory, for example zoology, ethology and biology. That there are connections between the natural and social sciences in theorizing and understanding human behaviour is best demonstrated by the development in recent years of 'hybrid' disciplines such as social biology and evolutionary psychology. Little use has been made to date of the natural sciences or the newer hybrid disciplines in developing HRD but they may become more significant in the future. Similarly, there are those who would wish to see a greater influence of the arts and humanities in HRD. This is part of a wider concern about the apparent failure of business schools to provide relevant ideas to actual business practice. There is a claim that the need to conform to rigorous models of scientific research loses the connection to the realities of practice (Ghoshal, 2005). Thus research into the practice of HRD can reveal the very human processes of talk, persuasion, use of rhetoric and storytelling in bringing about HRD activities and the valuing of such activities (Gold and Smith, 2003).

Contexts of practice

So far we have examined the origins and underlying academic disciplines of HRD and found that those questions are not easily settled. The same is true when we look at the contexts of HRD practice. The definition given earlier from Nadler illustrates this quite clearly. It specifically mentions and so focuses on 'employers'. An alternative definition provides a different view and different possibilities:

> HRD is constituted by planned interventions in organizational and individual learning processes. (Stewart, 2007, p. 66)

This definition allows for several additional contexts. First, the term 'organization' is not limited to those who engage in an employment relationship with individuals. Therefore, according to this definition, HRD can be and is practised by more than 'employers'. An example might be charitable organizations that rely on voluntary workers rather than employees. Another might be purely voluntary organizations such as interest or community groups. Second, the focus on 'planned interventions in individual learning processes' opens up a wide range of possibilities. These might include voluntary groups such as the Scout movement or local youth clubs. It might also be said to encompass what happens in schools during compulsory education. A more widely held view is that HRD does encompass further and higher education, since these two contexts have a firm focus on and purpose of planned interventions in individual learning processes (see, for example, Stewart and Knowles, 2003; Stewart and Harte, 2008).

The possible contexts of compulsory, further and higher education support a view that policies pursed by national governments are also a context of HRD practice. This context is associated with a number of different terms including national policies, vocational education and training (VET) and National HRD (NHRD). The latter term has recently become popular through the work of McLean (2004) in the USA, but VET is more common in Europe, including the UK. This focus on government interventions also raises the question of communities and whole societies being a context of HRD practice. There are other arguments to support this, for example much of the early work of OD practitioners in the USA and the UK centred on communities and community issues such as race relations. If we accept that HRD encompasses and includes OD, as suggested by McLagan (1989),

> **ACTIVITY**
>
> A number of government departments play a role in national HRD considerations. For example, go to www.berr.gov.uk/ for the Department for Business, Enterprise and Regulatory Reform and www.dius.gov.uk/ for the Department for Innovation, Universities and Skills. These departments cover policy in England but for Scotland, go to www.scotland.gov.uk/Topics/Education, for Wales, go to http://new.wales.gov.uk/topics/educationandskills/?lang=en and for Northern Ireland, go to www.delni.gov.uk/index/publications/pubs-sectoral/skills-strategy-ni.htm.

those early programmes and others like them today are yet another context of HRD practice.

This brief discussion illustrates a number of important points. First, the definition of HRD that is adopted will influence and shape the contexts in which HRD is understood to be practised. The definition offered by Stewart might include families as a context of HRD practice, since parents engage in planned interventions in the learning processes of their children, but Nadler's definition would certainly exclude such a context. It might be reasonably argued that taking Stewart's definition to include families would be stretching the concept of HRD too far, and, in contrast, that Nadler's definition is too restrictive and excludes areas of legitimate interest to researchers and professional practitioners alike. Second, 'professional practice' may be both helpful and legitimate as the defining feature determining contexts. Thus, where professionals with expertise in developing human resources work and practise determines the contexts of HRD practice. Adopting this suggestion as a guiding principle would allow for those contexts suggested in this section but it would not stop debate. For example, many who work in higher education, although their job and title includes the word 'lecturer', would not see themselves as HRD practitioners and so would argue against such a label. But their job and everyday work is certainly included in Stewart's definition, irrespective of their particular subject, for example lecturers in mathematics, physics, history and sociology are all engaged in the common task of designing and delivering planned interventions in learning processes. Such lecturers might argue that they are primarily specialists in their subject. A counterargument might accept that premise but then point out that they need also to be specialists in supporting and facilitating learning since they work in education.

A final point to arise from the discussion of contexts of practice is that HRD has historically and traditionally been associated with training in work organizations and as a tool of management in that context, but as it has developed as an academic subject, the contexts of practice have been broadened to encompass arenas not previously seen as legitimate. We can now say with confidence that HRD occurs in informal as well as formal organizations, at national and perhaps supranational as well as organization levels and, with the rise of personal coaching, for example, also at individual levels outside organization contexts, especially since individuals are increasingly encouraged to become lifelong learners.

reflective questions

1. How do the academic disciplines drawn on in researching and theorizing HRD influence the definition and meaning of the term?
2. Based on your understanding so far of the meaning of the term HRD, which academic disciplines have been and are most significant in shaping current definitions and meanings?
3. How does the definition of HRD influence contexts of practice? Which contexts of practice do you consider to be legitimate and why?

Key debates and emerging themes

We have seen that there are a number of areas of debate within HRD as both a field of academic enquiry and professional practice. These can be summarized as follows:

- Defining and attaching meaning to the term
- The possibility of theorizing HRD
- Assuming the possibility of theorizing, actual theories of HRD
- The significance, role and impact of various established academic disciplines in HRD theorizing
- The number and location of legitimate areas of HRD practice.

Some of these debates have been engaged in since the emergence of the term 'HRD', for example defining and attaching meaning to the term. Some are more recent and are still, to some extent, emerging themes, for example the possibility of theorizing HRD, which has, in chronological terms, actually emerged after early attempts to produce theories of HRD. This final section will identify a number of additional emerging themes in HRD debates.

The first theme is that of HRD in the development of small and medium-sized enterprises (SMEs). Debates here centre on at least three factors. The first is the extent to which HRD is practised in SMEs and the extent to which HRD theorizing has taken enough account of the different and variable contexts of small organizations (see Stewart and Beaver, 2004). The second factor is that of SME development in the sense of supporting and facilitating the establishment of new businesses and social enterprises. The key question here is what if any role is there for HRD and HRD practitioners in that process, especially in light of the growing consensus that learning and development in SMEs are best considered as informal processes (CBI, 2003)? The final focus is the role of higher education institutions in developing enterprising characteristics in university graduates. Related to this is the debate on the precise meaning of enterprise development in that context (Stewart and Harte, 2008).

A second emerging theme for debate is the value of adopting more precise foci for HRD research and practice. Such foci can be sector, function or method specific. Examples of the first of these include the public as opposed to the private sector, or even more specific sectors within that (see, for example, Sambrook and Stewart, 2007). An example of the second is Leadership Development, which has in recent years attracted a good deal of research by HRD academics and specialization by HRD professionals. The third focus can be illustrated by a profusion of both research and practice interest in recent years in coaching as a method within HRD. All these varying foci and examples raise a similar question: is HRD different and therefore worthy of special attention in different sectors or functions, or when particular methods are adopted? This is not a question to be addressed in this chapter, but it is one that a full reading of the book may at least help to answer.

The third emerging theme and area of debate is the difference between HRD and its relationship with other foci of academic research and professional practice. We have already mentioned the relationship with HRM but there are others such as 'learning organization', 'Organizational Learning' and 'Knowledge Management'.

All these share similarities with HRD, in that they have emerged as terms used in academic contexts as titles of departments and professorships, have their own academic and professional journals and also are applied in practice with people holding jobs in work organizations and government agencies with those or similar words used in their titles. The main issue is that the terms focus both academic enquiry and professional practice on the same social practices as does HRD (Stewart, 2005). The questions that arise therefore include: to what extent and how are they different from and the same as HRD?

The final emerging theme and area of debate is the most recent and is referred to as 'Critical HRD' (CHRD). This focus has emerged partly in response to the rise of critical management studies, although some of the themes addressed in CHRD such as ethics have a longer history than critical management as an area of debate (see, for example, Stewart, 1998; McGoldrick et al., 2004). CHRD questions the traditional and taken-for-granted assumptions of the purpose, nature, application and activities of HRD and raises issues to do with legitimacy, power, control and the economic and social context of HRD theory and practice. The term 'CHRD' became established in several academic conferences of the late 1990s and early 2000s and has led to a number of special editions of journals (Trehan et al., 2004, 2006) as well as edited collections in books (Elliott and Turnbull, 2005; Rigg et al., 2007).

CHRD does not represent a separate and particular strand in HRD research and practice, but provides alternative perspectives that can and do inform mainstream HRD theory and practice. Thus you will not find chapters on CHRD as such in this book, but you will find chapters that are informed to varying extents and in varying ways by work done by academics within CHRD. You will also find chapters that address some of the other emerging themes and areas of debate identified here. For example, there are chapters devoted to specific functions such as leadership and with specific contexts such as small businesses. The book therefore provides and examines current knowledge on emerging as well as established themes in HRD, and in doing so, also reviews and evaluates current debates on all those themes. To help to prepare you for getting the most out of the rest of the book, answer the Discussion questions below before moving on with your reading of the book.

Summary

- This chapter has introduced the term 'HRD' and briefly examined its origins and history as well as its core academic disciplines, contexts of practice and emerging themes and debates. We can conclude that HRD is not a simple or straightforward term and that it has no settled meaning.

- As a recent and abstract human construct, HRD is also subject to continuous and continuing debate. Such debate encompasses not just its definition and meaning but also the possibility of any theory of HRD as well as some additional emerging themes.

- There is a key debate among HRD professionals and academics between those who adopt a 'performative' focus for HRD and those who adopt a 'learning' focus.

- HRD is concerned with human behaviour and so disciplines in the social sciences concerned with understanding and explaining that behaviour are of some potential relevance to HRD.

- HRD is not restricted to work organizations and there has been growing interest in the practice of HRD in a range of contexts such as charities and voluntary contexts.
- At a national level, HRD is now a crucial emerging consideration, with a focus on government interventions in pursuit of national economic and social agendas.
- There are emerging themes of enquiry, practice and debate, which include sector-, function- and method-specific practice as well as the notion of Critical HRD.

DISCUSSION QUESTIONS

1. What does the term HRD mean to you?
2. How would you differentiate HRD from training and development in work organizations?
3. What is the value, if any, of using the term 'HRD' instead of training and development?
4. What is the value, if any, of the term 'CHRD'?
5. How does HRD relate to the term 'HRM'? How is it similar and different?
6. Which of the emerging themes within HRD research and writing are the most important and why?

Further reading

Lee, M.M., Stewart, J. and Woodall, J. (eds) (2004) *New Frontiers in Human Resource Development*, London, Routledge.
Lepak, D.P. and Snell, S.A. (1999) The human resource architecture: toward a theory of human capital allocation and development, *Academy of Management Review*, **24**(1): 31–48.
Stewart, J. and McGoldrick, J. (1996) *Human Resource Development: Perspectives, Strategies and Practice*, London, Pitman.
Swanson, R.A. (2001) Human resource development and its underlying theory, *Human Resource Development International*, **4**(3): 299–312.

References

Becker, G.S. (1964) *Human Capital*, New York, National Bureau of Economic Research.
Blake, R. (1995) Memories of HRD, *Training and Development*, **49**(3): 22–8.
Bratton, J. and Gold, J. (2007) *Human Resource Management: Theory and Practice*, Basingstoke, Palgrave Macmillan.
CBI (Confederation of British Industry) (2003) *Informality Works: A New Approach to Training for SMEs*, London, CBI.
Elliott, C. and Turnbull, S. (eds) (2005) *Critical Thinking in Human Resource Development*, London, Routledge.
Ghoshal, S. (2005) Bad management theories are destroying good management practices, *Academy of Management Learning and Education*, **4**(1): 75–81.
Gold, J. and Smith, V. (2003) Advances towards a learning movement: translations at work, *Human Resource Development International*, **6**(2): 139–52.
Harrison, R. (2005) *Learning and Development*, 4th edn, London, CIPD.

Kuchinke, K.P. and Han, H.-Y. (2005) Should caring be viewed as a competence? (Re-)Opening the dialogue over the limitations of competency frameworks in HRD, *Human Resource Development International*, **8**(3): 385–9.

Lee, M.M. (2004) A refusal to define HRD, in M.M. Lee, J. Stewart and J. Woodall (eds) *New Frontiers in Human Resource Development*, London, Routledge.

Lynham, S.A. (2000) Theory building in the human resource development profession, *Human Resource Development Quarterly*, **11**(2): 159–78.

McGoldrick, J. and Stewart, J. (1996) The HRM–HRD nexus, in J. Stewart and J. McGoldrick (eds) *HRD: Perspectives, Strategies and Practice*, London, Pitman.

McGoldrick, J., Stewart, J., Watson, S. (eds) (2004) *Understanding Human Resource Development: A Research Based Approach*, London, Routledge.

McLagan, P. (1989) *Models for HRD Practice*, Alexandra, VA, ASTD Press.

McLean, G.N. (2004) National human resource development: what in the world is it?, *Advances in Developing Human Resources*, **6**(3): 269–75.

Mankin, D. (2001) A model for human resource development, *Human Resource Development International*, **4**(1): 65–85.

Marquardt, M., Berger, N. and Loan, P. (2004) *HRD in the Age of Globalization: A Practical Guide to Workplace Learning in the Third Millennium*, New York, Basic Books.

Mumford, A. (ed.) (1986) *Handbook of Management Development*, 2nd edn, Aldershot, Gower.

Nadler, L. (1970) *Developing Human Resources*, Austin, Learning Concepts.

Nadler, L. and Nadler, Z. (1989) *Developing Human Resources*, 3rd edn, San Francisco, Jossey-Bass.

Oxtoby, B. and Coster, P. (1992) HRD: a sticky label, *Training and Development*, **10**(9): 31–2.

Rigg, C., Stewart, J. and Trehan, K. (2007) *Critical Human Resource Development: Beyond Orthodoxy*, Harlow, FT/Prentice Hall.

Sambrook, S. and Stewart, J. (2005) A critical review of researching human resource development: the case of a pan-European project, in C. Elliott and S. Turnbull (eds) *Critical Thinking in Human Resource Development*, London, Routledge.

Sambrook, S. and Stewart, J. (2007) HRD in health and social care, in S. Sambrook and J. Stewart (eds) *Human Resource Development in the Public Sector*, London, Routledge.

Stewart, J. (1989) Bringing about organisation change: a framework, *Journal of European Industrial Training*, **13**(6): 31–5.

Stewart, J. (1992) Towards a model of HRD, *Training and Development*, **10**(10): 26–9.

Stewart, J. (1998) Intervention and assessment: the ethics of HRD, *Human Resource Development International*, **1**(1): 16–22.

Stewart, J. (1999) *Employee Development Practice*, London, FT/Pitman.

Stewart, J. (2005) The current state and status of HRD research, *Learning Organisation Journal*, **12**(1): 90–5.

Stewart, J. (2007) The ethics of HRD, in C. Rigg, J. Stewart and K. Trehan (eds) *Critical Human Resource Development: Beyond Orthodoxy*, Harlow, Prentice Hall.

Stewart, J. and Beaver, G. (eds) (2004) *HRD in Small Organisations: Research and Practice*, London, Routledge.

Stewart, J. and Harte, V. (2008) Enterprise education and its impact on career intentions, paper presented at the 9th International Conference on HRD Research and Practice across Europe, IESEG School of Management, Lille, 21–23 May.

Stewart, J. and Knowles, V. (2003) Mentoring in undergraduate business management programmes, *Journal of European Industrial Training*, **27**(3): 147–59.

Stewart, J. and McGoldrick, J. (1996) *Human Resource Development: Perspectives, Strategies and Practice*, London, Pitman.

Swanson, R.A. (2001) Human resource development and its underlying theory, *Human Resource Development International*, **4**(3): 299–312.

Trehan, K., Rigg, C. and Stewart, J. (2004) Special issue on Critical Human Resource Development, *Journal of European Industrial Training*, **28**(8/9): 611–24.

Trehan, K., Rigg, C. and Stewart, J. (2006) Special issue on Critical HRD, *International Journal of Training and Development*, **10**(1): 4–15.

Walton. J. (1999) *Strategic Human Resource Development*, London, FT/Prentice Hall.

CHAPTER 14

Strategic HRD and the Learning and Development Function

Jim Stewart, Paul Iles, Jeff Gold, Rick Holden, Helen Rodgers and Hazel Kershaw-Solomon

CHAPTER OUTLINE

- Introduction
- SHRD and HRD strategy
- HRD and change
- The HRD function
- Summary

CHAPTER LEARNING OUTCOMES

After studying this chapter, you should be able to:

- Explain the meaning of Strategic HRD (SHRD)
- Explain the key ideas informing an HRD strategy and policy
- Understand the link between change and HRD
- Assess the role of the learning and development professional

Introduction

In a statement in the Foreword of the Leitch (2006) review of skills, it was suggested that:

> Without increased skills, we would condemn ourselves to a lingering decline in competitiveness, diminishing economic growth and a bleaker future for all.

This argument can be combined with significant changes in technology, global markets and customer requirements and such disturbances as the 'credit crunch' in

2008 and resource costs. As a consequence, HRD needs to be considered strategically by governments, organizations and individuals. Indeed, it is suggested that the move to make HRD more strategic provides a clear signal that learning and development are important. Bratton and Gold (2007) provide the following indicators of this move:

1. HRD emphasizes 'investment' in people rather than training as a 'cost', allowing a longer term perspective on outcomes and value-added.
2. HRD feeds other HRM polices such as recruitment for skills and retaining and rewarding talented employees as part of a qualitative difference between organizations and the development of a primary internal market with attention to continuous learning.
3. HRD is a key feature of a 'high road' HRM strategy (Cooke, 2000), which seeks to engender loyalty and commitment among employees. Through learning by employees, organization strategy itself can be transformed.

By adopting a more strategic view of HRD, organizations can consider learning at individual, group and organizational levels and as a source of competitive advantage. Learning occurs throughout the organization and is seen as a way of coping with change and generating innovation. Thus, Prahalad and Hamel (1990, p. 82) argue, 'collective learning' is an aspect of an organization's core competencies that other organizations cannot easily copy, and Ashton and Felstead (1995, p. 235) regard investment in skills as a 'litmus test' for a change in the way people are managed. One vital image that has emerged over the past decade is that of high performance working based on high-level skills and high discretion in work performance and decision making (ILO, 2000).

If HRD strategically becomes the concern of everyone, this has implications for those who specialize in its practice, and there has been growing interest in the profession of HRD. After many years of low interest and awareness, a growing number of HRD practitioners are seeking to advance their status through membership of the CIPD (Gold et al., 2003). In addition, there is more attention to the theoretical foundations of professional status, with journals and conferences devoted to HRD as a separate field of study rather than a small part of HRM. In this chapter, we will seek to explore the connection between Strategic HRD (SHRD) and the HRD function. First, we will consider strategy and the formation of HRD policies and plans, and then the link to change as a crucial source of understanding in SHRD. Finally, we will explore how the HRD function can benefit or otherwise from the enhanced status of HRD.

SHRD and HRD strategy

Attaching the word 'strategy' to organization functions is now so common that it is in danger of becoming meaningless. The word itself is associated with its own function of strategic management, which in these terms is seen to be a central part of general and senior management, for example a function of chief executives, managing directors, chief operating officers and other similar titles. It is also associated with the specialist and non-specialist contributions to organization management of top and senior functional managers, especially those with responsibility for finance, operations and perhaps marketing. The concern of top and senior managers with strategy follows from the history and development of the concept, which is mainly the application of economic theory to long-range planning and the long-term survival and prosperity in economic terms of business and commercial organizations. As with any and every other aspect and function of management, strategy has seen developments in theory and practice through academic research and academic and practitioner writing and publications.

In conventional terms, strategic management is concerned with ensuring the long-term survival of organizations. The key outcome of strategic management is a set of strategies that are themselves plans, programmes and activities and the resource allocations to support them. Strategies are based on an analysis of external and internal factors and a 'matching' process to ensure that the organization continues to be successful, especially in relation to formulating and achieving appropriate organizational-level performance goals and objectives in the face of competition from other organizations operating in the same markets. While it is of some value, it is a limited perspective on the meaning of strategy. What emerges from it for HRD is a view that top managers set out a vision and mission for an organization and develop organization or 'corporate' goals and strategy from which are derived business strategy and then functional strategy, including a strategy for HRD. This suggests a linear and static process, where fixed plans for HRD are formulated to contribute to the achievement of the business strategy, which in turn contributes to the achievement of the corporate strategy.

The logic of this understanding of strategic management and strategy is that HRD strategy is impossible in the absence of corporate and business strategy and that the purpose of HRD strategy is to support, or serve, business strategy. Stewart and McGoldrick (1996) adopt a different view of the strategic management process, which allows for a more proactive and processual contribution from HRD. In their nonlinear model of the strategy process, the focus is first on what they refer to as the 'strategic direction' of a given organization. This suggests the possibility of differences between what actually happens in practice in relation to long-term survival and what was and is determined and planned by top and senior managers. Stewart and McGoldrick go on to argue that strategic direction is the result of the interplay of a number of internal factors, the most significant of which are culture, leadership, the commitment of employees, and the approaches and responses to changed and changing internal and external conditions. They further argue that HRD in theory and practice has a major influence on each of these factors:

- shaping organizational culture
- developing current and future leaders
- building commitment among organization members
- anticipating and managing responses to changed conditions.

Thus, HRD is a strategic function as it has a significant impact on long-term survival. This view is supported by the work of Fredericks and Stewart (1996), who examine the connection between strategy and HRD from a processual rather than a functional perspective and argue that there are clear and mutually influencing relationships between organization structure (internally facing), organization strategy (externally facing), the actions and behaviours of organization members, management/leadership style and HRD policies and practices. So both pieces of work suggest that HRD is in and of itself strategic, since its practices have an impact on long-term survival.

SHRD

The previous point raises the question of whether there is any place for the concept of SHRD. If, as suggested above, HRD is by definition strategic, is there a need for and can there be any meaning attached to the concept of 'SHRD'? Many would argue such a need and therefore a distinction between HRD and SHRD, prominent among them Garavan (1991, 2007) and Walton (1999). Early work on SHRD by these authors adopted the conventional view of strategic management as being a long-term planning function in the hands (or perhaps brains) of top and senior managers. More recent work, summarized and applied by Garavan (2007), attempts to integrate both functional and processual perspectives on strategy to argue a meaning and space for SHRD. The main premise remains that HRD can be practised at an operational level without having connections with or relevance to corporate and business strategy or impact on long-term survival. This being the case, SHRD is distinguished from HRD, according to Garavan (2007, p. 11), because 'SHRD is a multi-level concept whose contribution to the organization is to enhance its performance in the long term'. It is perhaps a pity that in support of this claim, Garavan then quotes and cites the work of York, who actually writes about HRD rather than SHRD, rather suggesting that York is of the view that HRD is strategic in and of itself. This said, Garavan provides a detailed analysis of the literature on SHRD over the past 15 years as the basis for a persuasive argument on the nature and meaning of SHRD as a conceptual understanding of professional practice. His work does, however, leave the question of a clear distinction between HRD and SHRD open.

HRD strategies and plans

Despite the uncertainties over HRD and SHRD, it is nonetheless useful to apply the concept of 'strategy' in relation to HRD practice. In common with Stewart (1999), we adopt here a meaning in common usage, that an HRD strategy is a course of action intended to have long-term rather than short-term impact on significant rather than marginal areas of performance at organizational rather than individual level. The particular course of action will also have been arrived at through a series of decisions resulting from analysis of external as well as internal factors and be intended to directly contribute to matching organizational capability to changed and changing market conditions in order to achieve competitive advantage. If the particular organization in question does not operate in a market and so does not have competitors, the purpose will be related to whatever conditions affect long-term survival, for example satisfying funding and political stakeholders in the case of a public or quasi-public sector organization such as a university.

So HRD strategies are programmes and activities that make a contribution to long-term survival. Cultural change programmes around, for example, developing high levels of customer service through attitudes and values as well as knowledge and skills are a clear example of an HRD strategy. Others commonly include leadership and/or talent management programmes designed and intended to ensure a sufficient quantity and quality of future senior and top managers over, say, a 5-, 10- or 20-year period. Here 'quality' usually refers to a set of behavioural descriptors that reflect and express organizational values so as to ensure consistency and continuity in managerial and leadership style. Programmes to support the development of particular organizational forms, such as a 'learning organization', can also be described as HRD strategy. The use of the word 'support' here is significant. HRD strategies are commonly components in a range of programmes and activities designed and intended to bring about the kinds of changes implicit in these examples. Other components will usually include related HR strategies in, for example, employer branding in support of recruitment and selection, job and work design, employee reward and performance management. These HRD and HR strategies will in turn be linked with business strategy, for example the development of new products and/or distribution channels that require new and different competencies. It should be clear from this that the meaning being attached to the notion of strategy here is consistent with the conventional view, which leads to HRD being seen as the 'servant' of corporate and business strategy. HRD in Practice 14.1 provides an example of how one organization gave more strategic importance to HRD.

HRD in Practice 14.1 Security firm focuses on learning

Learning and development will be top of the agenda for G4S Security Services (UK) this year, according to its new HR director. Valerie Dale, who took up the post in January, explained: 'Learning and development is something that needs to be properly embedded in the company's culture. We need to look at how we can be better, quicker and slicker on the development side.'

Dale intends to introduce cross-divisional placements within G4S Security Services, a division of FTSE 100 firm G4S, saying: 'We want to try to move away from the traditional chalk and talk method.' Dale explained that encouraging cross-functional placements – for example HR employees spending time in the finance department – was 'a healthy thing to do ... It can be used to build up a rapport and there's the opportunity to resolve one another's problems. It's a great career development opportunity.'

Dale added that she would like to oversee the development of better qualifications for the industry, providing skills for life. She said that there was 'a good business proposition there in terms of credibility'.

A UK leadership programme for senior members is also being set up and is expected to launch later this month. Dale said: 'That's an extremely important

> strategy for us. It's vital that leaders are leading and are not being dictatorial through being led by market forces.'
>
> Dale is also considering using reward to encourage development. She explained: 'The old days of long service rewards are dead and buried. We should have some based on development, looking at recognized milestones and stepping stones.'
>
> *Source*: Adapted from Chubb, L. (2008) *People Management*, 6 March.

Designing and implementing programmes that meet the characteristics described here are not the only contribution of HRD practice. Other programmes and activities will need to be designed, implemented and conducted. They may not have long-term impact or be focused on significant aspirations and ambitions but they will nevertheless constitute an important contribution. We might signal the difference by the term 'plan' rather than the word 'strategy'. HRD plans will then be concerned with shorter time horizons, usually a year, and will cover a number and range of programmes and activities. The focus of these programmes and activities will be 'operational' and intended to ensure that the day-to-day work of the organization can be accomplished. Examples might include:

- programmes to train new starters to replace staff losses as a result of labour turnover
- programmes to develop knowledge and skills associated with some new technology or system
- programmes to develop better teamwork
- programmes of supervisory or management development to prepare individuals for promotion in the immediate or short term.

Another useful way of distinguishing between HRD strategies and plans is to apply the notions of 'maintenance' and 'change'. These have been applied to HRD practice for many years and one example is the work of Fredericks and Stewart (1996) referred to above. The basic idea is that HRD 'maintenance' programmes and activities are intended to keep the organization as it is, and effective and efficient at what it currently does. This is achieved by HRD plans. In contrast to this, HRD 'change' programmes are designed and intended to make the organization different and develop it to be able to do new and different things effectively and efficiently. This is achieved by HRD strategies. We will examine the application of this notion later in the chapter when we look at the connections between HRD and organizational change. Before that, there is one further related concept to be explained.

HRD policy

HRD policy is different from both strategy and plans. As we have seen, the latter two concepts are applied to programmes and activities – what HRD professionals do. Policy is a concept used to describe the framework within which decisions about programmes and activities are taken and which guides those decisions and their implementation. So policy is a set of principles that govern decisions and actions (Stewart, 1999). Such principles are not universal givens, however; they have to be determined and thus are a matter of human choice and decision. We will now describe a common process of determining policy as well as common features and content of HRD policy.

When looking at determining policy, it is as well to recognize that the process is not always and does not have to be a formal or deliberate process. Policy, like strategy, can emerge and be the cumulative result of ad hoc processes and decisions. Whether the result of formal and planned processes or an emergent and evolving process, there will be a number of factors influencing the formulation and content of HRD policy. These include:

External factors:

- Government policies and programmes
- Technological developments
- Social conditions, for example demographics and norms
- Competitor and stakeholder actions.

Internal factors:

- Organizational history and traditions
- Structure and culture
- Levels of management support
- Current performance and expected future performance
- Other organizational policies, especially related HR policies.

This list is taken from Stewart (1999) and he makes the important point that the factors do not operate separately and independently of each other. They all interact with and influence the impact of each other in complex processes that are hard to identify. One consequence of this is that even when policy making is planned and formalized, it will always be an iterative process. As well as being influenced by the factors identified above, policy making will also be influenced by the preferences, interests and needs of a variety of different groups involved in determining policy. These commonly include:

- Senior managers
- HRD professionals
- Trades unions representatives
- Other professional staff, especially HR and financial officers.

The specific content of any HRD policy will reflect the particular influence of the factors and groups identified here and how they interact. Resulting policies will commonly comprise a written statement of principles informing and shaping decisions in relation to a range of HRD applications. These will normally include the following:

- A statement of purpose and objectives
- A statement of priorities

- Roles and responsibilities of various groups and parties, for example senior managers, line managers, HRD professionals and individual employees
- Cost allocation policy and process
- Place of and access to records
- Application of policy to various different categories of employees
- Application of policy to various different approaches to and types of HRD practice, for example educational programmes and other forms of external development versus internal programmes.

It will be clear that there are connections between the concepts discussed so far. There is a need for some level of consistency and congruence between strategy, plans and policy. But this is not always the case in practice, since practice is not a matter of the simple application of theory or logic – organizations are much messier than that. What we have set out so far in this chapter represents what would be a textbook approach.

HRD and change

The formation of strategies in organizations of whatever kind have an inevitable link to change. Strategies are often a response to perceived change in the environment but they also set in motion desired changes within the organization. We know that the rate of change is never constant (Tushman et al., 1986) and that the effects of change can be studied over different timescales and at different levels – individual, group or team, department, whole organization, societal, national and international. In organizations, change is not always seen as an HRD issue, and whether change links to HRD depends on the various ways in which those who make strategy see learning as a key response. Gold and Smith (2003) found that some managers saw the need for change in terms of HRD as a principal component. In addition, it becomes possible for HRD specialists to have a role as facilitators or 'change agents' in ensuring that change can be managed and provide learning opportunities for others (McCracken and Wallace, 2000).

Types of change

It is not unusual to suggest that change and learning are the same thing. Certainly there seems to be some connection but we feel it is important to maintain some separation. We can think of some examples where change occurs, for example the installation of new equipment or a new procedure, but no one learns in terms of developing new skills or gaining knowledge. We can also find examples of people finding new possibilities for change that emerge from their learning at work. The latter possibility has been increasingly recognized as a source of new knowledge gained by individuals and shared with others, which can be captured for change in the organization as whole, but which can so easily be missed by managers (Bartlett and Ghoshal, 1997).

One thing that is clear – not all change is the same. Here we can make use of a distinction suggested by Hayes (2007) between 'incremental' and 'transformational' change. We present this as a dimension, as shown in Figure 14.1.

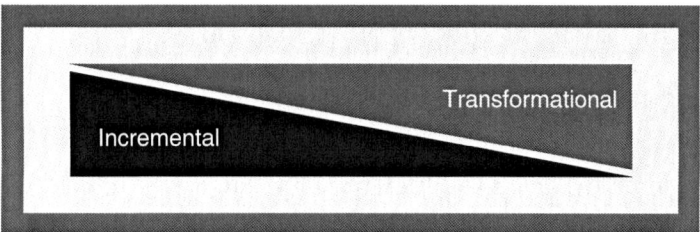

Figure 14.1 Incremental and transformational change

Incremental change occurs over a period of time but on a regular and continuous basis. However, such changes may hardly be noticed except that people are 'doing things better' through a process of 'tinkering, adaptation and modification' (Hayes 2007, p. 12). There is a link between change and continuous improvement and this is sometimes formalized in continuous improvement teams (CITs) and the Japanese Total Quality Management (TQM) principle of kaizan. This approach to change is connected to Toyota's lean manufacturing system, where changes for improvement are identified and implemented quickly by those closest to the work (Wall, 2005). As the small changes accumulate over time, it might be possible to identify some kind of transformation.

> **ACTIVITY**
>
> Kaizan is a development from TQM and you might like to explore some of the tools available to help people learn about improvement at work. Go to www.ifm.eng.cam.ac.uk/dstools/represent/tqm.html. Which of these tools could be used in your work?

One of the features of incremental change is that there is less difficulty or 'hassle' in making the changes identified (Buchanan and Boddy, 1992), whereas transformational change is considered to be a disturbance to the present and the creation of new dynamics that requires a break with the past. Rather than doing things better, the key question is: what can be done differently? For example, a manufacturing engineering company that shifts its purpose towards a design company because of the cost of manufacturing clearly makes a choice to change the path of its future development rather than remain in manufacturing.

How people in organizations understand the need for change also provides a close connection to the forms of learning suggested by Argyris and Schön (1978). First, single-loop learning is concerned with detecting errors and correcting them. There is no opportunity to challenge how things are done but incremental changes become possible. By contrast, there is double-loop learning, which challenges accepted practices based on particular assumptions that can be reconsidered. This can lead to new ideas and new practices. Bartunck and Moch (1987) use similar terms to describe frameworks of understanding for change. First-order change is concerned with incremental change that matches the shared understanding of those involved, while second-order change modifies how understanding occurs. They also add third-order change, which is concerned with developing the capacity to understand events as they occur, transcending single or particular ways of understanding to consider a variety of possibilities.

Hayes (2007) also considers how some organizations anticipate the need for change. They are 'proactive' in seeking opportunities for change, which they can initiate, as well as understanding threats, for which they can prepare. By contrast, and this is probably more common, organizations might only change when they have to – such organizations are 'reactive'.

Models of change management

Given the variation in types of change, it has become quite normal in the past 20 years to veer towards the transformational view, which provides a link to ideas about leaders who, through their vision, can inspire and motivate others for change (Stewart and McGoldrick, 1996). Transformational leaders connect strategy to culture and commitment. It is not surprising that one of the most well-known change models in organizations is concerned with 'leading change', based on the work of John Kotter. Kotter (1996, p. 35) put strong emphasis on the leading of change:

> Leadership defines what the future should look like, aligns people with that vision, and inspires them to make it happen.

The organizations he studied failed to achieve transformational change because of mistakes, which provided eight steps that leaders could follow to ensure success. These steps are:

- Establish a sense of urgency
- Form a powerful guiding coalition
- Create a vision
- Communicate the vision
- Empower others to act
- Create short-term wins
- Consolidate and build
- Institutionalize the new approaches.

While focusing on leaders, the model is very much in tune with other models of change based on the view that stages or steps can be used to guide change. Probably the most well-known and earliest model was by Kurt Lewin (1951), whose stages involved:

- *Unfreezing:* reducing those forces that maintain behaviour in its present form, and recognition of the need for change and improvement to occur
- *Movement:* development of new attitudes or behaviour and implementation of the change
- *Refreezing:* stabilizing change at the new level and reinforcement through supporting mechanisms, for example policies, structure or norms.

There is a range of other change models that provide stages or steps and this tends to reinforce the view that change can be planned or programmed and managed. Change could also be seen as a single disturbance to an organization, perhaps as part of a change in strategy, with a restoration of some kind of equilibrium in due course. HRD activities can also be part of the plan, provided at the appropriate stage in line with the strategy for change. For example, if a policy is implemented on discipline at work, training could be provided to enable new skills and behaviours to be learned and then reinforced through coaching and monitoring. Such steps can be easily predicted and built into the plan.

By contrast, and increasingly accepted as normal, change is seen as continuous and/or rather unpredictable. Weick (2000), for example, suggests that Lewin's stages should be freeze-rebalance-unfreeze, where the first step is to investigate and make visible what is happening, with rebalance concerned with reinterpreting and reordering activities. Unfreeze means to allow change to continue in an emergent way. Others such as Buchanan and Storey (1997, p. 127) see change as 'messy and untidy', with projects rarely following predictable stages. History, culture and contextual factors all have a role to play, so it becomes difficult to provide 'universal rules' for change management and leadership (Pettigrew and Whipp, 1993, p. 105). One organization we have worked with at least recognized this dilemma by advising change managers to build 'surprise, unpredictability and planning for the unplanned' into their models.

Most views of change recognize the importance of communication and one model seems to acknowledge this explicitly. Ford and Ford (2003) present a view of change as concerned with the shifting of current reality towards the creation of a new one. Since any organization of any size is composed of different groups and individuals, each with their own version of reality, it is the job of those leading change to 'author' new realities and this is achieved principally through conversations. This is a crucial feature where conversations between individuals and groups at work make and remake the realities they experience. People tell stories to each other about what is right and wrong and this includes why a particular project or process of change should or should not be considered worthy. Indeed, the whole organization can be considered as a network of conversation, which establishes the context, culture and history for change to occur or not. This puts great onus on change leaders to hold conversations with others and present good arguments for what they are seeking to achieve. Ford and Ford (2003) suggest a model composed of different conversations that need to be held. These are:

- *Initiative conversations:* asserting that there is an opportunity for change
- *Conversations for understanding:* explaining why change is needed and what would indicate satisfactory achievement, resulting in the involvement of others who know what they must do
- *Conversations for performance:* taking action and making things happen
- *Conversations for closure:* asserting what has been achieved and recognition of contributions.

This model should not be seen as another series of steps but rather as guidance to those leading and managing change of how it is only by talking with others that they can understand the variety of meanings present, which may help or hinder the change sought. They also need to present arguments and respond to counterarguments based on learning about the variety of meanings present in any situation.

> **reflective question**
>
> For those seeking to lead change projects, what are the implications of groups and individuals holding different views of reality?

Change agents, skills and interventions

Different types of change and different models for implementing change require a variety of skills and knowledge of tools and techniques by those expected to lead and manage change. During the 1980s, this role was closely associated with transformational leaders who were expected to become 'change masters' (Kanter, 1985), relying on their charisma and vision to act as change champions and leaders of change. More recently, Kotter (2008) reasserts the importance of leaders to establish a sense of urgency as the first stage of his model. During the 1990s and 2000s, this role was expected to become part of the work of managers throughout the organization and functional specialists such as HRD practitioners as change agents. In addition, experts in change could also be employed from consultancies outside the organization. Whoever undertakes such a role, there are some key questions to consider:

- How do individuals behave in times of change?
- Does theory inform our understanding of human change processes?
- What interventions are needed in the change process?
- What are the keys to successful and sustainable change?

If you look at any organization behaviour textbook in relation to change, you will see that, from a personal perspective, change is often difficult, largely influenced by emotions and can require an involved process of individual readjustment and reframing of a person's work context and orientation. Individual reactions to change are many and varied depending on a complex interaction of history, context, situation and individual orientation to change and work. People frequently experience a complicated mix of both positive and negative responses to change. In addition, the flow of responses may fluctuate and intensify over time and may be connected to the way in which change is presented by managers and colleagues at work over time (Balogun et al., 2008). The responses to change at any given point in time include:

- resentment
- frustration
- anxiety
- dissatisfaction

- fear
- insecurity.

This list is not exhaustive but does show the range of responses to a situation of change and the potential for 'disaffection' (Kanter, 1985) or indeed resistance to a change process.

The potential and real difficulties in change at work have been recognized for many years. As a consequence, a wide range of intervention tools and techniques have been developed for change agents during the 1950s and 60s, as part of OD. This takes a whole organization approach to planned change and builds on the work of Lewin, whose change model we referred to above. In OD, change agents seek to diagnose problems and find interventions that are appropriate to assist the 'change effort' (Beckhard 1969, p. 101). Diagnosis will involve collecting data, possibly through surveys and interviews, before developing plans for intervention to improve the situation. The aim is to find a degree of consensus between different groups and individuals, finding and building common ground where conflict and disagreement exists. Schein (1969) sees the change agent as a process consultant who 'facilitates' interventions in an unbiased and positive way. We can see how such a view informs the way HRD and other initiatives that seek to promote learning at work are now implemented, which will be considered throughout this book, for example teamwork, Investors in People, management and leadership development and so on. Among those who work in the field of HRD, the roles of change agent and facilitator are seen as the most important (Nijhof and de Rijk, 1997).

As facilitators of change, there has been considerable attention given to the skills that need to be learned and practice. For example, Buchanan and Boddy (1992) provide a list of competencies for effective change agents, which include:

- clarity of specifying goals
- team-building activities
- communication skills
- negotiation skills
- influencing skills to gain commitment to goals.

Many organizations also specify facilitating change as a skill for managers. For example, a large UK financial services organization identifies 'driving change' as one of the competencies managers require.

ACTIVITY

You can learn more about OD by visiting the USA's OD Institute website – www.odinstitute.org/.

For useful materials on change, project management and competencies for change, go to the UK's Improvement and Development Agency website – www.idea.gov.uk/idk/core/page.do?pageId=5817020.

The HRD function

We noted above that while a degree of conceptual ambiguity exists as regards HRD and SHRD, it is nonetheless useful to think about the concept of strategy in relation to HRD practice. A degree of consensus exists among leading practitioners and academics that HRD can, and should, operate strategically within an organization. However, exactly what such practice should look like, how the function should be positioned and managed in terms of such a responsibility remains problematic. Certainly there is little empirical evidence to suggest that there may be a 'one size fits all'. This said, there are a number of critical questions that can legitimately be raised about the positioning, role and management of the function which are pertinent to all organizations, irrespective of size, sector and so on.

The HRD landscape is shifting. The CIPD talks about a shift from 'training' to 'learning' (Sloman, 2005), e-learning has transformed the provision in some organizations (for example BA), and there is a real claim that in recent years the HRD profession has acquired and consolidated a credible position distinct from HRM (see, for example, Gold et al., 2003). This said, it remains unclear as to the extent to which the changing landscape is being driven by a new 'breed' of HRD practitioners or whether HRD is responding to a set of forces both within and external to the organization (see, for example, Hendry et al., 1988; Gold and Smith, 2003). This ambiguity is reflected in the two ideas we explore below about how we might begin to think about the changing role of the HRD function. Each of these notions seeks to capture critical elements of the shifting landscape of HRD and offer a conceptual vehicle for onward travel.

Business partner

In abstract, the idea of a business partner is simple. In order to engage appropriately with the strategic development of the organization, HRD operates as a 'partner' alongside the various business units and as an agent to facilitate change in the organization. The word 'partner' is crucial, implying that HRD has an equal, credible and legitimate role to play in relation to the most important business decisions taken by the organization. The HRD function becomes responsible for aligning HRD with the business strategy and ensuring that HRD can add value at any level within the organization. In this model, HRD has a key leadership role, working in collaboration with other senior figures to help determine the vision and direction of the organization (Ulrich, 1997). Gubbins and Garavan (2007) add the word 'Strategic' and position the 'Strategic Business Partner' model on the right-hand side of a chart, which seeks to 'map' the changing nature of HRD professional roles from the traditional role – training intervention focused – to one of 'transformational strategic partner' – shown in Figure 14.2. This is not exactly a neat, linear continuum but it does usefully capture the point that the journey away from this traditional role may well involve a range of different pathways and configurations. (See Analoui (1994) for further discussion of the more 'traditional' and 'transactional' roles, and Gilley and Maycunich Gilley (2003) for the more 'transformational' roles.)

STRATEGIC HRD AND THE LEARNING AND DEVELOPMENT FUNCTION

		Change Agent	
Facilitator	Performance Engineer	HRD Consultant	
Instructional Designer	Organisational Architect	Strategic Business Partner	
Activity-based	*Maintenance*	Results-based	Results-based
Transactional	*Transactional*	Transformational	Transformational
Maintenance	Change		Interventionist
Traditional methods	*Traditional*	Interventionist	Change
One-way customer service Model			Two-way customer service Model
Short-term relationships			Long-term relationships

Figure 14.2 Shifting roles of the HRD professional
Source: Gubbins and Garavan (2007).

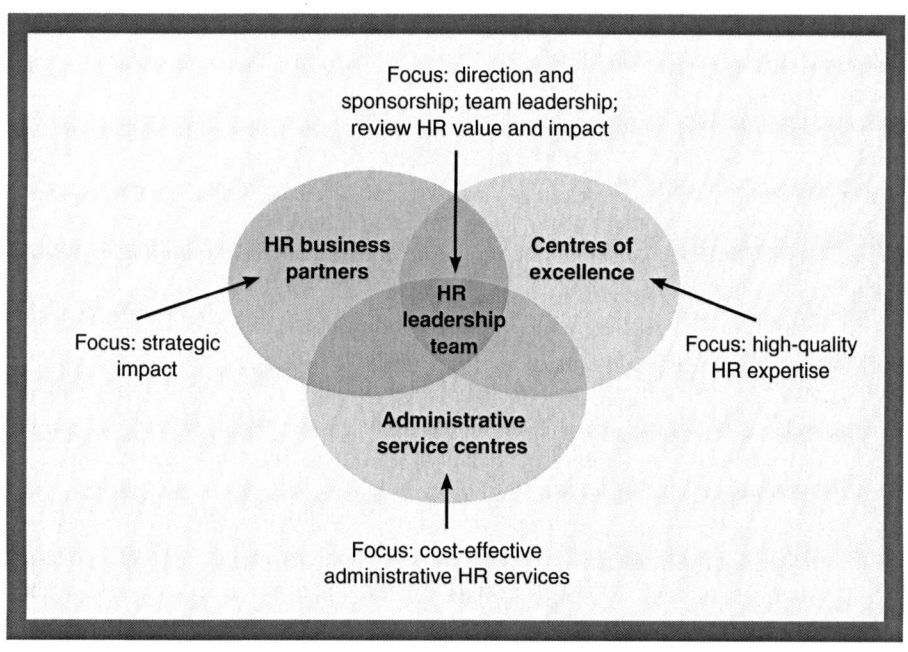

Figure 14.3 The business partner model in the UK civil service
Source: Civil service (2005).

It is important to note that the business partner model may well seek to integrate a number of subfunctions. Three such subfunctions might be:

- *shared services:* routine 'transactional' services across organizations, for example standard training programmes
- *centres of excellence:* small teams of experts with specialist knowledge of cutting-edge HRD solutions, for example 'electronic' knowledge management, mentoring
- *strategic partners:* HR professionals working closely with business leaders influencing strategy and steering its implementation.

The essence of the business partner model is captured in Figure 14.3, which forms the basis for how the civil service, drawing on the work of Ulrich (1997), seeks to put the business partner model into practice within HR.

The corporate university

Some of the biggest companies in the world have established corporate universities (CUs) in recent years, for example BAE Systems, Motorola, McDonald's, Heineken, Lloyds TSB. Gibb (2008, p. 143) offers the following description of a corporate university:

> The CU shapes corporate culture by fostering leadership, creative thinking and problem solving. Strategic is the key word. The CU provides strategically relevant (learning) solutions for each job family within a corporation. It aspires to create a strategic learning organization that functions as the umbrella for a company's total education requirements.

Paton et al. (2007) seek to identify the key features that make corporate universities distinctive. Three are suggested:

1. *Corporate-level initiatives in large, highly complex and differentiated settings:* CUs will have a presence on the board. They may be distinct from the HRD function within large business units. They aim to deliver a specific corporate contribution, avoiding replication or duplication with what is managed or delivered at a local level.
2. *The pursuit of continuing corporate alignment:* The CU is seen as a vehicle by which control of HRD activities, broadly interpreted, can most effectively be aligned with strategic priorities, such as post-merger integration, customer loyalty, developing leadership.
3. *The raising of standards, expectations and impact:* For Paton et al. (2007), it is the CU that can really reflect the strategic priority afforded to learning. Issues might be ensuring the highest quality of provision including harnessing the best available technology to create a virtual learning platform across global sites.

A fourth feature of the model, of course, is the use of the term 'university'. Advocates of CUs claim this provides the critical symbolic factor. It raises the status of organizational learning to its very highest level. For example, Motorola defends its decision to create a corporate university, arguing:

> Motorola management has always tried to use words in ways that force people to rethink their assumptions. The term university will arouse curiosity and, we hope, raise the expectations of our workforce and our training and education staff. We could have called it an educational resource facility but who would that have electrified? (Wiggenhorn, 1990)

One further feature of a CU is a possible influence beyond the boundary of the organization. In other words, the CU may seek to influence the training and development of the entire value chain, including customers and suppliers. An example is shown in HRD in Practice 14.2.

HRD in Practice 14.2   The Motorola University

The Motorola University is one of the most well-known CUs and is the inventor and creator of Six Sigma, in 1986, and holds the registered trademark for this quality improvement methodology. It offers green and black belt certification for Six Sigma and claims to 'practice what it preaches before it preaches it'. Based on the ability to apply the methodology internally, the Motorola University is able to update materials based on 'best practices'. Over $17bn in savings within Motorola have been documented, and in recent years, this has been extended to customers and suppliers.

John Emling, vice president of operations at the Kaydon Corporation, reports the benefits of working with Motorola University:

We were practicing Lean in many of our plants, but we knew we could get more impact than Lean was delivering. Motorola University helped us integrate our lean techniques into an overall Six Sigma Business Improvement Methodology. Their coaching and customer support made it easy to ramp up to full adoption of Six Sigma without over investing in infrastructure. Their training and project coaching was solid. But most importantly, through their help in adopting the Six Sigma Management System, we are delivering sustainable bottom line impact to Kaydon shareholders.

Source: www.motorola.com/motorolauniversity.jsp

Critics of CUs (see, for example, Walton, 2005) have been concerned that most are simply rebadged training departments. This is an important point. It is easy to give the HRD function a new name but if its actual practice is little different, then the role has not changed.

HRD positioning and management

With this in mind, if we now try and translate this conceptual thinking into the implications for the positioning and day-to-day management of the HRD function, two important sets of questions arise: first in terms of a centralizing–decentralizing tension and second in relation to the capabilities of those aspiring to purportedly 'new' HRD roles. Hirsh and Tamkin's (2005) research sought to ascertain how, in practice, organizations align their HRD activity with business needs. Their findings uncover some underlying 'dilemmas'. For example, they note that business needs can be both corporate and local, but which of these should influence what happens in terms of HRD practice at ground level? If line managers are taking greater responsibility for the training and development of their teams, this will act as a force towards devolvement including devolved budgets. A desire for 'just in time training' and tailored learning closer to the job reinforces such pressures. However, Hirsh and Tamkin's research shows that, for large organizations in particular, a perceived need to measure and control spend 'and to focus on corporate priorities' creates a powerful 'centralizing effect' (p. 33). Shared service initiatives, operating a call centre-type role, further reinforce centralizing tendencies and plans.

Hirsh and Tamkin (2005) report the case of Diageo, one of the world's leading drinks businesses. Diageo provides an interesting example of how a company has sought to deal with the corporate–local tension. A corporate policy is to devolve and embed training and learning throughout the business. However, Diageo differentiates between resources for strategic, company-wide priorities and those for more local and operational needs. A process called the 'organization and people review' aims to join and integrate the top-down view with the bottom-up view. HRD operates with local mangers to identify capability issues. This information is then 'amalgamated upwards' and a corporate perspective added at group level. This might be conceived of as an example of what Gibb (2008, p. 158) calls a 'hub and spoke' model.

ACTIVITY

'If only you'd asked us sooner' (Sloman, 2006, p. 13)

This is a reflection from the CIPD following its 2006 survey on learning and development. A key finding was that learning, training and development professionals do not have enough involvement in organizational change projects. Sloman notes: 'If the learning, training and development function isn't perceived as a key stakeholder, we won't be involved in the crucial decisions. As a result we'll only contribute late in the process ... if at all.' Hence the title of the reflection.

Think about the title of the reflection and the key finding raised from the survey. How does this capture some of the issues we have been discussing in terms of a shifting landscape and a model of the HRD role to reflect and drive this?

Visit the CIPD's website and view the most recent survey findings – www.cipd.co.uk/subjects/lrnanddev/general/_reftrendtd.htm?IsSrchRes=1.

Also visit the Institute for Employment Studies website – www.employment-studies.co.uk/pubs – for a fuller discussion of Hirsh and Tamkin's research.

Numerous questions of capability flow from the different ways of thinking about how HRD might be positioned. Two of some significance are noted below; one external to the function and the other much closer to home.

One of the anticipated challenges noted by advocates of the business partner model concerns line management. If, as part of an intimate engagement with strategy, an implication is that line management take on board a much greater responsibility for the day-to-day, week-by-week development of their staff (the devolvement of responsibility discussed above), have they the capability to fulfil such a responsibility effectively? A recurrent concern flagged by the CIPD as a result of its annual learning and development survey work has been this very theme. Reflecting on the 2007 survey findings, Wain (2007, p. 25) notes, for example, that as only 6% of organizations reward managers for developing their people, 'no wonder it's not top priority for the other 94%'.

Second, to play any kind of leadership role at the strategic centre of the organization clearly has implications for the capabilities of senior HRD professionals. Two are considered critical; first, power and influence, and second, learning expertise. Stewart and McGoldrick (1996) argue that 'a strategy for augmenting influence is virtually imperative if the HRD department is to survive' and the reader will note that we have been discussing a role that is much more than mere 'survival'.

The following extract, drawn from research undertaken with HRD practitioners about the 'politics' of their role (Holden and Griggs, 2008), illustrates the lived experience of one HRD manager who works for a large UK car dealership as she seeks to develop a strategic presence within the organization:

> I do go to Board meetings but I'm not a director ... I mean I influence as much as I can but it's hard work, it really wears you down. I've tried to make HRD a lever of change and I have driven a lot through but it's a battle, it's a real struggle ... you've got to be permanently selling it and by nature HR people are not salespeople. It's the art of balancing what we need operationally, today, now, with what's best for the business in the longer term ... And one of the problems here is that if you're not an accountant you don't fit ... they're so insular they won't look outside the motor trade and so I can't say 'Look, it works here' ... they just won't see it ... and of course we're women ... I'm sorry but that's the case and all the other directors are men.

Reflecting on the factors that may enhance and detract from a high level of power and influence within an organization, the issue of gendered power relations in HRD raises some important questions (Hanscome and Cervero, 2003). The majority of HRD professionals in the UK are female.

In relation to learning, the necessary expertise goes beyond a technical proficiency in identifying and managing learning needs and provision. The strategic HRD role requires an understanding of knowledge management and organizational learning and, increasingly, an appreciation of how technology may be utilized as a strategic learning tool.

Pettinger (2002) combines the two factors of influence and expertise in a simple matrix, shown in Figure 14.4.

Before we conclude this chapter, two important additional considerations need to be addressed.

Outsourcing

Over recent years, a growing trend has been for various training tasks to be undertaken by external organizations. According to a survey by Capita Learning & Development

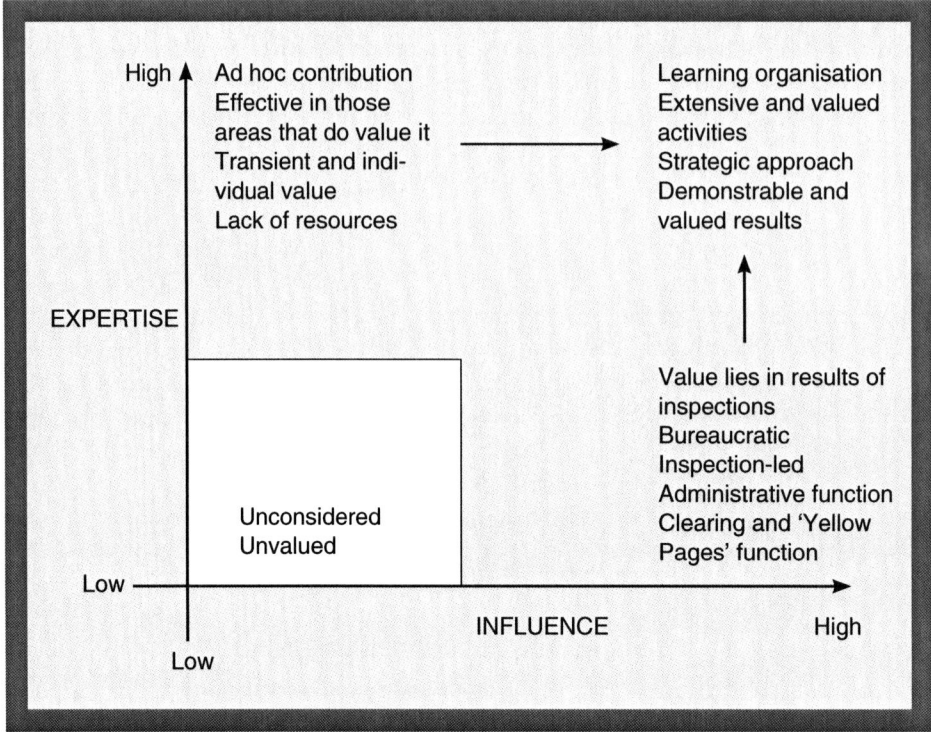

Figure 14.4 The balance of expertise and influence
Source: Pettinger (2002).

(www.capita-ld.co.uk/) in 2005, two in five UK organizations now outsource training in one way or another. This might simply be to an external provider of training programmes. Here Richman and Trondsen (2004) suggest the term 'out-tasking' might be more appropriate. Alternatively, comprehensive outsourcing may see an external contractor take complete control of an organization's total HRD function. Simmonds and Gibson (2008) identify the impetus for outsourcing as cost, competence and capacity. They cite the example of Unilever, which has taken transactional activities and delivery outside, with transformational and strategic activities remaining in Unilever's remit. While the authors identify a set of problems with any outsourcing of HRD, they suggest that the administrative, operational and transactional-type activities can be overcome, but less so the strategic. A critical research need is to explore those organizations that have taken or are taking this step (Woodal et al., 2002).

Competing on costs not skills

We noted above a variety of ways that in practice an HRD function may move away from a model based on ad hoc training activity or planned maintenance (Fonda and Hayes, 1988). Nonetheless, an underlying assumption has been the aspiration to see the HRD function develop into a strategic player and where learning is seen as critical for organizational growth and prosperity. The flaw in this assumption is the lack of evidence that all organizations necessarily see it as appropriate to compete through the development of human capital. As Keep (2005) rightly reminds us, much work undertaken by organizations does not sit comfortably with the rhetoric of the knowledge economy (see also Grugulis, 2007). Rather, it is highly routinized, involves low discretion and relatively low skills. Keep (2005) argues that in some sectors, cost-based competition is still the strategic driving force, with a consequent pressure to deskill rather than upskill. This presents corporate HRD managers with a dilemma. They are caught at the pinch point between, on the one hand, wider public policy goals in terms of skills and education, together with rhetoric from their own profession, and, on the other hand, the hard business realities and competitive pressures of the sector and market in which they operate. Of course, it could still be argued that the function is engaging strategically with the business goals of the organization when it refuses demands for training and opportunities for skill enhancement, but clearly the enhanced status given to learning within, say, the corporate university model is inappropriate. It follows, therefore, that if we equate 'best practice' HRD with the kinds of models and developments discussed above, this is likely to remain, as Keep (2005) eloquently puts it, a 'minority sport'.

Summary

- Conventional views on strategy are based on top managers setting out a vision and mission for an organization and developing organization or 'corporate' goals and strategy from which are derived business strategy and then functional strategy, including a strategy for HRD.

- An alternative view is that HRD can have a key role to play in shaping organizational culture, developing current and future leaders, building commitment among organization members and anticipating and managing responses to changed conditions to ensure long-term survival.

- HRD strategy is a course of action that is intended to have a long-term rather than a short-term impact on significant rather than marginal areas of performance at organizational rather than individual level.

- HRD plans are concerned with shorter time horizons, usually a year, and will cover a number and range of programmes and activities. The focus of these programmes and activities will be 'operational' and intended to ensure that the day-to-day work of the organization can be accomplished.

- HRD policy describes the framework within which decisions about programmes and activities are taken and which guides those decisions and their implementation.

- Organization strategies imply change but are not always linked to HRD.

- Types of change can vary between incremental and transformational. Organizations can be proactive or reactive in anticipating the need for change.

- Various models of change inform the skills needed to manage and implement change at work.

- Change agents need to use ideas and tools for intervention in change projects and facilitate intervention in an unbiased and positive way.

- HRD practitioners can operate as a business partner to align HRD with business strategy.
- Many large organizations have developed corporate universities to raise the status of learning.
- The HRD role in organizations must manage key dilemmas relating to centralizing and decentralizing HRD activities and the balance between expertise and influence.
- Recent years have seen a trend toward outsourcing HRD activities such as training.

DISCUSSION QUESTIONS

1. Can HRD ever be considered strategic?
2. Investment or cost? How important is this 'litmus test' for HRD and why?
3. Is HRD necessary for long-term organization survival?
4. Does all change lead to learning?
5. What are the key skills of a change agent?
6. What value is the business partner model for HRD in practice?

Further reading

Chia, R. (2002) 'Rhizomic' model of organizational change and transformation: perspective from a metaphysics of change, *British Journal of Management*, **10**(3): 209–27.

Gold, J., Rodgers, H. and Smith, V. (2003) What is the future for the human resource development professional? A UK perspective, *Human Resource Development International*, **6**(4): 437–55.

Horwitz, F.M. (1999) The emergence of strategic training and development: the current state of play, *Journal of European Industrial Training*, **23**(4/5): 180–90.

Oliver, J. (2008) Action learning enabled strategy making, *Action Learning: Research and Practice*, **5**(2): 149–58.

Watson, S., Maxwell, G.A. and Farquharson, L. (2007) Line managers' views on adopting human resource roles: the case of Hilton (UK) hotels, *Employee Relations*, **29**(1): 30–49.

References

Analoui, F. (1994) Training and development: the role of trainers, *Journal of Management Development*, **13**(9): 61–72.

Argyris, C. and Schön, D. (1978) *Organizational Learning: A Theory of Action Perspective*, Reading, MA, Addison Wesley.

Ashton, D. and Felstead, A. (1995) Training and development, in D. Storey (ed.) *Human Resource Management: A Critical Text*, London, Routledge.

Balogun, J., Hope Hailey, V. and Johnson, G. (2008) *Exploring Strategic Change*, London, Pearson Education.

Bartlett, C. and Ghoshal, S. (1997) The myth of the generic manager: new personal competencies for new management roles, *California Management Review*, **40**(1): 92–116.

Bartunek, J.M. and Moch, M.K. (1987) First-order, second-order, and third-order change and organization development interventions: a cognitive approach, *Journal of Applied Behavioral Science*, **23**(4): 483–500.

Beckhard, R. (1969) *Organizational Development: Strategies and Models*, Reading, MA, Addison.

Bratton, J. and Gold, J. (2007) *Human Resource Management: Theory and Practice*, 4th edn, Basingstoke, Palgrave Macmillan.

Buchanan, D. and Boddy, D. (1992) *The Expertise of the Change Agent: Public Performance and Backstage Activity*, London, Prentice Hall.

Buchanan, D. and Storey, J. (1997) Role taking and role switching in organizational change: the four pluralities, in I. McLoughlin and M. Harris (eds) *Innovation, Organizational Change and Technology*, London, International Thomson.

Civil Service (2005) Modernising People Management, HR Business Partner Guide, http://hr.civilservice.gov.uk/downloads/bp_guide.pdf.

Cooke, F.L. (2000) Human resource strategy to improve organisational performance: a route for British firms?, Working Paper 9, ESRC Future of Work Programme, ESRC, Swindon.

Fonda, N. and Hayes, C. (1988) Education, training and business performance, *Oxford Review of Economic Policy*, **4**(3).

Ford, J. and Ford, L. (2003) Conversations and the authoring of change, in D. Holman and R. Thorpe (eds) *Management and Language*, London, Sage.

Fredericks, J. and Stewart, J. (1996) The strategy-HRD connection, in J. Stewart and J. McGoldrick (eds) *Human Resource Development: Perspectives, Strategies and Practice*, London, Pitman.

Garavan, T. (1991) Strategic human resource development, *Journal of European Industrial Training*, **15**(1): 17–31.

Garavan, T. (2007) A strategic perspective on human resource development, *Advances in Developing Human Resources*, **9**(1): 11–30.

Gibb, S. (2008) *Human Resource Development: Process, Practices and Perspectives*, 2nd edn, Basingstoke, Palgrave Macmillan.

Gilley, J.W. and Maycunich Gilley, A. (2003) *Strategically Integrated HRD: Six Transformational Roles in Creating Results-driven Programmes*, 2nd edn, Cambridge, Perseus.

Gold, J. and Smith, V. (2003) Advances towards a learning movement: translations at work, *Human Resource Development International*, **6**(2): 139–52.

Gold, J., Rodgers, H. and Smith, V. (2003) What is the future for the human resource development professional? A UK perspective, *Human Resource Development International*, **6**(4): 437–55.

Grugulis, I. (2007) *Skills, Training and Human Resource Development*, Basingstoke, Palgrave Macmillan.

Gubbins, C. and Garavan, T. (2007) The changing context and role of the HRD professional, 8th International Conference on HRD Research and Practice across Europe, Oxford, June.

Hanscome, L. and Cervero, R. (2003) The impact of gendered power relations in HRD, *Human Resource Development International*, **6**(4): 509–25.

Hayes, J. (2007) *The Theory and Practice of Change Management*, Basingstoke, Palgrave Macmillan.

Hendry, C., Pettigrew, A. and Sparrow, P.R. (1988) The forces that trigger training, *Personnel Management*, **20**(12): 28–32.

Hirsh, W. and Tamkin, P. (2005) *Planning Training for your Business*, report no. 422, Brighton, Institute of Employment Studies.

Holden, R. and Griggs, V. (2008) Teaching the politics of HRD: problems and possibilities, 9th International Conference on HRD Research and Practice across Europe, Lille, May.

ILO (International Labour Office) (2000) *High Performance Work Research: Project Case Studies*, Geneva, ILO.

Kanter, R.M. (1985) *The Change Masters: Corporate Entrepreneurs at Work*, London, Taylor and Francis.

Keep, E. (2005) The firm, society and social inclusion: addressing the societal value of HRD, keynote address, 6th International Conference on HRD Research and Practice across Europe, Leeds, May.

Kotter, J.P. (1996) *Leading Change*, Boston, MA, Harvard Business Press.

Kotter, J.P. (2008) *A Sense of Urgency*, Boston, MA, Harvard Business Press.

Leitch, S. (2006) *Prosperity for all in the Global Economy: World Class Skills*, London, HM Treasury.

Lewin, K. (1951) *Field Theory in Social Science*, New York, Harper and Row.

McCracken, M. and Wallace, M. (2000) Towards a redefinition of strategic HRD, *Journal of European Industrial Training*, **24**(5): 281–90.

Nijhof, W.J. and de Rijk, R.N. (1997) Roles, competences and outputs of HRD practitioners: a comparative study in four European countries, *Journal of European Industrial Training*, **21**(6/7): 247–55.

Paton, R., Peters, G., Storey, J. and Taylor, S. (2007) *Handbook of Corporate University Development*, London, Gower.

Pettigrew, A. and Whipp, R. (1993) *Managing Change for Competitive Success*, London, Wiley.

Pettinger, R. (2002) *Mastering Employee Development*, Basingstoke, Palgrave – now Palgrave Macmillan.

Prahalad, C.K. and Hamel, G. (1990) The core competence of the corporation, *Harvard Business Review*, **90**(3): 79–91.

Richman, H. and Trondsen, E. (2004) Outsourcing: what can it do to your job?, *Training and Development*, **58**(10): 68–73.

Schein, E. (1969) *Process Consultation: Its Role in Organization Development*, Reading, MA, Addison-Wesley.

Simmonds, D. and Gibson, R. (2008) A model for outsourcing HRD, *Journal of European Industrial Training*, **32**(1): 4–18.

Sloman, M. (2005) *Training to Learning: Change Agenda*, London, CIPD.

Sloman, M. (2006) If only you'd asked us sooner: involvement of learning and development professionals in organizational change, in CIPD, *Latest Trends in Learning Training and Development*, London, CIPD.

Stewart J. (1999) *Employee Development Practice,* London, FT/Pitman.

Stewart, J. and McGoldrick, J.A. (1996) *Human Resource Development: Perspectives, Strategies and Practice*, London, Pitman.

Tushman, M.L., Newman, W.H. and Romanelli, E. (1986) Convergence and upheaval: managing the unsteady pace of organizational evolution, *California Management Review*, **29**: 22–39.

Ulrich, D. (1997) *Human Resource Champions: The Next Agenda for Adding Value and Delivering Results*, Boston, Harvard Business School Press.

Wain, D. (2007) *Lies, Damned Lies and a Few Home Truths: Reflections on the 2007 Learning and Development Survey*, London, CIPD.

Wall, S.J. (2005) The protean organization: learning to love change, *Organizational Dynamics*, **34**(1): 37–46.

Walton, J. (2005) Would the real corporate university please stand up, *Journal of European Industrial Training*, **29**(1): 7–20.

Weick, K.E. (2000) Emergent change as universal in organizations, in M. Beer and N. Nohria (eds) *Breaking the Code of Change*, Boston, MA, Harvard Business School Press.

Wiggenhorn, W. (1990) Motorola U: when training becomes an education, *Harvard Business Review*, **68**(4): 71–83.

Woodall, J., Gourlay, S. and Short, D. (2002) Trends in outsourcing HRD in the UK: the implications for strategic HRD, *International Journal of Human Resource Development and Management*, **2**(1/2): 50–63.

CHAPTER 15
The Design and Delivery of Training

Catherine Glaister, Rick Holden, Vivienne Griggs and Patrick McCauley

CHAPTER OUTLINE

- Introduction
- Designing training
- Training and learning methods
- Trends and issues
- Summary

CHAPTER LEARNING OUTCOMES

After studying this chapter, you should be able to:

- Understand the relationship between the identification of training needs and the subsequent design and delivery of training and learning
- Identify and explain the range of factors that will influence decisions about training and learning strategies and methods
- Juxtapose ideas about, and principles of, effective learning with practical considerations such as trainee characteristics, costs, trainer capabilities
- Identify a wide range of training and learning methods available to meet identified needs and explain the relative strengths and weaknesses of these approaches
- Understand the decisions necessary to determine fit for purpose training and learning solutions

Introduction

Lucy Kellaway (2005), writing in the *Financial Times*, argues that the real issue in training is not that employers do not spend enough on training, 'but that they do not pitch it right'. This captures the essence of this chapter. It is about the design

Source: ©Roger Beale.

and delivery of effective training and learning. The observant reader will have noticed we have complemented the term 'training' with that of 'learning'. We noted the issue of a potentially confusing terminology. We noted our position that a 'training' method was not necessarily the same as a 'learning' method. Our position in this chapter is that if we only consider possible 'training' solutions, we are potentially ignoring a range of interventions that are more appropriately labelled 'learning'. Thus, in this chapter, the terms are deliberately used interchangeably, to convey that a broad range of solutions may need to be part of decision making. For a fuller discussion on this issue, see the CIPD publication *Training to Learning* (Sloman, 2005).

We examined the importance of carefully identifying training needs before committing resources to meet those needs. An analysis of the job or task provides the cornerstone for progressing towards interventions, which will, in time, meet and remove any training gap. Building on this framework, this chapter explores a range of factors to address in the design of training and learning – such as the characteristics of the trainees, and how best to utilize our understanding of what we know about how individuals and groups learn most effectively. Inevitably, issues of cost and available resources are also part of these design considerations. The second half of the chapter looks at how these various design considerations can be translated into practice. What alternative methods of delivery might be possible? Can a skill need be effectively delivered using e-learning, and what implications does a preferred method of delivery have in terms of trainer capabilities?

While the chapter unfolds in this way, there is clearly an inextricable relationship between design and delivery. The choice of a particular method, or combination of methods, needs to be fit for purpose. A particular strategy might appear highly appropriate in terms of its ability to meet the main objectives, but is unrealistic in terms of costs or because it requires considerable time away from work, which is likely to be opposed and resisted by those involved. Many a training intervention has floundered because those responsible for its design and delivery had not thought carefully enough about the cultural context in which the programme was being implemented.

The case of Harvey Nicholls (HRD in Practice 15.1) provides an interesting example of the how one large UK retailer seeks to put training into practice. The reader might usefully reflect back to this case throughout our more detailed discussion of design and delivery practice issues as they unfold in the remainder of the chapter.

HRD in Practice 15.1   Learning and development at Harvey Nichols

According to its website (www.harveynicholscareers.com): 'Harvey Nichols is an international luxury lifestyle store, renowned both in the UK and internationally for the breadth and depth of its exclusive fashion merchandise', with stores in the UK and abroad.

The embedding of clear brand values – providing a feel-good experience, being exclusive but accessible, and providing fashion leadership – into everyday performance and behaviours within the company was seen as key to business success. Originating from a project begun in 2003, project teams involving representatives from all levels of the business undertook extensive consultation and developed a set of people values and behaviours.

People values	*Behaviours*
Eager to engage with customers in order to deliver a great experience	Being welcoming – using eye contact and positive body language
Willing to go the extra mile	Actively helping customers and colleagues
Enthusiastic and positive	Listening to customers and colleagues
People who like people	Looking for how to say 'yes'
Strong clear communicators	Encouraging colleagues to work as a team

A creative approach to learning and development has since played a key role in making the people values and behaviours a reality within the business. Together with the incorporation of desirable behaviours within the performance management system itself, a top-down cascade approach was introduced, beginning with launch events held by directors. These included role plays of desirable and undesirable behaviours. Subsequently, for departmental managers, there were a series of one-day 'train the trainer' courses to equip them with the skills to help them train their staff on a day-to-day, week-by-week basis, using discussions and workplace-based training exercises.

In this way, Harvey Nichols was signalling its desire to move away from generic training courses for all sales assistants. Traditional training was rejected and replaced with methods that allowed for immediate feedback, ongoing support, and flexibility, recognizing the difficulty of precisely defining the skills involved in 'reading the customer'. Transfer of training problems and barriers were thus minimized.

> To complement the training and development initiatives, Harvey Nichols launched the 'Brand Champion Scheme'. Staff were asked to identify examples of the values and behaviours in action by nominating peers for rewards based on exceptional performance. With this in place to reward excellence, attention was also placed on how to ensure development of poorer performance. Again, a belief in the importance of workplace learning underpinned the approach, with a further development of the line manager's skill in workplace coaching.
>
> *Source*: Adapted from Sloman (2005).

Designing training

Training provision is big business in the UK. According to the *National Employers Skills Survey 2007*, the UK spent over £36bn on training activity in 2007 (LSC, 2008). There is no shortage of training providers anxious to get organizations to sign up to their particular set of training solutions. Yet for all this activity and hype, there are nagging doubts as to whether the money spent on training is always well spent. Of course, one of the difficulties here is that we lack sound ways and means to ascertain value for money. Other reasons for legitimate concerns are a failure to identify needs effectively and a failure to design appropriate training to meet the identified training needs. It is the latter issue that we will address in this chapter. In practice, it is a little more complex than this.

ACTIVITY

Consider the following scenario:

> Thornlea is a family-controlled, medium-sized, 'high-spec' engineering company specializing in components for the defence industry. Although profitable, recent market pressures have resulted in a new business plan, which has seen a layer of the organizational hierarchy removed. The eight supervisors are now known as 'team leaders' but have received no guidance as to whether they should be doing anything differently. When the suppliers of new computer-controlled machinery were delivering on-the-job training, there were few problems, but since they have left, supervisors, or rather the team leaders, complain that they aren't equipped to handle the problems.

Is it obvious how such training needs may best be met?

While the broad thrust of the required training at Thornlea is reasonably clear, how best to meet this need raises all kinds of questions. Should the training be completed away from work? This is not a big company – is there someone within the organization (perhaps a senior manager) capable of leading such a training effort or will external help be needed? Is the nature of the training more focused on skills or knowledge? Among the eight supervisors, are there not likely to be differences (age, experience, personality) that might need to be taken on board in any training provision? Thus there is a mix of issues and questions facing whoever assumes the responsibility for some sort of training effort to meet this need.

In Figure 15.1, a range of 'design' issues is summarized. Careful analysis of these is important, both in terms of choosing an appropriate training strategy and then planning and designing it. We would argue this is the case for formal training events as well as less traditional options including workplace learning. An initial distinction is useful. The spheres labelled 1, 2 and 3 are what we would describe as 'design principles'. Spheres 4, 5 and 6 are a number of (potentially) 'complicating factors'. At the heart of design principles are issues about purpose (for example what we hope to achieve) and harnessing our understanding of the learning process. The pressure on many organizations today means that they may well start with the complicating factors. A trainer might ask: 'How much can I spend on this?' and then work backwards. However, acknowledging a consensus among professional bodies such as the CIPD and the Institute of Training and Occupational Learning, good practice suggests that organizations should begin with the former and then address the complicating factors. This is the path we will follow. We begin with purpose and objectives.

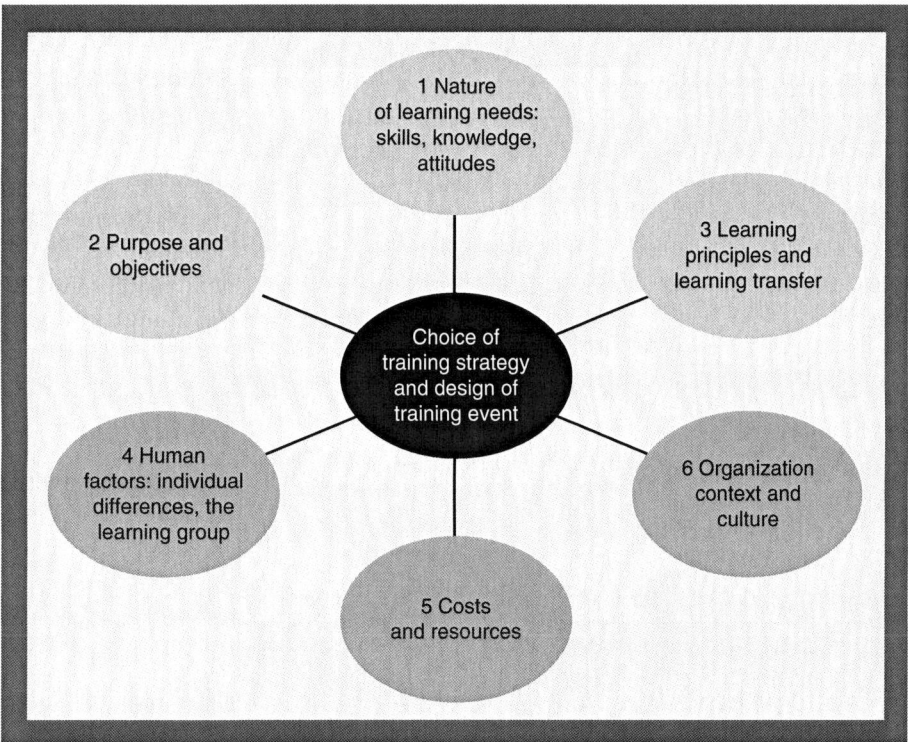

Figure 15.1 A training design framework

Purpose and objectives

A well-prepared statement of intent ('The purpose of this training is to ... '), together with a set of unambiguous objectives, is important for three reasons:

1. It provides the link between the training needs analysis and the design and delivery of training, enabling the trainer/manager to consider which path to follow in order to achieve the end goal.
2. It reduces uncertainty and doubt on behalf of prospective trainees.
3. It offers a basis upon which evaluation can subsequently be undertaken.

The acronym SMART offers a highly practical tool to help to determine the appropriate objectives. It stands for:

- Specific – objectives should specify what they want to achieve
- Measurable – the extent to which objectives have been met
- Achievable – are the objectives achievable and attainable?
- Realistic – are the objectives realistically achievable with the available resources?
- Time – within what time frame are objectives to be achieved?

SMART objectives are not the preserve of the training world. The example below shows how the SMART criteria have been used to formulate a training objective in the area of financial accounting, helping the trainer/manager to address design and delivery issues.

> By the end of a two-hour workshop, trainees will be able to create a profit and loss spreadsheet using Excel 2007 and utilize summation and subtraction formulae with complete accuracy.

Drawing on the work of Bloom (1956) and his development of taxonomies of learning in the areas of knowledge, skills and attitudes, it is important to acknowledge that while it may be relatively straightforward to construct a SMART objective for a basic skill or knowledge need, this becomes more difficult for attitudes and more complex combinations of knowledge and skill. A good example is the construction of objectives for leadership training and development.

ACTIVITY

Working with a partner, visit the website of the training provider, Fenman, and look particularly at the section devoted to training objectives – www.fenman.co.uk/cat/product_info/training_objectives.pdf.

Consider the following questions:

1. What sort of words are best suited to objectives and what words are best avoided?

2. What may make the setting of SMART objectives difficult? Think, for example, about a scenario requiring leadership training for senior managers.
3. Write a SMART objective for a student about to go on a three-month placement as part of their degree.

Learning principles and transfer of learning

The subject of learning is vast and complex, and has a huge literature. Consider for a moment the amount of learning achieved by a three-year old child, without any engagement in the processes so favoured by the institutions established as the guardians and gatekeepers of learning – schools, universities, training centres and so on.

In this chapter, our approach to the bewildering array of avenues one could take in pursuit of 'understanding learning' is characterized by two key criteria:

- learning is central to effective training
- pragmatism.

Thus, with acknowledgement, but little more, to the body of knowledge about learning, we move to identify a set of learning principles – a set of rules or guidelines that can usefully guide the design of learning events at a practical and workable level. Two illustrations help us make this point. Skinner (1950) is known for his work with rats and pigeons. Through the judicious provision of food to 'reward' appropriate behaviour, Skinner, in effect, 'trained' pigeons to dance and play ping pong. For our purposes here, it is the principle that learning is likely to be more effective when it is reinforced through appropriate reward. Our second illustration draws on research into individual differences. One such difference might be that we learn in different ways, with different styles (Kolb, 1984; Honey and Mumford, 1992). The learning principle here is that learning is likely to be more effective when it is geared to the individual.

Thus, the psychology and sociology of learning have yielded a number of general principles that apply to most learning situations. These principles are that learning is likely to be more effective when:

- clear goals and targets are established
- it is carefully and thoughtfully sequenced and structured
- learners receive relevant feedback
- it is appropriately rewarded and reinforced
- the learner is actively involved
- it engages understanding
- it is meaningful to the individual/group in terms of their job responsibilities.

One observation on these principles might be that they are little more than common sense, or, more critically, 'they are too obvious'. However, our experience of teaching trainers over the past 20 years suggests that whatever the level of common sense and however obvious they may appear to be at first sight, they have had a rather disappointing impact on the average trainer or manager in industry. There is a further point. Taken singly, a point such as the provision of feedback may be obvious. But when taken in combination, some considerable complexity results – which is far from obvious and requires much thought and consideration. Beard and Wilson (2006) generate a helpful way to think about how trainers (and managers with responsibility for training) might engage with important learning principles in their design and delivery of training. They use the analogy of a combination lock to create a diagnostic tool. Unpicking a combination lock is complex, and much the same is the case for training and learning. Their 'Learning Combination Lock' consists of six 'dials':

1. *The learning environment* – for example training rooms, space, organizational culture
2. *Learning activities* – for example individual/collaborative, passive/active
3. *Communicating through the senses* – for example visuals, sounds
4. *Emotions in learning* – for example nervousness, antipathy, aggression
5. *Stimulating intelligence* – for example logical, spatial, interpersonal
6. *Understanding ways of learning* – for example activist, pragmatist, intuitive.

Thus, adjustment of each of the dials, depending on the situation, provides a systematic approach for considering the learning design – in effect, it enables the trainer or manager to 'unlock the door' of individual learning. (Go to www.engsc.ac.uk/resources/learning/experiential.asp for more details.)

If training has taken place away from work, how learning will be transferred back to a work situation is a further important consideration impacting on design, and should not be left to chance. Transfer of learning is a key problem in HRD (Cromwell and Kolb, 2004). It could be argued that effective transfer of learning is most likely when the learning principles are satisfied but this may not suffice. One of the most significant models of training transfer in HRD has been provided by Baldwin and Ford (1988), shown in Figure 15.2. The model identifies six linkages that are required for the achievement of the learning and retention of new knowledge and skills and their application into various activities at work (generalization) and further application over time (maintenance).

The particular nature of the work environment, the opportunities to use the learning and the level of support within the workplace to assist application from managers and others are all factors worth some consideration. Trainees might be encouraged to consider what they think might arise by way of transfer and to develop action plans accordingly. Recently, Holton et al. (2007) have developed a Learning Transfer System Inventory (LTSI) to help organizations identify the key barriers to transfer.

reflective questions

Imagine you work in a busy city-centre restaurant three nights each week. The manager has arranged for you to attend a food hygiene training course.

1. What principles of learning do you hope will be reflected in the training?
2. How might the transfer of learning be enhanced?

THE DESIGN AND DELIVERY OF TRAINING

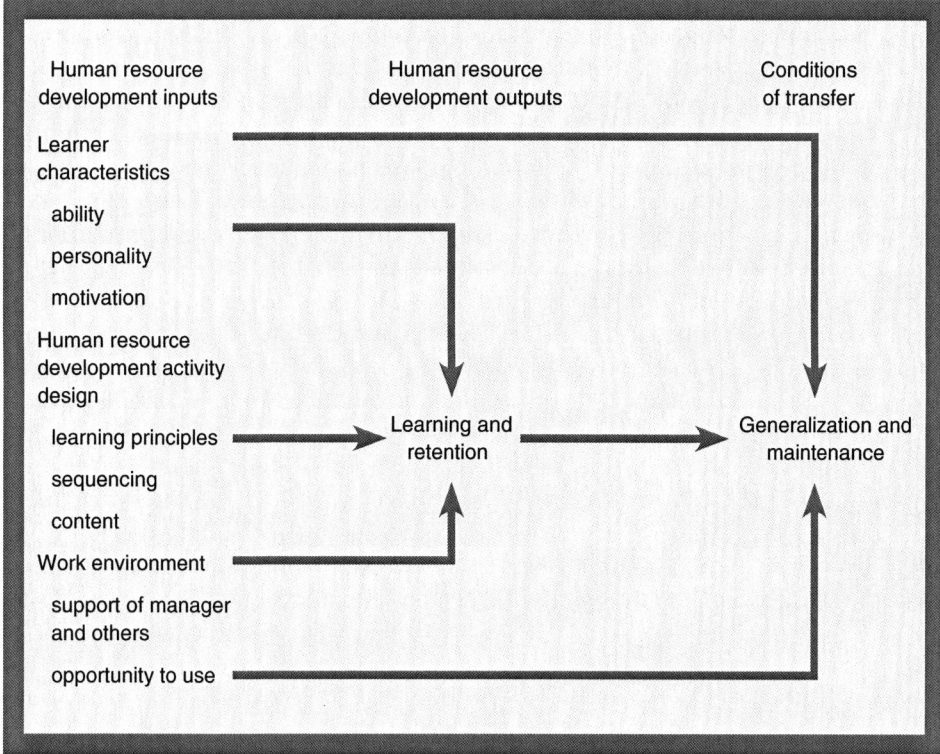

Figure 15.2 A model of the transfer of training
Source: Adapted from Baldwin and Ford (1988).

We move now to the first of our 'complicating factors', a range of 'human' or people issues.

Human factors

It is perhaps a little unfair to regard people as a complicating factor but consider the following short case, which demonstrates why we have taken this stance.

ACTIVITY

The reluctant learner

Reflecting on the first of a two-day in-house 'effective communication' course, the two trainers consider that it has been a successful day. They felt the objectives had largely been met – apart, that is, from Joanna. From the outset, Joanna had been 'troublesome'. She arrived a little late. She interrupted proceedings several times only to make comments about the poor communication skills of certain managers in the organization. For the first group exercise after lunch, she seemed to be on another planet and was clearly all packed up and ready to leave half an hour before the scheduled finish time. The trainers resolve to have a quiet word with Joanna first thing the next morning. After some hesitancy, Joanna opens up. She feels she has been sent on the course unnecessarily. She acknowledges a clash with her boss but feels that it is him, not her, that needs training. No consultation about the course was undertaken – she simply received an email on Monday saying 'Attend on Wednesday.' To cap it all, Wednesday was Joanna's birthday.

1. What do you consider to be the main problems here?
2. Why should this have an impact on the learning process?
3. What principles of learning are involved?

The case of the reluctant learner illustrates how individual differences due to their circumstances and characteristics can cause difficulties. Knowles' work on adult learning (see, for example, Knowles and Swanson, 2005) indicates that individual differences, in terms of motivation to learn and the extent to which individuals are self-directed and 'ready to learn', are likely to be particularly relevant in relation to achieving success in any training intervention. The way in which training needs are identified may also be an important influence in terms of motivation and readiness to learn. For example, an ambitious high performer, who has been identified as having potential for promotion and has been sent on a programme to help them achieve their aims, would arguably have a different mindset to an individual with problematic performance issues (Joanna perhaps?), who has been sent on a programme in order to address these.

There is a range of other factors, including learning styles, which we have already noted as an important principle of learning. The phrase 'I'm too old to learn' is still commonly heard and reflects two further potentially important differences. First, research evidence suggests that cognitive capabilities such as short-term memory and information processing do decline with age (Stammers and Patrick, 1975). Second, and possibly more importantly, is the individual's 'perception' that they are too old to learn, which links back to our point about an individual's learning 'disposition'. Previous experiences of learning, positive or negative, in terms of education more generally and learning at work in particular add further complexity. Buckley and Caple (2007) also suggest the importance of background and emotional disposition (including culture and social class) as factors influencing learning.

Acknowledgment and recognition of individual differences are clearly important in any consideration of how best to meet an identified training need. If training is one to one (discussed later in this chapter), there may be some real prospect of this being taken on board. But, much training takes place in a group context.

reflective questions

1. What particular challenges might a lecturer face when teaching groups of students?
2. Are these similar for a trainer working within, for example, a chain of hotels or for a large car dealership?

Clearly a group is simply a collection of individuals and hence the differences and issues discussed above may be compounded. While there is much truth in the phrase 'know your audience', there are likely to be practical issues in terms of the amount of information available to the trainer/manager in terms of design and, critically, the extent to which individual differences can be catered for in a group situation. This said, some training needs can only really be tackled through groupwork. Furthermore, many trainers would argue that groups can be fun to work with. If the dynamics of a group situation can be effectively harnessed by the trainer, a richer learning experience may well result.

Thus far we have considered the trainee, whether as an individual or in a group context. What about the trainer? Just as a group of trainees may reflect a complicated mix of individual differences, so might any group of trainers. These will include levels and nature of competence, nature of skills (stand up delivery versus facilitation, skills to assess and so on), motivation and orientation. Honey (2007), in an extension to his work on learning styles, notes that trainers also have 'styles' and suggests that there may be a tendency to use them as an excuse: 'I'm an activist so I work best with learners who are also activist. That's just the way I am.' Trainers who are best equipped to help diverse learners are those who:

- know their own strengths and how this translates into their approach and style
- are alert to differences among their participants
- adjust their approach style to cater for a range of different learning style preferences.

Costs and resources

From time to time we hear of stories where obscene amounts of money appear to have been spent on some training provision or seemingly bizarre events organized in the name of 'good training'. Kellaway (2000), for example, describes what she terms the 'ultimate nightmare in training programmes'. For a full week, a group of managers are transported to a training centre where they must relinquish every aspect of their ordinary lives and set up their own micro-society. Some are stripped of their belongings and labelled 'immigrants'. Others are chosen to form the 'elite' and enjoy a lavish lifestyle. The rest are designated 'middles' and are threatened by the underclass and harassed by the elite. After several days of bitter warfare, the 'game' comes to an end and the remaining days are spent analysing what has transpired.

> **reflective questions**
>
> Kellaway called this course 'The Course from Hell'.
>
> 1. Why do you think she has concerns about such a programme?
> 2. What might have been the rationale of the course designers?

Kellaway despairs at the expense of such provision, when the clues to improved managerial performance 'are not in simplified models of societies' but 'right under our noses'. Such an example suggests an almost unlimited HRD budget. In reality, most organizations are not like this. Resources for HRD are scarce and must be negotiated. It is not uncommon to hear of organizations cutting their budget when times are tough. This is why we refer to costs and resources as a complicating factor. Contrast the situation facing the trainer in two organizations with which the authors have close links – the Skipton Building Society, the sixth largest society in the UK, and Elite Packaging, a relatively small company that packages and distributes items to contract. The Skipton head office has a suite of comfortable, well-equipped training rooms, with state-of-the-art connections to web-based learning. In contrast, Elite Packaging, although it takes training seriously, has no dedicated training resources and must use the canteen for any group-based training sessions. So, while there may be sound reasons, in terms of learning principles, group size, learning environment and so on, to develop an intensive three-day team-building programme, with group sizes of no more than 12, some of these aspirations may have to be sacrificed in the face of budgetary constraints. At worst, for example, a company may decide that it cannot afford a tailor-made two-day interpersonal skills programme with active involvement on behalf of participants and must fall back on a generic e-learning package simply because of cost/resource constraints.

A key factor affecting the level of resources available to an HRD department will be the maturity and status of the function within the organization and the extent to which HRD is considered as input or a direct outcome of strategic considerations (Coleman and Keep, 2001).

Organizational context

Our final issue concerns the organizational context into which any training intervention is to be introduced, and the level of harmony and integration between learning and key aspects of organizational context, which will either help or hinder progress. This will include, crucially, the level of vertical integration between organizational strategy and HR strategy, and the extent to which HR strategies and approaches are themselves horizontally integrated and aligned to support and reinforce each other. The role of performance management processes, and the relationship between these and learning interventions, is worthy of particular consideration. Harrison (2005) argues that one outcome of a performance management system should be to ensure continuous learning and development, as well as being a tool to assist in the identification of training needs. In other words, there is the potential for a performance management process to be a development tool in its own right. Processes such as the provision of multisource feedback and appraisal can potentially add further value here. While the adoption of performance management by organizations is widespread, however, the nature of such systems varies significantly and may be a factor to consider in the selection of a particular development solution.

A further crucial aspect of context is organizational culture. Look back for a moment to the cartoon at the start of this chapter. Let's assume that the training need for some kind of teamwork is a legitimately identified need. The training implemented has clearly forced individuals to get 'upfront and personal' with members of their work team. But the boss has a problem. He is worried how others will view these kinds of techniques. One could almost hear him saying 'This isn't the sort of thing we do around here.' The practice may conflict with the values and beliefs that characterize the workplace or wider organization. This is not the place to discuss organizational culture in depth, suffice it to say that organizational culture can be the vital link between learners, the learning content and the transfer of learning into the workplace. Of course, there is a tension here. As noted by Swart et al. (2004), learning has a critical role to play in the development of organizational culture, yet organizational values, defence routines and taken-for-granted ways of working can provide real impediments and barriers to new learning. A paradox may result: 'Because of the way this organization learns, it cannot learn'.

In sum, organizational context provides a crucial backdrop to the success of any training intervention. A critical analysis at an early stage, to identify barriers and enablers within the reality of the work situation, that is, where the training ultimately needs to be applied, will be important in influencing choice and ultimately success. By identifying and harnessing 'enablers', such as senior management support or a motivated body of line managers, the chances of successful learning can be maximized. In contrast, the identification of problems and barriers at an early stage allows these to be acknowledged and mediated against.

The discussion above presents a complex web of factors to be considered when deciding which particular learning intervention is best suited to addressing a particular learning need, and the subsequent planning and design. It is important to recognize that these factors will not all be of equal weight in any given situation, and that the specific context surrounding a learning need, and the priorities within this, will be of key importance. What is really driving investment in a particular training programme?

> **reflective question**
>
> Think back to the case of Harvey Nichols in HRD in Practice 15.1.
>
> Which of the factors explored above, and summarized in Figure 15.1, were particularly important in influencing the design of the learning programmes chosen?

Training and learning methods

We turn now to how these various design issues can be acknowledged, addressed and utilized in the delivery of training and learning. We seek to provide an overview of the broad range of learning solutions, many of which can be creatively blended together to provide bespoke solutions to meet individual, team and organizational needs.

In providing an overview of the options available, it is worth noting that these have been categorized by many different authors according to different criteria. Marchington and Wilkinson (1996) aim to provide a framework to assist in the analysis of learning methods, and differentiate according to two main criteria:

1. the extent to which methods are individually or group based
2. the extent to which they are self-directed and participative (andragogical) or have high levels of control by tutors, trainers and other experts (pedagogical).

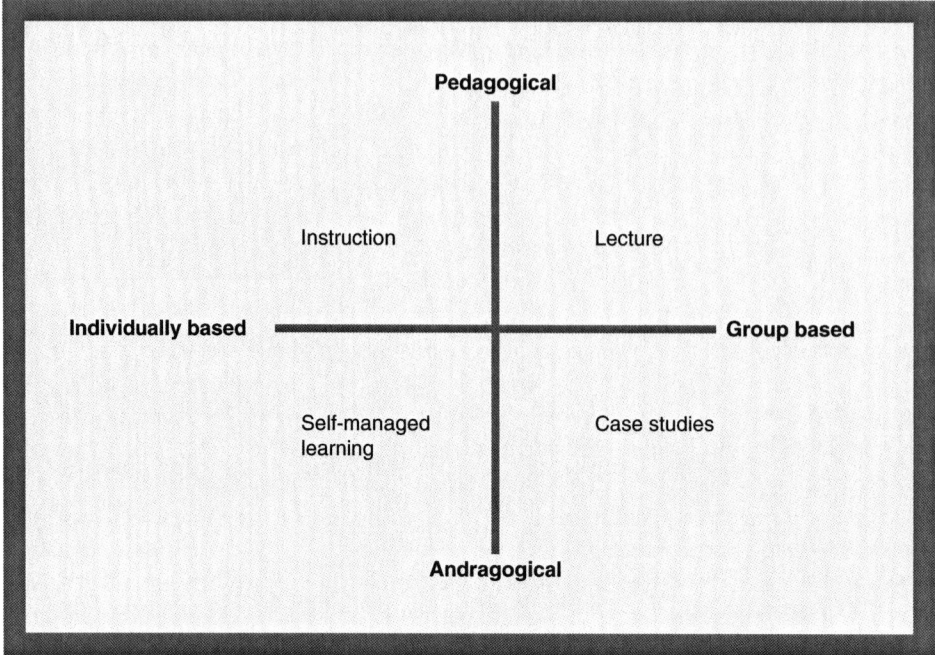

Figure 15.3 A framework of training and learning methods
Source: Adapted from Marchington and Wilkinson (1996).

These are represented visually as two axes, shown in Figure 15.3, and you are invited to position methods within the diagram.

Focusing on the issue of control, Hackett (2003) provides an analysis of the extent to which training methods are trainer or learner centred and concludes that three main categories exist:

1. *Training-centred methods* such as the lecture, which has the obvious advantage of high levels of control by the trainer over content and pace of delivery.
2. *Learner-centred methods* such as self-development questionnaires and learning logs, which hand over this control, to a greater or lesser extent, to the learner.
3. *Coaching*, which Hackett claims is the only method to allow a 'learning partnership' to develop between trainer and learner.

No categorization of methods is perfect. Our approach draws on Mumford's (1997) review of methods in terms of their relationship to work. We suggest two broad categories of options, off the job and integrated, considering each method in terms of how it is distinct from, or integrated with, the actual performance of work-related tasks:

- *Off-the-job learning options:* lectures, discussions, case studies, role plays, business games, group dynamics, e-learning and off-the-job skill instruction. These methods tend to be constructed purely for the purpose of learning, rather than to achieve a task or workplace activity. They may be delivered either internally or externally. They include methods that may be delivered as part of a larger programme or course, or as a stand-alone option. The focus tends to be trainer centred rather than learner centred. Table 15.1 has more details, including the strengths and weaknesses of each option.

- *Integrated learning methods:* on-the-job training, coaching, shadowing, mentoring, exercise/project work, action learning, job rotation and secondment. These methods combine a concern for learning with the performance of tasks/workplace activities. They tend to enlist the support of 'helpers' to aid in the learning process, and are heavily dependent on the appropriate learning climate for success. They tend to be learner centred with the opportunity for recognition of individual needs, and based on experiential learning, harnessing the emotions and senses as well as cognitive capabilities. Table 15.2 has more details, including the strengths and weaknesses of each option.

The CIPD defines training as 'an instructor led, content based intervention, leading to desired changes in behaviour' and learning as 'a self directed, work-based process, leading to increased adaptive potential' (Sloman, 2005). According to this, the off-the-job learning options would mostly be considered as 'training', and the integrated options as 'learning'.

ACTIVITY

Form a group of four. It is likely that you will be familiar with at least some of the methods outlined in Tables 15.1 and 15.2. Think about the different methods you have experienced within university and outside. Do you rate some as more effective than others? Why? Discuss your findings.

Trends and issues

The continued popularity of traditional 'off-the-job' provision

Despite the promotion of creative, more learner-centred and work-based options by HR theorists and indeed the CIPD, respondents to the CIPD (2007a) *Learning and Development Survey* still rated formal training courses as one of the most effective methods of learning, with instructor-led, off-the-job training being one of the most frequently used methods. Bearing in mind that the targeted respondents were those who hold roles as learning, training and development managers, a significant gap between rhetoric and reality is suggested. Commenting on the adoption of particular methods in his critique of the survey, Wain (2007, p. 23) notes that 'irrespective of claims to the contrary, formal and traditional approaches remain highly significant in learning and development practice'.

So why do traditional methods remain so popular? It is important, first, to recognize that such approaches do have value, and the way they are designed, adopted

Table 15.1 Off-the-job methods

Method	Description	Benefits and strengths	Problems/points to watch
Lecture	A structured talk or presentation to convey required information, for example product knowledge, new policy/procedure	Suitable for large audiences. A cost-effective way of communicating key information. Sequence and structure can be carefully thought through. Trainer centred, with high degree of control over content	Limited opportunity for participation – communication tends to be one way, although questions may be usefully integrated. Ability of participants to assimilate and understand material may not extend much beyond 30 minutes. Heavily dependent on the quality of the delivery
Discussion	Free exchange of information and ideas, but working to a clear brief provided by the trainer, for example a discussion of barriers to effective internal communications	Seeks involvement of the trainee. Suitable where subject matter involves opinion, 'grey' areas. Also when attitudes need to be addressed. Good for getting engagement as regards application of learning and feedback to trainer	Discussions often stray off the point. Superficial discussion may be unhelpful, vague and woolly. Control issues need careful thought by trainer. Some degree of prior knowledge may be required to make discussion useful rather than purely opinion based
Case study	Presentation of scenario (real or fictitious) describing organizational practice and behaviour. Trainees are asked to analyse the documented problem and/or reflect on described practice, for example an unfair dismissal case, a financial problem, departmental reorganization	Seeks involvement of the trainee. Suitable where a careful look at the problem or set of circumstances, free from pressures of an actual event, is beneficial. Provides opportunities for exchange of ideas and encourages consideration of alternative solutions. Tests trainees' ability to apply theory to practice. Can provide examples of organizational good practice	Decisions taken in case study settings are removed from the reality of decision making. Unrealistic scenarios may predominate. Quality of debrief crucial for effectiveness. Overuse can result in trainees treating as a 'mechanistic' exercise
Role play	Trainees enact a role they may have to play at work, for example interviewing a customer or negotiating an agreement. Other trainees, or actors, may be employed to play the role of significant others to enhance credibility	Involves the trainee. Good for training where suitable behaviour needs practising. Trainee can practise, in a 'safe' environment, and receive personal feedback. Role plays that are videoed offer a particularly valuable resource for reflection and managing feedback	Some trainees may be fearful/embarrassed. Unreal situations may encourage atypical behaviours unlikely to be seen in reality. Requires clear purpose, sound briefs and good facilitation on behalf of trainer. Can be time-consuming and resource demanding
Business game	Trainees manage a range of organizational issues or problems on the basis of information given to them. Outcomes of decisions are fed back to trainees to influence subsequent decision making. Sophisticated games may be computer assisted	Involves trainees, practically, in dealing with management problems. Simulation of a real-life problem or scenario aids transfer of learning. Enables theory to be put into practice and consequences reflected upon	Limited or unreal outcomes from decisions made may undermine value of method. May result in trainee disengagement. Extent to which 'game' reflects reality is critical

Group dynamics	Trainees are put into groups to carry out a simulated exercise and behaviour is examined, for example group decision making, intergroup conflict, intragroup communication	Potentially powerful way to understand self and impact of self on others and vice versa. Increases insight and understanding of working with other people and getting work done through other people	Learning can be hurtful as well as helpful – the facilitator's role is critical in managing this. High levels of skills required on behalf of the facilitators. Danger of trainees treating exercises as just a bit of fun and/or opting out. Invariably time-consuming and resource demanding
E-learning	Learning is delivered through the internet or intranet	Can effectively overcome time, place, pace issues and barriers. Good for material that can be broken down into distinct blocks and is not subject to interpretation or change. Sophisticated technological applications enable high risk training to be undertaken safely and effectively, for example flight simulation. Usefully used as part of blended solutions	Much e-learning is little more than electronic page turning. May not be fit for purpose. Can isolate trainees. To cope effectively with skills requires sophisticated applications that are expensive. Learner support should not be ignored
Off-the-job skill instruction	A skill is taught by explanation, demonstration and practice, for example how to operate a computer	Most suitable for a wide range of psychomotor skills. Particularly good where task analysis reveals potential difficulties or blocks to achieving mastery	Part or whole approach may cause trainer difficulty re most appropriate strategy. Trainee likely to experience difficulty if asked to absorb large chunks of information or procedures before opportunity for practice. A good employee does not necessarily make a good instructor

Table 15.2 Integrated methods

Method	Description	Benefits and strengths	Problems/points to watch
On-the-job training	Sometimes referred to as 'sitting by Nellie'. Training is undertaken at the workplace, often involving demonstration followed by supervised practice. Often used for semi-skilled jobs but potential for developing individual skills in all types of work	Can effectively integrate work and learning. Realistic and immediate. Transfer problems minimized	Potential to learn good habits as well as bad. Choice of 'Nellie' is critical. To do well requires planning and an understanding of trainee/learner
Coaching	An individual meets a coach on a one-to-one basis to work on a range of work-related issues, some of which may also include personal factors. Distinct from mentoring with its focus on specific behavioural change and/or performance improvement, for example customer service telephone training, leadership development	Targets individual needs. Enables trainee to practise skills in real situations under supervision and monitoring. Good for situations where trainee may be experiencing difficulties or problems. Potentially good role for line manager to adopt. Cost-effective and promotes devolvement of learning responsibility. Facilitates learning transfer	Not a substitute for basic skills and knowledge. Can be time-consuming and resource demanding. Frequently line mangers require coaching skills, so further resources are required. Trainees can become overdependent on coach. An appropriate (open) work culture/learning climate will enhance likelihood of success
Shadowing	Trainees observe a skilled, experienced practitioner at work, and discuss their perceptions with the practitioner. Process should require shadow to reflect on experience	Integrates work and learning. Enables trainee to witness first hand real day-to-day jobs and tasks being performed. Promotes wider participation in learning effort beyond HRD	Tends to be time-consuming and can slow down the person being shadowed. Real work can be mundane and boring, so the learning may be mundane and boring. Requires some structure, for example building in regular reflection and review
Mentoring	An appointed mentor supports and encourages trainee to manage their own personal development. The mentor, usually a senior professional or manager, helps the mentee find the right direction and developmental solutions to career and other issues	Develops the individual rather than training them. Particularly suitable for aspects of career development. Enables person to question assumptions, shift mental context. Good for addressing attitudes and feelings as regards work problems, issues and so on. Can assist individual to address organizational politics	Not appropriate for helping to enhance specific skills re performance. Time-consuming and resource demanding. Best over a longish period. Good mentors are hard to find. Mentoring relationships can be difficult and uneasy. Important that a mentor understands self before they mentor others
Exercise/project	Trainees asked to undertake a particular work-related task leading to a required outcome, for example computerizing client records or setting up a staff absence control system	Suitable for any situation where trainee might benefit from practice following knowledge and theory input. Can be individual or group based. Much scope for the imaginative trainer to design appropriate and challenging exercises to test and further develop trainees' capabilities	Unrealistic exercises risk disengagement. Should be challenging but attainable. Design critical to ensure sufficient focus on learning rather than just on task

Action learning	Individuals work in groups, addressing real organizational problems. Emphasizes the importance of crucial questioning and reflection in learning. Can be project based	Integrates work and learning. Maximizes opportunities for experiential and social learning. Harnesses the power of critical reflection and learning as a force for individual and organizational change	If participants do not have a genuine organizational problem to focus on, initiatives may fail. Benefits from strong facilitation. Needs champions and sponsors within the organization for success
Job rotation	Moving around a number of jobs to build experience across job roles. Often a feature of graduate training programmes	Provides broad experience and awareness of aspects of a number of roles in a shorter period of time than via natural progression. Should broaden perspective and outlook. Chance to develop new skills, knowledge and networks	May prove frustrating, as potentially insufficient time to deliver in roles experienced. Resource hungry due to learning curves. Consistency of learning support via different line managers may vary
Secondment	Trainee spends a substantial period of time (typically 3–12 months) in a different job or with different responsibilities from normal. No special arrangements – just normal work	Provides experience of a new role and environment. Opportunities to develop new knowledge, skills, outlook and networks	Potential problems may arise in identifying appropriate job or role. Responsibility for learning and critical reflection lie solely with individual. Tensions may arise on resumption of old role

and applied can be specifically tailored to meet organizational needs. The fact that a learning solution is conducted away from the job itself can be a real advantage. This is well illustrated in the case of role play, often used as a way of practising skills in a safe environment where it is important for the individual and the organization that mistakes are not made in reality, because of the scale or serious nature of potential negative consequences. Activities such as union negotiations and interviewing can fall into this category, as can work involving more vulnerable groups, with role play being used within criminal justice training programmes. Companies such as BT and HBOS have used professional actors in role-playing situations to provide additional realism and credibility to the training.

Nonetheless, it is somewhat puzzling that in the face of a plethora of alternative methods, many of which may well be more appropriate to meet the identified need, the traditional off-the-job course remains so popular. One explanation may lie in the approach organizations take to learning and development generally, and the nature of training needs identified and invested in. Drawing on Fonda and Hayes' (1986) typology where learning and development is not well developed within an organization and training needs are identified in an ad hoc way to meet immediate needs – for example the provision of health and safety training in response to a number of accidents, or customer care training in response to a number of complaints – traditional training packages may provide quick, cheap, easy and accessible ways of meeting those needs, and evidence that such needs have been addressed. This latter point reflects the pressure many organizations face to provide simple measures of their training effort. Annual reports regularly refer to an average number of 'training days' received by employees.

The more complex and advanced levels of skills needed on the part of trainers/facilitators to deliver alternative options may also play a part, as may the need to 'fit' learning solutions within the broader learning climate and culture within organizations. In other words, it may be indicative of a lack of capability and imagination on the part of the HR and training and development staff within them. Such a weakness is likely to be compounded if such staff perceive obstacles and barriers in trying to 'sell' new approaches to senior managers often steeped in traditional training practice.

ACTIVITY

In groups of three, visit the following website devoted to experiential learning – www.learningandteaching.info/learning/experience.htm.

Using material from this website, critically assess how the experiential learning cycle might be used as a basis for reducing the reliance on traditional off-the-job training.

The rise of e-learning

While the off-the-job course remains popular, there has been a shift in exactly how such provision is delivered. The ability to harness IT as a delivery tool in training and learning has witnessed considerable growth in recent years. E-learning and web-based training materials have been extensively adopted by a wide range of organizations including the education sector itself. Here it is appropriate to note two key points.

First, some organizations have acted in significant ways on the basis of the enormous potential they see in such delivery. Consider the examples in HRD in Practice 15.2.

HRD in Practice 15.2   Three examples of e-learning

Yorkshire Bank

The National Australia Group, Europe, of which the Yorkshire Bank is a part, has introduced a 'Learning Campus' containing more than 30 modules of e-learning material covering the areas of legislative and compliance training. While it estimated an approximate cost of £10.7m per year had the material been delivered via workshops, delivery via the e-learning platform allowed the training to reach all staff in the UK at an estimated total spend of £230,000 (£2 per employee).

Hilton Hotels

Hilton Hotels has a 'Hilton University' website (www.hiltonuniversity.com). This states: 'E-learning is our innovative web-based training system that lets you choose what, where and when you learn.' According to the website, between 2002 and 2005, nearly 10,000 Hilton people completed over 100,000 e-learning programmes and 93% of these learners said they would recommend this form of learning to their friends and colleagues. The strongest 'likes' were the chance to learn at a time, place and speed that suited the learner.

Learn Direct

Learn Direct was developed by the University for Industry, with a remit from the UK government to provide high-quality, post-16 learning, which:

- Reaches those with few or no skills and qualifications who are unlikely to participate in traditional forms of learning
- Equips people with the skills they need for employability, thereby strengthening the skills of the workforce and increasing productivity
- Is delivered innovatively through the use of new technologies.

According to its website (www.learndirect.co.uk), Learn Direct offers around 500 different courses covering a range of subjects, including management, IT, skills for life and languages, at all levels. More than three-quarters of the training courses are available online.

The second point to note is that despite the apparently glowing testimony of the participants on the Hilton Hotel's e-learning programmes, its overall effectiveness as a training method is far from proven. A key factor here may be the extent to which a lot of e-learning fails to address the basic principles of learning discussed earlier in this chapter. In other words, much e-learning can be little more than electronic page turning – not interactive and not geared to the needs of the individual trainee or learner (see, for example, Tynjala and Hakkinen, 2005; Gibb, 2008).

Flavour of the month: coaching and mentoring?

Traditionally viewed as a relatively directive way of improving performance of a work-related task, the field of coaching has expanded considerably to address longer term work and career development, structured and organic approaches. Defined by the CIPD as 'an activity where an individual meets with a coach on a one-to-one basis to work on a range of work-related issues, some of which may also include personal factors' (Knights and Poppleton, 2007, p. 2), the approach taken to coaching in organizations may vary greatly. A more traditional approach would be seen in a call centre environment such as BT where coaching on a one-to-one basis to improve call handling skills on the part of customer service advisers. In contrast, the fund manager M&G offers coaching as part of its talent management strategy, while the coaching offer at Orange is focused on career development. Here individuals are encouraged to nominate themselves for the coaching programme, with participants receiving three 90-minute sessions with an internal career coach (CIPD, 2007b). Whatever the aims, focus and design of a coaching initiative, the skills of the coach and climate in which the coaching is taking place will be key to its success.

Coaching skills are also potentially valuable within a mentoring relationship, although the focus will be different, with the strength of mentoring being its long-term holistic approach. Clutterbuck and Klasen (2002, p. 16) believe that:

> mentoring derives its immense effectiveness in employee learning and development from being an integrated method that flexibly combines elements of the four other one to one development approaches, coaching, counselling, networking/ facilitation and guardianship.

Often used to champion the needs of minority groups, its value to both mentors and mentees can be considerable. Cole (2005) discusses the case of a targeted mentoring programme introduced for black and minority ethnic health service employees. The scheme purports to offer mutual benefits, equipping the mentee to move up the NHS ladder and the mentor with a better understanding of the perspectives of ethnic minorities. Cole relates the experience of one mentee, Yvonne Coghill, who likened the mentoring to 'a laying on of hands' and reported that the impact on her self-confidence was 'transformational'. In another innovative initiative, Hampshire Constabulary has developed a gay mentoring scheme to help staff develop their careers. It reported that 90% of 2007 trainees opted for a mentor, with participants able to select a gay mentor if preferred (CIPD, 2008).

The best of both worlds: a blended approach?

Although loosely configured into a classification of 'off-the-job' and 'integrated' methods, this chapter has considered a wide range of potential training and learning methods. Of course, the most effective programmes tend to be those based on a sound analysis of learning needs and detailed consideration of the factors discussed earlier in the chapter. From this basis, effective solutions may well creatively combine a number of methods (see HRD in Practice 15.3). This is seen by the number of winners of the national training awards who have chosen to use some type of blended approach. (The website www.nationaltrainingawards.com/ gives details of previous winners and the rationale underpinning the programmes.)

> **HRD in Practice 15.3   The Bupa Personal Best programme**
>
> The Bupa care homes learning programme Personal Best is a good example of an organization using a blended approach to meet learning needs and enable its employees to 'go the extra mile' in terms of meeting the needs of residents. It was the overall winner of the CIPD People Management Award 2006. The programme delivered learning in the care homes themselves, using a modular approach, which included experiential learning, interviewing care home residents to develop a greater understanding and appreciation of their needs, and the development of individual action plans to specify actions to be taken in the future. One specific activity reported in *People Management* (Phillips, 2006) involved staff putting themselves in the place of residents, being lifted mechanically into bed and fed pureed food to learn for themselves what these experiences felt like. A series of customer service training modules has been developed to complement the Personal Best programme, and financial results were reported as being up 25% on the previous year.

Engaging 'hard to reach' groups

It is generally acknowledged that some methods of learning potentially act as barriers to some disenfranchised groups, who may be put off by the use of methods they associate with previous negative experiences. This is illustrated by the winner of the National Training Award 2005, the Lighthouse Project (www.thelighthouseproject.co.uk/), and which provides a good example of how the unique and individual nature of training needs will influence the methods chosen. This project was established in 1997 to meet the needs of severely disadvantaged groups, especially single parents, teenagers living alone and young families heavily dependent on benefits. Such groups lack basic skills and tend to be viewed as hard to reach and engage (see also Leitch, 2006). The Lighthouse Project identified a key reason as the inappropriate nature of the provision being offered, arguing for a more flexible and creative approach. It attempted, unsuccessfully, to source appropriate courses from local colleges, and then decided to design its own approach. This involved the delivery of the 'First Steps' programme in each of the project's four centres in the West Midlands. A number of sessions were delivered and adapted to meet individual needs, with the focus on 'achievement' providing the core of the programme. Participants were assessed continually by informal observation by tutors, and computer-generated evidence provided evidence of learning in literacy and numeracy, thus assisting in a level of accreditation towards a qualification.

Summary

- Effective and 'fit for purpose' training and learning require careful and thoughtful translation of identified needs into learning plans.

- This process is aided by the recognition of a range of factors, including the purpose and objectives of any training or learning intervention, an understanding of how learning principles can maximize effective learning, the characteristics of the learner or group of trainees, and the constraints of limited resources and organization context.

- Specific objectives, which can be clearly communicated and are measurable, avoid ambiguity and assist in designing fit for purpose training activity.

- Learning principles that can usefully be considered in the design of training or learning include:
    - learning is likely to be more effective when relevant feedback is provided
    - learning is likely to be more effective when the learner is actively involved.

- Fit for purpose training design can be considered as analogous to a combination lock – in the sense of good design 'unlocking' the door to individual learning.

- Groups of trainees, which reflect considerable individual differences, for example motivation, levels of experience, personality, can be problematic if available resources constrain the extent to which training can be 'tailored'.

- Training that is at odds with the culture of the organization will cause tensions and requires careful management.

- While resource constraints will influence what can be done in practice, a wide range of methods and practice is available to the trainer.

- A useful distinction is that between off-the-job learning options (including case studies, role play, business games) and integrated learning methods (including 'sitting by Nellie', action learning, coaching and mentoring).

- There is rarely one 'best' method. All methods have different strengths and weaknesses; the key is to match method(s) with needs.

- While a majority of organizations continue to make heavy use of off-the-job methods, recent years have seen methods such e-learning, coaching and mentoring rise in popularity.

- Blended learning, involving appropriate combinations of methods, is increasingly seen as the way forward, as this will enable more of the critical design factors to be addressed. Imaginative use of blended learning may well offer opportunities to meet the challenges of engaging 'hard to reach' or disenfranchised learners.

DISCUSSION QUESTIONS

1. What are three characteristics of SMART objectives? Why might setting objectives for interpersonal skills training be more difficult than for a range of PC training (Excel, Word and so on)?
2. What is a principle of learning? How can learning principles be integrated into the effective design of training or learning interventions? Which principles of learning are most relevant to you in your studies at university?

3. How might the notion of the 'integration of work and learning' be used to differentiate between different methods of training or learning?
4. What are two strengths and two weaknesses of e-learning?
5. Why are methods such as coaching and mentoring increasingly popular?
6. What is blended learning? Identify a training need where a blended learning solution might be most appropriate.

Further reading

Buckley, R. and Caple, J. (2007) *The Theory and Practice of Training*, 5th edn, London, Kogan Page.
Knowles, A. and Swanson, R.A. (2005) *The Adult Learner*, 6th edn, Burlington, MA, Elsevier.
Pettinger, R. (2002) *Mastering Employee Development*, Basingstoke, Palgrave – now Palgrave Macmillan.
Reid, M., Barrington, H. and Brown, M. (2004) *Human Resource Development: Beyond Training Interventions*, 7th edn, London, CIPD.
Sloman, M. (2005) *Training to Learning: Change Agenda*, London, CIPD.

References

Baldwin, T. and Ford, J.K. (1988) Transfer of training: a review and directions for future research, *Personnel Psychology*, **41**(1): 63–105.
Beard, C. and Wilson, J.P. (2006) *Experiential Learning: A Best Practice Handbook for Educators and Trainers*, London, Kogan Page.
Bloom, B.S. (ed.) (1956) *Taxonomy of Educational Objectives: The Classification of Educational Goals*, Handbook I, *Cognitive Domain*, New York, McKay.
Buckley, R. and Caple, J. (2007) *The Theory and Practice of Training*, 5th edn, London, Kogan Page.
CIPD (Chartered Institute of Personnel and Development) (2007a) *Learning and Development Survey*, London, CIPD.
CIPD (Chartered Institute of Personnel and Development) (2007b) 'What is on the job training?', fact sheet, London, CIPD.
CIPD (Chartered Institute of Personnel and Development) (2008) Police constabulary extends its gay mentoring scheme, *People Management*, **14**(7): 12.
Clutterbuck, D. and Klasen, N. (2002) *Implementing Mentoring Schemes*, Oxford, Butterworth Heinemann.
Cole, A. (2005) Minority support, *People Management*, **11**(19): 16–17.
Coleman, S. and Keep, E. (2001) *Background Literature Review for PIU Project on Workforce Development*, London, Cabinet Office.
Cromwell, S.E. and Kolb, J.A. (2004) An examination of work-environment support factors affecting transfer of supervisory skills training in the workplace, *Human Resource Development Quarterly*, **15**: 449–71.
Fonda, N. and Hayes, M. (1986) Is more training really necessary? *Personnel Management*.
Gibb, S. (2008) *Human Resource Development*, 2nd edn, Basingstoke, Palgrave Macmillan.
Hackett, P. (2003) *Training Practice*, London, CIPD.
Harrison, R. (2005) *Learning and Development*, London, CIPD.
Holton, E.F., Bates, R.A., Bookter, A.I. and Yamkovenko, V.B. (2007) Convergent and divergent validity of the learning transfer system inventory, *Human Resource Development Quarterly*, **18**(3): 385–419.

Honey, P. (2007) *The Trainer Styles Questionnaire,* Maidenhead, P. Honey.
Honey, P. and Mumford, A. (1992) *The Manual of Learning Styles*, Maidenhead, P. Honey.
Kellaway, L. (2000) *Sense and Nonsense in the Office*, London, FT/Prentice Hall.
Knights, A. and Poppleton, A. (2007) *Research Insight: Coaching in Organizations*, London, CIPD.
Knowles, A. and Swanson, R.A. (2005) *The Adult Learner*, 6th edn, Burlington, MA, Elsevier.
Kolb, D.A. (1984) *Experiential Learning: Experience as the Source of Learning and Development*, Englewood Cliffs, NJ, Prentice Hall.
Leitch, S. (2006) *Prosperity for all in the Global Economy: World Class Skills*, London, HM Treasury.
LSC (Learning and Skills Council) (2008) *National Employers Skills Survey 2007: Main Report*, London, LSC.
Marchington, M. and Wilkinson, A. (1996) *Core Personnel and Development*, London, IPD.
Mumford, A. (1997) *How to Choose the Right Development Method*, Maidenhead, P. Honey.
Phillips, L. (2006) BUPA stars, *People Management*, **12**(22): 30–3.
Skinner, B.F. (1950) Are theories of learning necessary?, *Psychological Review,* **57**: 193–216.
Sloman, M. (2005) *Training to Learning: Change Agenda*, London, CIPD.
Stammers, R. and Patrick, J. (1975) *The Psychology of Training*, London, Methuen.
Swart, J., Mann, C., Brown, S. and Price, A. (2004) *Human Resource Development: Strategy and Tactics*, Oxford, Butterworth Heinemann.
Tynjala, P. and Hakkinen, P. (2005) E-learning at work: theoretical underpinnings and pedagogical challenges, *Journal of Workplace Learning*, **17**(5/6): 318–36.
Wain, D. (2007) *Lies, Damned Lies and a few Home Truths: Reflections on the 2007 Learning and Development Survey*, London, CIPD.

CHAPTER 16
Evaluation of HRD
David Devins and Joanna Smith

CHAPTER OUTLINE

- Introduction
- Theoretical perspectives
- Evaluation of NHRD
- Evaluation of HRD in the workplace
- Future direction of evaluation
- Summary

CHAPTER LEARNING OUTCOMES

After studying this chapter, you should be able to:
- Explain the importance of evaluation in HRD
- Understand the key ideas and perspectives relating to evaluation
- Explain how evaluation is connected to HRD policy
- Assess various methods of evaluating HRD
- Examine the future direction of HRD evaluation

Introduction

Evaluation is a relatively young discipline, which has its roots in the work of Campbell and Stanley (1963), who were responsible for popularizing the distinction between experimental and quasi-experimental design. Over the years, the discipline has evolved and developed, and it is applied to many policies and practices, organizations, teams and individuals. It forms the core of many strategic planning processes, organizational development, HRD and individual development practices. In fact, some people suggest that there is very little that cannot be evaluated. One guru, when describing the scope of what can be evaluated, declared: '"Everything".

One can begin at the beginning of a dictionary and go through to the end, and every noun, common or proper, calls to mind a context in which evaluation would be appropriate' (Scriven, 1980, p. 4). While cautioning against this all-embracing view, it is clear that evaluation of one form or another has a key role to play in the field of HRD at a range of levels – national, sectoral, organizational, divisional, team and individual – along with a wide range of strategic, tactical and operational activities.

A key question to ask is: Why do evaluation? Sometimes, it is because we have to – there is a contractual obligation to undertake an evaluation. It is often the case that someone, somewhere has provided some resources and they want to know what their money has been spent on, if it has made a difference, or if it could have been spent more wisely elsewhere. Demonstrating the impact of an HRD intervention is an important part of reinforcing its value and utility. Equally, evaluation may be done because there is a wish to learn from experience and improve the design of a programme, policies or practices. We may want to involve others in reflecting on the process or performance of an intervention to build capacity and share understanding. Clearly there are many reasons why we should evaluate; however, evaluation is often lacking or may be done as an afterthought and the gains to be had from a well-designed and implemented evaluation will not be realized.

> **reflective questions**
>
> 1. In your experience, what type of things do you evaluate?
> 2. Why do you do it?
> 3. How do you do it?
>
> For further information about the evaluation community, see the UK's Evaluation Society – www.evaluation.org.uk/ – or the European Evaluation Society – www.europeanevaluation.org/.

Theoretical perspectives

There is no single universally accepted definition of the term 'evaluation', as the following selected quotes from the burgeoning evaluation literature illustrate:

> The process of determining the merit, worth or value of something or the product of that process. (Scriven, 1991, p. 139)
>
> Evaluation is the systematic application of social research procedures for assessing the conceptualization, design, implementation and utility of social intervention programmes. (Rossi and Freeman, 1993, p. 5)
>
> Evaluation is the systematic assessment of the operation and/or outcomes of a programme or policy, compared to a set of explicit or implicit standards as a means of contributing to the improvement of social policy. (Weiss, 1998, p. 4)

The definitions highlight some common themes associated with evaluation, emphasizing:

1. systematic approaches
2. some 'thing' (processes, projects, programmes or policies)
3. outcomes and impact
4. utility.

In this chapter, 'evaluation' is used as a general term that encompasses these attributes, which, as we will see, can be applied to a variety of aspects of HRD.

It should be noted, however, that there is a wide range of types of evaluation – ex ante, summative, formative, comprehensive evaluation, theory-driven evaluation, utilization focused evaluation and meta-evaluation, to name but a few. The following key terms highlight the focus of the different approaches:

- *Ex ante evaluation:* at the start of the project/programme (also known as formative)
- *Interim evaluation:* during the project/programme (formative and summative)
- *Ex post evaluation:* at the end of the programme (summative).

Adopting a particular approach to evaluation often means adopting a particular approach to research and a particular view of the world, which has, at its extremes, the notions of positivism underpinned by an experimental approach and relativism underpinned by a constructivist approach.

From its roots in positivism …

Underpinning much evaluation in the early days is the logic of experimentation. For more than 30 years, policy trials and rigorous social experiments have been a primary method of evaluating potential new policies, particularly in the USA, in advance of widespread policy implementation. These approaches generally involve the random assignment of individuals to treatment and control groups so that the impact of a policy intervention may be assessed. This approach is widely acknowledged as the 'gold standard' in terms of evaluation design. At its simplest, the logic of experimentation underpinning this approach involves a four-stage process:

1. Randomly assign research subjects to two or more matched groups
2. Apply a treatment (or in this case a policy instrument) to one group and not the other
3. Measure both groups before and after the treatment of one
4. Compare the changes in the treated and untreated groups.

The two groups are studied before and after the experimental treatment and at the same points in time, to allow comparisons and conclusions to be drawn about the effect of the intervention (see Figure 16.1). In this way, exogenous or confounding factors that might otherwise influence outcomes ought to be randomly distributed between the treatment and control group. As long as the samples in each group are large enough, differences in the outcomes of the two groups can be attributed to the 'treatment'.

	Before	After	
Experimental	X1	X2	Ediff = X2 − X1
Control	X*1	X*2	Cdiff = X*2 − X*1

Effect of intervention = difference between Ediff and Cdiff

Figure 16.1 Classic experimental design
Source: de Vaus (1993, p. 35).

The core element of this approach is the 'theory of causation'. It is argued that since the groups are randomly matched to begin with, the only difference between them is the application of the programme, and it is therefore only the treatment that can be responsible for the difference in outcomes. While one cannot observe causation, it has to be inferred from the repeated succession of one event by another. In a classic analysis, a causal relationship exists if:

- the cause preceded the effect
- the cause was related to the effect
- we can find no plausible alternative explanation for the effect other than the cause.

Perhaps importantly in the field of policy evaluation, experimental design does not explain why an effect takes place nor does it seek to understand why an intervention works or does not work (Pawson and Tilley, 1997). The unique strength of experimentation is in describing the consequences attributable to deliberately varying a treatment (that is, 'causal description'). In contrast, experiments do less well in clarifying the mechanisms through which, and the conditions under which, causal relationships hold (that is, 'causal explanation'). Causal explanation is an important route to the generalization of causal descriptions, because it identifies which features of the causal relationship are essential to transfer to other situations, an outcome of considerable interest to policy planners. What experiments do best is improve causal descriptions; they do less well at explaining causal relationships. The experimental method does not set out to explain why an intervention works, and the experimental paradigm has often struggled to deliver clear answers to the questions posed by policy planners and decision makers in terms of 'what works' – the programmes, projects or actions taken to develop human capital. To understand why there is an inconsistency of outcomes, different questions need to be asked in terms of 'why' or 'how' the processes have affected behaviours.

reflective questions

1. Why would you use a scientific approach?
2. Can you find a good example? (Google it.)
3. What value does it have in the HRD context?

... to constructivism

In the 1970s, many social science disciplines were gripped by the debate on positivism, and witnessed the rise of oppositional perspectives known variously as 'interpretative', 'phenomenological' or 'hermeneutical', for example. This coincided with a move towards the usefulness of evaluation as a means of informing decisions or, most optimistically, enlightening decision makers and those involved in the development and implementation of policies and programmes (Weiss, 1980). Together, the 'oppositional' perspectives and the pragmatic approach to evaluation led to an approach referred to as 'constructivism' (or sometimes 'constructionism').[1] The constructivist paradigm has its roots in anthropological traditions. Instead of focusing on explaining, this paradigm focuses on understanding the phenomenon being studied through ongoing and in-depth contact and relationships with those involved. Relying on qualitative data and rich descriptions, the constructivists' purpose is 'the collection of holistic world views, intact belief systems and complex inner psychic and interpersonal states' (Maxwell and Lincoln, 1990, p. 508). In other words, who are the people involved in the programme and what do the experiences mean to them?

While there are a number of approaches to social constructivism (Gergen, 1985, 1994; Pearce, 1992; Shotter, 1993; Burr, 1995), the key features are as follows:

- The use of language, organized into conversations, discourses, narratives, and stories, provides the means by which we come to experience our world and construct 'reality'. Thus language, as a social resource, has a central role in the making of phenomena that may come to be accepted as real.
- Meanings are made through a relational process between people that become embedded into ongoing ways of talking, which in turn may become accepted versions of reality in a particular local context. The taken-for-granted view of the world provides a variety of truths and facts about a reality, which may be 'highly circumscribed by culture, history or social context' (Gergen, 1985, p. 267). The extent to which meanings continue to be accepted depends not on empirical validity but the day-to-day workings of social processes in a particular time and place. What comes to be accepted as real serves a function within a particular historical and cultural context with no claim to 'truth' beyond the context.
- By participating in different relationships in different contexts, we acquire various ways of talking, which can be used for the achievement of valued ends in different situations. Meanings are unlikely to remain constant since, as a consequence of our participation in different relationships, versions of reality are always open to further or revised specification, offering the possibility of new meanings to emerge via a social process leading to a new or revised version of reality.

The idea is that initiatives and programmes that go under the microscope cannot and should not be treated as 'independent variables'. Rather, all policies and interventions are constituted in complex processes of human understanding and interaction. Proponents of the constructivist approach, such as Guba and Lincoln (1989), see evaluators as facilitating an exchange of meaning between stakeholders, where, through dialogue, stakeholders jointly construct a consensus about an intervention. Through this lens, programmes work through a process of reasoning, change, influence, negotiation, persuasion and choice. While traditional evaluation emphasizes outputs and outcomes, this form of evaluation emphasizes processes and particularly the myriad of stakeholders who may be involved in developing and implementing an intervention, strategy, programme or project.

> **reflective questions**
>
> 1. Why would you use a constructivist approach?
> 2. Can you find a good example? (Google it.)
> 3. What value does it have in the HRD context?

Somewhere between positivism and relativism

Throughout recent decades there have been heated exchanges between the proponents of positivist and constructionist approaches to evaluation. Between the extremes of positivism and constructivism lies a pluralist view of evaluation, which calls for both breadth and depth in programme evaluation (Cronbach, 1982).

This approach is taken further by Rossi and Freeman (1993), who highlight a threefold distinction of evaluation activities based on analysis related to the conceptualization and design of interventions, monitoring or programme implementation, and assessment of programme utility.

This has developed into theory-based evaluation based on the premise that interventions are based on a theory – either implicit or explicit – which explains how and why it will work. The key to understanding what really matters about a programme is through identifying this theory (sometimes referred to as the 'programme logic model'). By combining outcome data with an understanding of the process, a great deal can be learned about the programme's impact and its most influential factors (Weiss, 1995).

A more recent development has been the advent of realist evaluation (Pawson and Tilley, 1997), which seeks to position itself as a model of scientific explanation avoiding the traditional epistemological poles of positivism and relativism. Realism's key feature is its stress on the mechanics of explanation and its contribution to a progressive body of scientific knowledge.

> **reflective questions**
>
> 1. Are there any problems associated with combining outcome and process data?
> 2. What implications does it have for research methods?
> 3. Is this approach becoming more or less popular? Why/why not?

Evaluation of NHRD

Several models have been introduced to explore evaluation within the context of the organization and workplace training. However, much evaluation work today is conducted on national government programmes with government departments and quasi-government agencies. While it may be difficult to define and varies from country to country, the general focus of NHRD has developed out of a government interest in workforce development as a strategic issue. In the UK in particular, NHRD is often focused on the development and utilization of skills in order to enhance competitiveness and alleviate social exclusion. The system remains fragmented, with a range of government departments and agencies responsible for various aspects of the system. The UK government is committed to the vision outlined in the influential Leitch (2006) review of skills, which sees the UK becoming a world leader in skills by 2020. At the heart of this raised ambition for NHRD lies a shared responsibility for employers, individuals and government to increase action and investment in education and training. One of the key debates surrounding public policy intervention is whether and how much public intervention is needed. The Leitch review is a prime example of the use of evidence drawing on a range of research and evaluation studies, often commissioned by government departments or quasi-government agencies, to develop thinking and set the agenda.

ACTIVITY

Working with a partner, find out about NHRD in England. Go to the Department for Innovation, Universities and Skills – www.dius.gov.uk/ – and the UK Commission for Employment and Skills – www.ukces.org.uk/.

For Scotland, go to www.scotland.gov.uk/Topics/Education, for Wales, go to http://new.wales.gov.uk/topics/educationandskills/?lang=en, and for Northern Ireland, go to www.delni.gov.uk/index/publications/pubs-sectoral/skills-strategy-ni.htm.

Thinking about a policy or programme related to NHRD:

1. What was it seeking to achieve?
2. What actions were/are required to take it forward?
3. What factors are/were critical to its success?

Evaluation frameworks – the ROAMEF cycle

A framework is critical to the successful development and implementation of evaluation. There is a wide range of frameworks to be applied to appraise and evaluate policy and NHRD. An example of one endorsed by the government is provided in the *Green Book* (HM Treasury, 2003), which is a systematic approach used to guide national government appraisals and evaluation in the UK. It provides a useful overview to illustrate the key characteristics of evaluation throughout the policy process – important when considering evaluation within the context of NHRD – however, it is only one of a wide range of frameworks that may be used to evaluate public policy.

HRM / HRD IN ITS CONTEMPORARY CONTEXT

> **ACTIVITY**
>
> Working in groups of three, each person checks one of the following frameworks for evaluation:
>
> - http://ec.europa.eu/budget/sound_fin_mgt/eval_framework_en.htm – the European Commission
> - www.berr.gov.uk/files/file40324.pdf – *Evaluating Science and Society Initiatives*
> - www.wkkf.org/Pubs/Tools/Evaluation/Pub770.pdf – the *Kellogg Foundation Evaluation Handbook*.
>
> Identify the key features of each framework and share your results.

The basic model of evaluation outlined in the *Green Book* is the ROAMEF (rationale, objectives, appraisal, monitoring, evaluation and feedback) cycle, shown in Figure 16.2.

The underlying rationale for policy intervention is usually founded in market failure, or where there are clear government distributional objectives (societal equity) that need to be met. The Leitch (2006, p. 3) review of skills embodies this approach to NHRD, where government investment must focus on market failures, ensuring a basic platform of skills for all and targeting help where it is most needed.

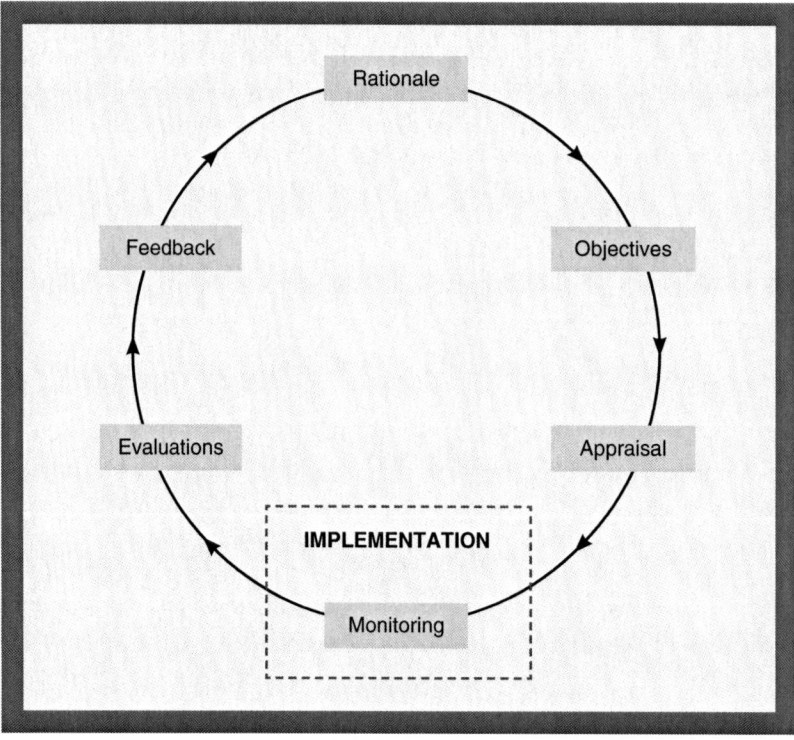

Figure 16.2 The ROAMEF cycle
Source: HM Treasury (2003, p. 3).

The *Green Book* outlines a circular process of evaluation, where the first step is based on a process or systems approach through an appraisal of the proposed intervention (ex ante evaluation). Towards the end of the process, an outcomes-oriented evaluation (ex post evaluation) is prescribed to determine whether the intervention has worked and, if so, to what extent.

Rationale

The Leitch review (2006) marshals both research and evaluation evidence to highlight that a skilled workforce has positive impacts on high-level economic aims such as productivity and GDP growth. At the same time, it provides evidence of a major skills deficiency, which is reflected in qualification levels at various levels when international comparisons are made. There is further evidence of different forms of market failure exerting an influence on policy, including:

- *Externalities:* leading to an underinvestment in training by employers where employers are concerned that, once trained, an employee will leave the firm before the firm has recouped its investment
- *Imperfect information:* leading to employees being unable to judge the quality of their training or appreciate the benefits
- *Credit market imperfections:* where low-paid employees in particular are likely to be credit constrained or unable to pay for training.

These market failures mean that the level of training provided by the market is likely to be inefficiently low from society's point of view. Well-designed interventions, engaging employers and providing high-quality flexible approaches to skills development, may help to bridge the gaps and improve NHRD.

Objectives

If an intervention is worthwhile, the objectives of the new policy, programme or project need to be clearly stated. Objectives may be expressed in general terms so that a range of options to meet them can be considered. There is usually a hierarchy of outcomes, outputs and targets that should be clearly set out. Objectives and their targets should be SMART:

- Specific
- Measurable
- Achievable
- Realistic
- Time bound.

An illustration of such an approach may propose an objective related to the development of skills, linked to an output in terms of number of training places and/or numbers completing training, which in turn may be linked to an outcome associated with the value of extra human capital or earnings capacity.

Appraisal

The purpose of appraisal is to help to develop an intervention that meets the objectives of government action. Appraisal emphasizes consideration of the costs and benefits of different intervention models (including a 'do nothing' model), with a view to identifying an approach that represents value for money. A key element of the appraisal is the treatment of uncertainty about the future, and techniques such as sensitivity and scenario analysis and methods may be used.

At the heart of appraisal lies the valuing of the costs and benefits of identified options. This can be a far from straightforward process, as the relevant costs and benefits to government and society of all options should be valued and the net benefits or costs calculated. As suggested earlier, HRD-related intervention at the micro- and macro-level needs to show a return like other expenditures and is often viewed as a cost rather than an investment. Costs can be expressed in terms of relevant opportunity costs, fixed, variable, semi-variable and step costs, and inputs may come from accountants, economists and other specialists depending on the type of appraisal. Benefits can be expressed in terms of taking into account the direct effects of interventions as well as wider societal effects using real or estimated market prices, or the results of commissioned research to ascertain the benefits associated with an intervention. Various other adjustments to the value of costs and benefits may be made to take account of equity, inflation and discounting.

Some form of appraisal of risk should also be part of this stage of the evaluation process and account for the overoptimism that characterizes many project appraisers, as well as assessing uncertainties associated with the development and implementation of the intervention.

> **reflective questions**
>
> 1. What is the purpose of appraisal?
> 2. Who should undertake appraisal?
> 3. What are the weaknesses of the *Green Book* approach to appraisal?

Monitoring

All organizations keep records and notes and discuss what they are doing. This simple administration becomes monitoring when it encompasses the systematic collection of data, particularly relating to the financial management and outcomes of a policy, programme or project during implementation. It is a key element of performance management, which seeks to ensure the successful implementation of an HRD intervention. An effective monitoring system will:

- ensure that management information is measuring what is important in terms of inputs (such as costs), outputs, outcomes and impact
- put in place controls to ensure that the data are accurate
- provide regular financial and progress reports.

Monitoring will help to answer questions at various points in the life of a project, such as: How well are we doing? What difference are we making?

> **reflective questions**
>
> 1. Why should we monitor?
> 2. Who should monitor?
> 3. What is the difference between monitoring and evaluation?

Evaluation

The section below on evaluation in the workplace provides a more detailed introduction to various models of evaluation of HRD and provides an opportunity to explore further the nature of evaluation within the organization context. However, within the ROAMEF cycle, evaluation is identified as a discrete activity to be completed towards the end, or at the end, of a programme. The main aim of this stage is to examine what has happened against what was expected to happen. A key element of this is to establish what would have happened in the absence of the intervention (the counterfactual). Other important concepts to consider when analysing data as part of an evaluation are additionality, displacement and deadweight. (Descriptions of these and many other concepts relevant to evaluation are available in the evaluation glossaries at www.oecd.org/dataoecd/29/21/2754804.pdf and www.un.org/Depts/oios/mecd/mecd_glossary/index.htm.)

Feedback

Feedback is a critical part of the process, as without it, recognition of the value of an intervention, potential improvements to the process identified though the evaluation, and the value of the evaluation itself will not be recognized. For some time, the challenge of connecting the outcomes of research and evaluation processes with the inputs that professionals and politicians use in making judgements and taking decisions has been recognized (Davies et al., 2000; Nutley et al., 2003) and forms an important dimension of the future of evaluation related to HRD intervention, which we will return to towards the end of this chapter.

Some observations on the ROAMEF approach

The ROAMEF framework, or variations of it, has become a central part of the approach to evaluation adopted by many organizations, especially those in the public sector, as a way of judging the success or otherwise of interventions. As well as being systematic and logical, the model is systemic as the feedback loop provides information about activities so that necessary improvements may be identified.

There are some obvious consequences for this model for the evaluation of NHRD. One of these is that evaluation appears as a distinct stage of the process and its placement towards the end of the process tends to mean that, in some instances, evaluation is something of an afterthought. In this case, evaluation tends to be completed towards the end of the programme, with a certain degree of pressure to undertake the activity quickly to come to a judgement on the 'success' or otherwise of the programme. However, as outlined above, it can encourage reflection and various types of evaluation and appraisal activities throughout the policy-making process (similar to the CIRO model outlined below). Furthermore, by adopting an approach that takes account of the interests of various stakeholders and cultural and contextual factors as part of the evaluation process, a more responsive approach can be adopted to evaluation (Stake, 2004). This shifts the emphasis of evaluation away from 'proving' towards feedback and learning.

Evaluation of HRD in the workplace

HRD is a collective process involving a range of people and activities. The purpose of evaluation will vary depending on the objectives of relevant stakeholders. Good workplace evaluation will engage stakeholders at the ex ante, interim and ex post stages outlined above. Harrison (2005, p. 144) argues for a participatory approach to evaluation 'that has been produced in collaboration with key partners'. However, the objectives of different stakeholders may vary and any evaluation may need to adopt a range of methods and measures to evaluate the success in meeting such objectives. Examples of varying stakeholder objectives for training for middle managers are outlined in Table 16.1. We will return to these later.

It is important that HRD practitioners are aware of the philosophical constructs of the positivist and constructivist approaches to evaluation. However, Kenny et al. (1979) caution those involved with the practical aspects of evaluation to take a pragmatic approach. They argue that a rigorous scientific approach, however desirable, is not practicable in most workplace settings. If evaluation does not take place and/or is not subject to some rigour, the success or otherwise of training and development interventions undertaken by organizations remains unmeasured and unproven. It can be safely asserted that Kenny et al.'s writings are no less relevant today. There is access to greater quantities and (it is hoped) greater quality of data from which to evaluate. The need to justify and measure success has arguably never been more at the forefront of business and society's thinking. Edwards (2005) recognizes the current societal phenomenon of measuring performance and satisfaction, from the success of schools and the individual child's progress within them, to how happy we are with our hotel bed, bus or burger. She notes that this process of measurement is prevalent within the workplace via competence frameworks and staff appraisals. Phillips (1994a, 1994b) identifies the dangers of such a climate as being self-fulfilling – evaluation for evaluation's sake.

Table 16.1 Stakeholder objectives for training middle managers

Stakeholder	Possible objectives
Individual	Obtain formal qualification to improve promotion prospects within or outside the organization
Line manager	Develop independence and confidence in role and reduce reliance on them as middle manager becomes more autonomous
HR department	Ensure consistency between managers and ensure all such managers are working within a common competency framework
Finance department	Provide positive financial return on investment
Senior management team	Improve overall organizational performance and meet strategic organizational objectives

EVALUATION OF HRD

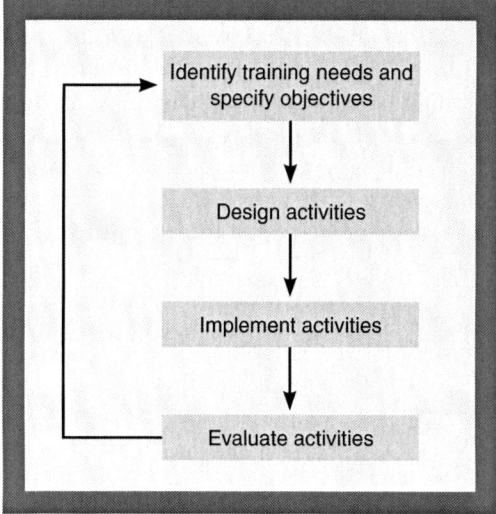

Figure 16.3 A four-stage training model

Evaluation fits within the four-stage training model, and shown in Figure 16.3.

The potential danger here is to consider evaluation as the last activity of the cycle, that is, we evaluate at the end of a training and development intervention. The references made earlier to ex ante, interim and ex post should mean embedding evaluation as a continuing process throughout the cycle.

With the macro- and micro-contexts of evaluation of workplace training and development interventions in mind, it is appropriate to consider the purpose of evaluation and then critique some established models of evaluation in the workplace.

Purpose of evaluation

The evaluation of HRD activity at work involves the collection and interpretation of data. The results of this process can be used for a variety of purposes according to particular needs. For example, senior managers might need evidence that a programme of learning on customer service was having a measurable impact on performance.

Easterby-Smith (1994) identifies four distinct purposes of evaluation:

1. *Proving:* This shows that something happened. It may justify the costs of training, provide evidence for its ongoing delivery, and confirm it was the right thing to do (or, of course, the converse of these).
2. *Improving:* This identifies how the training intervention might be improved. The tendency is for this to be measured and acted on after the training has been completed. However, noting the need for ex ante and interim evaluation, this could be done at various stages of delivery.
3. *Learning:* Participants in HRD activities can review what they are learning, considering how to make changes in the context of the activity but also what might be used at work or in the future.

4. *Controlling:* This is often the focus of training departments. Evaluation results help to control the quality of training providers, the costs and the behaviour of the participants. Easterby-Smith (1994, p. 19) notes the proliferation of such a purpose, particularly in large public sector organizations such as the police. The need to ensure consistency between central and regional (or in the case of education, individual local schools) is growing, as the tension to allow autonomy and yet ensure national standards increases.

In addition to these purposes, it is also suggested that because evaluation is concerned with the collection and interpretation of data, the results can be used to persuade and influence others of the value of HRD activities (Mumford and Gold, 2004). It is a reminder that information can be used for a variety of purposes, as a representation of the facts or a version of events, told from a particular point of view (Clarke, 1999).

Evaluation models

Kirkpatrick's evaluation model

In 1959, Kirkpatrick published articles outlining techniques for evaluating training programmes. These articles described a four-level process for the evaluation of training. This process has been commonly referred to as the Kirkpatrick model. The four levels are shown in Figure 16.4.

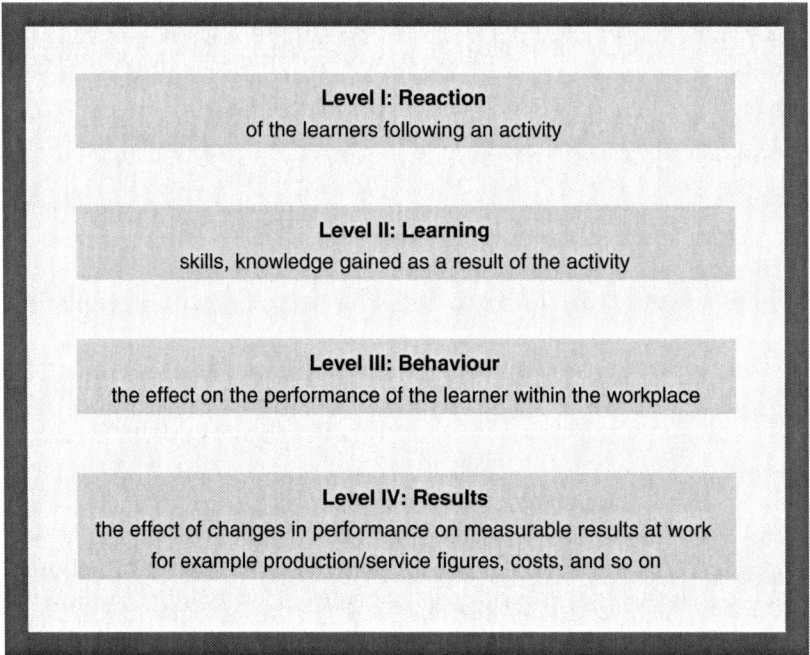

Figure 16.4 Levels of evaluation for training
Source: Adapted from Kirkpatrick (1998).

EVALUATION OF HRD

This all seems quite logical and sensible but, as HRD in Practice 16.1 shows, it can be difficult to implement.

Basarab, cited in Kirkpatrick (1998), notes that the first two levels of the model refer to internal drivers for the training department to evaluate the effectiveness of its provision. The second two levels refer to external drivers, which evaluate the participants' contribution to business operations and overall organizational success.

Reaction

This first level measures the participants' reactions to the training and development intervention they have experienced. Typically, data are collected ex post, via 'happy sheets' or other forms of what Kirkpatrick (1998, p. 20) refers to as measures of 'customer satisfaction'. Figure 16.5 provides an example.

HRD in Practice 16.1   Evaluation is a tricky business

Rose spent three months evaluating evaluation activity and processes at National Westminster Bank. As a large organization with many operating divisions, the bank had around 12 different and separate HRD departments and functions. Rose found that most had the same simplistic approach – end of course questionnaires ruled, and most were read by the HRD staff involved in the delivery and then filed. No analysis or reporting occurred, except in a few isolated examples. Rose also established the reasons for this:

1. No higher level evaluation occurred because it was considered too time and resource intensive to do so.
2. No information beyond learner satisfaction was ever asked for by senior or operational managers.
3. HRD staff had what they believed they needed to validate and improve their work and performance.

Because Rose investigated evaluation as part of the requirement of her professional qualification, she became an expert on the research and writing on evaluation and so reckoned the situation she found was untenable. She designed a corporate approach to evaluation for implementation across the bank and then spent the next nine months getting it accepted corporately and in each of the bank's divisions. The approach didn't go into return on investment or anything overly sophisticated. But it did achieve the generation of data on changes in work behaviour and performance following learning and development events, and also the production of evaluation reports for every activity, which fed into quarterly and annual divisional and corporate reports on the value of investing in employee development. An improvement on what previously existed was achieved.

Performance and Development Review Training

Please give your views and comments regarding your day						
Excellent 4	Very good 3		Satisfied 2		Not satisfied 1 (please give details)	
How did you rate the content of the programme?			4	3	2	1
Comments						
How did you rate the facilitator?			4	3	2	1
Comments						
How did you rate the quality of handouts information?			4	3	2	1
Comments						
How did you rate the venue?			4	3	2	1
Comments						
How was the quality of catering?			4	3	2	1
Comments						
Were your overall objectives met?			4	3	2	1
Your objectives were:						
Any other comments:						

Thank you for your feedback

Figure 16.5 Reaction-level evaluation sheet

The reasons for measuring reactions are varied. It can help to measure what is learned by participants. It measures an emotional response, which, although not scientifically proven as accurate, does give relatively quick data from which to evaluate the effectiveness of the intervention. Both Kirkpatrick (1998) and Alliger et al. (1997) caution those interpreting data that positive reactions do not always equal a good training experience and negative reactions do not always equal a poor one. A baseline conclusion could be that positive reactions do not guarantee learning, but do make participants more amenable to further training and may encourage learning. Participants may also be more positive in their recounting of the experience to their manager and peers, thereby influencing future participants' expectations. Conversely, a negative reaction may disengage a participant from learning and future training activities. The 'bad publicity' such reactions may produce in the wider workplace will not help the efforts of a training department when it promotes such interventions in the future.

Bramley (1999, p. 367) suggests that some basic questions should be asked before reaction data are gathered. What information is needed? How can it be collected? It is suggested that happy sheets do not predict learning or changes to behaviour. These sheets are therefore limited to collecting data on only the first level of Kirkpatrick's model. Bramley (1999) also suggests that for repeat interventions to different groups of participants, the gauging of reactions only needs to be done a few times. Unless the intervention changes, the range of reactions is likely to be the same.

This critique of Kirkpatrick's first level supports the suggestion above that the evaluation made at this level is an internal driver for the training department. Positive reactions can justify the intervention and garner support and funding for its repetition. Negative reactions can improve the quality of the intervention, from redesigning training aspects to changing the sandwiches served at lunchtime. The quality of the intervention can be improved prior to delivery. Reactions can also be gathered from participants during the training intervention. This may be done via interim 'happy sheets' or more qualitative focus groups. If there is a danger of negative reactions, such timely evaluation allows providers to amend and correct perceived shortcomings before the end of the event. This may result in more positive reactions later. Alliger et al. (1997) note that the 'usefulness' of learning is important for the application of training in the workplace. They urge designers to consider this at the planning stage. This relates to the need to engage relevant stakeholders from the outset in training intervention design. Workplace constraints and the perceptions of workers, when they return to their roles, are key to ensuring that these do not become blocks to effective learning and transfer of behaviour.

ACTIVITY

Working with a partner, consider the following questions:

1. How important are emotional reactions as measures of a successful training intervention?
2. Do you agree with Bramley that such data need only be collected a few times for the same event?

Learning

Tests of learning are undertaken to achieve educational and professional qualifications via assessments. The evaluation of learning from training interventions can follow the same process; however, this is often not designed into such interventions. It may be undesirable from the participants' viewpoint, too costly to administrate, or the learning taking place may be deemed too difficult to measure. Some interventions require assessment. Training to drive a forklift truck or to be a workplace first aider needs certification via formal testing. Other interventions, for example coaching or diversity training, may have more subjective outcomes, which do not require testing and can be difficult, if not impossible, to assess. There is also an argument that what is tested is not necessarily what is actually learned as a result of an intervention. Bramley (1999, p. 368) cautions that 'participation in an event does not equal learning'. A formula for measuring how much participants have learned can be expressed as the gain ratio:

$$\text{Gain ratio} \frac{\text{Post-test} - \text{Pre-test}}{\text{Possible} - \text{Pre-test}} \times 100$$

Bramley (1999, p. 369) suggests that 'the average gain ratio across the group is a measure of the efficiency of the programme'. He argues that a group average of over 70% is needed to be efficient. If the percentage is lower, Bramley suggests splitting the group into those with pre-knowledge and those without. The ratios may vary and show the intervention is appropriate for one group but not another. There is another danger with high pre-knowledge. The success of individuals' test results may be high, but this shows the extent of their prior learning, not the success of this specific training intervention. The importance of effective training needs analysis and a link to job analysis is critical here to the efficiency of the intervention.

Behaviour

Although evaluation of learning can evidence the extent to which something is learned, it will not predict the extent to which such learning will be used effectively in the workplace. The third element of Kirkpatrick's model seeks to address this. Bramley (1999) suggests a worker's performance is a combination of their ability and motivation and the opportunity to display such learning. He argues for the 'hardwiring' of learning when applied in the workplace. Rock (2006) provides extensive physiological evidence for the importance of using the hardwired brain as opposed to using 'working memory'. The latter requires great physical and mental energy. For example, the first time someone drives a car, the levels of concentration and effort are significantly greater than for someone who has driven the same route for many years. So in the workplace, learning that can be regularly practised and re-enforced is likely to result in changed behaviour.

This assumes that the worker has learned well from the training intervention, and that their ability to apply the learning to the workplace is within their mental and physical capacity. For example, an update on employment law may inform line managers of their legal rights and responsibilities to help them manage their staff more effectively, but it alone is unlikely to equip them to represent the work organization in legal proceedings. Workers may be more motivated to apply learning if they see an immediate benefit to themselves and, if they are turned into business objectives, to the overall success of the organization. If changed behaviour is likely to result in a pay increase or promotion, it too is likely to be more motivating and therefore more readily applied.

However, workers need opportunities to apply their learning. Recruitment and selection training may only be applied once or twice a year by some participants, as job vacancies to which they may appoint come up infrequently. Opportunities may also be limited by an organization's culture. A training intervention that encourages creativity and enterprise may be stifled in the workplace by hierarchical organizational structures and an autocratic management style. Those having undertaken diversity training may be ridiculed in the workplace for perceived 'political correctness'. Unless such participants are confident of the messages learned, they may suppress any application in order to retain the respect of immediate work colleagues.

In order to maximize the application of learning, Bramley (1999, p. 370) recommends the use of practical 'performance tests', rather than written assessments, when evaluating at the learning level of Kirkpatrick's model. A study by Rouiller and Goldstein (1993, cited in Bramley 1999, p. 374) identified seven scales to measure the 'transfer climate'. The emphasis was on how line managers can influence the adoption of new behaviours after training. The scales focused on:

- goal setting
- the closeness of training behaviour to normal behaviour
- whether equipment was available in the workplace
- the autonomy of those trained to handle problems
- the degree of negative and positive feedback
- the impact of no feedback because line managers were too busy to provide it
- the degree of ridicule those trained received if they applied their learning.

From Rouiller and Goldstein's studies, the tests at the end of the training intervention only predicted 8% of participants' behaviour transfer scores (that is, participants could score highly in the test but perform badly in the workplace). The transfer climate measure, described above, predicted 46% (see Bramley, 1999, p. 374).

Results

This level of the Kirkpatrick model is the most obviously business focused. It evaluates the extent to which a training intervention has had a positive impact on overall organizational success. Bloom (1964, cited in Wilson, 2005, p. 411) refers to the 'impact of learners' understanding, behaviour or attitudes'. The key here is to define what impact is sought from the training at its earliest development stage. Why has the intervention been commissioned? Who decided it should take place? What were the learning objectives? How do these objectives impact on organizational success? How will that success be measured?

Some outcomes of training interventions may be difficult if not impossible to measure (Edwards, 2005). Some interventions can give results that are relatively easy to measure numerically. Examples include the reduction in accidents following health and safety training, or an increase in sales after sales training. However, other interventions, such as coaching programmes for managers or diversity training, produce more subtle changes to behaviour and attitude, which may take years for statistical evidence of effectiveness to show.

reflective question

How would you measure the results of diversity training?

It may be helpful, given the complex nature of evaluating results, to establish how this level will be measured at the design stage of training. To be truly effective, such measurements should be the decision of the relevant stakeholders. Referring back to Table 16.1, the differing objectives of each stakeholder need different measurements of effectiveness. Table 16.2 suggests what these might be.

There is no end to the possible measures of effective results an organization could choose. However, to carry out all those suggested above would take significant time and expense. The key is to decide the measures at the planning stage and focus on these. The danger of this is that the measures chosen may not be the right ones. The cost of analysing data to provide evidence of results also needs to be factored in. One model for considering a range of measures of results is Kaplan and Norton's (1992) balanced scorecard. This combines financial and non-financial measures.

> **ACTIVITY**
>
> Working with a partner, go to www.balancedscorecard.org, the home page of Balanced Scorecard Institute. Explore how the process of the balanced scorecard might be used to measure results of HRD activity.

Another danger when trying to extract the direct cause and effect of HRD interventions is that extraneous factors may influence results. The improved market share may be due to better management training, but could be attributed to fail-

Table 16.2 Evaluation of development training for middle managers

Stakeholder	Possible objectives	Measurement of results
Individual	Obtain formal qualification to improve promotion prospects within or outside the organization	Awarded formal qualification – x% of participants obtain formal qualification
Line manager	Develop independence and confidence in role and reduce reliance on them as middle manager becomes more autonomous	Less line management time spent in support of middle managers
		No costs (financial or reputation) to the organization as a result of middle managers' autonomous decisions
		Financial savings to organization as line managers able to focus on own tasks
HR department	Ensure consistency between managers and that all such managers are working within a common competency framework	Fewer examples of middle managers operating outside organizational policies and processes – x% compliance with company rules – measure increase from baseline pre-training
Finance department	Provide positive financial return on investment	Financial benefits (more sales, profit, less wastage) outweigh cost of programme
Senior management team	Improve overall organizational performance and meet strategic organizational objectives	Improved business reputation, higher market share, better labour turnover, reduced absenteeism, organizational objectives met on time (or early)

ings by an organization's competitors. Higher labour turnover after a training programme could evidence the unplanned result that managers have been trained for promotion, which they find sooner from other employers. The impact of government policies, the economic environment, and supplier and competitor behaviour are all examples of external factors that could influence results.

However, such limitations should not stop this level of evaluation from being attempted. It provides a direct link back to why the intervention was identified at the outset. It offers evidence for improvement or modification. It could provide justification to the training department and other stakeholders that the intervention is worthwhile and should be continued. Without such a business focus, any evaluation may 'miss the point' and, as Phillips (1994a) states, become evaluation for evaluation's sake.

reflective questions

Think about some workplace training you have done or the course you are studying:
1. How would you evaluate its effectiveness?
2. How does your employer or course provider evaluate its effectiveness?
3. Does one aspect of Kirkpatrick's model apply more than the others?

The CIRO evaluation model

Harrison (2005, p. 144) offers an overall critique of the Kirkpatrick model, cautioning its use in the workplace: 'All generic models must be tailored to fit specific needs, and even Kirkpatrick does not always suit context.' This omission is arguably overcome by the use of another evaluation model, the CIRO, which refers to:

- Context
- Inputs
- Reactions
- Outcomes.

The model was developed by Warr et al. (1970) and Hamblin (1994), originally for the evaluation of management training. It supports the arguments made earlier in this chapter that evaluation activities should take place before, during and after the intervention.

Context

This is the ex ante aspect of evaluation. It aims to evaluate the context in which the training intervention took place. It will review the objectives and purpose of the training. Why was it commissioned? Who supported the intervention (and possibly, who did not)? It will evaluate how effective the preparation was for training. What briefings and support were put in place to ensure the training would meet its objectives? It should identify what worked and how the preparation and planning could be improved for future delivery. The context may also be wider in terms of the business climate in operation at the time of the intervention. If the training was delivered at a time of great success, would its outcomes be different at times of difficulty? Would managers be equally keen to release staff and engage in motivational activity to encourage behavioural change if the operating environment was less positive? Techniques for data collection would include interviews, questionnaires, briefings, written tests and feedback from others ahead of development.

Inputs

This evaluates the resources required to deliver the training intervention. There are tangible costs such as materials, external training consultant fees, room hire and subsistence. Harrison (2005, p. 145) recommends accurate records are kept as these costs are incurred for review after the event. There should be a measure between the resources used and the extent to which they met the learning objectives set at the 'context' stage above. It is important to account for hidden costs such as staff time away from their job. The opportunity cost of not undertaking the training should be higher than the cost of taking staff out of the workplace for hours or days, in order to justify its efficiency and effectiveness. It could be argued that this is attempting to 'measure the unmeasurable' (Edwards, 2005, p. 407). Measuring the cost of not doing something can be difficult to predict. Techniques for data collection would include session reviews, questionnaires, written or practical tests, feedback from others during events, and interviews.

Reactions

In many respects, this is similar in definition to the same term used in the Kirkpatrick model. It measures the emotional responses of participants to the training they have experienced. A broader range of reactions might be included here. For example, the reactions of the deliverers of the training and those of the managers, peers and subordinates to an individual's training will all inform the evaluation process. Harrison (2005, p. 145) notes that there should not be 'an indiscriminate use of happy sheets', but that such data collection must be used and relate back to the objectives of the training. Techniques for data collection would include questionnaires and interviews.

Outcomes

This stage of the CIRO model initially sounds similar to the results level of the Kirkpatrick model. However, Hamblin (1994) developed a four-level structure of analysis for outcomes. These levels integrate the internal and external drivers identified by Basarab above. Indeed, Warr et al. referred to a continuum of immediate, intermediate and ultimate outcomes (see Harrison 2005, p. 146). Hamblin's four levels are:

1. *The learner level:* measures what is learned by individuals, not unlike the learning level of Kirkpatrick's model.
2. *The workplace level:* measures changes in job behaviour (again not unlike the behaviour aspect of Kirkpatrick). Measurement may be in the form of appraisal, observation and from discussions with the individual, their peers and line manager.

3. *The team/departmental/unit level:* Hamblin includes within this level the operational measures (for example increases in production, reduced wastage) that can be attributed to a specific department.
4. *The organizational level:* these are the broader outcomes that may take time (years, possibly) to evaluate fully. It could include hard measures of increased share price or market share, or it could be softer outcomes of culture change, which, of course, could lead to the former.

Techniques for data collection would include questionnaires, interviews, debriefing meetings, feedback from others relating to behaviour and performance, measurements of performance and results achieved. HRD in Practice 16.2 shows the approach taken to data collection for a large programme of development for SME managers.

HRD in Practice 16.2   A development programme for SME managers

The development programme took place across England from September 2004 until April 2006 and allowed managers to obtain a grant of up to £1,000 towards any development identified following an in-depth assessment.

The aims of the evaluation were to:

- measure the impact of the programme on the participants' own performance
- measure the impact of the programme on their respective organizations
- assess how effective the brokerage models have been from the customer perspective
- inform policy on the way in which leadership and management provision can be embedded in Train to Gain.

The methodology consisted of:

- a postal/email survey of all local LSCs and Business Links
- six partnership case studies and telephone follow-up with ten Business Links
- stakeholder interviews with programme managers at the Centre for Enterprise
- a telephone survey of 500 participants on the programme and in-depth case studies with 20 participants
- a telephone survey of 216 intermediary organizations and a control group survey with 100 organizations.

Source: LSC (2006).

ACTIVITY

Working in groups of three, consider how you would evaluate a training event on communication for 10 participants in a management consultancy team. The task is to show that the three-hour event has had an impact on the participants and performance. Go to www.lancs.ac.uk/fss/projects/edres/ltsn-eval/ for a site devoted to resources for evaluators.

These evaluation models provide a systematic route for gathering data relating to HRD activities, allowing the purpose of evaluation to be met. There are limitations, in that the models are stronger when activities are clearly identified and completed in a limited time frame, such as training courses. HRD involves a wider view of learning at work and beyond, however, and there is often a time-lag between learning events and use. For example, completion of a professional qualification, such as the Chartered Institute of Marketing, may not lead to an immediate impact at work.

A further difficulty arises from the range of variables that affect learning at work, where it becomes more precarious to attempt to link impact at the different levels implied by the models above. For example, reactions to an HRD event may be strong but participants find they are prevented from applying learning to their work, because of the opinions of their fellow workers, the requirements of their managers, or the way the work is defined. These are features of an organization's learning climate.

Responsive models

The different purposes of evaluation and the difficulties of applying systematic models of evaluation have resulted in a number of approaches to evaluation, which take more account of the interests of different stakeholders and their requirements. Such approaches are referred to as 'responsive evaluation' (Stake, 2004) and give more attention to cultural and context factors and providing feedback for ongoing learning.

One approach, presented by Patton (1997), focuses on utilization by those who have an interest in what is happening, so that they can make decisions based on evaluation information as it emerges. The role of the evaluator is to facilitate such judgements 'rather than acting as a distant, independent judge'.

Another approach is concerned to make action possible, especially where learning is concerned with dealing with complex and difficult issues. This is referred to as 'action evaluation' (Rothman, 1997). Stakeholders can set goals, expressing values and motivations which can be shared with others in a project, and allowing for agreement on direction. Actions can be set and evaluated on a continuous basis.

ACTIVITY

Go to www.beyondintractability.org/essay/action_evaluation/ to find out more about action evaluation.

For more resources on helping learners to actively review HRD activities, go to www.reviewing.co.uk/.

Evaluation and organization change

Throughout this book, links have been made with the pressures on many organizations to change, leading to new definitions of what organizations do and how work is defined. For example, increasingly work is team based and requires interaction with others in different locations physically and virtually within and between organizations. Further, such work is frequently knowledge based and relies on the interactions of professionals and experts. Therefore organizations need to see change continuous with learning as a crucial capability to achieve this.

A number of approaches to supporting change through learning and evaluation have been presented. For example, Preskill and Torres (1999) present a model of evaluative enquiry based on key ideas relating to reflection, dialogue and the use of questions between change participants and stakeholders to surface assumptions and clarify values. The purpose of evaluation is to support learning and respond to the emerging patterns of information needs for decision making. The process is ongoing and becomes part of work practices on a continuous basis. In a similar vein, Rix and Gold (2000) develop the idea of a reflective infrastructure to support change agents leading complex projects, where evaluation is completed throughout the project and data are interpreted and fed back to help improve the operation of the project, especially where difficulties occur.

Future direction of evaluation

Evaluation continues to develop and evolve as a discipline and a practice in response to new threats and challenges. Globalization will continue to influence organizations and evaluation practice and the need to build evaluation capacity and to share experiences on an international scale will require new competencies and set new ethical challenges at both the macro- and the micro-level. A recent CIPD report (2008) identified future changes in terms of, for example, the prevalence of coaching and e-learning as key learning and development practices, and employers' preferences for the development of skills such as interpersonal skills and communications skills, and evaluation models and methods will need to take account of these developments as they evolve. For some time, the challenge of connecting the outcomes of research and evaluation processes with the inputs that professionals and politicians use in making judgements and taking decisions has been recognized in the literature, and if evaluation is to have an impact on policy and practice, there remains a need to develop approaches that facilitate this. A key challenge will be to incorporate these developments into the future education and training of evaluators and those who plan to undertake evaluations of HRD activity at the macro- and micro-levels. There have been some calls for professionalizing evaluators and providing standards and/or competencies to underpin their learning and development (Russ-Eft, 2008).

In April 2007, the CIPD published a report, *The Value of Learning: A New Model of Value and Evaluation* (Anderson, 2007). In many respects, the concerns of those evaluating learning in the workplace remain unchanged to those addressed by the models discussed earlier. However, the emphasis of this report by Anderson is keenly focused on the external aspects of the evaluation of learning. The concept of return on investment is not new. Phillips and Phillips (2001) stressed the need in some work organizations for a positive business return on the investment made in training the workforce. Kearns (2005) sought to find a calculation process to measure the economic return of individual learning. In simple terms, such measurements could be seen as a more sophisticated version of cost–benefit analysis. The focus for the early 21st century is the externality of training's success. Any benefits to the individual learner or training department are viewed as relatively insignificant if the training does not benefit the whole organization.

As identified by Anderson (2007), the benefit is the extent to which training interventions are aligned with, and help achieve, the strategic objectives of the organization. She dismisses a 'one size fits all set of metrics' (p. 2). Three key elements are identified for successful training and meaningful evaluation:

- the previously noted alignment
- the use of a number of evaluation methods
- working out which approaches are right for specific organizations.

What appears to frustrate many HRD professionals is the belief that training interventions in their organizations cannot be fully measured. In a CIPD survey (2006), 80% believed that their training interventions delivered far more than they could prove. However, only 36% of organizations surveyed specifically sought to evaluate training inputs against bottom line outputs. Detailed evaluation appears too time-consuming and of little interest to line managers. This appears contradictory to the earlier exhortations to involve line managers, as one of many stakeholders, in the evaluation process from the outset.

This is where the future of evaluation looks destined to change. Organizations are more concerned with investing in their 'human capital' (Anderson, 2007, p. 3). One perpetual feature of people is their potential to be both an asset and a liability. This can depend on their personal behaviour, response to management and general attitude to work. Using the 'capital' concept, the implication is of human resources as investments. In order to improve the return on this expensive investment, it needs to be nurtured – only then can this asset be truly appreciated. If it is starved of investment (that is, development), it may well turn out to be a costly liability for the organization. This is a significant change to the historical view of training in many organizations. When times were hard, the training investment was often the first to be cut. Organizations have woken up to the dangers of this short-termism.

Anderson identifies two new models of evaluation that emphasize the importance of strategic alignment and the definition of value in different organizations. The first, the value and evaluation process, is a linear model noting three elements, shown in Figure 16.6.

The second model consolidates the concept of return on investment. It also affirms the position of the graduate recruiters by introducing the concept of 'return on expectation'. The model identifies four values and evaluation practices that organizations may use, shown in Figure 16.7.

Each approach to evaluation could be used exclusively or in conjunction with other approaches, subject to the needs of the organization, its strategic objectives, and the way training and development interventions are then aligned. Each approach identifies a different emphasis in the business; from short-term to long-term measures and from learning metrics to senior management commitment to evidence organizational strategic success.

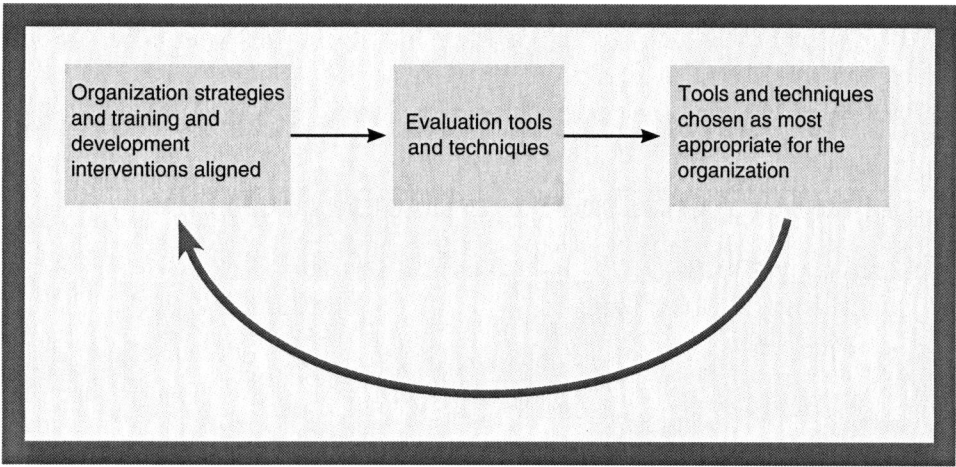

Figure 16.6 Value and evaluation process
Source: Adapted from Anderson (2007, p. 5).

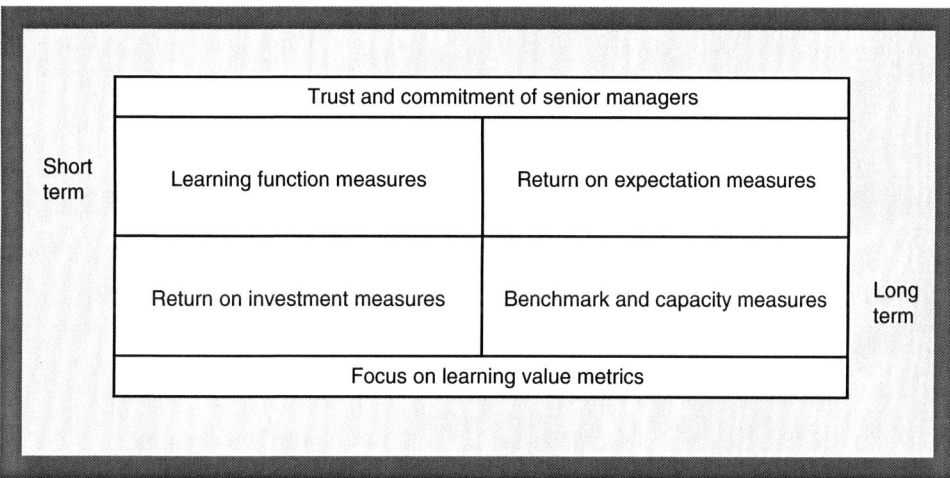

Figure 16.7 Measures of returns model
Source: Adapted from Anderson (2007, p. 11).

Summary

- Evaluation has a key role to play in the field of HRD at a range of levels – national, sectoral, organizational, divisional, team and individual – along with a wide range of strategic, tactical and operational activities.

- Common themes associated with evaluation emphasize systematic approaches, something to evaluate such as processes, projects, programmes or policies, outcomes, impact and utility.

- The logic of experimentation underpins much evaluation theory but recent years have seen a shift towards a more pragmatic approach and a more pluralist view of evaluation.

- Evaluation of NHRD programmes is guided by a systematic approach referred to as the ROAMEF (rationale, objectives, appraisal, monitoring, evaluation and feedback) cycle.
- In the workplace, evaluation of HRD activity at work involves the collection and interpretation of data for a variety of purposes.
- The Kirkpatrick model describes a four-level process for the evaluation of training that underpins systematic approaches to evaluation. Other models give more attention to the importance of context in providing the rationale for training and the support that may or may not be provided.
- Different purposes of evaluation and the difficulties of applying systematic models of evaluation have resulted in a number of approaches to evaluation that take more account of the interests of different stakeholders and their requirements.
- Evaluation can be a vital part of change projects.
- Future approaches to evaluation need to ensure that HRD activities are aligned with and help to achieve strategic objectives.

DISCUSSION QUESTIONS

1. Can the value of HRD activity be proven?
2. Can evaluation ensure that public funds are spent efficiently and for the benefit of society?
3. How can different interests in HRD activity be satisfied in the workplace?
4. Should evaluation become a profession?
5. What is the value of evaluation in change projects at work?

Further reading

Hale, R. (2003) How training can add real value to the business, part 1, *Industrial and Commercial Training*, **35**(1): 29–32.

Holton, E. and Naquin, S. (2005) A critical analysis of HRD evaluation models from a decision-making perspective, *Human Resource Development Quarterly*, **16**(2): 257–80.

Russ-Eft, D. and Preskill, H. (2005) In search of the holy grail: return on investment evaluation in human resource development, *Advances in Developing Human Resources*, **7**(1): 71–85.

Tamkin, P., Yarnell, J. and Kerrin, M. (2002) *Kirkpatrick and Beyond: A Review of Models of Training Evaluation*, Brighton, Institute of Employment Studies.

Note

1. There are important differences between constructivism and constructionism. However, we do not intend to explore these differences here. See Patton (2002) for a fuller explanation.

CASE STUDY

Tackling a training and learning problem: the case of the Hull dinner ladies

Wide public interest in school dinners followed Jamie Oliver's campaign to raise awareness about the unhealthy provision and his attempts to change attitudes and behaviour in relation to healthy food in Britain's schools. Interestingly, it also raised the profile of another group of workers – dinner ladies – often unrecognized and undervalued in our society. Nora, one of the dinner ladies featured, became a star in her own right, and the issue of 'lunchtime supervisors' – to give them their 'proper' title – was brought into the public consciousness.

Following the campaign, Hull City Council began a free school dinner programme, offering free school meals to all primary school children. As part of the monitoring of the project, it was highlighted that there was a lack of training for lunchtime supervisors. Lunchtime supervisors provide supervision for children during the lunch break, both in the dining hall and outside in the playground, and should be distinguished from the catering staff who prepare and serve the food. Existing training was ad hoc and had no long-term impact on performance. In the absence of teaching staff during the hour and a half lunch break, the lunchtime supervisors are often in charge of the school and the pupils. In order to investigate the perceived lack of training, Hull City Council commissioned the University of Hull to undertake a study of the training needs of lunchtime supervisors in 71 Hull primary schools.

All 71 schools were sent a survey to hand out to their lunchtime supervisors, asking questions about their role, their likes and dislikes, what they found challenging and the support they received. Six schools were selected to take part in a more in-depth study – chosen to vary in size, location and economic prosperity of the area. A representative from Hull University interviewed both the head teachers and the lunchtime supervisors over a period of several months. She spent a week working as a lunchtime supervisor and spoke to lunchtime supervisors, in groups and one to one, to understand what was required in the role and how the role was managed. A number of needs were identified:

- Head teachers wanted supervisors to be trained in playing with children to encourage playground activities
- The lunchtime supervisors themselves identified managing behaviour and resolving conflict as a key requirement
- The project manager highlighted developing confidence, understanding the role and understanding children's needs as critical requirements.

Additionally, as part of the investigation, a number of other contextual factors were highlighted; factors which it was considered important to acknowledge and address to help ensure the success of any training intervention:

- The government, in the form of Ofsted, measures the quality of lunchtime supervision as one factor in its assessment of school performance
- Hull City Council reports difficulties in recruiting lunchtime supervisors with the right skills. The work is low paid and confined to the lunchtime period

- Many of the existing dinner ladies left school without qualifications. Few had undertaken any sort of formal learning since leaving school
- The role of lunchtime supervisors tends to be undervalued by head teachers, teachers, children and even the dinner ladies themselves
- There was a lack of integration of the dinner ladies with the wider school team, highlighting the need to address the profile of the role and the need to change perceptions
- Some existing dinner ladies have been in the role for more than 20 years and believe their experience is sufficient and they therefore do not require training
- A number of existing staff have other part-time jobs, thus limiting their availability for training.

Source: Stead, F., Griggs, V. and Holden, R.J. (2007) *The Case of the Hull Dinner Ladies: Interview with Faye Stead*, Leeds Metropolitan University.

Questions

1. Consider the activities undertaken by Hull University to investigate the training needs of the dinner ladies. Would you consider these to be organizational-, job- or individual-level analysis?
2. Why might a training programme focusing on the needs as identified in the case be unsuccessful or insufficient?

Activities

1. Draw on the data collected and presented in the case study and develop two key competencies for the lunchtime supervisors, illustrating the mix of knowledge, skill and attitude in each competency statement.
2. Develop an outline proposal to meet the training needs identified. Include in the proposal:
    - the method(s) to be used
    - how the proposed training will reflect important ideas about learning and key principles of learning
    - consideration of the characteristics of this particular group of trainees
    - where the training might take place and when
    - a consideration of resources and costs in relation to the proposed training.
3. Consider the evaluation of the proposed training. As in 2, develop an outline proposal, which addresses:
    - an appropriate framework for the approach to be adopted for the evaluation
    - how evaluation data might best be collected
    - the value of the training activity to different stakeholders
    - the extent to which the process of evaluation employed might further assist the learning of the dinner ladies.

References

Alliger, G.M., Tannenbaum, S.I., Bennett, W. et al. (1997) A meta-analysis of the relations among training criteria, *Personnel Psychology*, **50**: 341–58.

Anderson, V. (2007) *The Value of Learning: A New Model of Value and Evaluation*, London, CIPD.

Bramley, P. (1999) Evaluating training and development, in A. Landale (ed.) *Gower Handbook of Training and Development*, 3rd edn, Aldershot, Gower.

Burr, V. (1995) *Introduction to Social Constructionism*, London, Routledge.

Campbell, D.T. and Stanley, J.C. (1963) *Experimental and Quasi-experimental Designs for Research*, Chicago, Rand McNally.

CIPD (Chartered Institute of Personnel and Development) (2006) *The Changing Role of the Trainer: Building a Learning Culture in your Organization*, London, CIPD.

CIPD (Chartered Institute of Personnel and Development) (2008) *Learning and Development: Annual Survey Report 2008*, London, CIPD.

Clarke, A. (1999) *Evaluation Research*, London, Sage.

Cronbach, L. (1982) *Designing Evaluations of Educational and Social Programs*, San Francisco, CA, Jossey-Bass.

Davies, H., Laycock, G., Nutley, S. et al. (2000) A strategic approach to research and development, in H. Davies (ed.) *What Works?*, Bristol, Policy Press.

De Vaus (1993) *Surveys in Social Research*, 3rd edn, London, University College London.

Easterby-Smith, M. (1994) *Evaluating Management Development, Training and Education*, 2nd edn, Aldershot, Gower.

Edwards, Z.C. (2005) Evaluation and assessment, in J. Wilson (ed.) *Human Resource Development*, 2nd edn, London, Kogan Page.

Gergen, K.J. (1985) Social constructionist inquiry: context and implications, in K.J. Gergen and K. Davis (eds) *The Social Construction of the Person*, New York, Springer Verlag.

Gergen, K.J. (1994) *Relationships and Realities*, Cambridge, MA, Harvard University Press.

Guba, E.G. and Lincoln Y.S. (1989) *Fourth Generation Evaluation*, Newbury Park, CA, Sage.

Hamblin, A.C. (1994) *Evaluation and Control of Training*, Maidenhead, McGraw-Hill.

Harrison, R. (2005) *Learning and Development*, 4th edn, London, CIPD.

HM Treasury (2003) *The Green Book: Appraisal and Evaluation in Central Government*, London, TSO.

Kaplan, R.S. and Norton, D.P. (1992) The balanced scorecard: measures that drive performance, *Harvard Business Review*, **70**(1): 71–9.

Kearns, P. (2005) *Evaluating the ROI from Learning: How to Develop Value-based Training*, London, CIPD.

Kenny, J. Donnelly, E. and Reid, M. (1979) *Manpower Training and Development*, 2nd edn, London, IPM.

Kirkpatrick, D.L. (1998) *Evaluating Training Programs*, 2nd edn, San Francisco, CA, Berrett-Koehler.

Leitch, S. (2006) *Prosperity for all in the Global Economy: World Class Skills*, HM Treasury, www.hm-treasury.gov.uk/media/6/4/leitch_finalreport051206.pdf.

LSC (Learning and Skills Council) (2006) *Impact Evaluation of the National Phase of the Leadership and Management Development Programme*, Coventry, LSC National Office.

Maxwell, J.A. and Lincoln, Y.S. (1990) Methodology and epistemology for social science, *Harvard Educational Review*, **60**(4): 497–512.

Mumford, A. and Gold, J. (2004) *Management Development: Strategies for Action*, London, CIPD.

Nutley, S., Percy-Smith, J. and Solesbury, W. (2003) *Models of Research Impact: A Cross Sector Review of Literature and Practice*, London, Learning and Skills Development Agency.

Patton, M. (1997) *Utilization-focused Evaluation*, 3rd edn, Thousand Oaks, CA, Sage.

Patton, M.Q. (2002) *Qualitative Evaluation and Research Methods*, 2nd edn, Thousand Oaks, CA, Sage.

Pawson, R. and Tilley, N. (1997) *Realistic Evaluation*, London, Sage.

Pearce, W.B. (1992) A 'camper's guide' to constructionisms, *Human Systems*, **3**: 136–61.

Phillips, J.J. (1994a) *Measuring Return on Investment*, vol. 1, Alexandria, VA, American Society for Training and Development.

Phillips, J.J. (1994b) *Measuring Return on Investment*, vol. 2, Alexandria, VA, American Society for Training and Development.

Phillips, J.J. (1997) *Handbook of Training Evaluation and Measurement Methods*, Houston, TX, Butterworth-Heinemann.

Phillips, P.P. and Phillips, J.J. (2001) *Measuring Return on Investment,* vol. 3, Alexandria, VA, American Society of Training and Development.

Preskill, H.S. and Torres, R.T. (1999) *Evaluative Inquiry for Learning in Organizations*, Thousand Oaks, CA, Sage.

Rix, M. and Gold, J. (2000) With a little help from my academic friend: mentoring change agents, *Mentoring and Tutoring*, **8**(1): 47–62.

Rock, D. (2006) *Quiet Leadership: Six Steps to Transforming Performance at Work,* London, HarperCollins.

Rossi, P.H. and Freeman H.E. (1993) *Evaluation: A Systematic Approach*, London, Sage.

Rothman, J. (1997) *Resolving Identity-based Conflict in Nations, Organizations, and Communities*, San Francisco, Jossey-Bass.

Russ-Eft, D. (2008) Expanding scope of evaluation in today's organizations, paper presented at the International HRD Conference, Lille.

Scriven, M. (1980) *The Logic of Evaluation*, Inverness, CA, Edgepress.

Scriven, M. (1991) *Evaluation Thesaurus*, 4th edn, Thousand Oaks, CA, Sage.

Shotter, J. (1993) *Conversational Realities*, London, Sage.

Stake, R.E. (2004) *Standards Based and Responsive Evaluation*, Thousand Oaks, CA, Sage.

Warr, P.B., Bird, M.W. and Rackham, N. (1970) *Evaluation of Management Training*, Aldershot, Gower.

Weiss, C.H. (1980) Knowledge creep and decision accretion, *Knowledge: Creation, Diffusion, Utilisation*, **1**: 381–404.

Weiss, C.H. (1995) Nothing as practical as good theory: exploring theory-based evaluation for comprehensive community initiatives for children and families, in J. Connell, A.C. Kubisch, L.B. Schorr and C.H. Weiss (eds) *New Approaches to Evaluating Community Initiatives: Concepts, Methods and Contexts*, Washington DC, Aspen Institute.

Weiss, C.H. (1998) Have we learned anything new about evaluation?, *American Journal of Evaluation*, **19**(1): 21–33.

Wilson, J. (ed.) *Human Resource Development*, 2nd edn, London, Kogan Page.

CHAPTER 17
Workplace Learning and Knowledge Management

Jeff Gold, Rick Holden, Vivienne Griggs and Niki Kyriakidou

CHAPTER OUTLINE

- Introduction
- The organization as a learning system
- Organizational Learning
- Knowledge creation and management
- Summary

CHAPTER LEARNING OUTCOMES

After studying this chapter, you should be able to:

- Explain the meaning of workplace learning, Organizational Learning (OL) and Knowledge Management (KM)
- Understand key ideas relating to workplace learning such as the learning company
- Explain how knowledge is produced at work
- Understand how knowledge can be managed at work

Introduction

The idea of high performance working as a route to competitive advantage – in an era of constant change from technology, global and local competition and high standards set by stakeholders and customers – is based on relationships of trust and commitment from enthusiastic employees who are empowered to use high skills and discretion in their work (Ashton and Sung, 2002). For HRD, it is now accepted that narrow conceptions concerned with training and work skills are insufficient – we are in the age of the learner and learning (Sloman, 2003). There is a shift in emphasis to how learning is occurring throughout an organization with a collective core competence of learning (Prahalad and Hamel, 1990). However, between the individual and the collective idea of a workplace or organization, there are the opportunities and situational factors that contribute to or prevent people from learning. That is, to a greater or lesser extent, a workplace provides space, an environment and a climate for learning, where most people gain and apply skills and knowledge every day of their working lives (Billett, 2006). Throughout the 1990s, many managers and leaders in organizations were attracted to the idea that their organization should become a 'learning organization' or 'learning company' (Pedler et al., 1991). By the start of the 2000s, this aspiration was extended to consider the importance of knowledge, its creation and management, stimulated by the increasing realization that many organizations were knowledge based, knowledge was the key ingredient of products and services (OECD, 1996) and that as knowledge workers, employees are a vital source of an organization's intellectual capital (Edvinsson and Malone, 1997). In this chapter, we will consider how this move to a more collective organizational view of learning at work provides new possibilities for HRD.

The organization as a learning system

A long-standing conundrum that has bedevilled many HRD practitioners is that despite their efforts to deliver training efficiently, this might not result in learning in terms of sustained changes in skills, behaviour and attitudes. Mayo (2005, p. 19), for example, suggests that a 'frightening amount of training' does not result in learning, for two reasons. First, training can be divorced from the workplace and so become irrelevant for those attending. Second, the training might not be supported by the context and environment of the workplace. Does this seem familiar?

> **reflective questions**
>
> 1. How effective are you in using training to change what you do?
> 2. What helps and what hinders you?

Taylor (1991) argued against the narrow focus on training through systematic models, which are simple and easily understood, and only suitable in stable environments. Thus in recent years, as environments have been less stable and more unpredictable, there has been growing interest in considering the contextual issues that affect learning at work, such as the motivation and interests of learners, but also factors like history and the response of others, such as managers, leaders and fellow workers. These elements together constitute a 'learning culture' at work. To consider the various factors requires a more systemic approach to HRD (Chiaburu and Tekleab, 2005) and an understanding of the organization as a learning system or what is usually referred to as 'workplace learning'.

This can be quite a challenge to managers and others because of the lack of awareness of taken-for-granted assumptions that dominate life in organizations. For example,

Morgan's *Images of Organization* (2006) highlights the role of metaphor in explaining complex phenomena such as the workplace by crossing images and language. Thus an organization can be understood as a machine and this can feed into what decisions are made in the reality that follows. However, we must remember that metaphors are a way of talking and understanding and are not the reality – organizations are not machines but it can be useful to consider them as such. The danger arises, as Mintzberg (1990, p. 19) argued, when the idea of organization structure as 'machine bureaucracy' is accepted as the *only* way to structure an organization. In HRD, Marsick and Watkins (1999) have suggested that the machine metaphor lies behind the way learning is based on a deficit model of identifying gaps against a hard standard, with little room for considering attitudes, apart from how they can be manipulated to reinforce desired performance. One consequence is the way that accounting procedures reinforce the dominance of the machine metaphor by requiring measurement of the cause and effect links of HRD to the bottom line.

Workplace learning requires a challenge to the machine metaphor and attempts to employ alternative ways of understanding, with different metaphors such as organizations as systems. Thus, while the idea of workplace learning is hardly a new phenomenon, like many other aspects of what Gold and Smith (2003) have called the 'learning movement', there is often a link to how learning is a source of competitive advantage, especially in a knowledge-based economy (Harrison and Kessels, 2004); clearly, the implication is that learning is a good thing. One way of seeing the organization as a system for learning is by highlighting the interdependence between strategy, the role of managers and teams and knowledge transfer (Hirsh and Tamkin, 2005). Competency frameworks are often seen as a way of making such links manifest through performance management systems that declare development requirements that reflect business needs. However, research on the use of competencies suggests that the way they are used and the support that follows in learning is vital (Strebler et al., 1997), which highlights the working of what is referred to as the 'learning climate' or 'environment'. For example, based on research on apprentices, Fuller and Unwin (2003) suggest that a learning environment can be considered as more or less expansive or restrictive on a continuum. Expansive environments are characterized by access to learning and qualifications, career progression, the valuing of skills and knowledge and, crucially, managers as facilitators. It is not too difficult to work out the restrictive environment.

At the centre of an expansive learning environment lies the relationship between line managers and their staff. Recent research has again explored the importance of this relationship for learning and development (Hutchinson and Purcell, 2007). While it is often formal training programmes that are identified, it is managers who provide the structure and support that set the climate for learning, which also affects what happens after training has been completed, informally (Eraut et al., 1999). There is growing interest in selecting managers for the responsibility of supporting staff development and this includes allocating them the role of coach. Thus, the interdependent systemic view of workplace learning also seeks to engender a 'coaching culture', where, according to Clutterbuck and Megginson (2005, p. 44), coaching becomes the 'predominant style of managing and working together'. This view brings us closer to the performance of work and how this provides opportunities for learning (see below). Coaching is often associated with mentoring, although there are some differences, where mentoring usually focuses on longer term learning and development. It is usually carried out by someone more senior or experienced. HRD in Practice 17.1 shows how one organization used coaching to change the culture at work.

> **HRD in Practice 17.1 Coaching lifts morale at the Child Benefit Office**
>
> Managers at the beleaguered Child Benefit Office (CBO) no longer feel 'beaten into a place where they did what they were told' and this is thanks to coaching. Delegates at the CIPD's annual conference heard that staff morale has increased and firmly moved the CBO and its sister agency, the Tax Credit Office, away from a command and control culture.
>
> Richard Summersgill, director of Child Benefit and Tax Credit Operations, part of HM Revenue & Customs said: 'When we inherited the culture in 2005, we were widely perceived as a failing organization, we had lots of flailing in the press and tens of thousands of unhappy customers. Much of it was down to computers not doing what they were specified to do but it was a very difficult place for our people to work. Managers each day were getting different instructions; orders were being issued that had to be obeyed.'
>
> Andy Farrar, Sommersgill's deputy, added: 'We needed a major transformation programme that recognized and unleashed dormant talent. We saw coaching as the cornerstone of that transformation.' The CBO and Tax Credit Office have spent 'tens of thousands of pounds' on coaching, but, according to Summersgill, it has 'more than paid off'.
>
> *Source*: Adapted from Hall (2008).

ACTIVITY

Find out more about coaching at the International Coaching Federation – www.coachfederation.org.uk/. There is a free online journal on evidence-based coaching and mentoring at www.business.brookes.ac.uk/research/areas/coaching&mentoring/. The European Mentoring and Coaching Council's site is at www.emccouncil.org/.

Moving towards a more systemic understanding of the workplace as a space for learning also requires a consideration of how there are different interpretations of the various activities and processes of work. It is within such activities and processes that people learn what they are allowed to do and what they should not do. For example, changes in processes advocated by management as part of a 'lean' production development usually require learning but employees may be reluctant, seeing this as a threat to their skills and their relationships with others (Bratton, 2001). There is a significant degree of uncertainty in how learning can be brought about in

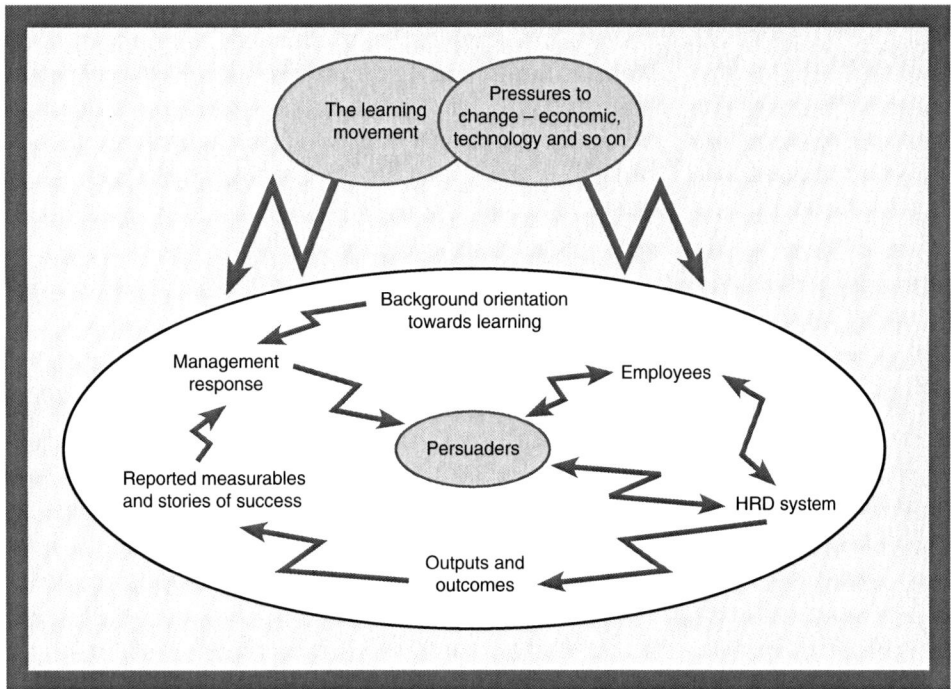

Figure 17.1 Contested possibilities in HRD
Source: Adapted from Gold and Smith (2003).

the workplace and Gold and Smith (2003) provide an image of the contested possibilities, shown in Figure 17.1.

This image begins to bring into play some of the less considered features of workplace learning. There is still a place for formality in the HRD system where training and other more recognized learning events are available and delivered. Outside the organization, in addition to the key considerations of pressures to change, there is also the learning movement, a part of the environment where recommendations, ideas and exhortations relating to learning and development are made but managers may or may not respond to these. It is suggested that some managers are more favourably disposed towards learning and development but this does not immediately become delivered learning. The jagged arrows indicate possible contests and the need for persuasion. Here there are key roles for managers as well as others who speak positively about learning, but there are also those who may not. Even if people complete activities, there is no certainty that learning follows (Antonacopoulou, 2001), nor that a precise cause and effect value can be shown – more likely is the spread of something good or otherwise by word-of-mouth storytelling.

reflective question

Does this image come close to the way ideas about learning are spread in your organization or any organization you know?

The informal system

A systemic view of workplace learning extends understanding to consider any learning that takes place in the context of the workplace, and this has to include much of what occurs as a response to work issues, including mistakes, accidents, problems or just simple incidental conversations – indeed, anything that occurs at work which instigates and sustains a change in knowledge, skills and attitudes. However, when this occurs, learning may not be the word used by those involved. Some of it remains implicit and tacit (Reber, 2003), with little or no conscious awareness that it has happened or is being used. Alternatively, there might be some incidental but just-about recognized reaction to events, or a more deliberate use of events for the purpose of learning. These three possibilities are presented as a typology of informal or, as preferred by Eraut (2000a), 'non-formal learning'. Whatever changes have been made can remain local and protected by those involved so that the benefits or otherwise do not move to other parts of the organization. The important contrast to formal HRD is the way that skills development takes place naturally (Stuart, 1984), in a non-contrived manner, in response to the issues that occur almost every day at work, mainly from the work itself, especially through interactions with others such as customers and fellow workers. This calls for an embellishment of the systemic metaphor with the idea of what Felstead et al. (2005) call 'learning as participation'. There is now much interest in the everyday processes of learning, much of it informal, through participation in work practice. The influence of the work of Russian psychologist Vygotsky (1978) and the social-cultural theory of human development is noticeable. The theory highlights how learning occurs through participation in action and interactions with others, who can provide support to learn new skills. This process focuses on how mediation occurs through the use of 'tools' such as language, social signs and symbols to create new understanding in individuals. The linking of individual learners to their social and cultural context is part of what Beckett and Hager (2002) see as an 'emerging paradigm' of learning, which is:

- organic and holistic
- contextual
- activity and experience based
- found in situations where learning is not the main aim
- activated by individual learners rather than by trainers or teachers
- often collaborative or collegial.

reflective questions

1. Do you often 'learn' when the main aim is not learning?
2. How influential are others in what you learn?

Fenwick (2008) has examined some of the key research in workplace learning over the past few years. The focus has been on the relationship between individual learning and the collective idea of the workplace. She found the idea of context to be particularly evident but with two contrasting possibilities of how the idea is understood. First, there is a view that context is a 'container' in which 'the individual moves' (p. 237). Within the container are the social and physical factors that make up an environment and this includes people and technology. It might also include the ways of talking and the various practices present. Second, there is the view of context as a 'web of relations', where individuals become inseparable from actions carried out jointly with others or a set of norms and values that are socially formed. This view is particularly pertinent to research on what are referred to as 'communities of practice' and a cultural view of organizing (see below). A key aspect of context relevant to both views is how power is analysed (Hager, 2004), although there is less research devoted to this.

However viewed, context is considered an essential component of models to take advantage of informal learning. For example, Marsick and Watkins (2001) provide a model for using informal and incidental learning, shown in Figure 17.2.

The model shows how context provides everyday possibilities for learning, which begins with some kind of trigger. This may take the form of a challenge or a problem, perhaps a surprise. These all serve to create sufficient dissatisfaction to require some kind of further examination and assessment. Such interpretation is also affected by context, which can promote or even inhibit the examination. Marsick and Watkins (2001, p. 29) point out that while the model suggests progression, making sense is more likely to proceed as 'ebb and flow' rather than as a sequence. For example, lack of time and space can inhibit the move from interpretation to alternatives. Context

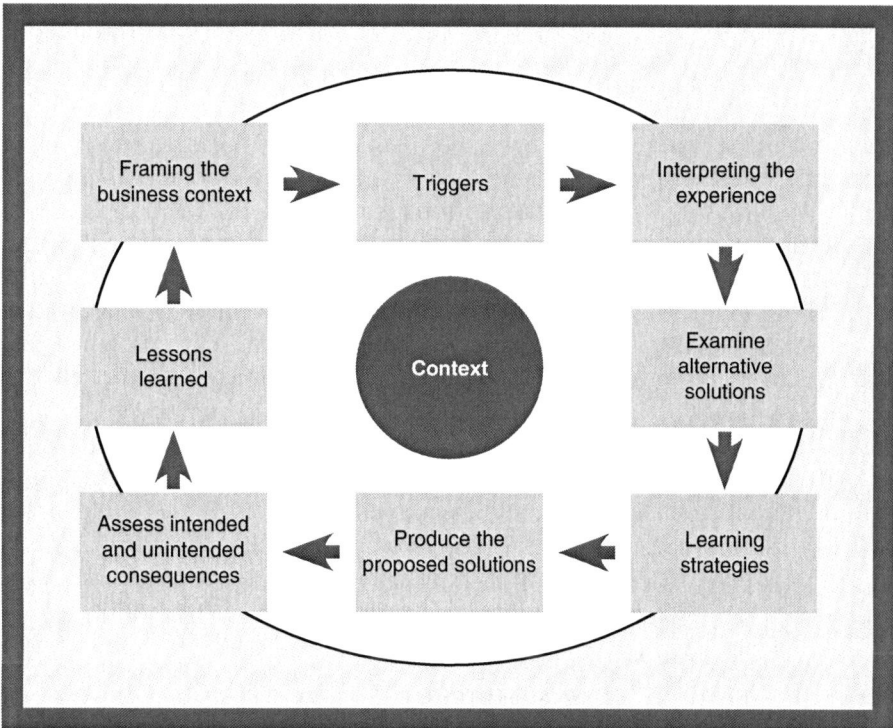

Figure 17.2 A model for informal and incidental learning
Source: Marsick and Watkins (2001, p. 29).

includes history, which influences the choice of alternatives, and implementation may require new skills or special permissions, perhaps redefining roles and responsibilities. There may also be variations in providing resources for ambiguous projects. However, if action can be taken, outcomes can be assessed and lessons learned for future actions. If sustained, these can also feed into the context for further learning in the future. In this way, informal learning becomes more explicit and is available to be used by organizations, a theme we will explore below.

Billett (2006) also seeks to make the learning as participation metaphor in workplace learning more explicit, arguing for a workplace curriculum. A key point is that all organizations require employees to learn, and that it is 'erroneous' (p. 9) to refer to workplaces as informal learning environments, since by necessity an organization provides workers with 'affordances' to engage with learning at work, so that they can fulfil their role as defined by the division of labour. This also engenders various contests about the composition of the curriculum reflecting differing interests and goals. For example, more experienced workers might limit participation if they perceive a threat from new workers. There may also be cultural and historical norms that prevent access to participation, for example the so-called glass ceiling for women managers (see Veale and Gold, 1998). Peers and colleagues will also have an impact on learning experiences, depending on the impact on their interests. Managers, as we identified above, can play a key role in supporting staff to engage with opportunities (they can also hinder this process), although as Billett (2006, p. 33) argues, 'individuals themselves will ultimately determine how they participate in and learn through what is afforded them'.

Organizational Learning

The learning as participation metaphor as an elaboration of the systemic metaphor connects with ideas that organizations are learning on a continuous basis in a variety of ways. Indeed, learning is so embedded in what people do, how they work and the systems that connect the parts together, it becomes possible to consider OL as the source of life at work (Gibb, 2002). There is a great deal of attraction in considering OL as crucial to securing competitive advantage and change. A key idea is that if current ways of working – the organization's routines that accumulate through the experience of everyday working and responding to problems – are less likely to secure competitive advantage or the future life of the organization, then new ways must be found and learned (Antonacopoulou et al., 2005). However, this is not easy and one of the most useful contributions in OL has been made by Argyris (1999) and Argyris and Schön (1996).[1] Where current ways of working are accepted, change only occurs in response to errors or problems that need to be corrected to bring things back to normal. This is referred to as 'single-loop learning' and is the most common form of OL. There is no challenge to accepted routines and ways of working based on embedded assumptions accepted by everyone. A commonly used analogy to understand this is the use of a thermostat in maintaining the temperature of a room. By contrast, if ways of working are simply insufficient in the face of more difficult problems, such as changes in markets or technology, single-loop learning will not be enough because the embedded assumptions remain in place. What is required is a challenge to these assumptions and principles of working, a process referred to as 'double-loop learning'. An example would be an engineering company that focused on manufacturing, which increasingly found itself outcompeted on cost by overseas competition. The challenge to assumptions resulted in a new focus on design engineering, using the knowledge of its workers, allowing manufacturing to switch to lower cost producers if necessary. As we will see below, there is strong link between OL and using knowledge as the source of competitive advantage.

OL is broadly a field of study of 'the learning processes of and within organizations' (Easterby-Smith and Lyles, 2003, p. 9), and while it has certainly been important in recent years, as Mirvis (1996) has indicated, the foundation of OL lies in the development of systems ideas dating back to the 16th century. However, it wasn't until the 1950s that systems ideas began to be used in considering organizations, for example as social systems and processors of information. These alternatives to the dominant machine metaphor of organizations are now themselves taken for granted. The idea that organizations learn, like humans, is embedded, and yet organizations are not humans, but the idea of learning is transposed to organizations as if they were humans. For example, Dixon (1994) adapts Kolb's learning cycle to form an organizational learning cycle based on the generation of information, its dissemination, integration and interpretation before its use in action. However, there are difficulties in moving from individual learning to other levels such as groups and teams and, of course, organizations. Fiol and Lyles (1985) argued that there was a lack of a clear definition of learning at levels beyond individuals and confusion with other terms such as adaptation and change.

One model of OL that attempts to link individual, group and organizational levels of analysis has been presented by Crossan et al. (1999). They argue that OL begins with learning at the individual level, then the group level before reaching the organizational level. There are four processes, working bidirectionally to create and apply knowledge. These processes, the '4Is model', are:

- *Intuiting:* individuals see patterns in their experience that provide new insights, which they translate into metaphors for possible communication to others.
- *Interpreting:* individuals explain their insights to themselves and then others, through talk, which then become possible ideas for application.
- *Integrating:* the group shares in the understanding and takes action as a consequence.
- *Institutionalizing:* the learning at individual and group levels becomes organizational through 'systems, structures, procedures and strategy' (p. 525) with which others can work.

Crossan et al. (1999) acknowledge that these processes, while forming a learning loop, are unlikely to flow without difficulty. For example, as outlined by Lawrence et al. (2005), power and politics are likely to play a role. Thus in the stages from intuition to interpretation, new ideas can be considered but take place against a background of what is rewarded and what is not. Any group will have a history of accepting or rejecting new ideas based on their interests. It is suggested that influence becomes crucial, requiring the control of resources, particular expertise that is seen as relevant and social skills that are in tune with cultures.

Another well-known OL model is Nonaka and Takeuchi's (1995) knowledge-creating model, as modified by Nonaka et al. (2000). The model is presented as a spiral of knowing that passes through conversion modes – these comprise the SECI model:

- *Socialization:* tacit knowledge of individuals shared with others
- *Externalization:* conversion of tacit knowledge into explicit metaphors, analogies, concepts and models
- *Combination:* new knowledge is combined with existing knowledge
- *Internalization:* whatever emerges from combination is enacted and becomes part of behaviour and accepted and so the process begins again.

Nonaka et al. (2000) also identify the importance of context, which can enable or inhibit the conversions. They conceptualize a context of shared space for knowledge creation, which they refer to as 'Ba'. This can be physical such as an office, or virtual, such as email or wiki, or mental, such as shared experiences. The nature of Ba varies with different phases. Thus Ba originates at the socialization phase, where face-to-face experiences are vital for the transfer of tacit knowledge.

ACTIVITY

Read more about Argyris at www.infed.org/thinkers/argyris.htm and Schön at www.infed.org/thinkers/et-schon.htm. Find out more about Nonaka's spiral and Ba at www.polia-consulting.com/A-Japanese-approach-of-KM-the-Ba.html.

These various OL models all imply or require some consideration of tacit knowledge, which, as we will consider below, is far from easy. There are other difficulties with OL models. For example, Weick and Westley (1996) suggest that the words 'organization learning' are an oxymoron, and are thus in contradiction. Preferring instead to consider the more active processes of learning and organizing since organization cannot be directly perceived, they also suggest using a cultural view of organizing to consider the dynamic of exploring and exploitation. This begins to tackle the assumption that organizations are single, unified entities. Yanow (2000) adopts a cultural view, for example, to consider the practice of groups and the values, beliefs and norms that are shared through talk, rituals, myths and stories. What we normally refer to as 'organizations' are composed of a variety of groups, practising or 'organizing' according to the local meanings and understanding created within the group. OL now becomes more concerned with this process of organizing, and learning at this local level can be as much about preserving what is valued and sustaining the life of the group as it is about change and innovation.

Communities of practice

The cultural view of OL connects with the importance of work practice as the source of knowing and the creation of knowledge, leading to the need for a practice-based understanding of how this occurs (Nicolini et al., 2003). For example, one of the most important contributions is the work on communities of practice (CoPs), where learning is mostly informal and improvisational, 'situated' in the practice of the work in a local context (Lave and Wenger, 1991). Learning occurs by becoming a participant in practice. Brown and Duguid (1991) use the idea of CoPs to show how the practice-based learning among technicians can be at variance to what others, such as managers outside the practice, consider to be the correct or 'espoused' way of doing things. It is practice in context that is learned, including the sharing of stories about practice and what is effective. This local knowledge can be very different to the abstract knowledge contained in work manuals or the talk of more senior managers. Yanow (2004, p. 12) highlights how local knowledge is frequently underprivileged in organizations at the expense of more theory-based and abstract knowledge, which is usually considered 'expert'. However, it is argued that local knowledge can also be expert. Thus salespersons and those working in the field are likely to learn about their practice of communicating with customers through their interactions, often in great detail. They learn about the lives and identities of those whom others might measure as numbers – both ways of understanding stem from different cultures that need to be considered in OL.

In recent years, CoPs have been recognized as a source of creativity and there has been an effort to formally recognize their value. In spite of the apparent informal and self-organizing quality around the demands of the situation, it is argued that they can be directed by managers and become more oriented towards 'their companies' success' (Wenger and Snyder, 2000, p. 145). There is widespread application of the idea of CoPs in the private and the public sector, often as part of KM techniques and toolkits.

However, there has also been criticism of the way CoPs have been commandeered by managers and consultants with too much focus on the formation of CoPs rather than the context of situated learning and the practice that occurs (Roberts, 2006). There is also a downplaying of the tensions, disagreements, contradictions and power issues in the way CoPs negotiate meanings (Marshall and Rollinson, 2004).

Nevertheless, research and debate continue about CoPs, and a crucial point remains concerning the importance of everyday practice that makes the life of any group at work, which is not always amenable to management control. Hager (2004) suggests that values of resistance to change and close boundaries are quite possible and presents a contrasting metaphor of construction, to bring together learners, context and articulation of learning.

The learning organization

Operationalizing CoPs has been one of the moves by managers in organizations to create learning organizations or learning companies. Thus while OL is a field of study, the learning organization (LO) is an attempt to make some of the ideas manifest in the workplace. In response, a range of models and formulas have been presented to provide guidance and even prescription. For example, in the UK, Pedler et al. (1991, p. 1) defined their version of the learning company as an 'organization which facilitates the learning of all its members and continuously transforms itself'. They included suggestions for the dimensions of a learning company, which provided differentiation from a non-learning company, including:

- A learning approach to strategy
- Participative policy making
- The use of ICT to inform and empower people
- Reward flexibility
- Self-development for all.

Of course, given the comments made earlier, it could be rather difficult to classify any organization as non-learning. Nevertheless, these dimensions give a flavour of the kinds of activities that could be pursued. Others, such as Peter Senge (1990a), suggested that learning organizations could be built on the basis of five disciplines:

- Personal mastery
- Shared vision
- Team learning
- Mental models
- Systems thinking.

Senge (1990b) was also keen to highlight the role of leaders as designers, teachers and stewards, whose job it was to challenge current mental models and support systemic thinking. In particular, leaders needed to work the idea of creative tension by developing a gap between current realities and feasible future possibilities. Thus the organization could engage with a generative learning process to create a new future, in contrast with adaptive learning, where the organization simply coped with the present.

Perhaps because of the idealistic nature of these models, there was little evidence of implementation and confusion on how to do this (Tsang, 1997). From the late 1990s, the idea of the LO remained popular and even appeared in government policy documents, along with other learning entities such as 'learning regions' or 'learning cities' (Longworth, 2006). The metaphor became one of a journey, possibly never completed but there is a retention of the persuasive appeal of the LO. Örtenblad (2004) suggests that the vagueness of the idea can be a source of creativity, although this is unlikely in bureaucratic structures. To help the journey of LOs, there are various diagnostic tools. For example, the Dimensions of the Learning Organization Questionnaire (DLOQ) is based on Watkins and Marsick's (1993) model, suggesting that the LO needs to consider dimensions at the people and the systems level (Yang et al., 2004). People-level dimensions include:

- Create continuous learning opportunities
- Promote enquiry and dialogue
- Encourage collaboration and team learning
- Empower people towards a collective vision

and the structural dimensions are:

- Connect the organization to its environment
- Establish systems to capture and share learning
- Provide strategic leadership for learning.

There are also outcome variables, such as the:

- Gain of organizational knowledge
- Increase of organization financial performance.

Another tool is provided by Garvin et al. (2008), who present three building blocks for measuring:

1. a supportive learning environment
2. concrete learning processes and practices
3. leadership behaviour that reinforces learning.

To some extent, the development of these tools is making the idea of the LO more meaningful, despite the scepticism among more critical observers (Sambrook and Stewart, 2002).

> **ACTIVITY**
>
> Go to www.partnersforlearning.com/instructions.html where you can find an online version of the DLOQ. Try another tool at www.conferenceboard.ca/human resource/LPI/what.asp.

Action learning

The LO as a journey chimes with a process of learning that focuses on groups with difficult work issues. This is 'action learning', originally developed by Revans (1982) as a counter to theory-led management development activities. There continues to be ongoing debate as to the meaning of action learning (Pedler et al., 2005), but the basic idea is that work problems are identified that are not easy to solve.

Not exactly a principle but an indication of Revans' approach to action learning is his learning statement of $L = P + Q$, where L = learning, P = programme knowledge/instruction and Q = questioning insight. Revans (1998) gave more prominence to Q, which for him also stood for quandary, quiz and query. Less attention is given to P, which also stood for platitude, package and sometimes poppycock. Learners, through questions and support in a group, reflect on questions and decide what action to take to solve real problems (McGill and Beaty, 1995). The process becomes continuous through the need to report back to the group, and reflect on the action, results achieved and, most crucially, learning. The curriculum is determined by the learner against the context of work practice (McLaughlin and Thorpe, 1993). As trust and confidence in the process grows, participants can potentially ask more critical questions and take more challenging actions (Miller, 2003).

Knowledge creation and management

Since the late 1980s, when writers such as Drucker (1988) identified the need to change from the mechanistic command and control organization towards an information-based organization, knowledge and its creation and management have been considered as the source of lasting competitive advantage. The emphasis on knowledge has spawned a plethora of terms such as 'knowledge workers', 'knowledge-intensive organizations', the 'knowledge-based' view of the firm, 'knowledge societies' and so on. Knowledge has been seen as the key ingredient of products and services (OECD, 1996), and those who make, manipulate and apply it are part of an organization's intellectual capital (Edvinsson and Mallone, 1997) and a reason for investing in HRD as part of an organization's human capital accumulation (Garavan et al., 2001).

Information as knowledge

Advances made in the application of ICT, especially over the internet, allow the digitization, storage, retrieval, analysis and communication of information. In addition, there has been a convergence around microtechnologies, computing, telecommunications, broadcasting and optical electronics to make what Castells (2000) has seen as the new 'age of information', with revolutionary consequences. Part of this revolution is the way that information-processing devices incorporate feedback that allows the accumulation and transfer of information.

> **reflective question**
>
> What assumptions are being made about the connection between information and knowledge?

It would seem that much of what is considered in KM is indistinguishable from information. For example, Mayo (1998, p. 36) defines KM as:

> the management of information, knowledge and experiences available to an organization – its creation, capture, storage, availability and utilization – in order that organizational activities build on what is already known and extend it further.

The information as knowledge equation is clearly prevalent in ICT-based commercial KM systems and more widely in a range of tools and devices. Even if the starting point is people, who learn something new, through codification and recording, this can be made available for searching by others anywhere in the world. This view of knowledge is clearly an option in deciding a strategy for managing knowledge (Hansen et al., 1999). Thus many organizations see KM as the installation of networked software and the allocation of roles to knowledge officers, company librarians, webmasters and information consultants. Capture and storage mean the resource can be counted as intellectual capital, even though there are many reasons why people in organizations may not use the KM tools available (Lubit, 2001). However, this is a partial view of knowledge and, as Machlup (1980, p. 27) reminds us, 'knowledge ... has several meanings'. Scarbrough and Swan (2001, p. 8) suggest that the systems and technologies of KM tend to 'gloss over the complex and intangible aspects of human behaviour', including learning in the workplace, where, we argue, much of what really counts for knowledge is created and used in practice. It becomes difficult to separate knowledge from those who know, what Tsoukas (2000) refers to as a 'knowing subject', who always exists in some place of action, embedded in some collective way of life.

Knowing-that and knowing-how

While any discussion on knowing and knowledge is fraught with difficulty, it is common to use a distinction first made by Ryle ([1949]1984) between 'knowing-that' and 'knowing-how'. The former is concerned with concepts and abstractions that can be made explicit and communicable, based on facts and explanations. For individuals, it is their 'embrained' knowledge (that is, knowledge dependent on their conceptual skills and cognitive abilities), as suggested by Blackler (1995). This form of knowledge is highly valued in our society and can become public, available in a codified form, and easily stored and transferred, for example in books, journals and papers from internet databases. As suggested above, this is barely distinguishable from information.

By contrast, knowing-how is personal, based on knowing what to do according to the requirements of the situation. According to Blackler (1995), this is 'embodied knowledge', and is related to doing and practice that can also become collective knowing-how, as embedded knowledge in organization routines and norms. Eraut (2000b, p. 128) suggests that dealing with new or unexpected events 'cannot be accomplished by procedural knowledge alone or by following a manual'. This kind of knowing is 'tacit' and it is generally accepted that without consideration of the tacit dimension in knowledge creation and management, there is little benefit from the accumulation of codified knowledge generated by advances in ICT. As identified earlier, it is also the source and potentially the outcome of OL models, such as that of Nonaka et al. (2000). According to Polanyi (1967), tacit knowing, the key source of this idea, is not easy to put into words. For example, we can usually pick out a face we know from a large crowd but it would be difficult to say how we do this. As Polanyi states: 'this knowledge cannot be put into words' (p. 6). This makes some of the claims relating to tacit knowledge and its role in KM problematic, or, as Beckett and Hager (2002, p. 120) point out, there is a 'multiply ambiguous' nature of tacit knowledge with a variety of meanings. Thus Collins (2001), who is concerned with the transferability of tacit knowledge in science, provides the following classification:

1. *Concealed knowledge:* 'the tricks of the trade', deliberately concealed and not passed on to others, or not included in journals with insufficient space for such details.
2. *Mismatched salience:* there are an indefinite number of potentially important variables in a new and difficult experiment and the two parties focus on different ones.
3. *Ostensive knowledge:* words, diagrams, or photographs cannot convey information that can be understood by direct pointing, demonstrating or feeling.
4. *Unrecognized knowledge:* work performed in a certain way without realizing the importance of this – others pick up the same habit during a visit, and neither party realizes that anything important has been passed on.

5. *'Uncognized/uncognizable' knowledge:* humans do things such as speak acceptably formed phrases in their native language without knowing how they do it.

Gourlay (2006, p. 67) seeks to remove some of the ambiguity by suggesting that we use the term 'tacit knowledge' in those situations where there is evidence of action or behaviour 'of which the actors could not give an account', which is closer to Polanyi's view considered above. He argues that managers can create the conditions for experiences to influence tacit knowledge but this can also 'be in a negative direction' (p. 67), as defensive routines. This view also has the potential to bring KM closer to learning and, as argued by Spender (2008), helps to move theory towards the creation of knowledge. He presents an emerging typology of KM – 'knowledge-as-data, knowledge-as-meaning and knowledge-as-practice' – and suggests that the latter is best placed to deal with uncertainties, failures, 'not-knowing or knowledge-absence' (p. 166) as the source of creativity and the development of a methodology to explore, understand and manage the constraints that people in organizations have to face.

> **ACTIVITY**
>
> Work with a partner. How much tacit knowing is there in reading this question? Share your comments.
>
> Try the following links to resources and publications on KM – www.kmresource.com/ and www.kmnetwork.com/. Go to www.localdirect.gov.uk/assets/other/cd4-local-directgov-knowledge/ to examine a KM guide, including the use of CoPs.

Increasingly, it would seem that the opportunities for learning and knowledge creation in response to failures and knowledge gaps are becoming more evident, requiring new ways of organizing as a response. For example, project-based organizing enables a response to customer demand that expects differentiated goods and services in sectors such as fashion, the arts, software, digital and multimedia (Sydow et al., 2004). Such products and services need to be customized through negotiation rather than standardized for a mass market, and therein lies the space for 'not-knowing' and creativity. To take advantage of these possibilities so that learning can be shared requires devices such as project reviews, critical incident logs and informal sharing of ideas (Brady and Davies, 2004). HRD in Practice 17.2 provides an example of how one company seeks to learn from projects.

In addition, it is not just within projects that knowledge can be created. As suggested by Newell et al. (2004), a team may not have all the relevant knowledge for its work and needs to network with others. This process draws on what Nahapiet and Ghoshal (1998, p. 243) call 'social capital', defined as the 'sum of the actual and potential resources, available through, and derived from, the network of relationships possessed by an individual or social unit'. The use of social capital

> **HRD in Practice 17.2   Learning in projects at Intraining NTP Consulting**
>
> First of all learning is a crucial part of what we do. Even when we have experience of a particular presenting issue, it is never exactly the same as our experience. Client briefs are always context specific and even if we are in familiar territory, there are always new facets to be considered.
>
> Managing knowledge is something close to our hearts and we try to focus on two aspects. Learning before, during and after a project and double-loop learning, that is, having learned from what is happening, digging deeper and looking for insights that at first sight might be hidden from view.
>
> While we are by no means perfect, we try to approach all our projects in this way. At the beginning of a project, we will pull the team together to decide on a methodology and try and draw the process. This draws out learning, before people can contribute to the diagrams based on their experience. We establish clear aims and objectives for the project for the client and any we might have. This approach also allows people who are not directly involved in the project to keep in touch and be brought in at a moment's notice to comment and review progress, ideas and problems so that a team approach is maintained.
>
> Evaluation is built into all our projects as a 'learning history', which is an ongoing review and at the end when the final report is delivered. We try to make sure that people working on a specific project are supported by the whole team without interfering with progress and creating a committee. In this way, everybody can keep in touch and learn from what is going on.
>
> *Source*: Mike Rix (2008, personal communication).

depends on trust and reciprocity. For sharing knowledge that feeds relationships to build social capital, there need to be opportunities to share knowledge, a degree of empathy, help and trust and a belief that the knowledge is accurate and reliable (von Krogh, 2003).

In addition to projects, customization can require an ongoing learning process between organizations and customers. Victor and Boynton (1998, p. 195) refer to this type of working as co-configuration:

> Mass customization ... requires the company to sense and respond to the individual customer's needs. But co-configuration work takes this relationship up one level – it brings the value of an intelligent and 'adapting' product.

As a way of working, co-configuration is synonymous with knowledge creation and knowledge sharing. It is oriented to both individuals and groups and has the potential to link learning at the individual level to that of the organization. Daniels (2004) identifies two features of learning for successful co-configuration. First, learning for co-configuration where different departments representing different specialisms find a mechanism for dialogue to negotiate their practices. Second, through interaction with customers and others, learning is articulated so that knowledge can be shared. Both processes become interdependent in a dialogue around customer and practice.

Summary

- Difficulties in implementing systematic models of training have led to an interest in understanding the contextual issues that affect learning at work. Understanding the organization as a learning system is referred to as 'workplace learning'.

- Workplace learning requires the use of different ways of understanding organizations and contrasts to the dominant image of organizations as machines.

- Informal learning at work includes much of what occurs as a response to work issues, including mistakes, accidents, problems or just simple incidental conversations, although changes that occur often remain protected by those who made them.

- There is growing interest in how organizations can take advantage of informal learning by emphasizing participation to make learning more explicit.

- OL is concerned with the routines of working that accumulate through experience of working and dealing with problems and finding new ways of working where required. It requires a consideration of learning at different levels of the organization.

- A cultural view of OL can lead to a consideration of communities of practice, where learning is informal and situated in practice.

- The LO and action learning are ways managers and others have tried to stimulate and take advantage of OL.

- Knowledge, its creation and management have been considered as the source of lasting competitive advantage. There are different ideas relating to the meaning of knowledge, such as the distinction between knowing-that and knowing-how.

- Tacit knowledge is considered important to models of KM but difficult to capture or even 'put into words'.

- Projects and customization require new ways of working, sharing knowledge and learning in an ongoing process.

DISCUSSION QUESTIONS

1. Should line managers take responsibility for HRD?
2. How can informal learning be considered in organizations?
3. Do organizations learn? Can such learning be used for competitive advantage?
4. Is the learning organization achievable?
5. Can tacit knowledge be understood?

Further reading

Bratton, J. (2004) *Workplace Learning: A Critical Introduction*, Aurora, Ontario, Garamond Press.
Bresnen, M. and Goussevskaia, A. (2004) Embedding new management knowledge in project-based organizations, *Organization Studies*, 25(9): 1535–55.
Davies, L. (2008) *Informal Learning*, Aldershot, Gower.
Duguid, P. (2005) 'The art of knowing': social and tacit dimensions of knowledge and the limits of the community of practice, *Information Society*, 21(2): 109–18.
Elkjaer, B. (2004) Organizational learning: the 'third way', *Management Learning*, 35(4): 419–34.

Pedler, M., Burgoyne, J.G. and Brook, C. (2005) What has action learning learned to become?, *Action Learning: Research and Practice*, **2**(1): 49–68.

Note

1. Argyris and Schön were themselves working with the ideas of Bateson (1972).

References

Antonacopoulou, E.P. (2001) The paradoxical nature of the relationship between training and learning, *Journal of Management Studies*, **38**(3): 327–50.

Antonacopoulou, E.P., Ferdinand, J., Graca, M. and Easterby-Smith, M. (2005) *Dynamic Capabilities and Organizational Learning: Socio-political Tensions in Organizational Renewal*, London, Advanced Institute of Management.

Argyris, C. (1999) *On Organizational Learning*, Oxford, Blackwell.

Argyris, C. and Schön, D.A. (1996) *Organizational Learning II*, Reading, MA, Addison-Wesley.

Ashton, D. and Sung, J. (2002) *High Performance Work Practices: A Comparative Analysis on Issues and Systems*, Geneva, International Labour Organization.

Bateson, G. (1972) *Steps to an Ecology of the Mind*, New York, Ballantine.

Beckett, D. and Hager, P. (2002) *Life, Work and Learning: Practice in Postmodernity*, London, Routledge.

Billett, S. (2006) Constituting the workplace curriculum, *Journal of Curriculum Studies*, **38**(1): 31–48.

Blackler, F. (1995) Knowledge, knowledge work and organizations: an overview and interpretation, *Organization Studies*, **16**(6): 1021–46.

Brady, T. and Davies, A. (2004) Building project capabilities: from exploratory to exploitative learning, *Organization Studies*, **25**(9): 1601–21.

Bratton, J. (2001) Why workers are reluctant learners: the case of the Canadian pulp and paper industry, *Journal of Workplace Learning*, **13**(7/8): 333–44.

Brown, J.S. and Duguid, P. (1991) Organizational learning and communities-of-practice: toward a unified view of working, learning, and innovation, *Organization Science*, **2**(1): 40–57.

Castells, M. (2000) *The Rise of Network Society*, Malden, MA, Blackwell.

Chiaburu, D. and Tekleab, A.G. (2005) Individual and contextual influences on multiple dimensions of training effectiveness, *Journal of European Industrial Training*, **29**: 604–23.

Clutterbuck, D. and Megginson, D. (2005) *Making Coaching Work*, London, CIPD.

Collins, H.M. (2001) Tacit knowledge, trust, and the Q of sapphire, *Social Studies of Science*, **31**(1): 71–85.

Crossan, M., Lane, H. and White, R. (1999). An organizational learning framework: from intuition to institution, *Academy of Management Review*, **24**: 522–37.

Daniels, H. (2004) Cultural historical activity theory and professional learning, *International Journal of Disability, Development and Education*, **51**(2): 185–200.

Dixon, N. (1994) *The Organizational Learning Cycle: How We Can Learn Collectively*, Maidenhead, McGraw-Hill.

Drucker, P. (1988) The coming of the new organization, *Harvard Business Review*, **66**(1): 45–53.

Easterby-Smith, M. and Lyles, M.A. (2003) Introduction: watersheds of organizational learning and knowledge management, in M. Easterby-Smith and M.A. Lyles (eds) *The Blackwell Handbook of Organizational Learning and Knowledge Management*, Oxford, Blackwell.

Edvinsson, L. and Malone, M.S. (1997) *Intellectual Capital*, New York, Harper Business.

Eraut, M. (2000a) Non-formal learning, implicit learning and tacit knowledge in professional work, in F. Coffield (ed.) *The Necessity of Informal Learning*, Bristol, Policy Press.

Eraut, M. (2000b) Non-formal learning and tacit knowledge in professional work, *British Journal of Educational Psychology*, **70**: 113–36.

Eraut, M., Alderton, J., Cole, G. and Senker, P. (1999) The impact of the manager on learning in the workplace, in F. Coffield (ed.) *Speaking Truth to Power,* Bristol, Policy Press.
Felstead, A., Fuller, A., Unwin, L. et al. (2005) Surveying the scene: learning metaphors, survey design and the workplace context, *Journal of Education and Work,* **18**(4): 359–83.
Fenwick, T. (2008) Understanding relations of individual collective learning in work: a review of research, *Management Learning,* **39**(3): 227–43.
Fiol, C.M. and Lyles, M.A (1985) Organizational learning, *Academy of Management Review,* **10**(4): 803–13.
Fuller, A. and Unwin, L. (2003) Learning as apprentices in the contemporary UK workplace: creating and managing expansive and restrictive participation, *Journal of Education and Work,* **16**(4): 407–26.
Garavan, T.N., Morley, M., Gunnigle, P. and Collins, E. (2001) Human capital accumulation: the role of human resource development, *Journal of European Industrial Training,* **25**(2/3/4): 48–68.
Garvin, D., Edmondson, A. and Gino, F. (2008) Is yours a learning organization?, *Harvard Business Review,* **86**(3): 109–16.
Gibb, S. (2002) *Learning and Development: Processes, Practices and Perspectives at Work,* Basingstoke, Palgrave Macmillan.
Gold, J. and Smith, V. (2003) Advances towards a learning movement: translations at work, *Human Resource Development International,* **6**(2): 139–52.
Gourlay, S. (2006) Towards conceptual clarity for 'tacit knowledge': a review of empirical studies, *Knowledge Management Research & Practice,* **4**(1): 60–9.
Hager, P. (2004) Lifelong learning in the workplace? Challenges and issues, *Journal of Workplace Learning,* **16**(1): 22–33.
Hall, L. (2008) Coaching lifts morale at Child Benefit Office, *People Management*, 2 October, p. 12.
Hansen, M.T., Nohria, N. and Tierney, T. (1999) What's your strategy for managing knowledge?, *Harvard Business Review,* **77**(2): 106–16.
Harrison, R. and Kessels, J. (2004) *Human Resource Development in a Knowledge Economy,* Basingstoke, Palgrave Macmillan.
Hirsh, W. and Tamkin, P. (2005) *Planning Training for your Business*, Brighton, Institute of Employment Studies.
Hutchinson, S. and Purcell, J. (2007) *Learning and the Line: The Role of Line Managers in Training, Learning and Development,* London, CIPD.
Lave, J. and Wenger, E. (1991) *Situated Learning: Legitimate Peripheral Participation,* Cambridge, Cambridge University Press.
Lawrence, T.B., Mauws, M.K., Dyck, B. and Kleysen, R.F. (2005) The politics of organizational learning: integrating power into the 4I framework, *Academy of Management Review,* **30**(1): 180–91.
Longworth, N. (2006) *Learning Cities, Learning Regions, Learning Communities,* London, Routledge.
Lubit, R. (2001) The keys to sustainable competitive advantage: tacit knowledge and knowledge management, *Organizational Dynamics,* **29**(3): 164–78.
Machlup, F. (1980) *Knowledge: Its Creation, Distribution, and Economic Significance,* vol. 1, *Knowledge and Knowledge Production,* Princeton, NJ, Princeton University Press.
McGill, I. and Beaty, L. (1995) *Action Learning,* London, Kogan Page.
McLaughlin, H. and Thorpe, R. (1993) Action learning – a paradigm in emergence: the problems facing a challenge to traditional management education and development, *British Journal of Management,* **4**(1): 19–27.
Marshall, N. and Rollinson, J. (2004) Maybe Bacon had a point: the politics of interpretation in collective sensemaking, *British Journal of Management,* **15**(Special 1): 71–86.
Marsick, V.J. and Watkins, K. (1999) Envisioning new organizations for learning, in D. Boud and J. Garrick (eds) *Understanding Learning at Work,* London, Routledge.
Marsick, V.J. and Watkins, K. (2001) Informal and incidental learning, *New Directions for Adult and Continuing Education,* **89**: 25–34.
Mayo, A. (1998) Memory bankers, *People Management,* 22 January: 34–8.
Mayo, A. (2005) What are the latest trends in training and development?, in CIPD, *Latest Trends in Learning, Training and Development,* London, CIPD.

Miller, P. (2003) Workplace learning by action learning: a practical example, *Journal of Workplace Learning*, **15**(1): 14–23.

Mintzberg, H. (1990) The design school: reconsidering the basic premises of strategic management, *Strategic Management Journal*, **11**(3): 171–95.

Mirvis, P.H. (1996) Historical foundations of organization learning, *Journal of Organizational Change Management*, **9**(1): 13–31.

Morgan, G. (2006) *Images of Organization*, London, Sage.

Nahapiet, J. and Ghoshal, S. (1998) Social capital, intellectual capital and the organizational advantage, *Academy of Management Review*, **23**(2): 242–66.

Newell, S., Tansley, C. and Huang, J. (2004) Social capital and knowledge integration in an ERP project team: the importance of bridging and bonding, *British Journal of Management*, **14**: S43–57.

Nicolini, D., Gherardi, S. and Yanow, D. (eds) (2003) *Knowing in Organizations: A Practice-based Approach*, New York, Armonk.

Nonaka, I. and Takeuchi, H. (1995) *The Knowledge-creating Company*, New York, Oxford University Press.

Nonaka, I., Toyama, R. and Konno, N. (2000) SECI, Ba and leadership: a unified model of dynamic knowledge creation, *Long Range Planning*, **33**: 5–34.

OECD (Organization for Economic Co-operation and Development) (1996) *The Knowledge-based Economy*, Paris, OECD.

Örtenblad, A. (2004) The learning organization: towards an integrated model, *Learning Organization*, **11**(2): 129–44.

Pedler, M., Burgoyne, J.G. and Boydell, T. (1991) *The Learning Company: A Strategy for Sustainable Development*, Cambridge, McGraw-Hill.

Pedler, M., Burgoyne, J. and Brook, C. (2005) What has action learning learned to become?, *Action Learning: Research and Practice*, **2**(1): 49–68.

Polanyi, M. (1967) *The Tacit Dimension*, Garden City, NY, Doubleday.

Prahalad, C.K. and Hamel, G. (1990) The core competence of the corporation, *Harvard Business Review*, **68**: 79–91.

Reber, A.S. (2003). Implicit learning and tacit knowledge, in B.J. Baars (ed.) *Essential Sources in the Scientific Study of Consciousness*, Boston, MIT Press.

Revans, R. (1982) *The Origins and Growth of Action Learning*, Lund, Studentlitteratur.

Revans, R. (1998) *ABC of Action Learning*, London, Lemons & Crane.

Roberts, J. (2006) Limits to communities of practice, *Journal of Management Studies*, **43**(3): 623–39.

Ryle, G. ([1949]1984) *The Concept of Mind*, Chicago, University of Chicago Press.

Sambrook, S. and Stewart, J. (2002) Reflections and discussion, in S. Tjepkema, J. Stewart, S. Sambrook et al. (eds) *HRD and Learning Organizations in Europe*, London, Routledge.

Scarbrough, H. and Swan, J. (2001) Explaining the diffusion of knowledge management: the role of fashion, *British Journal of Management*, **12**(1): 3–12.

Senge, P.M. (1990a) *The Fifth Discipline: The Art and Practice of the Learning Organization*, New York, Currency Doubleday.

Senge, P.M. (1990b) The leader's new work: building learning organizations, *Sloan Management Review*, **32**(1): 7–23.

Sloman, M. (2003) *Training in the Age of the Learner*, London, CIPD.

Spender, J.-C. (2008) Organizational learning and knowledge management: whence and whither?, *Management Learning*, **39**(2): 159–76.

Strebler, M., Robinson, D. and Heron, P. (1997) *Getting the Best out of your Competencies*, Brighton, Institute of Employment Studies.

Stuart, R. (1984) Towards re-establishing naturalism in management training and development, *Industrial and Commercial Training*, July/August: 19–21.

Sydow, J., Lindkvist, L. and DeFillippi, R. (2004) Project-based organizations, embeddedness and repositories of knowledge, *Organization Studies*, **25**(9): 1475–89.

Taylor, H. (1991) The systematic training model: corn circles in search of a spaceship?, *Management Education and Development*, **22**(4): 258–78.

Tsang, E.W. (1997) Organizational learning and the learning organization: a dichotomy between descriptive and prescriptive research, *Human Relations*, **50**: 73–89.

Tsoukas, H. (2000) Knowledge as action, organization as theory, *Emergence*, **2**(4): 104–12.

Veale, C. and Gold, J. (1998) Smashing into the glass ceiling for women managers, *Journal of Management Development*, **17**(1): 17–26.

Victor, B. and Boynton, A. (1998) *Invented Here: Maximizing your Organization's Internal Growth and Profitability*, Boston, Harvard Business School Press.

Von Krogh, G. (2003) Knowledge sharing and the communal resources, in M. Easterby-Smith and M.A. Lyles (eds) *The Blackwell Handbook of Organizational Learning and Knowledge Management*, Oxford, Blackwell.

Vygotsky, L. (1978) *Mind and Society: The Development of Higher Mental Processes*, Cambridge, MA, Harvard University Press.

Watkins, K.E. and Marsick, V.J. (1993) *Sculpting the Learning Organization: Lessons in the Art and Science of Systemic Change*, San Francisco, Jossey-Bass.

Weick, K. and Westley, F. (1996) Organizational learning: affirming an oxymoron, in S. Clegg, C. Hardy and W. Nord (eds) *Handbook of Organization Studies*, Thousand Oaks, CA, Sage.

Wenger, E.C. and Snyder, W.M. (2000) Communities of practice: the organizational frontier, *Harvard Business Review*, **78**(1): 139–45.

Yang, B., Watkins, K.E. and Marsick, V.J. (2004) The construct of the learning organization: dimensions, measurement, and validation, *Human Resource Development Quarterly*, **15**(1): 31–55.

Yanow, D. (2000) Seeing organizational learning: a 'cultural' view, *Organization*, **7**(2): 247–68.

Yanow, D. (2004) Translating local knowledge at organizational peripheries, *British Journal of Management*, **15**(S1): 9–25.

CHAPTER 18
Continuing Professional Development and Lifelong Learning

Jeff Gold and Joanna Smith

CHAPTER OUTLINE

- Introduction
- Key drivers
- Professional work and CPD
- Lifelong learning
- Summary

CHAPTER LEARNING OUTCOMES

After studying this chapter, you should be able to:

- Explain the meaning of continuing professional development (CPD) and lifelong learning (LL)
- Understand the key drivers for the necessity of CPD and LL
- Assess the benefits to individuals, society and groups and the economy, and the tensions between these
- Explain the nature of professional work and the various methods of CPD
- Assess the importance of LL and its practice

Introduction

For a number of years now, it has become axiomatic that learning should not cease once individuals have completed their period of formal education and training; instead, it is important for everyone to become a lifelong learner. Although the idea of learning throughout life has a long pedigree, especially among liberal-minded educationists, during the last quarter of the 20th century and into the 21st, Green (2002, p. 611) suggests that lifelong learning (LL) has become a 'dominant and organizing discourse in education and training policy'. Bagnall (2000, p. 20) states that LL 'is now featured in practically every imaginable agenda for social change, educational policy preamble and mission statement'. Impetus in the 1990s was provided by the OECD (1996a) and the European Commission (EC, 1995) and along with other terms such as 'learning companies', 'learning regions' and 'learning societies' (Coffield, 2000a), LL became seen as a response to significant changes in the way work is practised and the rapidity with which such changes impact on practice, with the concomitant effects on the requirements for skills and learning – this is the 'speed of change' argument for LL (Tamkin, 1997). Allied to this is the recognition that economic success can no longer rely on large numbers of the workforce with basic skills; instead, there is a need for people to reskill in line with the requirements of work or to aspire to move into more highly skilled work. The importance of skills for productivity was recognized by the Leitch review (2006) and the UK government's response to the review (DIUS, 2007) and, crucially, it was recognized that the gaps in learning and skills were a principal reason for a failure by organizations to compete in global markets but also for individuals to participate in economic activity. Thus, we can see how the LL movement embraces an economic imperative to compete globally as well as to enhance and widen participation and inclusion of greater numbers in the workforce. The latter is part of the social cohesion argument for LL, where through the acquisition of skills, individuals become more employable and are able to find work to match their talents, thereby contributing to and benefiting from social and economic prosperity. Further, they have the ability to manage their lives throughout their lives, 'from the cradle to the grave' – referred to as the 'life cycle' argument for LL. In addition, learning can spread to all contexts of life such as home, community as well as work – part of the 'life-wide' argument (EC, 2001).

In many of these arguments for LL, much is made of the developments in knowledge-intensive work as part of the knowledge economy and knowledge society (Rohrbach, 2007). For growing numbers of workers, knowledge is vital to the process of work and also the main constituent of the output of work, whether as a tangible product or intangible service. Increasingly, work occurs in knowledge-based organizations employing knowledge workers (Newell et al., 2002). Professional workers especially are able to make claims for their expertise in particular fields of knowledge work and such workers are usually members of a professional body that protects and enhances their professional status, for example solicitors belong to the Law Society. As we will explain below, a key characteristic of professional work is the command of an underpinning body of knowledge. Therefore, in response to the rapid changes in such knowledge that is vital for the claim of expert status, it has become increasingly recognized that all professionals need to undertake continuing professional development (CPD). Professional bodies such as the Law Society and the Chartered Institute of Personnel and Development (CIPD) seek to engender LL for their members as CPD as a representation of good professional practice (Roscoe, 2002). As a consequence, there are now various policies, approaches and methods that enable, support and sometimes pressurize professionals to build on their qualifications by undertaking CPD. In this chapter, we will consider how this occurs. We will first revisit some of the key drivers for CPD and LL. We will then explore the importance of CPD for professional work and the methods used before extending our analysis towards LL.

Key drivers

As with all arguments presented, those made in favour of LL and CPD, as well providing facts, are also attempts to persuade people to do something about their learning. If we have entered the 'risk society' (Beck, 1992), we apparently must do something about our learning. Such arguments therefore have a rhetorical quality (Edwards, 2001). Nevertheless, few can doubt that there are significant and interconnected technological, economic and social changes that underpin the arguments. Change was the principal reason presented in the Fryer report (NAGCELL, 1997), although it is also interesting to note that the report was cautious about learning being seen as the only response to change. It was, however, crucial to the development of government policy on LL in the UK. Of course, throughout history, people have learned to cope with change and, even today, many people are able to deal with change without reference to policies for LL or CPD. Such informal learning still represents the most common form of learning in all forms of work practice, although it is quite possible to use informal learning more deliberately and consciously (see Gold et al., 2007).

> **reflective questions**
>
> 1. What is your response to the idea of the 'risk society'?
> 2. How do you feel about the prospect that you must consider learning for the rest of your life?

The key dimensions of change that impact all areas of work are:

- globalization
- competition and deregulation
- technology
- knowledge
- social
- political.

We will provide brief coverage of each with consideration to LL and CPD.

Globalization

Changes in the global economy such as the growth of world trade and market liberalization accompanied by highly mobile capital, labour and information (Scase, 1999) are consistently invoked as a rationale for LL. The emerging economies of India, China and others are seen as a reason for western nations such as the UK to invest more in higher level or 'world class skills' (Leitch, 2006) in order to compete and innovate. It is argued that low-skill work will decline, which risks feeding a growing division and polarization between those with skills who are able to participate in the provision of high value-added services as part of the knowledge-driven economy and those who cannot. What is referred to as an 'hourglass' structure appears to be emerging in the labour market, where large numbers of workers are employed in low-skill occupations at low pay, while others such as professionals and knowledge workers enjoy high pay in high-skill occupations (Campbell et al., 2001; Moynagh and Worsley, 2005). On the grounds of participation and avoidance of division, it becomes crucial to enable a movement into higher skilled work and this puts a significant onus on how products and services are specified in terms of skill requirements. Wilson and Hogarth (2003) assert that higher specification denotes a more advanced level of production systems, which in turn demands a higher skill intensity in production and a higher demand for skills.

Competition and deregulation

This is strongly connected to globalization, where many jobs have been exposed to low-cost competition. However, even among professionals, who traditionally enjoyed a degree of protection from competitive forces, there is now recognition that a response must be made. For example, professionals and professional firms like lawyers and accountants are able to compete with each other and market their services. For example, auditing was a traditional service offered by accountants but competition and technological developments forced down profits, making it a low-cost service that could be provided by less expert staff (Powell et al., 1999). As a consequence, many accountancy firms have sought to provide high value-added services through an offer of consultancy (Hanlon, 1997), a process that has also fed the development of a 'new' profession – management consultancy – although some might question the professional status of such a process (see below). There have also been significant developments in the legal profession, where a recent review in England and Wales encouraged competition and the removal of restrictive barriers so that consumers can benefit (Clementi, 2004). It allowed non-lawyers to become partners in law firms and envisaged that law firms could consist of a range of legal professionals such as solicitors, barristers, licensed conveyancers and others (referred to as 'legal disciplinary practices'), and, in future, different professions will be able to establish a firm (referred to as 'multidisciplinary practices').

Many professionals such as lawyers, accountants and architects work for a firm. Traditionally, where competition between professionals was not accepted, such firms were organized as professional partnerships (Greenwood et al., 1990), with professionals left to develop roles according to preferences but with little strategic direction from partners. It has been suggested that competition and deregulation require a more commercial and market-oriented approach, giving more emphasis to managing, planning and strategy. Thus, according to Cooper et al. (1996), a new archetype of professional organization emerged, referred to as the 'managed professional business'.

Technology

There has always been a link between learning and changes in technology. However, the application of the microchip to so many domains of employment has been a fundamental cause of the necessity for LL and CPD. What are loosely referred to as the 'new technologies' have had an ongoing impact on workplace organization, size, design and production of products and services, location of production, the employment relationship and contract and so on. Castells (1996) highlights probably the most important feature of the IT revolution, through ICT, as knowledge generation combined with processing and communication devices, with a feedback loop that enables accumulation and production of further innovations. Developments in emerging technologies such as biotechnology and nanotechnology not only provide the opportunity for new products and services but also are considered to be drivers of change requiring new and different forms of expertise. For example, there is the emerging profession of the nanoscientist with the Institute of the Nanotechnology (www.nano.org.uk/).

Knowledge

The generative capacity of ICT is a fundamental feature of the knowledge-based economy allowing innovation in ideas, products and services, facilitated by the creation of knowledge networks (OECD, 1996b) where geography and distance provide no barriers to the sharing of knowledge. The focus on knowledge gives more emphasis to the skills of workers who can be recognized as knowledge workers, a key source of any organization's intellectual capital (Stewart, 1997). As we will show below, most claims for expertise made by professionals and others are based on a command of knowledge, although there are different kinds of knowledge that must be considered. However, for now, we will focus on the knowledge made available through ICT. Thus professionals who need to update their understanding increasingly turn to online and electronic sources, in contrast to a reliance on printed journals and books. For example, lawyers working in the employment field are able to join a mailing list to obtain the latest decisions from tribunals, which will affect their service to clients. They can also download seminars as part of their CPD (www.cpdwebinars.com/).

While knowledge provides the basis for expertise, it also becomes more possible to reconfigure work around different combinations of expert knowledge. For example, an implication of nanotechnology is the need to form multidisciplinary teams of scientists, engineers and medical researchers to share knowledge and create new solutions. Increasingly, experts will need to work across disciplinary boundaries though dialogue and negotiation (Daniels, 2004). In addition, since the solutions to many basic problems are now available online, experts and professionals will need to learn from customers and clients on how to provide value-added services that cannot be found elsewhere.

reflective questions

1. Why do we need doctors if we can access www.nhsdirect.nhs.uk/?
2. Do you need lecturers if you can download a podcast?
3. Do you need a lawyer if you can find out about employment law decisions at www.danielbarnett.co.uk/?

Social

There are trends and patterns emerging that affect the recognition of expertise and the granting of status. For example, a changing demographic profile has implications for the kinds of services that are needed and the skills to support their provision. One trend noted is the decline of deference to those in authority, including many professionals such as the health professions (Kuhlmann, 2006). This means that status, and often high fees, cannot be taken for granted. There is said to be a decline in the trust placed in professionals and a move towards making them more accountable, including a clearer demonstration that they are competent (Watkins and Drury, 1995).

With the availability of knowledge, status can be challenged and new claims for expert recognition can be made. It is increasingly being recognized that different generations have different expectations of services and how time between work and leisure is spent. The so-called 'generation Y' (Loughlin and Baring, 2001), for example, seem to want to spend their lives meaningfully and usefully, based on equity and fairness for which they are prepared to use collective strength – perhaps via an online facility (Zemke et al., 2000).

Political

The various factors above have forced governments and bodies such as professional associations to take a more strategic view of LL and CPD. There have been responses and reforms throughout the western world to education systems and qualifications as well as HRD (Eurydice, 2001). In the UK, and especially following the Fryer reports (NAGCELL, 1997, 1998), there has been a range of initiatives to engender a culture of LL so that everyone is oriented towards skill development in order to respond to and take advantage of change. In an age of skills shortages, there has been emphasis on removing the barriers of those excluded from opportunities, through discrimination or lack of self-belief, to become involved.

Despite the political pressure, the rhetorical quality of the arguments presented by governments is not necessarily translated into practice. For example, in the UK, policies that emphasize opportunities and learning can be hampered by the polarization of the high and low skills requirements of production and service provision (Green, 2006).

ACTIVITY

Find out about the latest developments in LL policy in England at www.lifelonglearninguk.org/. Go to www.lluk.org/, the website of the Sector Skills Council for those working in community learning and development, further education, higher education, libraries, archives and information services and work-based learning. For the Scottish strategy on lifelong learning, go to www.scotland.gov.uk/Publications/2003/02/16308/17750, and for Wales, go to www.elwa.ac.uk/ElwaWeb/elwa.aspx?pageid=2061.

Many professionals work in the public sector. For example, local government employs a variety of professional staff such as accountants, architects, social workers, teachers and so. Similarly, many professional staff can be found in the health service and the civil service. A discernable feature of work in such contexts is the various attempts to reform public services by giving more power to managers to complete change initiatives. Usually termed 'new public management' (Pollitt, 2000), it is recognized that there is significant potential for tension to arise between the values of professionals and the managerialist techniques employed. This is also bound to affect the learning and development of professionals in terms of which issues should be given prominence – professional or organizational. However, there is also recognition that professionals can become managers and leaders within the public sector, with more attention given to including such skills in their training (Gold, 2002). This may not prevent resentment among professionals who dislike attempts by others to direct their work (Exworthy and Halford, 1999).

Professionals may also resent attempts by their professional association to complete CPD. Although relatively unknown until the 1960s, most professional associations now have a CPD policy on the basis that the knowledge professionals use, the tasks performed and the roles completed become dated (Gear et al., 1994). Some professional associations, such as the Law Society, have a mandatory policy on CPD where lawyers are required to complete a minimum of 16 hours a year on activities recognized as CPD. This approach is referred to as a 'sanctions' model of CPD (Rapkins, 1995). Other associations, such as the Institute of Logistics and Transport, have a voluntary policy where the association suggests that members complete CPD but does not invoke sanctions against those who do not – referred to as a 'benefits' model. As we show below, the model adopted is a reflection of the status of a profession and the degree of guardianship provided by the professional association. While there does appear to be some confusion around policies, implementation and how CPD is undertaken (Woodall and Gourlay, 2004), there is considerable pressure on professionals to undertake CPD.

Professional work and CPD

In western societies, professional life and status are key attractors and in the UK it is estimated that around 20% of the workforce either hold or seek a professional qualification. The Skills Task Force (STF, 2000) identified a 50% rise in the professions from 1981 to 1998, with continued growth into the 2000s. Professionals are considered vital to support the growth in services but also manufacturing, where professionals are considered necessary for achieving technological and productivity gains. While professionals can be found in all advanced societies performing similar work (Brecher, 1999), in the UK, many professions have been a feature of life for over two centuries and some can trace their roots to pre-Enlightenment days. For example, law, medicine and the ministry have been termed the 'status professions', with their origins in medieval times as university disciplines to be studied by the sons of the aristocracy (Elliott, 1972). Since then, many areas of life have been professionalized and it is argued that this process has been a key contributor to the view of Britain as a meritocratic society (Perkin, 1989). There are currently over 350 professional associations in the UK (www.dfes.gov.uk/europeopen/eutouk/authorities_list.shtml lists all the regulated professional associations and provides links to all their websites). All professionals are recognized for their expertise because of the complexity of decisions faced by non-professionals in relation to particular aspects of life. According to Dietrich and Roberts (1997), this complexity of decisions provides the 'economic basis' for professionalism, where clients who are faced with ignorance seek the services of those they recognize as experts. Of course, more needs to done to arrive at fully fledged professionalism but through a recognition of expertise, organization and institutionalization into professional associations can follow (Witz, 1992). Over time, recognition of the need for particular kinds of expertise becomes more solid and grants power to those who have the credentials and command of the required knowledge to act and practise as professionals (Boreham, 1983).

> **reflective questions**
>
> 1. Is this explanation of professionalism one that matches the common understanding of those called 'professionals' in modern life?
> 2. What would be meant by someone acting 'unprofessionally'?

Freidson (2001) has presented an ideal type of professionalism composed of five interdependent elements:

1. specialized work that is grounded in a body of theoretically based discretionary knowledge and skill, which is given special status
2. an exclusive jurisdiction created and controlled by occupational negotiation
3. a sheltered position within labour markets based on the qualifying credentials of the occupation
4. a formal training programme to provide qualifying credentials
5. an ideology that asserts a commitment to quality and doing good.

You can use these elements to assess various claims for professionalism. For example, Gold et al. (2003) examined the status of HRD professionals. It was shown that HRD had partial claims for professionalism – an emerging body of theoretical knowledge that underpinned practice, with a growing number of dedicated journals and a growing importance attached to learning at work, which assisted HRD professionals in establishing an occupational division from others. However, it still remained possible for anyone to claim the ability to practise HRD, that is, membership of the relevant professional association, the CIPD, did not grant a licence to practise.

Professional knowledge

It should be clear from the above that knowledge plays a central role in professional work. Here it is customary to distinguish between what Eraut (2000a) refers to as 'public knowledge' and 'personal knowledge'. The former is knowledge that is explicit, communicable and provides the content of formal learning programmes, which lead to certification and professional accreditation. It can also be formally stated as 'codified knowledge' in abstract terms and abstraction distinguishes the professions from other groups (Abbott, 1988). Novices are accepted into the realm of a profession by proving their understanding of theories and models and their application within a range of practical situations. However, to progress from novice to expert requires learning within situations through practice and this is mostly achieved informally (Cheetham and Chivers, 2001). Such 'personal knowledge', although drawn from theories and models, is more extensive and accumulates as 'tacit knowledge'. This knowledge is highly situated, difficult to copy and, like all tacit knowledge, might even be difficult to talk about (Gourlay, 2006). As Eraut (2000a, p. 128) suggests, it 'cannot be accomplished by procedural knowledge alone or by following a manual'. Schön (1983) highlighted tacit knowledge as an aspect of 'reflection-in-action', which is the ability of professionals to respond spontaneously to surprise through improvisation, without thought. He contrasted such knowing with 'technical rationality', composed of formulable propositions within a distinct product of a body of knowledge aimed at problem solving, predictability and control.

These distinctions between codified and tacit knowledge do provide something of a complication for professionals and professional associations that seek to develop policies and requirements for CPD. Clearly, because abstract knowledge can be presented in codified form, through books, journal articles, websites and so on, it forms the basis of educational programmes for professional qualification and CPD. However, tacit knowledge is gained through practice, informally within various contexts, usually through interaction with others – clients, fellow professionals and so on. The difficulty here is recognizing or articulating that learning has occurred. However, for most professionals, it is the most common form of learning. As we shall see below, CPD presents professional associations and their members with a number of dilemmas and paradoxes (Megginson and Whitaker, 2003).

CPD policies and practices

In order to protect and advance the claims for expert status, most professional bodies have developed CPD policies for their members, undertaken following the completion of the initial qualification that allows entry to the profession. Madden and Mitchell (1993, p. 12) have defined CPD as:

> The maintenance and enhancement of the knowledge, expertise and competence of professionals throughout their careers, according to a plan formulated with regard to the needs of the professional, the employer and society.

As we can see from this definition, there are two key features of CPD. First, it is a planned and formulated process, and second, the focus is almost entirely on individual professionals. As we will see, on both counts, these features have been subjected to some criticisms in recent years.

Most professional associations seek to help their members 'manage' CPD by providing guidance on planning, implementing and monitoring. In this way, CPD models are similar to the systematic approaches to training based on a series of steps to follow (Grant et al., 1999). Figure 18.1 provides a CPD model showing a typical series of steps.

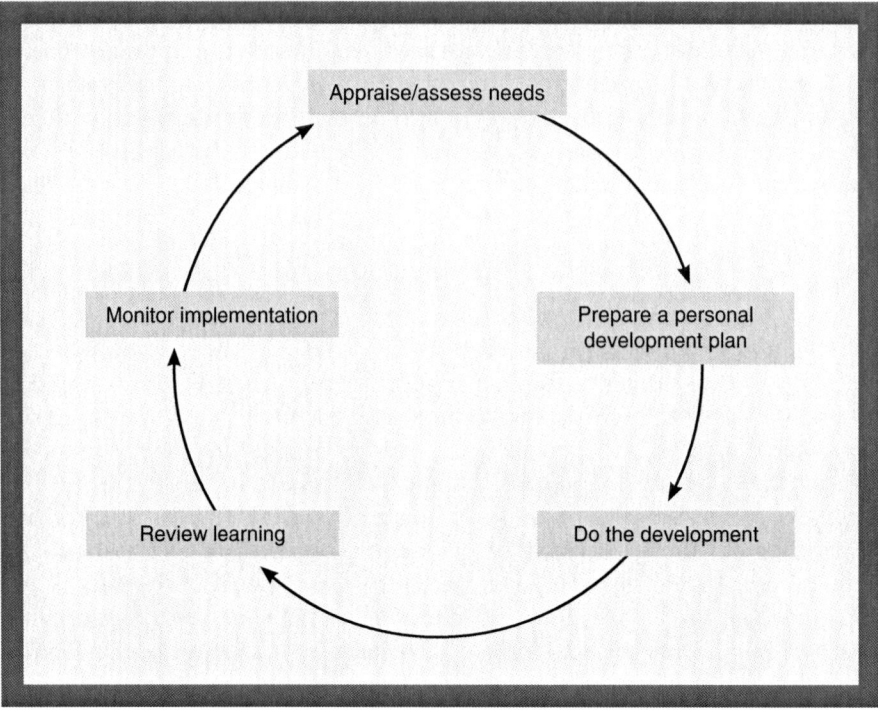

Figure 18.1 A CPD model

Although shown as a cycle, the usual starting point is an appraisal and assessment of needs. Because much professional work occurs in relationships with clients, it is difficult for those outside the relationship to make judgements about needs. Where performance is difficult to observe and is knowledge based, it is difficult to impose performance management processes such as appraisal and assessment from the outside (Reilly, 2005). It is therefore suggested that professionals should take responsibility to appraise and assess themselves. Of course, this also provides the potential for distortion in judgements. Also, many professionals work in organizations where, as part of a performance management system, they may be appraised and assessed by line managers for a variety of purposes including development. For example, Redman et al. (2000) examined appraisal in an NHS hospital and found strengths in personal development planning along with setting objectives, although there was some inconsistency in implementing the appraisal process. Nevertheless, professional associations are likely to focus on their members as individuals and make them responsible for their CPD. For example, the Institute of Chartered Accountants in England and Wales (ICAEW) requires its members to use their professional judgement to:

- reflect on the knowledge and skills required for their role
- consider the responsibilities and expectations placed upon them
- identify learning and development needs.

It is left to members to work out what needs should be met, but the ICAEW suggests that technical knowledge, business awareness, IT skills and 'soft' skills such as negotiation, time management and team leadership skills may be included. It is also left to members to identify how the needs are met by identifying particular inputs; we refer to this as the 'input approach' to CPD. The ICAEW offers the following suggestions, which are not untypical for CPD:

- focused discussion with colleagues
- online research
- reading
- study of regulations and standards
- researching a particular type of issue related to a role
- researching legislation applicable to a role.

Attending courses and seminars would also be typical for CPD, although the ICAEW does not specify the achievement of a certain number of hours or points nor a requirement to attend a certain number of courses or seminars. However, other professional associations are more prescriptive. For example, since 1985, CPD has been has been compulsory for members of the Law Society, with solicitors encouraged to take responsibility for their own development to meet the requirement of a minimum of 16 hours of CPD per year, of which at least 25% must consist of participation in accredited training courses for providers authorized by the Law Society (www.lawsociety.org.uk/professional/continuing/solicitors/cpdscheme.law). In addition, members are also required to attend a management course stage before the end of their third CPD year. Again, the policy sets out a wide range of activities that may be included, such as:

- work shadowing
- mentoring and coaching
- preparation and delivery of training courses
- distance learning and the use of audiovisual materials.

Depending on the power of the professional association, members may be required to complete a record of what inputs they identify and complete as part of their CPD. For example, the Law Society operates on an annual cycle and each solicitor returns a completed training record, an example of which is shown in Table 18.1.

We can notice the way such a record would require the specifying of particular inputs and conforms to a standard view of professional learning, where CPD is seen as a way of 'topping up' the initial period of compulsory education in qualifying as a professional. The record becomes a demonstration that CPD is being taken seriously (du Boulay, 2000).

This approach to managing CPD through the recording of inputs undertaken can be seen as a feature of control by professional associations. Taylor (1996), for example, suggests that monitoring is a feature of most CPD schemes and can become a pointless exercise, where the end becomes recording rather than the use of inputs by professionals in their work. This also raises the crucial issue for any training activity – the extent to which it is transferred to work practice. There have been some studies

Table 18.1 Sample training record for solicitors

Date	Training activity (for course attendance, indicate course title, provider name and reference, otherwise state how activity was undertaken)	Comments	Number of hours credit
10.11.03	Attendance at update on Revenue Law (inhouse) 123/ABCD video and discussion	Provided a review of the provisions in the budget which need to be taken into account when advising on personal investments and will planning	2 hours and 10 minutes
12.12.03	Time spent on building portfolio of evidence for NVQ in management	Prepared and gathered evidence in respect of units on budgeting and recruitment interviews	3 hours

Source: The Law Society.

of CPD that point to the difficulties of transfer. For example, Bolton (2002, p. 322) studied chiropractors' views of CPD and found little impact on practice. CPD was not seen as 'instrumental in improving the care of patients', even though they had positive views on what they did in CPD. Allery et al. (1997) studied 100 GPs and consultants and found that organized education only accounted for one-third of changes to practice and that most of these occurred through a combination of organizational and social factors. HRD in Practice 16.1 shows an example of how one professional, a leading solicitor in Leeds, took control of his own CPD.

HRD in Practice 18.1   CPD in the legal profession

'I am a Leeds-based lawyer with a long interest in and involvement with management. Like most lawyers, I am probably intelligent enough to know when I need external input or knowledge and arrogant enough to either ignore it or persuade myself that I can manage without it. Against that background, the hardest part of engaging in the CPD process leading to a Masters was acknowledging my need for such education and the considerable value it would add.

I have been delighted with the value that has been added both to my firm and to me personally by every stage of the programme; not only has the process been stimulating and thought-provoking, it has generated clear and tangible results in my firm in the form of real differences of approach and insights, which have informed and improved management processes.

An example of the direct application of the learning gained would be the impact of my investigation of leadership as a concept and the development of the theories surrounding it. Before beginning my exploration of this field, I would have put myself very much towards the 'command' style of leadership, although not quite at the extreme of that model. I am now a convert to and advocate of 'distributed leadership', and have already rolled out my first open space technology session and am exploring further ways of mining the pool of talent available within my firm.'

Source: Richard Marshall, Lupton Fawcett, Leeds (personal communication).

A criticism of input-driven approaches to CPD is that they pay insufficient attention to the context of practice and the ability and motivation of professionals to make attempts to change their practice. Eraut (2001, p. 8) considers many models of CPD as 'one-dimenional' because of the difficulty in considering application and continued learning. A further difficulty occurs for professionals who work in organizations that prioritize organizational needs against those of individual professionals and learners more generally (Jones and Fear, 1994).

Because there are restrictions with an input-driven approach to CPD, some models have also incorporated the outcomes of learning. This allows professionals to justify that learning has taken place through an impact on practice. This also allows CPD to be widened to include different forms of learning and how such learning might be shared with others as well as enhancing performance (Grant, 1999). One interesting development by a number of professional associations is to support CPD by the creation of online communities. For example, the CIPD (www.cipd.co.uk/community) has created a number of professional communities as well as providing downloads of tools and podcasts. The Institution of Engineering and Technology (www.kn.theiet.org/) has set up a knowledge network composed of different specialisms, which allows members to participate in online and physical events.

The shift towards outcomes does seem to have widened the scope of CPD and also recognizes that professional learning can occur within and from practice, including informal events and in collaboration with others (Cordingley et al., 2003). Thus, working with a mentor or coach and developing learning contracts can all be included. The onus is now on proving that learning has occurred. There is more attention to reflection, perhaps in learning logs or diaries as part of a process of continuous review as well as recording (Gibbons, 1995). We can see here the important influence of Kolb's (1984) learning cycle and Schön's (1983) notion of reflection-on-action and even critical reflection (Gold et al., 2002).

Nevertheless, despite the extension towards outcomes, there still remain problems, given the complexity of professional work. For example, many professionals achieve outcomes by working with others, so it becomes impossible to attribute outcomes achieved to a single professional, although CPD schemes focus on individual professionals as the learners. A further difficulty arises in who judges what counts as CPD. Professional associations are the main arbiters on the meaning of CPD for their members and this can create restrictions. For example, in a study of professional learning in context, Thorpe et al. (2004, p. 12) found that surprise, contradiction and ambiguity were not uncommon in informal learning at work. One recently qualified professional learned that, in contrast to her training, the work was more 'hands-on' with work 'piling up' and little 'time to reflect'. The importance of such features is that they are all part of the personal learning that we identified earlier as being crucial to working as a professional, which goes beyond the theories and procedures (Eraut, 2000a), although it might not be recognized by professional associations as CPD. Recently, Gold et al. (2007) explored what they called the 'missing perspective' in CPD – how professional learning occurs in the course of practice. Their study of solicitors in a law firm highlighted the significant and powerful ways in which professionals learned in their practice, which added to their knowledge and understanding, both explicitly and tacitly, but also generated new ideas and new understandings that provided an immediate and relevant form of CPD.

Lifelong learning

If CPD is concerned with professional learning, for everyone else there is LL. This is a simple idea, even a tautology, that everyone learns throughout their lives. In some respects, the idea of LL is broad and all-encompassing, stretching to any aspect of life where we learn to do something different – understand ideas and learn facts, skills and so on. As Field (2006, p. 2) states, LL 'covers pretty much everything – and rightly so'. Nevertheless, for the reasons we outlined earlier, LL has increasingly been seen as a requirement of participation in the knowledge society (Rohrbach, 2007) and as a contribution to social and economic wellbeing at home, in the community and at work. For example, in the UK, the Inquiry into the Future for Lifelong Learning (www.niace.org.uk/lifelonglearninginquiry/Default.htm) has identified the following themes as relevant to the future of policy and practice in LL:

- prosperity, employment and work
- demography and social structure
- wellbeing and happiness
- migration and communities
- technological change
- poverty reduction
- citizenship and belonging
- crime and social exclusion
- the roles of public, private and voluntary sectors
- environmental sustainability.

Models of lifelong learning

The broad view of LL finds much favour with writers and practitioners who have for many years taken a more humanist approach to learning and development. It is a model of LL that seeks to help people to participate in a free democracy, especially those who lack privileges in general education opportunities and other spheres of life. It is a model of emancipation and social justice (Schuetze and Casey, 2006), which can appear idealistic and utopian, although there are some clear influences of this model in policies that seek to support learning for disadvantaged communities. Schuetze and Casey identify two other models of LL that seek to enhance access and participation. These are a cultural model that aims to support individuals to seek fulfilment in life and self-realization and an 'open society' model in which LL is concerned with the development of a learning system for those who want to and are able to participate. As a contrast to each of these models, most policies relating to LL, while recognizing the wider meanings, tend to emphasize the importance of human capital development as part of an economic imperative for learning in the face of rapid technological advances and globalization of markets (Preston and Dyer, 2003). In reality, this narrows the focus and connects LL to NHRD agendas and models. This tends to see LL as an aspect of the VET system that is necessary to provide sufficient skills for a country to gain competitive advantage. The narrowness of the vocational slant but the prominence given to it often underlies some of the key debates around LL.

> **reflective question**
>
> To which of these models would you give prominence?

Skills and LL

The human capital model of LL underpins recent attempts in the UK to raise skill levels. For example, the Leitch review (2006) set 2020 as a target to achieve 'world leader' status, benchmarked by the upper quartile of OECD figures. This would be indicated by:

- 95% of working age adults achieving functional literacy and numeracy
- more than 90% of workforce adults qualified to at least level 2 where feasible
- shifting the balance of intermediate skills from level 2 to level 3 and improving the esteem, quantity and quality of intermediate skills
- more than 40% of the adult population qualified to level 4 and above.

We set out the key principles of the NQF based on NVQs or SVQs. Vital to the acceptance of this framework is the use of qualifications as a measurement by proxy of skills in an economy, a process referred to as 'credentialism'. An obvious criticism of using qualifications as a measurement tool is that it drives the system – in the sense that only qualifications count as learning. As Coffield (2000b, p. 5) argued, learners become 'intent on increasing their credentials rather than their understanding'. In most cases, informal learning is more likely, especially for adults in the work context, and this is not always amenable to certification (see below).

We also considered the academic/vocational divide in the UK, manifest in the different types of qualification available. This divide is a product of the UK's cultural and historical tradition, which has valued thinking over doing. However, there is a growing move to remove this divide and create a more unified pathway for learners to progress in paths of their choice. For example, in 2004, the NQF was extended to include academic qualifications up to doctorate level. This is shown in Table 18.2.

In September 2008, further revisions to the framework were introduced to help understanding and measurement (for further details, go to www.qca.org.uk/qca_19674.aspx). This will provide a credit value for how much time a qualification takes to complete – the size of a qualification, and how difficult it is – the difficulty as indicated by the level.

One of the key benefits of the revised framework is the clarity it provides for those seeking to move from vocational education into higher education. This is seen as part of an agenda to widen participation in higher education and a contributor to social justice as well as economic competitiveness. However, there is still a need for universities and colleges to consider how they can develop the curriculum to make their programmes more relevant to those seeking a vocational education. In the UK, Lifelong Learning Networks were established in 2005 to enhance progression opportunities for vocational learners, providing a 'bridge' from vocational education to higher education, covering nearly all universities and colleges. HRD in Practice 18.2 shows some examples of LL from the West Yorkshire Lifelong Learning Network.

Table 18.2 The revised 2004 National Qualifications Framework in the UK

National Qualifications Framework		Framework for higher education qualification levels
Original levels	Revised levels	
5 Level 5 NVQ Level 5 Diploma	8 Specialist awards	D (doctoral): doctorates
	7 Level 7 Diploma	M (masters): masters degrees, postgraduate certificates and diplomas
4 Level 4 NVQ	6 Level 6 Diploma	H (honours): bachelors degrees, graduate certificates and diplomas
Level 4 Diploma Level 4 BTEC Higher National Diploma Level 4 Certificate	5 Level 5 BTEC Higher National Diploma	I (intermediate): diplomas of higher education and further education, foundation degrees, higher national diplomas
	4 Level 4 Certificate	C (certificate): certificates of higher education
3 Level 3 Certificate Level 3 NVQ A levels		
2 Level 2 Diploma Level 2 NVQ GCSEs Grades A*–C		
1 Level 1 Certificate Level 1 NVQ GCSEs Grades D–G Entry Entry Level Certificate in Adult Literacy		

Source: www.qca.org.uk/libraryAssets/media/qca-06-2298-nqf-web.pdf.

HRD in Practice 18.2   LL in West Yorkshire

Lifelong learning, often used synonymously with adult education, continuing education and work-based learning, is a term that has been introduced quite recently in education-speak, but has a history going back centuries. Born out of the apprenticeship and Mechanics Institute movements, LL was associated with the development of the individual in terms of their work and personal prosperity. In the 20th century, it became more associated with political and social development, becoming embedded in community-based adult education. Into the 21st century, LL has once again become more associated with work. For many it provides a second chance. This is a typical case study.

As a mother and housewife, Sharon wondered what she was doing with her life. She enrolled on a foundation degree in e-technology at a local further education college, before progressing to an honours degree at university. With this achievement, she gained employment in a web-based e-learning company.

> For others, lifelong learning has simply been an opportunity to develop their own career, as this case study shows.
>
> Taking the opportunity of the new skills-based training introduced in the 1980s, Rachel took up a place on a youth training scheme in engineering. By studying part time at her local college and university, over the years she gained an ONC and HNC in Mechanical Engineering and is now studying for a BEng in Computer-aided Engineering. This commitment to learning has resulted in a successful career – from an engineering apprentice, she has progressed to become a general engineer and now a design engineer.
>
> In these cases, the individual and employer benefited from the learning that took place, but both case studies were from a time of economic growth. As we move into a recession and associated redundancies, LL will be needed to effect career changes needed for the individual to fit into the new economy.
>
> *Source*: Stephen Challenger, director, West Yorkshire Lifelong Learning Network (personal communication)
>
> Read more about Lifelong Learning Networks at www.hefce.ac.uk/widen/lln/ and www.lifelonglearningnetworks.org.uk/.

A key activity of the network is to set up progression agreements between institutions to allow recognition of credit for learning and transfer. It has also helped in the development of foundation degrees, which have been developed with employers and allow the combination of academic study and workplace learning, making them relevant to performance at work. These are mainly delivered in further education colleges but are validated by universities.

Foundation degrees are one of the ways, along with apprenticeships, in which the UK is seeking to stimulate interest in intermediate skills qualifications (Wilson et al., 2005) and to attract students from different backgrounds and non-traditional learners into higher education (www.fdf.ac.uk/ has more on foundation degrees). The supply of intermediate skills has for several years been identified as a source of weakness in the UK. For example, the National Skills Task Force (2000) found a mismatch in technical and craft jobs and had concerns about qualified adults when compared to France and Germany. Such skills are usually classified at level 3 in the NQF, and the National Skills Task Force suggested that intermediate skills needed to include communications, innovation and problem solving, in addition to the technical skills and personal attributes such as motivation, judgement, leadership and initiative. However, the precise meaning of intermediate skills will vary between occupations and sectors. This means that a term such as 'craft' in one sector might be more or less complex compared to other sectors and be categorized at different levels in the NQF (Smeaton and Hughes, 2003).

A crucial element in learning intermediate skills seems to be their development at work in a programme of structured learning. This immediately creates difficulties for those who do not have access to work contexts due to low educational attainment and a lack of basic skills. The Moser reports (1993, 1999) have sought to highlight these problems. In schools, there have been national literacy and numeracy strategies, but the Leitch report (2006) found that 6.8 million adults had numeracy problems and 5 million were not functionally literate. In response, the government has set a target of 95% of adults to have these basic skills by 2020 as part of its Skills for Life strategy (DfES, 2004) (see the Skills for Life Strategy Unit at www.dfes.gov.uk/readwriteplus/Who_We_Are). In addition, in order to encourage adults to undertake training, whether they are in employment or between jobs, there are plans for lifetime Skills Accounts, containing the power to purchase learning from a quality assured source. These appear similar to attempts to improve adult participation in learning through Individual Learning Accounts in 2000. These allowed individuals to choose programmes of subsidized learning and by 2001, there were 2.5 million members but the programme was suspended in October 2001 and then abolished due to evidence of abuse and fraud by some providers. Thursfield et al. (2002) were critical of their design and implementation, so it remains to be seen whether Skills Accounts will fare better.

Of course, most learning and development is undertaken in a work context, although much of it is not accredited. In 2005, according to the National Employers' Skills Survey (NESS, 2006), 61% of the workforce in England had received training in the previous 12 months but this varied according to organization size. Most of it will be concerned with improving skills or knowledge and there will be some connection to organization performance. This is most people's experience of LL and gives rise to Boshier's (1998) comment that LL is 'human resource development in drag'. However, this is not always the case and during the 1990s, some organizations began to provide employee-led development (ELD) schemes, which allowed employees to choose learning programmes that were not necessarily work related. Such attempts to stimulate adults to undertake learning have a long history in the UK (Corner, 1990), for example Cadbury's provided support for non-work-related learning in the early 20th century. Perhaps the most well-known recent scheme is the Ford Motor Company's Employee Development and Assistance Programme, developed in collaboration with trade unions in 1988, first in the US and then in the UK. Under the scheme, all employees are entitled to £200 a year for non-work-related learning and health/fitness sessions. The apparent success of this scheme, and growing enthusiasm for ideas like the learning company in the 1990s, saw a growth of such schemes and support from the government (DfEE, 1997). Holden and Hamblett (1998) point to the assumption that ELD is a 'good thing' based on a mutuality of interests between employers and employees, allowing the establishment of a learning culture at work. However, the idea that ELD can eventually link to organization success and competitive advantage is seen as problematic and avoids difficult considerations of how skills are formed and products and services are specified and designed (Hamblett and Holden, 2000).

reflective question

If your employer offered you £200 for any non-work-related learning, would it increase your desire to learn at work?

While not all ELD schemes are collaboratively developed with trade unions, there is evidence that recognition of unions can lead to more effective HRD strategies (Green et al., 1999). Under the provisions of the Employment Act 2002, organizations can grant recognition to union learning representatives (ULRs), who can promote training and learning to union members and consult with employers on issues concerning training and learning. They can also establish learning agreements with employers to provide joint mechanisms for coordinating and monitoring learning activities. ULRs can also draw funding from a union learning fund (www.unionlearningfund.org.uk/) provided by the government for projects to promote workplace learning. Wood and Moore (2005) completed a survey of union learning and found positive outcomes for unions and employers, although this mainly occurred where there were already cooperative relations between unions and management.

Informal or non-formal learning

Most LL is recognized in formal terms – employees undertake training, students attend courses, apprentices complete qualifications and so on. However, a moment's reflection will soon reveal how much informal learning occurs, mainly through interactions with others on an everyday basis. Even on formal programmes, there is likely to be a great deal of interaction that is not strictly in line with the formal requirements but probably vital to it (Field, 2006). As we outlined earlier with professionals, personal learning acquired informally through practice, surprises and ambiguity in work are all part of the accumulation of experience. Such processes are also vital to LL more generally and this is becoming increasingly recognized. For example, in SMEs, informal learning – by exploring, experimenting, problem solving and mistakes – is now understood as a key feature of the 'world' of entrepreneurs (CEML, 2002). Marsick and Watkins (1990, p. 12) point to the need for informal learning to 'deliberately encourage' in order to make it more effective through processes such as mentoring, team working, providing feedback and trial and error working. They also highlight how much incidental learning occurs every day but this is usually unconscious.

Eraut (2000b, p. 12) sees the term 'informal learning' as too much of a 'catchall' label that covers all learning that is not formal, but the term is also confused with aspects of dress and ways of talking. He prefers the term 'non-formal learning' to contrast with formal learning. He sets out three types of non-formal learning:

1. *Implicit learning:* learning that occurs without intention and awareness at the time it has taken place but becomes part of experience, used unconsciously in future events.
2. *Reactive learning:* learning occurs spontaneously in response to events – there might be awareness that learning has occurred but there is little time to consider this except through reflection.
3. *Deliberative learning:* learning from events is recognized through reviewing and reflecting on actions, and time is provided to allow this to happen.

These views of learning are seen as a source of tacit knowledge, which has a particular value for organizations in the process of creating knowledge. For example, Nonaka and Takeuchi's (1995) knowledge-creating model begins with tacit knowledge by individuals that is then expressed to others, although there are doubts about the degree to which tacit knowledge can be expressed (Beckett and Hager, 2002). Nevertheless, in many organizations where knowledge is essential to the production and provision of services, proactive efforts are being made to surface knowledge from non-formal learning to provide new ways of doing things (Garvey and Williamson, 2002). Essential to this is knowledge sharing through reviewing and reflecting on experiences.

Review and reflection on experiences are often seen as key features of self-directed learning by adults who take responsibility for their own learning. Mezirow (1990), for example, sees critical reflection as a route to new ideas and 'transformative learning'. This requires a challenge to assumptions so that new possibilities can be identified. Self-directed learning is mainly characterized by projects where the learning is owned and controlled by the learner. The individual chooses what to learn, when to learn and how, and for many people such choices are available both formally and non-formally, according to preferences. Increasingly, individuals gain access to learning programmes through online sources and e-learning packages.

Summary

- LL has become a key idea in education and training policy, stimulated by the speed of change in knowledge-intensive work and technology. Professionals need to undertake CPD to preserve and advance their status as professionals.
- There are significant and interconnected technological, economic and social changes that underpin the arguments for LL and CPD.
- Professionals are considered vital in advanced societies and are recognized for their expertise because of the complexity of decisions faced by clients and consumers.
- Professional knowledge is composed of codified and abstracted knowledge and its application, which results in tacit knowledge.
- Most professional bodies have developed policies for CPD for their members in order to protect and advance claims for professional status.
- CPD is generally understood as a planned and formulated process of learning with an individual focus but there is growing interest in practice-based learning.
- LL has increasingly been seen as a requirement of participation in the knowledge society as well as a contribution to social and economic wellbeing where learning stretches to any aspect of life.
- LL underpins attempts to raise skill levels through credentialism, measured by qualifications gained at different levels.
- In the UK, there are difficulties of a vocational/academic divide in skills and qualifications, which policies are seeking to address.
- In the workplace, most LL is connected to improving skills or knowledge for organization performance but there are schemes that allow employees to undertake non-work-related learning.
- Informal and tacit learning are now recognized as vital features of LL.

> **DISCUSSION QUESTIONS**
>
> 1. Why should we all become lifelong learners?
> 2. Can we compel professionals to complete CPD?
> 3. How can professionals demonstrate that they are up to date in their knowledge and skills?
> 4. Should LL be work related?
> 5. Who should be responsible for LL?
> 6. Can informal learning be recognized more fully?

Further reading

Candy, P.C. (1991) *Self-Direction for Lifelong Learning*, San Francisco, Jossey-Bass.
Coffield, F. (1999) Breaking the consensus: lifelong learning as social control, *British Educational Research Journal*, 25(4): 479–99.
Kennedy, A. (2005) Models of continuing professional development: a framework for analysis, *Journal of In-service Education*, 31(2): 235–50.
Longworth, N. and Davies, W.K. (1996) *Lifelong Learning*, London, Kogan Page.
Sadler-Smith, E. and Smith, P. (2006) Technical rationality and professional artistry in HRD practice, *Human Resource Development International*, 9(2): 271–81.
Yeo, R.K. (2008) How does learning (not) take place in problem-based learning activities in workplace contexts?, *Human Resource Development International*, 11(3): 317–30.

References

Abbott, A. (1988) *The System of Professions*, Chicago, University of Chicago Press.
Allery, L.A., Owen, P.A and Robling, M.R. (1997) Why general practitioners and consultants change their clinical practice: a critical incident study, *British Medical Journal*, 314: 870–4.
Bagnall, R. (2000) Lifelong learning and the limits of economic determinism, *International Journal of Lifelong Education*, 19: 20–35.
Beck, U. (1992) *Risk Society: Towards A New Modernity*, London, Sage.
Beckett, D. and Hager, P. (2002) *Life, Work and Learning*, London, Routledge.
Bolton, J. (2002) Chiropractors' attitudes to, and perceptions of, the impact of continuing professional education on clinical practice, *Medical Education*, 36: 317–24.
Boreham, P. (1983) Indetermination: professional knowledge, organization and control, *Sociological Review*, 31: 693–718.
Boshier, R. (1998) Edgar Faure after 25 years, in J. Holford, P. Jarvis and C. Griffin (eds) *International Perspectives on Lifelong Learning*, London, Routledge.
Brecher, T. (1999) *Professional Practices: Commitment and Capability in a Changing Environment*, London, Transaction.
Campbell, M., Baldwin, S., Johnson, S. et al. (2001) *Skills in England 2001: The Research Report*, Nottingham, DfES.
Castells, M. (1996) *The Rise of the Network Society*, Oxford, Blackwell.
CEML (Council for Excellence in Management and Leadership) (2002) *Joining Entrepreneurs in their World*, London, CEML.
Cheetham, G. and Chivers, G. (2001) How professionals learn in practice, *Journal of European Industrial Training*, 24(7): 247–92.

Clementi, D. (2004) *Report of the Review of the Regulatory Framework for Legal Services in England and Wales*, London, Department for Constitutional Affairs.

Coffield, F. (2000a) Introduction: a critical analysis of the concept of a learning society, in F. Coffield (ed.) *Different Visions of a Learning Society*, Bristol, Policy Press.

Coffield, F. (2000b) The structure below the surface: reassessing the significance of informal learning, in F. Coffield (ed.) *The Necessity of Informal Learning*, Bristol, Policy Press.

Cooper, D., Greenwood, R., Hinings, C.R. and Brown, J. (1996) Sedimentation and transformation in organizational change: the case of Canadian law firms, *Organization Studies*, **17**(4): 623–47.

Cordingley, P., Bell, M., Rundell, B. et al. (2003) *The Impact of Collaborative CPD on Classroom Teaching and Learning: How Does Collaborative Continuing Professional Development (CPD) For Teachers of the 5–16 Age Range Affect Teaching and Learning?*, London, EPPI-Centre.

Corner, T.E. (1990) *Learning Opportunities for Adults*, London, Routledge & Kegan Paul.

Daniels, H. (2004) Cultural historical activity theory and professional learning, *International Journal of Disability, Development and Education*, **51**(2): 185–200.

DfEE (Department for Education and Employment) (1997) *Successful Strategies for Employee Development Schemes*, London, DfEE.

DfES (Department for Education and Skills) (2004) *Skills for Life: Improving Adult Literacy and Numeracy*, London, DfES.

Dietrich, M. and Roberts, J. (1997) Beyond the economics of professionalism, in J. Broadbent, M. Dietrich and J. Roberts (eds) *The End of the Professions?*, London, Routledge.

DIUS (Department of Innovation, Universities and Skills) (2007) *World Class Skills: Implementing the Leitch Review of Skills in England*, London, DIUS.

Du Boulay, C. (2000) From CME to CPD: getting better at getting better?, *British Medical Journal*, **320**: 393–4.

EC (European Commission) (1995) *Teaching and Learning: Towards the Learning Society*, White Paper, Brussels, EC.

EC (European Commission) (2001) *A Memorandum on Lifelong Learning*, Brussels, EC.

Edwards, R. (2001) Researching the rhetoric of lifelong learning, *Journal of Education Policy*, **16**(2): 103–12.

Elliott, P. (1972) *The Sociology of the Professions*, Basingstoke, Macmillan.

Eraut, M. (2000a) Non-formal learning and tacit knowledge in professional work, *British Journal of Educational Psychology*, **70**: 113–36.

Eraut, M. (2000b) Non-formal learning, implicit learning and tacit knowledge in professional work, in F. Coffield (ed.) *The Necessity of Informal Learning*, Bristol, Policy Press.

Eraut, M. (2001) Do continuing professional development models promote one-dimensional learning?, *Medical Education*, **35**: 8–11.

Eurydice (2001) *National Actions to Implement Lifelong Learning in Europe*, Brussels, Eurydice.

Exworthy, M. and Halford, S. (1999) Professionals and managers in a changing public sector: conflict, compromise and collaboration, in M. Exworthy and S. Halford (eds) *Professionals and the New Managerialism in the Public Sector*, Buckingham, Open University Press.

Field, J. (2006) *Lifelong Learning and the New Educational Order*, Stoke on Trent, Trentham Books.

Freidson, E. (2001) *Professionalism*, Cambridge, Polity Press.

Garvey, R. and Williamson, B. (2002) *Beyond Knowledge Management*, Harlow, Pearson.

Gear, J., McIntosh, A. and Squires, G. (1994) *Informal Learning in the Professions*, Department of Adult Education, University of Hull.

Gibbons, A. (1995) A personal approach to CPD, in S. Clyne (ed.) *Continuing Professional Development*, London, Kogan Page.

Gold, J. (2002) *Towards Management and Leadership in the Professions*, London, CEML.

Gold, J., Holman, D. and Thorpe, R. (2002) The role of argument analysis and story-telling in facilitating critical thinking, *Management Learning*, **33**: 371–88.

Gold, J., Rodgers, H. and Smith, V. (2003) What is the future for the human resource development professional? A UK perspective, *Human Resource Development International*, **6**(4): 437–56.

Gold, J., Thorpe, R., Woodall, J. and Sadler-Smith, E. (2007) Continuing professional development in the legal profession: a practice-based learning perspective, *Management Learning*, **38**(2): 235–50.

Gourlay, S. (2006) Towards conceptual clarity for 'tacit knowledge': a review of empirical studies, *Knowledge Management Research and Practice*, **4**: 60–9.
Grant, J. (1999) Measurement of learning outcome in continuing professional development, *Journal of Continuing Education in the Health Professions*, **19**: 214–21.
Grant, J., Chambers, E. and Jackson, G. (eds) (1999) *The Good CPD Guide: A Practical Guide to Managed CPD*, Sutton, Reed Business Information.
Green, A. (2002) The many faces of lifelong learning: recent education policy trends in Europe, *Journal of Education Policy*, **17**(6): 611–26.
Green, A. (2006) Models of lifelong learning and the 'knowledge society', *Journal of Comparative Education*, **36**(3): 307–25.
Green, F., Machin, S. and Wilkinson, D. (1999) Trade unions and training practices in British workplaces, *Industrial and Labor Relations Review*, **52**(2): 179–95.
Greenwood, R., Hinings, C.R. and Brown, J. (1990) 'P2 Form' strategic management: corporate practices in professional partnerships, *Academy of Management Journal*, **33**(4): 725–55.
Hamblett, J. and Holden, R. (2000) Employee-led development: another piece of left luggage?, *Personnel Review*, **29**(4): 509–20.
Hanlon, G. (1997) A shifting professionalism: accountancy, in J. Broadbent, M. Dietrich and J. Roberts (eds) *The End of the Professions?*, London, Routledge.
Holden, R. and Hamblett, J. (1998) Learning lessons from non-work related learning, *Journal of Workplace Learning*, **10**(5): 241–50.
Jones, N. and Fear, N. (1994) Continuing professional development: perspectives from human resource professionals, *Personnel Review*, **23**(8): 49–60.
Kolb, D. (1984) *Experiential Learning*, Englewood Cliffs, NJ, Prentice Hall.
Kuhlmann, E. (2006) Traces of doubt and sources of trust: health professions in an uncertain society, *Current Sociology*, **54**(4): 607–20.
Leitch, S. (2006) *Prosperity for all in the Global Economy: World Class Skills*, London, HM Treasury.
Loughlin, C. and Barling, J. (2001) Young workers' work values, attitudes, and behaviours, *Journal of Occupational and Organizational Psychology*, **74**(4): 543–58.
Madden, C.A. and Mitchell, V.A. (1993) *Professions, Standards and Competence: A Survey of Continuing Education for the Profession*, Department of Continuing Education, University of Bristol.
Marsick, V. and Watkins, K.E. (1990) Towards a theory of informal and incidental learning, in V. Marsick and K.E. Watkins (eds) *Informal and Incidental Learning in the Workplace*, London, Routledge.
Megginson, D. and Whitaker, V. (2003) *Continuing Professional Development*, London, CIPD.
Mezirow, J. (1990) *Fostering Critical Reflection*, San Francisco, Jossey-Bass.
Moser, C. (1993) *Learning to Succeed: A Radical Look at Education Today and a Strategy for the Future*, London, Heinemann.
Moser, C. (1999) *A Fresh Start: Improving Literacy and Numeracy*, London, DfEE.
Moynagh, M. and Worsley, R. (2005) *Working in the Twenty-first Century*, Leeds, ESRC Future of Work Programme.
NAGCELL (1997) *Learning for the 21st Century*, www.lifelonglearning.co.uk/nagcell/.
NAGCELL (1998) *Creating Learning Cultures: Next Steps in Achieving the Learning Age*, www.lifelonglearning.co.uk/nagcell2/index.htm.
National Skills Task Force (2000) *Skills for All: Research Report from the National Skills Task Force*, London, DfEE.
NESS (National Employers' Skills Survey) (2006) *National Employers' Skills Survey*, Coventry, Learning and Skills Council.
Newell, S., Robertson, M., Scarbrough, H. and Swann, J. (2002) *Managing Knowledge Work*, Basingstoke, Palgrave – now Palgrave Macmillan.
Nonaka, I. and Takeuchi, H. (1995) *The Knowledge-creating Company*, New York, Oxford University Press.
OECD (Organization for Economic Co-operation and Development) (1996a) *Lifelong Learning for All*, Paris, OECD.
OECD (Organization for Economic Co-operation and Development) (1996b) *The Knowledge-based Economy*, Paris, OECD.

Perkin, H. (1989) *The Rise of the Professional Society: England Since 1880*, London, Routledge.
Pollitt, C. (2000) Is the emperor in his new underwear?: An analysis of the impacts of public management reform, *Public Management*, **2**(2): 181–99.
Powell, M.J., Brock, D.M. and Hinings, C.R. (1999) The changing professional organization, in D.M Brock, M.J. Powell and C.R. Hinings (eds) *Restructuring the Professional Organization*, London, Routledge.
Preston, R. and Dyer, C. (2003) Human capital, social capital and lifelong learning: an editorial introduction, *Compare*, **33**(4): 429–36.
Rapkins, C. (1995) Professional bodies and continuing professional development, in S. Clyne (ed.) *Continuing Professional Development*, London, Kogan Page.
Redman, T., Snape, E., Thompson, D. and Ka-Ching Yan, F. (2000) Performance appraisal in an NHS hospital, *Human Resource Management Journal*, **10**(1): 48–62.
Reilly, P. (2005) Get the best from knowledge workers, *People Management*, 29 September: 52–3.
Rohrbach, D. (2007) The development of knowledge societies in 19 OECD countries between 1970 and 2002, *Social Science Information*, **46**(4): 655–89.
Roscoe, J. (2002) Continuing professional development in higher education, *Human Resource Development International*, **5**: 3–10.
Scase, R. (1999) *Britain Towards 2010: The Changing Business Environment*, London, ESRC.
Schön, D.A. (1983) *The Reflective Practitioner: How Professionals Think in Action*, London, Maurice Temple Smith.
Schuetze, H. and Casey, C. (2006) Models and meanings of lifelong learning: progress and barriers on the road to a learning society, *Compare*, **36**(3): 279–87.
Smeaton, B. and Hughes, M. (2003) *A Basis for Skills: Investigating Intermediate Skills*, London, Learning and Skills Development Agency.
Stewart, T.A. (1997) *Intellectual Capital: The New Wealth of Organizations*, New York, Doubleday.
STF (Skills Task Force) (2000) *Skills for All: Research Report from the National Skills Task Force*, London, DfEE.
Tamkin, P. (1997) Lifelong learning: a question of privilege?, *Industrial and Commercial Training*, **29**(6): 184–6.
Taylor, N. (1996) Professionalism and monitoring CPD: Kafka revisited, *Planning Practice and Research*, **11**(4): 379–89.
Thorpe, R., Woodall, J., Sadler-Smith, E. and Gold, J. (2004) Studying CPD in professional life, *British Journal of Occupational Learning*, **2**(2): 3–20.
Thursfield, D., Smith, V., Holden, R. and Hamblett, J. (2002) Individual learning accounts: honourable intentions, ignoble utility?, *Research in Post-compulsory Education*, **7**(2): 133–46.
Watkins, J. and Drury, L. (1995) The professions in the 1990s, in S. Clyne (ed.) *Continuing Professional Development*, London, Kogan Page.
Wilson, J.P., Blewitt, J. and Moody, D. (2005) Reconfiguring higher education: the case of foundation degrees, *Education and Training*, **47**(2): 112–23.
Wilson, R. and Hogarth, T. (eds) (2003) *Tackling the Low Skills Equilibrium: A Review of Issues and some new Evidence*, Coventry, University of Warwick, Institute of Employment Research.
Witz, A. (1992) *Professions and Patriarchy*, London, Routledge.
Wood, H. and Moore, S. (2005) *An Evaluation of the UK Union Learning Fund: Its Impact on Unions and Employers*, London Metropolitan University, Working Lives Research Institute.
Woodall, J. and Gourlay, S.N. (2004) The relationship between professional learning and continuing professional development in the UK: a critical review of the literature, in J. Woodall, M. Lee and J. Steward (eds) *New Frontiers in HRD*, London, Routledge.
Zemke, R., Raines, C. and Filipczak, B. (2000) *Generations at Work: Managing the Clash of Veterans, Boomers, Xers, and Nexters in your Workplace*, Washington, DC, American Management Association.

Index

3 (mobile phone company), 280
3M, 127
16 Personality Factor Test (16PF), 328, 329
16PF questionnaire, 298

A
Ability tests, 294, 295
Absenteeism, 60, 198
   diversity management, 144–145
   reward management, 399
   work–life balance, 166, 173–175, 178
Academic disciplines, 435–436
Academic titles, 432
Academy of Human Resource Development, 432
Accenture, 213
Acceptability in performance management, 358–360, 366–367, 368–369, 372, 374
Accountability, 150, 356
Accountants, competition, 550
Accounting, 229–231
Achievement tests, 328
Action evaluation, 516
Action learning, 485, 537
Added value, 9, 230
Administrative experts, 30
Advertising, 315–316, 320, 321
   in recruitment, 279
Affirmative action, 141–142, 143
Affordability, 388
Age, 4, 37, 272
   discrimination, 227
   Regulations, 14
Age and ageism, 54, 57, 64, 169–170
   diversity management, 140–141, 148, 155
   work–life balance, 166–167, 169–170, 172–173, 175, 180
Age Discrimination in Employment Act (1967) (USA), 170
Agency and agency theory, 314, 338, 390, 417
Alcoa, 252
Algorithm, 78–79
American Society of Training and Development, 433–434
Amersham International, 365
Annualized hours, 209
Antenatal care, 13
Anthropology, 435, 436
Application forms, 323
Appraisal, 556
   assessment online, 298–299
   culture, 122, 125–126
Apprenticeships, 565
Aptitude tests, 295, 328
Artefacts, 108, 110, 114, 120
Asia
   culture, 103
Assessment centres, 299–301, 331–332, 342
Assessment of needs, 556
Atomic Energy Authority, 365
Attitudes to work, 214–215
Attraction
   framework, 278
   recruitment, 271–284
Auditing, 550
Australian Cladding Company (ACC), 261–263
Austria, 211
Authenticity, 224
Automobile industry, 247
   Hyundai, 58

B
B & Q, 171
Ba, 534
Balanced scorecard (BSC), 358–359, 367, 403
Balanced Scorecard Institute, 512
Banking and finance, 182–185, 357
   HSBC, 145, 150
Barclays Bank, 225

Baringa Partners, 100, 124
Base pay, 386–387, 388, 393–399, 400–401, 416
Basic assumptions, 108, 110
BC Tel, 148
Behaviour
　human, 435, 436
Behaviour description interviews, 290
Behaviour observation scales (BOSs), 366, 375
Belbin Team Role, 298
Belgium, 281
Beliefs, 101, 103, 105, 108, 110, 112, 114
Benefits, 386–387, 399–400, 415–416
　flexible, 400
　voluntary, 399–400
Bentham, Jeremy, 118
Best fit approach, 83, 87–88, 90, 91, 125
Best practice approach, 4, 83, 87–88, 90, 91
Best Workplace Award, 100
Bias, 359, 361, 365, 366, 372
Big Outdoors, 130–131
Binge-working culture, 100
Biodata, 288–289, 327, 332
Biotechnology, 551
Bonus culture, 36, 105
Bonus payments, 402, 404
Boundaryless career, 221
BP, 271
Branding, 269, 270, 271, 277
British Airways, 121, 213, 281
British Psychological Society, 299
Broadbanding, 398
BT, 213, 217, 227, 228, 279
Bullying
　call centres, 211
Bupa, 111
　Personal Best (learning programme), 489
Business case approach, 140, 143
Business games, 482
Business partner model, 456–458
　line management responsibility for staff development, 460–461
　subfunctions, 458
　in UK civil service, 457
Business process re-engineering (BPR), 201
Business strategy, 445
Business-to-employee (B2E) portals, 205

C
Cadbury's, non-work-related learning, 564
Call centres, 180, 256
　bullying, 211
　India, 200
　staff turnover, 278
　surveillance, 117
　workforce planning, 210, 211, 212

Canada, 302
　culture, 106
　gender bias, 35
　sustainability, 127
Canterbury Hospital, 37–40
Capitalism, 5, 12, 29, 33, 37, 58, 59, 336
　employment relationship, 9
Capitalist modernity, 102
Career management, 202, 221, 223
　talent, 217
Career Value Map, 93
Carers, 166, 167, 173, 175, 177–178
　rights of, 208
Case studies, as training/learning method, 479–481
Casual or temporary workers, 254
Causation, theory of, 496
CCTV, 118
Centres of excellence, 458
Ceremonies, 114, 120
Challenge, 224
Change, 450–455
　continuous, 451
　conversations contributing to, 453
　facilitators of, 455
　first-order, 451–452
　incremental vs. transformational, 450–451
　leading change, 452
　vs. learning, 450
　proactive/reactive organizations, 452
　responses to, 454–455
　second-order, 451–452
　third-order, 451–452
　transformational, 450, 451
　types of, 450–451
Change agents, 30, 454–455
　competencies, 455
Change management, models of, 452–454
Change masters, 454
Change programmes, 448
Changing roles, 14
Chartered Institute of Personnel and Development (CIPD), 432, 444, 548
　online communities, 559
Chief Human Resources Officers (CHROs), 20
Child Benefit Office (CBO)
　coaching, 527–528
China
　manufacturing, 28
Chiropractors, views of CPD, 558
CHROs, 20
Clemenger, 407
Climate change, 4, 52
Climate compared with culture, 105
Clothing industry, 53

Coaching, 439, 480, 484, 488, 527–528
  Child Benefit Office, 528
  culture, 527–528
  definition, 488
  evidence-based, 528
Co-configuration, 541
Cognitive ability tests (CATs), 328
Cognitive dissonance theory, 361
Cognitive evaluation theory, 390–391
Collective bargaining
  employment relationship, 12
Collective bargaining, 392, 410, 413–414, 417
  SHRM, 89, 90
Collective learning, 444
Collective performance plans, 400–402, 403–404, 409
Collectivism, 6, 55, 58, 70, 103, 402, 403
Commissions, 401, 402
Commitment, 4, 8, 15
  attitudes, 215
  control, 10
  Guest model of HRM, 24, 25
  organizational culture, 100, 104, 112, 119
  staff turnover, 199–200
Commonwealth Bank, 252
Communication, 411–412
  change and, 453
  reward management, 386, 393, 411–412
Communities of practice (CoPs), 534–535
Community Environment Fund (CEF), 38
Competencies, 274, 275, 284, 292–293
  definition, 274
  examples, 275
Competency assessment, 397–399
Competency frameworks, 269–270, 275, 293, 527
Competition, 550
  on costs not skills, 462–463
Competitive advantage, 52, 62, 64
  SHRM, 77–78, 87, 90, 91
Competitive strategies, 82–84
Compliance, 24
Comprehensive Spending Review, 215
Compressed hours, 209
Computer software, 197, 204
Comte, Auguste, 32, 112
Confederation of British Industry (CBI), 227
Configurational approach, 83
Conflict, 10, 114, 116
  paradigm, 32, 34
Constructivism, 497–498
Construct theories, 361
Contextualization, 49–64, 357, 358
  case study, 50, 57, 65–66
Contingencies affecting management, 18

Contingency perspective, 76, 83, 87
Continuing professional
  benefits model, 553
  change, dimensions of, 549–553
  definition, 555–556
  development (CPD), 548
  discussion questions, 567
  further reading, 567
  input approach to, 557–558
  key drivers, 549–553
  key features, 555–556
  legal profession, 558
  missing perspective, 559
  model, 553
  online communities, 559
  policies and practices, 555–559
  political factors, 552–553
  professional work and, 553–559
  sanctions model, 553
  social trends, 552
  summary, 566–567
Continuous improvement teams (CITs), 451
Contract of Employment Acts (1963/1972), 14
Contracts of employment, 12, 15
Contract workers, 214
Control, 4
  commitment, 10
  culture, 114, 115, 116, 120
Conversations, change and, 453
Cooperation, 4, 10
Core workforce, 207, 253
Corporate Manslaughter and
  Corporate Homicide Act (2007), 14
Corporate Rabobank, 148
Corporate social responsibility (CSR), 166
Corporate social responsibility (CSR), 216
Corporate universities (CUs), 458
  description, 458
  key features, 458
  rebadged training departments, 459
Cost-based competition, 463
Cost leadership, 84
Costs
  recruitment, 272, 280
  selection, 284
  training, 284
Counterculture, 114
Creativity, 145, 150
Credentialism, 561
Credentials, 291–292
Critical HRD (CHRD), 440
Critical HRM (CHRM), 9, 37, 40
Critical perspectives, 114–117, 118
Critical reflection, 559, 566
Critique, 35–37
Cross-national HRM, 50

Culture, 17, 104, 105, 108–110, 112, 172–173, 357, 372–375, 435–436
   case studies, 65–69, 130–131, 183–184, 343
   change, 120–123
   changing values, 102
   contextualization, 50, 51–61, 62–63
   control, 114, 115, 116
   definition, 101
   diversity, 224, 228
   diversity management, 143–144, 148, 151–154
   dynamics, 101
   further reading, 133–134
   Hofstede's five dimensions, 54, 56
   HRD, 4
   management, 119–123
   measuring change, 124
   modernity, 101–105
   multiculturalism, 106–107
   offshoring, 258
   organizational, 478
   paradox, 128–129
   performance management, 352–357, 359, 361–364, 366, 368–370, 378–379
   perspectives, 112–119
   recruitment and selection, 315–316, 323, 334, 338, 343
   reward management, 388, 401, 403, 405, 409–410, 414–415, 418
   SHRM, 89
   summary, 132
   sustainability, 123, 125
   three levels, 108
   work–life balance, 166–167, 172–176, 178–180, 182–183
Curriculum vitae (CV), 284, 288–289, 323

D

DaimlerChrysler, 302
Decentralization, 17
Delayering, 216, 222
Deloitte, 93–96, 258
Delphi technique, 246–247
Demand forecasting, 246
Denmark, 211
Deregulation, 550
Develop, deploy and connect modes, 93–95
Development
   learning and, 444, 447–448
   reward to encourage, 448
Developmental rewards, 388, 389
Development centres, 300
Diageo, 460
Differentiation, 119
Differentiation strategy, 225
Dignity, 9–10

Dilemmas, 460–461
Dimensions of the Learning Organization Questionnaire (DLOQ), 536–537
Disability, 140, 155, 167, 170–171
Disability Discrimination Act (1995), 171
Disability Discrimination Act (2005), 14
Disability Equality Duty, 171
Discrimination, 57, 224, 226, 413
   diversity management, 140–141, 145, 146, 147, 148–149, 150
   gender, 103, 116, 119, 226
   job descriptions, 283
   legislation, 57, 171
   recruitment and selection, 314, 326, 328, 337
   Social Charter, 189
   work–life balance, 168–169, 170, 171
Discussions, 479
Disneyland, 108
Distributive justice, 361, 364, 409–410, 416
Divergence–convergence question, 374–375
Diversity, 50, 139–155, 224
   advantages, 145–146
   case study, 93–94
   cost, 145
   discourse, 141–144
   ethnic minority women, 151–154
   key concepts, 140–141
   management, 224–228
   positive action, 147
   relational framework, 144–145
   strategies, 148–151
   training, 147, 148, 150
Donovan Commission, 6
Double-loop learning, 533, 541
Downscoping, 253
Downsizing, 4, 195, 215, 244, 250–253, 259, 262
   BPR, 201
   psychological contract, 15
Downtime, 215
Durkheim, Emile, 32, 112, 113

E

E-assessment, 298
Ebco Industries, 148
Economic content, 54, 59–60, 61, 63, 68–69
Economic crisis (2008), 9, 116, 121, 194, 202
Economic relationship, 12
Economics, 435, 436
Ecosystem
   culture, 125, 128
E-HR, 205, 280
E-HRM, 60–61
E-learning, 205, 456, 480, 486–487
Emails, 118, 280, 284

Emotional intelligence, 297
Emotional labour, 120
Employee champions, 30
Employee grievances, 6
Employee involvement, 150, 405
Employee involvement and participation (EIP)
  culture, 126
Employee-led development (ELD), 564
Employee relations, 6, 8, 10
  culture, 126
Employee rights, 13
Employee role behaviours, 84, 88
Employee share option plans (ESOPs), 393, 400, 405–408, 413, 417
Employee value proposition (EVP), 270
Employment Act (1980), 14
Employment Act (1982), 14
Employment Act (1988), 14
Employment Act (1989), 14
Employment Act (1990), 14
Employment Act (2002), 14, 208, 564–565
Employment deal, 270
Employment Equality (Age) Regulations (2006), 170
Employment Equality (Age) Regulations, 14
Employment Equality (Belief) Regulations (2003), 14
Employment Equality (Religion or Belief) Regulations (2003), 172
Employment Equality (Sexual Orientation) Regulations (2003), 14, 171
Employment Protection (Consolidation) Act (1978), 14
Employment Protection Act (1975), 14
Employment relations, 412–414
  Brunei, 65–66, 70
  contextualization, 50, 54, 57, 58, 63
  human resource planning, 250–251, 255, 257–258
  SHRM, 79, 80
Employment Relations Act (2004), 14
Employment relationship, 12–16
  control and commitment, 10
  social, 13
Employment Rights (Disputes Resolution) Act (1998), 14
Employment rights, 13
Employment Rights Act (1996), 14
Employment tribunals, 4
Employment Tribunals Act (1996), 14
Engels, Friedrich, 115
England, 104
Enron, 362, 365
Enterprise resource planning (ESR), 205
Entrepreneurs, informal learning, 565

Environment
  Canterbury Hospital, 37–40
  recruitment, 273
  sustainability, 123, 125
Equal employment opportunity (EEO), 245, 257, 339
  diversity management, 140–141, 143–144, 154
Equality, 55–57
  work–life balance, 167–173, 176–178
Equality Act (2006), 14
Equality Act (2010), 140–141, 147, 168, 171, 172
Equality and Human Rights Commission, 228, 285
Equal opportunities, 116, 224, 227
Equal pay
  legislation, 14
Equal Pay Act (1970), 14
Equal Pay Directive (1975), 413
Equal Treatment in Employment and Occupation Directive (2000), 170
Equity theory, 390, 409
E-recruitment, 205, 280
E-rewards, 205
Ernst & Young, 301
Ethics, 5, 50
  culture, 110
  downsizing, 252–253
  performance management, 352–353, 354, 361–364
  recruitment and selection, 314, 315, 333, 336–337
  rewards and pay, 391
  SHRM, 76
Ethnic minorities, 224, 227
  career management, 221
Ethnic minority women, 140, 151–154
  case study, 157–159
  pay inequality, 396
  performance-related pay, 410
  sociocultural context, 55, 63
  work–life balance, 166, 167–169, 172–178, 179–180
Europe and the European Union (EU)
  culture, 103
  legislation, 13
  redundancy, 215
  Social Charter, 189
  sustainability, 127
  trade unions, 127
  working time, 208
European Evaluation Society, 494
European Mentoring and Coaching Council, 528
European Passengers Services Ltd, 300

Evaluation
    action evaluation, 516
    appraisal, 502
    approach, 495–496
    CIRO model, 513–515
    cost of, 502, 514
    definition, 493–494
    discussion questions, 520
    for evaluation's sake, 504
    ex ante (formative), 495, 501, 513
    experimentation, 495–496
    ex post (summative), 495, 501
    frameworks, 499
    further reading, 520
    future direction, 517
    of HRD, 493–521
    interim (formative/summative), 495
    Kirkpatrick model, 506–508
    measures of returns model, 519
    models, 506–517, 518–519
    monitoring, 502
    of NHRD, 498–499
    objectives (SMART), 501
    organization change and, 516–517
    pluralist approach, 498
    positivist vs. constructionist, 498
    programme logic model, 498
    purpose of, 506
    rationale, 501
    realist, 498
    reasons for doing, 494
    responsive, 516
    risk appraisal, 502
    ROAMEF cycle, 499–504
    summary, 519–520
    types of, 495
    value and evaluation process, 517
    in the workplace, 504–506
Evaluation Society, 494
E-working, 205
Exercises, 484
Exit interviews, 199
Expatriates, 50, 63
    case study, 342–345
    expectancy theory, 390–391, 404, 409
    external recruitment, 319–321
    extrinsic rewards, 388–391, 408, 417
    performance management, 352–353
    recruitment and selection, 315, 333–334
    reward management, 387, 414–416, 421–424
    work–life balance, 179–180
Experiential learning, 486
Experiential learning cycle (Kolb), 533
Experimentation, evaluation and, 495–496
Expertise and influence, balance of, 461–462
Eysenck Personality Questionnaire, 329

F
Facebook, 281
Face validity, 294
Factory/Factories Acts, 14
Fairness, 287, 371, 373
    reward management, 386, 387, 396, 408, 416
Family and work, 16
Fantastic Holdings, 407
Fattal Holding, 85–86
Feedback, 255, 372
    case study, 342–345
    performance management, 356, 360, 364–365, 367–368, 372, 375–376
    recruitment and selection, 315–316, 320, 321
    reward management, 389, 390, 402
    in ROAMEF cycle, 500
Femininity, 56, 103, 117
Feminism, 32, 34, 114, 116, 118, 151–154
Financial flexibility, 254
Fixed-term contracts, 208, 214
Flexibility and flexible working, 145, 173–176, 206–217, 253–255, 400
    benefits, 400
    case study, 182–185
    Guest model, 24–25
    HRP, 244, 253–255, 259
    job descriptions, 283
    performance management, 366
    recruitment and selection, 338
    reward management, 389–390, 398, 399
    types, 207
    women, 226
    work–life balance, 166, 173–175, 176, 179–180
Flexi-time, 209
Fombrun, Tichy and Devanna model, 22
Ford Motor Company, 227
Ford Motor Company, Employee Programme, 564
Formal appraisals, 364–365, 372
Formalization, 314
Foucauldian analysis, 36
Foucault, Michel, 118, 393
Foundation, The, 378–379
Foundation degrees, 562
France
    culture, 106
Freedom of association, 58
Freelancing, 210
Friedan, Betty, 34
Fringe benefits, 399
Fryer reports, 549, 552
Functional flexibility, 254

G

G4S Security Services, 447–448
Gain-sharing, 401, 405
Gardner Smith, 407
Gate Gourmet, 213
Gender, 35, 151–154, 167–169, 224, 227
   case studies, 157–158, 182–185
   culture, 103, 116, 119
   Deloitte, 93–96
   discrimination, 103, 116, 119, 226
   diversity management, 140, 142–148, 150, 155
Gendered power relations, 461
Gender Equality Duty, 168
Gender Recognition Act (2004), 14
General Electric, 353, 365
General mental ability (GMA) tests, 328–329, 332
General Teaching Council for Scotland, 203
Generation X, 224
Generation Y, 224, 273, 552
Geography, 435, 436
Germany, 211
   culture, 106
Glass ceiling, 221, 227, 532
Globalization, 51–53, 60, 62, 243
   culture, 103
   HRM models, 28–29
   latent tensions, 50
   and lifelong learning, 549–550
   performance management, 352, 354, 371, 372–375
   recruitment and selection, 338
   work–life balance, 166
Global professionals, 354
Globe Ground India (GGI), 389
Goal-based bonuses, 401–402
Goal-setting, 366–367, 390, 405
Goal-sharing, 401, 404, 405
Goldman Sachs, 258
Google, 278
Government departments, 437
Government Employee Management System (GEMS), 66, 69
Graduates
   recruitment, 268, 273, 301
Great Depression, 5
Green Book, 499
Green concerns
   culture, 123–127
Grievance process, 6
Group dynamics, 480
Guardian Media Group, 228
Guest model of HRM, 24–25
   components, 24–25
Gulf of Mexico oil spill, 271

H

Harassment
   sexual, 119
Harvard model, 22–24
Harvey Nichols, learning and development, 469–470, 479
Headcount, 203–204
Health, safety and wellness
   legislation, 14
Health and Safety at Work etc. Act (1974), 14
Health insurance, 174, 388, 399
High-performance practices
   diversity, 228
High-performance work systems, 120
   call centres, 211
High-road strategy, 200–201
Hilton Hotels, e-learning, 487
History of HRM, 4–8
Hoffman, Gary, 202
Holden, 246, 247, 252
Home-based approach, 415
Home-working, 209, 210
Host-based approach (going rate), 416
Host country nationals (HCNs), 353–354
   reward management, 414–416, 421–422
HRD policy, 448–450, 463
   content, 449–450
   factors influencing, 449
   groups involved in determining, 449
   HRD strategies, 444–446, 446–447
   meaning, 446
   programmes and activities, 447
HRM cycle, 22
HRM definition, 8, 9
HRM dimensions, 18, 19
HRM scope and functions, 16–19
HRM theory, 19, 23, 29–31
HSBC Bank, 145, 150
Hull dinner ladies training, case study, 521–522
Human behaviour, 435, 436
Human capital, 10, 230, 436
   development, 560
Human capital advantage (HCA), 81–82
Human capital monitor, 230
Human process advantage (HPA), 81–82
Human resource accounting (HRA), 229
Human resource acquisition, 145
Human resource advantage, 82
Human Resource Development (HRD), 4, 6–8
   contexts of practice, 437–438
   Critical (CHRD), 440
   definitions, 432–434, 437, 438
   history and origins, 433–435
   meaning of, 432
   national, *see* National HRD

Human Resource Development (HRD) – (*continued*)
  performative vs. learning focus, 433
  plans, 446, 463
  positioning and management, 459–463
  relationship with education, training and development, 434
  vs. Strategic HRD (SHRD), 434
  subject of academic enquiry vs. area of professional practice, 431
  see also HRD policy; HRD strategies
Human resource information systems (HRIS), 203–204, 205
Human Resource Management (HRM), 434
  'high road' strategy, 444
Human resource meaning, 10–11
Human resource planning (HRP), 195, 200–202, 202
Human resource practices, 200
Human resource specialists, 18, 19
Human resources planning (HRP), 243–262
  approaches, 244–250
  case study, 261–263
  mini case study, 256
  strategic role, 250–259
Human resources strategy fit, 82
Human rights, 5
Hummel, Tania, 272
Hyundai, 58–59

I
IBM, 103, 175
Immigrant labour, 338, 339
Improvement and Development Agency, 455
Incentives, 400–404, 409, 413, 416
Indeterminacy, 9
India
  call centres, 200
  manufacturing, 28
  outsourcing, 28, 212
Individual difference hypothesis, 319–320
Individualism, 7–8, 103, 287
Individual Learning Accounts, 564
Individual performance plans, 401–403, 404, 409
Induction, 315
Industrial relations, 6, 13, 27
Industrial Relations Act (1971), 14
Industrial Revolution, 6
Industrial Training Act (1965), 14
Influence
  and expertise, balance of, 460–461
  power and, 460–461
  Informal appraisals, 364, 372

Information
  as knowledge, 538–539
  new age of, 538–539
Information and communication technology (ICT), 204–206
  teleworking, 209–211
Information technology (IT), 60–61, 62
  Brunei, 65, 68, 70
Innovation, 54, 62, 66, 149, 150
  SHRM, 80, 82, 83, 84
Inquiry into the Future for Lifelong Learning, 560
Institute for Employment Studies, 460
Institute of Chartered Accountants in England and Wales (ICAEW), 556–557
Institute of Logistics and Transport, 553
Institute of Nanotechnology, 551
Institution of Engineering and Technology, knowledge network, 559
Integration
  culture, 112, 119
Integrity and honesty tests, 333
Intellectual capital, 229–230
Intelligence tests, 296
Internal recruitment, 321
International Coaching Federation, 528
International human resource management (IHRM), 16–17, 18
International Labour Organization (ILO), 446
International Monetary Fund (IMF), 103
Internet, 205, 298
  culture, 129
  recruitment, 271, 279, 281, 283
  teleworking, 209–211
Internships, 281
Interviews
  exit, 199
  selection, 284–285, 288, 289, 290–292
Interviews, 323–326, 342
Intraining NTP Consulting, 541
Intrinsic rewards, 389–391, 408–409, 417
Inventories (questionnaires), 294, 295
Investment, return on, 436
Ireland, 228

J
Japan
  culture, 102, 104
  Fukushima nuclear plant, 9
Job analysis, 244, 249–250, 269, 274, 282–284, 315, 316–318, 319
  techniques, 274, 275
Job and work design, 82
Job applicant variables, 318–319, 320, 321, 325
Job assessment software, 275
Job-based pay, 393, 394–396, 401, 410, 413, 417

Job boards, 280
Job description, 282–284, 317, 319, 335–336
Job evaluation, 394, 395–397
Job rotation, 438
Job-sharing, 209
Journals, 435

K
Kaizan, 451
Kaminski, Ron, 127
Keynesianism, 6–7, 8
Keystone XL, 127
Knowledge, 551
  abstract, 554–555
  codified vs. tacit, 554–555
  concealed, 539
  embedded, 539
  embodied, 539
  embrained, 539
  information as, 538–539
  knowing-how, 539–541
  knowing-that, 539–541
  mismatched salience, 539
  ostensive, 539
  professional, 554–555
  public vs. personal, 554–555
  tacit, 540, 542, 554–555, 565
  uncognized/uncognizable, 540
  unrecognized, 539
Knowledge-based organizations, 548
Knowledge-creating model, 565–566
Knowledge creation, 538–541
  shared space (Ba) for, 534
Knowledge Management (KM), 439–440, 537–541
  definition, 537–538
  discussion questions, 542
  further reading, 542–543
  summary, 542
  Knowledge networks, 551
  Knowledge sharing, 566
  Knowledge society, 560
  Knowledge work and workers, 199
  South, 204
Kolb's experiential learning cycle, 533, 559
Kyoto Protocol (1997), 52, 64

L
Labour market, hourglass structure, 549–550
Language, 102, 104, 108, 114, 120
Latin America, 226
Law Society, 548, 553, 557
Leaders
  transformational, 451
Leadership commitment, 149

Leadership Development (LD), 439–440
Lean Lease, 407
Learn Direct, e-learning, 487
Learners, reluctant, 477
Learning
  action learning, 437
  age and, 476
  agreements, 565
  vs. change, 448
  cities, 536
  climate, 527
  for co-configuration, 541
  collective, 444
  company, 535–536
  complicating factors, 475–477
  context, 530–531, 534, 535
  contracts, 559
  culture, 526
  definition, 480
  deliberative, 565
  and development, 444, 447–448
  double-loop, 451, 533, 541
  emerging paradigm of, 530
  enablers, 479
  environment, 527
  experiential, 481
  expertise, 461
  factors influencing, 476
  gain ratio, 510
  human factors, 475–477
  implicit, 565
  informal, 531, 542, 561, 565–566
  informal and incidental, 531–532
  informal vs. formal, 565–566
  Learning Combination Lock, 474
  life-long, 222
  movement, 527
  non-formal, 530
  as participation, 530, 532
  principles, 473–474
  in projects, 541
  reactive, 565
  regions, 536
  reward, 473
  shift from training, 456
  single-loop, 451, 532–533
  vs. training, 468
  transfer of, 474
  transformative, 566
  trigger, 531
  workplace, 126
  see also E-learning; Lifelong learning; Organizational Learning; Workplace learning
Learning and development
  Harvey Nichols, 469–470, 478

Learning cycles
  Kolb's, 533, 559
Learning methods, 432–435, 489
  framework, 433
  integrated, 481, 484–485
  on-the-job, 482–483
  'hard to reach' groups, 489
Learning organizations (LOs), 439–440, 535–536
  Dimensions of the Learning Organization Questionnaire (DLOQ), 536–537
  disciplines, 536
Learning system organization as, 526–531
  see also Organizational Learning
Learning Transfer System Inventory (LTSI), 474
Leaver profiling, 199
Lecturers, 438
Lectures, 438
Legal and political context, 54, 57–58, 61, 63
  Brunei, 65, 67–69
Legal disciplinary practices, 550
Legal profession
  competition, 550
  CPD in, 550–551
Legal relationship, 13
Legislation, 13
  diversity, 224
  employment relationship, 12–16
  European, 17
  health and safety, 17
Legislation and regulation, 176–178, 375
  contextualization, 50, 52, 53–54, 57–58
  diversity management, 140–141, 143, 144, 154
  HRP, 244, 249, 258–259
  performance management, 355, 375
  recruitment and selection, 338, 339
  reward management, 387, 393, 399, 412–414
  working hours, 52, 53, 177, 178
  work–life balance, 166–168, 172, 179–180
Leitch report/review of skills, 443, 499, 500, 501, 548, 561, 564
Lifelong learning (LL), 222, 547, 560–566
  change, dimensions of, 549–553
  discussion questions, 567
  formal vs. informal, 565–566
  further reading, 567
  globalization and, 550
  human capital model, 561
  Inquiry into the Future for Lifelong Learning, 560
  key drivers, 549–553
  life cycle argument, 548
  models, 560–561
  policy/strategy in UK, 552–553
  political factors, 552–553
  relevant themes, 559
  skills, 561–565
  social cohesion argument, 548
  social trends, 552
  speed of change argument, 548
  summary, 566
  in West Yorkshire, 561–562
Lifelong Learning Networks, 561–562
Lighthouse Project, 489
Line management, responsibility for staff development in business partner model, 460–461
Line managers, 17
  Storey model, 26, 27
LinkedIn, 281
Lloyds TSB, 298, 300
Long-term orientation, 56
Low-road strategy, 200, 201
Lufthansa, 389

M
Machine bureaucracy, 527
Machine metaphor, 527
Macho, 226
Macmillan Publishers, 272
Macquarie Group, 258
Macroenvironment
  contextualization, 50, 54, 63, 70
Maintenance programmes, 448
Malay Islamic Monarchy (MIB), 65, 67, 70
Managed professional businesses, 550
Management-by-objectives (MBO), 365, 366, 367
Management consultancy, 550
Managerialist perspective, 112–114, 287
Managers and management, 9–10
  employment relationship, 10–11
  surveillance, 117
Manpower planning, 195–200
  computer software, 197–198
  definition, 195–196
  diagnostic approach, 198–199
  stages, 196–197
  supply and demand, 196–197
Mansour, Mohamed, 124
Manufacturing, 28, 244
Market disciplines, 7
Marketing, 145
Market surveys, 395
Marx, Karl, 33, 115
Marzipan layer, 285–286
Masculinity, 56, 103, 117, 119, 357
Maternity rights, 13, 208–209
Maynard, Kelly, 131
McDonald's, 279
Measurement of diversity, 150

Medtronic Incorporated, 366
Mentoring, 217, 484, 488, 528
Merit bonuses, 402
Merit pay plans, 401–402
Merkel, Chancellor Angela, 106
Merrill Lynch, 281
Metaphor, 527
Micro HRM (MHRM), 16
Microprocessor technology, 62
Minimum wage, 57, 58, 245, 293
Mission statements, 279
MobilCom, 342
Mobility and mobile working, 210
Models of HRM, 7–8, 22–31
   advancing economies, 28–29
   Fombrun, Tichy and Devanna, 22
   generic and organization-specific Guest, 24–25
   hard version, 7
   Harvard, 22–24
   soft version, 7
   Storey, 26–27
   Ulrich, 29–31
   Warwick, 25–26
Modernity, 101–105
Mohair, 58
Monster, 280
Morrisons, 276, 277
Moser reports, 563
Motivation, 15, 61, 77
   performance management, 355, 366, 369–370
   reward management, 386–387, 390–393, 398–399, 401, 408, 417
Motorola University, 459
MRF, 59
Multiculturalism, 106–107
Multidisciplinary practices, 550
Multinational companies (MNCs), 356–357
   Chinese, 374, 387, 421–424
   culture, 102, 119
   performance management, 352, 356–358, 360–370, 372–375
   recruitment and selection, 269
   recruitment and selection, 339, 342–345
   reward management, 387, 414-416, 421–424
   SHRM, 89
   work–life balance, 175, 179–180
Multiple regression, 246–247
Multisite working, 210
Multisource feedback (360 degree appraisal), 367–370
Myers, Sarah, 220
Myers–Briggs personality test, 379
Myers–Briggs Type Indicator, 297

N

Nadler, Leonard, 433
Nando's, 218
Nanotechnology, 551
National Employers' Skills Survey, 564
National Health Service (NHS), 203, 204
   culture, 108, 109, 112, 113
   equality and diversity, 228
National HRD (NHRD), 437
   evaluation of, 498–499
National Minimum Wage (Enforcement) Act (2003), 14
National Minimum Wage Act (1998), 14
National Qualification Framework (NQF) revised, 561
National Skills Task Force, 563
Natural sciences, 436
Neo-liberalism, 7–8
Netherlands, The, 211
   culture, 106
Networking, 217
Networks
   knowledge networks, 551
New Labour, 13
New public management, 553
New Zealand, 222
   Canterbury Hospital, 37–39
Nicol, Heather, 39
Nicol, Hugo, 226
Non-cash rewards, 403, 417
Normative model, 7
Northern Ireland, 104
Northern Rock, 202
Norway, 178
Nuclear accidents
   Japan, 9
Numerical flexibility, 254

O

Occupational Personality Questionnaire, 298
Offshoring, 212–213
Offshoring tasks, 258
Oil pipeline, 127
Oil spill disaster, 271
Onboarding, 278
OneSteel, 407
Online performance management, 376
Online testing, 298–299
Organic solidarity, 32
Organizational culture, 478–479
Organizational Development Institute (USA), 455
Organizational flexibility, 145
Organizational justice theory, 361

Organizational Learning (OL), 439–440, 532–537
  4Is model, 533
  communities of practice (CoPs), 535
  discussion questions, 542
  further reading, 542–543
  knowledge-creating model, 534
  SECI model, 534
  summary, 542
Organization Development (OD), 433, 436
Organizations, proactive/reactive, 452
Orientation to work, 16
Outsourcing, 4, 17, 212–213, 338, 461
  China, 28
  India, 28, 212
  recruitment, 273
  of training, 45
Oxfam, 103

P
Paid leave, 399, 415
Panel interviews, 324
Panopticon, 118
Paradigms, 31–35
Paradox, 33, 35–37
  culture, 128–129
Parent country nationals (PCNs), 353–354
Parents, 167, 172–173, 173, 175, 176–177
  case study, 249–250
Parochialism, 50, 51
Parsons, Talcott, 32, 112
Partnerships, professional, 550
Part-time workers, 199–200, 208
Paternity rights, 208
Pay
  women, 226
Pay dispersion, 395
Pay–effort bargain, 12
Pay variability, 410, 412
Peace Corps, 368
Peer appraisals, 369
People, 4, 9, 194–195, 230
Performance
  and diversity, 149
  employee turnover, 199–200
Performance appraisals, 54, 352–353, 354–355, 356–377
  culture, 122, 125–126, 357
  main approaches, 364–367
Performance contracts, 283
Performance management, 245, 351, 353, 364, 366, 368–370, 374
  case study, 378
  characteristics, 354–358
  criteria, 358–361
  cycle, 354

ethics, 353, 354, 361–364
international context, 372–375
main approaches, 364–367
mini case studies, 362–363, 373
multisource feedback, 367–370
purpose, 355–358
strategic importance, 353
strategies to improve, 370–372
Performance-related pay
  and criticisms, 408–411
  and rewards, 386, 388–391, 393, 400–411, 416
Perilya, 407
Peripheral workforce, 207, 253
Personality
  tests, 271, 294–295
Personality tests, 328, 329, 332
  faking, 331
Person-based pay, 393–394, 397, 413, 417
Person–job fit, 315–316, 318, 321, 336
Personnel management, 4, 7, 24, 27
Pharmaceutical industry, 78, 335–336
Piece rates, 401, 402
Placements, 281
Planning, 194, 200–202
  manpower, 195–200
  people, 194–195
Planning, organizing, directing, controlling (PODC) tradition, 11
Pluralism, 6, 25
  recruitment and selection, 314, 337, 338
  reward management, 386, 392
Politics, 435, 436
  and performance management, 371
Pollution
  culture, 125–126
Portfolio career, 221
Positive action, 147, 155
Positive discrimination, 224
Positivism, 32
Power, 14, 18, 34, 436
  culture, 129
  and influence, 461
  selection, 287
Power distance, 56, 70
  performance management, 357, 364, 367–368
Power relationships, 153
Pre-employment activities, 301–302
Pregnancy, 13
Pre-screening, 315, 320, 323
Proaction, 79, 85, 94
Problem-solving, 77, 145, 145–146, 397
  Brunei, 67, 70
Procedural flexibility, 254
Procedural justice, 361, 364, 410

Proctor and Gamble, 145
Productivity, 50, 60, 149
  downsizing, 251, 253
  expatriates, 334
  performance management, 372–375
  reward management, 400, 405
  SHRM, 76, 82–83, 88
  work–life balance, 166, 168–170, 176, 178, 180
Professional associations
  CPD policies, 553
  online communities, 559
  in the UK, 553–554
Professionalism, 553–555
  economic basis for, 554
  HRD professionals, 554
  ideal type, 554
Professional knowledge, 554–555
Professional partnerships, 550
Professional practice, 438
Professionals
  decline in trust placed in, 552
  HRD professionals, 457, 461
  and professionalism, 18, 19
  in the public sector, 553
  women in HRD, 461
Professional work, CPD, 553–559
Profit-sharing, 404
  reward management, 393, 401, 404, 413
Projects, 484
Protean career, 222
Psychological contract, 14–15, 18, 214
  culture, 119
  definition, 14
Psychology, 435–436
Psychometric testing, 268, 287, 294–302, 327–331, 340
Public sector
  culture, 129
  professionals in, 553
  workforce planning, 194, 203, 204–206, 215
Public sector, 65–71

Q
Qualitative demand forecasting, 246–247
Quality in Guest model, 24–25
Quality scouts, 279
Quantitative demand forecasting, 246

R
Race and ethnicity, 172–173
  case study, 157–159
  diversity management, 140–147, 151–154, 155
  work–life balance, 166, 172–173, 174, 176, 182
Race and racism, 224, 227
Race Equality Duty, 172
Race Relations (Amendment) Act (2000), 140, 172
Race Relations Act (1976), 14, 140, 147, 172
Ranking, 365, 366
Rationality, technical, 555
Real estate, 359, 364
Realistic information hypothesis, 319
Realistic job previews (RJPs), 301–302, 321–322, 333
Recession, 4, 31, 53, 60, 251
  downsizing, 195
  laying off staff, 128, 129, 215
  recruitment and selection, 268, 271–272, 279, 284–285, 301–302
  talent management, 217, 220
  workforce planning, 194–195, 215, 217, 221
Recruitment, 16, 268–271
  advertising, 279
  case study, 302–304
  channels, 279–281
  diversity, 301–302
  further reading, 306
  graduates, 268, 273, 301
  internal, 280
  older employees, 279
  person–environment fit, 277
  person–job fit, 279
  person–organization fit, 277–278, 336–337
  person–team fit, 277
  planning, 194–195
  policies, 268–271
  psychometric testing, 268, 287, 294–302
  selection, 284–285
  stages, 269
  strategic view, 274
  summary, 304–305
  traditional approaches, 268
Recruitment agencies, 268, 279
Recruitment and selection, 150, 313
  Brunei, 66, 67, 70
  case study, 342–345
  contextualization, 54, 57, 60, 61
  critical perspective, 338–339
  Deloitte, 93
  diversity management, 145, 147, 148, 150–151
  ethics, 314, 315, 333, 337
  expatriates, 315, 333–335
  methods, 319–321
  mini case study, 326
  process model, 318–319
  recruiter effect, 320–321
  selection methods, 323–326
  SHRM, 77, 78
  stages, 315–337
  validity and reliability, 359

Recruitment ratio, 284
Redundancy, 215–217
Re-engineering, 201
References, 323, 342
Reflection, 559
   critical, 559, 566
Reflection-in-action, 555
Reflection-on-action, 559
Reflexivity, 315, 338
Region-based approach, 415, 416
Reinforcement theory, 390
Reliability, 288, 289, 295, 358, 359–360, 366, 369
Religion, 167, 172–173
   diversity management, 140, 152
Reputation for corporate social performance (RCSP), 252–253, 259
Research and practice, foci for, 439
Resource-based views (RBVs), 76, 80–81, 86–87, 89, 90–91
Responsive evaluation, 516
Restructuring, 244, 250–251
Résumés, 288–289
Retail, 157–158, 245
Return on investment, 436
Rewards and pay, 77
   base, 393–399
   benefits plans, 399–400
   case studies, 65, 421–424
   communication, 411–412
   contextualization, 56, 57, 59
   critical perspective, 391–393
   downsizing, 250–251, 252
   employment relations, 412–414
   ethics, 392
   HRP, 245, 254
   international, 414–416
   intrinsic and extrinsic, 388–391
   management, 385–427
   nature and purpose, 387–388
   performance management, 354–355, 356, 357, 361, 366, 374
   performance-related, 386, 388, 393, 400–411
Rewards and reward management
   income, 5
Reward systems
   culture, 125–127
Rights, 5, 10–11, 13, 208
Risk appraisal, 502
Risk society, 549
Rituals, 108, 110, 120
ROAMEF cycle, 499–504
Role play, 482, 486

S

Salary sacrifice, 407
Schools in England, 373
Scientific management systems, 76
Scotland, 104, 203
Secondment, 485
Secrecy, 387, 411
Sector Skills Councils, 552
Selection, 284–294
   assessment centres, 299–301
   case study, 302–304
   culture, 121, 125
   further reading, 306
   online testing, 298–299
   policies, 268–271
   power dimensions, 287
   psychometric tests, 268, 287, 294–302
   realistic job previews (RJPs), 301–302
   stages, 268–269
   summary, 304–305
   techniques, 287, 288, 299
   traditional approaches, 268
   validity, 288, 289, 290, 294, 296, 297
Selection interviews, 284, 288, 289, 292–294
   behavioural, 292–293
   comprehensive structured, 292
   information elicited, 232, 289
   order and involvement, 289
   situational, 290–292
   videos, 289
Self-assessment, 368–369, 370
Self-managed teams, 18
Self-reporting, 297
Services industry, 245
Sex Discrimination Act (1975), 14, 116, 140, 147, 168
Sex Discrimination Act (1986), 14
Sexual harassment, 119
Sexual orientation, 140, 171–172
Sexual orientation, 224, 227
Shadowing, 484
Shared services, 458
Share grant plans, 406
Shareholders and shareholder value, 5
Share purchase plans, 406–408
Shift working, 209
Short-term orientation, 56–57
Siemens, 302
Singapore, 204
Single-loop learning, 451, 532
Situational interviews, 324
Six Sigma, 62
Skills
   career management, 221, 222
   intermediate, 563
   LL and, 561–565
   natural development, 530
   off-the-job instruction, 483

workforce planning, 202, 204
world leader status, 561
Skills Accounts, 564
Skill set, 397
Skills for Life Strategy Unit, 564
Skill shortages, 244, 248
Sky, 220
Small and medium-sized enterprises (SMEs), 17
   development programme for managers, 515
   enterprises (SMEs), 439
   informal learning, 565
   performance management, 365, 375
SMART objectives, 472, 501
SMEs, *see* Small and medium-sized enterprises
Social capital, 199, 540
   development, 218
Social Charter (EU), 189
Social contract, 5, 7
Social equity approach, 140, 143
Socialization, 102, 121
Social networks, 121
Social psychology, 435, 436
Social rewards, 389
Social sciences, 435, 436
Social systems theory, 32
Sociocultural context, 54, 55–57, 61, 63
   Brunei, 66–67
Sociological imagination, 9
Sociology, 435, 436
Solicitors, training record, 557
Somerfield, 171
South Korea, 204
Specificity, 358
Staff turnover, 145, 386
Staff turnover, 197, 199–200
   call centres, 278
   cost, 284
Staggered hours, 209
Stakeholder interests in Harvard model, 23
Starbucks, 103
Status professions, 553
StepStone, 280
Stopforth, Keith, 111
Storey model of HRM, 26–29
Strategic alignment, 355, 358–359, 358, 388
Strategic business partners, 31, 456, 458
Strategic congruence, 358, 366
Strategic direction of organization, 445
Strategic HRD (SHRD) vs. HRD, 434, 446
Strategic HRM (SHRM), 75–98, 352
   case study, 93–96
   defined, 80
   mini case study, 78–79, 85–86
Strategic human resource management (SHRM), 16–17
Strategic management, 445

Strategic partner model, 29–31
Strategic plan, 149
Strategy, 445
   business strategy, 445
   see also HRD strategies
Stress, 410
   downsizing, 251
   expatriates, 335
   work–life balance, 166, 173, 174, 178, 180
Stress in the workplace
   teleworking, 210
Strikes, 213
Structural-functionalism, 32–33, 112, 114
Subcultures, 113, 114
Subjective career, 222
Subjectivity, 314, 338
Subordinates as sources, 368–370
Subsidiaries
   managers, 353–354
Succession planning, 150, 202, 218–219
Sugar, Lord Alan, 267–268
Superannuation, 388, 399, 415
Supervisor as source, 367–368, 369
Supply and demand, 195–197
Supply and demand of labour, 60, 68, 246
   HRP, 244–245, 246, 249, 253, 258, 259
Supply forecasting, 248
Surveillance, 117
Survivor syndrome, 216
Sustainability, 9, 17
   Canterbury Hospital, 37–40
   culture, 121, 125–127
Sweden, 211
   HR accounting, 229
Symbolic-interactionist approach, 114
Symbols, 101–102

T
Tacit knowledge, 555, 565
Taiwan, 204
Talent Attraction Program, 93
Talent management (TM), 195, 202, 217–224, 244, 255–258, 260
   case study, 261–263
Tax Credit Office, coaching, 528
Taylor, FW and Taylorism, 76
Technical rationality, 555
Technological context, 60–61, 63
   Brunei, 69, 70
Technology
   learning and, 550–551
   new technologies, 550–551
Telecommunications, 53
Telecommuting, 335
Telephone hacking, 5

INDEX

Teleworking, 209–212, 211
  stress, 210
  types, 210
Telstra, 407
Tempest, Jonathan, 131
Termination or dismissal
  redundancy, 53, 57
Term-time working, 175
Tesco, 148
Thatcher, Margaret and Thatcherism, 7
Theoretical perspective, 12, 21, 100
Theory Y, 23
Third country nationals (TCNs), 353, 414, 416
TNNB, 231–232
Tokenism, 146, 158
Total Quality Management (TQM), 62, 451
  SHRM, 77, 83
Trades Union Congress (TUC), 127
Trade Union Act (1984), 14
Trade Union and Labour Relations (Consolidation) Act (1992), 14
Trade Union and Labour Relations Acts (1974/1976), 14
Trade Union Reform and Employment Rights Act (1993), 14
Trade unions, 6, 90, 246
  contextualization, 58, 59, 60, 70
  culture, 128
  and ELD schemes, 564
  employment relationship, 11, 13
  Europe, 127
  legislation, 13
  neo-liberalism, 7–8
  recruitment and selection, 339
  reward management, 392, 413, 414, 417
  strikes, 213
  sustainability, 127
Traditional personnel management, 76–78
Trainers, 477
Training
  at National Westminster Bank, 507
  behaviour evaluation, 506, 510–511
  context evaluation, 513–514
  cost, 284
  costs and resources, 477–478
  definition
  evaluation levels, 506
  external influences on results interpretation, 513
  four-stage model, 512
  in group context, 477
  HR planning, 200
  Hull dinner ladies, case study, 521–522
  human factors, 475–477
  inputs evaluation, 514
  integrated methods, 484–485
  Kirkpatrick evaluation model, 506–507
  vs. learning, 468
  learning evaluation, 506, 509–510
  for middle managers, 504, 512
  objectives, 472
  organizational context, 478–479
  organizational culture, 478–479
  outcomes evaluation, 514–515
  outsourcing of, 461–462
  purpose of, 472
  reaction evaluation, 506, 507–509, 514
  results evaluation, 506, 511–512
  shift to learning, 456
  staff turnover, 200
  sustainability, 126
  transfer of, 475
Training, development and learning
  case studies, 69–70
  contextualization, 54, 55, 57, 60, 69
  diversity management, 147, 148, 150–151
  HRP, 248, 251, 254, 255–258
  performance management, 356, 357, 361, 368, 375–376
  reward management, 389
  SHRM, 77, 78, 83
  work–life balance, 170
Training design, 470–479
  complicating factors, 471
  discussion questions, 490–491
  framework, 471
  further reading, 491
  principles, 471
  statement of intent, 472
  summary, 490
Training methods, 479–481, 488
  coaching, *see* Coaching
  framework, 480
  learner-centred, 480
  off-the-job, 480–481, 486
  training-centred, 480
Transnational companies
  contextualization, 50, 52, 53, 63
Transparency, 387, 396, 411, 412
Travelscence, 362–363
Treaty of Amsterdam (1999), 413
Trend projection, 246
Trust, 119, 371
  performance management, 371, 376
Twitter, 281

U

Ulrich's model, 29–31
Uncertainty avoidance, 56, 402
Unemployment, 53, 60, 61, 202
Unilever, outsourcing, 462
Union learning representatives (ULRs), 565

INDEX

Unitarism, 7, 15, 24, 338
  reward management, 392, 417
United Kingdom
  call centres, 210, 211
  career management, 222–223
  culture, 104, 106
  diversity, 227–228, 230
  flexibility, 207
  legislation, 13
  redundancy, 215–217, 216
  selection, 284, 295
  Social Charter, 189
United Nations, 103
United States Air Force, 149
United States of America
  call centres, 211
  credentials, 291
  culture, 103, 104, 127
  sustainability, 126, 127
Universal Declaration of Human Rights, 5
Universalism
  SHRM, 76, 83, 87
Universities, academics in, 432
University Forum for Human Resource Development, 432
Utilitarianism, 228, 287

V

Validation feedback loops, 316
Validity, 336, 358, 359, 366, 369
Validity coefficient, 288
Validity in selection, 288, 289, 292, 295, 296, 297
Values, 102–104, 108, 110, 113, 114, 120
Vision statements, 276
Vocational education and training (VET), 437
  credential ism, 561
Vocational qualifications, 275
Vygotsky, Lev, 530

W

Wage indexation, 412
Wages Act (1986), 13
Wales, 104
WalMart, 108
Warwick model, 25–26
Watson and Hamilton lawyers, 302–304
Watson-Glaser test, 296
Weber, Max, 33–34, 36, 112
Weberism, 76
Well-being, 166, 178
Whitbread, 280
Windows Meeting Space, 210
Wollstonecraft, Mary, 34
Women
  career management, 221
  diversity, 226
  feminism, 32, 34, 114, 116, 118
  glass ceiling, 221, 285
  HRD professionals in the UK, 461
  maternity rights, 13
  pay, 226
Work and Families Act (2006), 13, 177, 208
Work and work systems
  home, 209, 210, 212
Workforce numbers, 194, 195, 201–202, 202, 203
Workforce planning, 194, 195, 202–206
  case study, 231–233
  flexibility, 206–217
  further reading, 235
  human resource, 200–202
  manpower, 195–200
  people, 194–195
  summary, 233–234
Workforce reduction, 244, 248
Working conditions, 245, 254, 395
Working hours
  legislation, 52, 53, 177, 178–179
  work–life balance, 177, 178–179, 180
Working time, 208
Working Time Directive, 178
Working Time Regulations (1998), 177, 178
Work–life balance (WlB), 167, 257
  age, 169–170, 173, 176, 181
  career management, 233
  case study, 182–185
  culture, 100
  disability, 170–171
  flexibility, 206, 207, 209, 210
  flexible working, 166, 169–170, 173–176, 181
  gender, 166, 167–169, 172, 174, 176, 181
  international and context considerations, 179–180
  legislation, 176–178
  race and ethnicity, 166, 172–173, 176, 181
  recruitment and selection, 335
  reward management, 389, 400
  sexual orientation, 171–172
  well-being and health, 178
Workplace Employment Relations Surveys, 208
Workplace learning, 526–532
  contested possibilities, 529
  discussion questions, 542
  further reading, 542–543
  informal (non-formal), 530–532
  summary, 542
  sustainability, 126
Work samples, 332–333

Y

Yorkshire Bank, e-learning, 487